W9-BRT-853

Supporting
Windows NT® & 2000
Workstation & Server

ISBN 0-13-083068-2

9 780130 830685

PRENTICE HALL PTR MICROSOFT® TECHNOLOGIES SERIES

PRENTICE HALL PTR MICROSOFT® TECHNOLOGIES SERIES

Jim Mohr

Supporting Windows NT® & 2000 Workstation & Server

PH
PTR

Prentice Hall PTR
Upper Saddle River, NJ 07458
www.phptr.com

Editorial/production supervision: *Vincent Janoski*
Acquisitions editor: *Mike Meehan*
Marketing manager: *Bryan Gambrel*
Manufacturing manager: *Maura Goldstaub*
Cover design director: *Jerry Votta*

© 2000 by James Mohr

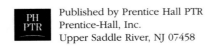 Published by Prentice Hall PTR
Prentice-Hall, Inc.
Upper Saddle River, NJ 07458

Prentice Hall books are widely used by corporations and government agencies
for training, marketEditorial/productioning, and resale.

The publisher offers discounts on this book when ordered in bulk quantities.
For more information, contact: Corporate Sales Department, Phone: 800-382-3419;
Fax: 201-236-7141; E-mail: corpsales@prenhall.com; or write: Prentice Hall PTR,
Corp. Sales Dept., One Lake Street, Upper Saddle River, NJ 07458.

All products or services mentioned in this book are the trademarks or service marks of their
respective companies or organizations. Screen shots reprinted by permission from Microsoft
Corporation.

All rights reserved. No part of this book may be reproduced, in any form or by any means, without
permission in writing from the publisher.

Printed in the United States of America
10 9 8 7 6 5 4 3 2 1

ISBN   0-13-083068-2

Prentice-Hall International (UK) Limited, *London*
Prentice-Hall of Australia Pty. Limited, *Sydney*
Prentice-Hall Canada Inc., *Toronto*
Prentice-Hall Hispanoamericana, S.A., *Mexico*
Prentice-Hall of India Private Limited, *New Delhi*
Prentice-Hall of Japan, Inc., *Tokyo*
Pearson Education Asia Pte. Ltd.
Editora Prentice-Hall do Brasil, Ltda., *Rio de Janeiro*

For Karen Delaney
*Thanks for being everything one could
ask for in a big sister*

C O N T E N T S

Welcome and thanks! First, I need to say right up front that this book is not specifically about administering a Windows NT or Windows 2000 system (or any other version, for that matter). Although I talk about many administrative functions and describe the use of some of the tools, I do not go into detail about every program, what fields to fill in, what check boxes to mark, and so forth. If you are looking for a book to help you pass any of the Microsoft certification tests, you would be better off putting this book back on the shelf and looking elsewhere.

On the other hand, if you are concerned with the processes involved in the day-to-day operation of supporting users in a Windows NT environment, look no further. This is the book for you. As the title says, this book is about supporting Windows. Supporting users in a Windows environment (or any environment for that matter) is more than knowing which programs to start for particular administrative functions or knowing which buttons to push. There are so many aspects that go beyond clicking the right button in a specific program. Because of this, much of what I will discuss could be applied in any computer environment. In fact, much of it could be applied to any service-oriented field.

The material in this book is based on almost 15 years' experience in support and related fields. It began when I worked in a liaison office while in the U.S. Army. Dealing with border incidents, traffic accidents, and bar fights is very similar to doing computer tech support, although reinstalling is not an option when a tank plows into a farmer's barn.

Next, I worked in tech support for a major software vendor. When I picked up the phone, I often had no idea what the call was about, what kind of computer the person had, nor anything about the particular environment. Proper organization on the part of both the support department and each individual was vital for the survival of the company.

Currently, I am working for a manufacturer of industrial machinery. We have about 1000 users spread out all over the world, ranging from single-person offices running Windows 95 on a laptop to over 500 users in the company's headquarters, where I am. As a result, I have dealt with support issues in a wide range of environments.

I have found that aspects of each can be applied to the others, as the goal is always to either solve a particular problem or provide someone with a particular service. What I have done in this book is to address these issues in a way that particularly apply to support users in a Windows NT environment.

One of the key aspects of all of these jobs is providing the service the users need without its becoming a burden or unmanageable. In every case, you are often presented with conflicting priorities, none of which is better than the others. Sometimes, you need to base your decision on intuition or simply pick the lesser of two evils. Therefore, I have tried to present both sides of the issue, because what is the lesser evil in one company is not the same as somewhere else.

The book is broken into three parts. In Chapters 1–5, I talk about the framework. These are the issues that form the foundation of your information technology department (IT, or whatever it is called) and therefore is the basis of your user support. Chapters 6–13 are the processes you go through to support your users. Finally, Chapters 14–16 are details of what most people think of when they talk about "user support."

Once again, I need to say that this book does not cover every minute detail of the topics I discuss. That would take volumes and volumes of material. Besides, that isn't the goal of this book nor is it necessary. What I have done is to pick out those areas that I feel have the greatest impact on both the users and your ability to support them. There are also a few scattered places that have less of an overall impact, but ones I feel are often ignored, overlooked, or done inefficiently (at least in my opinion).

Some of you are going to look at the topics and wonder why I chose that one and not something else, if you think something else is more important. Well, the blunt answer is that it is a matter of personal opinion. I am basing these decisions on my own personal experience supporting users in a Windows NT environment as well as conversations with a number of people who do the same job in other companies. Unfortunately, I was not able to talk to someone in every possible situation. As a result, it is possible (if not probable) that there are certain aspects of your company where it might have been better to talk in more detail about something other than what I did. This is unavoidable without turning this book into an encyclopedia.

One place you might notice this is in the Chapter 5: Hardware Configuration. There are many other kinds of hardware you can connect to your machine that I didn't discuss. Some are very basic like floppies, mice, or modems. I had to weigh the number of issues that are involved, how often problems can crop up, and how significant these issues and problems are. The result is that I left off a little bit of hardware. I apologize to anyone who might have felt let out.

The same basic principle applies to the products I talk about. There are many, many, many more products on the market. Not just those in a particular category, but there are also a number of product categories that I did not talk about at all. Here again, I talked about those categories that have the largest impact on users.

On the other hand, there a few products that are in the category of "nice to have" but are not really essential for business. However, in these cases, I was so impressed with the products that I just had to mention them. Besides, the goal is to help your users work more efficiently, which I believe these products do.

There is also the level of the products I talked about. There are a number of products on the market that are designed more for large companies (i.e., "enterprise-grade"). I did not talk about products at this level for three main reasons. First, although these products generally work on a client–server basis, the basic functionality is same as single-seat products, which are intended for smaller companies. In discussing these products, I still provide you an overview of the available functionality. Second, it would not be very cost effective for a small company to buy one of the enterprise-level products, although there still is a great deal of benefit for large companies to buy stand-alone products. Finally, there is an issue of space, both in the book and on the accompanying CD. It would not have been possible to provide demo versions of more than a handful of these enterprise-level products. Instead, I was able to give you a wider range of products to look at.

Please keep in mind that time passes while writing a book and technology changes faster than many writers would like. From the time I started writing this book until the time I finished it, the computer industry went through many changes. Even between the time the book was finished and first hit the bookstores, the technology wouldhave changed. That's the nature of the business.

As a result, there are probably many aspects of the technology that I could not discuss simply because things changed too quickly. Because this book is not about "technologies," but more about "processes," I hope you will see that what's missing of the technology (perhaps) makes this book incomplete and not useless.

Acknowledgments

A book of this scope is not a one-person project. It is unbelievable how many people were so willing to help me with this project.

First, I would like to thank my loving wife, Anja, and two wonderful sons, Daniel and David, for doing without me once again.

Thanks to Tillman Dickson for giving me some great tips on how to make this a better book.

Of course, a great deal of thanks go out to my editor at Prentice Hall, Mike Meehan, and his executive assistant, Bart Blanken, for helping me get the things I needed, when I needed them.

A lot of thanks also go to Vince Janoski and the rest of the Prentice Hall production staff for getting this book together.

I would also like to thank the following people for providing me with materials and support for this project: Dave Anderson, creator of the PC Technology Web Site; Cindy Cooper of 3Com; Dr. Mudge of l0pht Heavy Industries; Willemijn Houtman of Microtek; Elain Smith of Quarterdeck Corporation; Alois Schalk and Edwin Cooke of Brother International; Bettina Jetter of MindJet LLC; Brain Holt and Emily Voisin of KeyStone Learning Systems; Chris Rogers of WRQ; Drew Praire of Advanced Micro Devices; Eric Brown and Kimberly Waldschmidt of Adaptec, Inc.; Frank Loehmann of StarDivision GmbH; Gail Wetmore and Jim Alexander of KnowledgeBroker, Inc Genevieve Halderman of Symantec Corporation; Jason Ferris of Micro2000, Inc.; Jeremy Cope and Lisa Edrieda of Adobe Systems Europe Limited; Jim Zimmermann of Windsor Techologies; Jobee Knight of Executive Software International; Laura Shook and Jeff Hurley of Cerious Software, Inc.; Lisa Woo-Bloxberg, formerly of Netscape Communications; Matthew Boucher and Colleen Cronin of Dragon Systems, Inc.; Nicole Milne of SyQuest Technology; Patrick Crisp of Caere Corporation; Paul Farr and Tim Davis of Network Associates; Reed Terry and Melissa Schmidt of LearnKey, Inc.; Alex Eckelberry of Mijenix; CorporationSarah Grossman of S&S Public Relations; Stuart Young of Transcender; Susanne Buti of Waggener Edstrom; Tammie Kocher of Viagrafix; Tyler Smith of KeyLabs; Tyson Heyn of Seagate; Dave Stockley, formerly of Brother International; Melissa Trotter of Micro House International; Mike Bradshaw of Connect Public Relations; David Walsh of NetObjects, Inc.; Melanie Sautner and Anette Weidner of Brodeur Kohtes & Klewes Komminkations GmbH; Monika Rhein of Brose Fahrzeugteil GmbH; Stefan Zapf of Zapf Creations.

I would also like to thank: Allaire Corporation; Ipswitch, Inc.; Corel Corporation; and Visio Corporation.

Plus, there are a number of people who helped out who either specifically wished to be anonymous—or I forgot to mention them: I am also grateful for your assistance. For those I forgot, I humbly apologize.

As usual, all the mistakes are mine. When you find any, please drop me a line and let me know. Even if you don't find any, I would still appreciate your dropping me a line and letting me know what you think.

Jim Mohr
Untersiemau, Germany
jimmo@jimmo.com

Windows
NT Basics

Introduction to Operating Systems

It is a common occurrence to find users who are not even aware of what operating system they are running. On occasion, you also find an administrator who may know the name of the operating system but nothing about its inner workings. For many, they have no time, as they are often clerical workers or other personnel who were reluctantly appointed to be the system administrator.

Microsoft has sold Windows NT as a system that is easy to use and to administer. Although this is true to some extent, few operating systems are easy to use or to administer when things go wrong. I know many administrators whose most common administrative tool is the big red switch at the back of the computer. They do not know enough about computers, let alone Windows NT, to do much else. Fortunately, this corrects the symptoms in most cases, but it does not solve the underlying problem.

Being able to run or work on a Windows NT system does not mean you have to understand the intricate details of how it functions internally. However, there are some operating system concepts that will help you and your users not only interact better with the system, but also serve as the foundation for many of the issues we're going to cover in this book.

In this chapter, we are going to go through the *basics* of what makes an operating system. First, we will talk about what an operating system is and why it is important. We are also going to address how the different components work and work together.

My goal is not to make you an expert on operating system concepts. Instead, I want to provide you with a starting point from which we can go on to other topics. If you want to go into more details about operating systems I would suggest *Modern Operating Systems* by Andrew Tanenbaum, published by Prentice Hall, and *Operating System Concepts* by Silberschatz, Peterson, and Galvin, published by Addison-Wesley. For an excellent examination of Windows internals, take a look at *Inside Windows NT* by Helen Custer, from Microsoft Press.

What is an Operating System?

In simple terms, the operating system is a manager. It manages all the resources available on a computer. These resources can be the hard disk, a printer, or the monitor screen. Even memory is a resource that needs to be managed. Within an operating system are the management functions that determine who gets to read data from the hard disk, what file is going to be printed next, what characters appear on the screen, and how much memory a certain program gets.

Once upon a time, there was no such thing as operating systems. The computers of 40 years ago ran one program at a time. The computer programmer would load the program he (they were almost universally male at that time) had written and run it. If there was a mistake that caused the program to stop sooner than expected, the programmer had to start over. Since there were many other people waiting for their turn to try their programs, it may have been several days before the first programmer got a another chance to run his deck of cards through the machine. Even if the program did run correctly, the programmer probably never got to work on the machine directly. The program (punched cards) was fed into the computer by an operator who then passed the printed output back to the programmer several hours later.

As technology advanced, many such programs, or jobs, were all loaded onto a single tape. This tape was then loaded and manipulated by another program, which was the ancestor of today's operating systems. This program would monitor the behavior of the running program, and if it misbehaved (crashed), the monitor could then immediately load and run another. Such programs were called (logically) monitors.

In the 1960s, technology and operating system theory advanced to the point that many different programs could be held in memory at once. This was the concept of "multiprogramming." If one program needed to wait for some external event, such as the tape to rewind to the right spot, another program could have access to the CPU. This improved performance dramatically and allowed the CPU to be busy almost 100% of the time.

By the end of the 1960s, something wonderful happened: UNIX was born. It began as a one-man project designed by Ken Thompson of Bell Labs and has grown to become the most widely used operating system. In the time since UNIX was first developed, it has gone through many different generations and even mutations. Some differ substantially from the original version, like BSD (Berkeley Software Distribution) UNIX or Linux. Others still contain major portions that are based on the original source code. (A friend of mine described UNIX as the only operating system where you can throw the manual onto the keyboard and get a real command.)

In the early 1990s, Microsoft introduced its new operating system, Windows NT. Windows NT is one of many operating systems, such as DOS, VMS, OS/360, and CP/M. It performs many of the same tasks in very similar ways. It is the manager and administrator of all of the system resources and facilities. Without it, nothing works. Despite this, most users can go on indefinitely without knowing even which operating system they are on, let alone the basics of how an operating system works.

For example, if you own a car, you don't really need to know the details of the internal combustion engine to understand that this is what makes the car move forward. You don't need to know the principles of hydraulics to understand what isn't happening if pressing the brake pedal has no effect.

An operating system is like that. You can work productively for years without even knowing what operating system you're running on, let alone how it works. Sometimes things go wrong. In many companies, you are given a number to call when problems arise, you tell them what happened, and they deal with it.

If the computer is not backed up within a few minutes, you get upset and call back, demanding to know when "that damned thing will be up and running again." When the technician (or whoever has to deal with the problem) tries to explain what is happening and what is being done to correct the problem, the response is usually along the lines of, "Well, yeah, I need it backed up now."

The problem is that many people heard the explanation, but didn't understand it. It is not unexpected for people to not want to acknowledge they didn't understand the answer. Instead, they try to deflect the other person's attention away from that fact. Had they understood the explanation, they would be in a better position to understand what the technician was doing, and that the problem was actually being worked on.

By having a working knowledge of the principles of an operating system, you are in a better position to understand not only the problems that can arise, but also what steps are necessary to find a solution. There is also the attitude that you have a better relationship with things you understand. Like in a car, if you see steam pouring out from under the hood, you know that you need to add water. This logic also applies to an operating system.

In this section, that's what we're going to talk about. What goes into an operating system and what does it do? How does it do it? How are you, the user, affected by all this?

Because of advances in both hardware design and performance, computers are able to process increasingly larger amounts of information. The speed at which computer transactions occur is often talked about in terms of billionths of a second. Because of this speed, today's computers can give the appearance of doing many things simultaneously by actually switching back and forth between each task extremely fast. This is the concept of multitasking. That is, the computer is working on multiple tasks at the same time.

Another function of the operating system is to keep track of what each program is doing. That is, the operating system needs to keep track of whose program, or task, is currently writing its file to the printer, which program needs to read a certain spot on the hard disk, etc. This is the concept of *multi-user,* as multiple users have access to the same resources.

Processes

One of the basic concepts of an operating system is the process. If we think of the program as the file stored on the hard disk or floppy and the process as the program stored in memory, we can better understand the difference between a *program* and a *process*. Although these two terms are often interchanged or even misused in "casual" conversation, the difference is very important for issues that we talk about later.

A process is more than just a program. Especially in a multitasking operating system such as Windows NT, there is much more to consider. Each program has a set of data that it uses to do what it requires. Often this data is not part of the program. For example, if you are using a text editor, the file you are editing is not part of the program on disk but is part of the process in memory. If someone else were to be using the same editor, both of you would be using the same program. However, each of you would have a different process in memory. How this looks graphically is seen in Figure 1–1.

Although Windows NT is not a multi-user operating system like UNIX, many different users can still access resources on the system at the same time, or the system can be doing things on their behalf. In other words, the users all have processes that are in memory at the same time. The system needs to keep track of what user is running what process, which terminal the process is being run on, and what other resources the process has (such as open files). All of this is part of the process, or task, as it is often called in Windows NT.

When you log on, you might want to start MS Word. As you are writing your letter, you notice you need information out of a database, so you start up MS Access. The database is large, so it takes awhile to find what you

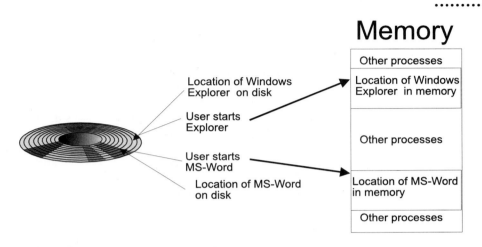

FIGURE 1–1   From program to process.

want, so you go back to the letter. As you continue to edit, you delete words, insert new lines, sort your text, and write it occasionally to the disk. All this time, the database search is continuing. Someone else on the system may be accessing a file in a directory you share. Another is using a printer on your system. No one seems to notice that there are other people using the system. For them, the processor is working for them alone. Well, that's the way it seems.

As I am writing this sentence, the operating system needs to know whether the keys I press are part of the text or are commands I want to pass to the editor. Each keystroke needs to be interpreted. Despite the fact that I can clip along at about 30 words per minute, the central processing unit (CPU) is spending approximately 95% of its time doing nothing.

The reason for this is that for a computer, the time between successive keystrokes is an eternity. Let's take my Intel Pentium, running at a clock speed of 133 MHz as an example. The clock speed of 133 MHz means that there are 133 million(!) clock cycles per second. Because the Pentium gets close to one instruction per clock cycle, this means that within 1 second, the CPU can execute close to 133 million instructions! No wonder it is spending most of its time idle. (Note: This is an oversimplification of what is actually happening.)

A single computer instruction doesn't really do much by itself. However, being able to do 133 million little things in 1 second allows the CPU to give the user an impression of being the only person on the system. Actually, it is simply switching between the different processes so fast that no one is aware of it happening.

Compare this with an operating system such as standard Windows (not Windows NT). The program will hang on to the CPU until it decides to give it up. An ill-behaved program can hold on to the CPU forever. This is the cause of many system hangs, because nothing, not even the operating system itself, can gain control of the CPU.

Depending on the load of the system (how busy it is) a process may get several time-slices per second. However, after it has run through its time-slice, the operating system checks to see if some other process needs a turn. If so, that process gets to run for a time-slice, and then it's someone else's turn: maybe the first process, maybe a new one.

As your process is running, it will be given full use of the CPU for the entire time-slice unless one of three things happens. Your process may need to wait for some event. For example, the editor I am writing this text in is waiting for me to type in characters. I said that I type about 30 words per minute, so if we assume an average of 6 letters per word, that's 180 characters per minute or 3 characters per second. That means that on the average, a character is pressed once every 1/3 of a second. Assuming a time-slice is 1/100th of a second, over 30 processes can have a turn on the CPU between each keystroke! Rather than tying everything up, the program waits until the next key is pressed. It puts itself to sleep until it is awakened by some external event, such as my pressing a key. Compare this with a "busy loop," where the process keeps checking for a key being pressed.

File Access

When I want to write to the disk to save my file, it may appear that it happens instantaneously, but like the "complete-use-of-the-CPU myth," this is only appearance. The system will gather requests to write to or read from the disk and do it in chunks. This is much more efficient than satisfying everyone's request when they ask for it.

Gathering up requests and accessing the disk at once has another advantage. Often-times, for example, the data that was just written are needed again in a database application. If the system were to write everything to the disk immediately, you would have to perform another read to get back that same data. Instead, the system holds that data in a special buffer; it "caches" that data in the buffer.

If a file is being written to or read from, the system first checks the cache. If on a read, it finds what it's looking for in that buffer, it has just saved itself a trip to the disk. Because the cache is in memory, it is substantially faster to read from memory than from the disk. Writes are normally written to the buffer cache, which is then written out in larger chunks. If the data being written already exists in the buffer cache, it is overwritten.

When your process is running and you make a request to read from the hard disk, you can't do anything until you have completed the write to the disk. If you haven't completed your time-slice yet, it would be a waste not to let someone else have a turn. That's exactly what the system does. If you decided you need access to some resource that the system cannot immediately give to you, you are "put to sleep" to wait. It is said that you are put to sleep waiting on an event: the event being the disk access. This is the second case where you may not get your full time on the CPU.

The third way that you might not get your full time-slice is the result of an external event as well. If a device (such as a keyboard, the clock, hard disk, etc.) needs to communicate with the operating system, it signals this need through the use of an interrupt (which behaves somewhat like an alarm). When an interrupt is generated, the CPU itself will stop execution of the process and immediately start executing a routine in the operating system to handle interrupts. Once the operating system has satisfied this interrupt, it returns to its regularly scheduled process. (Note: Things are much more complicated than that. The "priority" of both the interrupt and the process are factors here.)

As I mentioned earlier, there are certain things that the operating system keeps track of when a process is running. The information the operating system is keeping track of is referred to as the process's context. This might be the terminal you are running on or what files you have open. The context even includes the internal state of the CPU; that is, what the content of each register is.

What happens when a process's time-slice has run out or for some other reason another process gets to run? Well, if things go right (and they usually do), eventually that process gets another turn. However, to do things right, the process must be allowed to return to the exact place where it left off. Any difference could result in disaster.

You may have heard of the classic banking problem of deducting an amount from an account. If the process returned to the balance that preceded the deduction, it would have deducted it twice. If the deduction hadn't yet been made, but the process started up again at a point after it would have made the deduction, it appears as if the deduction was made. Good for you, not so good for the bank. Therefore, everything must be put back the way it was.

The processors used by Windows NT have built-in capabilities to manage both multiple users and multiple tasks. We will get into the details of this in later chapters. For now, just be aware of the fact that the CPU assists the operating system in managing users and processes.

In addition to user processes, such as Windows Explorer, word processors, and databases, there are system processes that are running. These are processes that were started by the system. They deal with security, mail, printing, and other tasks that we take for granted. In principle, both user and system processes are identical. However, system processes can run at much higher priorities and therefore run more often than user processes.

I have talked to customers who have complained about the system grinding to a halt although they had nothing running. The misconception is that because they didn't "see" any process running, it must not be taking up any resources. (Out of sight, out of mind.) The issue here is that, even though the process is running in the background and you can't see it, it still behaves like any other process, taking up memory and other resources.

Windows NT Internals

Windows NT is provided in two versions: Workstation and Server. For most users, there is no noticeable functionality difference; rather, the differences lay in areas that are of more interest to administrators. Windows NT workstations can function either as clients within a network consisting of one or more Window NT servers, or they can be part of a peer-to-peer network, such as a workgroup. Servers provide additional functionality, such as maintaining domain-wide user and security information as well as providing authentication services. In addition, the Windows NT Server allows unlimited connection, whereas the Workstation is limited to 10.

Although a Windows NT Server can be configured in "stand-alone" mode to function within a workgroup, it can best show its functionality as part of a domain. A Workgroup is a logical collection of machines that share resources. Normally, workgroups are created by the computers within a single department or within a company, if it is small enough. Each computer can make available to as well as share resources from all the other computers. In essence, all computers are of equal status. Within a company, different departments may be workgroups and each may have a unique name to identify the workgroup. Because each computer is independent, each is responsible for authenticating users itself.

Like a workgroup, a domain is a logical collection of computers that share resources. One of the key differences is that there is a single server that is responsible for managing security and other user-related information for the domain. This server allows logon validation, by which a user logs into the domain and not into just a single computer.

Microsoft has called Windows NT a "multiple-personality operating system," as it was designed to support more than one application programming interface (API). This makes it is easier to provide emulation for older OS environments as well as the ability to more easily add new interfaces without requiring major changes to the system. The technique that Windows NT uses is called a "microkernel" and was influenced by the Mach microkernel developed at Carnegie Mellon University. (The *kernel* is the central part of operating system.)

Windows was designed as a module operating system. This has advantages in both the development and actual operation of the system. A substantial number of operating system components were implemented as modules and as such have well-defined interfaces that other modules can easily use. From a design standpoint, this enables new components to be added to the system without affecting the existing modules. For example, a new file system driver could be added without affecting the other file system drivers.

In addition, the total amount of code needed is smaller. Many functions need only be implemented once and are shared by the other modules. If changes are made to that function, only one set of instructions needs to be changed. Provided it maintains the same interface, the other modules are not even aware of the change.

The other major advantage is when the system is running. Because certain code is shared, it does not need to be loaded more than once. First, that saves memory, as there are not multiple copies of certain functions in memory. Second, it saves time, as the functions do not need to be loaded repeatedly.

Although all versions of Windows support multitasking, the major difference is that Windows 3.1x, along with Windows 95 and Windows 98, implement *non-preemptive* or *cooperative* multitasking, which means that each program must *voluntarily* give up control of the processor to allow other programs a chance to run. If a program fails to voluntarily yield control to other programs, the system will stop responding to user actions and will appear to be hung. Windows NT resolves this problem by implementing the same type of preemptive multitasking as had already been available on UNIX machines for many years.

The operating system fully controls which program runs at any given time and for how long. Each program is allowed to run for its time-slice, and when the time-slice expires, someone else has a turn. Windows NT saves the necessary information about the executing program's state to allow it to continue where it left off.

In addition to being a preemptive multitasking operating system, Windows NT is also *multithreaded*. A thread is often referred to as a "lightweight" process. In some aspects, a thread (or lightweight process) is the same as a normal process. In both cases, the processor state is maintained, along with both a user and a kernel stack. (The stack is an area of memory used to keep track of which function have been called, as well as the values of different variables.)

One key difference is that threads do not have their own address space or access tokens. Instead, all threads of a process share the same memory, access tokens, resource handles, and others. This simplifies programming in one regard, because the data can be shared without any new data structures. However, it is up to the programmer to ensure that the threads do not interfere with one another—which makes the programming trickier.

One aspect of this is the very nature of threads. They have no separate data space and therefore have the same access rights to the data and other parts of memory of other threads of the same process. This makes it easier to share data but also makes it easier to corrupt it.

To avoid this problem, programmers need to work with what are called "critical sections" of code. When one thread is in a critical section, it needs to ensure that no other thread can access the data in any way. It is not sufficient to simply say that other threads cannot change the data, as they may expect the data to be in one state when the thread in the critical section changes it: In other words, access to a object must be *synchronized* between threads. Windows NT accomplishes this all through the use of *synchronization objects*.

Windows NT actually uses different kinds of synchronization objects depending on the needs of the programmer. In addition, the testing and setting of the synchronization object can be done automatically; that is, in one uninterruptible step. If a thread is waiting for a synchronization object, it will be "suspended" until the other thread has completed its critical section. However, it is up to the programmer to create the synchronization object when the program is initialized.

Because no additional structures are needed, threads have an advantage over normal processes. No time needs to be spent creating the new structures to be able to share this information; it simply is available. Also, threads do not have their own address space and are therefore easier (and quicker) to create.

As one would expect, threads are treated like objects, just as processes are. Both processes and threads are managed by the Process Manager. The function of the Process Manager includes creation, management, and destruction of processes and threads.

Although you may not realize it, you use threads with a large number of applications. The most common example is printing a document while you continue to use your word processor. Although you could pass the file (data) to another process, using threads makes this much more efficient for the reasons just discussed.

Like processes, only one thread can use the processor at any given time. However, what happens if you have multiple processors? Windows NT, like many UNIX dialects, has a built-in capability to use multiple processors. If you do have multiple processors, different processes can be running on each processor at any given time. Taking this one step further, different threads could be on different processes at the same time, thus significantly speeding up the execution of your program.

Threads (and therefore processes) under Windows NT operate in a number of different states. The three most significant are running, ready, and waiting. When a thread is running, it is currently using the processor. In a single processor environment, only a single process can be in the running state at any given time.

Ready means that the thread is ready to run. This means that it has all the resources it needs and is just waiting for its turn. As with UNIX, the thread that runs is determined by a scheduling algorithm which is based on the original priority of the process and therefore each respective thread thread.

When a thread is waiting, there is some event that needs to occur before it can be ready again. As with UNIX, that event can be anything from waiting for a key to be pressed to waiting for a synchronization object to become unlocked.

One aspect of the modular design of Windows NT shows itself in the kernel, which provides the means for a certain activity but does not itself decide when these activities should take place. In other words, it provides the mechanism to do some task but not when it occurs: This is accomplished through the various *kernel objects*, two of which are the process object and the thread object. These are very similar objects, but they *are* different. Therefore, they must be treated differently by the kernel.

Task Priorities and Resources

You can see what tasks are currently running on your system as well as their priorities by using the Task Manager. Either right-click the taskbar and select the "Task Manager" entry or press CTRL-ALT-DEL and click the "Task Manager" button. When the window appears, click the "Processes" tab. This will show something similar to Figure 1–2.

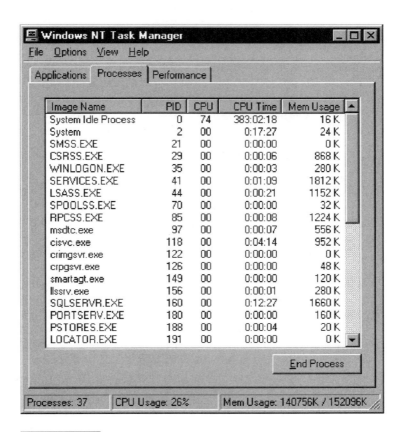

FIGURE 1–2   Task Manager processes.

Name: the program that was started to create the process

PID: the process ID

CPU %: average CPU usage for that process

CPU Time: total amount of time that process has been on the CPU since the system started

Memory: amount of virtual memory that the processes is currently using

Under the view menu, you can select addition columns to display. I rarely have used any other ones, and a discussion of them goes beyond the scope of this book. However, sometimes I include the Base Priority column to see the priorities of the various processes. You can change a process's priority by right-clicking the process name and selecting the appropriate menu entry. Be extremely careful with this, as you can cause major problems if the wrong processes have too high a priority.

At the bottom of the screen you see the total number of processes, the average CPU usage (not including the idle process and the memory usage). The first value is the total memory usage followed by the maximum available memory.

Environment Subsystems

One of the key design goals of Windows NT was compatibility with existing applications. If Microsoft had decided to ignore this issue and concentrate solely on performance, most (if not all) of the existing Windows and DOS applications would have become useless. Because this would have meant purchasing new applications, business might have opted to move completely away from Microsoft.

While still improving performance considerably, Microsoft was able to accomplish the goal of compatibility by implementing a set of operating system "environment emulators." These are the so-called environment subsystems that form the intermediate layer between user applications and the core of the NT operating system. Because of module design of the operating system, Windows NT is capable of supporting Windows/DOS, OS/2, and POSIX applications.

The Windows NT environment subsystems run as user-mode processes. In addition, the environment subsystems are also multithreaded. Many of the functionality provided by the environment subsystems are only available through system-level processes on other operating systems. On the one hand, this provides an additional level of protection, as less of the system is running in the highest privileged mode. However, in order for Windows NT to access the lower-level function, a context switch may be necessary. Due to the time involved to make the context switch, performance *may* suffer.

These are also responsible for defining the syntax used for device and file names that the calling process uses. For example, the Win32 subsystem uses the "MS-DOS-style" syntax (C:\dir\filename.typ), whereas the POSIX subsystem uses file name syntax similar to that of UNIX (/dir/filename). The

MS-DOS-style device names (like A:, B:, C:) are actually symbolic links within the Windows NT I/O system. Windows NT actually uses names like "Floppy0" or "Disk1" to access devices.

Essentially, each program is bound to a *single* environment subsystem. Therefore, you cannot mix calls between subsystems. For example, a POSIX program cannot call services defined by the Win32 subsystem or vice versa. This presents problems when one subsystem provides features that another needs.

The interaction between the application at the appropriate environment subsystems is like a client-server system. Here, the client is the user application, and the server is the environment subsystems. When a user application wishes to utilize some low-level aspect of the system (i.e., the hardware), two things can happen. If the call is mapped directly to a part of the operating system called the Windows NT Executive service, then it is done so. However, if the call needs to be serviced by an environment subsystem, then the appropriate environment subsystem (i.e., Win32, POSIX) is called.

One example where the *same* environment subsystem is used is when a new process is created. Typically, a process will create another process that uses the same environment subsystem. For example, a POSIX program will normally create another POSIX program. Because the POSIX environment subsystem needs to be aware of all POSIX processes, it is called to create a new one.

On the other hand, *only* the Win32 subsystem can write to the screen. Therefore, all processes must call the Win32 environment subsystem to process screen I/O. In both cases, a context switch occurs that allows the appropriate subsystem to run. This obviously decreases the performance of the system. (A context switch is the process by which the system takes one taks off the CPU to let another one run.)

Note that this problem does not exist in most UNIX versions. When a process is accessing the hardware, it is still running within its own context. Granted, it may be running in kernel mode, but the system is still running the original process. To solve this problem, Windows NT uses the technique of *shared memory* (also available in UNIX for years). This is a portion of memory that is accessible to both the application and the appropriate environment subsystem. Therefore, the system does not spend time copying the data that need to be accessed by both the application and the environment subsystem.

Another benefit is achieved by changing the process scheduler slightly. Remember that threads are an integral part of Windows NT. The client thread of the applications only needs to call the server thread in the environment subsystem. Because no new process is created, the process scheduler does not need to schedule asnew process.

Remember that the Win32 subsystem controls the display. Any time an application wants to write to the display, the Win32 subsystem needs to be called. Instead of calling the Win32 for every screen update, all graphics calls are buffered. For example, if you wanted to create a new window of a particular size, location, background color, and so forth, each of these would require different calls. By waiting and "batching" the calls together, you can save time.

MS-DOS and 16-bit Windows programs actually run as a Win32 process. The program that creates the virtual MS-DOS environments for these to run in (NTVDM.EXE) is a Win32 program. A virtual DOS machine (VDM) is created for the program, so it thinks that it is running on a machine by itself. However, the virtual machine is a normal 32-bit Windows NT process and is subject to the same rules of preemptive multitasking as is other programs. However, this only applies to MS-DOS programs. By default, Windows applications share a common virtual machine and are still subjected to nonpreemptive multitasking. However, each application can be configured to run within its *own* virtual machine. When calls are made to the 16-bit Windows API, they are translated into 32-bit calls so that they can be executed by the Win32 subsystem.

Essentially, a VDM emulates an 80286 machine running DOS. MS-DOS applications normally own the machine and can do anything they want, including directly accessing the hardware and even overwriting memory used by the system. Therefore, an extra level of protection is need. For this reason, Windows NT implemented the VDM mechanism to protect the system from errant MS-DOS applications. When a DOS program running in a VMD "misbehaves," the worse that can happen is that it crashes its own VDM. Other processes are not affected.

Although the MS-DOS application tries to access hardware directly, it cannot: Windows NT prevents this. As with other aspects, Windows NT provides a set of virtual device drivers. Any attempt to access the hardware must pass through this virtual machine. The virtual machine is then able to intercept the calls and process them with appropriate Windows NT virtual device drivers.

To run 16-bit Windows applications, NT uses a VDM that contains an extra software layer called the Win16 on Win32 (WOW) layer. Although the VDM for Windows shares some of the code for MS-DOS VDM, all Windows applications share the same VDM. The reason this is done is to simulate the environment that 16-bit Windows applications run in. Because Windows applications might want to communicate with one another, a single VDM is used. Each 16-bit application runs as a thread of the VDM; however, the WOW layers ensures that only one of these threads is running at any given time.

Along with the benefits that the single VDM brings, it also brings disadvantages. Even though it is running as a thread of the VDM, a 16-bit application can completely take over the VDM, just like it can take over a regular Windows machine. Because it is running as a thread of the VDM, it has access to all the memory of the VDM and therefore to the other 16-bit applications (which run in that same VDM), just as with a regular Windows machine. (Windows NT will multi-task the VDM, just like any other process.)

NT Executive

One of the most important aspects of Windows NT is the NT Executive. Here lies most of the functions that we normally call the "operating system." This includes memory and process management, preemptive multitasking, I/O, security, and interprocess communication. Each component of NT Executive provides a set of functions, referred to as "native services" or "executive services." These services form the API to NT Executive. Application programs on Windows NT do not call NT Executive, but rather "system service" calls go through another layer of code that maps the user interface to the appropriate Windows NT Executive service.

NT Executive sits on top of the kernel and the Hardware Abstraction Layer (HAL), which then provides the lowest level functions, such as directly accessing the hardware. Because of this separation, the majority of NT Executive code can be hardware independent and therefore easily ported to different hardware platforms.

The HAL is the lowest level of the Windows NT operating system (see Figure 1–3). It is said to "virtualize" hardware interfaces, as the actual interface to the hardware is hidden from the programmer. It is no longer necessary to know the details of a specific type of hardware, but rather just the interface provided by the HAL. This allows Windows NT to be portable from one hardware platform to another.

The HAL is a kernel-mode set of hardware access and manipulating routines. Many are provided by Microsoft, but due to the modular nature of Windows NT, these can also be provided by the hardware manufacturer. The HAL is part of NT Executive and lies at the lowest level between the hardware and the rest of the operating system.

The reason it is called such is that the HAL hides, or *abstracts*, the details of the hardware behind standard entry points. As a result, different platforms and architectures look alike to the operating system and therefore to the programmer. Because the programming interface is the same, much of

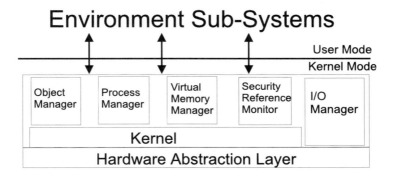

FIGURE 1–3 The layers of Windows NT.

the code is the same between hardware platforms. Hardware-dependent details, such as I/O interfaces, interrupt controllers, and multiprocessor communication mechanisms become hidden and become less of a concern to the programmers.

This is also a disadvantage to the system administrator, as there is no longer a direct connection to the hardware. Should an application have difficulty accessing a specific piece of hardware, it is not possible to access the hardware without going through the programming interface. Although it may make programming easier, it does make troubleshooting hardware more difficult.

Windows NT does not provide compatibility with device drivers written for MS-DOS or Windows. This does not mean that specific hardware will not work with Windows NT, but rather that a new driver needs to be specifically written for NT. Because the device driver architecture is modular in design, device drivers can be broken up into layers of smaller independent device drivers. Parts of a driver that provide common functionality need only be written once. This code can then be shared among various components, making the kernel smaller.

Because NT Executive runs in kernel mode, it has *complete* access to all the system resources, including all of memory, and can therefore issue any machine instructions that it wants. All other code, including that of the environment subsystems, runs in user mode and can only access memory that NT Executive has given it permission to access.

When a subsystem calls an executive service, the call is "trapped" and sent to NT Executive. The processor is switched from user to kernel mode so that NT Executive can issue the instructions and access the memory it needs to execute the requested service. Once the service is complete, NT Executive switches the processor back to user mode and returns control to the subsystem.

Note that the kernel is not an independent module but is part of NT Executive. In addition to managing the thread scheduling, the kernel is responsible for many other aspects of the system. The kernel is also treated specially, in that it can neither be paged to disk nor can it be preempted. So that the kernel does not take up too much space, it is made as compact as possible. Also, to keep it from using up too much CPU time, it is made as fast as possible.

Memory Management

Virtual memory on a Windows NT machine is handled by a component of NT Executive called the virtual memory manager. As with other operating systems, the job of the virtual memory manager is to manage the relationship between the memory seen by the application (virtual memory) and the memory seen by the system (physical memory). Because Windows NT is intended to run multiple processes simultaneously, the virtual memory manager must not only protect processes from one another, but it must also protect the operating system from the applications. In addition, the virtual memory manager was designed to be able to run on different hardware platforms, regardless of what memory addressing scheme they use.

One of the major drawbacks of MS-DOS and Windows 3.1x are that they are 16-bit systems. As a result, they need to utilize a *segmented memory model*. This means memory is accessed in small, 64-KB chunks called *segments*. Windows NT followed the lead of UNIX vendors by switching to a *flat memory model*. This means that memory is seen as one large chunk. As of this writing, Windows NT is still a 32-bit operating system, meaning that it can access 2^{32} or 4 GBs of memory. (Note that Microsoft has promised a 64-bit version of Windows NT sometime after the initial release of Windows 2000).

Both the Intel and Alpha family of processors (the only ones that Windows NT is currently being developed for) provide certain protections for the system. When these protections are enabled, the CPU will prevent processes from accessing memory they are not allowed to. Within the 4-GB flat memory, the upper 2 GBs can only be accessed by code within NT Executive. Because this is also where NT Executive resides, it is safe from all processes running in user mode.

Separate tables are maintained for each process, which translates the virtual memory that the process sees to the physical memory that the system sees. The virtual memory manager is responsible for ensuring that the translation is done correctly. By accessing physical memory only through these tables, the virtual memory manager can ensure that two processes do not have access to each other's physical memory.

What happens when two processes *need* to access the same physical memory? There are methods of sharing data between running processes. The most obvious way is a file on the disk somewhere. However, this requires going through the file system and hardware drivers as well as locating some mechanism to tell the other process where the memory lies. The processes can send signals to one another, but these are extremely limited. The best alternative in many cases is to simply share a region of memory.

The virtual memory manager takes care of this by changing the appropriate entries in the address translation tables so that both processes point to the same location. In addition, the NT Executive provides *synchronization objects* that the two processes use to ensure that they both get the memory location that they need.

When physical memory runs low, it is the job of the virtual memory manager to free up space. Memory is accessed in units called *pages*. Although different page sizes are possible on some platforms, Windows NT universally uses a 4-KB page. This helps to make the porting to other operating system easier, as the Intel i386 family also uses 4-KB pages.

Windows NT uses a temporary storage area on the hard disk to store pages of processes that are currently not running. This is called *page file* (sometimes referred to as a paging file). Because both physical memory and the page file are accessed in 4-KB pages, copying files back and forth is fairly easy.

Changing the Size of the Paging File

Although there is no real substitute for RAM, you can often increase performance by increasing the amount of virtual memory available. This is done by increasing the size of the paging file. Start the System applet in the Control Panel and Select the "Performance" tab. This brings you to Figure 1—4.

In the top part you see a list of only the *local* drives, as you cannot put a paging file on a network drive. By selecting the appropriate drive letter, you can set the minimum and maximum size of your paging file.

If you have multiple hard disks, you can improve performance by having a paging file on each drive. Even though the system is reading from one drive, it can make a request of the second drive.(Note that this only works for SCSI drives, not (E)IDE.)

You can also increase speed by creating a paging file that does not change its size; that is, where the minimum and maximum are the same size. To increase speed even further, this should be done on a partition that has very little fragmentation. You can completely move the paging file to a different partition, defragment the first drive, then move the paging file back. The system will then create a single file that is unfragmented.

Note that you can also change the maximum size of your registry here as well.

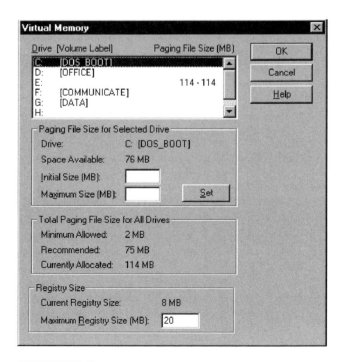

FIGURE 1—4   Virtual memory configuration.

When pages are copied from memory to a page file, the address translation tables for the process are marked to indicate that these pages are not in physical memory. When an application attempts to access a page that is not in physical memory, a fault occurs. The virtual memory manager needs to determine if the fault was generated because the page was never in physical memory or was copied to the swap file. Once the page is copied back into physical memory, the address translation table is marked to indicate its new location.

Windows NT uses another mechanism from UNIX to improve efficiency: *mapped file I/O*. In essence, this is a process by which a file on the file system is treated as if located in memory. All or part of the file is mapped to a range of virtual memory within the process. The process can then access the file as if located in memory and does not have to go through the same process to open, access, and then close the file.

Conceptually, there is nothing different between memory-mapped I/O and the use of the paging file. In both cases, a file on the hard disk is treated as an extension of virtual memory. For this reason, mapped file I/O is managed by the Windows NT virtual memory manager.

This process can come in handy when the size of the file to be read is larger than the size of physical RAM and the paging file combined. Normally, the system would not be able to load the entire file. Instead, only those pieces that are currently being used are loaded into memory. The system then loads or writes pages just as it would with the paging file.

When deciding what pages to pull into memory, the virtual memory manager uses three policies. The first is called "fetch." This occurs when a page is first accessed. In general, the system will wait until an attempt is made to access a page before it is loaded into memory. Based on the principle of locality, it is likely that the next page (or pages) will be needed as well. Windows NT takes advantage of this principle by loading several pages at once. Because it is likely that subsequent pages will be needed, why wait?

The term "placement" refers to the process by which the virtual memory manager stores a page in physical RAM by loading each page into the first free page in RAM. There is no need to store pages in contiguous locations in RAM. Because there is no physical movement, accessing memory locations is the same no matter where the memory is located. The physical location is given to the address decode circuits on the motherboard, and the contents are returned. Although most modern computers also take advantage of the locality principle and return more than what is actually requested (i.e., pipeline burst cache), the speed at which the memory is accessed is independent of the physical location.

If there is no more room in physical memory, (i.e., no free pages) the virtual memory manager has to make room. It uses its "replacement policy" to determine what pages should be replaced. Windows NT uses a very simple replacement scheme: first-in, first out (FIFO). This means that pages that have been in memory the longest (they were the first ones in) are replaced with newer pages (they are the first to be paged out). This has the disadvantage that pages that are pulled in first, but used regularly have a greater chance of being paged out.

The Kernel's Dispatcher and Process Scheduling

The Windows NT dispatcher schedules threads to run on the processor. Windows NT uses a 32-level priority (0–31), where the higher the number, the higher the priority. Only processes that are ready to run can be scheduled to run, even if they should have the highest priority. For example, if a process were waiting for data from the hard disk, it would not be scheduled to run.

When a process or thread starts up, it has a specific "base priority." The dispatcher adjusts the priority based on the thread's behavior. Interactive threads, such as a word processor, spend a lot of their time waiting (i.e., for actions such as key presses.) Because they regularly give up their time on the CPU voluntarily, the dispatcher may return the favor by increasing their priority. Therefore, when the user finally does press a key, it is responded to almost immediately. Threads that do not give up the processor voluntarily (e.g., large database queries) may have their priority decreased. Which thread actually gets to run is very straightforward: The process that is ready to run and has the highest priority will run.

Certain threads are referred to as "real-time" threads, and they run at the same priority for the entire time they are running. Real-time threads will have a priority between 16 and 31, which means they are on the upper half (highest priority) of the scale. These are normally used to control or monitor systems that require responses and precisely measured times.

In contrast with real-time threads, there are "variable priority" threads. As their name implies, their priority can change while they are running. While the thread is running, the dispatcher can change a variable thread priority by up to two levels above or below its base priority.

The hardware clock generates an interrupt at regular intervals. The kernel dispatcher is called and schedules the thread with the highest priority. However, it is possible that the process that was running gets to continue running. This happens frequently, when a thread is running at high priority and all of the other threads are running at a lower priority. Even if the system were to decrease the priority of that thread, it would continue at that priority for as long as it is active.

Changing Default Task Priority

Windows NT does allow you to adjust the priority, although this ability is very limited compared with that of UNIX. Changing the default priority is done from the system applet in the Control Panel under the tab "Performance" (see Figure 1–5).

Here you can set the "boost" that foreground (active) applications get. The Windows NT default is that foreground applications get the highest priority, which means that their base priority is increased by two levels.

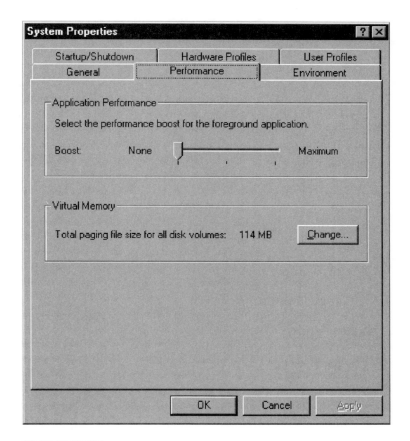

FIGURE 1-5   Performance in system applets.

Although this type of scheduling is simple to program and does well in many cases, it does have limitations. Obviously, a thread with a real-time priority could "hog" the CPU so that no other process can run. This might be fine in some circumstances, but a programmer could decide to put a thread at a real-time priority, even though it doesn't need one. The result is that this single thread could take complete control over the system. The priority calculation is much more complicated; however, the intent is to allow everyone their fair share of time on the CPU.

Input/Output

Accessing peripheral devices was one area that the Window NT designers really had to clean house. The routines used to access hardware in MS-DOS, and therefore Windows 3.x, had some *major* limitations. Written in 80 x 806 assembly language, they are not portable at all. Assembly language often makes for faster code, but each time it is brought to a new hardware platform, the code must be rewritten from scratch.

Another problem is the sheer age of the MS-DOS drivers. At the time they were written, most programmers were not thinking along the lines of objects or modules. As a result, there is a lot of repetitive code.

If moved to the Windows NT environment, these drivers would be completely inappropriate. In addition to the problems that existed under DOS, these drivers are not designed to work in a multitasking environment. Windows had to do a lot of work to get these drivers to function correctly, even in the nonpreemptive environment of Windows 3.x. Needless to say, these types of drivers would be totally useless in the multiprocessor environment of Windows NT.

As you may have guessed by now, I/O under Windows NT is composed of several modules. These are coordinated by the *I/O manager,* which is part of NT Executive. One of the primary functions of the I/O manager is to manage communication between the various drivers. To do this properly, each driver must maintain the standard interface that the I/O manager used, no matter what physical device is being accessed.

At the lowest level are the device drivers that actually talk to the hardware. These need to know about all of the physical characteristics of the hardware. In few cases the code can be shared, so there is a driver for each device. Not only for each *kind* of device, but a different device driver for each manufacturer and sometimes even for each model.

Above the device drivers are higher level drivers that applications are more likely to use to interface with user applications. When they access hardware, what they are actually doing is passing a *logical* request. The I/O manager then processes the request and passes it to the appropriate physical device driver.

As previously discussed, Windows NT relies heavily on modular and layered drivers. The Windows NT I/O subsystem also takes advantage of the benefits of this scheme. Within the I/O subsystem, however, the advantages of this modular approach become even more apparent. Because changes in one module rarely have an impact on other modules, new or updated hardware drivers can be implemented without affecting the other layers. A good example of this would be the development of a new kind of hard disk that requires a new driver. The file system driver does not need to be changed; only the driver directly accessing the hardware does. Another example would be a situation such as: I have two partitions, one formatted as the DOS File Allocation Table (FAT) and the other as the NT File System (NTFS). Both the FAT file system and the NTFS must access the same hardware. Although being accessed twice (once for each file system driver), the hardware driver need only be loaded once.

When a process makes an I/O request, it does so through the appropriate environment subsystem, which then issues the request to the I/O subsystem. Upon receipt of the request, the I/O manager creates one or more so-called *I/O request packets,* which it transfers back and forth between the different driver layers. These packets will be different for different drivers, so it is the responsibility of the I/O manager to know how to create the packets for each driver.

For example, an application wishes to read a file from an NTFS on the hard disk. It makes the request of the Win32 environment subsystem, which communicates with the I/O request manager. The I/O request manager creates the I/O request pack and hands it to the NTFS. The NTFS driver then *calls back* to the I/O manager, whereupon the I/O manager calls the device drivers that actually manipulate the hardware. Each of these layers must send return status to the previous layers (which is done in reverse order) until the status is finally passed back to the original application.

Depending on the application, it can continue working while the I/O request is being processed. This process is called *asynchronous I/O*. In such cases, the I/O manager does not wait for the task to complete but will return to the calling environmental subsystem immediately rather than waiting for the file system and hard device to complete their work. This request is put into a queue and processed later.

Another advantage of this mechanism is that I/O requests can be handled in a more-efficient order and not necessarily in the order in which they were received. This way, similar requests can be gathered together (e.g., all requests from the hard disk). Once the request has been satisfied, the calling process is signaled that the task has been completed.

This has an obvious advantage when writing to the disk. Because the process relies on the system to write the data to the disk, it can continue working without any problem. However, with reads, the process needs to be a lot more careful. Granted, it could continue working (or perhaps running only a single thread), but it must be sure that the data are available before the process attempts to use it.

File Systems

Windows NT supports a number of different file systems. Because compatibility with older Microsoft systems was important in the development of Windows NT, it is not surprising that Windows NT supports the MS-DOS FAT file system as well as the OS/2 High-Performance File System (HPFS) and the standard CD-ROM file system (ISO9660). A new file system that Windows NT brings with it is the NTFS, which provides many advanced features.

Compatibility with older systems is not the only reason you would choose one file system over another. The NTFS offers a wide range of advantages over the FAT file system, but there are cases when you might prefer the FAT to the NTFS. Because I support users running Windows for Workgroups as well as Windows NT, I need to have access to both. Therefore, I cannot create an NTFS-only file system. In my case, it is simpler to leave the C: drive as FAT.

In addition, on many machines I use, I run different versions of UNIX (SCO, Solaris, Linux); the only file system that is compatible with all three is the FAT.

The File Allocation Table (FAT) File System

To better understand the advantage of the NTFS, we need to compare it with something else we know. Therefore, I am going to first talk about the MS-DOS FAT file system. Although it does offer some advantages, the HPFS in OS/2 is beyond the scope of this book. In addition, the driver is not included if you install Windows NT 4.0 from scratch; only when you upgrade from 3.51.

The fact that the FAT is a very simple file system is one reason why it is supported by so many operating systems. It is often referred to, although incorrectly, as simply FAT and not as the FAT File System. The actual file allocation table is a structure that is used to manage the file system. Because the file system is characterized by how access is made through the FAT, it is properly referred to as the FAT file system.

The smallest unit of space on a hard disk or floppy is a *block*. On most media today, whether for a DOS PC or a Sun Workstation, the block size is 512 bytes of data. Due to the nature of the FAT, it manages the blocks in larger groups called *clusters*. How many blocks are contained within the cluster is dependent on the size of the hard disk. (Note: As a safety measure, there are actually two copies of the FAT in case one gets damaged.)

One of the major limitations of the FAT is its size. The FAT stems from the ancient history of computers when the largest number anyone could imagine was 64 KBs. As a result, there is a maximum of 64-KB entries in the FAT. This means that there can be, at most, a total of 64-KB files and directories on the FAT file system. This means that the larger the hard disk or floppy, the larger the cluster. For example, if the file system were 64 MB, then 64-KB entries would mean that a cluster would be 1 KB in size. If the system were 640 MBs, each cluster would be 10 KBs in size. The file system is 10 times as large, so the cluster need to be 10 times as large. This limitation is not based on the total size of the hard disk but rather on a single partition. (Microsoft increased the limit of the FAT in Windows 95 with the FAT32 filesystem, but this is not supported by Windows NT.)

Actually, it does work exactly this way. Cluster sizes are in powers of 2 KBs, such as 2 KBs, 4 KBs, 8 KBs, and so forth. For example, I have a 500-MB hard disk with a single partition and each of the clusters are 8 KBs in size, whereas on the 640-MB file system mentioned above, the cluster would actually be 16 KBs. On my 2-GB hard disk, each cluster is 32 KBs! If I have a file that is only 10 KBs, I lose 22 KBs, because the remainder of the cluster is unused. If the file is 33 KBs, I lose 31 KBs, as the entire first 32-KB cluster is used, but only 1 KB of the second is used. Therefore, the last 31 KBs is left unused. In one case, converting one 500-MB partition to two 250-MB partitions, I ended up with over 70 MBs more free space!

Another limitation shows itself when trying to implement the FAT file system in a multiuser environment. There is nothing built into the file system to deal with security. Although I could make a file read-only, anyone with access to the system could change this and then write to the file.

The FAT file system also has a limitation on the names that can be used for files. Each file name is made up of two parts: the name and an extension (.). The name can be up to eight characters and can be composed of ASCII characters (with a few exceptions). There is a separator between the name and the extension, but this is not an actual part of the file name within the FAT. The extension can be up to three characters long, but there does not have to be an extension. By convention, this naming scheme is referred to as the "8.3 file naming convention."

If you have a small hard disk (e.g., under 250 MBs), then the FAT file system may be useful, because there is little space wasted on administrative overhead. However, as the size of the disk increases, so does the size of the clusters, and you end up losing the space that you would otherwise save.

As I mentioned, The FAT file system is named for its method of organization, the file allocation table (FAT). The FAT resides at the beginning of the volume and essentially contains pointers to the data on the hard disk. The FAT file system has several disadvantages as a result of its design. It was originally designed for small disks and had a simple folder structure. Although more-efficient and therefore more-complex file systems were available at the time, the FAT file system provided the necessary functionality in the least amount of space.

Despite common misconception, the FAT file system provides a limited safety mechanism. There are actually two copies of the FAT on the system. Should the primary one become damaged, it can be rebuilt using the second one. In addition, should the file system become corrupted, the information in both FATs can be compared and return the file systems to a reasonable state.

At the beginning of a FAT formatted partition is the partition boot sector, similar to that found on any other file system. Following that are the two copies of the FATs. Following the second FAT is the root directory, followed by all remaining files and directories.

The root directory has the same structure and content as any other directory on the system. The only difference is that the root directory is at a specific location and has a limited (fixed) size. A hard disk can contain up to 512 entries, including files and other directories. Root directories contain entries for each file and directory that it contains. Each entry is 32 bytes long and contains the following information:

- Name (8.3 format)
- Attribute byte
- Create time (24 bits)
- Create date (16 bits)

- Last access date (16 bits)
- Last modified time (16 bits)
- Last modified date (16 bits)
- Starting cluster number in the FAT (16 bits)
- File size (32 bits)

There is no attempt on the part of the system to organize the FAT file system. Files are allocated on a first-come, first-served basis. After time, as files are removed and new ones are created, files become scattered around the disk, as the system searches for free space to write the files. The result is that the file system becomes "fragmented." This happens as a result of the FAT file system design. As mentioned, the starting cluster for each file is contained within the directory. The entry in the FAT that corresponds to that cluster then contains a pointer to the next cluster. It then contains a pointer to the next cluster and so on. The last cluster contains the value 0xFFFF, which indicates that this is the last cluster.

To support long file names, Windows NT (as well as Windows 95) uses the attributes in a way that does not interfere with MS-DOS. When a file is created with a long file name, Windows NT creates the standard 8.3 file name but uses addition directory entries to store the long file name. One entry is used for each 13 characters in the file name. Based on how the volume, read-only, system, and hidden file attributes are set in the subsequent directory entries, Windows NT determines the long name of the file. (Generally if all 4 bits are set, MS-DOS will ignore these files.)

In addition, Windows NT can create names that do not adhere to the other MS-DOS limitations, such as which characters can be used. Therefore, the names stored in the subsequent directory entries are in Unicode. Also, both Windows NT and Windows 95 use the same algorithm to create long files names. Therefore, if you have a dual-boot system (where you can boot either Windows 95 or Windows NT), they will both be able to read the long file names on a FAT partition.

NTFS

The NTFS offers some significant advantages over the FAT file system. In addition to increased reliability and performance, the NTFS does not suffer from the limitations of the FAT file system. In addition, the NTFS supports more file attributes, such as those related to security, and was designed to allow additional attributes that were not thought of when the file system was first designed.

The NTFS is said to be "recoverable" because it keeps track of activity on the hard disk. This activity is referred to as "transactions," which are kept in a transaction log. This makes recovering from a system crash or other problem simple in that the system need only check the transaction log and use it for recovery purposes. The system is "rolled back" to the last "commit" point, which is a place where the system wrote everything to disk. When a check is performed on the FAT file system, the consistency of pointers within all of the directory is checked along with file tables and the actual allocation. For example, it checks that entries in all directories actually point to data on the disk.

One of the most welcome additions in the NTFS was the extending of file name length to 255 characters as well as allowing new characters such as spaces. However, the NTFS still does not support all the functionality of most UNIX file systems. For example, the NTFS will generally preserve the case when you create a new file, but it is still case insensitive. Therefore, NT FILE.TXT and file.txt are the same file but would be different on UNIX, as they should be.

An interesting aspect of the NTFS is the fact that *all* space on the partition that is in use is part of a file. This includes the bootstrap information and the system files used to implement the NTFS structure. When the partition is formatted for an NTFS, it is said that it contains an NTFS "volume."

The Master File Table (MFT) is the central management unit on an NTFS and contains at least one record for each file on the volume, including one for *itself*. Each record is 2 KBs in size, which means that there is a lot more space necessary on an NTFS just to manage the files. This makes an NTFS appear very much like a relational database. Each file is identified by a file number, which is created from the position of the file in the MFT. Each file also has a sequence number and a set of attributes.

Another interesting aspect is that the NTFS uses a clustering scheme similar to that of the FAT and is always multiples of the sector size on the physical medium. One important aspect is that you are not limited to 64-KBs entries in some table. Instead, you can choose a cluster size of 512, 1024, 2048, or 4096 bytes. Therefore, prior to formatting the disk, you can give some consideration to the kind of data that will be stored there. If you expect a lot of small files, you should consider a small cluster size. However, larger cluster size means access times are reduced, because there are less data to search.

The file system driver accesses files by their cluster number and is therefore unaware of the sector size or any other information about the physical drive. When accessing the disk, the logical cluster number is multiplied by the cluster factor. This makes accessing the files on the disk faster.

The NTFS boot sector is located at the beginning of the volume, with a duplicate located in the middle of the volume. It contains various information about the volume, including the start location of the Master File Table (MFT) and the Master File Table Mirror (MFT2) as well as the number of sector in the volume.

Unlike the directory entry of many other file systems such as the FAT, the filename is an attribute of the file and not just an entry within a directory. In fact, the NTFS will have multiple entries for each directory entry. This is how it can have hard links as are available on UNIX systems. However, this is only supported by the POSIX environment subsystem, so it is not available from most Windows applications. Among the other information contained within the file is a header, standard information, security descriptor, and the data. The structure of the MFT is shown in Figure 1–6.

IMAGE OF MFT

- Header (H)
- Standard Information (SI)
- Security Descriptor (SD)
- File Name (FN)
- Data

Let's assume we have a file that is approximately 1500 bytes long. This size added to the information stored with the MFT record is less than the 2-KB size of the record. Therefore, the data together with the attributes can be stored within single MFT records.

The first 16 records of the MFT are reserved for special system information, the first of which describes the MFT itself. The second record is a MFT record that points to mirror of the MFT, in case the first MFT becomes corrupt. The location of both the MFT and the MFT mirror are stored within the boot record. To increase recoverability even further, a duplicate of the boot sector is located at the logical center of the disk.

Starting with the seventeenth record, you have the records that point to the files within the file systems. Like many other systems, the NTFS also sees directories as files, which just happen to have a specific structure. Instead of what we humans consider to be data, the data for a directory are indexes into other locations within the MFT. Like files, small directories are kept within the data portion of the MFT record (See Figure 1–7). With larger directories, the indexes point to other records and then point to the actual file indexes.

The scheme provides some speed enhancements over the FAT and many UNIX file systems for smaller files. In both the FAT and UNIX file systems, finding the data is a two-step process. First, the system locations the appropriate entry for a file (such as in the node table under UNIX) then needs to find the physical location on the hard disk. With the NTFS, the moment the entry in the MFT is found, the data are located as well.

H SI FN   Data   SD

H - Header
S - Standard Information
FN - File Name
D - Data
SD - Security Descriptioon

FIGURE 1–6   The Windows NT MFT.

FIGURE 1-7   MFT record for a small file or directory.

If the data cannot fit into a single record, the data portion of the records contains pointers to the actual data on the disk. This pointer is called a virtual cluster number (Vcn) and points to the first cluster in each of what is called a *data run* or simply *run* as well as to the number of contiguous clusters in each of the runs. If the file is so large, it may be that there are so many runs that pointing to all of them would be more than can fit in the data record. The data record will then point to another MFT record, which then points to the data.

NTFS ATTRIBUTES

Each NTFS file consists of one or more *attributes*. Each attribute consists of an attribute type, length, value, and optionally an attribute name. Attributes are ordered by attribute type, and some attribute types can appear many times.

With the NTFS, there are both system-defined and user-defined attributes. It is through these attributes that *every* aspect of the file is accessed, including the data. This is because file data are just an attribute of the file. This data attribute contains what we normally think of as data as well as the normal file sizes and sizes for all attributes.

System-defined attributes are defined by the NTFS volume structure and have fixed names and attribute type codes. The name and format of user-defined attributes are determined solely by users, with the attribute type codes established uniquely for each NTFS volume.

Attributes are stored either as *resident* or *nonresident*. When an attribute is stored within the MFT record, it is considered resident. However, it can happen that the attribute is too large to fit within the MFT. In this case, the attribute is stored elsewhere and therefore considered nonresident.

SOME SYSTEM-DEFINED ATTRIBUTES

- **Attribute List**—defines the valid attributes for this particular file
- **File Name**—contains the long file name and the file number of the parent directory file. Must always be a resident attribute
- **MS-DOS Name**—contains the 8.3 file name as well as the case-insensitive file name
- **Security Descriptor**—attribute the contains the file's Access Control List (ACL) and audit field (activities on this file to be audited)
- **Reference Count**—similar to the reference count in UNIX. This is basically the number of "directories" that contain this particular file

SECURITY ON THE NTFS

Like other aspects of Windows NT, security information for the NTFS is stored in ACLs. Each entry in an ACL is referred to as an Access Control Entry (ACE). ACEs are ordered (sorted) first by those that deny access, then by those that grant access. In this way, if you are denied access to any object by an ACE, it will be found first before any that grant you access. In addition, you need to keep in mind that "deny" will always override "allow" if there is ever a conflict.

When an object is created, one or more ACLs are usually assigned to that object. Windows NT uses a scheme of "ACL inheritance," which is intended to allow access control information to be passed on to subsequent objects. Using the concept of *containers*, a Windows NT ACL can be thought of as three separate ACLs:

1. **Effective ACL**—ACL pertaining to the container object
2. **Object Inherit ACL**—ACL to be inherited by sub-noncontainer objects.
3. **Container Inherit**—ACL to be inherited by subcontainer objects, such as subdirectories.

When a new object is created, what access is given will be determined by a couple of things. First, what kind of object it is. If the new object is a noncontainer (i.e., a file), it may have a different ACL than if it were a container (i.e., a directory). For example, when a new file is created, the effective ACL of the file is the same as the Object Inherit ACL. Because the new object is not a container, the Container Inherit ACL has no effect (not inherited).

If the new object is a container (i.e., directory), the process is slightly more complicated. The Object Inherit ACL is simply transferred to the new object. That is, the Object Inherit ACL of the parent object becomes the Object Inherit ACL of the child. The Container Inherit ACL will become *both* the Effective *and* Container Inherit ACL for the new container. Essentially, this means that all directories and subdirectories end up with the same ACL (provided no one changes things).

Although it seems that there are three separate ACLs for each object, there is actually only one. Each ACE can be defined to have different inheritance characteristics. That is, it can be marked for no inheritance or inheritance by subcontainers, noncontainer objects, or both.

In general, children inherit the properties of their parent, whether or not an object is created new and when it is copied/moved. For example, if you are inside of MS Word and create a new file, it inherits the security properties of the directory. If you create a new directory inside of MS Word (or something like Windows Explorer), the new directory also inherits the permissions. If copied, files and directories inherit the permissions of their new parent. This is because they are new objects. However, if files or directories are *moved*, they retain their original permissions.

NTFS STRATEGY: RECOVERABLE FILE SYSTEM

There are several mechanisms within the NTFS that help ensure recoverability in the event of a system crash. To aid in this, the NTFS is *transaction* based. A transaction is a collection of smaller actions, all of which must either be completed, or none can. Each action on the system that modifies it in some way is considered a transaction. Transactions are logged, which helps in recovering the file system.

When a file is changed, the Log File Service logs all redo and undo information for that transaction. Redo information is essentially the information needed to repeat the action, and undo information is the information needed to make the system think that nothing has happened.

After a transaction is logged, it is passed to the Cache Manager, which checks the Memory Manager for free memory resources. If the resources are available, the Cache Manager sends the transaction instructions to the NTFS to make the requested changes to the file. If not, the Memory Manager needs to free up resources.

If the transaction completes successfully, the transaction (file update) is committed. If the transaction is incomplete, the NTFS will roll back the transaction by following the instructions in the undo information. If the NTFS detects an error in the transaction, the transaction will be ended and then also rolled back using the undo information.

The cache is used to slightly speed up performance. Keep in mind the logging requires a certain amount of time and therefore slightly decreases system performance. Windows NT uses something called a "lazy commit," which is similar to a "lazy write." Instead of writing the commitment information to the disk, it is cached and written to the log as a background process. If the system crashes before the commit has been logged, when the system restarts the NTFS checks the transaction log to see whether or not it was successfully completed. If not, the NTFS will undo the transaction.

At regular intervals (8 seconds), the NTFS checks the status of the lazy writer in the cache and marks it a *checkpoint* in the log file. If the system crashes following the checkpoint, the system knows to back up to that specific checkpoint for recovery purposes. Because the system does not have to figure out how far transactions were made, checkpointing results in faster recovery times.

NTFS ADVANTAGES

The NTFS file system is best for use on partitions of about 400 MBs or more, because performance does not degrade with larger partition sizes under the NTFS as it does under the FAT file system.

The NTFS enables you to assign permissions to individual files, so you can specify who is allowed various kinds of access to a file or directory. The NTFS offers more permissions than the FAT file system, and you can set permissions for individual users or groups of users. The FAT file system only provides permissions at the directory level, and FAT permissions either allow or deny access to all users. However, there is no file encryption built into the NTFS. Therefore, someone can start the system under MS-DOS or another operating system and then use a low-level disk editing utility to view data stored on an NTFS partition.

The recoverability designed into the NTFS file system is such that a user should seldom have to run any disk repair utility on an NTFS partition. In the event of a system crash, the NTFS uses its log file and checkpoint information to automatically restore the consistency of the file system.

Even with these benefits, the NTFS is still subject to fragmentation. Unlike memory, if parts of files are stored in different physical locations on the hard disk, it takes longer to read the file. Unfortunately, Microsoft has not provided any defragmentation software for Windows NT, which is available in abundance for Windows 95/98.

Fortunately, Executive Software (*www.executive.com*) provides a solution with their Diskeeper products. There are both workstation and server versions of the software, which can be configured to automatically defragment the system as it is running. The functionality of Diskeeper is so well proven that Microsoft will reportedly include it as a standard component of Windows 2000. A lite version is provided on the accompanying CD for you to try out.

The System Registry

In Windows 3.1, configuration information was stored in various files spread out all over the system. Although they generally had the common extension (.INI), it was often difficult to figure out exactly which file was responsible for which aspect of the configuration. Windows NT changed that by introducing the concept of the system registry. Windows registry is a central repository for all of the systems configuration information.

The registry is a kind of hierarchically organized database. It is grouped into several groups of entries, which are referred to as *hives*. These contain keys, which themselves can contain subkeys. It is within these keys and subkeys where the information is actually stored. The function of each hive is shown in Table 1–1.

Each hive is contained in a separate file as well as in a single .log file. Normally, the system related hives are found in the directory %SYSTEMROOT%\system32\config and the user-related hives are in %SYSTEMROOT%\profiles*username* (where *username* is the name of the respective user; see Table 1–2) . The system hives have the name DEFAULT, SAM, SECURITY, SOFTWARE, and SYSTEM. The following table contains the names of the hives and in which files they reside.

The system administrator can specify the amount of space that the registry uses on the hard disk. Sometimes the default of 2 MBs is insufficient, so

TABLE 1–1	Function of the Registry Hives
Name of the Primary Key	**Description**
HKEY_LOCAL_MACHINE	Contains information about the local machine
HKEY_CLASSES_ROOT	Contains information about file association and Object Linking & Embedding (OLE)
HKEY_CURRENT_USER	Contains information about the current user
HKEY_USERS	Contains information for all user profiles, including the current user
HKEY_CURRENT_CONFIG	Contains information about the current hardware configuration

the space needs to be increased. This is only really necessary on the domain controllers, because they contain the user account information, which grows a lot faster than other configuration information. When the system gets close to using up the allocated space, it generates a message that gives you enough time to make the necessary changes.

When the system is first installed, a base copy of the registry is loaded, and changes are made based on what configuration options you chose. Each time the system is changed, such as when hardware or software is installed, the registry gets changed. Even when you boot your system, the NTDE-TECT.COM program can make changes to the registry.

Viewing the Registry

The registry can be viewed or changed directly using REGEDT32.EXE (Figure 1–8). Note that each hive controls *many* different aspects of your system. If you must edit the registry by hand, make sure you make a copy before you start.

Each key consists of three components: the key name, the data type, and the value. How long the value can be and in what format it is is dependent on the data type. You can have such data types as binary data, text strings, and multipart text.

TABLE 1–2	Registry Hives and Their Associated Files
Registry Hive	**File name**
HKEY_LOCAL_MACHINE\SAM	Sam and Sam.log
HKEY_LOCAL_MACHINE\SECURITY	Security and Security.log
HKEY_LOCAL_MACHINE\SOFTWARE	Software and Software.log
HKEY_LOCAL_MACHINE\SYSTEM	System and System.log
HKEY_CURRENT_USER	Ntuser.dat and Ntuser.dat.log
HKEY_USERS\.DEFAULT	Default and Default.log

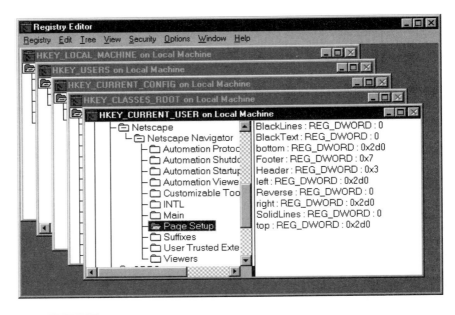

FIGURE 1–8   Registry editor.

Be extremely careful when you make changes directly to the registry, because you can make your system nonbootable.

Starting Windows

The process of turning on your computer and having it jump through its hoops to bring up the operating system is called *booting*. This derives from the term *bootstrapping*. This is an allusion to the idea that a computer pulls itself up by its bootstraps, in that smaller pieces of simple code start larger, more complex ones to get the system running.

The process a computer goes through is similar between the different computer types, whether it is a PC, Macintosh, or SPARC Workstation. In the next section, I will be talking specifically about the PC. However the concepts are still valid for other machines.

The very first thing that happens is the Power-On Self-Test (POST). Here, the hardware is checking itself to see that things are all right. One thing that is done is to compare the hardware settings in the CMOS (Complementary Metal-Oxide Semiconductor) to what is physically on the system. Some errors, like the floppy types not matching, are annoying, but your system still can boot. Others, like the lack of a video card, can keep the system from continuing. Oftentimes, there is nothing to indicate what the problem is, except for a few little "beeps." On some systems, you can configure the system to behave differently for different errors or problems it detects in the CMOS.

Once the POST is completed, the hardware jumps to a specific, predefined location in RAM. The instructions that are located here are relatively simple and basically tell the hardware to go look for a boot device. Depending on how your CMOS is configured, first your floppy is checked and then your hard disk.

When a boot device is found (let's assume that it's a hard disk), the hardware is told to go to the 0th (first) sector (cylinder 0, head 0, sector 0), then load and execute the instructions there. This is the master boot record (MBR), sometimes called the master boot block. This code is small enough to fit into one block but is intelligent enough to read the partition table (located just past the master boot block) and find the active partition. Once it finds the active partition, it begins reading and executing the instructions contained within the first block.

It is at this point that viruses can affect/infect a Windows NT system. The master boot block is the same format for essentially all PC-based operating systems. All the master boot block does is to find and execute code at the beginning of the active partition. Instead, the master boot block could contain code that told it to go to the very last sector of the hard disk and execute the code there. If that last sector contained code that told the system to find and execute code at the beginning of the active partition, you would never know anything was wrong.

Let's assume that the instructions at the very end of the disk are larger than a single, 512-byte sector. If they took up a couple of kilobytes, you could get some fairly complicated code. Because it as at the end of the disk, you would probably never know it was there. What if that code checked the date in the CMOS, and if the day of the week was Friday and the day of the month was the 13th, it would erase the first few kilobytes of your hard disk? If that were the case, then your system would be infected with the Friday the 13th virus, and you could no longer boot your hard disk.

Viruses that behave in this way are called "boot viruses," because they affect the master boot block and can only damage your system if this is the disk you are booting from. These kinds of viruses can affect all PC-based systems. Some computers will allow you to configure the CMOS so that you cannot write to the master boot block. Although this is a good safeguard against older viruses, the newer ones can change the CMOS to allow writing to master boot block. So, just because you have enabled this feature, it does not mean your system is safe. Therefore, you need to be especially careful when booting from floppies.

Now back to our story. . . .

As I mentioned, the code in the master boot block finds the active partition and begins executing the code there. On an MS-DOS system, these are the IO.SYS and MSDOS.SYS files. On an NT system, this is the NTLDR, which reads the contents of the BOOT.INI file and provides you with the various boot options. In addition, it is also the responsibility of the NTLDR program to switch x86-based CPUs from real mode to 32-bit, protected mode.

If you choose to boot into DOS or Windows at this point, the NTLDR program loads the file BOOTSECT.DOS and runs it. This file is a copy of the boot sector that existed before you installed Windows NT (assuming you installed NT on top of DOS or Windows). If you select to boot Windows NT, NTLDR loads the programmer NTDETECT.COM, which is responsible for detecting your hardware. If you have configured multiple hardware profiles, it is NTDETECT.COM that provides you the choices. Next, NTDETECT.COM loads program NTOSKRNL.EXE and passes it the information it has collected about your hardware. However, on RISC-based computers, the OSLOADER carries out all of the functions.

Network Basics

Long ago (at least in terms of the history of electronic data processing), having two computers at the same time was something you read about in science fiction novels. As systems became more common, the time did come when a company or university would have two computers. The need then arose that data be exchanged between the two machines. This was the beginning of SNEAKER-Net (Slow, Non-Electrical Activity, Keeping Everyone Running), which was developed in the 1950s. With SNEAKER-Net, the technician would copy data onto a tape or other media and, by using his sneakers would run the tape over to the other machine to be loaded. In many organizations, SNEAKER-Net is still employed today as this is often the only type of network they *think* they can afford.

In 1976, researchers at AT&T Bell Laboratories came to the rescue. This was the development of a serial line protocol to exchange data between UNIX machines, which came to be known as UUCP, for Unix-to-Unix Copy. Over the years, there were several changes, upgrades revisions, and so forth.

Although UUCP was a good thing, it was limited by the speed of the serial line connecting the two computers. Because the system could only be as fast as it's slowest component, there needed to be a way to speed up that slowest component. Well, serial line speeds increased, but that still was not enough. In the 1970s, Xerox came out with Ethernet, which made high-speed communication between computers possible. It was now possible for users to access remote computers and expect response times comparable to being logged in locally, rather than experiencing delays as was common with the serial line communication of the day. (We'll get into more details on Ethernet later.)

Today, there are dozens of networking methods, with an alphabet soup of acronyms that makes even the most experienced administrator dizzy. Unfortunately, you need networking functionality to really be able to take advantage of the system. Therefore, we need to talk about some of the more common concepts and protocols.

Before we talk about the details of networking, we should first talk about the process of network communication. Let's take a process such as copying a file from the server to your local machine. On the surface, the process seems to be identical with copying a file between two directories on the local machine. However, there is a lot more going on behind the scenes.

Although it may appear as if there is a constant flow of information between your local machine and the remote one, this is not what is happening. At any given time, there may be dozens, if not hundreds of programs using the network. You see what appears to be a constant flow of data. However, things actually happen so fast, you are not aware of the changes. Because only one can use the network at a time, there needs to be some mechanism to allow each program to have its turn.

Think back to our discussion on Windows NT basics. When we need something from the hard disk, the system does not read everything at once. If it did, one process could hog the computer if it needed to read in a large file. Instead, disk requests are sent in smaller chunks, and the program only thinks that it gets everything it wants. Something similar is done with network connections.

Computers are like human beings in that they need to speak the same language in order to communicate. Regardless of how they are connected, be it serial or Ethernet, the computers must know how to talk to one another. The communication is carried out in a pre-defined manner, called a protocol. Like the protocols that diplomats and politicians go through, computer protocols determine how each side behaves and how it should react to behavior by its counterpart. Roughly speaking, even the interaction between the computer and the hardware, such as the hard disk, can be considered a protocol.

The most common protocol used in computers today is Transmission Control Protocol/Internet Protocol (TCP/IP). Although, Windows NT originally used the NetBEUI protocol, as of Windows NT 4.0, the default is TCP/IP. It is more accurate to call TCP/IP a protocol suite, or protocol family. This is because TCP/IP actually consists of several different protocols. Even the name consists of two different protocols: Transmission Control Protocol and Internet Protocol.

TCP/IP is often referred to as protocol suite, as it contains many different protocols and therefore many different ways for computers to talk to one another. However, TCP/IP is not the only protocol suite. There are dozens, if not hundreds of different ones, although only a small portion have gained wide acceptance. Windows NT only uses a few, although the TCP/IP family is what is delivered by default and most commonly used.

Although the name refers to two specific protocols, TCP/IP usually refers to an entire suite of protocols and programs. The result of many years of planning and discussion, the TCP/IP suite includes a set of standards that specify how computers ought to communicate. By following these standards, computers "speak" the same language and can therefore communicate. In addition to the actual means of communication, the TCP/IP suite defines conventions for connecting different networks and routing traffic through routers, bridges and other types of connections.

The TCP/IP suite is result of a Defense Advanced Research Projects Agency (DARPA) research project on network connectivity. However, its availability has made it the most commonly installed network software. Many versions provide source-code that resides in the public domain, allowing users to adapt it to many new systems. Most vendors of network hardware (e.g., bridges, routers) support the TCP/IP suite.

Whereas the data being transferred to and from the hard disk is talked about in terms of blocks, the unit of information transfer across a network connection is referred to as a packet. Depending on the program you are using, this packet can be a different size. In any event, they are small enough to send across the network fast enough, so that no single process can hog the network. In addition, the packets go across the network so fast that you don't notice that your data is broken into packets. This is similar to the way the CPU manages processes. Each one gets a very small turn on the processor. Because it switches so fast between processes, it only seems like you have the processor to yourself.

If we take a and look at the process of network communication more abstractly, we see it composed of of different componets, each portion supported by and supporting another. We can say that each portion sits on top of another. Or in other words, the protocols are stacked on top of each other. Therefore, TCP/IP is often referred to as a protocol stack. To see how these layers look graphically, take a look at Figure 2–1.

Each portion of the stack is referred to as a layer. At the bottom of the stack is the layer that is responsible for the physical connection between the two computers. This is the physical layer. Sitting on top of the physical layer is layer that is responsible for the network portion of the stack. That is, it ensures that packets either stay on the network or get to the right network. Once it has found the right network, this layer ensures that packets get to the right network address. This is the network layer.

On top of the network layer is the layer that ensures that the packets have been transmitted correctly. That is, there are no errors and all packets

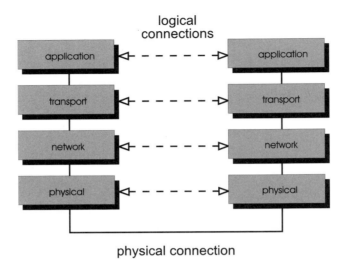

logical
connections

physical connection

FIGURE 2–1 Network layers.

have been received. This is the transport layer. Finally, at the top of all of this is the layer that the user sees. Because the programs that we use are often called applications, this upper layer is called the application layer.

Conceptually, each layer is talking to its counterpart on the other system. For example, the HTTP layer used by your Web browser is talking with the HTTP layer on the server. TCP on the remote machine sends an acknowledgment to TCP on the local machine when it receives a packet. IP on the local machine gets information from IP on the remote machine that tells it that this packet is destined for the local machine. Then there are the network interface cards that communicate with one another using their specific language.

This communication between corresponding layers is all conceptual. The actual communication takes place between the different layers on each machine, not the corresponding layers on both machines. It is not until the information is passed to the physical layer that communication between the machines takes place.

When the application layer has data to send, it prepends an application header onto the data it needs to send. This header contains information necessary for the application to get the data to the right part of the application on the receiving side. The application then calls up TCP to send the information along. TCP wraps that data into a TCP packet, which contains a TCP header followed by the application data (including header). TCP then hands the packet (also called a TCP segment) to IP. Like the layers before it, IP wraps the packet up and prepends an IP header, to create an IP datagram. Finally, IP hands it off to the hardware driver. If Ethernet, this includes both an Ethernet header and Ethernet trailer. This creates an Ethernet frame. How the encapsulation looks graphically, take a look at Figure 2–2.

As we see, it is the TCP layer that the application talks to. TCP sticks the data from the application into a kind of envelope (the process is called encapsulation) and passes it to the IP layer. Just as the operating system has a mechanism to keep track of which area of memory belongs to what processes, the network has a means of keeping track of what data belongs to what process. This is the job of TCP. It is the also the responsibility of TCP to ensure that the packets are delivered with the correct contents and then to put them in the right order. (Encapsulation is shown graphically in Figure 2–2.)

Error detection is the job of the TCP envelope, which contains a checksum of the data contained within the packet. This checksum information sits in the packet header and is checked on all packets. If the checksum doesn't match the contents of the packet or the packet doesn't arrive at all, it is the job of TCP to ensure that packet is resent. On the sending end, TCP waits for an acknowledgment that each packet has been received. If it hasn't received one within a specific period, it will resend that packet. Because of this checksum and the resending of packets, TCP is considered a reliable connection.

Another protocol that is often used is the User Datagram Protocol (UDP). Like TCP, UDP sits on top of IP. However, UDP provides a connectionless transport between applications. It is up to the applications using UDP to provide their own mechanism to ensure delivery and correct sequencing of

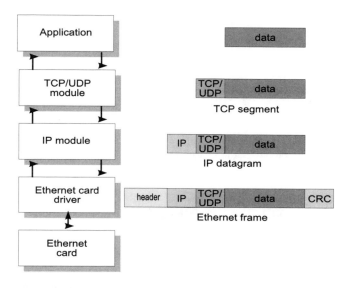

FIGURE 2–2   Encapsulation.

packets. Because it can be either broadcast or multicast, UDP also offers one-to-many services. Because there is no checking by UDP, it is also considered unreliable.

Closest to the hardware level, IP is a protocol that provides the delivery mechanism for the protocols. The IP layer serves the same function as your house addresses, telling the upper layers how to get where they need to go. In fact, the information used by IP to get the pieces of information to their destination are called IP addresses. However, IP does not guarantee that the packets arrive in the right order or that they arrive at all. Just like a letter to your house requires it to be addressed in order to ensure that it gets delivered with the content in-tact, IP depends on the upper layers to ensure the integrity and sequencing of the packets. Therefore, IP is considered unreliable.

Because the hardware, that is, the network cards do the actual, physical transfer of the packets, it is important that they can be addressed somehow. Each card has its own, unique identifier. This is the Media Access Control address, or MAC, address. The MAC address is a 48-bit number that is usually represented by six pairs of hexadecimal numbers separated by (usually) dashes or colons. Each manufacturer of network card is assigned a specific range of addresses, which usually are specified by the first three pairs of numbers. Each card has its own individual address: the MAC address.

When sending a packet, the IP layer has to figure out how to send the packet. If the destination is on a different physical network, then IP needs to send it to the appropriate gateway. However, if the destination machine is on the local network, the IP layers uses the Address Resolution Protocol (ARP) to determine what the MAC address of the Ethernet card is with that IP address.

To figure this out, ARP will broadcast an ARP packet across the entire network asking which MAC address belongs to a particular IP address. Although every machine gets this broadcast, only the one out there that matches will respond. This is then stored by the IP layer in its internal ARP table.

Checking Network Interfaces with arp

It is often very useful to know where Windows thinks it should be sending packets. Often you believe a certain machine has a specific IP address. Using the arp command, you can see what network card Windows sees as belonging to a specific IP address.

```
arp -a
```

This would give you a response similar to:

```
siemau 194.113.47.147 at 0:0:2:c:8c:d2
```

This has the general format:

```
<machine name> (IP address) at <MAC address>
```

Because the ARP table is cached, IP does not have to send out an ARP request every time it needs to make a connection. Instead, it can quickly look in the ARP table to make the IP-MAC translation. Then, the packet is sent to the appropriate machine.

Status and error information is exchanged between machines through the Internet Control Message Protocol (ICMP). This information can be used by other protocols to recover from transmission problems or by system administrators to detect problems in the network. One of the most commonly used diagnostic tools, "ping," makes use of ICMP.

At the bottom of the pile is the hardware or link layer. As I mentioned before, this can be represented by many different kinds of physical connections: Ethernet, tokenring, fiber optics, ISDN, RS—232, to name a few.

This four-layer model is common when referring to computer networks. This is the model that is most commonly used and the one that I will use through the book. There is another model that consists of seven layers. This is referred to as the OSI model, but we won't be using it here.

Network Services

As the name implies, a network service is simply a service that provides some sort of functionality of a network. There are many services that provide functionality, such as access to files, electronic mail, networking printing, and so forth. Other products, such as database applications, may have one central machine containing all the data, and access is gained from the other machines via TCP/IP. Often this access is invisible to the user who just sees the "front end" of the database.

This configuration, where one machine contains the data or resource that another machine uses, is very common in computer networking. The machine with the resource that it is providing to other machines is referred to as the *server,* because it is serving the resource to the other machine. The machine that is using the resource is called the *client.* This model, where one machine is the server and the other is the client is referred to as a client-server model.

Another common network model is the peer-to-peer model. In this model, there is no one central machine that has all the resources. Instead, all machines are on equal status. Oftentimes, these two models sort of blend together. In Windows networks, it is possible to have multiple servers, each providing many of the same resources. It can also happen that multiple machines all have resources that the others need, so everyone is acting as both a client and a server, similar to peer-to-peer, which is common in Microsoft Windows and Windows for Workgroups networks.

How to See What Services Are Running

Start the Network applet in the Control Panel and click the "Services" tab. This brings you to something like Figure 2–3.

Here you can add or remove networking services as needed. In some cases, you can double-click the service and configure various options. If there is nothing to configure for that service you get an appropriate message.

Unfortunately, not all services can be viewed through the network applet. Some have to be accessed through the Server Manager, which is normally in the Administration Tools group. Single

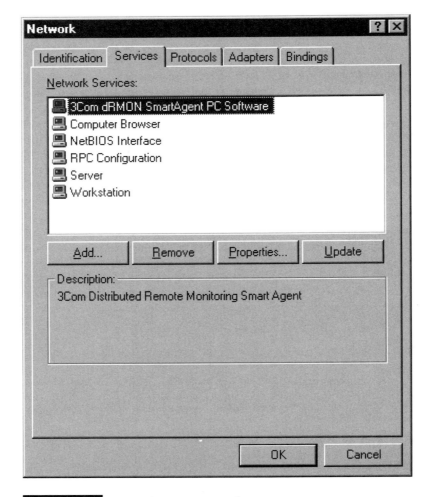

FIGURE 2–3   Network services window.

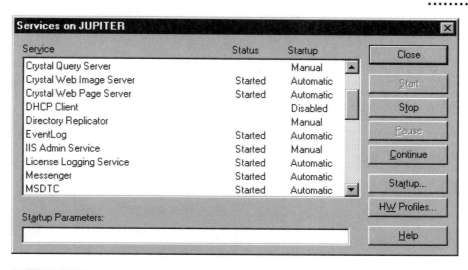

Service	Status	Startup
Crystal Query Server		Manual
Crystal Web Image Server	Started	Automatic
Crystal Web Page Server	Started	Automatic
DHCP Client		Disabled
Directory Replicator		Manual
EventLog	Started	Automatic
IIS Admin Service	Started	Manual
License Logging Service	Started	Automatic
Messenger	Started	Automatic
MSDTC	Started	Automatic

FIGURE 2–4   Server Manager services window.

click the server you want then select "Services" from the "Computer" menu. This brings you to something like Figure 2–4.

By double-clicking on the respective service, you can configure how the service starts and whether it logs in as a particular user.

IP Addressing

In today's world of inter-connected computers, you may have a connection to hundred of thousands of other machines. Granted, there is no single cable connecting all of these computers; however, there is a logical connection in that you can use the telnet program from your PC in California and connect to a machine in Germany. The problem is, how do the packets get from one end to another? Added to that, how do you keep your local network in California from getting overloaded with packets that are being sent between machines in Germany and at the same time making sure that those telnet packets do get through? The answer is provided IP.

Just as a street address is not always sufficient to get your letter delivered, so is the IP not always sufficient to get the packet delivered. If I sent you a letter, it could be sent to a single, central post office, whose job it was to distribute mail throughout the entire United States. Because of the incredibly large number of pieces of mail, this is impractical. Instead, there are thousands of offices, all over the country, whose job it is to route the mail for us.

If we lived in a small town, the local post office could catch a letter destined for a local address before it goes further. Mail with addresses outside town could be sent to other post offices to be processed.

A similar situation applies to IP addresses. In local, self-contained networks, the IP address alone is sufficient. However, when multiple networks are combined, machines spend more time trying to figure out if the packet belongs to them than actually processing information. The solution is a network mask. Just as a zip code tells a postal worker whether to process a particular piece of mail locally or not, the network mask (or netmask) tells machines whether or not they can simply ignore a packet or need to process it further. How this works, we'll get to in a moment.

Every machine on the network needs to have its own, unique IP address. Just like every house has a unique mail address. If that network is connected to the rest of the world, that address must not only be unique within the local network, but unique within the rest of the world as well. As of this writing, IP addresses are 32-bit values. They are usually represented by four sets of numbers, ranging from 0–255 separated by dots (.). This is referred to as dotted-decimal notation. In dotted-decimal notation, an address might look like this:

```
147.132.42.18
```

Because each of these numbers ranges between 0 and 255, they can be represented by 8 bits and are therefore referred to as an octet. This IP address is often thought of as being composed of a network portion (at the beginning) and a node (or machine) portion at the end. This would be comparable to writing a street address as:

```
95061.Main_Street.42
```

Where 95061 is the zip code and Main Street is the street and 42 is the address on that street. The reason we write the street address in this fashion, is that it's common to think of the IP address as moving from the general to the more-specific.

Currently, there are three classes of networks in common use, which are broken down by both the range used in the first octet and the number of octets used to identify the network. Class A networks are the largest and use the first octet as the network address. Networks in the class will have the first octet in the range 1–126. Class B networks use the first two octets, with the first being in the range 128–192. The smallest networks, Class C, use the first three octets in the network address and with the first in the range 192–223. How IP addresses are broken down by the different network classes is shown in Table 2–1.

There are a couple of things I would like to point out about this table. First, the network address 127 represents the local computer, regardless of what network it is really on. This is helpful for testing as well as for many internal operations. Network addresses 224 and above are reserved for special

	TABLE 2-1	IP Address Breakdown by Network			
Class	**Range within 1st octet**	**Network ID**	**Host ID**	**Possible Networks**	**Possible Hosts per Network**
A	1–126	a	b.c.d	126	16,777,214
B	128–191	a.b	c.d	16,384	65,534
C	192–223	a.b.c	d	2,097,151	254

purposes such as multicast addresses. The terms "possible networks" and "possible hosts per network" are those that are calculated mathematically. In some cases, 0 and 255 are not acceptable values for either the network address or the host address.

Keep in mind that a Class A address does not necessarily mean that there are 16 million hosts on a single network. This would be impossible to administrate and would overburden most network technologies. What normally happens is that a single entity, such as Hewlett-Packard, is given a Class A address. They will then break it down further into smaller subnets. We'll get into more details about this shortly.

A network host uses the network ID and host ID to determine which packets it should receive or ignore and to determine the scope of its transmissions (only nodes with the same network ID accept one another's IP-level broadcasts). Because the sender's IP address is included in every outgoing IP packet, it is useful for the receiving computer system to derive the originating network ID and host ID from the IP address field. This is done by using subnet masks, as described in the following section.

In some cases, there is no need to have unique IP addresses, because the network will never be connected to the rest of the world; for example, in a factory where the machines communicate with one another via TCP/IP. There is no reason for these machines to be accessible from the Internet. Therefore, there is no need for them to have an official IP address.

You could just randomly assign IP addresses to these machines and hope that your router is configured correctly not to route the packets from these machines. One slip and you have the potential for not only messing up your own network, but someone else's as well.

The solution was provided in RFC-1918. Here, three sets of IP address were defined for use in "private" networks. These won't be routed, and there is no need to coordinate their use with any of the registrations agencies. The IP addresses are:

```
10.0.0.0     -  10.255.255.255
172.16.0.0   -  172.31.255.255
192.168.0.0  -  192.168.255.255
```

As you can see, that there is just a single Class A address, but 16 Class B and 255 Class C networks. Therefore, no matter what size your network is, you can find a private network for your needs.

Subnet Masks

SUBNET MASKS

Subnet masks are 32-bit values that allow the recipient of IP packets to distinguish the network ID portion of the IP address from the host ID. Like an IP address, the value of a subnet mask is frequently represented in dotted decimal notation. Subnet masks are determined by assigning 1s to bits that belong to the network ID and 0s to the bits that belong to the host ID. Once the bits are in place, the 32-bit value is converted to dotted decimal notation, as shown in Table 2–2.

The result allows TCP/IP to determine the host and network IDs of the local computer. For example, when the IP address is 102.54.94.97 and the subnet mask is 255.255.0.0, the network ID is 102.54 and the host ID is 94.97.

Keep in mind that all of this with the subnet masks is the principle and not necessarily the practice. If you (meaning your company) has been assigned a Class B address, then the first two octets are assigned to you. You could then break down the Class B net into Class C nets. If we take a look at Table 2–1, we see that there are 65,534 possible nodes in that network. That is really too many to manage.

However, if we considered each of the third octets to represent a subnet of our Class B network, they would all have 254 possible nodes per subnet. This is basically what a Class C net is anyway. We can then assign each subnet to a department or building and then assign one person to manage each of the Class C subnets, which is a little easier to do.

To keep the different Class C subnets from interfering with one another, we give each subnet a Class C subnet mask, although the first octet is in the range for a Class B network. That way, machines on this subnet are only concerned with packets for the subnet. We can also physically break down the subnets throught the use of a gateway or router between the subnets. That way, the physical network is not overburdened with traffic from 65,534 machines.

TABLE 2–2	Default Subnet Masks for Standard IP Address Classes	
Address Class	**Bits for Subnet Mask**	**Subnet Mask**
Class A	1111111 00000000 00000000 00000000	255.0.0.0
Class B	1111111 11111111 00000000 00000000	255.255.0.0
Class C	11111111 11111111 11111111 00000000	255.255.255.0

Let's look at an example. Assume your company uses the Class B address 172.16.0.0. The different departments within the company are assigned a Class C address that might look like this:

```
172.16.144.0
```

Although the first octet (172) says that this is a Class B address, it is really the subnet mask that makes that determination. In this case, our subnet mask would be:

```
255.255.255.0
```

Therefore, any packet that is destined for an address other than one starting with 172.16.144.0 is not on this network.

It is the responsibility of IP to ensure that each packet ends up going to the right machine. This is accomplished, in part, by assigned a unique address to each machine. This address is referred to as the IP address. Each network gets a set of these IP addresses that are within a specific range. In general, packets that are destined for an IP address within that range will stay within the local network. Only when a packet is destined for somewhere outside of the local network is it "allowed" to pass.

In other words, IP is responsible for the delivery of the packet. It functions similar to the post office, whereby you have both a sending and receiving address. Oftentimes you have many more letters than a single mail bag can handle. The mail carrier (or someone else at the post office) will break down the number of letters into sets small enough to fit in a bag. This is what IP does.

Because there are many people using the line at once, IP will break down the TCP packets into units of a specific size. Although often referred to also as packets, the more correct terminology is to referr to IP packets as datagrams. Just like bags of mail need to go from one post office to the next to reach their final destination, IP datagrams must often go through different machines to reach their final destination.

Saying that IP routing can be accomplished completely in software isn't entirely accurate. Although no physical router is needed, IP can't send a packet to someplace where there is no physical connection. This is normally accomplished by an additional network card. With two (or more) network cards, a single machine can be connected to multiple networks. The IP layer on that one machine can then be used to route IP packets between the two networks.

Once configured (how that's done, we'll talk about later), IP maintains a table of routing information, called (logically) a routing table. Every time the IP layer receives a packet, it checks the destination address

Routing

I mentioned a moment ago that IP is an unreliable, connectionless protocol. That is, it contains no provision to ensure that the packet arrives correctly at the destination nor is there anything that guarantees that when packets do arrive they arrive in the correct order. Although IP is responsible to ensure that the packets get to the right machine, it has essentially no understanding of the physical connection between the two machines. IP will happily run on machines that are connected with something as simple as a telephone wire to something as complex as satellites. IP depends on some other means to "physically" carry it across the network.

What this means is that the system administrator (or network administrator) is responsible for laying the "map" that is used to define which network addresses go with what sets of machines and what IP addresses are assigned to individual machines.

One important job that IP does is routing, that is, getting the packet to the right machine. If the source and destination machines are directly connected, that is, on the same network, then routing is easy: Essentially, there isn't any. IP sees this fact and simply hands the packets off to the data link layer. Otherwise, IP has to figure out how and where to send it.

Usually the 'how' is over a router. A router is some piece of hardware that acts like an air traffic controller and sends one packet off one way and others off a different way. Often routers are separate pieces of equipment that can be configured in very detailed ways. The disadvantage to this is that with power comes price. The ability to configure a router in many different ways usually means a high price tag. Fortunately, many operating systems, including Linux, allow IP to serve as router-software, thereby avoiding the cost of router hardware.

In comparison to the router is the concept of a gateway. Like a router, a gateway has knowledge of other networks and how to reach them. In general, we can think of a router as a special piece of hardware that does the work for us. In fact, there are companies that sell equipment called routers. A gateway is more of a concept, in that it is the means by which you go from one network to another. Today, the distinction between a router and a gateway is blurred. Originally, a gateway was a machine that converted from one protocol to another. However, in common usage today, routers can serve as gateways, and gateways can serve as routers.

The path the packet takes from one machine to the next is called a route. Although each machine can maintain static routes for specific destinations, the default gateway is usually used to find remote destinations. (The default gateway is needed only for computers that are part of an internetwork.) If you have a gateway connected to several other networks, there will (probably) be route definitions for each of those other networks.

Let's look at this process as if we were sending a letter, as we did a little while ago. Each letter we send has an envelope that contains a message. On the envelope we write the source and destination addresses. When we mail the letter, it gets to the post office and the person sorting the mail checks the destination zip code. If it's the same as the local zip code, the envelope is sent to one of the carriers for delivery. If the zip code is different, then it is sent to some other location. Perhaps all nonlocal mail is sent to the same place.

If you live across the country from me, the letter probably doesn't go directly from my local post office to yours (assuming I don't live in San Francisco and you don't live in New York). The same applies to IP packets. My letter first goes to my local post office, and if it is destined for a local address it is processed there. If not, it is sent along to a larger post office. If I sent a letter from Santa Cruz, CA destined for Annsville, PA, it would probably go first to San Francisco and then to New York (or Philadelphia) before it gets sent to Annsville.

Again, the same applies to IP packets. If I were communicating with a network on the other side of the country, my machine needs to know how to get to the other one. This is the concept of a "gateway." A gateway is the first step in the path, or "route," to the remote machine. Just as there are a couple of post offices between Santa Cruz and Annsville, there can be multiple gateways between computers.

Because San Francisco is the closest "major" city to Santa Cruz, it is possible that all mail bound for points beyond must first go through there. What if I lived in Fresno, which is about halfway between San Francisco and Los Angeles? If I sent a letter to Annsville, it could go through Los Angeles, or it could go through San Francisco. To make things easy, it might always get sent through San Francisco if not destined for a local address. What if the letter is bound for Los Angeles? It seems silly to go through San Francisco first when it is bound for L.A. At the post office in Fresno, they might have a special procedure that says all remote mail goes through San Francisco, except for those with a zip code in a special range.

Here, too, the same applies to IP addresses. One machine may be defined as the "default" gateway, but if an IP packet was bound for a particular network, it could be told to use a completely different gateway (See Figure 2–5). Which gateway to use to get to a particular machine or network is the concept of "routes." If I want all remotely bound packets to use a particular route, I add that route as a default to my machine. If packets bound for a particular network are to go via a different route, I can add that route as well.

When IP prepares to send a "message," it inserts the local (source) and destination address IP addresses in the IP header. It then checks whether the network ID of the destination and source match (the zip codes). If so, the packet is sent directly to the destination, because it is on the local network. If the network IDs don't match, the routing table is examined for static routes. If none is found, the packet is forwarded to the default gateway.

The default gateway is a computer or other network device, such as a router, that is connected to the local subnet and other networks that have knowledge of the network IDs for other networks and how to reach them. Because the default gateway knows how to reach the other networks, it can forward the packet, either to other gateways or directly to that machine, if the gateway is on the same network as the destination. This process is known as routing.

Setting the Default Route

If your machines are configured to use DHCP, the default gateway is automatically configured. Otherwise, it is configured through the Network applet in the Control Panel. Select the Protocol tab and double-click the TCP/IP entry. This brings you to something like Figure 2–6.

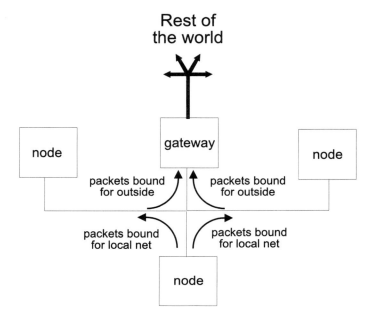

FIGURE 2–5   Network gateway.

Input the IP address of the default gateway in the appropriate field.

To see what the system currently *thinks* the routes are, use the command "route print", which gives you something like this:

```
===========================================================================
Interface List
0x1 ...................... MS TCP Loopback interface
0x2 ...00 60 97 77 b8 cd ... 3Com 3C90x Ethernet Adapter
===========================================================================
===========================================================================
Active Routes:
Network Destination        Netmask          Gateway       Interface  Metric
0.0.0.0                    0.0.0.0    192.168.42.3   192.168.42.3       1
127.0.0.0                255.0.0.0      127.0.0.1      127.0.0.1       1
192.168.42.0         255.255.255.0    192.168.42.3   192.168.42.3       1
192.168.42.3       255.255.255.255      127.0.0.1      127.0.0.1       1
192.168.42.255     255.255.255.255    192.168.42.3   192.168.42.3       1
224.0.0.0                224.0.0.0    192.168.42.3   192.168.42.3       1
255.255.255.255    255.255.255.255    192.168.42.3   192.168.42.3       1
===========================================================================
```

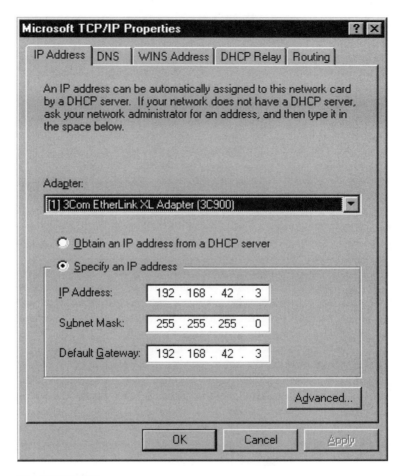

FIGURE 2–6   TCP/IP configuration window.

If you only have a single network, there is no reason to have a gateway, as each machine is directly connected to every other. It's possible that you only want certain machines within your network to go beyond the local net to the outside. In this case, these machines can have a default (or static) route default, whereas the others have none. However, users can add routes themselves by using the route command.

As you move about the network, dynamic entries are created by the routing protocol that you use (most commonly routed). The routing protocol communicates with it counterpart on other machines and adds entries to the routing tables automatically.

Finding Other Machines

As we discussed previously, a computer needs to know how contact another computer on the network. This is done using the IP address. However, the IP address is not very user friendly, so we give computers (as well as other network devices) names that we can easily recognize. The problem is that the computer still needs a way to contact the remote computer. Therefore, there needs to be a conversion of some kind between the name and the IP address. This is the process of name resolution.

The simplest way of doing name resolution is by having a file that contains all of the associations. When you wish to contact a particular machine by its name, the computer looks in the table for the IP address associated with that name. With this mechanism, you would need to copy this file to all of your computers. If you only have a handful of computers, then even if you added a new one, the work necessary to add the name machine to the list is minimal.

What if you have hundreds or thousands of computers in your network? It is impractical to make changes on each machine whenever a new computer is added, even if you were to automate the process (such as through logon scripts). Then there is the issue of networks over which you have no control. If you want to connect to a machine on the Internet, you need to know it's IP address. Because you have no way of knowing the IP address of every machine on the Internet, you need some method of resolving the name in other networks. This is the function of the Domain Name Service (DNS).

When you first install Windows NT, you are given the choice of whether you want to enable DNS or not. When you do, you input the name of any number of servers you wish to query. When you want to find out the IP address of a machine, you ask (query) a particular DNS server, which gives you an answer.

Even though the server you query appears to be giving you the answer, the information may actually come from a different server; that server may actually be asking another machine for the information. This is obviously the case on the Internet, where it is impossible for a single machine to maintain the information for every machine. The DNS server that you query knows how to obtain the information from other servers, which pass the information eitherback to you directly or to the server which you queried.

The second is the hosts file, normally located in %SYSTEMROOT%\system32\config. This is a standard ASCII file with the same structure as under UNIX. The hosts file is used for TCP/IP connectivity when you do not use DNS.

So, when do you use DNS over the hosts? Well, it's up to you. The first question I would ask is, "Are you connecting to the Internet?" If the answer is "yes", "maybe," or "someday," then definitely set up DNS. DNS functions somewhat like directory assistance from the phone company. If your local directory assistance doesn't have the number, you can contact one in the area you are looking. If your name server doesn't have the answer, it will query other name servers for that information (assuming you told it to do so).

If you are never going to go into the Internet, then the answer is up to you. If you only have two machines in your network, the trouble setting up DNS is not worth it. On the other hand, if you have a dozen or more machines, then setting it up makes life easier in the long run. However, how many companies can definitively say that they will never be on the Internet? However, with just a handful of computers, you could continue to use either of the other two alternatives until you decide to connect to the Internet.

There are several key concepts that need to be discussed before we dive into DNS. The first is DNS, like so many other aspects of TCP/IP, is client–server oriented. We have the name server containing the IP addresses and names that serves information to the clients. Next, we need to think about DNS operating in an environment similar to a directory tree. All machines that fall under DNS can be thought of as files in this directory tree structure. These machines are often referred to as nodes. Like directories and file names, there is a hierarchy of names with the tree. This is often referred to as the domain name space.

A branch of the DNS tree is referred to as a domain. A domain is simply a collection of computers that is managed by a single organization. This organization can be a company, university, or even a government agency. The organization has a name that it is known by to the outside world. In conjunction with the domains of the individual organizations, there are things called top-level domains. These are broken down by the function of the domains under it.

Originally, there were just a handful of top-level domains, plus individual domains for each country. Note that the top-level domains we talked about a moment ago are no longer the only ones available. You can now register your own top-level domain. The original top level domains are:

> com—Commercial
>
> edu—Educational
>
> gov—Government
>
> net—Network
>
> mil—Military
>
> org—Non-profit organizations

Each domain will fall within one of these top-level domains. For example, there is the domain prenhall (for Prentice Hall), which falls under the commercial top-level domain. It is thus designated as prenhall.com. The domain assigned to the White House is whitehouse.gov. The domain assigned to the University of California at Santa Cruz is ucsc.edu. (Note that the dot is used to separate the individual components in the machine's domain and name.)

Keep in mind that these domains are used primarily within the United States. Even though a foreign subsidiary might belong to one of these top-level domains, for the most part, the top-level domain within most non-U.S. countries is the country code. For example, the geographical domain Germany is indicated by the domain abbreviation de (for Deutschland). There are exceptions, however. I do know some German companies within the .com domain. There are also geographic domains within the United States, such as ca.us for California as compared to just .ca for Canada. This is often for very small domains or nonorganizations, such as individuals.

In many places, they will use a combination of the upper-level domains that are used in the United States and their own country code. For example, the domain name of an Internet provider in Singapore is singnet.com.sg. (where sg is the country code for Singapore). You can see how the domains fit together graphically in Figure 2–7.

Within each domain, there may be subdomains. However, there there don't have to be. You usually find subdomains in larger domains in an effort to break down the administration into smaller units. For example, if you had a set of machines that were for use by Or, if your company had a subdomain for sales, it might be sales.yourdomain.com.

Keep in mind that these are just the domain names, not the machine or node name. Within a domain, there can be (in principle) any number of machines. A machine sitting on the desk in the Oval Office might be called boss1. Its full name, including domain, would be boss1.pres.whitehouse.gov. A machine in your sales department called darkstar would then be darkstar.sales.yourdomain.com.

Up to now, I have only seen a machine name with five components: the machine name, two subdomains, the company domain, and then the top-level domain. On the other hand, if there was no sales subdomain, and

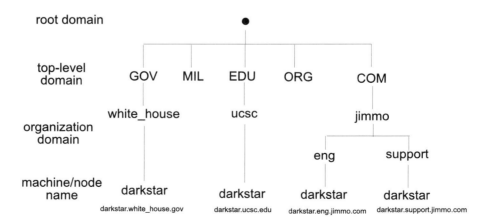

FIGURE 2–7 Internet domains.

everything were under the yourdomain.com domain, the machine's name would be: darkstar.yourdomain.com.

You may often see the fully qualified domain name (FQDN) of a machine listed like this:

```
darkstar.yourdomain.com.
```

Including the trailing dot(.). That dot indicates the root domain. This has no name other than root domain or . (read "dot"). Very similar to the way the root directory has no name other than root or /. In some cases, this dot is optional. However, there are cases where is it required, and we'll get to those in the section on configuring DNS.

Like files, it is possible that two machines have the same name. The only criterion for files is that their full path be unique. The same applies to machines. For example, there might be a machine darkstar at the White House. (Maybe Bill's a closet Dead Head.) Its FQDN would be darkstar.whitehouse.gov. This is obviously not the same machine as darkstar.yourdomain.com, any more than 1033 Main Street in Santa Cruz is the same as 1033 Main Street in Annsville. Even something like darkstar.support.yourdomain.com is different from darkstar.sales.yourdomain.com.

A zone is a grouping of machines that may or may not be the same as a domain. This is the set of machines over which a particular name server has authority and maintains the data. In our example above, there might be a zone for support, even if there was no subdomain. On the other hand, there might be a team.support.yourdomain.com domain, but the zone is still yourdomain.com. Therefore, zones can be subordinate or superior to domains. Basically, zones are used to make the job of managing the name server easier. Therefore, what constitutes a zone depends on your specific circumstances.

In DNS, there are a couple different types of servers. A primary server is the master server for one or more DNS zones. Each server maintains the database files and is considered the authority for this zone. It may also periodically transfer data to a secondary server, if one exists for that zone.

For example, the primary server for the yourdomain.com domain needs to know about the machines within the support.yourdomain.com domain. It could serve as a secondary server to the support.yourdomain.com domain, whereby it would maintain all the records for the machines within that subdomain. If, on the other hand, it servers as a "stub" server, the primary for the yourdomain.com need only know how to get to the primary for the support.yourdomain.com subdomain. Note here that it is possible for a server to be primary in one zone and secondary in another.

By moving responsibility to the subzone, the administrator of the parent zone does not need to concern him or herself with changing the configurations files when a machine is added or removed within the subzone. As long as the address of subzone primary server matches the stub server entry, all is well.

A secondary server takes over for the primary should the primary go down or be otherwise inaccessible. A secondary server maintains copies of the database files and "refreshes" them at predetermined intervals. If it cannot reach the primary to refresh its files, it will keep trying at (again) predetermined intervals. If after another predetermined time, the secondary still cannot reach the primary, the secondary considers its data invalid and flushes it.

Caching-only servers save data in a cache file only until those data expire. The expiration time is based on a field within the data that is received from another server. This is called the time-to-live. Time-to-live is a regularly occurring concept within DNS.

A slave server can be a primary, secondary, or caching-only server. If it cannot satisfy the query locally, it will pass, or forward, the request to a fixed list of forwarders (forwarding server), rather than interacting directly with the primary name servers of other zones. These requests are recursive, which means that the forwarder must answer either with the requested information or by saying it doesn't know. The requesting machine then asks the next server, then the next, and then the next until it finally runs out of servers to check or gets an answer. Slave servers never attempt to contact servers other than the forwarders.

The concept of recursive requests is in contrast to (the concept of) iterative requests. Here the queried server either gives an answer or tells the requesting machine where it should look next. For example, darkstar asks iguana, the primary server for support.yourdomain.com for some information. In a recursive query, iguana asks boomer, the primary server for yourdomain.com and passes the information back to darkstar. In a iterative query, iguana tells darkstar about boomer, and darkstar then goes to ask boomer. This process of asking name servers for information, whether recursive or iterative, is called resolution.

Keep in mind that there is client software running on the server. When an application needs information, the client DNS server asks the server for the information, despite the fact that the server is running on the same machine. Applications don't access the server directly.

There is also the concept of a root server, which is a server. These are servers located at the top of the domain tree and maintain information about the top-level zone. Root servers are positioned at the top, or root, of the DNS hierarchy, and maintain data about each of the top-level zones.

Checking Name Resolution with nslookup

You can check what DNS thinks are the correct values by using the nslookup command followed by either the machine name or IP address. This gives you something like this:

```
Server:  alf020.kaeser-net.de
Address: 194.76.160.20
Name:    alf023.kaeser-net.de
Address: 130.1.20.23
```

Windows has a similar functionality with its Windows Internet Naming Service (WINS). One of the key differences is that DNS is static, in that you need to manage the database by hand, adding and removing entries as necessary. On the other hand, WINS is dynamic, whereby the machines register themselves with a central WINS server and in general require less administration.

There are a couple of major problems with WINS. First, it is a Windows protocol, and most of the servers on the Internet are not Windows machines. The purpose of WINS is to resolve NetBIOS names into IP addresses. Therefore, despite the name, WINS is not very useful on the Internet. Therefore, if you want to connect to the Internet, you either use DNS or use two protocols (WINS internally and NDS for the Internet).

DNS has the advantage that it is hierarchically based. You create zones for which a particular machine (or set of machines) is responsible. WINS has a flat structure and with large number of machine resolution can take longer. Because WINS uses the NetBIOS names, the names themselves have a flat structure and are limited to just 15 characters, whereas the DNS names use the Internet standard, which is hierarchical.

Windows 2000 promises to correct many of the shortcomings of the Windows name resolution mechanisms. A better integration between WINS and DNS has been announced to ease the administration of system where both are used.

Windows Network Protocols

In contrast to operating systems, such as Unix, where network functionality grew onto the system, Windows NT was built from the very beginning to be a network-capable operating system. Although Windows NT has always supported TCP/IP, its primary protocol was originally NetBIOS. With the NetBEUI protocol, NetBIOS builds the basis for all Microsoft products, including the older Lan Manager and Windows for Workgroups.

The abbreviation NetBIOS is simply an extension of the BIOS (basic input/output services), which you know from the computer hardware. With the "net" at the beginning, NetBIOS is the basic input and output services for the work. NetBIOS provides the functionality that the BIOS provides the hardware so that you get the same (or at least similar) functionality and network, which you have with hardware.

Originally NetBIOS was physically on the network card. Over the years, it grew to be an application programming interface (API). Therefore, there are functions in the various programming languages with options to access NetBIOS functionality, without having to access the hardware directly.

The extension to NetBIOS is the NetBIOS Expanded User Interface or NetBEUI. It is incorrect to say that NetBEUI is simply the successor to NetBIOS. NetBEUI *contains* NetBIOS. Additional components of NetBEUI all are the Server Message B-block protocol (SMB) and the NetBIOS frame protocol (NBF). Like NetBIOS, SMB is an API, which provides access to network services.

One advantage of NetBIOS is that it is a quick and compact protocol and uses less memory than does TCP/IP. The major disadvantage is that it cannot be routed. NetBIOS is therefore dependent on the underlying network. The reason is simply that NetBIOS is completely dependent on the underlying physical network address. Therefore, it does not function over serial or point-to-point connections.

What happens in the network when a computer "registers" itself explains this dependency? When the Windows computer starts, it sends out a knee registration request. If the name of this computer is not yet registered in network, it is allowed to participate in a network using this name. This name then becomes the "address" of computer. That means that all future messages are sent to this name. This is in contrast to IP, where the messages are sent to the IP address and not to the name. However, like TCP/IP, both the recipient's and sender's name are present in each packet.

For both the user and the administrator this process is simpler. First, it is much easier to identify which machines are which. Although a 1:1 relationship can be established between the IP address and the computer itself, it is much simpler to just name the computer, and this name is what is used to identify the computer in the network. In contrast, a computer on an IP network can be identified by both its IP address and its name (which is then translated to the IP address).

The second advantage is probably more important for the administrators. Because there's no central management of the names (such as the hosts file or DNS), there is less administrative work. The computers register themselves. The administrator needs to pay attention during installation to make sure that there are no two computers with the same name.

On smaller networks, this solution is acceptable. However, as the network grows, so does the administration work. In order to ensure that each name remains unique, there needs to be some kind of central administration. For example, in one company where I worked, there were a number of computers that were used by several different people. Therefore, it did not make sense to give the computer a name such as Joe or Mary. Instead, the computers were given names such as PC 479 and next one PC 480. Because these were the names used in our inventory, it assured us of unique names. In addition, this naming scheme was easily transferred to a TCP/IP network.

The problem arises when you need to connect to computers outside of your local network, such as across the Internet. In order to make this possible, Microsoft would've had to completely change all of its network protocols in order to follow the standards of the rest of the world. Instead of doing that, they added that additional extension to NetBIOS. This is referred

to as NetBIOS over TCP/IP (NBT). At the same time, Microsoft allowed Net-
BIOS to work on the same computer across the same network as other protocols. The result was an independence from the underlying network. This
means that NetBIOS simply becomes an "application," which runs on top of
TCP/IP. The NetBIOS packets are encapsulated within TCP packets and then
sent across IP.

Although NBT is defined in RFC1001 and RC1002 and many other companies have implemented it, Microsoft added ideas and uses a slightly modified version of NBT. Microsoft NBT uses the broadcast node (B-node) architecture. This mean that messages used to resolve names are sent across the
network using a broadcast (that is, sent to every machine). To reduce the
burden on the network, Microsoft made still another change: the LMHOSTS
file. This is similar to the hosts file in that it makes the translation between
gain and IP address. In this case, it is making the translation between the Net-
BIOS name and the IP address.

Browser Service

The browser service is one of the most important services provided on a
Windows NT network. Like browsing in your local bookstore, browsing in
the computer network allows you to find something without specifically
knowing its name. This is similar to what one does on NBT Internet, and
therefore the program that is used to access information on the Internet is
called a browser.

The browser service on a Windows NT computer provides you the ability to "browse" through the various computers on your network and to look
for specific resources. This is the fairly efficient method of finding resources
when you do not immediately know the name.

The Windows NT computer browser service manages a list of all available resources on the network. Applications (for example MS Word, Windows Explorer, etc.) take advantage of the service when they are looking for
resources. Because this list is managed centrally, you save both computer
processing power and memory. Not every computer is required to maintain a
copy of the list in memory or need to spend time keeping it up to date. Instead, there is a single computer that queries the list as needed. In essence,
this is the same way that DNS works, but for a different purpose.

As with DNS, different computers can play different roles in this
scheme. The master browser is the computer that maintains the Master list. It
is responsible to collect all the information and to create the list. It is also responsible to distribute the list to the backup browsers.

Both the master and backup browsers can be read for this information.
The system administrator can define a computer as the "preferred" master
browser. When the computer started, it declares itself master browser for the

workgroup or domain. If another computer has already declared itself as master browser, an election takes place. This election ensures that there is only one master browser and that information remain consistent. Election can also take place when a computer cannot find the master browser.

When an election takes place, an election packet is sent via broadcast across the network. Because the packet is broadcast, each browser receives this packet. Within the packet is a value that states the precedents of that browser. If the browser has a higher value than the packet receives, it replaces the current value with its own value, and we send the packet until a master browser has been elected.

When a computer starts on which the server service is running, it reports to the master browser that it is a member of the workgroup or domain. The server service does not mean that the computer is a server such as a Primary Domain Controller (PDC) or Backup Domain Controller (BDC) , but rather it can provide resources, which other computers can take advantage of. Note that this does not mean that this particular computer is actually providing resources, but rather just that the server service is running.

When a client wishes to use a particular resource, it asks the master browser for a list of the backup browsers. The backup browsers spread the load so the master is not overburdened. If there is no backup browser, the work is done by the master browser.

In Windows 3.1 and Windows NT 3.51, you had to connect to the resource before you could use it. That meant you had to connect the shared directory to a specific drive letter or a network printer to a specific local board before you could use it. In Windows 95/98/NT and later you have the "network neighborhood," which you see in the Windows Explorer. Through this, you are able to access network resources without first connecting to them in the traditional sent.

Figure 2–8 shows you the network neighborhood on a Windows NT computer. Here you see all of the available domains and shared resources. Directories can be opened and the files accessed just as you normally would. If you have a larger domain with a lot of computers and resources, it is cumbersome to put through all of the different computers looking for a resource that you need repeatedly. However, if you will need a particular resource once (or infrequently), this is extremely efficient.

Windows NT Domains

In order to simplify administration, Microsoft developed the concept of domains. As with the Internet domains before it, Windows NT domains are logical collections of machines. In addition, machines in a domain can all be in the same room or spread out around the world.

Like an Internet domain, a Windows NT domain can be any size. You can start with a single server and a few workstations and end up with a network of several servers and hundreds of workstations. However, no matter

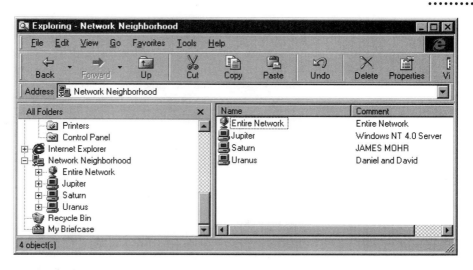

FIGURE 2-8   The Windows network neighborhood.

where they exist in the world, they are administered from a central location and therefore the domain forms the central administration unit in a Windows NT network.

Also keep in mind that a domain is not necessarily related to a physical location. It is possible to have a single domain spread out over multiple physical locations, just as it is possible to have multiple domains at one site. In fact, I have worked in companies were both situations existed. That is, domains were spread out across multiple physical locations and a large site had multiple domains.

Also, Windows NT domains are similar conceptually to an Internet domain; there are a number things to remember. First, a single machine can belong to both a Windows NT domain and an Internet domain. In addition, the two domains need not be identical. It is possible (actually likely) that a single Internet domain consists of multiple NT domains. Although less likely, it is also possible that a single NT domain can consist of multiple Internet domains.

One key difference to Internet domains is that Windows NT domains are the most powerful administrative units within a Windows network. In an Internet domain, it is possible that there is no administrative body responsible for all of the machines. In each case, it is possible that there are completely separate groups of users. In order to access resources on other machines, multiple-user accounts may be necessary. In contrast, there is a central user database within a Windows NT domain. Normally, users will logon to the domain and not locally onto their machine. It is then a server within the domain that allows or denies access.

Another key aspect is that Windows NT domains can be configured to trust one another. Once this *trust relationship* has been established, you can grant access to files and directories to users and groups in other domains. The domains providing resources are referred to as "resource domains," and those with the user databases are called "user domains."

In addition to being able to allow users in other domains to access resources, you can also include groups from other domains in local groups. We used this to include the Domain Admins group (the domain administrators) from the headquarters in the local administrators group. This meant that the administrators in the headquarters were essentially administrators in all of the other domains. This saved a great deal of time, as it was not necessary to contact someone in the local office to perform certain tasks.

Although you can have multiple servers within a domain, there will always be one tht take the dominant role and becomes the Primary Domain Controller (PDC). Here all of the user account information and security information is stored, which allows access to the network. However, access for each individual object, such as directory or printer, is stored on the machine where that object resides. To avoid any conflicts, a domain will always consist of just a single PDC.

Another kind of server is the Backup Domain Controller (BDC). The only reason it needs to be labeled as "backup" is that the PDC is the authority in terms of user and group information. It is possible that the BDC is the primary server for all of the other activity on the network. This also means that it is entirely possible that the BDC is a much more powerful machine than the primary.

When changes are made to the user database on the PDC, the changes are passed on to the BDC. It is therefore possible that the BDC provides user authentication within the domain and thus reduces the load on the PDC. The user is then given a token, which serves as identification during that session. Part of this token is also the name of the domain the user belongs to. When the user tries to access a resource in another domain, the server in that domain uses the token to verify the user's ID with the original server.

This "pass-through" authentication is a great advantage for the users. Because the server in the resource domain does the checking, the user only needs a single account. There is therefore no need to logon multiple times to access resources on different machines.

Whether a machine becomes a PDC, BDC, or even a stand-alone server is decided during the installation. The first server in a domain *must* be configured as the primary, as the BDCs need to contact the PDC to get the necessary logon information. If there is no PDC, there is no information to get. When the PDC is installed, you can say that the domain is "created."

Although you can have only a single PDC, you can have as many BDCs as you want. As with domains in general, the servers can be spread out over multiple physical locations as well as servers from multiple domains in a single location. In one company, we had eight BDCs in seven different locations. At one location, we had the PDC from two different domains, although one of the domains was literally on the other side of the world. The reason this was done was to speed up administration activity.

Although the PDCs were either in the headquarters or in a specific office, each branch had its own BDC. This was useful because of the time needed to do the authentication across the WAN: Because the BDC in the local office could do the authentication, there was no real need to have the PDC on-site.

In the same company, we also had situations where the local office comprised its own domain. This actually made the administration easier, as these were larger offices, which had their own system administrators. They could take over a lot of the work we had to do for other domains.

Basically, the resources that users needed (directories, printers, etc.) existed on the local server. Even though it was a BDC, the local server was almost always the first to answer logon requests. Therefore, there was basically no delay. However, if the BDC in the branch office was down, it took a considerable amount of time to get a response from the primary, but it was still possible.

Because the administrators in the headquarters were all part of the Domain Admins group that was included in the local Administrators group, we could administer any server anywhere in the world. This was only possible by establishing a trust relationship between the two domains. Therefore, there was a trust relation between the central domain and the domains for the various branch offices.

There are actually two kinds of trust relationships. Either each domain trusts the other, or only one domain is trusted. For example, it is possible that the headquarters is trusted by all of the domains, but none of the domains is trusted by the headquarters. This means that users from the headquarters can access resources in the other domains, but users in the branch offices cannot use resources in the headquarters.

Note also that the trust relationship is not transitive. For example, in one company, we configured the domains so that each domain trusted and was trusted by the headquarters. However, few of the branch offices trusted one another. This was simply a security issue and had nothing to do with the individuals in each office. However, there were several cases where information was regularly exchanged between different offices, so a trust relationship was established.

Keep in mind that having mutual trust among all domains can become an administrative nightmare. Because the trust is not transitive and must be established in *both* directions, there will be two trust relationships between any pair of domains. With just four domains, there are six pairs. That means there are 12 trust relationships. Generalized, there are $n(n-1)$ trust relationships. This means that with 10 domains, there are 90 trust relationships. With 25 domains, there are 600 trust relationships. It is therefore extremely beneficial to plan your domain concept from the beginning.

This brings us to the different kinds of domain configurations. The simplest is a single domain model. Here, all machines belong to a single domain. This really only makes sense in smaller organizations in a single physical locations.

Next is the master domain model. Here, the master domain contains all of the user information; subsequent domains contain resources. Access to these resources is defined by the users in the master domain. This requires at least a trust relationship whereby the master (user) domain is trusted by the resource domains.

Finally, there is the multiple master domain model. Here, there are multiple user databases, managed by the PDC in each of the respective domains. These domains (as well as others) can then serve as resource domains.

Network Hardware

The saying that the chain is only as strong as its weakest link definitely applies to the network. For a network operating system like Windows NT, the network hardware can become a deciding factor in terms of how well it performs (or at least how the performance is perceived). It is therefore essential that your network hardware not only handle the load now, but also as you network grows.

One of the problems I encountered during my research is that there is so much material available on so many different products. In addition, networking covers such a wide range of products, you could write an entire book just on the networking aspects. In fact, there are a number of good books that do just that.

Because I cannot talk about every aspect, I decided that I would address the most primary concern to users and that is the network interface card (NIC), which is the first piece of hardware in the long journey between workstation and server. In addition, a few of the most common pieces of hardware on this journey are routers, bridges, hubs, and switches (if you have a twisted pair network).

As its name implies, a *router* routes the traffic along the network. However, there is more to it than just deciding what path to take. Instead, modern routers have the ability to determine if the packet should be sent at all. This can be determined by which port as well as which machine sent or is to receive the packet. For example, it is common to have routers that only allow connections to a specific machine using only the HTTP or SMTP (email) protocols. Other protocols or even these protocols to other machines are blocked. This is the basic functionality of a firewall.

Typically, routers are a connection between two separate networks. Depending on the router itself, you could have several different networks connected to the same router. In fact, it is possible to have different kinds of physical networks connected to the routers, such as having both serial and twisted pair.

Thin Wire Versus Twisted Pair

The fact that twisted pair cabling is less expensive than thin wire is deceiving. For a given length of cable, the cable itself and the connectors are cheaper. However, you must keep in mind that there will be a cable from the hub to each node, including the server. In contrast, thin wire cables are laid *between* the nodes.

Let's take an example with a server and four computers, spaced evenly every 10 feet. You could get away with just 40 feet of thin wire cable, as you need 10 feet from the server to the first machine, another 10 feet from the first to the second, and so on.

With twisted pair, let's assume that the hub is right next to the top of the server, so the cable length can be ignored. You need 10 feet of cable to the first computer, but 20 feet to the second, 30 feet to the third, and 40 feet to the fourth. This means a total of 100 feet. The more computers you have, the greater the difference in cable lengths.

In addition, there is more work. You cannot just move from computer to computer, adding cable as you go. You lay the cable from the hub to the first computer, then go back to the hub. You lay the cable from the hub to the second computer, then go back to the hub, and so forth.

One the other hand, twisted pair is a fair bit safer. As I mentioned, if the connection to one computer goes down, the rest can still work.

A *hub* is often called a repeater, because it serves as a hub for the network cables as well as "repeats" the signal, allowing you to transmit over greater distances. A hub is needed when you are using twisted pair cables, and every node (client and server) must be connected to a hub. Because a hub sits at the bottom of the protocol stack, it transmits every type of packet.

Typically, hubs are used to organize the nodes on your network into physical groups. However, it does not perform any logical functions, such as determining routes to take. (That's what a router does.) Despite this, most hubs are capable of doing collision detection.

A modification of a hub is a *bridge*. Bridges allow you to physically separate network segments and can extend the length of your cables. The difference lies in the fact that the bridge determines if a packet is intended for a machine on the same segment or not. If it is, it can be ignored and not passed through to other segments.

The key lies in what is called a *collision domain*. In essence, this is the set of nodes that sends out packets, which collide with one another. The more collisions you have, the worse your network performance becomes, because it means you have more network traffic, and other machines need to wait. By grouping machines into groups that communicate with one another, you reduce the collisions with unrelated machines.

Because bridges block the packets for the local collision domain, each domain has fewer collisions. Keep in mind that this only works when there is a lot of traffic between the nodes, such as in a work group. If you have a strictly client–server model, a bridge may not bring you much advantage.

Another way of significantly reducing collisions is by using a *switch*. The difference is that the switch analyzes packets to determine the destination and makes a virtual connection between the two ports, thus reducing the number of collisions. Using the store-and-forward method, packets are stored within the switch before being sent along. The cut-through method reads just the header to determine the destination.

An important aspect to look at is, obviously, the transfer speed of the card. One common problem I have seen in companies without a dedicated IT organization (and in some cases with one) is forgetting the saying about the weakest link. This happens when they buy 10-Mbit cards for their workstations (or are perhaps using older models) but install a 100-Mbit card in their server. The problem is that the server can only send at 10 Mbits, because that's what the clients can handle.

As we discussed previously, the two most common Ethernet types are twisted pair and thin-wire. Traditional Ethernet was limited to only 10 Mbits and is slowly being replaced with FastEthernet, which can handle 100 Mbits. The problem is that you may not be able to use other existing network components such as cables if you were using thin wire. The reason is simply that thin wire is unable to transmit at the higher speed. On the other hand, twisted pair can handle it (provided you use the right kind of cable).

One place this is commonly noticed is the connectors on the network cards themselves. You will often find many cards designated 10/100 or something in their name. As you might guess, this indicates they can handle either 10 or 100 Mbits, depending on the speed of the hub to which they are connected. I have seen some cards that require you to set the speed either in software or hardware.

However, my 3Com cards detect the speed the hub uses and adjust automatically. In my office at home, I have three computers, all hooked through a 10-Mbit hub. Because very little data are going through the network, this was sufficient as well as less expensive. Even so, my 3Com cards are all 10/100 and adjust to the slower speed. When I upgrade to a faster up, I do not need to replace the cards or do any configuration. I just plug the cables into the new hub and go.

This may sound like a minor point, and it is for my three-node network. However, at work, with hundreds of nodes, it becomes a major issue. Imagine having to change the hardware settings on hundreds of PCs. That means opening the case, pulling out the card, setting the jumper, putting the card back in, and then closing the case. Granted, most newer cards are Plug and Play, but are you sure yours is?

Some cards, like my 3Com Fast EtherLink XL 3C905B-COMBO, have connectors for thin wire, thick-wire, and twisted pair, but only the twisted-pair connector allows you to use the 100-Mbit connector. Note also that most of the 3Com Fast EtherLink 10/100 cards just have the twisted-pair connector.

Keep in mind that even if you do use the twisted-pair connector, you are limited by the speed of the other hardware. I chose a 10-Mbit hub because I did not want or need to spend the extra money for a 100-Mbit hub. Even in a business, you may not need more. If all of your applications are installed locally, with only the data on the server, you probably won't even come close to needing even the 10Mbit hub. This is especially true if you break down your network into subnets, which are separated by routers.

However, speed is not the only consideration, particularly in a server. Take the analogy of a 100-mile race between a Ferrari and a Geo Metro. The winner is fairly obvious, unless you take a Ferrari loaded with bricks and has to refuel every mile. In some cases, you might have a Ferrari network card that is slowed down by other things.

There are several things your card can do, such as what my 3Com 3C980-TX Fast EtherLink Server NIC does. The first is the ability to combine multiple cards into a single virtual interface. One card is processing the packet while the other is receiving, for example. The load is balanced between the cards to ensure that one is not overburdened.

The next feature is what 3Com calls *self-healing drivers*. Here the card monitors and action is taken based on what it finds. One simple example would be shutting down one card in a virtual set if it appeared to be causing too many errors.

Throughput (the true measure of speed) is increased by using 3Com's Parallel Tasking. Traditionally, networks cards transfer data between the card and memory in one direction at a time. 3Com cards can transmit in both directions. In addition, there was a previous limitation with PCI cards that could transmit a maximum of 64 bytes at once. The newest 3Com cards have increased this to the maximum 1514 of a standard Ethernet packet. This meant that with previous cards, where it might need up to 24 buy cycles to transmit the data, the 3Com card can do it in a single cycle.

A moment ago, I mentioned cases where people would install 100-Mbit cards in their server and 10-Mbit cards in their clients'. In those cases, they actually had 10 M-bit hubs, so the problem was as much an issue with the hub as with the speed of the client cards. In some cases, it actually makes sense to configure your system like that, but you need a hub that can handle the job.

One solution to this is the 3Com SuperStack II Dual Speed Hub. The key is part of the name: "dual speed." As its name implies, it can actually handle both 10-Mbit and 100-Mbit connections. It is able to sense the speed on the port and adjust itself *for that port*. This means that the connection between the server could be running at 100 Mbits, with the connection between the hub and clients running at 10 Mbits (or maybe just some of the clients).

This ends up increasing overall performance, as the hub can operate in duplex mode. That is, it can send and receive at the same time. 10-Mbit data are being sent to the hub as it is sending 100-Mbit data to the server.

Some vendors try to save a little by making hubs that "pretend" to run at both 10 and 100 Mbits. This is done by having a single port that can handle the 100 Mbits, which is typically connected to the server. However, this means that if you ever upgrade a single client, you have to upgrade the up as well. The 3Com solutions automatically make the change for you.

One thing to keep in mind here is the cabling. FastEthernet requires what is referred to as category 5 cabling. However, 10 Mbit can handle category 3 or 4. Although you can certainly connect your network using category 3 cable, the number of errors increases dramatically. Packets need to get resent, and it can actually turn out to be slower than running at 10 Mbits. The 3Com Super-Stack addresses this issue by monitoring the frequency and type of errors. Should the errors be too high, it will automatically lower the speed to 10 Mbits.

Twisted Pair Cables

TP Cabling consists of four twister pairs of wire (hence the name). The wires themselves are 24 American Wire Gauge (AWG), which has an impedance of 100 Ohms. Each end of the wire has an eight-position modular jack, similar to what you find in a telephone (which only has four wires). As of this writing, there are three categories in common use:

- CAT 3 — up to 16 MHz

- CAT 4 — up to 20 MHz

- CAT 5 — up to 100 MHz

In principle, routers have the same limitations as hubs, in that they can limit well as are limited by the other network components. However, there are several features that we ought to take a look at.

One feature provided by 3Com's NETBuilder routers is what is referred to as *bandwidth grooming*. Among other things, this allows you to prioritized the traffic on your network, based on a number of different criteria. For example, you define higher priority to specific protocols or specific ports (or both). This is useful when defining priority based on a specific application, type of connection and many other cases.

In addition, the NETBuilder series features dual processors. While one processor is handling tradition routing functions such processing the packets. The second processor concerns itself with the "grooming" functions, which greatly increases the overall performance.

There is also the issue of security. Many people think of router security only in terms of connections to the Internet. However, some companies are concerned with internal security as well. For example, it is possible with the NETBuilder routers to disallow connections from the warehouse to the main server, except for specifically defined ports. This might give them access to the main database application but prevent them from poking around the file system.

One thing to keep in mind that there are a number of differences between the behavior of a Wide Area Network (WAN) and a Local Area Network (LAN). In my opinion, the two most significant aspects are that a WAN has slower speeds and the routing of the packets is the dominant behavior as compared to fast speeds and switching for the LAN. Even if your internal network only runs at 10 Mbps, it is still 160 times faster than a typical 64-Kbps WAN connection.

The result of all of this is that you typically have different kinds of equipment for both. In addition, because of the slower speeds, a WAN has less bandwidth and you are "encouraged" to reduce unnecessary traffic. This is where routing comes in. You want to limit unnecessary and even unwanted traffic. For example, we talked above about the ability of 3Com routers to direct traffic based on specific ports. In some cases, you may want to turn off specific ports to certain network segments to reduce the traffic, although other ports (and therefore other protocols) are allowed. One common thing is to restrict broadcast traffic, which the 3Com routers can do.

Another thing we discussed was the ability of the 3Com routers to prioritize the packets. I have worked in places using a database application that always accessed the server in a specific port range. To ensure proper response times, this range of ports could be given priority over something like file data transfer. Files going across the WAN were typically lower priority than the database application. The 3Com router thus allows you to manage the performance on each network segment.

A shoot-off of this is "protocol reservation." As its name implies, a certain portion of the bandwidth is reserved for specific protocols. That means that no matter what other traffic is on the link, the reserved portion will always be available for that protocol.

Another thing to consider is how the routing information is transferred between routers. Many routers use what is called "distance vector routing," where the router can determine the shortest path between two nodes. However, you may not want the router to choose the shortest path, because "short" means the number of nodes it goes through (or hops) and not the length of the cable or the speed. Often such routers will exchange information even though the network has not changed. In essence, this wastes bandwidth.

Instead, to limit bandwidth, you want all packets going to a particular subnet to *always* use a predefined route. This is the basis behind "link-state" routing. Although this is requires more computational power than distance vector routing, it also requires a lot less bandwidth. Because routes are calculated, less data is transferred, so when a link goes down, the updated information reaches the affected routers more quickly and the new route in effect more quickly, as the computation is faster than the network.

Another core aspect of the vendor you chose is the after-sales service. For most companies, the primary concern is the warranty. That is, what happens when a card malfunctions. Most warranties last a year, which is normally long enough to identify any manufacturing defects. However, even within the warranty period, you will generally find that you will either have to return the card to the reseller or return it directly to the manufacturer. Therefore, it is a good idea to have enough spares on hand. Although you might be able to work out an arrangement with either the vendor or reseller to send you a replacement before they receive the defective card, you are still out of work for a couple days, so spares are still a good idea.

For larger companies, there may be some greater need, especially when planning extensive enhancement to the existing network. Many vendors of networking technology provide consulting services to assist you in a wide range of areas involving your network. This can be anything from an evaluation of your existing network to complete project management in which the vendor manages every aspect from the planning through the implementation, testing, and beyond.

Getting professional services from a vendor is a two-edged sword. On the one hand, they are obviously interested in having you purchase their products and may push something on you, which you do not need On the other hand, if you have already chosen them for the products you will implement, they are in a better position to help you implement the products correctly.

As one of the pioneers with many network technologies, 3Com has been at the forefront of the network technologies as well as network-related services. For starters, 3Com provides a detailed network analysis. This is important if you have already identified that your network is having problems and need assistance tracking down the problems or implementing the correct solution. This is also extremely useful if you are planning network improvements and are looking for the best places to implement the changes.

You can start with the 3Com Network Performance Check. As its name implies, this service will conduct a performance analysis of your system and report on any areas that either should or could be improved. One problem I regularly see is that the system administrators do not have the experience to analyze their network performance properly to make the appropriate changes. Often the solution is to throw enough hardware at the problem until it goes away. This often means more work and usually means much more money than implementing the correct solution the first time, and you will probably not have a complete solution. In addition, the analysis will show areas that could need changes for increased performance in the future as the network expands.

The larger your network, the greater I feel the need for services like this. The sheer number of different components complicates the matter to such an extent that most administrators are covered in a mountain of statistics. Having experienced engineers visit your site, collect the data, and analyze it is generally more efficient. Plus, sticking with one vendor standardizes the hardware, which makes administering it, and even troubleshotting it, much easier.

One key aspect is the tools the engineers bring with them. Most companies cannot afford the expensive equipment required to gather the necessary data. In addition, I have seen cases myself, where for a novice the data indicated a specific problem. However, with a more-detailed analysis, the actual problem turned out to be something different.

At the high end of the scale, 3Com offers project management services that start with the basic analysis and end up with a finished project, complete with documentation. Based on the information obtained through the network analysis, the 3Ccom project engineers can make detailed specification of your project and allow you to decide which changes should be made. Based on your choices, the project is implemented, tested, and reevaluated to ensure it meets the promised specifications.

One of the key aspects here is the documentation of the project. I have worked with consultants before, who have simply submitted a project report when finished, which contained little detail of the work accomplished. This makes questioning the bill they send you difficult. In addition, how can you really be expected to manage your system if you are not told anything about it?

Another aspect that the 3Com project management emphasizes is regular reporting. Here again, I can speak from experience about how important it is to be kept abreast of what is happening. I have been involved in projects where nothing was mentioned until the project was completed. They only *thought* they understood the project. The result was something completely different. Therefore, having the project team provide regular *written* reports is an absolute must.

You will also find a wide ranges of services that lie somewhere in the middle. Such services include network design service, which plans the layout of a network to meet your needs. Should your current network be sufficient but is lacking a little fine tuning, 3Com also provides network configuration services.

Extended support options are also available for your needs. These range anywhere from traditional telephone support to a 4-hour on-site response time. In addition, 3Com provides access to their on-line knowledge base for free.

The Computer Itself

··

If the hardware doesn't work, the operating system won't work and neither will the users. Although Admins may not need to know the name or number of each chip on the motherboard, they should at least know about basic issues like the different kinds of RAM and whether their hard disk is EIDE or SCSI.

These may seem like mundane issues, which every administrator should know. However, I have worked in companies where they didn't. Other people were responsible for the hardware, so they didn't bother. Depending on your organization, there may be administrators that ever actually touch the hardware. In one company where I worked, we had a separate team that was responsible for installing all of the machines, including those for the administrators. There was little communication, which meant the administrator had to figure out what was in the machine on his own.

Just knowing the type of hard disk in your machine is not necessarily an indication that you know what the characteristics are. However, in order to be able to support users, you will need to know what different kinds of hardware are available, what their characteristics are, and how you can choose the right hardware for each situation.

That's exactly what we are going to be talking about in this chapter.

This section should serve as a background for many issues I've covered elsewhere. This chapter is designed to familiarize you with the concepts rather than make you an expert on any aspect of the hardware. If you want to read more about PC hardware, an excellent book is *the Winn Rosch Hardware Bible* from Brady Books. (It's more than 1000 pages and, as of this writing is in its third edition.)

In the following sections, I will be talking primarily about Intel-based PC hardware. Many of the concepts are the same as on Alpha machines, but when I talk about specific interactions with the hardware, they may only apply to the PC. Despite the fact that Windows NT runs on both Intel and Alpha, neither Windows 95 nor Windows 98 run on Alpha. Therefore, to cover this machine as well without turning this into a book on PC hardware, I will restrict myself primarily to Intel.

Basic Input/Output Services and the System Bus

A key concept for this discussion is the bus. So, just what is a bus? In computer terms, it has a similar meaning as your local county public transit—it is used to move something from one place to another. The county transit bus moves people; a computer bus moves information.

The information is transmitted along the bus as electric signals. If you have ever opened up a computer, you probably saw that there is one central printed circuit board with the CPU, the expansion cards, and several chips sticking out of it. The electronic connection between these parts is referred to as a bus.

The signals that move along a computer bus come in two basic forms: control and data. Control signals do just that: They control things. Data signals are just that: data. I will get to how this happens and what each part does as we move along.

In today's PC computer market, there are several buses, many of which have the same functions but approach things quite differently. In this section, I am going to talk about the different bus types, what goes on between the different devices on the bus, and what the main components are that communicate along the bus.

Despite differences in bus types, certain aspects of the hardware are common with among all PCs. The Basic Input-Output Service (BIOS), interrupts, Direct Memory Access channels, and base addresses are just a few.

The standard BIOS for PCs is the IBM BIOS, but that's simply because "PC" is an IBM standard. However, "standard" does not mean "most common," as there are several other BIOS vendors, such as Phoenix and AMI.

DOS or a DOS application makes device-independent calls to the BIOS to transfer data. The BIOS then translates this into device-dependent instructions. For example, DOS (or the application) requests that the hard disk read a certain block of data. The application does not care what kind of hard disk hardware there is, nor should it. It is BIOS's job to make that translation to something the specific hard disk can understand.

In Windows NT, on the other hand, a special program called a device driver handles the functions of the BIOS. As we talked about in the section on the kernel, device drivers are sets of routines that directly access the hardware, just as the BIOS does.

The fact that Windows NT bypasses the BIOS and goes directly to the hardware is one reason why some hardware drivers will work under DOS but not under Windows NT. In some instances, the BIOS has been specially designed for the machine on which it runs. Because of this, it can speak the same dialect of "machine language" that the rest of the hardware speaks. However, because Windows NT does not speak the same dialect, things get lost in the translation.

The Expansion Bus

It is generally understood that the speed and capabilities of the CPU are directly related to the performance of the system as a whole. In fact, the CPU is a major selling point of PCs, especially among less-experienced users. One aspect of the machine that is less understood and therefore less likely to be an issue is the expansion bus.

The *expansion bus,* simply put, is the set of connections and slots that enable users to add to, or expand, their system. Although it's not really an "expansion" of the system, you often find video cards and hard disk controllers attached to the "expansion" bus.

Anyone who has opened a computer case has seen parts of the expansion bus. The slots used to connect cards to the system are part of this bus. Note that people will often refer to this bus as "the bus." Though it will be understood what is meant, there are other buses on the system. Just keep this in mind as you go through this chapter.

Most people are aware of the differences in CPUs, whether the CPU is 16-bit or 32-bit, what the speed of the processor is, whether there is a math coprocessor, and so on. The concepts of BIOS and interrupts are also commonly understood.

One part of the machine's hardware that is somewhat less known and often causes confusion is the bus architecture. This is the basic way in which the hardware components (usually on the motherboard) all fit together. Windows NT will run on several different kinds of buses. The most common are those in PCs, which I will talk about first. (Note: Here I am referring to the main system bus, although all versions of Windows can access devices on other buses.)

The three major types of bus architectures used are the Industry Standard Architecture (ISA), the Extended Industry Standard Architecture (EISA), and the Micro-Channel Architecture (MCA). Both ISA and EISA machines are manufactured by a wide range of companies, but only a few (primarily IBM) manufacture MCA machines. As of this writing, no commercial distributions are available for MCA, but a development project is underway.

In addition to these three architectures, a few other bus types can be used in conjunction with or to supplement the three, including the Small Computer System Interface (SCSI), Peripheral Component Interconnect (PCI), and the Advanced Graphics Port (AGP).

PCI and the newer AGP exist as separate buses on the computer motherboard (although SCSI controllers are sometimes built directly onto the motherboard). Expansion cards exist for both of these types of buses. You will usually find any one of them in addition to either ISA or EISA. In many cases, however, you can also find both, or your may find both PCI and AGP in addition to the primary bus. It is also possible to have machines that only have PCI, because it is a true system bus. Because of the advantages of the PCI-Bus, some manufacturers are beginning to manufacture machines with only the PCI-Bus. However, as of this writing, only a few machines provide PCI-only expansion buses.

SCSI, on the other hand, complements the existing bus architecture by adding an additional hardware controller to the system. There are SCSI controllers (more commonly referred to as host adapters) that fit in ISA, EISA, MCA, PCI, or AGP slots.

Industry Standard Architecture (ISA)

As I mentioned before, most people are generally aware of the relationship between CPU performance and system performance. However, every system is only as strong as its weakest component. Therefore, the expansion bus also sets limits on the system performance.

There were several drawbacks with the original expansion bus in the original IBM PC. First, it was limited to only 8 data lines, which meant that only 8 bits could be transferred at a time. Second, the expansion bus was, in a way, directly connected to the CPU. Therefore, it operated at the same speed as the CPU, which meant that to improve performance with the CPU, the expansion bus had to be altered as well. The result would have been that existing expansion cards would be obsolete.

In the early days of PC computing, IBM was not known to want to cut its own throat. It had already developed quite a following with the IBM PC among users and developers. If it decided to change the design of the expansion bus, developers would have to reinvent the wheel, and users would have to buy all new equipment. There was the risk that users and developers would switch to another platform instead of sticking with IBM.

Rather than risk that, IBM decided that backward compatibility was a paramount issue. One key change was severing the direct connection between the expansion bus and CPU. As a result, expansion boards could operate at a different speed than the CPU, enabling users to keep existing hardware and enabling manufacturers to keep producing their expansion cards. As a result, the IBM standard became the industry standard, and the bus architecture became known as the Industry Standard Architecture, or ISA.

In addition to this change, IBM added more address and data lines. They doubled the data lines to 16 and increased the address lines to 24. This meant that the system could address up to 16 MB of memory, the maximum that the 80286 CPU (Intel's newest central processor at the time) could handle.

When the 80386 came out, the connection between the CPU and bus clocks were severed completely, because no expansion board could operate at the 16 MHz or more than the 80386 could. The bus speed does not need to be an exact fraction of the CPU speed, but an attempt has been made to keep it there, because by keeping the bus and CPU synchronized, it is easier to transfer data. The CPU will only accept data when it coincides with its own clock. If an attempt is made to speed the bus a little, the data must wait until the right moment in the CPU's clock cycle to pass the data. Therefore, nothing has been gained by making it faster.

One method used to speed up the transfer of data is Direct Memory Access, or DMA. Although DMA existed in the IBM XT, the ISA-Bus provided some extra lines. DMA enables the system to move data from place to place without the intervention of the CPU. In that way, data can be transferred from, let's say, the hard disk to memory while the CPU is working on something else. Keep in mind that to make the transfer, the DMA controller must have complete control of both the data and the address lines, so the CPU itself cannot access memory at this time. What DMA access looks like graphically we see in Figure 3–1.

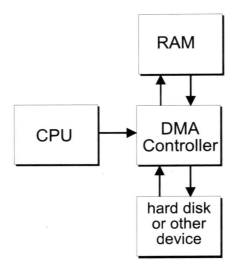

FIGURE 3–1   Direct memory access.

Let's step back a minute. It is somewhat incorrect to say that a DMA transfer occurs without intervention from the CPU, as it is the CPU that must initiate the transfer. Once the transfer is started, however, the CPU is free to continue with other activities. DMA controllers on ISA-Bus machines use "pass-through" or "fly-by" transfers. That is, the data are not latched or held internally but rather is simply passed through the controller. If it were latched, two cycles would be needed: one to latch into the DMA controller and another to pass it to the device or memory (depending on which way it was headed).

Devices tell the DMA controller that they wish to make DMA transfers through one of three "DMA Request" lines, numbered 1–3. Each of these lines is given a priority based on its number, 1 being the highest. The ISA-Bus includes two sets of DMA controllers: four 8-bit channels and four 16-bit channels. The channels are labeled 0–7, 0 having the highest priority.

Each device on the system capable of doing DMA transfers is given its own DMA channel. The channel is set on the expansion board, usually by means of jumpers. The pins to which these jumpers are connected are usually labeled DRQ, for DMA Request.

The two DMA controllers (both Intel 8237), each with four DMA channels, are cascaded together. The master DMA controller is the one connected directly to the CPU. One of its DMA channels is used to connect to the slave controller. Because of this, there are actually only seven channels available.

Anyone who has cared for a baby knows what an interrupt-driven operating system like Windows goes through on a regular basis. Just like a baby when it needs its diaper changed, when a device on the expansion bus needs servicing, it tells the system by generating an interrupt (the baby cries). For example, when the hard disk has transferred the requested data to or from memory, it signals the CPU by means of an interrupt. When keys are pressed on the keyboard, the keyboard interface also generates an interrupt.

On receiving such an interrupt, the system executes a set of functions commonly referred to as an Interrupt Service Routine, or ISR. Because the reaction to a key being pressed on the keyboard is different from the reaction when data are transferred from the hard disk, there needs to be different ISRs for each device. Although the behavior of ISRs is different under DOS than UNIX, their functionality is basically the same.

On the CPU, there is a single interrupt request line. This does not mean that every device on the system is connected to the CPU via this single line, however. Just as a DMA controller handles DMA requests, an interrupt controller handles interrupt requests. This is the Intel 8259 Programmable Interrupt Controller (PIC).

On the original IBM PC, there were five "Interrupt Request" lines, numbered 2–7. Here again, the higher the number, the lower the priority. (Interrupts 0 and 1 are used internally and are not available for expansion cards.)

The ISA-Bus also added an additional PIC, which is "cascaded" off the first PIC. With this addition, there were now 16 interrupt values on the system. However, not all of these were available to devices. Interrupts 0 and 1 were still used internally, but so were interrupts 8 and 13. Interrupt 2 was something special. It, too, was reserved for system use, but instead of being a device of some kind, an interrupt on line 2 actually meant that an interrupt was coming from the second PIC, similar to the way cascading works on the DMA controller.

A question I brought up when I first started learning about interrupts was, "What happens when the system is servicing an interrupt and another one comes in?" Two mechanisms can help in this situation.

Remember that the 8259 is a "programmable" interrupt controller. There is a machine instruction called Clear Interrupt Enable (CLI). If a program is executing what is called a critical section of code (a section that should not be stopped in the middle), the programmer can call the CLI instruction and disable acknowledgment of all incoming interrupts. As soon as the critical section is finished and closed, the program should execute a Set Interrupt Enable, or STI, instruction shortly afterward.

I say "should" because the programmer doesn't have to do this. A CLI instruction could be in the middle of a program somewhere, and if the STI is never called, no more interrupts will be serviced. Nothing, aside from common sense, prevents the programmer from doing this. Should the program take too long before it calls the STI, interrupts could get lost. This is common on busy systems when characters from the keyboard "disappear."

The second mechanism is that the interrupts are priority based. The lower the interrupt request level, or IRQ, the higher the priority. This has an interesting side effect, because the second PIC (or slave) is bridged off the first PIC (or master) at IRQ 2. The interrupts on the first PIC are numbered 0–7, and on the second PIC, the interrupts are numbered 8–15. However, the slave PIC is attached to the master at interrupt 2. Therefore, the actual priority is 0, 1, 8–15, 3–7.

There's one thing you should consider when dealing with interrupts. On XT machines, IRQ 2 was a valid interrupt. Now on AT machines, IRQ 2 is bridged to the second PIC. So, to ensure that devices configured to IRQ 2 work properly, the IRQ 2 pin on all of the expansion slots are connected to the IRQ 9 input of the second PIC. In addition, all the devices attached to the second PIC are associated with an IRQ value where they are attached to the PIC, and they generate an IRQ 2 on the first PIC.

The PICs on an ISA machine are edge triggered, which means that they react only when the interrupt signal is making the transition from low to high, that is, when it is on a transition edge. This becomes an issue when you attempt to share interrupts, that is, where two devices use the same interrupt.

Assume you have both a serial port and floppy controller at interrupt 6. If the serial port generates an interrupt, the system will "service" it. If the floppy controller generates an interrupt before the system has finished servicing the interrupt for the serial port, the interrupt from the floppy is lost. There is another way to react to interrupts called "level triggered," which I will get to shortly.

As I mentioned earlier, a primary consideration in the design of the AT Bus (as the changed PC-Bus came to be called) was that it maintain compatibility with its predecessors. It maintains compatibility with the PC expansion cards but takes advantage of 16-bit technology. To do this, connectors were not changed, only added. Therefore, you could slide cards designed for the 8-bit PC-Bus right into a 16-bit slot on the ISA-Bus, and no one would know the difference.

Micro-Channel Architecture (MCA)

The introduction of IBM's Micro-Channel Architecture (MCA) was a redesign of the entire bus architecture. Although IBM developed the original AT architecture, which later became ISA, many companies produced machines that followed this standard. The introduction of MCA meant that IBM could produce machines to which it alone had the patent rights.

One of the most obvious differences is the smaller slots required for MCA cards. ISA cards are 4.75" x 13.5", compared with the 3.5" x 11.5" MCA cards. As a result, the same number of cards can fit into a smaller area. The drawback was that ISA cards could not fit into MCA slots, and MCA cards could not fit into ISA slots. Although this might seem as though IBM had decided to cut its own throat, the changes they made in creating MCA made it very appealing.

Part of the decrease in size was a result of surface mount components, or surface mount technology (SMT). Previously, cards used "through-hole" mounting, in which holes were drilled through the system board (hence the name). Chips were mounted in these holes or into holders that were mounted in the holes. Surface mount does not use this and as a result looks "flattened" by comparison. This saves not only space, but also time and money, as SMT cards are easier to produce. In addition, the spacing between the pins on the card (0.050") corresponds to the spacing on the chips, which makes designing the boards much easier.

Micro-Channel also increases speed, because there is a ground on every fourth pin, which reduces interference, and as a result, the MCA-Bus can operate at ten times the speed of non-MCA machines and still comply with FCC regulations in terms of radio frequency interference.

Another major improvement was the expansion of the data bus to 32 bits. This meant that machines were no longer limited to 16 MB of memory but could now access 4 GB.

One key change in the MCA architecture was the concept of hardware-mediated bus arbitration. With ISA machines, devices could share the bus, and the OS was required to arbitrate who got a turn. With MCA, that arbitration is done at the hardware level, freeing the OS to work on other things. This also enables multiple processors to use the bus. To implement this, the bus has several new lines. Four lines determine the arbitration bus priority level, which represents the 16 different priority levels that a device could have. Who gets the bus depends on the priority.

From the user's perspective, the installation of MCA cards is much easier than that of ISA cards due to the introduction of the Programmable Option Select (POS). With POS, the entire hardware configuration is stored in the CMOS. When new cards are added, you are required to run the machine's reference disk. In addition, each card comes with an options disk that contains configuration information for the card. With the combination of reference disk and options disk, conflicts are all but eliminated.

Part of the MCA spec is that each card has its own unique identifying number encoded into the firmware. When the system boots, the settings in the CMOS are compared to the cards that are found on the bus. If one has been added or removed, the system requires you to boot using the reference disk to ensure that things are set up correctly.

As I mentioned, on each options disk is the necessary configuration information. This information is contained within the Adapter Description File (ADF). The ADF contains all the necessary information for your system to recognize the expansion card. Because it is only a few kilobytes big, many ADF files can be stored on a floppy. This is useful in situations like those we had in tech support. There were several MCA machines in the department with dozens of expansion cards, each with its own ADF file. Rather than having copies of each disk, the analysts who supported MCA machines (myself included) each had a single disk with all the ADF files. (Eventually that, too, became burdensome, so we copied the ADF files into a central directory where we could copy them as needed.) Any time we needed to add a new card to our machines for testing, we didn't need to worry about the ADF files, because they were all in one place.

Because each device has its own identification number, and this number is stored in the ADF, the reference diskette can find the appropriate number with no problem. All ADF files have names such as @BFDF.ADF, so it isn't obvious what kind of card the ADF file is for just by looking at the name. However, because the ADF files are simply text files, you can easily figure out which file is which by looking at the contents.

Unlike ISA machines, the MCA architecture enables interrupt sharing. Because many expansion boards are limited to a small range of interrupts, it is often difficult, if not impossible, to configure every combination on your system. Interrupt sharing is possible on MCA machines, because they use something called level-triggered interrupts, or level-sensitive interrupts.

With edge-triggered interrupts, or edge-sensitive interrupts (the standard on ISA buses), an interrupt is generated and is then dropped. This sets a flag in the PIC, which figures out which device generated the interrupt and services it. If interrupts were shared with edge-triggered interrupts, any interrupt that arrived between the time the first interrupt is generated and serviced would be lost, because the PIC has no means of knowing that a second interrupt occurred. All the PIC sees is that an interrupt occurred. Figure 3–2 shows how all of these elements relate to one another in time.

With level-triggered interrupts, when an interrupt is generated, it is held high until the PIC forces it low after the interrupt has been serviced. If another device were on the same interrupt, the PIC would try to pull down the interrupt line; however, the second device would keep it high. The PIC would then see that it was high and would be able to service the second device.

Despite the many obvious advantages of the MCA, there are a few drawbacks. One primary drawback is the interchangeability of expansion cards between architectures. MCA cards can only fit in MCA machines. However, it is possible to use an ISA card in an EISA machine, and EISA machines are what I will talk about next.

Extended Industry Standard Architecture (EISA)

To break the hold that IBM had on the 32-bit bus market with the Micro-Channel Architecture, a consortium of computer companies, lead by Compaq, issued their own standard in September 1988. This new standard was an extension of the ISA-Bus architecture and was (logically) called the Extended Industry Standard Architecture (EISA). EISA offered many of the same features as MCA but with a different approach.

Although EISA provides some major improvements, it has maintained backward compatibility with ISA boards. Therefore, existing ISA boards can be used in EISA machines. In some cases, such boards can even take advantage of the features that EISA offers.

To maintain this compatibility, EISA boards are the same size as their ISA counterparts and provide connections to the bus in the same locations. The original designed called for an extension of the bus slot, similar to the way the AT slots were an extension on the XT slots. However, this was deemed impractical, because some hardware vendors had additional contacts that extended beyond the ends of the slots. There was also the issue that in most cases, the slots would extend the entire length of the motherboard, which meant that the motherboard would need to be either longer or wider to handle the longer slots.

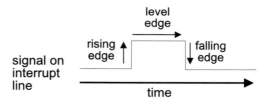

FIGURE 3–2   Interrupt signal.

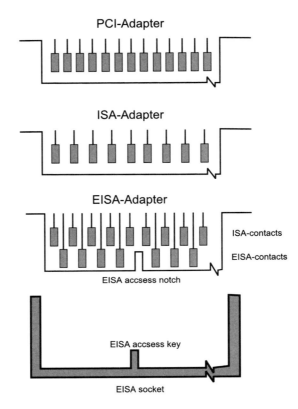

PCI-Adapter

ISA-Adapter

EISA-Adapter

ISA-contacts

EISA-contacts

EISA accsess notch

EISA accsess key

EISA socket

FIGURE 3–3 Comparison of ISA and EISA connections.

Instead, the current spec calls for the additional connections to be intertwined with the old ones and extend lower. In what used to be gaps between
the connectors are now leads to the new connectors. Therefore, EISA slots
are deeper than are those for ISA machines. Looking at EISA cards, you can
easily tell them from ISA cards by the two rows of connectors. Figure 3–3
shows what the ISA and EISA connections look like. Note that the adapters
are not to scale.

Another major improvement of EISA over ISA is the issue of bus arbitration. Bus arbitration is the process by which devices "discuss" whose turn it is
on the bus and then let one of them go. In XT and AT class machines, the
CPU completely managed control of the bus. EISA includes additional control
hardware to take this job away from the CPU, which does two important
things. First, the CPU is now "free" to carry on more important work, and second, the CPU gets to use the bus only when its turn comes around.

Hmmm. Does that sound right? Because the CPU is the single most important piece of hardware on the system, shouldn't it get the bus whenever it needs it? Well, yes and no. The key issue of contention is the use of the word "single." EISA was designed with multiprocessing in mind; that is, computers with more than one CPU. If there is more than one CPU, which one is more important?

The term used here is bus arbitration. Each of the six devices that EISA allows to take control of the bus has its own priority level. A device signals its desire for the bus by sending a signal to the Centralized Arbitration Control (CAC) unit. If conflicts arise (e.g., multiple requests), the CAC unit resolves them according to the priority of the requesting devices. Certain activity such as DMA and memory refresh have the highest priority, with the CPU following close behind. Such devices are called "bus mastering devices" or "bus masters," because they become the master of the bus.

The EISA DMA controller was designed for devices that cannot take advantage of the bus mastering capabilities of EISA. The DMA controller supports ISA, with ISA timing and 24-bit addressing as the default mode. However, it can be configured by EISA devices to take full advantage of the 32-bit capabilities.

Another advantage that EISA has is the concept of dual buses. Because cache memory is considered a basic part of the EISA specification, the CPU can often continue working for some time, even if it does not have access to the bus.

A major drawback of EISA (compared with MCA) is that to maintain the compatibility to ISA, EISA speed improvements cannot extend into memory. This is because the ISA-Bus cannot handle the speed requirements of the high-speed CPUs. Therefore, EISA requires separate memory buses. This results in every manufacturer having its own memory expansion cards.

In the discussion on ISA, I talked about the problems with sharing level-triggered interrupts. MCA, on the other hand, uses edge-triggered interrupts, which enables interrupt sharing. EISA uses a combination of the two. Obviously, EISA needs to support edge-triggered interrupts to maintain compatibility with ISA cards. However, it enables EISA boards to configure that particular interrupt as either edge- or level-triggered.

As with MCA, EISA enables each board to be identified at boot up. Each manufacturer is assigned a prefix code to make the identification of the board easier. EISA also provides a configuration utility similar to the MCA reference disk to enable configuration of the cards. In addition, EISA supports automatic configuration, which enables the system to recognize the hardware at boot-up and configure itself accordingly. This can present problems for a Windows system, because drivers in the kernel rely on the configuration to remain constant. Because each slot on an EISA machine is given a particular range of base addresses, it is necessary to modify the kernel before making such changes. This is often referred to as the EISA-config, EISA Configuration Utility (ECU).

Peripheral Component Interconnect (PCI)

More and more machines found on the market today are including PCI local buses. One advantage that PCI offers over other bus types is the higher performance, automatic configuration of peripheral cards, and superior compatibility. A major drawback with the other bus types (ISA, EISA, MCA) is the I/O bottleneck. Local buses overcome this by accessing memory using the same signal lines as the CPU. As a result, they can operate at the full speed of the CPU as well as utilize the 32-bit data path. Therefore, the card and not the bus limit I/O performance.

Although PCI is referred to as a local bus, it actually lies somewhere "above" the system bus. As a result, it is often referred to as a "mezzanine bus" and has electronic "bridges" between the system bus and the expansion bus. As a result, the PCI-Bus can support up to five PCI devices, whereas the older VESA Local Bus can only support two or three. In addition, the PCI-Bus can reach transfer speeds four times that of EISA or MCA. (Note that as of this writing, VESA Local Bus [VLB] appears to be a dying technology, being taken over by PCI).

Even though PCI is called a mezzanine bus, it could replace ISA-, EISA-, or MCA-Buses, although in most cases, PCI is offered as a *supplement* to the existing bus type. If you look at a motherboard with PCI slots, you will see that they are completely separate from the other slots, whereas VLB slots are extensions of the existing slots. (You see this graphically in Figure 3–4.)

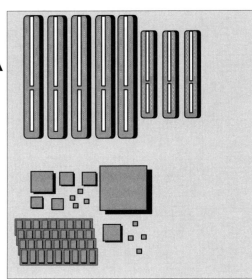

ISA or EISA
bus slots

PCI
slots

FIGURE 3–4   Comparison of ISA/EISA bus slots to PCI slots.

Another advantage of PCI over the VLB is the VLB cannot keep up with the speed of the faster CPUs, especially if multiple VLB devices are on the system. Because PCI works with the CPU, it is much more suited to multitasking operating systems like Windows NT, whereas the CPU cannot work independently if a VLB device is running.

Like EISA and MCA, PCI boards have configuration information built into the card. As the computer is booting, the system can configure each card individually based on system resources. This configuration is done "around" existing ISA, EISA, and MCA cards on your system.

To overcome PCI's shortcoming in transferring data, Intel (the designer and chief proponent of PCI) has come up with PCI-specific chip sets that enable data to be stored on the PCI controller, freeing the CPU to do other work. Although this may delay the start of the transfer, once the data flow starts, the transfer should continue uninterrupted.

Another of PCI's shortcomings is that although you can swap ISA and EISA cards for VLB cards without any major problems, this is not so for PCI cards. Significant changes must be made to both the kernel and device drivers to account for the differences.

Also, although the number of PCI boards is growing rapidly, it is still a very small fraction of the number of ISA boards available. However, it is becoming more common to find PCI-Bus slots in a PC. PCI has become a de facto standard, if not de jure.

On the other hand, the PCI-Bus is not processor dependent; you can install PCI in Pentium machines as well as in Alpha machines. You can therefore run the same SCSI host adapter (or whatever). Because it is 64 bits wide, neither the Pentium nor Alphas are slowed down (too much) by the bus.

Universal Serial Bus (USB)

Although not supported in Windows NT 4.0, the Universal Serial Bus (USB) brings the concept of "plug-and-play" to a new level. The USB is an expansion bus, which is intended for peripheral devices that are *outside* of the computer, such as keyboards, scanners, mice, and even hard disks. When a USB device is attached to the bus, it announces itself, and the system automatically loads and configures the driver without the need to reboot the system. The USB also eliminates the need for many of expansion cards, as the devices can now all be connected to the USB.

There are three types of USB devices. The USB controller on the computer itself is referred to as either the host, root, root tier, or root hub. This controls all of the activity on the USB. The second kind of device is a hub. Like network hubs, a USB hub server has intermediate connection points for the various devices. Hubs can either be self-powered or draw their power from the USB itself. Other hubs can also be connected to that; you can (theoretically) build complex tree structures. Note also that the host can also server as a hub.

Finally we get to the devices themselves. These are often referred to as "nodes," once again taking the terminology from networking.

Accelerated Graphics Port (AGP)

The latest entrant to the alphabet soup of bus types is the Accelerated Graphics Port (AGP). As its name implies, AGP is intended as a bus for graphics cards. Although PCI is more than sufficient for most users needs, there are some shortcoming with high-end applications. The need for something like AGP arises from problems when creating 3-D graphics, which use a "texture map" to get the necessary effects. The problem lies in the fact that most video cards deal with at most 8 MB, but texture maps are reaching 10 or even 20 MB (probably more by the time this book is published.).

Added to this memory limitation is the bandwidth required to quickly transfer that amount of data. To get real-time 3-D graphics, you need far better throughput than loading a document into WordPerfect. Added to this fact is that there is just a single PCI bus, which makes it even more of a bottleneck.

In essence, the AGP is a high-speed path between system memory and the video controller. It is no longer necessary to store things such as the texture maps in the system memory rather than in the limited space of the video card. Because data transfer can be up to four times that of the PCI bus, AGP provide even better performance.

The Small Computer Systems Interface (SCSI)

The SCSI-Bus is an extension of your existing bus. A controller card, called a host adapter, is placed into one of your expansion slots. A ribbon cable that contains both data and control signals then connects the host adapter to your peripheral devices.

There are several advantages to having SCSI in your system. If you have a limited number of bus slots, adding a single SCSI host adapter enables you to add up to seven more devices by taking up only one slot with older SCSI systems and up to 15 devices with Wide SCSI. SCSI has higher throughput than either IDE or ESDI. SCSI also supports many more different types of devices and is much better suited for multi-tasking environments

There are several different types of SCSI devices. The original SCSI specification is commonly referred to as SCSI-1. The next specification, SCSI-2, offered increased speed and performance as well as new commands, making some of the previously optional features mandatory.

SCSI-3 offered more than just speed and performance increases. One significant change is increasing the number of bits used to identify the SCSI ID, so that SCSI-3 can support up to 16 devices per bus instead of the previous eight. In addition, SCSI-3 includes support for other cable types, such as fiber channel.

Fast SCSI increases throughput to more than 10 Mbps. Fast-Wide SCSI provides a wider data path and throughput of up to 40 Mbps and up to 16 devices. Note that the devices for SCSI-3 and Fast SCSI must support the higher SCSI IDs. Ultra SCSI uses the same command set as SCSI-2 but increases the transfer rate to 40 Mbps.

Twin-Channel is not so much an improvement in the SCSI technology as it is an aid to the frustrated system administrator. One common problem has always been the lack of expansion slots on your system. Even though SCSI-3 might provide support for more devices on a single bus, if you do not have devices that support this, you will need to attach them to a different bus. Twin-Channel provides the solution to this problem with two channels on a single host adapter. That is, by taking up the space of a single expansion card, you can have twice as many devices.

Each SCSI device has its own controller and can send, receive, and execute SCSI commands. As long as it communicates with the host adapter using proper SCSI commands, internal data manipulation is not an issue. In fact, most SCSI hard disks have an IDE controller with a SCSI interface built onto them.

Because there is a standard set of SCSI commands, new and different kinds of devices can be added to the SCSI family with little trouble. However, IDE and ESDI are limited to disk-type devices. Because the SCSI commands need to be "translated" by the device, there is a slight overhead, which is compensated for by the fact that SCSI devices are intrinsically faster than non-SCSI devices. SCSI devices also have higher data integrity than non-SCSI devices. The SCSI cable consists of 50 or more pins, half of which are ground. Because every pin has its own ground, it is less prone to interference and therefore it has higher data integrity.

On each SCSI host adapter are two connectors. One connector is at the top of the card (opposite the bus connectors) and is used for internal devices. A flat ribbon cable is used to connect each device to the host adapter. On internal SCSI devices, only one connector is on the device itself. Should you have external SCSI devices, there is a second connector on the end of the card (where it attaches to the chassis). Here SCSI devices are "daisy-chained" together.

The SCSI-Bus must be closed to work correctly. By this, I mean that each end of the bus must be terminated. There is usually a set of resistors (or slots for resistors) on each device. The devices at either end of the SCSI-Bus must have such resistors. This process is referred to as terminating the bus, and the resistors are called terminating resistors. The details of this we will get to shortly.

Each SCSI device is "identified" by a unique pair of addresses, which are the controller addresses that are also referred to as the SCSI ID. This pair of addresses is usually set by jumpers or dip switches on the device itself. Keep in mind that the ID is something that is set on the device itself and is not related to location on the bus. Note that in Figure 3–5, the SCSI ID of the

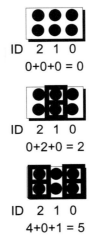

ID   2   1   0
0+0+0 = 0

ID   2   1   0
0+2+0 = 2

ID   2   1   0

FIGURE 3-5   Examples of binary for SCSI Ids.   4+0+1 = 5

devices are ordered ID 0, 6, and 5. Also, the SCSI ID is often set using a combination of jumpers with no 1:1 relationship. (That is a pair of pins labeled ID
0 through ID 7.) Therefore, you should always read the hardware documentation to determine how to set the ID.

    This sounds pretty obvious, but some people double check. They make
assumptions about what they see on the device regarding how the ID is set
and do not fully understand what it means. For example, I had an Archive
5150 SCSI tape drive. On the back are three jumpers, labeled 0, 1, and 2. I
have had customers call in with similar hardware who had their SCSI tape
drive set at 2. After configuring the tape drive and rebooting, they still
couldn't access the tape drive. Nothing else was set at ID 2, so there were no
conflicts. The system could access other devices on the SCSI-Bus, so the host
adapter was probably okay. Different SCSI devices can be plugged into the
same spot on the SCSI cable, so it wasn't the cable. The SCSI-Bus was terminated correctly, so that wasn't the problem.

    Rather than simply giving up and saying that it was a hardware prob-
lem, I suggested that the customer change the SCSI ID to 3 or 4 to see if that
would work. Well, the customer couldn't, because the jumpers on the back
only allowed him to change the SCSI ID to 0, 1, or 2. It then dawned on me
what the problem was: The jumpers in the back are in binary! To set the ID
to 2, the jumper needs to be on jumper 1, not jumper 2. Once the customer
switched it to jumper 1 and rebooted, all was well. (Note: I helped this customer before I bought the Archive tape drive. When I got my drive home and
wanted to check the SCSI ID, I saw only three jumpers. I then did something
that would appall most users: I read the manual! Sure enough, it explained
that the jumpers for the SCSI ID were binary.)

    An additional problem to this whole SCSI ID business is that manufac-
turers are not consistent among each other. Some might label the jumpers (or

switches) 0, 1, and 2. Others label them 1, 2, and 4. Still others label them ID0, ID1, and ID2. I have even seen some with a dial on them with 8 settings, which makes configuration a lot easier. The key is that no matter how they are labeled, the three pins or switches are binary, and their values are added to give you the SCSI ID.

Let's look at Figure 3–5, which represents the jumper settings on a SCSI device. In the first example, none of the jumpers is set, so the SCSI ID is 0. In the second example, the jumper labeled 1 is set. This is 21 or 2, so the ID here is 2. In the last example, the jumpers labeled 2 and 0 are set, which is 22 + 20 = 4 + 1, or 5.

On an AT-Bus, the number of devices added is limited only by the number of slots (granted, the AT-Bus is limited in how far away the slot can be from the CPU and therefore is limited in the number of slots). On a SCSI-Bus, however, there can be only seven devices in addition to the host adapter. Whereas devices on the AT-Bus are distinguished by their base addresses, devices on the SCSI-Bus are distinguished by their ID number.

ID numbers range from 0 to 7 and, unlike base addresses, the higher the ID, the higher the priority. Therefore, the ID of the host adapter should always be a 7. Because it manages all the other devices, it should have the highest priority. On the newer Wide SCSI-Buses, there can be up to 15 devices, plus the host adapter, with SCSI IDs ranging from 0 to 15.

Now back to our story. . . .

In theory, a single-channel SCSI host adapter can support 56 devices. Devices called bridge adapters connect devices without embedded controllers to the SCSI-Bus. Devices attached to the bridge adapter have LUNs between 0 and 7. If there are seven bridge adapters, each with eight LUNs (relating to eight devices), 56 total devices are therefore possible.

The original SCSI-1 spec only defined the connection to hard disks. The SCSI-2 spec has extended this connection to such devices as CD-ROMS, tape drives, scanners, and printers. Provided these devices all adhere to the SCSI-2 standard, they can even be mixed and matched with older SCSI-1 hard disks.

One common problem with external SCSI devices is that the power supply is external as well. If you are booting your system with the power to that external device turned off, once the kernel gets past the initialization routines for that device (the hardware screen), it can no longer recognize that device. The only solution is to reboot. To prevent this problem, it is a good idea to keep all your SCSI devices internally. (This doesn't help for scanners and printers.)

Although the number of host adapter manufacturers has steadily decreased in the past few years, Adaptec, the premier name in host adapters, has bought up both Trantor and Future Domain. Adaptec's biggest competitor for years, Buslogic, was no longer able to compete and was taken over by Mylex (a motherboard manufacturer, among other things). Despite the decrease in number of manufacturers, the number of models is still overwhelming.

Most host adapter manufacturers provide more than just a single model—many provide models for the entire spectrum of buses and SCSI types. ISA, EISA, PCI, Fast SCSI, Wide SCSI, and Ultra SCSI are part of the alphabet soup of SCSI devices. You can connect Wide SCSI disks onto a Fast SCSI adapter, although it will still only get 8 bits instead of the Wide SCSI's 16 bits, so it therefore only gets 10 Mbps compared with 20 Mbps per second of Wide SCSI.

Ultra SCSI disks can also be connected with the same limitations. (It is an 8-bit bus.) It can also handle Ultra-Wide SCSI and get 40 Mbps. This is not too big of an issue, as most of the devices available today can only handle 10 Mbps.

When looking at the performance of a SCSI device, you need to be careful of the manufacturer's test results—they can be deceiving. If a test reads 200 MB from the disk in 10 seconds, you get an average of 20 Mbps. What if those 100 MB are all from the same track? The disk hardware reads the track and keeps it in its own cache. When the host adapter requests a new block from that track, the hard disk doesn't need to find the block on the disk. Instead, it delivers it from the cache. This dramatically decreases the access time and increases the apparent transfer rate of the drive. The manufacturer can say, in all honesty, that the host adapter has a transfer rate of 20 Mbps, though the drive can only do half of this at most. Again, the chain is only as strong as its weakest link.

This does not mean that Wide SCSI or Ultra SCSI is only useful for the companies' marketing departments. SCSI has the advantage of being able to talk to multiple devices. For example, it can request data from one drive and, rather than waiting for the data, free the SCSI-Bus (disconnect). When the drive (or other device) is ready, it requests the bus again (reconnect), and the data are transferred. While the drive searches for the data, the host adapter can request data from another device. While this device is looking for the data, the first device can transfer the data to the host adapter. Being able to read or write devices like this means that a host adapter could get a sustained transfer rate of more that what individual devices can handle. (Note that both the host adapter and device must support disconnect/reconnect.)

Wide SCSI gets its performance gain by the fact it is wide (16 bits vs. 8 bits). Ultra SCSI, on the other hand, gets the increase through a shorter cycle time. This is an important aspect, because this makes for a steeper edge on the signal (the time from a low to high signal is much shorter and vice versa). This means that the SCSI-Bus has higher requirements regarding the cabling.

Internal devices usually are connected by flat cable ribbons and present few new problems with Fast SCSI. The maximum length of the cable is half of what it could be with older SCSI devices, and you must follow the specs exactly. Round cables for external devices have to be created specifically for Ultra SCSI and are therefore more expensive. Although the actual data transfer rate between the host adapter and the device is only as high as the device can handle, the steepness of the edges is the same. This means that if you connect Fast SCSI devices to Ultra SCSI host adapters, you still need the special Ultra SCSI cables.

Another consideration is that Ultra SCSI requires active termination. On the host adapter side, this isn't a problem, because the host adapters are designed to give active termination. However, many older devices support only passive termination and therefore can't work on Ultra SCSI host adapters. This really comes into play when larger amounts of data are being transferred.

PCI devices can generally behave as either masters or slaves. For slave devices, the CPU is responsible for all the activity. This is a disadvantage for slave devices, because the CPU is often busy transferring data and issuing commands instead of doing other work. This is really an issue in multitasking operating systems that have "better" things to do. Master devices, on the other hand, have an advantage here. The CPU only needs to tell them where to transfer the data, and they do the work themselves.

Regardless of whether a device acts as a master or slave, it will take up an interrupt line. Single function devices, such as host adapters, are given the interrupt INT-A. This means that the actual IRQ (between 5 and 15) will be determined by the system BIOS.

Generally, you can say that a higher throughput is required on a file server as compared with a workstation. Although there are applications like CAD or video processing, which require more throughput on a workstation than do other kinds of applications, the majority of the work is done by the server. Therefore, it is extremely important to consider the performance of your hard disk and similar devices on the server.

Despite reaching comparable prices and sizes, ATA hard disks are suited for work in a server, because they do not have the throughput of SCSI. As we discussed previously, SCSI has the advantage of being able to have two devices communicate with each other directly without the need to go through the CPU. In addition, while waiting for one device to find the data, it can "disconnect" itself, and you can make a request of another device on the same SCSI bus. This is especially important on servers, as they usually have multiple disks as well as other kinds of devices.

Here again, the chain to your hard disk is only as strong as the weakest link. Therefore, you need to have a SCSI host adapter that can keep up with the hard disk.

As an example, let's take my Adaptec 2940U2W host adapter, which I have in my primary workstation. This is an Ultra2 SCSI device, which gives me a maximum transfer rate of 80 Mbps. One neat aspect of this host adapter is that it uses a technology Adaptec calls "SpeedFlex." Internally, there are three connectors: one for Ultra2 SCSI (80 Mbps), one for Ultra-Wide SCSI (40 Mbps), and one for Ultra SCSI (20 Mbps). Externally, you have two connectors: one 68-pin for Ultra2 SCSI and one 50-pin for Ultra SCSI. Therefore, you get the maximum throughput, no matter what kind of device is connect to the host adapter. In addition, one aspect of the SpeedFlex technology is that it can operate the different buses at the different speeds simultaneously, so there is no performance lost on one bus because of a slow device on another bus.

The "W" at the end of the host adapter name means that it has the Ultra-Wide SCSI connector. Adaptec also produces the 2940U2, which has the same specifications, but without the internal Ultra-Wide SCSI connector and without the external Ultra2 connector. Note that in each case, devices supporting older SCSI standards can still be connected.

In my server, I have an Adaptec 3940U2, which is also an Ultra2 SCSI adapter. One key difference is that this adapter is *twin-channel*. That means I have two SCSI buses running off the same host adapter. This is extremely useful when you have more devices that will fit on a single bus plus added speed. Both of these aspects make this the perfect adapter for a Windows NT server. Another important difference is that the Adaptec 3940U2 supports 64-bit PCI, although it is still capable with 32-bit PCI.

One thing to note is that all of the devices support up to 15 devices (plus the host adapter per channel). This means that the twin-channel 3940U2 can connect up to 30 devices. In addition, all devices support cables up to 12 meters long.

On one machine, I have an Adaptec 1542 CF host adapter. The Adaptec 1540 is a SCSI-1- and SCSI-2-compliant ISA host adapter, which has an 8-bit data bus and a maximum transfer rate of 10 Mbps. This is a perfect host adapter for workstations that require less performance.

Initially, I wanted to say "low-end," but that tends to create false impressions of something of lesser quality. This definitely does not apply to the Adaptec 1540 family (or to any of the Adaptec products for that matter). A few months ago, I replaced the 1542CF I had for 6 years because the built-in floppy controller was no longer working correctly. The host adapter was working fine. I just couldn't access my floppy drive.

A few weeks later, I put the adapter back into the machine, because it is the only one with the external connector my CD-ROM changer had. Rather than buying an adapter for the connector, I put in my old Adaptec 1542 CF, and it has run perfectly ever since.

All of the Adaptec host adapters support what is called "scatter gather." Here, requests for data on the hard disk that are "scattered" all over the drive are "gathered" together in order that they be more efficiently processed.

This is similar to a way an elevator works. Image that four people get into an elevator. The first one presses the button for Floor 12, the next one for Floor 16, the next one for Floor 3, and the last one wants Floor 8. Although the person wanting to go to Floor 12 was there first, the elevator stops at Floor 3 first, then Floor 8 before continuing to Floor 12. This is much more efficient than going to each floor in the order the buttons were pressed.

Accessing a hard disk is similar. On active systems, there will be several requests waiting to process. Adaptec host adapters will sort the requests based on their physical location on the hard disk. Interestingly enough, Adaptec refers to this as an "elevator sort."

Termination

It's fine to say that the SCSI-Bus needs to be terminated. However, that doesn't help your understanding of the issue. As with other kinds of devices, SCSI devices react to the commands sent along the cable to them. Unless otherwise impeded, the signals reach the end of the cable and bounce back. In such cases, there are two outcomes, both of which are undesirable: Either the bounced signal interferes with the valid one, or the devices react to a second (unique in its mind) command. By placing a terminator at the end of the bus, the signals are "absorbed" and, therefore, don't bounce back.

Figures 3–6 and 3–7 show examples of how the SCSI-Bus should be terminated. Note that Figure 3–6 says that it is an example of "all external devices." Keep in mind that the principle is still the same for internal devices. If all the devices are internal, then the host adapter would be still be terminated, as would the last device in the chain.

If you don't have any external devices (or only have external devices), the host adapter is at one end of the bus. Therefore, it too must be terminated. Many host adapters today have the ability to be terminated in software, so there is no need for terminating resistors (also known as resistor packs).

With Ultra SCSI, termination plays an more important role. A steeper edge means that the reflection has a stronger effect than with Fast SCSI. Moreover, a faster cycle means that the bus is more sensitive to interference. In principle, SCSI termination, even with Ultra SCSI, is simple: Both ends of the bus (that is, the physical ends of the bus) must be terminated.

If you have fewer devices than connectors on your SCSI cable, I advise you to connect devices at both ends of the cable, terminating both of them. Loose ends can definitely lead to problems with reflection. By having devices

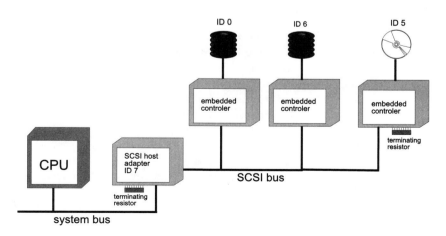

FIGURE 3–6 Example of SCSI bus with all external devices.

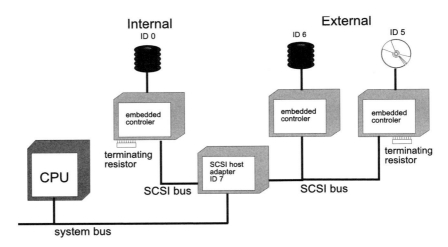

FIGURE 3–7 Example of SCSI bus with both external and internal devices.

at the physical ends of the cable, there is no question which device is at the end of the bus. Keep in mind that the order of the devices on the bus is independent of this.

You run into problems when the device has no possibility of being terminated or functions only with passive termination. Although no termination is rarely found, many (especially older) devices support only passive termination. Such devices include a lot of CD-ROMs and tape drives. Read the hardware documentation to find out what type of termination your drive supports or contact the manufacturer before you purchase the drive.

You need to be careful with some hard disks. There is often a jumper labeled TERM, which does not enable/disable the termination, but rather enables/disables the power for the active termination.

If you do have a device with active termination, this device belongs at one end of the SCSI cable. The other end is usually the host adapter. PCI host adapters are almost exclusively produced with active termination.

If both external and internal devices are present, the host adapter must not be terminated, because it is now in the middle of the bus and no longer at the end. The termination is now on the device at the end of the other cable. Note that older, 50-pin Centronics connectors are almost exclusively passive terminators. Therefore, if you replace your existing host adapter with an Ultra-SCSI adapter, you really should change the termination to active.

Wide SCSI presents its own termination and cabling problems. On most Wide-SCSI host adapters, you'll find an 8-bit and 16-bit connector, both of which you can use. However, keep in mind that both must be terminated.

....

Memory

Memory is the part of the computer where your program and data reside while they are being processed by the CPU. Contrast this to a hard disk or floppy, where the program is sitting on the disk and is not being used. (Of course, with operating systems like Windows, parts of both the program and the data can be stored on the disk, even as the program is running.) There are two types of memory that are most commonly talked about: RAM and cache.

RAM

A computer stores the data it works with in three ways, often referred to as memory. Long-term memory, which remains in the system even when there is no power, is called nonvolatile memory and exists in such places as hard disks or floppies, which are often referred to as secondary storage. Short-term memory, or volatile memory, is stored in memory chips called RAM (random-access memory). RAM is often referred to as primary storage. The third class of memory is often ignored, or at least is not often thought of. This type of memory exists in hardware on the system but does not disappear when power is turned off. This is called ROM, or read-only memory.

I need to clarify one thing before we go on. Read-only memory is, as it says, read-only. For the most part, you cannot write to it. However, like random-access memory, the locations within it can be accessed in a "random" order, that is, at the discretion of the programmer. Also, read-only memory isn't always read-only, but that's a different story that goes beyond the scope of this book.

The best way to refer to memory to keep things clear (at least the best way in my opinion) is to refer to the memory we traditionally call RAM as "main" memory. This is where our programs and the operating system actually reside.

There are two broad classes of memory: Dynamic RAM, or DRAM (pronounced dee-ram), and Static RAM, or SRAM (pronounced es-ram). DRAM is composed of tiny capacitors that can hold their charge only a short while before they require a "boost." SRAM is static because it does not require an extra power supply to keep its charge. As a result of the way it works internally, SRAM is faster and more expensive than DRAM. Because of the cost, the RAM that composes main memory is typically DRAM.

DRAM chips hold memory in ranges of 64 K to 16 MB and more. In older systems, individual DRAM chips were laid out in parallel rows called banks. The chips themselves were called DIPPs, for Dual In-Line Pin Package. These look like the average, run-of-the-mill computer chip, with two rows of parallel pins, one row on each side of the chip. If memory ever went bad in one of these banks, it was usually necessary to replace (or test) dozens of individual chips. Because the maximum for most of these chips was 256 K (32 KB), it took 32 of them for each megabyte!

On newer systems, the DIPP chips have been replaced by Single In-Line Memory Modules, or SIMMs. Technological advances have decreased the size considerably. Whereas a few years ago, you needed an area the size of standard piece of binder paper to hold just a few megabytes, today's SIMMs can squeeze twice as much into an area the size of a stick of gum.

SIMMs come in powers of 2 MB (1, 2, 4, 8, etc.,) and are generally arranged in banks of four or eight. Because of the way the memory is accessed, you sometimes cannot mix sizes. That is, if you have four 2-MB SIMMs, you cannot simply add an 8-MB SIMM to get 16 MB. Bear this in mind when you order your system or order more memory. You should first check the documentation that came with the motherboard or the manufacturer.

Many hardware salespeople are not aware of this distinction. Therefore, if you order a system with 8 MB that's "expandable" to 128 MB, you may be in for a big surprise. True, there are eight slots that can contain 16MB each. However, if the vendor fills all eight slots with 1-MB SIMMs to give you your 8 MB, you may have to throw everything out if you ever want to increase your RAM.

However, this is not always the case. My motherboard has some strange configurations. The memory slots on my motherboard consist of two banks of four slots each, which is typical of many machines. Originally, I had one bank completely full with four 4-MB SIMMs. I could have increased this by 1 MB by filling the first bank with four 256-K SIMMs and moving the four 4-MB SIMMs to the second bank. However, if I wanted to move up to 20 MB, I could use 1 MB instead of 256 K. So, here is one example where everything does not have to match. In the end, I added four 4-MB SIMMs to bring my total up to 32 MB. The moral of the story: Read the manual!

Another issue that you should consider with SIMMs is that the motherboard design may require you to put in memory in multiples of either two or four because this is the way the motherboard accesses that memory. Potentially, a 32-bit machine could read a byte from four SIMMs at once, essentially reading the full 32 bits in one read. Keep in mind that the 32 bits are probably not being read simultaneously. However, being able to read them in succession is faster that reading one bank and then waiting for it to reset.

Even so, this requires special circuitry for each of the slots, called address decode logic. The address decode logic receives a memory address from the CPU and determines which SIMM it's in and where it is on the SIMM. In other words, it decodes the address to determine which SIMM is needed for a particular physical address.

This extra circuitry makes the machine more expensive because this is not just an issue with the memory but with the motherboard design as well. Accessing memory in this fashion is called "page mode" because the memory is broken into sets of bytes, or pages. Because the address decode logic is designed to access memory in only one way, the memory that is installed must fit the way it is read. For example, my motherboard requires each bank to be either completely filled or completely empty. Now, this requires a little bit of explanation.

As I mentioned earlier, DRAM consists of little capacitors for each bit of information. If the capacitor is charged, then the bit is 1; if there is no charge, the bit is 0. Capacitors have a tendency to drain over time, and for capacitors this small, that time is very short. Therefore, they must be regularly (or dynamically) recharged.

When a memory location is read, there must be some way of determining whether there is a charge in the capacitor. The only way to do that is to discharge the capacitor. If the capacitor can be discharged, that means that there was a charge to begin with and the system knows the bit was 1. Once discharged, internal circuitry recharges the capacitor.

Now, assume that the system wanted to read two consecutive bytes from a single SIMM. Because there is no practical way for the address decode logic to tell that the second read is not just a re-read of the first byte, the system must wait until the first byte has recharged itself. Only then can the second byte be read.

By taking advantage of the fact that programs run sequential and rarely read the same byte more than once at any given time, the memory subsystem can interleave its reads. That is, while the first bank is recharging, it can be reading from the second, and while the second is recharging, it can be reading from the third, and so on. Because subsequent reads must wait until the previous read has completed, this method is obviously not as fast as simultaneous reads. This is referred to as "interleaved" or "banked" memory.

Because all of these issues are motherboard dependent, it best to check the hardware documentation when you change or add memory. Additionally, you may need to adjust settings, or jumpers, on the motherboard to tell it how much RAM you have and in what configuration.

Another issue that addresses speed is the physical layout of the SIMM. SIMMs are often described as being arranged in a "by-9" or "by-36" configuration, which refers to the number of bits that are immediately accessible. So, in a "by-9" configuration, 9 bits are immediately accessible, with 1 bit used for parity. In a "by-36" configuration, 36 bits are available with 4 bits for parity (one for each 8 bits). The "by-9" configuration comes on SIMMs with 30 pins, where the "by-36" configuration comes on SIMMs with 72 pins. The 72-pin SIMMs can read 32 bits simultaneously, so they are even faster than 30-pin SIMMs at the same speed. Figure 3–8 shows give you a comparison of the older SIMMs and PS/2 SIMMs.

There are also different physical sizes for the SIMM. The 30-pin SIMMs are slightly smaller than 72-pin SIMMs. The larger, 72-pin variety are called PS/2 SIMMs because they are used in IBM's PS/2 machines. As well as being slightly larger, the PS/2 SIMM has a notch in the center so it is impossible to mix up the two. In both cases, there is a notch on one end that fits into a key

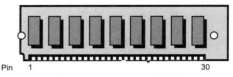

Pin   1   30

Standard 30-pin SIMM

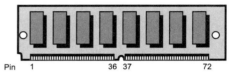

FIGURE 3–8 Comparison of 30-pin and 72-pin SIMMs.

Pin   1   36 37   72

72-pin PS/2 SIMM

in the slot on the motherboard, which makes putting the SIMM in backward almost impossible.

SIMMs come in several different speeds. The most common today are between 60 and 80 nanoseconds. Although there is usually no harm in mixing speeds, there is little to be gained. However, I want to emphasize the word usually. Mixing speeds has been known to cause panics. Therefore, if you mix speeds, it is best keep all the SIMMs within a single bank at a single speed. If your machine does not have multiple banks, then it is best not to mix speeds. Even if you do, remember that the system is only as fast as its slowest component.

Several years ago, the computer industry has begun to shift away from the old SIMMs toward extended data out RAM or EDORAM. Although, EDO-RAM was initially more expensive than SIMM, the demand for EDORAM has been such that the price difference disappeared.

The principle behind EDORAM is an extension of the fast-page-mode (FPM) RAM. With FPM RAM, you rely on the fact that memory is generally read sequentially. Because you don't really need to wait for each memory location to recharge itself, you can read the next location without waiting. Because you have to wait until the signal is stabilized, though, there is still some wait, though it is much less of a wait than waiting for the memory to recharge. At CPU speeds greater than 33 MHz, the CPU requests memory faster than memory can deliver it, and the CPU needs to wait.

EDORAM works by "latching" the memory, which means adding secondary memory cells. These detect the data being out from memory and store the signals so the CPU can retrieve it. This works at bus speeds of 66 MHz. This process can be made even faster by including "burst" EDORAM, which extends the locality principle even further. Because the system is going to read sequentially, why doesn't it anticipate the processor and read more than just that single location? In some cases, the system will read 128 bits at once.

Part of the reason why EDORAM hasn't simply taken over the market is the similar to the reason why PS/2 didn't take over standard SIMMs: The hardware needed to support them is different. You cannot just install EDO-RAM in your machine and expect it to work-you need a special chip set on your motherboard. One such chip set is the Intel Triton chip set.

A newer memory type are the dual in-line memory modules or DIMMs. These look similar to the SIMM, but are generally larger. One key difference is that although both SIMMs and DIMMs have contacts on both sides of the board, the pins on opposite sides of the DIMMs are electrically isolated from each other, which creates two separate contacts. In addition, unlike SIMMs, you do not need to have pairs of DIMMS in your machine.

Cache Memory

Based on the principle of spatial locality, a program is more likely to spend its time executing code around the same set of instructions. This is demonstrated by the tests that have shown that most programs spend 80 percent of their time executing 20 percent of their code. Cache memory takes advantage of that.

Cache memory, or sometimes just cache, is a small set of very-high-speed memory. Typically, it uses SRAM, which can be up to ten times more expensive than DRAM, which usually makes it prohibitive for anything other than cache.

When the IBM PC first came out, DRAM was fast enough to keep up with even the fastest processor. However, as CPU technology increased, so did its speed. Soon, the CPU began to outrun its memory. The advances in CPU technology could not be used unless the system was filled with the more expensive, faster SRAM.

The solution to this was a compromise. Using the locality principle, manufacturers of fast 386 and 486 machines began to include a set of cache memory consisting of SRAM but still populated main memory with the slower, less expensive DRAM.

To better understand the advantages of this scheme, let's cover the principle of locality in a little more detail. For a computer program, we deal with two types of locality: temporal (time) and spatial (space). Because programs tend to run in loops (repeating the same instructions), the same set of instructions must be read over and over. The longer a set of instructions is in memory without being used, the less likely it is to be used again. This is the principle of temporal locality. What cache memory does is enable us to keep those regularly used instructions "closer" to the CPU, making access to them much faster. This is shown graphically in Figure 3–9.

Spatial locality is the relationship between consecutively executed instructions. I just said that a program spends more of its time executing the same set of instructions. Therefore, in all likelihood, the next instruction the program will execute lies in the next memory location. By filling cache with

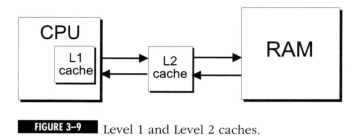

FIGURE 3–9 Level 1 and Level 2 caches.

more than just one instruction at a time, the principle of spatial locality can be used.

Is there really such a major advantage to cache memory? Cache performance is evaluated in terms of cache hits. A hit occurs when the CPU requests a memory location that is already in cache (that is, it does not have to go to main memory to get it). Because most programs run in loops (including the OS), the principle of locality results in a hit ratio of 85 to 95 percent. Not bad!

On most 486 machines and all subsequent CPUs, two levels of cache are used: level 1 cache and level 2 cache. Level 1 cache is internal to the CPU. Although nothing (other than cost) prevents it from being any larger, Intel has limited the level 1 cache in the 486 K to 8 K.

The level 2 cache is the kind that you buy separately from your machine (although with the Pentium Pro and the Pentium II/III, the L2 cache is part of the CPU package.) It is often part of the ad you see in the paper and is usually what people are talking about when they say how much cache is in their systems. Level 2 cache is external to the CPU and can be increased at any time, whereas level 1 cache is an integral part of the CPU and the only way to get more is to buy a different CPU. Typical sizes of level 2 cache range from 64 KB to 256 KB, usually in increments of 64 KB.

There is one major problem with dealing with cache memory: the issue of consistency. What happens when main memory is updated and cache is not? What happens when cache is updated and main memory is not? This is where the cache's write policy comes in.

The write policy determines if and when the contents of the cache are written back to memory. The write-through cache simply writes the data through the cache directly into memory. This slows writes, but the data are consistent. Buffered write-through is a slight modification of this, in which data are collected and everything is written at once. Write-back improves cache performance by writing to main memory only when necessary. Write-dirty is when it writes to main memory only when it has been modified.

Cache (or main memory, for that matter) is referred to as "dirty" when it is written to. Unfortunately, the system has no way of telling whether anything has changed, just that it is being written to. Therefore it is possible, but not likely, that a block of cache is written back to memory even if it is not actually dirty.

Another aspect of cache is its organization. Without going into detail (that would take most of a chapter itself), I can generalize by saying there are four different types of cache organization.

The first kind is fully associative, which means that every entry in the cache has a slot in the "cache directory" to indicate where it came from in memory. Usually these are not individual bytes, but chunks of four bytes or more. Because each slot in the cache has a separate directory slot, any location in RAM can be placed anywhere in the cache. This is the simplest scheme but also the slowest because each cache directory entry must be searched until a match (if any) is found. Therefore, this kind of cache is often limited to just 4 K.

The second type of cache organization is direct-mapped or one-way set associative cache, which requires that only a single directory entry be searched. This speeds up access time considerably. The location in the cache is related on the location in memory and is usually based on blocks of memory equal to the size of the cache. For example, if the cache could hold 4-K 32-bit (4-byte) entries, then the block with which each entry is associated is also 4 K x 32 bits. The first 32 bits in each block are read into the first slot of the cache, the second 32 bits in each block are read into the second slot, and so on. The size of each entry, or line, usually ranges from 4 to 16 bytes.

There is a mechanism called a tag, which tells us which block this came from. Also, because of the very nature of this method, the cache cannot hold data from multiple blocks for the same offset. If, for example, slot 1 was already filled with the data from block 1 and a program wanted to read the data at the same location from block 2, the data in the cache would be overwritten. Therefore, the shortcoming in this scheme is that when data are read at intervals that are the size of these blocks, the cache is constantly overwritten. Keep in mind that this does not occur too often due to the principle of spatial locality.

The third type of cache organization is an extension of the one-way set associative cache, called the two-way set associative. Here, there are two entries per slot. Again, data can end up in only a particular slot, but there are two places to go within that slot. Granted, the system is slowed a little because it has to look at the tags for both slots, but this scheme allows data at the same offset from multiple blocks to be in the cache at the same time. This is also extended to four-way set associative cache. In fact, the cache internal to 486 and Pentium has a four-way set associate cache.

Although this is interesting (at least to me), you may be asking yourself, "Why is this memory stuff important to me as a system administrator?" First, knowing about the differences in RAM (main memory) can aid you in making decisions about your upgrade. Also, as I mentioned earlier, it may be necessary to set switches on the motherboard if you change memory configuration.

Knowledge about cache memory is important for the same reason because you may be the one who will adjust it. On many machines, the write policy can be adjusted through the CMOS. For example, on my machine, I have a choice of write-back, write-through, and write-dirty. Depending on the applications you are running, you may want to change the write policy to improve performance.

Parity

In most memory today, an extra bit is added for each byte. This is a parity bit. Parity is a simple way of detecting errors within a memory chip (among other things). If an odd number of bits is set, the parity bit will be set to make the total number of bits set an even number (most memory uses even parity). For example, if three bits are set, the parity bit will also be set to make the total bits set four.

When data are written, the number of set bits is calculated and the parity bit is set accordingly. When the data are read, the parity bit is also read. If the total number of bits set is even, all is well. However, if an odd number of data bits is set and the parity bit is not set, or if an even number of data bits is set and the parity bit is set, a parity error has occurred.

When a parity error occurs in memory, the state of the system is uncertain. To prevent any further problems, the parity checking logic generates a Nonmaskable Interrupt (NMI), and the CPU immediately jumps to special codes called NMI service routines.

When Windows is interrupted with an NMI as the result of a parity error, it too realizes things are not good, and the system panics. The panic causes the system to stop everything and shut down. Certain machines support ECC (Error Correcting Code) RAM, which corrects parity problems before it kills your system.

The Central Processing Unit

Sometimes people just don't understand. At first, I thought that they "didn't have a clue," but that's was really the problem. They had a clue, but a single clue doesn't solve a crime, nor does it help you run a Windows system. You can easily copy a program from a Windows NT system running on an Intel machine to another one running on an Alpha. So you click in the name of the program and nothing happens, or you get an error about incorrect format.

The problem is comparable to German and English. Although both use (basically) the same alphabet, words (sets of characters) written in German are not understandable by someone reading them as English, and vice versa. Sets of machine instructions that are designed to be interpreted under Intel will not be understood under Alpha. (Actually, the problem is a little more complicated, but you get the basic idea.)

In this section, I will talk about the CPU, the brains of the outfit. It is perfectly reasonable for users and administrators alike to have no understanding of what the CPU does internally. However, a basic knowledge of some of the key issues is important so you can completely understand some of the issues I'll get into elsewhere.

It's like trying to tune-up your car. You don't really need to know how oxygen mixes with gasoline to be able to adjust the carburetor. However, knowing that it happens makes adjusting the carburetor that much easier.

I won't go into detail about the CPU's instruction cycle, that is, how it receives and executes instructions. Though I'm interested in things like that and would love to talk about them, it isn't really necessary to understand what we need to talk about here. Instead, I am going to talk mostly about how the CPU enables the operating system to create a scheme whereby many programs can be in memory simultaneously. These are the concepts of paging and multitasking.

In the next section, I will go into a little depth about the Intel process and how Windows NT interacts with it. Afterwards, I will talk briefly about the DEC Alpha to give you an idea of what it is about. Because of the number of Intel distributions and Intel-based machines, I won't go into the same depth for the Alpha. The concepts a basically the same, though the names of registers, etc., are different.

Intel Processors

Although it is an interesting subject, the ancient history of microprocessors is not really important to the issues at hand. It might be nice to learn how the young PC grew from a small, budding 4-bit system to the gigantic, strapping 64-bit Pentium. However, there are many books that have covered this subject and unfortunately, I don't have the space. Besides, the Intel chips on which Windows NT runs, are only the 80386 (or 100-percent compatible clones) and higher processors.

So, instead of setting the way-back machine to Charles Babbage and his Analytic Engine, we leap ahead to 1985 and the introduction of the Intel 80386. Even compared to its immediate predecessor, the 80286, the 80386 (386 for short) was a powerhouse. Not only could it handle twice the amount of data at once (now 32 bits), but its speed rapidly increased far beyond that of the 286.

New advances were added to increase the 386's power. Internal registers were added and their size was increased. Built into the 386 was the concept of virtual memory, which was a way to make it appear as though there was much more memory on system than there actually was. This substantially increased the system efficiency. Another major advance was the inclusion of a 16-byte, pre-fetch cache. With this, the CPU could load instructions before it actually processed them, thereby speeding things up even more. Then the most obvious speed increase came when the speed of the processor was increased from 8 MHz to 16 MHz.

Although the 386 had major advantages over its predecessors, at first its cost seemed relatively prohibitive. To allow users access to the multitasking capability and still make the chip fit within their customers' budgets, Intel made an interesting compromise: By making a new chip in which the interface to the bus was 16-bits instead of 32-bits, Intel made their chip a fair bit cheaper.

Internally, this new chip, designated the 80386SX, is identical to the standard 386. All the registers are there and it is fully 32 bits wide. However, data and instructions are accessed 16 bits at a time, therefore requiring two bus accesses to fill the registers. Despite this shortcoming, the 80386SX is still faster than the 286.

Perhaps the most significant advance of the 386 for many systems was its paging abilities. I talked a little about paging in the section on operating system basics, so you already have a general idea of what paging is about. I will also go into more detail about paging in the section on the kernel. However, I will talk about it a little here so you can fully understand the power that the 386 has given us and see how the CPU helps the OS.

Because Windows NT was first released for the 386 (but doesn't support it any more), I won't go into anymore detail about the 286 or the differences between the 286 and 386. Instead, I will just describe the CPU Windows NT uses as sort of an abstract entity. In addition, because most of what I will be talking about is valid for the 486 and Pentium as well as the 386, I will simply call it "the CPU" instead of 386, 486, Pentium, Pentium Pro, etc.

Windows NT will also run on non-Intel CPUs, such as those from AMD or Cyrix. However, the issues I am going to talk about are all common to Intel-based or Intel-derived CPUs.

I need to take a side step here for a minute. On PC-Buses, multiple things are happening at once. The CPU is busily processing while much of the hardware is being access via DMA. Although these multiple tasks are occurring simultaneously on the system, this is not what is referred to as multitasking.

When I talk about multitasking, I am referring to multiple processes being in memory at the same time. Because of the time the computer takes to switch between these processes, or tasks, is much shorter than the human brain can recognize, it appears as though the processes are running simultaneously. In reality, each process gets to use the CPU and other system resources for a brief time and then it's another process's turn.

As it runs, the process could use any part of the system memory it needs. The problem with this is that a portion of RAM that one process wants may already contain code from another process. Rather than allowing each process to access any part of memory it wants, protections keep one program from overwriting another one. This protection is built in as part of the CPU and is called, quite logically, "protected mode." Without it, Windows NT could not function.

Note, however, that just because the CPU is in protected mode does not necessarily mean that the protections are being utilized. It simply means that the operating system can take advantage of the built-in abilities if it wants.

Although this capability is built into the CPU, it is not the default mode. Instead, the CPU starts in what I like to call "DOS-compatibility mode." However, the correct term is "real mode." Real mode is a real danger to an operating system like Windows NT. In this mode, there are no protections (which makes sense because protections exist only in protected mode). A process running in real mode has complete control over the entire system and can do anything it wants. Therefore, trying to run a multi-user system on a real-mode system would be a nightmare. All the protections would have to be built into the process because the operating system wouldn't be able to prevent a process from doing what it wanted.

A third mode, called "virtual mode," is also built in. In virtual mode, the CPU behaves to a limited degree as though it is in real mode. However, when a process attempts to directly access registers or hardware, the instruction is caught, or trapped, and the operating system is allowed to take over.

Let's get back to protected mode because this is what makes multitasking possible. When in protected mode, the CPU can use virtual memory. As I mentioned, this is a way to trick the system into thinking that there is more memory than there really is. There are two ways of doing this. The first is called swapping, in which the entire process is loaded into memory. It is allowed to run its course for a certain amount of time. When its turn is over, another process is allowed to run. What happens when there is not enough room for both process to be in memory at the same time? The only solution is that the first process is copied out to a special part of the hard disk called the swap space, or swap device. Then, the next process is loaded into memory and allowed its turn. The second is called paging and we will get to it in a minute.

Because it takes such a large portion of the system resources to swap processes in and out of memory, virtual memory can be very inefficient, especially when you have a lot of processes running. So let's take this a step further. What happens if there are too many process and the system spends all of its time swapping? Not good.

To avoid this problem, a mechanism was devised whereby only those parts of the process that are needed are in memory. As it goes about its business, a program may only need to access a small portion of its code. As I mentioned earlier, empirical tests show that a program spends 80 percent of its time executing 20 percent of its code. So why bother bringing in those parts that aren't being used? Why not wait and see whether they are used?

To make things more efficient, only those parts of the program that are needed (or expected to be needed) are brought into memory. Rather than accessing memory in random units, the memory is divided into 4-K chunks, called pages. Although there is nothing magic about 4 K per se, this value is easily manipulated. In the CPU, data are referenced in 32-bit (4-K) chunks, and 1 K (1,024 bits) of each chunk is a page (4,096 bits). Later you will see how this helps things work out.

As I mentioned, only that part of the process currently being used needs to be in memory. When the process wants to read something that is not currently in RAM, it needs to go out to the hard disk to pull in the other parts of the process; that is, it goes out and reads in new pages. This process is called paging. When the process attempts to read from a part of the process that is not in physical memory, a "page fault" occurs.

One thing you must bear in mind is that a process can jump around a lot. Functions are called, sending the process off somewhere completely different. It is possible—likely, for that matter—that the page containing the memory location to which the process needs to jump is not currently in memory. Because it is trying to read a part of the process not in physical memory, this, too, is called a page fault. As memory fills up, pages that haven't been used in some time are replaced by new ones. (I'll talk much more about this whole business later.)

Assume that a process has just made a call to a function somewhere else in the code and the page it needed is brought into memory. Now there are two pages of the process from completely different parts of the code. Should the process take another jump or return from the function, it needs to know whether it is going into memory. The operating system could keep track of this, but it doesn't need to—the CPU will keep track for it.

Stop here for a minute! This is not entirely true. The OS must first set up the structures that the CPU uses. However, the CPU uses these structures to determine whether a section of a program is in memory. Although not part of the CPU, but rather RAM, the CPU administers the RAM utilization through page tables. As their names imply, page tables are simply tables of pages. In other words, they are memory locations in which other memory locations are stored.

Confused? I was at first, so let's look at this concept another way. Each running process has a certain part of its code currently in memory. The system uses these page tables to keep track of what is currently in memory and where it is located. To limit the amount the CPU has to work, each of these page tables is only 4 K, or one page, in size. Because each page contains a set of 32-bit addresses, a page table can contain only 1,024 entries.

Although this would imply that a process can only have 4 K x 1,024, or 4 MB, loaded at a time, there is more to it. Page tables are grouped into page directories. Like the page table, the entries in a page directory point to memory locations. However, rather than pointing to a part of the process, page directories point to page tables. Again, to reduce the CPU's work, a page directory is only one page. Because each entry in the page directory points to a page, this means that a process can only have 1,024 page tables.

Is this enough? Let's see. A page is 4 K or 4,096 bytes, which is 2^{12}. Each page table can refer to 1,024 pages, which is 2^{10}. Each page directory can refer to 1,024 page tables, which is also 2^{10}. Multiplying this out, we have

$$(\text{page size}) \times (\text{pages in page table}) \times (\text{page tables in page directory})$$

or

$$(2^{12}) \times (2^{10}) \times (2^{10}) = 2^{32}$$

Because the CPU is only capable of accessing 2^{32} bytes, this scheme allows access to every possible memory address that the system can generate.

Built into the CPU is a special unit that is responsible for making the translation from the virtual address of the process to physical pages in memory. This special unit is called (what else?) the paging unit. To understand more about the work that the paging unit saves the operating system or other parts of the CPU, let's see how the address is translated.

When paging is turned on, the paging unit receives a 32-bit value that represents a virtual memory location within a process. The paging unit takes theses values and translates them, as shown in Figure 3–10. At the top of the figure, we see that the virtual address is handed to the paging unit, which converts it to a linear address. This is not the physical address in memory. As you see, the 32-bit linear address is broken down into three components. The first 10 bits (22-31) are offset into the page directory. The location in memory of the page directory is determined by the Page Directory Base Register (PDBR).

The page directory entry contains 4 bits that point to a specific page table. The entry in the page table, as you see, is determined by bits 12–21. Here again, we have 10 bits, which means each entry is 32 bits. These 32-bit entries point to a specific page in physical memory. Which byte is referenced in physical memory is determined by the offset portion of the linear address, which are bits 0–11. These 12 bits represent the 4,096 bytes (4 K) in each physical page.

Keep in mind a couple of things. First, page tables and page directories are not part of the CPU. They can't be. If a page directory were full, it would contain 1,024 references to 4 K chunks of memory. For the page tables alone, you would need 4 MB! Because this would create a CPU hundreds of times larger than it is now, page tables and directories are stored in RAM.

Next, page tables and page directories are abstract concepts that the CPU knows how to utilize. They occupy physical RAM, and operating systems such as Windows NT know how to switch this capability on within the CPU. All the CPU does is the "translation" work. When it starts, Windows NT turns this capability on and sets up all the structures. These structures are then handed off to the CPU, where the paging unit does the work.

As I said, a process with all of its page directory entries full would require 4 MB just for the page tables. This implies that the entire process is somewhere in memory. Because each of the page table entries points to physical pages in RAM, you would need 16 GB of RAM. Not that I would

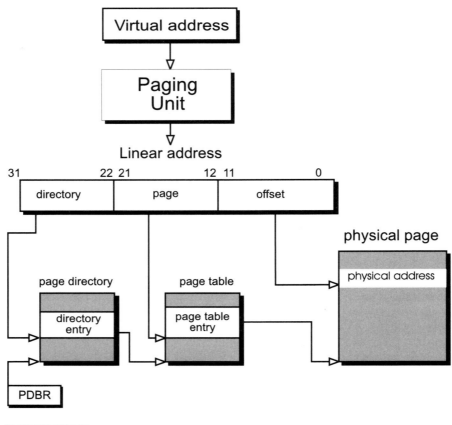

FIGURE 3–10   Translation of virtual-to-physical address.

mind having that much RAM, though it is a bit costly and even if you had 16 MB SIMMs, you would need 1000 of them.

    Like pages of the process, it's possible that a linear address passed to the paging unit translates to a page table or even a page directory that was not in memory. Because the system is trying to access a page (which contains a page table and not part of the process) that is not in memory, a page fault occurs and the system must go get that page.

    Because page tables and the page directory are not really part of the process but are important only to the operating system, a page fault causes these structures to be created rather than read in from the hard disk or elsewhere. In fact, as the process starts up, all is without form and is void: no pages, no page tables, and no page directory.

    The system accesses a memory location as it starts the process. The system translates the address, as I described above, and tries to read the page directory. It's not there. A page fault occurs and the page directory must be created. Now that the directory is there, the system finds the entry that points to the page table. Because no page tables exist, the slot is empty and another page fault occurs. So, the system needs to create a page table. The entry in the page table for the physical page is found to be empty, and so yet another page fault occurs. Finally, the system can read in the page that was referenced in the first place.

This whole process sounds a bit cumbersome, but bear in mind that this amount of page faulting only occurs as the process is starting. Once the table is created for a given process, it won't page fault again on that table. Based on the principle of locality, the page tables will hold enough entries for a while, unless, of course, the process bounces around a lot.

The potential for bouncing around brings up an interesting aspect of page tables. Because page tables translate to physical RAM in the same way all the time, virtual addresses in the same area of the process end up in the same page tables. Therefore, page tables fill up because the process is more likely to execute code in the same part of a process rather than elsewhere (this is spatial locality).

There is something here that bothered me in the beginning and may still bother you. As I have described, each time a memory reference is made, the CPU has to look at the page directory, then a page table, then calculate the physical address. This means that for every memory reference, the CPU has to make two more references just to find out where the next instruction or data is coming from. I though that was pretty stupid.

Well, so did the designers of the CPU. They have included a functional unit called the Translation Lookaside Buffer, or TLB. The TLB contains 32 entries and, as the internal and external caches point to sets of instructions, points to pages. If a page that is being searched is in the TLB, a TLB hit occurs (just like a cache hit). As a result of the principle of spatial locality, there is a 98% hit rate using the TLB.

When you think about it, this makes a lot of sense. The CPU does not just execute one instruction for a program then switch to something else—it executes hundreds or even thousands of instructions before it is another program's turn. If each page contains 1,024 instructions and the CPU executes 1000 before it's another program's turn, all 1000 will most likely be in the same page. Therefore, they are all TLB hits.

If we put all of these components together, we get an operating system that works together with the hardware to provide a multitasking, multi-user system. Unfortunately, what I talked about here are just the basics. I could spend a whole book just talking about the relationship between the operating system and the CPU and still not be done.

Recent Advances

One thing I didn't talk about was the difference between the 80386, 80486, and Pentium. With each new processor comes new instructions. The 80486 added an instruction pipeline to improve the performance to the point where the CPU could average almost one instruction per cycle. The Pentium has dual instruction paths (pipelines) to increase the speed even more. It also contains branch prediction logic, which is used to "guess" where the next instruction should come from.

The Pentium (as well as the newer PentiumPro) has a few new features that make for significantly better performance. This first feature is multiple instruction paths or pipelines, which allow the CPU to work on multiple instructions at the same time. In some cases, the CPU will have to wait to finish one before working on the other, though this is not always necessary.

The second improvement is called dynamic execution. Normally, instructions are executed one after other. If the execution order is changed, the whole program is changed. Well, not exactly. In some instances, upcoming instructions are not based on previous instructions, so the processor can "jump ahead" and start executing the executions before others are finished.

The next advance is branch prediction. Based on previous activity, the CPU can expect certain behavior to continue. For example, the odds are that once the CPU is in a loop, the loop will be repeated. With more than one pipeline executing instruction, multiple possibilities can be attempted. This is not always right, but is right more than 75% of the time!

The PentiumPro (P6) introduced the concept of data flow analysis. Here, instructions are executed as they are ready, not necessarily in the order in which they appear in the program. Often, the result is available before it normally would be. The P6 also introduced speculative execution, in which the CPU takes a guess at or anticipates what is coming.

The P6 is also new in that it is actually two separate chips. However, the function of the second chip is the level-2 cache. Both an external bus and a "private" bus connect the CPU to the level-2 cache, and both of these are 64 bits.

Both the Socket and the CPU itself changed with the Pentium II processor. Instead of a processor with pins sticking out all over the bottom, the Pentium II uses a Single Edge Contact Cartridge (SECC). This reportedly eliminates the need for resigning the socket with every new CPU generation. In addition, the CPU is encased in plastic, which protects the CPU during handling. Starting at "only," the Pentium II can reach speeds of up to 450 MHz.

Improving performance even further, the Pentium II has increased the internal, level-one cache to 32 K, with 16 K for data and 16 K for instructions. Technically, it may be appropriate to call the level-two cache internal, as the 512-K L2 cache is included within the SECC, making access faster than for a traditional L2 cache. The Dual Independent Bus (DIB) architecture provides for higher throughput, as there are separate system and cache buses.

The Pentium II also increases performance internally through changes to the processor logic. Using *Multiple Branch Prediction*, the Pentium predicts the flow of instructions through several branches. Because computers usually process instructions in loops (i.e., repeatedly), it is generally easy to guess what the computer will do next. By predicting multiple branches, the processor reduces "wrong guesses."

Processor "management" has become an important part of the Pentium II. A Built-In Self-Test (BIST) is included, which is used to test things like the cache and the TLB. It also includes a diode within the case to monitor the processor's temperature.

The Pentium II Xeon Processor added a "system bus management interface," which allows the CPU to communicate with other system management components (hardware and software). The thermal sensor, which was already present in the Pentium II, as well as the new Processor Information ROM (PI ROM) and the Scratch EEPROM, use this bus.

The PI ROM contains various pieces of information about the CPU, like the CPU ID, voltage tolerances, and other technical information. The Scratch EEPROM is shipped blank from Intel but is intended for system manufacturers to include whatever information they want to, such as an inventory of the other components, service information, system default, and so forth.

Like the Pentium II, the latest (as of this writing) processor, the Pentium III also comes in the SECC. It has increased the number of transistors from the 7.5 million in the Pentium II to over 9.5 million. Currently, the Pentium III comes in 450-MHz and 500-MHz models, with a 550-MHz model in the planning.

The Pentium II also includes the Internet Streaming SIMD Extensions, which consist of 70 new instructions that enhance imagining in general, as well as 3-D graphics, streaming audio and video, as well as speech recognition.

Intel also added a serial number to the Pentium II. This is extremely useful should the CPU itself get stolen or the computer get stolen, after the CPU has been installed. In addition, the CPU can be uniquely identified across the network, regardless of the network card or other components. This can be used in the future to prevent improper access to sensitive data, aid in asset management, and help in remote management and configuration.

Even today, people think that the PC CPU is synonymous with Intel; that is, if you are going to buy a CPU for your PC that it will be manufactured by Intel. This is not the case. Two manufactures, Advanced Micro Devices (ADM) and Cyrix, provide CPUs with comparable functionality. Like any other brand name, Intel CPUs are often more expensive than an equivalent from another company with the same performance.

AMD Processors

More than likely, you have seen the stickers on the front of computers saying "Intel Inside." As you might guess, this computer has an Intel processor. This sticker and the associated ad campaign is important for name recognition. For many people, the name Intel has become synonymous with CPUs for PCs.

Many people may have heard the name of other CPU vendors, but often feel they are simply cheap "clones." This is unfortunate, because the performance of these CPUs is comparable to the Intel CPUs. Although these other vendors generally release chips with the same performance several months after the comparable one from Intel, they are typically less expensive and therefore have a better price-performance ratio.

This is where business buyers really look. If a product provides the necessary performance and reliability at a lower price, it does not make business sense to pay for something just because it has an expensive television ad. Therefore, more and more businesses, including PC manufacturers, are switching to AMD CPUs.

One of the first successful "clones" of the Intel CPUs was the AMD AM5$_x$86. The first assumption is that the "5" in that its name indicates that it is a clone of the Intel Pentium. Instead, it is much better to think of the AM5$_x$86 as a high-end version of the 486. Tests have shown that a 133-MHz AM5$_x$86 will not quite outperform a 90-MHz Pentium but will outperform one at 70 MHz. Because of the reduced cost, you still get better performance dollar for dollar, despite the faster processor.

The AMD K5 was the first Pentium-class CPU developed by AMD. One interesting aspect of the K5 is that it "translates" the Intel instructions into fixed-length RISC instructions. This makes executing the instructions a lot faster, because the CPU does not need to waste time figuring out how long the instruction really is. In addition, because all instructions are the same length, they can be loaded more efficiently into the K5's six-stage instructions pipeline, which can process for instruction simultaneously.

Following the K5, AMD logically came out with the K6. One benefit of this CPU was the fact that it was the first on the market that used Intel's own MMX technology. In addition, the K6 has instruction pipelines, which are fed by a set of four instruction decoders. Like the K5, the K6 translates the Intel instructions into RISC instructions before executing them. Added to that, the K6 has separate instruction and data caches like the Pentium, but those in the K6 are four times as large (32 K).

The successor to the successful AMD-K6 series is the AMD-K6–2, which is the first CPU to offer AMD's 3DNow! technology. As you might guess from its name, 3DNow! improves system performance when displaying 3-D graphics, something Intel's MMX technology was not designed to do. However, MMX does provide some performance improvements, so the AMD-K6-2 includes MMX as well. As of this writing, the AMD-K6-2 is available in speeds from 300 to 475 MHz.

Next came the AMD-K6-III series. As with the AMD-K6-2, the AMD-K6-III series also provides AMD's 3DNow! technology. One of the most significant improvements is the additional CPU, which give it a "tri-level" cache, thus providing a maximum cache of 2.3 MB, which is more than four times as much as possible with the Intel Pentium III Processors. In addition, the L2 cache operates at the same speed as the CPU. This means the 450-MHz version has the potential to outperform a 500-MHz Pentium III.

The next step is the AMD-K7 processor. As of this writing, it has not yet been released, but the features announced by AMD are exciting. One important aspect is that it is expected to be the first CPU to support a 200-MHz system bus. This includes a nine-stage, superscalar execution pipeline, with a 128-K L1 cache. This is twice what is currently available.

Alpha Processors

The Alpha processor from the Digital Equipment Corporation (Now Compaq) is the only other non-Intel-based processor for which Windows NT is still being developed. The most significant difference between the Intel family and Alpha is that the Alpha is a Reduced Instruction Set Computer (RISC), as compared to the Intel, which is a Complex Instruction Set Computer (CISC). Without turning this book into a textbook on microprocessor design, I can simply say that the difference is that RISC has fewer instructions (the instruction set is reduced), and therefore it takes more instructions to do a specific job. A CISC processor has more instructions, and it takes fewer instructions to do the same job.

Imagine someone told you to stand up and open the door. The CISC instruction might simply say, "Go open the door." Using what's built into your CPU (your brain), you know to translate this to "stand up and open the door." On the other hand, the RISC instructions might be "Stand up. Turn left and take two paces forward. Turn right, and take three paces forward. Raise right hand, . . ." There might then be a CISC instruction that says, "Go open the window." However, the RISC instructions might be "Stand up. Turn left, and take two paces forward. Turn left, and take three paces forward, . . ."

Not only does the CISC give fewer instructions, it also requires less logic circuitry. As a result, an Alpha processor can run at higher speeds than an Intel. This does not make the Alpha intrinsically faster! Take our example. I simply tell you to open the window, and you do it. However, giving you each instruction individually takes more time. One significant difference is that when the PentiumPro broke the 200-MHz barrier two years ago, the Alphas were already more than twice that.

Even if the increase in clock speed is not considered, the design of the Alpha enables it to do more work per cycle. Several issues were addressed to help eliminate any aspect of the processor that would hinder multiple instruction issues. For example, there are no branch delay or skip instructions. As a result of its design, the Alpha (as of this writing) can get up to 10 new instructions per cycle.

In addition, the Alpha was designed to run with multiple processors, though that's not to say that it can't run as a single processor. The Alpha was designed with several instructions that simplify adding multiple processors.

Unlike other processors, this functionality was designed from the beginning and didn't have to be built onto an existing system.

One advantage of Alpha is that it doesn't have a lot of baggage to carry around. The Intel 80x86 family is based on the 8086 and is completely backward compatible. If you have an 8086 program, it will run on an PentiumPro. The Alpha was developed with a full 64-bit architecture, although it has a few 32-bit operations for backward compatibility.

Part of the 64-bit architecture is the Alpha's 64-bit virtual address space. All values (registers, addresses, integers, etc.) are operated on as full 64-bit quantities. Unlike with the Intel processors, there are no segmented addresses. In some cases, the operating system may restrict the number of bits that is used to translate the virtual address; however, at least 43 bits are used.

Like the Intel, Alpha's memory protection is done on a per-page basis. The design of the paging mechanism in Intel specifies a 4-K page, but the Alpha can have 8-K, 16-K, 32-K, or even 64-K pages. In addition, the Alpha uses many-to-one page mapping, as does the Intel, so that multiple processors can have a virtual memory address that references the same page in physical memory.

Motherboards

Even if you buy preconfigured computers, you should still consider what kind of motherboards you are getting. It is very common today to find a number of the devices, which were formally expansion cards, that are now integrated onto the motherboard. In many cases, the motherboard is smaller and therefore the total cost is reduced. However, this means if you wish to use something other than what the motherboard manufacturer has indeed provided for you, you'll need to spend additional money as well as need a way to disable the device on the motherboard.

The reason the motherboard becomes smaller is that it can "get away with" having fewer expansion bus slots. Because the hard disk controller, for example, is integrated onto the motherboard, you do not need to use an expansion slot for it. If this were a controller for IDE drives, you would be less likely to want to buy one of your own. However, if the SCSI host adapter is built-in, it's human nature to want to use something more powerful than the one that is provided. This means that you have to take one of the main expansion slots for the additional SCSI host adapter.

Another problem motherboard design brings with it is the placement of the integrated controllers. In some cases, I have found the plugs for such devices stuck between the expansion slots. Even though this does a great job of saving space, it makes it extremely difficult to access the pins. The only way to connect the cable to pins was to remove all of the cards. However, you had to be extremely careful when you put cards back in so as not to hold a cable off the pins. Although it is unlikely you will be changing expansion cards every day, the headache and wasted time often negates any benefit of having paid $10 less for the motherboard.

Most new motherboards that I have encountered, come with three PCI slots and at least three ISA slots. Some come with either an additional PCI or ISA slot, whereas some have an AGP slot. However, you can expect to have at least six expansion slots between PCI and ISA.

One thing you need to be careful about when shopping for motherboards is whether or not they support your chosen CPU. People do not often have a CPU before they have the motherboard (although I did once); you may have decided on a particular CPU before you bought the motherboard.

The days are gone in which you could simply by a "PC motherboard" and expect it to work with your CPU. The technology is changing so fast, and there are so many different kinds of CPUs on the market, you need to be absolutely sure the CPU is compatible with the motherboard. Most of the motherboard manufacturers have Web sites with a compatibility matrix. You can find out which CPUs are supported and which clock speeds.

Sockets

One thing to consider when buying a motherboard for your CPU is where you are going to plug in that CPU. Not all CPUs are alike and not all sockets for the CPUs are alike. As of this writing, nine different socket types (0-8) have been defined.

Socket Designation	Number of Pins	Pin Layout	Voltage	CPU	OverDrive Processors
0	168	In-line	5 V	486DX	DX2, DX4
1	169	In-line	5 V	486DX, 486SX	DX2, DX4
2	238	In-line	5 V	486DX, 486SX, DX2	DX2, DX4, Pentium
3	237	In-line	3 V or 5 V	486DX, 486SX, DX2, DX4	DX2, DX4, Pentium
4	273	In-line	5 V	60- and 66-MHz Pentium	Pentium
5	320	Staggered	3 V	Other Pentium	Pentium
6	235	In-line	3 V	DX4	Pentium
7	321	Staggered	3 V	Other Pentium	Pentium
8	387	Staggered	3 V	Pentium Pro	Pentium Pro

There are several things to note about this table. First, there was never an officially designated socket 0, but Intel made a line of sockets for 486 OverDrive processors that followed the Socket 0 design.

Second, the difference between an in-line and staggered pin layout is simply whether or not the pins line up in different rows.

The inner 169 pins of Socket 2 match those of socket 1, so you can simply plug in a CPU that is normally intended for Socket 1. The only difference is that the outer pins are open.

You will see that Socket 3 is the same size as Socket 2 but has one pin missing, and the "keying pins" are in different places. It supports CPUs with either 3 V or 5 V, and the rearranged keying pins help prevent someone from accidentally putting a 3-V CPU into a 5-V machine.

Socket 4 was for the first Pentiums, but is no longer used. It was followed by the Socket 5, which had a staggered pin layout. Socket 6 had a similar layout as Sockets 2 and 3 but was only able to handle the 486DX4.

Finally, we get to Socket 7, which is currently the most common for Pentium-based machines. The PentiumPro CPUs fit into Socket 8.

Computer Cases

A computer case is more that just something that protects the inside of your computer from spilled coffee and other dangers associated with the typical computer user. It also protects you from the inside of your computer. The 110 V flowing through the power supply (220 V in Europe and other countries) is not something you want to meet up with unexpectedly.

In addition, the computer case is both the skin and skeleton for your computer. It holds everything together and holds them in the proper location. Your motherboard is attached to the case, so the expansion slots need to be in the proper position when you insert a card, as the connectors on the end of the card are sticking out of the computer and not pointing in.

Fortunately, there is a standard in both motherboard and case design that helps keep things from pointing in the wrong direction. However, idiots are getting smarter ever day, so this system will never be idiot-proof.

One of the first things to look at is the physical construction of the case. Cases come in many different sizes and shapes. PC cases are normally thought of in terms of desktop, mini-tower, tower and maxi-tower, or something similar. As its name implies, a desktop case is one that is intended to sit on your desktop. The smaller the better. In fact, a new term "small-footprint" case is used to refer to cases that are even smaller than traditional desktop cases (XT, AT, and Mini-AT).

These cases lay flat on your desk and often have a set of four compartments (or *bays*) arranged in a 2″ x 2″ square to hold hard disks, floppy drives, and CD-ROM drives. The obvious limitation is expansion. The motherboard is often smaller, and therefore there is less room for expansion cards. Plus, there is not much extra room in the case if you wanted to add too much more.

Tower cases stand vertically, with the bays one on top of the other. With mini-towers, the case is small enough that it *might* fit on your desk, as this is generally just a rearrangement of the desktop case. That is, you have room for four devices. Big towers are just that. There are usually at least six bays for devices that could have some access slot at the front (i.e., floppy-drive, CD-ROM, tape drive, etc.). However, this space could also be used for a hard disk, as the cases are usually provide with some kind of plate covering the front. In addition, there is room for a couple more hard disks.

However, this is a classic case of not judging a book by its cover. I have seen large cases that had some really goofy construction. The result was few bays and a lot of wasted space.

In the last couple of years, server cases, which are a lot larger than tower cases, have made it to the market. These are normally the same height, but can be several times wider. There is room for a dozen or more hard disks, and many are designed explicitly with the goal of having a large number of disks that you set up in some kind of redundant array (RAID). However, in every case I have seen, these were delivered with a prebuilt system.

There are a couple of key aspects to consider when looking for a case. First, the case and the motherboard need to fit together. There are a number of motherboard types, and, for the most part, the holes in the motherboard match those in the case. There are usually more holes than you need, and some combination is likely to fit.

However, what you need to consider is that the motherboard should not lie completely flat against the case. It needs to be spaced above the case so that nothing metal on the case can touch the motherboard. This ensures that no short circuit is possible. Included with all of the motherboards I have purchased in recent years have been nylon spacers, which keep the motherboard away from the metal frame of the case.

The next aspect is the placement of the bays for the hard disks. I have met my share of cases, where you almost need to take the case apart in order to get to the bays. If this is the case, you can end up spending a lot of time replacing the drives and a lot of money on Band-Aids for your scraped knuckles.

If you have a tower case and can use one of the front-loading bays, it makes it much easy to get the drives into the bays. However, it may make getting the cables onto the drives another problem. Both of these issues become moot (for you) if you have someone else doing the maintenance. If, however, you are the ones building the machines or replacing defective drives, how hard it is to get access to the bays is an important consideration. DEC did it right for a few years until something caused them to change their minds. Drives were inserted into the case sideways and not front-to-back. Although they still lay flat, there was no problem getting the drives in and out. There were typically enough slots for four to six drives, and several pairs of brackets were provided that screwed onto the hard disk. With the brackets in place, the drives slid in, locked into place, with the plug end sticking out. It was also a simple matter to remove the drives when you needed to. Unfortunately, just prior to being purchased by Compaq, DEC changed the construction of their cases, and getting at the drives was almost impossible. In fact, I have yet to see worse placement than I saw on some of the cases.

Also, consider how easy it is to open *and* close the case. There should be no "trick" to opening closing the case. I have had some where you had to apply just the right amount of pressure on the top and bottom of the side panels that slid into the case from the back. First, this meant having to move the case far enough away from the wall so you had room to pull the sides off. Plus "just the right amount of pressure" was harder than it sounds.

The next important issue is cooling. Unless you are running an old 486, you probably have at least the fan on your CPU (as well as the one for the power supply). However, that may not be enough. All electronic devices generate heat, and it can build up pretty fast in the enclosed space of your computer case.

The most common way for the computer cases to get cooled is simply letting the hot air escape out the holes in the case. However, I have seen places were the computer is hidden under a desk, with almost no circulation and it overheated. Even if the computer is in the open, you may still not have enough circulation inside the computer, particularly if you have a lot of peripherals in your machine. If this is the case, you might want to consider getting a fan card. As its name implies, it is a fan that sits in one of your expansion slots and helps circulate air.

You should also consider the design of the case. I have seen many where an extra fan was built into the case that blew directly onto the hard disks. In other cases, an additional fan would blow onto the CPU.

RAID

RAID is an acronym for Redundant Array of Inexpensive Disks. Originally, the idea was that you would get better performance and reliability from several, less-expensive drives linked together than you would from a single, more-expensive drive. The key change in the entire concept is that hard disk prices have dropped so dramatically that RAID is no longer concerned with inexpensive drives. So much so that the "I" in RAID is often interpreted as meaning "Intelligent" rather than "Inexpensive."

In the original paper that defined RAID, there were five levels. Because that paper was written, the concept has been expanded and revised. In some cases, characteristics of the original levels are combined to form new levels.

Two concepts are key to understanding RAID. These are redundancy and parity. The concept of parity is no different than that used in serial communication, except for the fact that parity in a RAID system can be used to not only detect errors but also to correct them. This is because more than just a single bit is used per byte of data. The parity information is stored on a drive separate from the data. When an error is detected, the information is used from the good drives, plus the parity information to correct the error. It is also possible to have an entire drive fail completely and still be able to continue working. Usually the drive can be replaced and the information on it rebuilt, even while the system is running. Redundancy is the concept that all information is duplicated. If you have a system where one disk is an exact copy of another, one disk is redundant for the other.

A striped array is also referred to as RAID 0 or RAID Level 0. Here, portions of the data are written to and read from multiple disks in parallel. This greatly increases the speed at which data can be accessed. This is because half of the data are being read or written by each hard disk, which cuts the access time almost in half. The amount of data that is written to a single disk is referred to as the stripe width. For example, if single blocks are written to each disk, then the stripe width would be a block.

This type of virtual disk provides increased performance, because data are being read from multiple disks simultaneously. Because there is no parity to update when data are written, this is faster than system using parity. However, the drawback is that there is no redundancy. If one disk goes out, then data are probably lost. Such a system is more suited for organizations where speed is more important than reliability.

Keep in mind that data are written to all of the physical drives each time data are written to the logical disk. Therefore, the pieces must all be the same size. For example, you could not have one piece that was 500 MB and a second piece that was only 400 MB. (Where would the other 100 MB be written?) Here again, the total amount of space available is the sum of all the pieces.

Disk mirroring (also referred to as RAID 1) is where data from the first drive are duplicated on the second drive. When data are written to the primary drive, it is automatically written to the secondary drive as well. Although this slows things down a bit when data are written, when data are read it can be read from either disk, thus increasing performance. Mirrored systems are best employed where there is a large database application.

Availability of the data (transaction speed and reliability) is more important than storage efficiency. Another consideration is the speed of the system. Because it takes longer than normal to write data, mirrored systems are better suited to database applications, where queries are more common than updates.

The term used for RAID 4 is a block-interleaved undistributed parity array. Like RAID 0, RAID 4 is also based on striping, but redundancy is built-in, with parity information written to a separate drive. The term "undistributed" is used because a single drive is used to store the parity information. If one drive fails (or even a portion of the drive), the missing data can be created using the information on the parity disk. It is possible to continue working even with one drive inoperable, because the parity drive is used on-the-fly to recreate the data. Even data written to the disk are still valid because the parity information is updated as well. This is not intended as a means of running your system indefinitely with a drive missing, but rather it gives you the chance to stop your system gracefully.

RAID 5 (Figure 3–11) takes this one step further and distributes the parity information to all drives. For example, the parity drive for block 1 might be drive 5, but the parity drive for block 2 is drive 4. With RAID 4, the single parity drive was accessed on every single data write, which decreased overall performance. Because data and parity are interspersed on a RAID 5 system, no single drive is overburdened. In both cases, the parity information is generated during the write and should the drive go out, the missing data can be recreated. Here again, you can recreate the data while the system is running, if a hot spare is used.

As I mentioned before, some of the characteristics can be combined. For example, it is not uncommon to have stripped arrays mirrored as well. This provides the speed of a striped array with redundancy of a mirrored array, without the expense necessary to implement RAID 5. Such a system would probably be referred to as RAID 10 (RAID 1 plus RAID 0).

Regardless of how long your drives are supposed to last, they will eventually fail. The question is when. On a server, a crashed hard disk means that many if not all of your employees are unable to work until the drive is replaced. However, there are ways of limiting the effects the crash has in a cou-

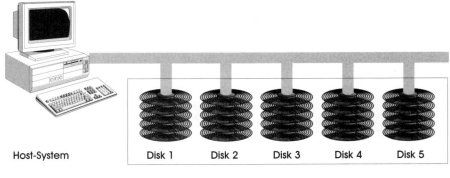

	Host-System	Disk 1	Disk 2	Disk 3	Disk 4	Disk 5

Stripe					
0	cluster 0	cluster 1	cluster 2	cluster 3	parity
1	cluster 4	cluster 5	cluster 6	parity	cluster 7
2	cluster 8	cluster 9	parity	cluster 10	cluster 11
3	cluster 12	parity	cluster 13	cluster 14	cluster 15
4	parity	cluster 16	cluster 17	cluster 18	cluster 19
5	cluster 20	cluster 21	cluster 22	cluster 23	parity

Striped with distributed parity
(RAID 5)

FIGURE 3–11   Raid 5.

ple of ways. First, you can keep the system from going down unexpectedly. Second, you can protect the data already on the drive.

The key issue with RAID is the mechanisms the system uses to portray the multiple drives as single one. The two solutions are, quite simply, hardware and software. With hardware RAID, the SCSI host adapter does all of the work. Basically, the operating system does not even see that there are multiple drives. Therefore, you can use hardware RAID with operating systems that do not have any support on their own.

On the other hand, software RAID is less expensive. The Windows NT Server comes with software, so there is no additional cost. However, to me this is no real advantage, as the initial hardware costs are a small fraction of the total cost of running the system. Maintenance and support play a much larger roll, so these ought to be considered before the cost of the actual hardware. In it's Annual Disaster Impact Research, Microsoft reports that on average, a downed server costs at least $10,000 *per hour*. Think about how many RAID controllers you can buy with that money.

In addition, the total cost of ownership also includes user productivity. Should a drive fail, performance degrades faster with a software solution than with a hardware solution.

Another thing to consider is that as of this writing, Windows NT does not support software RAID 5 for your boot drive. It can be mirrored, but replacing a failed drive means you have to make software changes, increasing the downtime further. With a hardware solution, the RAID array "appears" to be a single drive. Therefore, it does not matter what operating system is running.

Let's take an Adaptec AA-133SA RAID controller as an example. This is currently the top-end model and provides three Ultra SCSI channels, which means you could theoretically connect 45 devices to this single host adapter. Because each of the channels is Ultra SCSI, you have a maximum throughput of 120 Mbps. At the other end of the spectrum is the Adaptec AAA-131CA, which is designed more for high-end workstations, as it only supports mirroring and striping.

One thing to note is that the Adaptec RAID host adapters do not just provide the interface, which makes multiple drives appear as one. Instead, they all include a coprocessor, which increases the performance of the drives considerably.

However, providing data faster and redundancy in not all of it. Adaptec RAID controllers also have the ability to detect errors and in some cases correct errors on the hard disk. Many SCSI systems can already *detect* single-bit errors. However, using the parity information from the drives, the Adaptec RAID controllers can *correct* these single-bit errors. In addition, the Adaptec RAID controllers can also detect 4-bit errors.

You need to also keep in mind the fact that maintenance and administration are more costly than the initial hardware. Even though you have a RAID 5 array, you still need to replace the drive should it fail. This brings up two important aspects.

First, how well can your system detect the fact that a drive has failed? Whatever mechanisms you choose must be in a position to immediately notify the administrators should a drive fail.

The second aspect returns to the fact that maintenance and administration costs are much higher than are the cost of the initial hardware. If the hardware makes replacing the drive difficult, your increase your downtime, and therefore the maintenance costs increase. Adaptec has addressed this issue by allowing you to "hot swap" your drives. This means you can replace the defective drive on a *running* system, without have to shutdown the operating system.

Note that this also requires the case containing the RAID drive be accessible. If your drives are in the same case as the CPU (such as traditional tower cases), you often have difficulty getting to the drives. Removing one while the system is running is not practical. The solution is an external case, which is *specifically* designed for RAID.

Often you can configure the SCSI ID of the drive with dials on the cases itself, and sometimes the position in the case determines the SCSI ID. Typically, the drives are mounted onto rails, which slide into the case. Should one fail, you simple slide it out and replace it with the new drive.

Protecting your data and being able to replace the drive is just a start. The next level up is what is referred to as "hot spares." Here, you have addition drives already installed that are simply waiting for another to break down. As soon as a failure is detected, the RAID card simply replaces the failed drive with a spare drive, reconfigures the array to reflect the new drive, and the failure is reported to the administrator. Keep in mind that this must be completely supported in the hardware.

If you have an I/O-bound application, a failed drive decreases the performance. Instead of just delivering the data, your RAID array must calculate the missing data using the parity information, which means it has a slower response time in delivering the data. The degraded performance continues until you replace the drive. With a hot spare, the RAID array is rebuilding itself as it is delivering data. Although performance is obviously degraded, it is to a lesser extent than having to swap the drives manually.

If you have a CPU-bound application, you obtain substantial increases in performance over software solutions. If a drive fails, the operating system needs to perform the parity calculations in order to reconstruct the data. This keeps the CPU from doing the other tasks and performance is degraded. Because the Adaptec RAID controller does all of the work of reconstructing the data, the CPU doesn't even notice it. In fact, even while the system is running normally, the RAID controller is doing the partite calculations, so there is no performance lost here either.

In addition, the Adaptec RAID controllers can be configured to set the priority of performance versus availability. If performance is given a high priority, it will take longer to restore the data. If availability is given the higher priority, performance suffers. Either is valid, depending on your situation. It is also possible to give each the same priority.

Because the new drive contains no data, it must take the time to recreate the data using the parity information and the data from the other drives. During this time, performance will suffer as the system is working to restore the data on the failed drive.

Redundancy like this (and therefore the safety of your data) can be increased further by having redundant RAID 5 arrays. This is often referred to as RAID 50, as it is a combination of RAID 5 and RAID 0, although RAID 50 was not defined in the original RAID paper. Basically, this is a RAID array that is mirrored. Should a drive fail, not only can the data be recovered from the parity information, but it can also be copied from its mirror. Note that as of this writing, Windows NT does not support mirrored RAID 5. Therefore, you need a SCSI RAID controller that can.

Another important aspect is the administration of your RAID array. If you use the software solution provided by Windows NT, you are limited to just the Disk Manager, which has extremely limited management function. Many RAID products provide access to administration functions when the system boots, where you can configure the different aspects of the system. However, this does little good if you want to access the functions while the system is running.

The more sophisticated RAID controller, such as those from Adaptec, provide a GUI-based administration and maintenance tool, which you can access directly from Windows. Therefore, there is no need to shut down the system to access these functions. With the Adaptec product, you have access to the properties of both the physical as well as logical drivers, using a viewer with the same look-and-feel as the Windows Explorer. This makes accessing as well as viewing the information extremely easy.

Peripherals

Having a computer with the fastest CPU, full of the largest SIMM chips does not necessarily make for the best server. A computer is a system. As with any system, the whole is only as fast/strong as its slowest/weakest component. Therefore, providing users with the most efficient system means choosing peripherals that can provide them the level of performance they require. Note that this does not necessarily mean the fastest, as many users do not need the fastest equipment.

I consider peripheral devices as hardware that are separate from the motherboard and any of the associated buses. Granted, some motherboards have built-in video cards or hard-disk controllers; I still consider these devices peripherals. In many cases, it is a toss-up where you place something.

Hard Disks

A hard disk is composed of several (probably) aluminum-coated disks with either an "oxide" medium (the stuff on the disks) or "thin film" medium. Because "thin film" is thinner than oxide, the denser (that is, larger) hard disks are more likely to have thin film. Each disk is called a platter, and the more platters you have, the more data you can store.

Platters are usually the same size as floppies. Older platters were 5.25" round, and the newer ones are 3.5" round. (If someone knows the reason for this, I would love to hear it.) In the center of each platter is a hole though which the spindle sticks. In other words, the platters rotate around the spindle. The functionality is the same as with a phonograph record. (Remember those?)

The medium that coats the platters is very thin—about 30 millionths of an inch. The medium has magnetic properties that can change its alignment when it is exposed to a magnetic field. That magnetic field comes in the form of the hard-disk's read/write heads. It is the change in alignment of this magnetic media that enables data to be stored on the hard disk.

As I said earlier, a read/write head does just that: It reads and writes. There is usually one head per surface of the platters (top and bottom). That means that there are usually twice as many heads as platters. However, this is not always the case. Sometimes the top- and bottom-most surfaces do not have heads.

The head moves across the platters that are spinning several thousand times per minute (at least 60 times per second!). The gap between the head and platter is smaller than a human hair, smaller than a particle of smoke. For this reason, hard disks are manufactured and repaired in rooms where the number of particles in the air is fewer than 100 per cubic meter.

Because of this very small gap and the high speeds in which the platters are rotating, if the head comes into contact with the surface of a platter, the result is (aptly named) a head crash. More than likely this will cause some physical damage to your hard disk. (Imagine burying your face into an asphalt street going even only 20 mph!)

The heads move in and out across the platters by the older stepping motor or the new, more-efficient voice-coil motor. Stepping motors rotate and monitor their movement based on notches or indentations. Voice-coil motors operate on the same principle as a stereo speaker. A magnet inside the speaker causes the speaker cone to move in time to the music (or with the voice). Because there are no notches to determine movement, one surface of the platters is marked with special signals. Because the head above this surface has no write capabilities, this surface cannot be used for any other purpose.

The voice-coil motor enables finer control and is not subject to the problems of heat expanding the disk, because the marks are expanded as well. Another fringe benefit is that because the voice-coil operates on electricity, once power is removed, the disk moves back to its starting position, because it no longer is resisting a "retaining" spring. This is called "automatic head parking."

Physically, data are stored on the disk in concentric rings. The head does not spiral in like a phonograph record but rather moves in and out across the rings, which are called tracks. Because the heads move in unison across the surface of their respective platters, data are usually stored not in consecutive tracks but rather in the tracks that are positioned directly above or below them. The set of all tracks that are the same distance from the spindle is called a cylinder. Therefore, hard disks read from successive tracks on the same cylinder and not the same surface.

Think of it this way. As the disk is spinning under the head, it is busy reading data. If it needs to read more data than what fits on a single track, it has to get it from a different track. Assume data were read from consecutive tracks. When the disk finished reading from one track, it would have to move in (or out) to the next track before it could continue. Because tracks are rings and the end is the beginning, the delay in moving out (or in) one track causes the beginning of the next track to spin past the position of the head before the disk can start reading it. Therefore, the disk must wait until the beginning comes around again. Granted, you could stager the start of each track, but this makes seeking a particular spot much more difficult.

Let's now look at when data are read from consecutive tracks (that is, one complete cylinder is read before it goes on). Once the disk has read the entire contents of a track and has reached the end, the beginning of the track just below it is just now spinning under the head. Therefore, by switching the head it is reading from, the disk can begin to read (or write) as though nothing was different. No movement must take place and the reads occur much faster.

Each track is broken down into smaller chunks called sectors. The number of sectors into which each track is divided is called sectors per track, or sectors/track. Although any value is possible, common values for sectors/track are 17, 24, 32, and 64. (These are shown graphically in Figure 4–1.)

Each sector contains 512 bytes of data. However, each sector can contain up to 571 bytes of information. Each sector contains information that indicates the start and end of the sector, which is only ever changed by a low-level format. In addition, space is reserved for a checksum contained in the data portion of the sector. If the calculated checksum does not match the checksum in this field, the disk will report an error.

This difference between the total number of bytes per sector and the actual amount of data has been cause for a fair amount of grief. For example, in trying to sell you a hard disk, the salesperson might praise the tremendous amount of space that the hard disk has. You might be amazed at the low cost of a 1-GB drive.

There are two things to watch out for. Computers count in twos, humans count in tens. Despite what the salesperson wants you to believe (or believes himself), a hard disk with 1 billion bytes is not a 1-GB drive—it is only 10^9 bytes. One gigabyte means 2^{30} bytes. A hard disk with 10^9 (1 billion) is only about 950 MBs. This is 5% smaller!

The next thing is that the seller will often state is the *unformatted* storage capacity of a drive. This is the number that you would get if you multiplied all the sectors on the disk by 571 (see the preceding discussion). Therefore, the unformatted size is irrelevant to almost all users. Typical formatted

cylinders

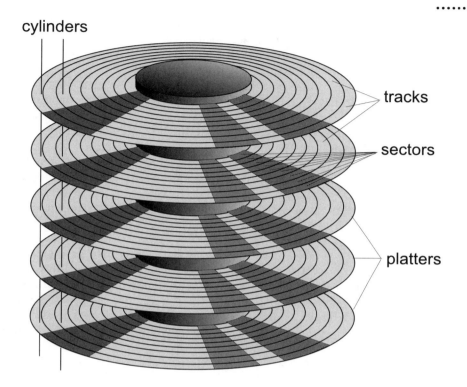

tracks

sectors

platters

FIGURE 4–1   Logical components of a hard disk.

modified frequency modulation (MFM) drives give the user 85% of the unformatted size, and run length limited (RLL) drives give the user about 89%. (MFM and RLL are formatting standards, the specifics of which are beyond the scope of this book.)

This brings up an interesting question. If the manufacturer is telling us the unformatted size, and the formatted size is about 85% for MFM and 89% for SCSI/IDE (using RLL), how can I figure out how much usable space there really is? Elementary, my dear Watson: It's a matter of multiplication.

Let's start at the beginning. Normally, when you get a hard disk, it comes with reference material that indicates how many cylinders, heads, and sectors per track there are (among other things). The set of all tracks at the same distance from the spindle is a cylinder. The number of cylinders is therefore simply the number of tracks, because a track is on one surface and a cylinder is all tracks at the same distance. Because you can only use those surfaces that have a head associated with them, you can calculate the number of total tracks by multiplying the number of cylinders by the number of heads. In other words, take the number of tracks on a surface and multiply it by the number of surfaces. This gives you the total number of tracks.

From our discussion of tracks, you know that each track is divided into a specific number of sectors. To find the total number of sectors, simply multiply the number of total tracks that we calculated above by the sectors per track. Once you have the total number of sectors, multiply this by 512 (the number of bytes of data in a sector). This gives us the total number of bytes on the hard disk. To figure out how may megabytes this is, simply divide this number by 1,048,576 (1024 × 1024 = 1 MB).

All PC-based operating systems need to break down the hard disk into units called partitions. A partition can be any size, from just a couple of megabytes to the entire disk. Each partition is defined in a partition table that appears at the very beginning of the disk. This partition table contains information about the kind of partition it is, where it starts, and where it ends. This table is the same whether you have a DOS-based PC, UNIX, or both.

Keep in mind that there can be only four partitions in total, because there are four entries in the table. DOS gets around this by creating logical partitions within one physical partition. This is a characteristic of DOS, not of the partition table. Both DOS and UNIX must first partition the drive before installing the operating system and provide the mechanism during the installation process in the form of the FDISK.EXE program under DOS or the Disk Manager under Windows NT.

To physically connect itself to the rest of the computer, the hard disk has five choices: ST506/412, ESDI (Enhanced Small Device Interface), SCSI (Small Computer System Interface), IDE (Integrated Drive Electronics), and the newest Enhanced IDE (EIDE). However, the interface the operating system sees for ST506/412 and IDE are identical, and there is no special option for an IDE drive. At the hardware level, though, there are some differences that I need to cover for completeness.

To be quite honest, only ESDI and ST506/412 are really disk interfaces. SCSI and IDE are referred to as "system-level interfaces," and they incorporate ESDI into the circuitry physically located on the drive.

The ST506/412 was developed by Seagate Technologies (hence the ST) for its ST506 hard disk, which had a whopping 5-MB formatted capacity. (This was in 1980 when 360 K was a big floppy.) Seagate later used the same interface in their ST412, which doubled the drive capacity (which is still less hard-disk space than I have RAM—Oh well). Other drive manufacturers decided to incorporate this technology, and over the years, it has become a standard. One of its major drawbacks is that it is a 15-year-old technology, which can no longer compete with the demands of today's hard-disk users.

In 1983, the Maxtor Corporation established the Enhanced Small Device Interface (ESDI) standard. The enhancements ESDI provided offered higher reliability, because Maxtor had built the encoder/decoder directly into the drive and therefore reduced the noise, high transfer rates, and the ability to get drive parameters directly from this disk. This meant that users no longer had to run the computer setup routines to tell the CMOS what kind of hard disk it had.

One drawback that I have found with ESDI drives is the physical connection between the controller and the drive itself. Two cables were needed: a 34-pin control cable and a 24-pin data cable. Although the cables are different sizes and can't (easily) be confused, the separation of control and data is something of which I was never a big fan. The connectors on the drive itself were usually split into two unequal halves. In the connector on the cable, a small piece of plastic called a key prevented the connector from being inserted improperly. Even if the key was missing, you could still tell which end was which because the pins on the hard disk were labeled and the first line on the cable had a colored stripe down its side. (This may not always be the case, but I have never seen a cable that wasn't colored like this.)

Another drawback that I have found is that the physical location on the cable determines which drive is which. The primary drive is located at the end of the cable, and the secondary drive is in the middle. The other issue is the number of cables: ESDI drives require three separate cables. Each drive has its own data cable and the drives share a common control cable.

Although originally introduced as the interface for hard cards (hard disks directly attached to expansion cards), the IDE interface has grown in popularity to the point where it is perhaps the most commonly used hard-disk interface today (rapidly being replaced by SCSI). As its name implies, the controller electronics are integrated onto the hard disk itself. The connection to the motherboard is made through a relatively small adapter, commonly referred to as a "paddle board." From here, a single cable attaches two hard disks in a daisy chain, which is similar to the way floppy drives are connected, and often, IDE controllers have connectors and control electronics for floppy drives as well.

IDE drives often play tricks on systems by presenting a different face to the outside world than is actually on the disk. For example, because IDE drives are already preformatted when they reach you, they can have more physical sectors in the outer tracks, thereby increasing the overall amount of space on the disk that can be used for storage. When a request is made to read a particular block of data on the drive, the IDE electronics translate this to the actual physical location.

Because IDE drives come preformatted, you should never low-level format an IDE drive unless you are specifically permitted to do so by the manufacturer. You could potentially wipe out the entire drive to the point at which point it must be returned to the factory for "repair." Certain drive manufacturers, such as Maxtor, provide low-level format routines that accurately and safely low-level format your drive. Most vendors that I am aware of today simply "zero" out the data blocks when doing a low-level format. However, don't take my word for it! Check the vendor.

The next great advance in hard-disk technology was SCSI. SCSI is not a disk interface, but rather a semiindependent bus. More than just hard disks can be attached to a SCSI-Bus. Because of its complex nature and the fact that it can support such a wide range of devices, I talked in more detail about SCSI earlier in this chapter. However, a few specific SCSI issues relate to hard disks in general and the interaction between SCSI and other types of drives.

The thing to note is that the BIOS inside the PC knows nothing about SCSI. Whether this is an oversight or intentional, I don't know. The SCSI spec is more than 10 years old, so there has been plenty of time to include it. Because the BIOS is fairly standard from machine to machine, including SCSI support might create problems for backward compatibility.

On the other hand, the BIOS is for DOS. DOS makes BIOS calls. To be able to access all the possible SCSI devices through the BIOS, it must be several times larger. Therefore, every PC-based operating system needs to have extra drivers to be able to access SCSI devices.

Because the BIOS does not understand about SCSI, you have to trick the PC's BIOS a little to boot from a SCSI device. By telling the PC's BIOS that no drives are installed as either C: or D:, you force it to quit before it looks for any of the other types. Once it quits, the BIOS on the SCSI host adapter has a chance to run.

The SCSI host adapter obviously knows how to boot from a SCSI hard disk and does so wonderfully. This is assuming that you enabled the BIOS on the host adapter. If not, you're hosed.

There is also the flip side of the coin. The official doctrine says that if you have a non-SCSI boot driver, you have to disable the SCSI BIOS, because this can cause problems. However, I run a number of systems that have IDE boot drives, and I still leave the SCSI BIOS enabled. NT normally reacts as though the SCSI BIOS was not enabled, so what to do? I suggest that you see what works. I can only add that if you have multiple host adapters, only one should have the BIOS enabled.

Another thing is that once the kernel boots from a SCSI device, you lose access to other kinds of drives. Just because it doesn't boot from the IDE (or whatever), does this mean you cannot access it at all? Unfortunately, yes. This is simply the way the kernel is designed. Once the kernel has determined that it has booted off a SCSI hard disk, it can no longer access a non-SCSI hard disk.

The newest member of the hard-disk family is EIDE. The most important aspect of this new hard-disk interface is its ability to access more than 504 MBs. This limitation is because the IDE interface can access only 1,024 cylinders, 16 heads, and 63 sectors per track. If you multiply this out using the formula I gave you earlier, you get 504 MBs.

EIDE also has other advantages, such as higher transfer rates, ability to connect more than just two hard disks, and attach more than just hard disks. One drawback the EIDE had at the beginning was part of its very nature. To overcome the hard-disk size limit that DOS had, EIDE drives employ a method called logical block addressing (LBA).

The idea behind LBA is that the system's BIOS would "rearrange" the drive geometry so that drives larger than 528 MBs could still boot. Because Windows NT does not use the BIOS to access the hard disk, the fact that the BIOS could handle the EIDE drive means nothing. New drivers needed to be added to account for this.

More and more you find the (E)IDE controllers built directly onto the motherboard. On the one hand, this is a good thing, because you do not need to use an expansion card slot for the controller. However, you need to be careful where it is located. I have had a few motherboards where the IDE controller was stuck between the PCI and ISA slots. This made it extremely difficult to access the pins without removing either of the cards in either the PCI or ISA slot (sometimes both).

Although this might not seem like a big deal, it may become one the next time you do anything with that machine. It is not uncommon when adding a hard disk or something else to the system that you accidentally pull on the hard-disk cable. All you need to do is pull it no more than quarter of an inch before some plugs are no longer connected to the pins. Because this connection is almost impossible to see, you don't notice that the cable has come loose. When you reboot the machine nothing works, as the system is getting signals through only some of the lines. If the pins for the IDE controller are out in the open, you may still pull on the cable, but it is easier to see and far easier to fix.

There is much more to choosing the right hard disk than its size. Although size determines how much data you can store, it tells you nothing about the speed at which you can access that data. How quickly you can access your data is the true measure of performance.

Unfortunately, there is no one absolute measure of hard-disk performance. The reason is simply that data access occurs in so many different ways that it is often difficult for even the experienced administrator to judge which drive is better. However, there are several different characteristics of hard disks, which, when viewed together, give you a good idea of the overall performance of a drive.

One characteristic that is often quoted is the *seek time*. This refers to the time needed to move the read/write head between tracks. If the data are not on the same track, it could mean moving the head a couple thousand tracks in either direction. Movement from one track to the adjacent one might take only 2 ms, whereas moving the entire diameter of the drive might take 20 ms.

So which one do you use? Typically, neither. When access times are specified, you normally see the *average* seek time. This is measured as the average time between randomly located tracks on the disk. Typical ranges at the time of this writing are between 8 and 14 ms. The problem is that disk access is often (usually?) not random. Depending on how you work, you read a large number of blocks at once, such as to load a WordPerfect file. Therefore, average seek time does not reflect access of large pieces of data.

Once the head has moved to the track you need, you are not necessarily ready to work. You need to wait until the right block is under the read/write head. The time the drive takes to reach that point is called *rotational latency*. The faster the drive speed, the more quickly the block is underneath the head. Therefore, rotational latency is directly related to the rotational speed (rpm) of your drive.

By increasing the rotational speed of a drive, you obviously decrease the time the drive has to wait. The fastest drives, as I am writing this, spin at least 10,000 times per minute, which means that an average rotational latency is about 4.2 ms.

You can also decrease the rotational latency by staggering the start of each track. This is especially effective when doing sequential reads across tracks. If the start of all tracks was at the same place, the head would move to the new track, and the start of the track would have already spin out from underneath. If the tracks are staggered, the head has to wait less time (less rotational latency) until the start of the track is underneath.

Think back to our discussion of hard disks and the concept of a cylinder. This is all of the tracks at the same distance from the spindle. To physically move heads from one track to another takes more time than simply switching the head you are using. However, because switching heads does not occur instantaneously, there is a certain amount of rotational latency. Therefore, the start of each track is staggered, because one moves up and down the cylinder as well as across the cylinders.

By decreasing the rotational latency, we increase the speed at which the head reaches the right position. Once we are there, we can begin reading; this is the average *access time*. This, too, is measured in milliseconds.

Still, this is not the complete measure of the performance of our drive. Although it is nice that the drive can quickly begin to read, this does not necessarily mean that it will read the data fast. The faster the hard disk can read the data, the faster your WordPerfect file is loaded. This is due to the *transfer rate*. This is normally measured in megabytes per second.

However, the actual transfer is not necessarily what the hard-disk manufacturer says it is. They may have given the transfer rate in terms of the maximum or average *sustained* transfer rate. This is important to understand. If you have one huge 200-MB file that you are reading on a new drive, the entire drive might be contiguous. Therefore, there is very little movement of the heads as the file is read. This would obviously increase the average transfer rate. However, if you have 200 1-MB files spread out all over the disk, you will definitely notice a lower transfer rate.

In addition, this is another case of the chain being as strong as its weakest link. The actual transfer rate is dependent on other factors as well. A slow hard-disk controller or slow system bus can make a fast hard disk display bad performance.

Another aspect is how much of the date is being reread. For example, if you read the same 1-MB file 200 times, the head won't move much. This is not a bad thing, as data are often read repeatedly. Hard-disk manufacturers are aware of this and therefore will add caches to the hard disk to improve performance. Data that are read from the hard disk can be stored in the cache, so if it is needed again, it can be accessed more quickly than if it must be first read from the drive. Data that are written may also be needed again, so it too can be reread from the cache.

This is also called a cache buffer, because it also serves to buffer the data. Sometimes the hard disk cannot keep up with the CPU. It may be that the disk is writing someone as new data comes in. Rather than making the CPU wait, the data are written to the cache, which the hard disk can read when it can. Other times, the CPU is busy elsewhere when the data from the hard disk is ready. The hard disk can write it to the buffer, and the CPU can take it when it can.

Finally, there is *data throughput*. This is a measure of the total amount of data the CPU can access in a given amount of time. Because the data are going through the hard-disk controller and through the system bus, this may not be a good measure of performance of the drive itself. However, if the other components can process the data as quickly as the drive can provide it, it is a good measure of the complete system.

This is why you will see references to Seagate drives on the Adaptec Web site. Adaptec understands the relationship among the components in your system. Therefore, they suggest drives that can keep up with the other components, such as the appropriate ones from Seagate.

Another aspect of the administration costs that a lot of people do not think about is the drive designation. Although calling a hard disk "Whirl-Wind" or "Falcon" might be pleasing to the marketing people or to the IT manager who has no clue about the technical details. However, the administrator is not interested in what name it has but rather the characteristics it has. If it takes a long time to figure out the characteristics, the total cost of ownership has increased.

How often have you had to wade through page after page on a company's Internet site to figure out how big a particular model was? Although many (most?) companies have a 1:1 relationship between the model designation and the characteristics, you have to first figure out the scheme, as often it is not posted anywhere on the site.

This is one reason why I keep coming back to Seagate. Without thinking, I can come up with the model number or something very close. The general format is:

```
ST<F><MB><INT>
```

where

> <F> = Form factor, such as 3″, 3″ half-high, 5″, etc.
> <MB> = Approximate size in megabytes
> <INT> = Interface

So, looking at my drive, which is a ST39140A, I can quickly tell that it is a form factor 3 (3″ drive and 1″ high), it has approximately 9140 MBs and an ATA interface. Granted, some of the abbreviations used for the interface take a little getting used to. However, the naming scheme is consistent and very easy to figure out.

As with other hardware, your choice of hard disk is also guided by the reputation of the company. This applies not only to what you have heard, but also to your own personal experiences. Often it is more than just having heard or read that a particular manufacturer is bad, but rather is an issue of being "sure." This is why I will never buy an IBM hard disk again. All three I have bought were defective. Although other people have claimed not to have problems with them, I do not want to risk my data on them. Three times is too much of a coincidence, and I would not feel safe if I installed an IBM hard disk on any of my machines, nor would I have a clear conscience if I installed it in a customer's machine.

On the other hand, I have had a proportionally large number of Seagate drives since I first started working with computers, none of which have ever given me problems. So far, all of my Seagate drives have been replaced with larger drives, not because they have failed, but because they have become too small. There are only so many bays in a computer case, and filling them up with small drives is not worth it. Instead, I got larger drives.

In addition to the size and speed of your drive, one important consideration is the interface to the hard disk. Typically, SCSI hard disks are more expensive than ATA drives, even if you ignore the extra costs for the SCSI host adapter. Even if you want to ignore the extra costs to acquire the drive, you need to consider the costs to install and manage the host adapter; the performance increase you get with SCSI is negligible for workstations. Generally, you do not need the extra throughput that SCSI can provide.

In most cases, space will be an issue. Although you need just a few hundred megabytes for the operating system, you are getting larger and larger applications, with dozens of components that quickly fill up space on your hard disk. Buying and installing a new ATA hard disk is generally simpler than adding a SCSI hard disk, particularly if your first hard disk is ATA. In addition, on newer system, you can have up to four ATA devices, including CD-ROM drives, which is generally sufficient for workstations as well as for mobile users.

On the other hand, if you are in an environment where you need more than four devices or need devices that do not support ATA, then you will have to go with SCSI. In addition, SCSI is basically a *must* when talking about your server. Size isn't an issue, as what is available is generally the same for ATA and SCSI. The key difference is performance. This is particularly important in a multiuser environment.

Let's take the Seagate Cheetah as an example. As of this writing, it is the fastest available on the market with 10,000 rpm. It has a maximum internal transfer rate of 306 Mbps, which means it is even faster than the 80 Mbps of the Ultra SCSI interface. This is a result of an average seek time of 6 ms and 2.99 average latency. This means the average access time is under 9 ms. To compensate, the Cheetah series has default buffer size of 1 MB. In addition, the throughput is too high to use anything other than SCSI or Fibre Channel, so it is not available with an ATA interface.

There are also a few other reasons why something like the Cheetah is the perfect solution for a server. First, it supports up to 15 devices on a single Wide SCSI bus. Using the Fibre Channel versions, you can get up to 126 devices, which are also hot swappable.

Another thing to consider is the maintenance and administration. Low-end Medalist drives have an expected mean-time between failures (MTBF) of 400,000 hours, which is about 45 years. The MTBF for the Cheetah is approximately 1,000,000 hours, over 100 years. No wonder I haven't ever had a hard-disk crash.

The Seagate drives also do something else to reduce maintenance and administration costs. First, there is a feature that Seagate calls SeaShield and is something other hard-disk manufacturers should adopt. This is simply a protective cover around the electronics that are exposed on other hard disks. This protects the electronics from static electrical discharge as well as from damage caused by bumping the drive against something. In addition, this cover provides the perfect space for installation instructions, such as the jumper settings. There is no need to go hunting around for the data sheet, which often isn't supplied with the drive. Talk about saving administration costs!

Some of you might be saying that names like Cheetah go against my desire to have understandable model names. My answer is that the opposite is true. As of this writing, Seagate has four primary *series*: Medalist, Medalist Pro, Barracuda, and Cheetah. These names simply denote the rotation rate, which is 5400, 7200, 7200 and 10,000 rpm, respectively. The Medalist is Ultra ATA. The Medalist Pro is either ATA or SCSI. The Barracuda and Cheetah are either SCSI or Fibre Channel. Okay, this requires you to use your brain a little, but it is far easier than many other vendors.

Tape Drives and Tape Loaders

Because this device has the potential for either saving your data or opening up career opportunities for you to flip burgers, knowing how to install and use them is an important part of your job as a system administrator. Because the tape device node is usually read/write, regular users can also back up their own data with it.

The first tape drives common among PC-based operating systems were 1/4-inch cartridge (QIC) tapes. QIC is not just an abbreviation for the size of the media; it is also a standard.

In principle, a QIC tape is like a music cassette. Both consist of a long, two-layer tape. The "backing" is usually made of cellulose acetate (photographic film) or polyester (1970s leisure suits), polyester being more common today. The "coating" is the actual media that holds the magnetic signals.

The difference is in the way the tapes are moved from the supply reel to the take-up reel. In cassette tapes, movement is accomplished by a capstan, and the tape is pinched between two rollers. QIC tapes spread the driving pressure out over a larger area by means of a drive belt. Additionally, more care is taken to ensure that the coating touches only the read/write heads. Another major difference is the size. QIC tapes are much larger than cassette tapes (and a little bit smaller than a VHS videotape).

Initially, the QIC tape was 300 feet long and held approximately 30 MBs of data. This was the DC300 tape. The tape that next appeared was the DC600, which was 600 feet long and could hold about 60 MBs. As with other technologies, tape drives got better and longer and were able to hold more data. The technology advanced to the point where the same tapes could be used in new drives and could store as much as twice as much as they could before.

There are currently several different QIC standards for writing to tape drives, depending on the tape and tape drive being used. Older, 60-MB drives used a QIC-24 format when writing to 60-MB tapes. Newer drives use the QIC-525 format to write to several different kinds of tapes. As a result, different tapes yield different capacity, depending on the drive on which they are written.

For example, I have an Archive 5150 tape drive that is "officially" designed to work with 150-MB tapes (DC6150). However, I can get 120 MBs from a DC600. Why? The DC600 is 600 feet long and the DC6150 is only 20 feet longer. A tape drive designed to use DC600 tapes only writes in 9 tracks, however, and a tape that uses DC6150s writes in 15 tracks. In fact, you can use many different combinations of tapes and drives.

One thing I would like to point out from a technical standpoint is that there is no difference between 150-MB and 250-MB QIC drives. When the QIC standard was enhanced to include 1000-foot tapes, 150-MB drives automatically became 250-MB drives.

A similar thing happened with 320-MB and 525-MB tapes. The QIC-320 standard was based on 600-foot tapes. However, the QIC committee decided to go with the QIC-525 standard based on 1000-foot tape. That's why a 600-foot tape writing with the QIC-525 standard writes 320 MBs.

Notice that this entire time, I never referred to QIC-02 tapes. That's because QIC-02 is not a tape standard, but a controller standard.

An interesting side note is just how the data are actually written to the tape. QIC tape drives use a system called "serpentine recording." Like a serpent, it winds its way back and forth along the length of the tape. It starts at one end and writes until it reaches the other end. The tape drive then reverses direction and begins to write toward the other end.

Other common tape drives are QIC-40 and QIC-80 tape drives, which provide 40 MBs and 80 MBs, respectively. These provide inexpensive backup solutions. These tape drives are connected to standard floppy controllers and, in most cases, the standard floppy cables can be used. The size of the tapes used for this kind of drive is about the same as a pack of cigarettes.

Aside from using the same type of controller, QIC-40/80 tape drives are similar to floppy drives in other ways as well. Both use modified frequency modulation (MFM) when writing to the device. Sectors are assigned in similar fashion, and each tape has the equivalent of a file allocation table to keep track of where each file is on the media.

QIC-40/80 tapes must be formatted before they are used, just like floppies. Because the size of data storage is substantially greater than for a floppy, formatting takes substantially longer. Depending on the speed of the tape drive, formatting can take up to an hour. Preformatted tapes are also available and, like their floppy counterparts, the prices are only slightly higher than unformatted tapes.

Because these tape drives run off the floppy controller, it is often a choice between a second floppy drive and a tape drive. The deciding factor is the floppy controller. Normally, floppy controllers can only handle two drives, so this is usually the limit.

However, this limit can be circumvented if the tape drive supports soft select (sometimes called "phantom select"), whereby the software chooses the device number for the tape drive as it is using it. The ability to soft select depends on the drive. Although more floppy tape drives support this capability, many of the older drives do not. I will get into more detail about this in the second part of the book when I talk about installing and using tape drives.

On larger systems, neither QIC nor minitapes can really handle the volume of data being stored. Even though some QIC tapes can store up to 1.3 GBs, they cannot compare with digital audio tape (DAT) devices. Such devices use Digital Data Storage (DDS) media. Rather than storing signals similar (or analogous) to those coming across the bus, DDS stores the data as a series of numbers or digits on the tape, hence, the name "digital." The result is much higher reliability.

Hewlett-Packard DAT drives can be divided into multiple logical tapes. This is useful when making backups if you want to store different file systems to different "tapes," and you don't want to use any extra physical tapes. Device nodes are created to represent these different logical tapes. DAT drives can quickly scan for the location of subsequent partitions (as they are called), making searches much faster than with backups to single tapes.

One thing to watch out for is that data written to DATs are not as standardized as data written to QIC tapes are. Therefore, it is possible that data written on one DAT drive cannot be read on another.

There are two reasons for this problem. This first is the blocking factor, which is the minimum space each file will take up. A 1-KB file with a blocking factor of 20 will have 19 KBs of wasted space. Such a situation is faster in that the tape drive is streaming more, although there is a lot of wasted space.

DAT drives use either a variable or fixed block size. Each drive has a default blocking factor that is determined by the drive itself.

Another problem is data compression, which, if it is done, is performed at the hardware level. Because there is no standard for data compression, it is very unlikely that two drives from different manufactures that both do data compression will be able to read each other's tapes.

Keep in mind that that's not all. There are many more standards that I didn't list here. One place to start is the QIC consortium's home page at www.qic.org, which lists dozens of tape standards and associated documents.

Before you buy a tape drive, be sure to find out how easy it to get the tapes and how expensive they are. I bought a tape drive once that was fairly inexpensive, but the tapes were hard to find and more expensive than others were. Eventually, I had to special order them from a distributor on the other side of the country, because my local vendor stopped carrying them (I was the only one who used them).

Tape Loaders

If you have a lot of data to backup, tape loaders can be a real timesaver. In essence, a tape loader is a single tape drive with the ability to store multiple tapes. Because the mechanism can load any tape you choose, they function similarly to music jukeboxes. As a result, tape loaders are sometimes called tape jukeboxes.

Most of the tape loaders I have seen come with either five or seven slots. You can fill up all of the slots on Monday and write to a different tape each day of the week. Although this saves time, I would still recommend taking the tape out every day and storing it separately from the machines.

Even so, I still feel it is a timesaver to fill the loader once on Monday for the week, particularly if you have a large pool of tapes. For example, at one company, we had enough tapes for a couple of months' worth of backups. Our backup software kept track of which tapes were in the drive as well as on which tape any given file resided. We checked once on Monday to see what tapes were needed for the week, filled up the loader and then simply removed each tape as it was used.

On Friday, we did a full backup of every file on the system. This required the loader be filled up completely, because we had so much data. Therefore, having the loader was a necessity for the weekend backups. Therefore, we simply used the available functionality during the week.

As the company and quantity of data grew, we eventually needed more tapes than could fit in a single loader. That meant we had to get a second loader for that machine. Although most of the more advanced backup packages can handle loaders, not all of them work well with multiple loaders. Therefore, you should check in advance before buying something that cannot grow with you.

Video Cards and Monitors

Without a video card and monitor, you don't see anything. In fact, every PC that I have ever seen won't even boot unless there is a video card in it. Granted, your computer could boot and even work without being attached to a monitor (and I have seen those), but it's no fun unless you get to see what's going on.

When PCs first hit the market, there was only one kind of video system. High resolution and millions of colors were something you read about in science fiction novels. Times changed and so did graphics adapters. The first dramatic change was with the introduction of color with IBM's color graphics adapter (CGA), which required a completely new (and incompatible) video subsystem. In an attempt to integrate color and monochrome systems, IBM came out with the enhanced graphics adapter (EGA).

But I'm not going to talk about those. Why? First, no one buys them anymore. I doubt that anyone still makes them. If you could find one, there would be no problem at all to install them and get them to work. The second reason why I am not going to talk about them is because they are not that common. Because "no one" uses them any more, the time I spend telling you why I won't tell you about them has already been too much.

What are we going to talk about instead? Well, the first thing is Video Graphics Array (VGA). VGA is the standard by which virtually all video card manufacturers base their products. Though enhancements to VGA (Super VGA or SVGA) exist, it is all based on VGA.

When talking about VGA, I first need to talk about some basics of video technology. The first issue is just how things work. Digital signals are sent by the operating system to the video card, which sends them through a digital-to-analog converter (DAC). Usually a single chip contains three DACs, one for each color (red, green, and blue, or RGB). The DAC has a look-up table that determines the voltage to be output on each line for the respective color.

The voltage that the DAC has found for a given color is sent to the three electron guns at the back of the monitor's cathode ray tube (CRT); again, one for each color. The intensity of the electron stream is a result of this voltage.

Some monitor manufacturers try to save money by using less-expensive components. The tradeoff is that the beams cannot scan every line during each pass. Instead, they scan every other line during the first pass, then scan the lines they missed during the second pass. This is called interlacing because the scan lines are interlaced. Although this provides higher resolutions in less-expensive monitors, the images will "flicker" because the phosphors begin to fade before they can be recharged. (This flickering gives me, and other people, headaches.)

For most users, the most important aspect is the resolution. Resolution determines the total number of pixels that can be shown on the screen. In graphics mode, standard VGA has a resolution of 640 pixels horizontally and 480 pixels vertically. By convention, you say that your resolution is 640-by-480.

A pixel is actually a set of three phosphors rather than just a single phosphor. So, in essence, a pixel is a single spot of color on the screen. What color is shown at any given location is an interaction between the operating system and the video card. Years ago, the operating system (or program) had to tell the video card where each dot on the screen was. It had an internal array (or table) of pixels, each containing the appropriate color values. Today, some video cards can be told to draw. They don't need to know that there is a row of red dots between points A and B. Instead, they are simply told to draw a red line from point A to point B. This results in faster graphics, because the video card has taken over much of the work.

In other cases, the system still needs to keep track of which colors are where. If we had a truly monochrome video system, any given pixel would either be on or off. Therefore, a single bit can be used to store that information. If we go up to 16 colors, we need 4 bits, or half a byte, of information (2^4 = 16). If we go to a whole byte, then we can have 256 colors at once (2^8). Many video cards use three bytes to store the color data, one for each of the primary colors (RGB). In this way, they can get more than 16 million colors!

Now, 16 million colors seem like a lot, and it is. However, it's actually too much. Humans cannot distinguish that many colors, so much of the ability is wasted. Add to that the fact that most monitors are limited to just a few hundred thousand colors. So, no matter what your friends tell you about how wonderful their video card is that does 16 million colors, you need not be impressed. The odds are the monitor can't handle them, and you certainly can't see them. (Note that I have heard from some people that this is a myth, but no one has been able to provide me with any sources to dispute this.)

However, don't think that the makings of video cards are trying to rip us off. In fact, it's easier to design cards that are multiples of whole bytes. If we had an 18-bit display (which is needed to get the 250 K of colors that monitors could handle), we either use 6 bits of three different bytes or two whole bytes and 2 bits of the third. Either way, things are wasted and you spend time processing the bits. If you know that you have to read three whole bytes, one for each color, then there is not as much processing.

How many pixels and how many colors a video card can show are independent of each other. When you bought it, your video card came with a certain amount of memory. The amount of memory it has limits the total number of pixels and colors you can have. If you take the standard resolution of a VGA card of 640 x 480 pixels, that's 307,200 pixels. If we want to show 16 colors, that's 307,200 x 4 bits or 1,228,800 bits. Dividing this by 8 gives you 153,600 bytes needed to display 640 x 480 in 16 colors. Because memory is usually produced in powers of two, the next smallest size is 256 K. Therefore, a video card with 256 K of memory is needed.

Maybe this is enough. For me, I don't get enough on the screen with 640 x 480, and only 16 colors looks terrible (at least to me). However, on a server, there is usually no need for anything better. Operating in text mode, your video card does fine.

. . . .

As I said, I am not happy with this—I want more. If I want to go up to the next highest resolution (800 x 600) with 16 colors, I need 240,000 bytes. I still have less than the 256 K I need for 640 x 480 and 16 colors. If, instead, I want 256 colors (which requires 8 bits per pixel), I need at least 480,000. I now need 512 K on the video card.

Now I buy a great big monitor and want something closer to "true color." Let's not get greedy, but say I wanted a resolution of 1,024 x 768 (the next highest) and "only" 65,635 colors. I now need 1,572,864 bytes of memory. Because my video card has only 1 MB of memory, I'm out of luck!

But wait a minute! Doesn't the VGA standard only support resolutions up to 640 x 480? True. However, the Video Electronics Standards Association (VESA) has defined resolutions more than 640 x 480 as Super VGA. In addition to the resolutions I mentioned previously (800 x 600 and 1,024 x 768), SVGA also includes 1,280 x 1,024 and 1,600 x 1,200.

Okay. The mere fact that you have a video card that handle SVGA resolutions does not mean you are going to get a decent picture (or at least not the picture you want). Any system is only as good as its worst component, and this also applies to your video system. It is therefore important to understand a characteristic of your monitor: pitch. I mentioned this briefly before, but it is important to talk about it further.

When shopping for a monitor, you will often see that among the characteristics used to sell it is the pitch. The values you would see could be something like .39 or .28, which is the spacing between the holes in the shadow mask, measured in millimeters. Therefore, a pitch of .28 is just more than 0.25 mm. The lower the pitch, the closer together the holes and the sharper the image. Even if you aren't using any graphics-oriented programs, it's worth the few extra dollars to get a lower pitch and the resulting sharper image.

Another important aspect is the "refresh rate." This is a measure of how fast the monitor can redraw the screen. You get the best image (less flicker) if you monitor can refresh at least 72 times a second or has a refresh rate of 72 Hz. Some monitors are produced with a constant refresh rate that cannot be change and are therefore less expensive than monitors with a variable refresh rate. Personally, I feel it is worth the extra money to get a monitor where you can change the refresh rate.

Printers

Although more and more companies are trying to transform into a "paperless office," you will undoubtedly see a printer somewhere. Even if the office is paperless internally, it will have to use paper of some kind to communicate with the rest of the world.

Printers come in many different shapes, sizes, formats, means of connection to the system, ways of printing characters, speeds, and so on. The two most common ways to connect printers are by serial port and parallel port. Windows NT also supports Hewlett-Packard Laser Jet printers equipped with JetDirect cards. These cards allow the printer to be attached directly to a network, thereby increasing its speed. I'll talk more about these later. In addition, at the time of this writing, SCSI printers have begun appearing on the market.

There are two kinds of printers, the daisy-wheel and chain printers, though once very common, are now making way for more advanced successors. The distinction these printers had is that they had preformed characters.

In the case of a daisy-wheel printer, printing was accomplished by means of a wheel, where the characters were at the end of thin "leaves," which formed the daisy shape. The wheel rotated very fast, and as the appropriate letter came into position, it was struck with a hammer that forced the leaf with the character on it against the ink ribbon, which then struck the paper. This mechanism uses the same principle as a normal typewriter. In fact, there are typewriters that use the same daisy-wheel principle.

Chain printers also have preformed letters. Instead of a wheel, however, the letters are on a long strip called a chain. Instead of rotating, the chain moves back and forth to bring the appropriate letter into position.

Although these printers are fairly quick, they are limited in what they can print. You could get pretty tricky in which characters you use and can come up with some rather cute pictures. However, these mechanisms aren't able to do anything very detailed.

The next step in printers was the impact dot-matrix printer. These, too, had hammers, but rather than striking preformed letters, the hammers themselves struck the ink ribbon. Instead of a single hammer, there was a column of usually 9 or 24 hammers, or pins. Such printers are called 9-pin or 24-pin printers.

As the printer prints, the heads move across the page and print out columns of dots. Depending on what character is to be printed, some of the pins do not strike the ink ribbon. For example, when a dash is printed, only the middle pin(s) strike the ribbon. When printing a more complex character like an ampersand (&), the pins strike at different times as the print head moves across the page.

As with monitors, the more dots you have, the sharper the image. Therefore, a 24-pin printer can produce a sharper image than one with only 9 pins. In most cases, the type of printer used is obvious the moment you see something printed with a 9-pin printer. Some 24-pin printers require a closer look before you can tell.

Next, printers began to get rid of the ink ribbon and replace the pins with little sprayers connected to a supply of ink. Instead of striking something, these sprayers squirt a little dot of ink onto the paper. The result, similar to that of an impact dot-matrix printer, is what an inkjet printer does.

Inkjet printers have two advantages over impact dot-matrix printers. First is the issue of noise. Because no pins are striking the ink ribbon, the inkjet printer is much quieter. Second, by extending the technology a little, the manufacturer increased the number of jets in each row. Also, instead of just squirting out black ink, you could squirt out colored ink, which is how many color printers work.

The drawback is the nature of the print process itself. Little sprayers squirting ink all over the place is messy. Without regular maintenance, ink jets can clog up.

Using a principle very similar to video systems, laser printers can obtain very high resolution. A laser inside the printer (hence the name) scans across a rotating drum that has been given a static-electric charge. When the laser hits a spot on the drum, that area loses its charge. Toner then spreads across the drum and sticks to those areas that retain the charge. Next, the drum rolls the paper across, smashing the toner onto the paper. Finally, the toner is fused into the paper by means of a heating element.

Although laser printers may appear to print a solid image, they still work with dots. The dots are substantially smaller than those of a 24-pin dot matrix are, but they are still dots. As with video systems, the more dots, the sharper the image. Because a laser is used to change the characteristics of the drum, the areas affected are very small. Therefore, with laser printers, you can get resolutions of even 300 dpi on even the least expensive printers. Newer printers are approaching 1,200 dpi, which is comparable to photographs.

Some laser printers, like HP's LaserJet, use a technology called resolution enhancement. Although there are still a limited number of dots per inch, the size of each dot can be altered, thereby changing the apparent resolution.

Keep in mind that printers have the same problem with resolution as video systems do. The more dots desired, the more memory is needed to process them. An 8 1/2" × 11" page with a resolution of 300 dpi takes almost 1 MB of memory to print.

With printers such as daisy-wheel and chain printers, you really don't have this issue. Even a buffer as small as 8 K is more than sufficient to hold a whole page of text, including control characters that can change the way the other characters appear. Even though such control characters may cause the text to be printed bold or underlined, they are relatively simple in nature. For example, underlining normally consists of printing the character, backing up one space, and then printing an underline.

Multiple-character sets or fonts are something that this kind of printer just can't handle. Different character sets (e.g., German) or changing the character's form (e.g., italic) can easily be accomplished when the letter is created "on-the-fly" with dot-matrix printers. All that is needed is to change the way the dots are positioned, which is usually accomplished by using escape sequences. First, an escape character (ASCII 27) is sent to the printer to tell it that the next character (or characters) is a command to change its behavior.

Different printers react differently to different escape sequences. Although there is a wide range of sets of escape sequences, the two most com-

· · · · · · · · · · · · ·

mon sets are those for IBM Proprinters and Epson printers. Most dot-matrix printers can be configured to behave like one of these. Some can be configured to behave like either one.

The shortcoming with this is that you are limited to a small range of character types and sizes. Some printers, like mine, can get around this limitation because they can print in graphics modes as well. By viewing the page as a one complete image composed of thousands of dots, they can get any font, any size, with any attribute (assuming the software can handle this). This is how printers like mine can print charts, tables, and, to some extent, pictures.

Viewing the page as a complete image works when you have graphics or diagrams, but it's a waste of memory when you're dealing with straight text. Therefore, most laser printers operate in character-mapped mode, in which the characters are stored in memory and are the dots are generated as the page goes through the printer.

Printers are controlled by other means than just escape sequences or treating the page as a single image. One most widely used means of control is Adobe System's Postscript page description language, which is as much a language as the programming languages C or Pascal, with syntax and vocabulary. To use it, both the software and the printer have to support it. However, the advantage is that many applications allow you to print Postscript to a file. That file can then be transferred to a remote site with a Postscript printer. The file is then sent to a printer (as raw data), and the output is the same as though it was printed directly from the application. The nice thing is that the remote site does not even have to have the same application as long as its printer is Postscript-capable.

Selecting the best printer is more than just choosing the one with the highest resolution and fastest print speed. Although these are two of the most commonly quoted characteristics, they do not represent everything you need to consider.

One commonly overlooked thing is administration. Most businesses are at a single site, with a handful of people. Even if everyone had their own printers, walking a few feet to figure out what's wrong or make changes is no big deal. However, if you are dealing with dozens or even hundreds of printers, spread out all over the world, physically going to the printer is not always practical.

In many cases, the only solution is to physically be at the printer, such as adding paper or changing the toner. You hope that the people on-site are capable of doing that much. However, there are a number of problems and configuration issues that most users are not able to handle. Because calling in a service technician for mundane issues might be too expensive, it would be helpful to be able to do some kind of administration remotely.

There are many printers on the market available that have built-in network cards, and others can be connected to printer servers to allow you to do certain administrative functions across the network. You simply use telnet to connect to a specific port where you get a command line interface to the configuration options. Although you can generally do all of the configuration across the network that you can directly, you still have the command line interface, which is typically not all that easy to use.

If you can build a telnet server into the printer (or print server), why can't you build in an HTTPD server? Well, that's what Brother did with a number of their printers. Using any standard browser that supports JavaScript, you can administer any of the Brother internal or external print servers.

Their external print servers are just like many others on the market in that you can match almost any printer to it. It has both twisted-pair and thin-wire connectors, which allows them to be placed in most any Windows NT network. In addition, the NC-2100h supports either 10- or 100-Mbit Ethernet, making it perfect for high-use printers.

The internal print server is basically an Ethernet card built into the printer, with the same connectors as the external version. These are essentially the same products with slightly different constructions, which means the administration is identical. As with the external printer, the Ethernet connector is auto sensing. In addition, both support a large list of network protocols, including:

- lpr/lpd
- HTTP
- BOOTP
- WINS, DHCP
- TELNET (with user-definable ports)
- SNMP (including proprietary MIB)
- SMTP, POP3
- IPX/SPX (NDS and Bindery)
- EtherTalk
- DLC/LLC
- NetBEUI
- NetBIOS support (TCP/IP and NetBEUI)
- Banyan Vines
- DEC LAT

One of the most interesting things for me was the inclusion of DHCP. I used network printers from other companies before, which only supported BOOTP. This meant that we either had to configure our UNIX machines to support BOOTP, just for these printers, or configure them by hand. With DHCP, you can configure all of your nodes using just a single protocol.

However, if you look at the list, the Brother print servers are not just limited to specific protocols. Basically, all of the most common protocols are supported, allowing the Brother printers to fit into any network environment. In addition, the Web configuration interface allows you to switch between Printer Control Language (PCL) and PostScript.

Near top end of the scale is the Brother HL 1660N, which is designed for very demanding businesses. It can provide resolutions as high as 1200 x 600 dpi, in 256 shades of gray. Although it has a default of only 4 MBs of RAM, it can be expanded to 66 MBs using *industry standard* SIMMs. This is an important issue, because some hardware manufacturers require you to buy your memory upgrades directly from them, although they are the same as what you buy from other places. The result is that you can pay as much as ten times the street price just to have the hardware vendor's name on it. I realize that many companies make most of their money through after-sales service, but this is ridiculous and unnecessary.

Even without addition memory, Brother has made a number of improvements to improve performance. For example, a 100-MHz RISC-based processor is included. Added to that, the Windows drivers include an extremely efficient compression algorithm that compresses the data prior to sending it across the network. This speeds up the transfer, thereby reducing the network load.

The HL-1660N is ready to work amazingly fast. Many printers can take several minutes to warm up, even if just in standby mode. However, the HL-1660N is usually up in about 1 minute, meaning basically no waiting when you walk from your desk to the printer. Keep in mind that if 10 people a day have to wait an average of 3 minutes for the printer to warm up, that's 2.5 hours a week or over 500 hours a year!

The speed of printing is also another factor is determining how much time your printer can save. Depending on the amount of text, resolution, and other factors, the HL-1660N can get up to 17 pages per minute or just under 4 seconds per page.

The HL-1660N can also help you save paper. When you print, you can tell the printer driver to print in "draft" mode, which decreases the resolution. This is useful for seeing exactly how the printout will look or in cases when high quality is not necessary. In addition, it supports 2-in-1 and 4-in-1 printing so you can get multiple pages of your document on a single piece of paper.

For business with less-demanding requirements and even for home users, Brother also produces a number of printers with slightly less speed and throughput. For example, the HL-1040 has a resolution of 600 dpi, but only prints about 10 pages per minute. It also includes an internal processor and supports Brothers data compression, thereby increasing throughput.

Brother also produces several color laser printers. The HL-2400C has a resolution of 300 x 300 dpi in color mode and 1200 x 600 dpi mono, with a throughput of 4 and 16 pages per minute, respectively. Once again, throughput is enhanced with an internal processor, this time with a SPARClite and a default of 32-MB RAM. The HL-2400CN is network ready and supports all of the features discussed previously, including SMTP and POP3, allowing you to automatically print out incoming mail.

If you work with people (like some I do), then you will appreciate the addition security features. The HL-2400C and the HL-2400CN both allow you to block access to the printer based on IP address. Therefore, you won't have certain users blocking the printer by outputting all of those images they downloaded from the Internet.

One group of users whose printer needs are often forgotten are those that are always on the road (out of sight, out of mind). If they are visiting a customer site, for example, it is either embarrassing or cumbersome to get the customer to make a printout for them. Therefore, it would be nice to have a portable printer. Many vendors provide solutions that require cumbersome parallel cables and the inconvenience of a bulky power supply.

Brother's answer to this is the MC-21P series of "mobile" inkjet color printers. Connectivity to the printer for both data and power is provided by a PCMCIA card. Although it can only get about 2.5 pages per minute, the convenience far outweighs the delay in getting your printout. In addition, the MC-21P can print on transparencies as well as on plain paper, which helps you make last -changes to your presentations, reports, and so forth.

From a business perspective, it is important to look at having a single company satisfy all of your printing needs. The larger your company, the greater the need is. With a handful of printers, the need is not as great. However, I can speak from experience when I say how hard it can be to manage a large number of different kinds of printers.

Keep in mind that you not only need to deal with different drivers, but with different quality of printouts and different components (i.e., toner cartridges). In addition, there is the issue of support. You need to keep track of different warranty information, different support numbers, as well as different problems. If you have discovered how to solve one specific problem on one printer, you will end up having to call another vendor when the problem arises on a different printer.

One thing that Brother printers and other devices emphasize is straight-through printing. This can make them slightly larger than similar devices from other vendors. However, I get annoyed when my pages come out with a slight curve to them.

Brother also provides multifunction printers, which are slightly different than their multifunction centers. As with the multifunction centers, these provide printer, scanner, and copier functionality, but no fax or other communication. The MFC-P2000, for example, is a laser printer that gets up to 10 pages per minutes with a resolution of 600 x 600, which is perfect for the small or home office. It can scan at the same resolution and comes with a copy of the Xerox TextBridge OCR soft. So, what do you get when you combine the functionality of a scanner with that of a printer? A copier, which is the third function the MFC-P2000 provides. It, too, has a built-in processor and warms up in less than 1 minute.

Keep in mind: This is not all that Brother has to offer. I barely touched on what printers and multifunction device are available. If I hadn't, I would have needed an entire book. To find the exact printer to suit your needs, check out the brother web site (www.brother.com).

There are also a number of inkjet printers that Brother produces. At the high end of the scale is the HS-5300. This gives you a resolution of 600 x 600, with a quality that is extremely close to that of a laser printer. It too comes with a built-in processor and default 24-MB RAM but can be increased to up to 72 MBs. As an upgrade option, you can get it with the NC-2010H network card, which then gives it the same functionality as any of the other Brother network capable printers.

It too, has the built-in compressor of the driver, which helps increase speed across the network. In addition, the ink cartridges are replaced through a panel in the front of the printer. No need to open up the cover and deal with the cartridge attached to the print head.

One important aspect that I often see overlooked with printers is the total cost of ownership. Some companies will consider it for their computers, but often overlook it for their printers. The reason is that often many people are unaware of what aspects can increase the total cost of owning a printer. One important aspect is the expendable materials that have to be replenished at regular intervals or the parts that can wear out and need to be replaced.

Let's take a laser printer as an example. As you print, you use toner, and eventually you will need to replace the toner cartridge. Normally, there is at least one cartridge provided by the vendor when you first purchase the printer, so you may not be aware of how much a new toner cartridge costs. In many cases, it can be anywhere from $50 to $100 or more. The more often you have to change the toner cartridge, the more you pay in total for the toner and the more the total cost of ownership.

Let's take two theoretical printers. One costs $300 and the other $500. Both have the exact same quality and speed, and each can print 10,000 pages before the toner needs to be replaced. You might think that $300 printer is less expensive. Let's assume that the toner cartridge for the $300 printer costs $70, but the one for the $500 printer costs only $50. You expect the printer to last 3 years, and in that time, you also expect to print over 200,000 copies. This means, you will need to buy 20 new cartridges. With a price difference of $20, that means you will pay $400 extra for the toner cartridges for the less-expensive printer. Therefore, the more-expensive printer actually comes out cheaper.

Unfortunately, the calculations are not always as easy as that. Often the total number of pages you can print with a single cartridge will differ from printer to printer. Therefore, you need to first make an estimate of how many pages you will print during the expected lifetime of the printer and then calculate how many cartridges you will need. In addition, you need to find out how long parts like the drum will last before it needs to be replaced. This also adds to the total cost. When you have done your calculations, the best choice is the printer that has the lowest cost *per page*.

This is one place where I often seen people complain about Brother printers. If you are using your printer at home with just a couple of dozen pages per month, then perhaps many of the Brother printers are not for you. However, once you start getting toward hundreds or thousands of pages per month, this is where Brother printers become extremely attractive. In some cases, a Brother printer can cost as little as half as much per page.

Another problem I often see is buying generic toner or ink. As with other products, generic or less-known printer supplies are often cheaper than their brand-name counterparts. I intentionally used the word "cheaper" here, as such products often take on the other meaning of "cheap." For example, I have found many vendors who sell ink for inkjet printers that has a lot higher water content than the ink from the printer vendor does. It doesn't dry as quickly and therefore produces a less-than-acceptable printout. (Maybe it's okay for a draft, but nothing you would want to send to a customer.)

However, this is not always the case, and it often depends on the paper. Therefore, you might want to test a single cartridge and package of paper before you buy them in bulk.

With color printers, another place to save money is if it is a color printer and there are separate cartridges for each color. If your company logo has red letters on a yellow background, then you might end up using more yellow and magenta. The cyan cartridge could be almost full, but you end up having to throw the ink away if there are separate cartridges.

You should also look into refills for the ink cartridges. This usually allows you to refill a specific color without having to replace the entire cartridge. However, this can be a messy job if you are not familiar with it. In addition, how easy it is to use the refills will be different from vendor to vendor. If you only do refills a few times a year, the savings compared with buying completely new cartridges may not be worth the hassle.

Hardware Configuration and Management

Standard Installation

I am a strong believer in standards. Although many of my coworkers are also strong believers in standards, I believe standards should be used to help the users get their job done and not to control them. I work with many people who see standards as hard rules that should always be adhered to except for the most extreme cases. On the other hand, I believe standards should be there to serve as a baseline from which changes can be made.

Many of my coworkers believe that because there are users who "play" with their computers, steps should be taken to prevent them from even trying. Unfortunately, they take this to extremes and apply it to everyone. Therefore, everyone is limited in what they can do. My attitude is that we should treat all users as adults until they prove the need to do otherwise. We'll get into more details of my philosophy as we move along.

In any event, you need to find standards for your systems. This starts as high up as the overall structure of your network, down to individual workstations, in some extent even what appears on the users' desktop. Standardization means that problems will almost by default be able to resolve easier. And when a user calls in with a particular problem, there is no need to guess what applications the user has available or how their desktop appears. Things that you need all are in their expected place, and you do not need to go hunting for them.

The workstation and server standards will change as technology changes. Therefore, you need to be flexible in what to define as the standard. For example, my first SCSI hard disk was 500 MBs. At that time, that was considered a large hard disk. Today, a small hard disk is anything under 2 GBs. Another thing to consider is the expanding requirements of the operating system. It seems like every new Microsoft operating system requires 50% more hard disk space and twice as much RAM. Therefore, the potential for change needs to be reflected within your standard.

My best suggestion is to define the minimum standard. That is, that a particular class of machine must have *at least* the configuration that you define.

Computer technology has reached the point where most users do not see the changes or do not notice the increase in performance of their machine from one generation to the next. In the early '90s, a jump in processor speed of 25 MHz was substantial because it basically doubled the speed of your system. At the end of the '90s, an increase of 25 MHz essentially goes unnoticed as it represents an increase in speed of less than 10%. For the most part, most people who do not even notice performance increases unless it is an increase of a least one third.

Even if you can attain performance increases that are noticeable by the user, you need to ask yourself whether the increase justifies the additional expense. On individual workstations, you may not have the return on investment in substantial amounts to justify the increase. However, on the server, even small increases may be worth the investment.

One very common misconception is that the faster CPU automatically equates to better performance. If you have an unlimited budget, then you might as well go ahead and buy the faster CPU. On the other hand, if the purse strings are tight, you need to look for the right places to spend your money.

Network Standardization

Perhaps the first thing you need to agree on is the network protocols that you use. Although Windows NT started using TCP/IP as its standard protocol beginning with version 4.00, previous versions did not. If you work in a company where your network has grown rather then having been planned, you may have encountered a situation where two networks in your company were incompatible. If your company is like some where I have worked, both sides will fight vehemently to maintain their standard. The only solution is that company management "dictates" the standard.

So what should that standard be?

Windows NT supports the three most common network protocols called TCP/IP, NetBEUI, and IPX SPX. If your computers are connected to the Internet, they will have to support TCP/IP to some degree. If not, NetBEUI may be the solution due to lower overhead. If you have servers running Novell, then maybe IPX SPX will be a requirement.

Personally, I feel that if at all possible, you should just run TCP/IP. The first reason is the need for TCP/IP when connecting to the Internet. The next is that so many diagnostic and administration tools expect or even require a TCP/IP network. Even though you may decide not to implement any such tools at the moment, you probably will sometime in the future. Starting with a TCP/IP network at the beginning is much easier than converting later.

Concurrently with the decision as to which protocol you'll use, you also need to decide the physical aspects of your network. If you will be running Ethernet, you'll need to decide whether to use thick wire, a thin wire, or twisted pair. Thick wire has the advantage of being able to travel longer distances. Thin wire has the advantage of being extremely inexpensive. (It is often referred to as "cheaper—net"). Twisted pair has the advantage that local disturbances (i.e., breaks in the line) affect just single machines.

One common configuration is to have thick wire running from the server to more distant parts of the company, where they are connected to twisted pair hubs. Individual machines are then connected to these hubs.

Companies where there is a larger physical separation between the server and workstations are becoming more and more common. For example, I have worked in companies where the distance between the server and/or remote PCs was well over a mile. To bridge this gap, fiber distributed data interface (FDDI) was used. To improve performance between the servers, asynchronous transfer mode (ATM) was used.

At the next level, the naming of the PCs themselves needed to be standardized. In smaller companies, it may be okay to name the machines after their user, but this becomes an administrative nightmare in larger networks. To me, the most logical naming scheme is to name machines based on their function as well as their IP address. For example, you may have a machine that is used for CAD applications. If it has an IP address of 42 the machine name would be CAD 42.

Note that using this naming scheme prevents the use of all of the dynamic aspects of the dynamic host configration protocol (DHCP). That is, the names will be assigned statically. This is okay. When you are troubleshooting a network connection, there is an immediate association between the machine's IP address and its name. When the machine was first installed, the little sticker is placed on the front like a name tag. When the user calls with a problem, the name tag is red, and the analyst knows immediately the IP address of that machine. There is no need to start any other tools to find out.

Some people may insist that matching the name to the IP address is not necessary because you can reach the machine either with its name or its IP address. However, this is often part of the problem. It is possible using DHCP to assign the computer name along with the IP address. In such cases, it is much harder for the user to determine what the name of other computer is, which wastes a great deal of time when trying to solve problems. In addition, DHCP is not foolproof. In my experience, there are cases where the names were duplicated when they're assigned dynamically. Although the IP address was unique, the duplicate names made troubleshooting extremely difficult.

I found the most successful solution is to enable DHCP but to assign IP addresses statically. This means that every machine can be installed and configured identically. We can therefore spend less time during the installation configuring the machine and continue to maintain our standard.

Standard Naming

If your company is large enough, that is, you have a large number of PCs, you should also consider assigning IP addresses based on physical location. Many companies already do this, in that their network is broken into a number of subnets. However, I know some companies that take a single class B network and distribute the IP addresses seemingly at random.

This can be a problem when need is assigned based on how the computer is used. For example, let's assume CAD machines all start with the letters CAD. The machine CAD42 has a host IP address of 1.42. The machine CAD 342 has a host IP address of 2.42. It is entirely possible that these two machines sit in the same office, because the base server has a similar function. However, the machines with the IP addresses 1.43 and 2.43 are in completely different parts of the building.

With the two CAD machines, it may be fairly easy to tell where they are physically located. However, there is no easy way of telling where the other two machines are located. If specific IP networks where in two specific physical locations (such as floors or buildings), it would be a lot easier to tell where they are physically located. For example, the network 192.168.1 may be the first floor in the network; 192.168.2 could be the second floor.

If you have not been assigned the appropriate addresses to allow you to do this, you can use any one of the networks that have been reserved for internal use, which are not used on the Internet. You essentially have an unlimited number of networks to choose from, which can be used to fit any physical layout.

Using twisted pair cables, you can take this one step further. The sockets in the walls will most likely need to be numbered in order to find its counterpart on the hub. It is a fairly simple matter to assign numbers to the sockets that are directly related to the IP address. In fact, because the number of private networks available to you is essentially unlimited, the IP address can not only reflect the general part of the building, such as the floor, it can even tell you which room.

You may decide to use a private class A address. This could be submitted into the large number of class B addresses, which would indicate a particular floor or section of the building. These class B addresses could then be assigned to even smaller units. By looking at the IP address you can immediately tell in which room to computer is. Even if your company's layout in a large open space, you can still uniquely locate a particular machine using this method.

At the server level, your standard should define the minimum characteristics each server should have. Because computer technology changes so quickly, this standard will need to be reviewed at regular intervals. However, there are a number of aspects that remain relatively constant that you should define as minimum for your server. In general, CPU performance is less of an issue for file or print servers as it is for a database server or any other machine that needs to do a lot of processing. In order to save money, as well as increase overall performance, it is generally a good idea to separate servers based on their function. For example, one server is responsible for buyout and print services and another houses your Internet server.

When doing an upgrade of a system, many more things need to be considered than when doing a fresh install. The most obvious thing is the data on the machine. Unless you decide to reformat the hard disk, the data are generally safe. However, I don't like to take chances with data, particularly if it is unnecessary. This is, therefore, one very strong motivation for storing all data on the server.

By storing all of the data on the server, , you not only help ensure the safety of your data, but you also make upgrading workstations much easier. I am not a big fan of in-place upgrades. Given the choice, I much prefer a fresh installation. Even in cases where the software requires a copying of the previous version, I prefer to install a fresh copy of the previous version and then the new version on top of that. There are several techniques that you can use to simplify the installation of a large number of machines.

One thing to consider is just how you name your workstations and servers. With five employees, you might consider naming them things like Chris, John, Sandra, Mary, and Steve, to match the names of your employees. However, what do you do if you have 500 employees? The question then arises, "Which machine is Steve 3?" Even if your user's name was Steve M., identifying the machine is more difficult.

Although it is less friendly, I have found that from the administration standpoint it is easier to give machine names like PC 21. Naming workstations like this brings two key advantages. First, machines are not bound to particular users. Remember that workstations are designed for the task of the person using them. If Chris were doing simple data entry, he would have a low-end machine. What happens when he gets promoted and begins to write letters, faxes, and other things that require a more powerful machine?

If he gets a new machine, that machine will need to be named Chris. The old machine will need to be renamed. On the other hand, if Chris was using PC 21 and was promoted, his new machine would be PC 42, for example. There would be no needed to rename the machine!

The second advantage is when assigning IP addresses. It makes sense to assign PC 21 the IP address 21 (e.g., 192. 168. 42. 21.) If, for example, a user has trouble connecting to the network from PC 21, I know immediately what the IP address is. I can then try to connect to the IP address, without worrying if there is a problem with the name-to-IP-address translation. Obviously, the name-to-IP-address translation *could* be a problem.

In one company, we took this so far as to explicitly assign IP addresses using DHCP. This may sound like we are defeating the purpose of DHCP by assigning addresses statically. However, there is a certain logic. First, it makes installation easier. Each machine is told to use DHCP. Therefore, we do not need to assign the IP address directly on machine. This makes "cloning" machines much easier. Plus, with the 1:1 assignment of the PC name-to-IP-address administration is easier.

You could take the naming one step further by assigning names that indicate something of the function of the workstation. For example, PC 42 could be a standard workstation, whereas CAD 42 would be a CAD workstation. If the standard workstations in the CAD workstations were on different networks, naming them like this would be okay. However, you do not have the same one-to-one assignment of PC naming IP address if they're on the same network. Therefore, you could have machines PC 42 and CAD 142 with the host IP addresses above 42 and 142, respectively. This means that there's a likelihood you'll have holes in your names (for example, no PC 57–PC 88). However, this is acceptable, as your machines are easier to manage in general.

Installation

If you don't get the installation right, you can forget about managing that system efficiently. Therefore, it is vital to do a correct installation, which means detailing the steps you take in advance of the installation.

The first step in this is to define what each of the workstations is. It makes least sense to describe your workstations if you only have a single type. For example, if your office consists of five people that are just doing clerkal work, they probably all have the exact same kind of machines. Therefore, it may not be necessary to describe in detail the components of each system. Even so, I have found it useful to define what the standard workstation is. This helps in the decision making later when a new PC needs to be purchased, for example.

However, if there are several different kinds of machines, it is useful to describe each type of machine. For example, you might have 10 workstations for normal clerical work and one for graphical work, such as publicity or marketing. Here too, it is useful in the decision making later when a new workstation needs to be obtained.

The problem becomes even more dramatic and more important when you have hundreds or even thousands of workstations to deal with. You may have a half dozen different kinds of workstations. For example, there might be one workstation for users doing very basic data input. In essence, all they really needed is the operating system and the one application they're using. The next class out might be a person who also does basic data entry but also writes letters or faxes. Therefore, they need a word processing program in addition to the database application. Potentially, they would need more memory.

You might help employees that do know clerical work but are responsible for creating the documentation for your products. They are using, for example, high-end desktop publishing applications, such as Adobe Frame-Maker. Although they are using just a single application, they need a more powerful CPU, more memory, and probably more hard disk space than the typical clerical user.

If your company consists of several hundred employees, you might have your own marketing or publicity department. These people will need a computer that is possibly even more powerful than those used by the people doing desktop publishing. In addition, it is also possible that they will need a much more powerful video card, such as one with 4 or even 8 MBs of video RAM.

Depending on your company, each person too might be filling a particular Java position. The personnel or human resources department may have detailed exactly what are the responsibilities for each position. You could take this one step further by including what kind of workstations they need to do their job. When a new person is hired, the human resources department notifies the IT department, who is then responsible to ensure that this user has the correct workstation.

If your company consists of more than just one physical location, this standard should be applied to all offices. This too is very useful, particularly if you have a centralized support organization. For example, all the branch offices get their support from headquarters. In such cases, IS personnel at the headquarters knows exactly what machines exist in the branch offices. This makes supporting them much easier.

One thing I would like to point out is that this standard should be fairly general. By this I mean that you should not name the specific plans and specific models of computers. Instead, you should describe a class of machine. For example, a clerical workstation should consist of a Pentium 120 MHz with 32 MBs of RAM, 1024-by -768 video card and 17-inch monitor, and a 2-GB hard disk (assuming you can find one that small). You would then describe the graphics workstation as requiring a 266-MHz Pentium Pro, with 128 MBs of RAM, a 1600-by-1200 video card with 8 MBs of video RAM, and a 6-GB SCSI hard disk.

Obviously, the exact details of each machine will depend on your organization. The key is that you define what the standards are. This makes administration and purchasing much, much easier.

The next step is a description of the installation itself. That is, the exact steps you take when you install the workstations. Experience has taught me that does not do any harm to include too much information. The reason is that you are not writing this documentation for yourself and your coworkers, per se, but rather for posterity. That is, people who come into your organization some time in the future. You do not know what their skill level it is. Therefore, you do not know in advance how detailed you have to be. The easiest solution is to be as detailed as possible in the beginning to avoid problems later.

For example, if you are installing on the new machine, these instructions could say to create a new partition using the DOS fdisk.exe commands and detail the steps to use fdisk.exe. You could then go into the details of a formatting the disk and installing Windows 95 or Windows 98. If, for example, you were installing Windows NT, you would describe the installation process, stating that the file system should be formatted as in Windows NT File System (NTFS). I personally believe that you should describe every single step, take nothing for granted, and be as detailed as possible. Once again, it is better to list too much information here than to deal with the problems later.

Among the things that you should list are not only the physical aspects of the installation (e.g., partitions, file system type), but also configuration of the software: for example, what protocols to install, the name of the domain, what user account to use when connecting to the domain, and so forth. Experience has taught me that the easiest thing to do is to list every single step of the installation and what values to input at each step.

In many cases, much of the configuration is done after the system is installed (at least, it is separate from the installation of the operating system). Take for example, creating the user. This modeling includes creation of the user accounts, but also adding the user to the appropriate groups, creating the user's own directory, defining a logon script, and so forth.

At this point, I need to sidestep for a moment. In some organizations, the person doing the installation of the workstation is not the same person who creates the user account. However, both have to be done. The person who was responsible for installing the workstation was notified by the human resources department. He, in turn, notified the person who created the user account and notified the person who was responsible for managing the software licenses.

This does not mean that the steps to create a new user or record the use of software license are not documented. These are all part of the installation process. Therefore, you could have them all in a single document. On the other hand, you simply couldn't make references from one document to the other. For example, at the end of the documents describing the installation process, you could simply mention that a new user name needs to be created, and the software usage needs to be reported and make a reference to the appropriate documentation.

Remember that not all workstations are alike. You'll have clerical workstations and desktop publishing workstations and graphic workstations. Each will need to be installed differently. That is, each will have different software. You need to describe the installation process for each software product. Here, too, you need to be as detailed as possible! Describe each step of the installation, including all of the necessary values to input. Although you may not need to describe things like "input serial number here," you will need to describe what installation directory should be used. This may sound like ridiculously simple information. However, if you have 10 workstations with 10 different installations, directory support will be a nightmare!

Describing the hardware and software standard and installation of software does not apply just to the workstations. It also applies to the servers. Here too, you may have different kinds of servers. For example, the server or servers in your headquarters will be of a different class than the server in a branch office supporting just five people. You'll then need to define classes of servers based on what work is being done at the particular office. For example, in one company where I worked, we had two offices that each had about 100 employees. However, one was actually a production site and had different requirements than the other office. Therefore, it needed a different kind of server.

Part of the workstation standard is the software that is installed. Originally, Microsoft allowed you to install one copy of the software on the server, provided you paid for a license for each user that accessed the software. Not only is Microsoft becoming less and less happy with this procedure, it is becoming less and less necessary. This dates back to the time when 500 MBs was a large hard disk. Today you are lucky if you can find a hard disk smaller than 2 Bytes. It is therefore no longer necessary to install the software on the server. In fact, experience has shown me that it is much simpler to install *everything* on the local hard drive.

Another thing to consider is updates. It is less a concern when you update applications, but it is a major concern when updating the operating system. In one company, we had a policy that said that during installation, the hard disk would be formatted and the operating system would be installed from scratch since we were not very big fans of upgrading an operating system. Experience taught us that too much is left lying around that could cause problems later on. Therefore, on every operating system installation was a fresh install.

The question is what to do with data on the local hard disk. If you have a workgroup with no server, then you'll probably have data on the local hard disk. You need to have a procedure in place that addresses the local data. For example, in one company, we had a "Round Robin" backup scheme. Machine A backed up to machine B, which backed up to machine C, which backed up to machine A. Therefore, the data were on two machines. We could then install one machine and then restore the data from the machine where we did the backup.

In offices that were large enough to have their own server, we made a rule that said no data were to be stored on the local workstation. This was a company-wide rule that every branch office manager knew. When it came time to upgrade the operating system, we simply overrode the hard disk. Any data that were lost was the fault of the person using that workstation.

I know this sounds a little cold, but everyone knew the policy. It was much more efficient to have them restore all of the data on the server than on the workstation. First, we did a backup of the server and not the workstations. Second, there was essentially no information that could be considered "private." Therefore, the information needed to be accessible by everyone. The logical place to put it was on the server. In addition, when it came time to upgrade the workstations, we did not have to go to each machine and check if there was any local data. We simply took it for granted that there was none. Again, it was the user's fault if they stored data on the local machine.

Part of the standard is defining what operating system will go on each machine. Neither Windows 95 nor Windows 98 has anywhere near the level of security possible with Windows NT. Therefore, you need to consider how important security is for you. Some people believe that it is okay to have Windows NT on the server and Windows 95 or Windows 98 on the workstations. However, the adage that the strength of a chain is defined by its weakest link applies particularly to security. It is possible for someone to introduce a program onto the workstations to gather information from the server when the legitimate user logs on. Therefore, if security is at all an issue, you should seriously consider installing Windows NT on every machine.

An argument against this is that Windows NT is more expensive. The question you need to answer is how expensive is it if someone either destroys, or worse steals, your company data. The difference in price almost becomes not worth discussing.

You also need to consider the extra administration required by a mixed network. The administration of Windows NT and Windows 95/98 is different enough to consider having only a single operating system.

Although most newer programs come with an uninstall program, they sometimes leave things lying around. Therefore, you may consider an additional software product that monitors the installation and records the changes; for example, Symantec's CleanSweep. If you plan to use programs like this, I would suggest that they be one of the very first things that you install on each machine. That way they can monitor the installation of everything that you install.

In one company, we found that it was easier to install most every product on every machine. Access was then defined based on group membership. We then had fewer machines to administer. For example, we had a complete office license for *each* user; however, we only had enough licenses for our fax product for about 10% of the users (no more were needed). However, each machine had the fax software loaded on it. You can only access the fax software if you were a member of the appropriate group.

The software that you install on each of the different workstation type will obviously be different. As we mentioned, you might have one workstation type for your desktop publishing and other for your graphics. Because they will be using different software, the software that is installed and the way it is installed will be different for different workstations.

Another thing that seems fairly obvious is that users should get only the software that they need, not what they want. This needs to be made a part of the company policy. For example, the company's policy states that each user gets a computer based on the job position that they fill. As I mentioned, which job position determines the kind of computer they have, therefore, the software they have. It should be made a matter of policy that only when the job position changes does the user get different software.

If you do have a situation where a user does need a different kind of software than what is appropriate for the job position, you have two alternatives. The first is to create a new job position that has a new set of software. Next, the job position remains the same, but you make an exception and say this user gets this additional software. In some companies, the personnel department might have enough influence to dictate that only the first alternative is appropriate.

Installation Instructions

The more machines you have, the greater the need to document your installation procedures. Even without a standard installation, step-by-step instructions can be a great time-saver. There will be specific information such as IP configuration or the naming conventions that will be standardized. Therefore, it makes sense to have this information as well as the steps needed to configure the machine well documented.

Many companies are extremely strict in their standards. There is basically no deviation, and there is almost nothing the users can configure on their machines. Other companies allow much more freedom. For example, I worked with one company that gave their users free rein. That is, they could configure their systems any way they wanted. Granted, there were aspects defined in the company policy, such as network configuration; however, much of the rest was up to them. If they got approval to purchase new software, they could install it if they wanted. They were even allowed to install games, which they could play during their breaks.

If they messed up their machine, they were given a disk and instructions on how to reinstall the machine themselves. If they did it too often, their manager would probably get annoyed, but not the IS department. It was not the job of the IS department to dictate how people should work. No one was told they could not bring a potted plant to work. However, the third time it got knocked over onto the monthly report, someone might bring up the point. The same thing applied to the PCs.

The key was having a standard that was documented. When the user had the disk in their hand, they simply followed the steps and within half an hour they were back to work.

Written installation procedures also help the administrators or whoever is installing the machines. Granted, these people should know what they are doing, but I can speak from experience when I say how useful written instructions are. I have installed well over 100 Windows NT machines in a dozen countries, all with the same basic configuration. The written instructions have always served as a checklist to make sure I did everything I was supposed to. When the trip is costing the company thousands of dollars, you want to make sure you don't have to come back to fix your mistakes.

Although it may seem pretty obvious, one thing that needs to be emphasized is that all your installation instructions and procedures should be localized. But this does not necessarily mean that means to translate the instructions into every language. Instead, the instructions need to fit the local environment. For example, in one company, we developed an automated installation script. The first time we sent the script along with the CD to a branch office it failed miserably. The reason was the office where we created the script and CD was in Germany, and the office where the install was done was in Belgium. Not only was the language different, but the keyboard layout was different as well.

Laptops

Laptops present their own set of problems. Conventionally, laptops are best suited for those users that are constantly working when traveling. Because laptops fulfil a different requirement than standard workstations, you must define a new standard type of PCs. Potentially, you'll also need to define multiple standards for different kind of laptops. For example, your sales force that is constantly on the road and needs to be able to make connections to their office regularly will probably need some kind of communications software. With Windows NT, this could be accomplished through the remote access server (RAS).

You'll probably have to determine what software will be used to make the connection; and you'll also have to determine what kind of hardware you'll use to make the connection. For example, you might consider that the 28.8-MHz modem is sufficient in most cases. However, in other cases an ISDN connection is required. Obviously, this will depend on the availability of ISDN in your area.

The another key aspect of laptops is security. First there's the physical security of the laptop. Users need to be instructed on the proper security concerning the laptops. For example, they should never leave the laptops unattended. Even though this may sound like an obvious statement, some users do not take the same kind of care of laptops as they do with their own equipment. In some companies, the may be the"owner" of the laptop. They are therefore responsible for the safety of laptop. In some extreme cases, if negligence can be proven, the loss of the laptop can result in termination. A less severe reaction would be to make the user pay for the laptop.

Because of its security features, NT is a perfect operating system for a laptop. Even if the laptop were to be stolen, the thief would have a harder time accessing the information on the laptop than if it were Windows 95/98. (Note that without an encrypted file system, once the laptop is stolen, the thief will eventually be able to gain access to the data.)

Another aspect of the security of the laptop is the security of the data. This brings up the question of doing backups of the laptop. The first question is just how much data need to be backed up. If the only data that are changing is a customer database, for example, like something stored in Synamtec's ACT! program, that is generally small enough to fit on a diskette. If not, the database could be compressed to fit on diskette.

Alternatively, you could provide a means for doing a backup onto an external device. Although a tape backup would probably not be cost effective, you might consider one of the devices that use removable media. For example, on one system, I have an EZFlyer 230MB drive from SyQuest. This drive attaches to the parallel port, and although slower than a normal hard disk, it provides an excellent means for backing up my data. In addition, this drive can be used to exchange large amounts of data between the office and a laptop; for example, large PowerPoint presentations where it is impossible to fit them onto a single floppy.

In some cases, you might have a pool of laptops that are used for those people that leave the office on an irregular basis. There is no need for them to have a specific laptop assigned to them. However, when they do go on the road, they need to have the access to a computer. Cases like this have their own set of problems.

A set of rules needs to be defined for using the laptops. For example, users should not install their own software. In addition, if using Windows NT, you can disable the floppy through the software. If necessary, floppies on the laptops can be fitted with floppy locks to prevent users from installing unauthorized software.

You should define and stick to a policy to both check out and check in for the laptops. This means that when a user borrows a laptop, he is required to check that all components are present and to sign a receipt for the laptop. Upon return, your IS department should inspect the laptop to see that it is in good working order and that all components are still present. I believe that the company policy should be that the person borrowing the laptop is responsible for returning it in one piece. Although the sounds like an obvious statement, some companies do not take action if a laptop is returned damaged or has missing pieces. This is the same thing as not making the user responsible for using the laptop.

As an alternative to laptops, you might want to consider personal data assistants (PDAs). These are the electronic equivalents of something like the Time Manager organizer. Many of these have the additional advantage of being able to exchange data with your desktop machine. If all the user needs is an efficient way of storing information, PDAs are an effective alternative to a laptop.

Halfway between PDAs and laptops are the newer handheld or palmtop computers. These run a special version of Windows called Windows CE. In addition, there are a number of commercial software products available for Windows CE, such as Act! From Symantec.

Fresh Install Versus Updates

One of the primary reasons why I like to do a fresh install is that it is not always clear what effects the upgrade will have on the other components. Rather than trying to figure out what effects an operating system upgrade has on the installed software and what effects a software update has on the operating system, I much prefer to start with a clean system.

In smaller companies, this is not always an option. There is no one who's primary responsibility is the administration of the computer systems, and therefore you cannot take the time to install all of the parts from scratch. However, it is much more efficient in large organizations to have a fresh system, with as few upgrades as possible.

Let's look at this issue for a moment. Let's assume you are the administrator of a system with 200 computers. Some of them get software upgrades, some of them have already had the newer version for awhile and some of them need to be replaced. The question is: which are which? Granted, good inventory software can gather and record much of this information for you. However, not all of the necessary information will be recorded. You can save yourself the great deal of time by knowing that all of the computers have a standard installation.

If circumstances require that you do an upgrade rather than a new installation, it might be worthwhile to investigate exactly what changes are made to your system during the upgrade. Should you encounter problems after the upgrade, knowing what changes have been made may help you in localizing the problem.

To this end, there are several products on the market that can help you. For example, Quarterdeck Remove-It from Symantec and Uninstaller from Network Associates (formerly CyberMedia) are just two examples. Both of these products monitor the installation of software and record changes. In many cases, copies are made of system files. When you need to remove a software product, this record of the changes is extremely useful and ensures that everything is returned to its original state. We will go into more detail of these products later on.

When you install an NT service pack, you have the option of creating an "uninstall" directory. As its name implies, this directory is used when you need to uninstall the service pack. Problems can occur when you need to install something by itself or update something that the service pack does. In any number of cases, the service pack contains a newer version of a particular component, while the other product (such as Microsoft Office) contains a version that is newer than what was already installed. This requires that you reinstall the service pack after you install the new version of Office. If you create an uninstall directory, you end up overriding the save files with the files from the previous installation of the service pack. Therefore, you need to be careful, when installing a service pack again, that you do not create the uninstall directory.

The Server

Backup Server

Time is money. If your server is down and your people are not working, you are paying them for doing nothing. You need to do your best to keep them working, which means keeping your server running. If a single workstation crashes, you might be able to handle a single person sitting idle. However, the effects could be devastating if the server were down for an extended period of time.

In order to plan for a potential loss of the server, you need to look at the services that it provides. If you are running with a domain model, that is, a central user database, then your server needs to provide authentication services for the workstations. If the server should fail, another computer needs to take over the work (assuming the data are not all on that single server, which would make logging on a moot point). If you have a workgroup, then logon services are provided by the local workstations.

If your server provides either file or print services, these need to be replaced. As we will see in a moment, having the primary server crash does not necessarily mean that the data are inaccessible. In addition, depending on your configuration, having the server down does not mean loss of printing services. Should you be running a database on your server, this needs to be replaced as well. Finally, there are other network services such as WINS, DNS, DHCP, and so forth.

A crash is not the only time the server goes down. Although Windows 2000 promises to require less rebooting than previous versions, adding most hardware and many software changes will still require a reboot. If you work a 24 x 7 schedule, you need to consider what will happen when the server goes down.

The next thing to consider is how long it will take to get things backed up. If the server crashes or freezes (hangs) and needs to be rebooted, the best you can hope for is at least 10 minutes. However, in such cases, the biggest problem is lost work as a result of the crash. First, people need to wait until the server is running again. Second, they need to repeat all the work they did just prior to the crash.

If the server cannot simply be rebooted, you may have some major problems. If you are in a small company, you *might* be able to handle a couple of days of down time. However, mid-sized and large companies should be backed up within an hour or so or they probably won't survive. Keep in mind all of the employees that *cannot* work when the server was down. I have worked in places that have sent employees home because they couldn't work.

So what can you do? Well, quite a bit depending on how much you want to spend as well as how much down time you can afford.

One solution is to have a backup server available. This could be a traditional Windows NT backup domain controller (BDC), or it could be a separate set of hardware, not yet connected to the network. A BDC could take over logon authentication, WINS, DHCP, and other network functions, should the primary server fail. Whether the server is taken down for maintenance or crashes, this solution provides a fair level of protection with limited costs. Plus, the BDC can take over some of the normal work from the primary domain controller (PDC), such as providing file and print services.

In the case of the BDC, it can be configured as the secondary WINS, DNS, or DHCP server. Should the primary be unavailable, these services switch over to the secondary without the administrators doing anything.

One of the biggest problems is the data. The data can only exist physically in one location. It is possible to store all of the data in an external case and simply switch cables when the primary server goes down. The drive letters on the workstations will be connected to specific directories on the server. Some mechanism needs to be in place to make the switch.

One solution would be to connect the drives using a logon script (more on that in the section on user and group management). It would then call another script that does the actual connection between the drive letters and the shared directories. You then change a single line in the logon script that calls a different script to connect the drive letters to the new server.

One major problem with this is some foolish behavior on the part of many applications, specifically MS Office. MS –Word, for example, stores the path to the workgroup templates using the universal naming convention (UNC) name (i.e., \\server\\path) and not the drive letter. Although you define a specific drive when defining the directory, MS Office changes it to the UNC name. If that machine is down, you don't have access to your workgroup templates.

Even with this built-in limitation of MS Word and other applications, I still recommend connecting the same drive letters to the same shares. It makes it much simpler to recover from a crashed server. The directories for the templates can be changed relatively quickly.

One of the differences between a BDC and a second set of hardware is that you save the cost of the Windows NT license. This is cheaper than the cost of the server hardware, and because the hardware would be sitting in the corner doing nothing, it may be worth the extra expense of the license to have the backup server and then the immediate recoverability of much of the functionality.

On the other hand, having both a running BDC and an extra set of hardware is even better. The primary server could be reinstalled and restored from tape, while the backup server takes over the functionality temporarily. The primary could be repaired and then restored to its original state.

Clusters

Another alternative is a server-mirroring software such as Octopus, from Octopus Technologies. Here a server is configured as a traditional BDC. The software then mirrors all the data and certain configuration information to the backup server with a slight delay. If the primary server crashed, the backup is rebooted and becomes the primary with just a very slight delay. Within a few minutes, everything is back to normal (at least from the users' perspective.

The major drawback is that everything needs to be duplicated. You need two servers, twice the storage space, two Windows NT licenses, and, of course, the Octopus software. There is also the issue of the decreased performance of both servers, as they have to spend time copying the files. In addition, the network is loaded more because the data are copied from one machine to the other. However, the primary benefit of quick, easy recovery with minimal data loss is at least worth the consideration.

The next step up is a true cluster. Here, two servers are configured to share common data storage across a SCSI bus. Should one server fail, the other one is there to take over the work. All services are redundant, and the failover happens almost instantly, so the users do not see the change. Because the two machines are seen as a single one by the other computers on the network, there is no loss of work. When the failed server is restored to operation, everything returns to the way it was.

This has the obvious advantage of no down time. The major drawback is that it is expensive. Because you have two machines doing the work of one, you are essentially paying twice as much for your server. Because the software is actually installed on two machines, you may be required to pay for each license. Check with the vendor to be sure. Then there is the cost of the clustering software.

Another problem is that there is extremely little hardware support. For the most part, you cannot just buy a stack of components off the shelf and expect everything to be fine. You will probably have to buy a pair of servers that have been especially designed to be used as a cluster. This makes upgrading the hardware difficult.

Documenting Servers

When documenting the current state of your computer network, you obviously need to consider your servers. Like workstations, you need to detail the hardware as well as the software components of each server. It is not sufficient to simply say that Windows NT is running on a server. Instead, you need to say explicitly which version. For example, you need to say Windows NT 4.0, with SP4.

Describing the server is just the beginning. Just because you know what hardware and software the server houses, you do not necessarily know what function that server performs within the company. It might be obvious, for example, if only one server, has Microsoft Exchange, installed. However, two servers that are almost identically configured might have different functions. For example, one is the application server and the other is the file and print server. It is therefore essential that you list the task that each server performs with the description of the hardware and software.

Part of the description of the server is exactly how it is configured. For example, you need to mention such things as whether it is the primary domain controller, what its IP address and netmask are, what machine it uses as its WINS server, what software is installed, and how they are configured.

Extremely important are those aspects that are presented to the outside world. For example, what shares are provided. This not only includes their names but also what directories are being shared as well as the permissions on the share.

The key motivation is getting your system backed up and running when it crashes. A good backup scheme can protect you in many cases, but there are times when it cannot, particularly if you need to replace the hardware. This means that a lot of configuration will need to be repeated. If you have standard configuration between servers, it is easy to look at another server and "copy" the configuration. However, what about those cases when you cannot simply copy the configuration? If you do not properly document the configuration, a great deal of time will be wasted during which users cannot work.

Regardless of the size of your company, I recommend to maintain some kind of hardware database. In a small company, this could be something as simple as an XL spreadsheet. In larger companies, this could be something as complex as an SQL server database. In any case, the information used is the same for every company. For example, your database should maintain the manufacturer, the model number, serial number, and the description of the component. I would also recommend that the database include the location of the hardware. I have found that including location of the hardware is important for troubleshooting during the period, for example, when a number of users report network holdings to the main location; it might help you determine the cause of the problem.

You should define some policies about who has access to the database. Although there is generally no problem with people reading the database, I do not recommended that a large number of people be able to make changes. You should define the specific functions to specific areas of the database. For example, when each new piece of equipment is ordered, an entry is made to indicate the order. Another entry is made when the equipment is delivered. Finally, when the equipment is assigned to a user, another entry is made. If each of these three tasks is handled by three different people, they normally do not mean to make changes in the other areas. On the other hand, if your company is small enough, the person ordering, receiving, and assigning the hardware may be the same person.

The Right Hardware

Purchase

There are three different ways of getting your workstations and servers. Each has its own advantages and disadvantages: The first is to build all of your machines from scratch. This can be cheaper in terms of actual cash outlay for the hardware. However, you also need to consider that a lot more time will be spent putting the pieces together. The second alternative is to buy whenever computers happen to be on sale when you need them. This saves you the to time of putting together the machine as well as savess you money. The downside is that you end up with as many different configurations as you have machines. This means additional administrator work to manage all of these different configurations.

Finally, there is drawing all of your hardware from a single vendor. This helps standardize your machines, while at the same time shifting a lot of the work to the vendor. In many cases, you may not work with the vendor directly, but rather with a distributor or reseller. In essence, this has the same advantages and disadvantages of dealing with the vendor directly.

Which of these methods you choose will depend solely on your unique circumstances. Although building machines from scratch may not be the best solution for smaller companies, you may discover a financial advantage in purchasing them all from the same vendor. In order to get the best deal, you'll need to negotiate with each vendor individually. What additional services are provided vary sporadically from company to company. Because it requires a fair bit of administrative work, let's look at some of the issues involved in dealing with a single vendor.

You can obviously save yourself a great deal of administrative work by simply buying the same brand and model from your local computer superstore. However, this defeats the purpose and loses many of the benefits of going directly through the vendor or through one of their official resellers.

The first thing that you will be missing is having a personal contact within the company. Although it is possible to get an individual account representative when buying through one of a large chain stores, you do not get the same level of personalized service. This is an important issue in that part of what you're trying to do is to shift much of the responsibility onto your supplier. It is possible that the local retailer is in a position to support you, so it is worth investigating.

There is a large variation in the sales program and services the vendors will provide. This not only depends on the vendors themselves, but also of the size of your company. You are obviously in a much better position to make "demands" of the vendor if you're planning to purchase several hundred machines. However, even in smaller units, you have a great deal of negotiating power. Remember, there are dozens of computer vendors. If the first one cannot or will not meet your needs, the logical alternative is to go somewhere else. Depending on your area, you may even find companies that will build the machines for you.

One thing that is often forgotten is that buying the computer outright is just one alternative. Some companies will rent the computers to you. Others will lease them. Still others have programs in which you can buy the computers outright at the end of the lease. Although this is slightly more expensive then buying the computers outright due to the amount you need to pay in interest, you can end up saving money, because the vendor is responsible for getting the computer repaired. Depending on your contract, the vendor may be obligated to provide you with a replacement while your computer is being repaired.

Another benefit in purchasing from the vendor is that you commonly get quantity discounts. This does not mean you're required to buy a large number of computers at once, rather you need to buy them within a specific time frame such as six months or a year. In addition, the software may also be part of the deal. Normally, you can't lease the software, but you can spread out the purchase price of the software over the lifetime of the lease.

One thing to look at in the leasing contract is whether or not hardware upgrades are included in the lease. One possibility is that you can upgrade the hardware for a moderate payment. This keeps you up-to-date without making you go bankrupt.

Standard machines from brand-name companies are often not as standard as one might think. I once worked on a server from DEC (now Compaq) which had a defective drive in a mirror set. When the replacement drive was sent, we discovered that it was smaller than the original, although it had the exact same part number. The drive was from a different manufacturer, who had a slightly smaller size than the other. If the drive were bigger, it would not have been a problem. However, we could not simply recreate the mirror set after adding the new drive. Instead, we had to install and format the new drive, copy all the data to it, and use it as the base for the new mirror set. This meant that some of the space on the older drive was lost.

This example is not intended to demonstrate problems with brand-name computers, nor is it intended to put either DEC or Compaq in a bad light. Instead, it is intended to point out that there are things that you need to look out for. In this case, the new drive was not an adequate replacement for the old one. If the vendor is not willing to provide to an appropriate replacement, then you might want to consider looking for a new vendor.

The steps to take when a machine or component needs to be replaced should be formally documented. Every administrator should be in the position to replace or repair machines as needed. This is not to say that every administrator has the ability to get out the soldering iron and fix damaged cards.

Instead, the administrators should be a position to get the machine repaired. Your company may be different in that there is a special group that is responsible for repairing PCs. However, the principal stays the same—period.

Another important aspect of standardization is defining exactly what information will be kept, where it will be stored, and which format the data will be in. If different groups use different formats to store their information, sharing becomes difficult and in many cases impossible. This may be as simple as creating a database to which everyone has access, but you also need to ensure that the databases all are compatible.

Part of this is determining who has what access to what information. Although everyone on your help desk (if you have one) should at least be able to read this information, it is not absolutely necessary that they be able to update or change it. If multiple people all are allowed to change this information, then the procedures need to be documented.

Depending on the number of users in your company, you probably will end up with several different kinds of standard workstations. Each will depend on the type of work that is done on that machine. For example, you might have machines that are used solely to input data into the database and others that are used for your technical applications. By defining a standard you are likely to find that repairing or replacing the machines is much easier. You know which components go into that machine, so you can simply order that exact same part. You know what the standard workstation is so you do not need to waste time trying to figure out what the replacement machine should need.

Because your business depends on getting work done, it is not unreasonable to expect timely deliveries of your computers. Therefore, you should consider including penalties for late delivery in the contract. Some vendors can take 6 weeks or longer to deliver their machines. If you plan delivery on a specific date and that date is not met, you may be out some money. Why shouldn't the vendor take responsibility?

In one instance, we were repeatedly promised delivery to one of our branch offices by a specific date. Because the installation was being done by administrators from the head office, plane and hotel reservations needed to be made and work schedules needed to be adjusted. Two days before the scheduled to depart, the vendor announced they would not be able to deliver on time (although we had ordered six weeks earlier). Because we planned well enough in advance, we got a substantial discount on all our airline tickets. However, 2 days before the flight, the tickets were neither refundable nor could they be changed. This was money that was lost due to problems within the vendor's organization, and therefore they should be responsible for the damages.

I've worked with contracts that have had penalties for late delivery. In one case, the contract went so for as to stipulate that all machines had to be up and running for the contract to be considered fulfilled. For each machine that was not running, the specific penalty would be applied. In one case, ten

PCs that were leased were delivered, but the server was not. This meant that neither the server nor any of the workstations were operational. Bad planning on the part of the vendor resulted in a tenfold penalty.

Even if you do not lose money because of nonrefundable airline tickets, you do lose time and sometimes money when deliveries are not made on time. If users are waiting for the machines, they cannot work as effectively as they should be able to. You have increased administrative costs for the time you spend tracking down the status of the order. If the machines are replacements for existing computers, you have the problem of different users running different software. These problems can be compounded when you have a large number of machines spread out across multiple deliveries. You have the extra administrative burden of ensuring everything is delivered properly.

In such cases, it stays in your best interest to have the contract stipulate what things cause a contract violation and what the penalty is in each case. And you should also stipulate what your responsibilities are, for example, for making arrangements with an ISP.

When deciding on vendors, one thing to ask is how long they will guarantee the delivery of specific equipment. It defeats the purpose of standardization if you get different machines with each order. One vendor I work with changed models every 3–4 months. With a 6–8 week delivery time, orders made 2 months apart had a great chance of not being the same model.

An argument in favor of the vendor might be that this was necessary in order to keep up with the technology. To some extent this is true, but it makes managing standard PCs extremely difficult. If you are contractually obligated to purchase a specific number of machines within a specific period of time, it is not unreasonable to expect that the vendor be obligated to provide you the same product during the lifetime of the contract.

Due to the frequent changes in the computer market, it might not be possible to completely guarantee the availability of machines over the course of the year. Therefore, you'll need to work closely with your vendor to see that they come as close as possible.

Another key aspect of all of this is deciding where you can get your workstations and servers. There are three different approaches you can take, each with its own advantages and disadvantages. If you have enough people you could build all of your machines from scratch; that is, order all of the components separately and install them yourself. This has the advantage that you know *exactly* what is in each machine. The problem is the amount of time it takes to build each machine individually. On the other hand, this can be less expensive than ordering prebuilt machines.

Next, you could simply buy the most cost-effective PC available; for example, from your local computer discount store. Alternatively, there are many places that will build machines to suit your needs. Here, you get exactly what you want, and you know exactly what is in the machine.

The next alternative is to buy machines from one of the major vendors; for example, NEC. These machines might be slightly more expensive than the ones you buy from your computer discount store. I say "might" because it all depends on the quantity you are buying. For example, it may not be beneficial to buy five machines from a major vendor like this. It might be cheaper to buy all five from a single computer discount store. The best saying is for you to define a standard and to determine which of the two alternatives is less expensive.

However, we come to the magic phrase: total cost of ownership (TCO). Eventually, the computer will need to be repaired. The question is, What kind of service are you getting from the computer discount store as compared to the major vendor? Even if you are not buying hundreds of computers at a time, you can still get good support from the major vendors. Obviously, the quicker and more detailed the support, the more you are liable to pay.

However, I need to warn you here. Just because you're buying workstations or servers from one of the major vendors, it does not mean that what you're getting will be consistent. One prime example is DEC (now Compaq). I have encountered two major problems when ordering machines from DEC. First, you cannot always be sure that the components are consistent even within a particular model; that is, the description of two machines may be identical. However, they could have different motherboards, different video cards, or different hard disks.

This makes mass installations of machines extremely difficult. For example, if you are expecting a particular video card to be in a machine, the installation may not work correctly because of the different video card. This problem can even be more dramatic when dealing with hard disks., for example the differing sizes for drive having the same model numbers as we discussed before.

Another advantage of having a single vendor is that you have a single point of contact. If something goes wrong, for example, a computer breaks down, you know exactly who to call. On the other hand, if you have machines from different manufacturers, you need to first check to see who the manufacturer is of the computer in question. In addition, if you have warranty or maintenance contracts, you'll need ten separate contracts, one for each of the different vendors. A side benefit of having a single vendor with a single maintenance or support contract is that you build up a relationship with the company. Depending on the company, this can lead to sometimes getting more benefits than are defined in your contract.

One thing that we have found out is vital when ordering hardware is that the invoice should be as detailed as the original order. For example, if you ordered an Adaptec 2940 PCI host adapter, then this should be listed on the invoice. In some cases, I have received invoices that simply stated that there was a SCSI host adapter. This is **not** enough, especially later when you need to make warranty claims. Also, simply stating that there is 32 MBs of RAM is not enough. The invoice should state exactly what you get, like 60-ns EDO RAM.

Sometimes buying hardware is more than just finding the fastest or largest for the best price. Often, it is a question of "peace of mind." It's like accident insurance. You know to be careful, but sometimes accidents happen. That's why it's called "accident" insurance. In essence, you are betting against yourself. However, the costs of being wrong are not worth the risk. Therefore, you pay a little extra each month, "just in case." Even if you never have to use it, there is the peace of mind of knowing that *if* something were to happen, you would be covered.

I take this same approach to hardware. For example, I will never again put an IBM hard disk in any machine and I advise you never to do it yourself. In the space of about a year, I had three different IBM hard disks, all with similar problems. The first was a DORS 2-GB SCSI drive. It repeatedly reported read and write errors. I brought it to my dealer, who kept it for several days to "test" it. After 3 days of not being able to work, I got the same drive back with the report that the dealer could not recreate the problem.

When I put it back in the machine, I got the same problems. At that point the first thought was a defective controller or cable, but the drive reported the same problems on a completely different machine.

Next was a DHEA 6.4-GB ATA drive. I brought it home, plugged it in, and it wasn't recognized at all. By that time the dealer was closed, so I had to wait until the next day. In this case, they could easily recreate the problem, because it wasn't recognized on their machine either. They gave me a new one, which I installed. A couple of months later the same read and write errors started appearing as with the IBM DORS drive.

One day when I turned on the machine, the system reported that it could not find the primary hard disk (which was the IBM DHEA drive). Although I could boot from a floppy and access the hard disk, I could not read anything from the root directory. When I ran CHKDSK.EXE, I was left with about three directories that were *not* damaged. All others were now in the root directory with names like DIR00001.

Needless to say, this forced me to reinstall Windows 95, dozens of applications, and to reconfigure the entire system. This cost me 2 days (actually two evenings) until I was back at a place where I could work effectively. However, it was more than a week until I had reinstalled all the applications.

Two months later, it happened again. The primary hard disk was not recognized, and I could not access the root directory when I booted from a floppy. A low-level format revealed a dozen bad tracks. Obviously after the low-level format I had to reinstall the system and my applications and reconfigure everything.

This taught me three important lessons. First, even if the data are on a different system and backed-up regularly, a crash of the primary hard disk means a lot of time is wasted reinstalling everything. Therefore, you need some mechanism to quickly reinstall and reconfigure your system. Some of these techniques we will get to in later chapters.

The second lesson I learned is to get a dealer that won't spend my time "testing" the drive and then return it to me when he cannot find any problems. If the problems are intermittent, the dealer should expect that the problem cannot be recreated so easily. In my opinion, the dealer should simply give you a replacement and be the one who has to deal with the manufacturer. For private customers, the dealer may not be so willing to go out of the way. However, if you are a business spending hundreds of thousands of dollars a year, they *must* be willing to make the extra effort.

The last lesson is never to put an IBM drive in my machine again. IBM "claims" that they have a large number of drives in all sorts of machines and do not all have these problems. There are probably many of you, who are reading this who have not had the same experience. In fact, I know people who swear by them. However, I am not willing to take the risk, just like I am not willing to take the risk of driving without insurance. The consequences of being wrong are too high.

Every single IBM drive I have had has exhibited some kind of problem that put my data at risk. Even if a drive from another vendor costs $20 or even $50 more than one from IBM, I am willing to pay it for the peace of mind of not having to worry about whether the system will boot the next time I turn it on or that the data actually get written to the drive.

So to whom do you go for hardware? There are two main approaches that you can take when purchasing hardware. Either you buy complete systems or you buy components. If you buy components, you may not be the one who installs everything. However, you decide exactly what goes into the machines.

Having a single source for both hardware and software has a number of advantages. For example, it is more likely that you'll have one set of drivers for that hardware. However, a single vendor does not guarantee a single set of drivers.

An additional advantage is that you have much less to learn when buying hardware from single vendor. This is because the construction of the machines and components is generally the same. Again, this is not an absolute. Because the hardware is similar with each machine, the administrators and users do not need to relearn each time a new piece of hardware is acquired.

On the other hard, sticking with a single vendor can become a trap. Can you really wait 6 weeks for your machines? In one company where I worked, we stuck with a single vendor who could not promise delivery in less than 6 weeks. The IS manager thought it was more beneficial to have 100%-standard PCs than having no PC at all, even though the machines differed from country to country and sometimes even between deliveries.

In one company, they had the best of both worlds. PCs were grouped into classes with similar characteristics. However, being 100% identical was not as important as having a machine. Therefore, the company stuck with three vendors. If the first one could not deliver fast enough, they went to the second.

Note that this requires a little discipline on the part of the administrators. They needed to keep track of which machine had which configuration. However, with any of the asset management tools available on the market this is fairly easy.

Going to three vendors also has the added advantage of being better able to dictate prices. Obviously, if you must have the machine within a specific amount of time, you will probably end up paying more. However, if you are willing to wait a little, you might be able to cut a good deal. For example, if one vendor says they can deliver in 4 weeks and another says they can deliver in 2 weeks, you might be able to get a good deal by waiting the extra 2 weeks. Remember: supply and demand. You are supplying the money, so you can make demands.

Another alternative is to have your machines built for you specifically. You supply the criteria to someone who builds the machines for you. This has a better chance of getting you exactly the configuration you want. Even if you do not get the exact parts you wanted, you know exactly what is in the machines, which is the goal of all of this.

Repair

You might find it useful to develop a "maintenance pool" for your workstations. This pool consists of complete PCs as well as a number of pool copies of the different kinds of hardware. Standardization of your machines means that you need to have fewer different models and different brands of hardware. This allows you to choose between replacing the entire machine or just individual components.

In some cases, it is not necessary to have exactly matched hardware such as hard disks. However, with devices that require a specific driver, such as hard disk controllers or network interface cards, it is in your best interest to standardize this as much as possible.

If your hardware pool is designed to swap out the defective machine, repair it, and then return it to its original owner, you can decrease the number of spares you need by using removable media, such as from SyQuest. Your maintenance pool consists both of mid- to high-end machines, each with its own SyQuest drive. When you need to exchange machines, it does not matter who needs the machine; you simply take one from the pool and stick in the appropriate drive.

The downside of this is that it requires much greater standardization of hardware, and there is the additional expense of the SyQuest drives. These have a much higher cost per megabyte than standard hard disks. Alternatively, you could simply swap out the hard disks and save on the cost of the SyQuest drives. The downside of this is the additional time it takes to install the hard disk. On the other hand, as hardware prices continue to sink, having a few extra computers on hand probably isn't enough to make you go bankrupt.

If you have a maintenance contract with your computer vendor, you should really investigate how things are handled internally weigh all in advance of your first call. In some cases, the sales and support organizations may have the same company name, but are two separate entities, which have a hard time communicating with each other. I have experienced it myself that after purchasing a large number of computers from one vendor, we could not get any work done on them, because the sales organization had not yet submitted the necessary paperwork.

Depending on how much the salesperson pushes the after-sales service aspects of their company, you might want to try getting a penalty clause built in should the vendor not repair or replace the equipment within the time they promised. When they say that a particular service contract "guarantees" a specific response time, what does this actually mean? If a tangible product such as a computer fails to meet the guarantee, you can always return it. How do you return a promised level of support?

Just like when the computer is not delivered on time, having nonfunctioning computers can cost you money in terms of loss of productivity. If you don't pay for the computers like you promised you would, the vendor can simply re-possess it. What are your options? You could go to another vendor the next time, but you already lost the money. If the vendor wants your business, some kind of tangible penalty should be applied if they do not fulfil their obligations.

The repair or replacement of defective machines is another place where you can save time, at least from the users' perspective. This is one of the strongest motivations for having standard PCs. Should the machine go down you can swap the machine in just a few minutes, allowing the user to get back to work. You can then repair the machine or replace defective components at your leisure.

In some companies, assets such as computers are assigned to specific departments or even individuals. Therefore, you may need to return that computer to its original owner. However, if that's not the case, the repaired machine can then be used as a replacement the next time a computer goes down.

If your workstations are standardized, it is much easier to keep a stock of spare parts on hand. Swapping a defective component is often as cost effective as replacing entire machines, especially if you do not have the money for machines that are not regularly being used.

Regardless of how you obtain your hardware, you should always have spares on hand. This is not as easy when you get your computers from major vendors as it is when you build the machines yourself or order them to be built for you. Often, when you order from major vendors, the description may simply be something like "3.4-GB SCSI hard disk." This tells you nothing about the manufacturer. With hard disks this is often less of a problem.

However, with other pieces of hardware the difference becomes more critical. For example, if your network card fails you would want to replace it with the same kind of card. This enables you to simply remove the old card and insert the new card without having to install a new driver.

I need to emphasize the need to have the spares on hand as opposed to ordering them from the vendor. Even if your vendor promises a 1-day turnaround, this usually means one business day. Therefore, if the hard disk dies on Friday, you may not be able to continue work until Monday. If Monday is a holiday, you may not get it until Tuesday. Your business week may not be the same as the vendor's.

If your company uses standard computer configurations, there may actually not be any need to have spares of individual components. Instead you might want to consider having spares of *entire* machines. In one company I worked, we had a few spares for each of the different classes. When one computer failed, we simply replaced it with a comparable machine. Because all of the data were stored on the server, the only thing the user lost was configuration settings. However, using Windows NT profiles and in some cases file replication, even that was kept to a minimum. The result was we were able to replace the computer in less than 10 minutes. That meant the user was back to work in 10 minutes. If we were to replace components, it could take anywhere from a half-hour to 2 hours or even longer.

Which method is most effective will depend on your company. The larger the company, the more likely you would want to employ a system by which you replace the entire computer. This is simply because there are more problems occurring in a larger company. You will need to make replacements more often. Therefore you will need to limit the down time for the users.

If you do decide for a system where you swap components, I would recommend having *several* spares of each type of components. Once again, standardization of hardware is vital to make the system more manageable. You must be able to swap out like components. You do not know in advance when a component will fail and which component it will be. What do you do if you have only a single spare and the same component decides to break on two machines on the same day?

The odds are generally low for such things, but how much money do you stand to lose if you are wrong? If you have standard machines from a single vendor (or just a few vendors), the vendor may have bought a whole batch of defective parts. Remember, they are trying to keep their costs low and do not always put in brand name components. The more components that are defective, the greater the likelihood that even more will have problems.

What you do with the defective computer will be determined by your company's policy. In some companies, the computer is repaired and the old one is returned to the user. This is because there is a 1:1 assignment between computers and the users. In other companies, where there is no 1:1 assignment, there is no need for the old computer to be returned to a specific user. Therefore, it is returned to the computer pool and waits to be used as a replacement somewhere else.

Hardware Diagnostic Tools

Because the world is not perfect, you will eventually have to deal with a crashed system. In many cases, how the system behaves when it boots (or doesn't boot) will give you an indication of what is going on. However, it also will happen that there is nothing that specifically identifies the problem. It is also possible that your system boots fine, but exhibits odd behavior as it is running. The most common solution for this kind of problem on Windows machines is to reinstall. However, this only corrects the problem if it is related to the software. What about hardware problems?

There are a number of hardware diagnostic tools on the market. Some run under Windows, whereas others have their own "operating system" which you can boot, allowing you to directly access the hardware. Those that run as stand alone products, typically have a much wider range of tests they can conduct because they are not limited by the operating system. Keep in mind that this is more that just reporting the IRQ or base address of the devices. These products actually test the various components of your system.

Personally, I think you should use tools that run under the operating system in conjunction with stand-alone products. It is possible that you might get incorrect results if you are running under any operating system as it often "interprets" the information for you. Although this is useful for "configuration" issues, defects and other problems are often missed.

There are also a few products that come with interface cards that are inserted into the bus, allowing you to diagnose problems even when your system cannot boot. These have a small digital display on the card that shows you the power-on self test (POST) code being sent across the bus. Based on the code, you can determine where the problem lies.

In general, the software products have a common set of tests they run through. The tests normally include:

- System board
- Video alignment aids
- Video adapter
- Parallel port
- Serial port
- Floppy disk drive
- Hard disk tests (0 & 1)
- Main memory tests

One of the key features to look at is the extent to which you can configure these tests. This might mean defining a specific set of tests to run as well as how many times to run each test. Both are important aspects. If you already have an idea of where the problem is, you should not have to wait for the program to run through unnecessary tests. Also, with hardware you often have sporadic problems. Therefore, you might have to run the test continually for an extended length of time before the problem reappears.

Another thing to look at is what values or configuration settings can be changed. Keep in mind that changing settings is not always a good thing, particularly if a novice is running the tests.

Micro 2000

If you are concerned with diagnosing PC hardware problems, take a look at the wide range of products that Micro 2000 has to offer. The products range from self-booting diagnostic tools to POST reader cards to remote diagnostics and beyond.

Micro-Scope is their self-booting diagnostic tool that can run on any PC. Regardless of the CPU manufacturer (Intel, Cyrix, or AMD) or bus (ISA, EISA, MCA, PCI, and PCMCIA), Micro-Scope can identify problems on your PC. Version 7 (the newest, as of this writing) contains tests for your CD-ROM drive, without the need to load DOS-based CD-ROM drivers, something that many other diagnostic tools do not have. In addition, the version 7 also contains support for the AMD K6-II and Intel Xeon processor, even those with a clock speed above 500 MHz. Upgrades for new processors are available for download from the Internet.

Many tools simply report on the problems they find. However, Micro-Scope not only allows you to make changes, but also gives you detailed benchmarks of your system. This is useful when you "feel" something is wrong with your machine, but there is no identifiable hardware problem. With the report generated by the benchmark, you can see if the machine is performing as it should.

During the testing, Micro-Scope examines the CMOS and POST information. Anything that is inaccurate or questionable is flagged, allowing you to change it as needed. Part of this is being able to accurately identify your hardware, including brand name and model. This is extremely useful when buying brand name computers, which normally do not tell you exactly what components you have.

Micro-Scope supports all common bus types including ISA, EISA, PCI and Microchannel. You can even display the POST registers on IBM PS/2 systems, including all slots, which adapters are in which slot, which adapter description file (ADF) to use, and whether the ADF is loaded.

In addition to being able to diagnose CD-ROM problems, Micro-Scope can test many other multimedia components, such as DVD drives and sound cards. It has full synthesizer tests and can test the volume and left–right channels of your sound card.

Tests can be run once or repeatedly, the results of which can either be printed out or saved to disk (or just viewed on-screen if you want). In addition, you can use the print screen capability to print directly from the application.

As with other products, Micro-Scope will thoroughly check your memory, using all of the common tests (checkerboard, walking-ones, etc.). Low memory is tested before the entire program is loaded, which is then relocated in memory to enable you to test all of your memory, regardless of how much you have. In addition, Micro-Scope will tell you exactly what bank is failing. This includes the ability to test internal and external system cache as well as video RAM up to 64 MBs.

Another bonus is the tools Micro-Scope has for data recovery. It can identify and correct many problems in the master boot record of your hard disk. It also includes an editor to allow you to make changes yourself anywhere on the disk (assuming you have the knowledge to do it).

In addition, to free download of patches, Micro-Scope comes with lifetime technical support. After using the program, I find it difficult to conceive of a reason why someone would need to call tech support, as it is so intuitive, but the offer is nice. The product package contains both 3.5″ and 5.25″ disks, a user's manual, as well as 9-pin serial, 25-pin serial, and 25-pin parallel loopback connectors, to diagnose serial and parallel port problems.

Unfortunately, something like Micro-Scope cannot always do the job. This happens when your system just won't boot for any number of reasons. Using a diskette with its own operating system does no good, because the computer does not get that far to boot from anywhere. This is where Micro 2000's product POST-Probe comes in handy.

As its name implies, POST-Probe monitors the POST codes being sent across your system bus as the computer is booting. It can fit into any ISA, EISA, PCU, or MCA slot (although it requires the included adapter for the MCA). These codes are displayed on two seven-segment displays, indicating what the POST is testing at the moment. There are also four LEDs that monitor the power, as well as four voltage pads (+5 VDC, −5 VDC, +12 VDC, −12 VDC, and an additional 3.3 V for PCI) to test the system using a voltmeter.

There are additional LEDs that monitor clock signals, the RESET signal, and I/O reads and writes. You can therefore use POST-Probe after your system is running to identify other bus problems and possible problems with specific cards.

When your system stops, the last code displayed gives you an indication of what is wrong. Although the code does not always tell you the exact place where there is a problem, the included user's manual lists the phases of the POST. By looking at the steps around where it stopped, I have never not found the problem. In one instance, I accidentally loosened the cable to my hard disk. When I tried to boot nothing happened. Using the POST-Probe, I quickly found the problem.

As I will talk about in later chapters, I am a stickler for documentation. I am really impressed with the POST-Probe manual. It is written in an easy-to-understand language. POST failure codes are on the left side of each page, with the description the device or chip that is causing the problem. This helps in finding and understanding the problem.

For the true professional, Micro 2000 has combined Micro-Scope and POST-Probe into a single product, which they call the Universal Diagnostics Toolkit. Both products are combined in the full version within a case, which is not only large enough to hold both products, but tools and many other things. Each product has the same lifetime technical support as the stand-alone versions.

Micro 2000's product Burn-In takes much of the functionality of Micro-Scope to the next level. As its name implies, it is used to conduct "burn-in" tests of computers. This can be either new machines or ones that you have repaired. This is an extremely useful tool to prevent deploying products that will only cause you problems down the road. Particularly in cases where machines have multiple problems and only one is correct, burn-in tests can save you a great deal of both time and money.

Like Micro-Scope, Burn-In is compatible with all CPU manufacturers and system buses. In addition, Burn-In performs all of the same tests that Micro-Scope does.

Burn-In has a couple of very useful features for companies that install a large number of PCs at once. First, the tests can be run without a monitor or keyboard, therefore, you need a lot less space, allowing you to simply stack up the PCs and run a large number of tests at once. Using the floppy drive light and speaker, the program sends a few signals to the technician when it needs a "scratch" disk or the loopback plugs. Other than that, the program runs completely on its own, saving the results to disk.

As the tests are run, Burn-In writes a complete log to the scratch disk you provided. Because the log is in ASCII, you can read it with any text editor. In addition, the log is being updated the entire time. Therefore, if something should happen to the machine (like someone accidentally pulling the plug), Burn-In will be able to continue where it left off.

In addition, you only need to run the setup once. The test configuration is then saved and performed the same way each time the disk is booted. If the program determines that hardware is not present for a test is it was selected to do, that test is simply skipped, without the need to configure the test for different hardware variations.

TuffTEST

TuffTEST from Windsor Technologies is a powerful and very inexpensive stand-alone diagnostic tool. Although you could order it with all of the packaging, you can save time, money, and trees by ordering and then downloading it from the Web. As of this writing, it is just $9.95, which is a fraction of most other products.

One key aspect is that it is designed specifically for users with less experience. Although it has most of the features of high-end tools, the emphasis is on ease of use as well as providing the user with sufficient information to diagnose the problem.

This is a stand-alone product, in that it can be booted from a floppy. This sounds confusing at first, because you download it from the Internet. What you download is a program that allows you to create the bootable floppies. Once booted, TuffTEST "takes over" the computer, without the need for an operating system like DOS or Windows. As I mentioned before, often this yields more accurate results. TuffTEST has its own set of device drivers, which can access hardware directly.

Windsor boasts that TuffTEST is "safe for use by anyone." This is because none of the tests changes data on the hard disk. In addition, the program is so configured that once it boots, it will wait 10 seconds for a menu selection, and if no key is pressed, it runs through the complete suite of tests.

Another advantage of TuffTEST is that it is completely written in assembly language, which means more compact code and faster execution. In addition, it takes up just 125 KBs of memory, which is actually relocated when the program runs. This ensures that every memory location tests. In other cases, the program is actually too large to be able to check *all* of memory.

TuffTEST is not just a diagnostic tool, as it can also display all of your hardware configuration information. This information can then be printed or saved to the disk. Each saved session contains the test results as well as the system configuration. Because you can save up to five previous sessions, you can compare the results from multiple tests.

Higher up on the scale is TuffTEST PRO which is intended for the professional. This has the same basic functionality plus you can edit your configuration and make other changes to your system. Like TuffTEST, TuffTEST PRO is a stand-alone product, meaning you boot your operating system from the diskette and it becomes your operating system.

In addition, there are a number of tests that TuffTEST PRO has that are not included in TuffTEST. For example, TuffTEST PRO can report in the switch positions on your motherboard, conduct I/O tests on your serial and parallel ports (with an included loopback plug), determine the optimal interleave and low-level your hard disk, and many other tests.

One of the most interesting aspects of TuffTEST is the sales approach. You can order a packaged version of the product, including a printed manual, if you feel it is necessary. However, there really is no need. The on-line manual contains all of the necessary information, plus the product is extremely intuitive.

Lifetime support is provided for *free*. However, the product is so easy to use it is hard to think of a reason why you would need to call them. In addition, updates range from free for minor changes to a slight fee for major new releases.

Other Goodies

The PC Technology Guide

If you feel you are overwhelmed by all the different hardware technologies, you're not alone. Quite frankly, there are a lot of different kinds of hardware, and it is extremely difficult to be really familiar with all of it, especially if you have other duties to perform. However, at one time or another you're going to need to know about different kinds of hardware, so you will either need to learn it all yourself, hire someone who already knows it all, or find a source of information that can deliver the necessary information efficiently.

In this context, efficiency has two key aspects. The first is related to speed. If it takes tomorrow to get the information you need (like leafing through stacks and stacks of old magazines), it is not very efficient. Even if you *know* that the information is in that stack "somewhere," it does you little good if you spend hours or even days looking for it.

Second, efficiency is also related to the amount of information available to you. This does not mean you need access to all of the material ever written about PC hardware. Instead, the opposite is more often true. That is, sometimes the information available is just too much. You cannot see the forest for the trees. If the amount of information keeps you from getting at what you need, it is not very efficient.

I often encounter "information overload" when I'm confronted by new technology. I'm interested in learning what it's all about and browse the Web site of a vendor who offers this technology. It is loaded with technology briefs, press releases, white papers, and many other documents describing the technology. Unfortunately, more often than not, where I would expect to find a description of the technology, I end up with what equates to nothing more than the marketing blurb about how wonderfully this company has implemented the technology.

Even if there are technical details about the technology, I'm often confronted with a problem with new technology that there is often not enough background information for me to understand what the paper's talking about. So I have to go running to some other site to find out the technical background to understand the technical background of this new technology.

Therefore, when I came across the PC technology guide Web site (*www.pctechguide.com*), I was amazed to find so much useful information in one place. The site explicitly states it is "aimed more at the PC hobbiest than the IT professional." However, I feel that the authors "aim" is off as this site provides a wealth of information for the hobbiest *and* the IT professional.

One key issue that is overlooked by many people is just what "IT professional" means today. As late as the mid-'90s, an IT professional had to be a jack-of-all-trades. You had to know about hardware, operating systems, networking, programming, and all of the other areas that fall under the heading of "information technology." Today, people within the IT profession are becoming more and more specialized. It is not unreasonable to find an outstanding database administrator who knows little about the underlying hardware. He or she does not need to know this, as the operating system should provide the necessary level of abstraction.

Therefore, something like the PC technology guide provides an outstanding resource for anyone, *including* IT professionals who need to find out more information about the hardware technology aspects of IT. Plus, it is loaded with detailed images, which help you to understand the technology being discussed. Being Web pages has the added advantage of having links to different places on the site. Therefore, you do not need to go hunting to define details. You just click on the link and you are there.

The site's author, Dave Anderson, has also considered the wishes of people who want continual access to the information. Dave provides the PC technology guide on CD, which you can order on the Web site. This is definitely well worth the money. For less than the cost of any good book on the subject, you have immediate access to the information you need. Because it only takes up about 25 MBs, including all of the information stored in MS Word documents, there is no reason not to copy it to your hard disk.

Although a separate browser is provided with the product that allows you to access the pages, I prefer using a separate browser such as Netscape Navigator. By purchasing a site license, you could easily link in the PC technology guide into your intranet, making it available to all of your users. In addition, regular updates of the CD are provided.

LearnKey

Until recently, there was no certification that identified a person as being qualified to work with PC hardware. You could become a Microsoft Certified Systems Engineer (MCSE) or Certified Novell Engineer (CNE), but there was no equivalent for PC hardware. That was until the introduction of the A+ Exams, which is sponsored by the Computing Technology Industry Association (CompTIA), an organization composed of many computer industry leaders. Now you have the same level of certification for hardware and software.

When hiring someone new, having the A+ certification gives you an indication of what they know. For your own employees, you might think that this certification has little value. However, I tend to disagree, because it provides the company with several benefits. First, you have established criteria by which you can judge the skill level of your employees. You may even considering using the A+ certification as one of the criterion for promotion. Another key advantage is that it helps you define what level of knowledge is necessary to do the job. If your system administrators are required to pass the A+ exam, you know what level of knowledge they have.

Not everyone can pass the A+ exams the first time. This is not because the exam is inherently difficult, but it does cover a wide range of topics, going fairly deep into the material. In order to avoid the costs of taking the exam and not passing, you should consider training in advance. Although you can get a list of the material for the test from CompTIA, you will have to gather the necessary study materials on your own. The solution is to get a prepackaged training course.

Although A+ training is available from several companies, my personal favorite is the CD training from LearnKey. The material is basically the same for all products, because it is all based on the same test. However, I find the way the material is presented from LearnKey is by far the most useful. For the A+ exam, the course consists of seven CDs.

In addition, you can also obtain test preparation software that does a much more thorough job of evaluating your preparedness for the exam. The training CDs themselves also provide an overview of what will be on the exams, so you know exactly what to concentrate on as well has how much each area is weighted.

For me, the most significant is the level of interactivity. Being a CD, you can more easily move to a specific topic, and the A+ training from LearnKey is no exception. In fact, I have found that the LearnKey courses have much more precise control over where you can jump to than most other products.

Figure 5–1 shows you the main window. At the bottom are the main topics discussed in the course. Clicking on one brings you to that topic. At the bottom left is an Index of the main topics in the course. On the right are several control buttons. The Directory button shows you all of the videos contained on the CD. The Challenge button is used to access interactive exercises on the topic. Depending on the subject, this could either be a short quiz or an interactive exercise.

A nice feature is the on-line glossary, which is accessed through the search button. You often encounter terms that are defined in other modules

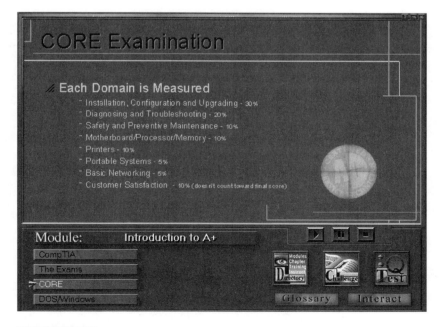

FIGURE 5–1 LearnKey Main Screen

or you are not sure what they mean. With the on-line glossary, you do not need to stop your training session to find the definition.

You also have a pre- and posttest as well other training courses. Both cover the same level of material, but the pretest is designed to give you a feeling for the material as well as help you decide whether you need to review the module or not. Even though I passed all of the pretests, there were a number of questions that I got wrong, which encouraged me to study the material (can you identify the first CPU to run at 3.3 V?).

Even if you do not plan to take the A+ exam, I found the training material to be extremely useful, although there was a lot of material that I really don't need on a daily basis (like the first CPU to run at 3.3 V).

Security

Any computer system has a set of security issues that needs to be considered. Regardless of what mechanisms are in place, the basic concepts are the same. In fact, the security of a computer system is very much like the security of your house, just as running a computer system is like running a household. You only want to let those people in who should be allowed in and you only want people accessing resources that they should. (Do you really want your three-year-old playing with your collection of Dresden porcelain?)

The term *security* is common enough. On a personal basis, we think of it as freedom from risk or danger, being safe. We might also think of this as the methods we undertake to prevent someone from breaking into our house. In computer science terms, both of these ideas are applicable, depending on what you are referring to.

If we talk about being safe from risk when working with computers, we are often talking about things like regular backups and reliable hardware. Although these are very important issues, these are not what is generally meant when referring to security. On computer systems, security is more along the lines of preventing someone from breaking in. The definition can be expanded by saying computer security is preventing someone from doing something that they are not allowed to do. This could be anything from reading other people's mail to stopping the printers.

In this section, I'm going to be talking about what mechanisms exist to keep people from poking around and doing things they shouldn't. I'll talk about what tools Windows provides to control access, change what users can access, and how to make sure users are not even trying to do things they shouldn't.

Real Threats

One thing that I enjoyed most about one job I had was that I was one of the few people that most of the end users felt comfortable talking to. One day I was approached about how we required passwords to be changed every couple of months. Computers are to be used, not to keep people out. Many people were annoyed that they even had passwords, let alone had to change them regularly. The biggest problem is not that the users were right, but that users, as well as many system administrators, don't understand the dangers involved without the protection of passwords, let alone other protections.

The stereotypical image of a pair of teenage computer enthusiasts breaking into a military computer and almost starting a war may be good for Hollywood, but the times have changed. Yes, there are still those kinds of hackers running around, but they are not likely to break into systems with the more advanced security techniques employed today, because most of the security is good enough. But then again, it may not be.

Hacking has become an almost cult phenomenon with newsgroups, magazines, and even their own language. The people who belong to this culture are not only equipped with the latest technology, they also have an almost never-ending list of new security holes that they can use to break into a system. Because they spend much of their free time trying to break into systems, they may have found some of the security holes themselves. However, the techniques they use go beyond just the list of known holes (though these are probably things that they try first). Instead, there is a methodology to the attack.

Today, many hackers are not just randomly trying systems across the country. Instead, there is usually some motivation for attacking a particular site. It may be just the notoriety of being the first to break into the crystal palace that is some major corporation. In some cases, this is what these people do for a living. The ability to break into a competitor's computer system and look over the shoulder of its research and development people may be worth the investment of hiring a hacker.

As we all know from many of the detective shows we see on TV, criminals are caught because of the clues they leave behind. This also applies to the computer hacker. Hackers breaking into a computer are less likely to leave evidence that can be traced directly back to them. It is usually a case in which the perpetrator is caught in the act during a subsequent break-in. Then there is the added problem of criminal jurisdiction, because the hacker could just as easily be on the other side of the world as on the other side of town.

Just knowing that you should lock your front door or buckle your seat belt is enough for many people to do it. However, I am not one of those people. Understanding that someone could walk away with my TV or that my head could go flying through the windshield is what motivates *me* to do what I should do. I am also less likely to forget or not to do it one time because it's inconvenient. I take the same approach to computer security: I want to know why. Once I know why, I am less likely to forget.

Most system administrators are aware that there needs to be "security" on their systems. I put it in quotes because it is often just a phrase brought up at staff meetings. When addressed, security often just means forcing users to change their password at regular intervals or making sure that users were logged out when they go home. One company where I worked forced users to change their passwords every 6 weeks, but the root password was only changed when someone left the company. (It was too inconvenient.) Added to that, the root password for all the machines were variations on a single theme, so once you figured out one, it was easy to figure out the rest.

With all the talk of the Internet, the kind of security most often in peoples' minds is the attack from outside. Although this is a very real threat, it is not the only one. Personal experience has taught me that inside attacks can be just as devastating.

In this same MIS shop, everyone had the root password to every machine (also the administrator password on our NT machines). There were people who only administered the UNIX machines and others who only administered the NT machines. However, they had the passwords to all machines. One employee was not satisfied with the speed with which the hardware vendor was reacting to a problem he was having with one of the NT machines. Because it was the same vendor for the UNIX machines, he decided to "motivate" them to make a personal call.

On several irregular occasions, this employee stopped the Oracle database process. Because almost everyone used that database, the company was brought to a standstill for the couple of hours it took to discover the problem, reboot the system, and clean up. Eventually he was caught, but not after causing tens (if not hundreds) of thousands of dollars worth of damage.

Keeping the UNIX root password from him would have probably prevented him from doing this exact thing. However, he could have done other things to damage the company if that was his intent. Nothing can prevent this kind of act. However, if passwords are limited and something goes wrong, it is not so easy for the guilty party to deny it.

In the beginning, I was a firm believer that information about security holes should be kept secret (security by obscurity). I had an obligation as the all-knowing guru to protect the innocent system administrators in the world. Therefore, I felt it was improper to discuss these issues publicly.

As I began to read more about security, I discovered that I was one of the few people who shared this belief. Most of the books and articles that I read presented the material as "Here's the threat and here's what you can do about it." By not only knowing that there is a threat but why it is a threat, you can correct the problem as well as identify other potential problems that may not have been discussed.

On any computer system, there is always the danger that something can be compromised. Now, the word "danger" can span a whole spectrum of meaning, and it all depends on what you are talking about. It might be dangerous to leave a bowl of sugar on the counter where your two-year-old can reach it, just as it might be dangerous to walk through Chernobyl without a radiation suit. It's purely a matter of scale.

The dangers involved with an insecure computer system are like that. If someone found out the password of another user on our system, the danger of damage is low. On the other hand, if someone found out a password for a computer at the CIA, the danger is greater.

The damage caused can also span the entire spectrum. Sometimes there is no real damage. Someone who breaks into a system might simply be curious and want to look around. This is comparable to having someone wandering through your living room.

The "worm" that Robert Morris let loose on the Internet in 1988 was such an event. His intent was not to cause damage, but things went awry. Although little real damage was done, it "infected" 2,100–2,600 computers. Many machines were brought to a standstill, as file systems filled up and systems could no longer write their log files and were busy running the processes that the worm started. In the end, it has been estimated that between $1 and $100 million was lost due to time spent cleaning up and the loss in productivity when the systems were down. Even with the lowest estimates, the loss was stunning.

On the other end of the spectrum is the case that was documented by Cliff Stoll in his book, *The Cuckoo's Egg*. The information that these intruders from West Germany had gathered from more than 450 government and military computers was sold to the Soviet KGB. There were a few convictions, and one of the prime suspects was found burned to death in a wooded area near his home.

Computer intruders also have the ability to cause physical damage. A virus that's introduced to a system, acting as a file server for DOS PCs, could change the scan rate of the monitor, which can cause it to explode. One computer that Cliff Stoll was monitoring that was broken into was used to regulate the radiation doses given to cancer patients. If the computer behaved unexpectedly as a result of the hackers actions, it could have meant the death of a patient.

In any information system, whether it is a computer or filing cabinet, there are some basic security issues that need to be considered. First, there is one aspect of security that no operating system can help you with: the physical security of your system. You might have implemented all the security that your system provides, but if someone can walk off with your computer, even the highest levels of operating system security won't do any good, just as a security policy in an office has no effect if someone can just walk away with sensitive files.

One more commonly ignored aspect of security, in general, is the power of small pieces of information. As individual items, these pieces may have no significance at all. However, when taken in context, they can have far-reaching implications. Police use this same concept to investigate crimes, and intelligence agencies like the CIA use it as well. Extending this to the business world, such techniques are useful for corporate spies.

There are other cases in which security is important in business. What if someone came along and changed an important piece of information; for example, an employee who thinks he is underpaid may want to change it? Whether this information is on paper or in a computer, the integrity of the data is an important part of security. Along the same lines is the consistency of the data. You want the same behavior from the system in identical situations. For example, if salary is based on position, inconsistent data could mean that the night watchman suddenly gets paid as much as the company president.

When preparing one company for connection to the Internet, I checked the security on the system and found dozens of holes. Keep in mind that this was actually my first attempt at being a hacker. Added to that, I exploited no real bug in the software; instead, I just took advantage of "features" that were not considered in a security context. By using just the tools and programs that the system provides, I was able to gain complete access to the system. Once the system is compromised, the danger of further compromise grows steady. The only safe thing to do is to reinstall from scratch.

I do not mean to scare you when I say that every system has the potential for being broken into. In the end, every security-related decision and every function in the program was written by a human. The security could be mathematically tested, but who is to say that the mathematical test is not flawed?

The first step in stopping the would-be intruder is to keep him or her from getting to your system in the first place. This is similar to having a lock on your front door. You could go to the extreme of fencing off your property, hiring full-time guards, and installing video cameras and alarms, but this is too extreme for most people. First, they probably can't afford it. Second, the threat is not that great, compared to the costs.

But what about your business? The potential loss from someone breaking in can be devastating. Corporate spies can clean out your sensitive data or a disgruntled former (or current) employee can wipe out your entire system.

If there is a physical connection to the outside, there is the potential that someone could break in. However, once you have made the decision to connect to the Internet (and you really should), you need to be much more aware of security than when you network was isolated.

When an attacker improperly accesses a system, he or she may not necessarily continue with the attack immediately after gaining access. Instead, he or she might create backdoors to gain access to the system at a later time. He or she might be able to create users, new shares, or change the associations between particular file types and the appropriate applications. He or she can also use one machine to gain information about other machines and the network in general.

The severity of this problem can be demonstrated by what I found at one company for which I was working. In preparing for connecting the company to the Internet, I conducted a security check of the internal network. I wanted to see just how far I could get.

One of the first steps that a burglar takes before he breaks in is to case the joint. He may observe it for several days or weeks before making his move. To make his presence less conspicuous, he may watch several scattered locations and then choose the easiest target (or may choose all of them in turn). A computer break-in is basically the same. The only difference is the tools the burglar uses and the information that is collected. In both cases, however, the more careless you are as the potential victim, the easier time the burglar has in gathering the information and breaking in.

Because you are not trying to keep someone from breaking into your house, let's talk about the tools that a hacker would use to break into your computer system. One of the most innocuous and most dangerous tools is net.exe, with all its various options. You can see all of the shares a particular server has with "net use." You can get a list of user and group names with "net user" and "net group". These functions are *not* secure and any user can access this information.

Although there is not much that a hacker could *do* with these programs even on insecure systems, a great deal of information can be gathered. As I mentioned earlier, most people overlook the dangers of small pieces of information. Using "net group," I can find out the names of the administrators; using "net user," I can then find information about their account.

Net Commands

Both the net user and net group commands can provide you with very useful information about the users on your system. The net user command gives you details about specific users, such when they last logged in, their logon script, when their password expires, to what groups they belong and so forth.

Using the "net view" command or even the computer browser, you can see whatever comment is listed. If it says something like "Jim Mohr, System Administration", it would be a perfect target for a hacker. Using "net user," the hacker can easily figure out where my home directory is.

One common tactic used works on the belief that an account that is not used too often will have an easily guessed password. Based on my experience, this seems to be true. Usually, people who don't use their computer accounts are not as aware of the security issues and are more than likely to choose a password that is easy to remember and therefore easy to guess. Finding out when someone last logged in can be done with "net user." What are good passwords and what are not is something I'll get into in a minute.

Dictionary Attack

One very common attack is the dictionary attack. Here the hacker uses common words, encrypts them using the same method as Windows NT uses and then compares the two. By default, only administrators can access the data file containing the user information. However, using a LINUX boot disk, a hacker could get to it with no problem. In addition, tools such as l0phtcrack can "sniff" the network and read the passwords as they float by across the network.

I put together a dictionary of about 1.5 million words in English, German, and French. It took less than an hour to encrypt through these words and compare them with the passwords. I ended up with 25% of the company. The newest version of l0phtcrack has features that will tack on a specified number of additional characters to the words in the dictionary before encrypting them. For example, if the word in the dictionary was boardwalk and l0phtcrack is set to try up to four additional characters, it will try things like boardwalk7, boardwalk?-, boardwalk3%+, and so forth. Because the LAN Manager hash that NT uses splits the password into two seven-character blocks before it encrypts it, the characters "boardwa" are encrypted the same all the time. Therefore, programs like l0phtcrack only need to encrypt the last part, which makes things go a lot faster.

Windows NT provides the ability to enforce certain password restrictions. However, l0phtcrack can be configured to use a "brute force" approach, in which it simply tries every combination of characters. Passwords of four characters or less can be cracked in a matter of minutes. It might take a few weeks to crack longer passwords, but it will eventually. The question is "How long?" Therefore, you need to come up with a strategy that increases the time it takes for a hacker to crack the password.

An analysis of the passwords showed some interesting things. One person chose as a password the geographic area for which he was responsible. His girlfriend, the personal secretary of the company president, chose his name as her password. Other people chose their first name, their spouse's first name, and other easy-to-guess passwords. One even chose 123456.

Because I used the same password in many different contexts, I went on the assumption that other people did the same. As you might expect, several people used the same password elsewhere. I tried some of these passwords in our bookkeeping and management software. Here, too, I was able to crack "only" about 20 passwords, including those of the head of the purchasing department and the head of sales.

One major flaw in the Windows NT security is that passwords are encrypted the same way all the time. That is, if two people have the same password, the encrypted password is the same! Because all the passwords were encrypted the same way, a hacker could sort the list of encrypted passwords and look for any that were duplicated. Even without something like l0pht-crack, the hacker would know that these are the same passwords. In my tests, I found about a two dozen that were all the same. Because it is unlikely that they all chose some random word, I guess that it had something to do with the company. As it turned out it was the company's name.

Add to that the fact that the very nature of NT allows remote access to the password information. Once I had gained administrator access, I was a member of the Domain Admins group and could therefore access the password database of other domains within our company. Actually, I do not have to gain access directly. The default security on a Windows NT system is so open, there are literally hundreds of opportunities for a hacker to create a Trojan horse to trick the administrator into giving him access to the user database (or the entire file).

Trojan Horses

Tricking someone into giving access to the system does not necessarily mean you call them and ask them to do it for you. There are a lot of other ways to do it. The traditional way is to use what is called a "Trojan horse". Like the historical horse of the same name, this is used to gain access to a system disguised as something else. In many cases, a Trojan horse is disguised as some program that a user would want to run. For example, a game or utility that the victim wants to install on a system. When it is run, it can do any one of a number of things that allow the hacker to gain access to the system later on.

Unfortunately, the default state of Windows NT security allows hackers literally hundreds of opportunities for planting a Trojan horse. This is because the default permissions on so many files and directories allows *anyone* full access. For example, there are numerous programs and DLLs that give full access to everyone. All any hacker would need to do would be to replace one of these files with a Trojan horse. This not only applies to programs and DLLs, but to anything that executes code.

Like the dictionary attack, Trojan horses are not something unique to other operating systems. In fact, by default, Windows NT is more susceptible to Trojan horses than any other system I know of. Microsoft did some very foolish things when it came to security on Windows NT. There are several commonly used programs that are FULL-CONTROL by everyone. In one instance, I took advantage of the order in which Windows NT executes programs to create a Trojan horse. Normally, one of the last places that Windows NT looks for a program is in the directories defined by the path. Therefore, by creating a Trojan horse version of something like NOTEPAD.EXE, it is very easy to get someone to execute another program for you, which then starts the real program by calling it explicitly (i.e., C:\WINNT\PROGRAM.EXE).

In addition, all users have the ability to change the file associations, which are then valid for all subsequent users. Anyone can change the association between common extensions like TXT or DOC so that some other program is executed. The next time someone on that machine double-clicks on a DOC file, the Trojan horse program is started.

If it's an administrator, the program is executed under his name and it is his name that goes into the system log as having added this user to the Administrators group, for example. In addition, you could create a second program that is called from the first, which then erases the first. The next time the program is started, it behaves as it should. In other words, the hacker is covering his tracks.

Windows NT Security Basics

There are a number of concepts and processes that are part of Windows NT security that most system administrators are unfamiliar with. In order to administer a Windows NT system properly and therefore support users efficiently, an understanding of these concepts is important. Although administrators have been relatively successful by simply sharing resources, creating users, setting permissions, and similar actions, an understanding of the basics is vital to utilizing the resources available to their fullest as well as protecting them.

Under Windows NT, accessing any resource involves two entities: subject and object. The subject is, in essence, the user. However, it is not always a user in the conventional sense. Instead, there are many system processes that are running within the context of a specific user, although that user may never have physically logged on to the system.. These may be any one of the built-in accounts, such as the system account, or they may be a "real" user. For example, if you start the services applet in the Control Panel, you can configure a service to run as a particular user.

Security on a Windows NT system is based on the premise that Windows NT can refer to every aspect of the system by some *unique identifier.* That identifier is basically the object's name. The object is what we normally think about when we're talking about resources. These can be files, printers, or any other resource the system has, such as memory. By referring to all aspects of the system as objects, Windows NT is able to provide the same security mechanisms regardless of whether it is a physical object such as a file or something less tangible like a process in memory.

With all things as objects, Windows NT is able to define specific access controls where one can define which subjects can access which object and what kind of access they have. What that access is and how it can be controlled is dependent on the object. For example, you can execute a file but not a printer. You can manage a printer but not a file.

One of the most commonly known aspects of Windows NT security is the security account manager (SAM). It is the responsibility of the SAM to maintain the user and group account information. This includes information on the local machine as well as within a domain. Therefore, there will be a

SAM for the local machine as well as both the primary and backup domain controllers. User and group information is stored within a database that is accessed by the SAM to provide authentication for users.

Access is not actually granted by the SAM. Instead, this is accomplished by the Local Security Authority (LSA). When the user logs in, the LSA generates what is called an "access token". This access token is what is used by the system to determine what access a particular user has. The user name is therefore not what the system uses to determine access. Although the user name and associated password are used to determine the initial access, the access token is assigned at logon and then used to determine access to various resources. This is why a user must logout and log back in when added to a new group.

Another component is the security reference monitor (SRM). In essence, the SRM is perhaps the key element in the entire Windows NT security steam. When a user tries to access a particular object on the system, the SRM will check to determine whether or not the user has the necessary authorization. In addition, if the action is being audited, the SRM will generate the appropriate message that will be logged by the LSA.

In order to access an object on any Windows NT machine, a user must first logon. In the conventional sense, this means entering a user name and password. However, the Windows NT single sign on (SSO) capability allows users to logon once, and it is the original logon process that logs the user on to other systems.

Users on a Windows NT system are identified not by their user name but rather by a unique number called the security identifier (SID). By using a hashing function that is based on the current system time, the amount of execution time the current process has used in users' mode, and computer or domain name, the SID is almost guaranteed to be unique. There is, however, an incredibly slight chance that the SID is repeated.

This has an advantage over other systems, like UNIX, where the user ID can be reused. In UNIX, it is possible to force users to have a specific user ID and therefore give them access to files they probably should not have. Because of this, it is also possible to give multiple users the same user ID, something that is impossible under Windows NT.

Windows Objects

Windows NT manages access to the various aspects of the system by referring to them as objects. The more common things that users access, like files, directories, and printers are seen by the system as objects. Even some of the more abstract resources, such as processes, threads, memory, and even windows are considered objects. In fact, all aspects of the operating system and not just those related to top security are treated as objects in one way or another.

In essence an object from the perspective of Windows NT security is the same as objects that we program with. An object contains functions and data and only those functions within the object can access that data. What goes on inside the function is irrelevant to you as you just want the data. This is also important to understand as there are many different kinds of objects and each will be accessed in a different way. For example both a file and a windows object can be written to. However a file cannot be resized but a window can. A window cannot be read but a file can.

One thing to note is that a program never accesses an object directly. Instead, the operating system itself does all the work. This ensures that the operating system can check each access to each object to see if it is authorized. In contrast, on a UNIX system, the system administrator has the ability to directly access things like the hard disk and avoid the security mechanisms built into the filesystem. This does not make UNIX less secure, as the administrator could write programs and change the security to allow him to do the same thing. However, this functionality is built into UNIX, without the need to write a special program.

One kind of object that you will often find is called a container. A container object is an object that contains other objects. One common example of a container is a directory, as it "contains" files and other directories. Because files do not contain other objects, a file is considered a noncontainer object. Later, when we talk about *inheritance*, the difference will become important.

Windows NT controls the access to all objects. Because all applications must go through the operating system to access any object, no matter who is running the process, the operating system will verify that access is allowed.

Because hardware devices are system resources, they too are treated like objects. Therefore, Windows NT controls access to them. Not only is this a security issue, but the operating system can also prevent conflicting accesses to hardware devices. In Windows NT, no program may directly access any hardware device but must go through the operating system. Although there are API calls to access them, a program is still going through the operating system. In many cases, there is no direct interface, such as the device nodes under UNIX.

Access to the system is provided to users based on their user ID. Although the mechanisms are much more complex, it is the ID that determines what type of access a user has to what objects. Because they are the types of objects most commonly dealt with, I will limit this discussion to accessing files and directories. However, the same principle applies to other objects.

Access Control Lists

Associated with each file and directory (as well as the share name of an object) is an access control list (ACL). This is a list of who has what kind of access. In contrast to standard UNIX permissions, the ACL can have a long list of different types of access. Because Windows NT can identify users, it knows what each user is allowed to do. It can then compare the ACL for an object with the user's access token to determine what kinds of accesses are allowed.

Because the permission is based on the user's identity and not on a password to the object, auditing of the object is possible. Take, for example, a door that has a regular key lock. It is impossible to tell exactly who opened the door, as all the keys are (normally) the same. On the other hand, if you have a card key, the card is registered to a particular user. When a door is opened, you know who did it.

It is this card key, or user token, that gives you access to a Windows NT system. Because you actually do not have a card key that you plug into your computer, the system needs some other way of determining who you are. In order to do that, you are given a user account and a password. Windows NT then requires that you input your user name and password to gain access to the system.

Keep in mind that once you have logged in, your ID is set as far as the system is concerned. If you are added to a new group while you are logged in, your current session is not aware of this. You then need to log out and then log back in.

When an object is created, the associated ACL is created with it. Initially, the owner of the object can define who has access and what kind of access is permitted on this object. This access is defined by changing the access control entries (ACEs) of the ACL. Each ACE contains an SID and the permissions that are allowed or denied that SID. The SID can either be a user or a group.

Most objects have a security descriptor that describes the security attributes for that object. Each security descriptor consists of four parts:

- owner SID: indicates the user or group who owns the object
- group SID: used only by the POSIX subsystem and ignored by the rest of Windows NT
- discretionary ACL: identifies the users and groups who are granted or denied specific access permissions
- system ACL: controls the auditing messages the system will generate

Discretionary ACLs are "discretionary" because how they are configured is at the discretion of (i.e., controlled by) the owner of the object. That is, the owner of an object can set the permissions to anything he wants. On the other hand, system ACLs are controlled by the system administrators and cannot be changed by the owner.

However, one needs to be careful with these terms. In principle, even the system ACLs can be considered discretionary, because they are at the discretion of the system administrator. In some systems, certain kinds of security are forced by the system, and the system administrator cannot change them. This is mandatory security.

Controlling Access

Before accessing an object in any manner, it first has to be opened. This is essentially the same process as when a file is opened, as files are just one kind of object. When the object is opened, a handle is passed to the process that opened it. Again, this handle is basically the same that a file handles and is a "token" that is used to uniquely identify your "connection" to the object. Keep in mind that your process can have several concurrent connections to a single object. Each will have its own handle. Normally, you will access the object in different ways depending on what kind of object it is. When you are finished using the object, you close it, essentially giving the handle back to the system.

When the object is first opened, the object manager asks the security reference monitor to determine if the process should be given the requested access. This is done by comparing the process with the ACL of the object. If there is insufficient authorization, the security reference monitor will fail the request. If granted access to the object, the object manager determines the resource usage for that process and can also fail the request if the process already uses too many resources (e.g., memory). When both the object manager and the security reference monitor have "approved" the request, the handle is passed back to the process.

When the process tries to access the object once it has received the handle, the object manager does not need to refer to the security reference monitor. That is, the ACL for the object is only checked when the handle is given. Instead, the object need only check to see if that action is among those rights permitted for that handle. This saves a lot of time as compared to checking the ACL for each access. This also means that one handle could be given to a process to access an object in one way (i.e., read), and another handle to access it in another way (i.e., write); even though the process can both read and write to the object, each handle is treated differently.

Keep in mind one important thing: The access rights contained within the handle remain with the handle until it is given up. If either the object's security descriptor or the process changes once the handle has been issued, the *original access* is still in effect. For example, if you open a file for which you only have read permissions, the owner cannot change it to read/write and expect you to be able to write to the file. You must first close the file and re-open it. If you are not a member of a group when you logon and the system administrator adds you to the group, you must log out and then back in before the change takes effect.

Note that the ACL is sorted so that "deny access" entries are listed before "grant access" entries. When you first open an object, the security reference monitor searches the ACL and compares it to the SID of the process. When a match is found, the search stops. Because the "deny access" entries are first, if one should deny access to the object, it will be found before any that grant access and access is denied. If there are no denies, but there is a grant, then access is granted. However, even if there are no entries that explicitly deny access, if no entry is found to grant access, then access is denied by default.

Because the ACL is searched by the security reference monitor for each specific kind of access requested, you do not need a single ACL entry to grant you all the access you need. For example, one ACE can grant you read access, whereas another can grant you write access. You therefore have read and write access.

What You Can Do about the Danger

You could create a fairly secure system simply by following any one of the numerous security checklists that are available in books or on the Internet, but there will be most likely something missing. Although many of them go into extreme detail in describing the steps necessary to secure the system, they can never be complete. The reason is quite simply that no two systems are identical. Therefore, it is virtually impossible for such checklists to cover *every* aspect of every system.

Don't just follow a checklist to secure your system. You must *know* and understand what the changes mean. You must *know* and understand what it takes to make a secure system and what the implications are. If your checklist is missing something, you may overlook it.

Does this mean that the only way for you to have a system secure is to hire an expensive security consultant? Although security consultants are a wise choice in situations where you do not have the skills to secure the system yourself, I've found that in many cases, companies have the skills but hire consultants anyway. This is nothing against consultants, but rather against managers who underestimate the abilities of their employees.

Part of this is the 80/20 rule. This means you can protect 80% of your system with 20% of the effort. Conversely, the other 80% of effort is required to protect that last 20% of your system. The result is that implementing the very basic security measures will be sufficient to protect most of your system. The rest will take a little more time and effort.

In my experience, you should not try to become a security expert, but rather you should try to become a hacker. By this I do not mean that you should try to break into other systems, but rather you should try to break into your *own*. By doing so, you accomplish three things. First, you learn more about security. In order to hack a system, you need to understand the security of that system. Because basic security concepts are the same on every system, you learn more about security in general.

The second thing you'll accomplish is that you'll probably find security holes or potential security holes that the checklists did not mention (at least, I did). When I hacked my own network, I found several places that the checklists overlooked. This was simply because we had configurations that were not discussed.

The third thing that you will accomplish is that you will begin to think like a hacker. This is perhaps the most important aspect of all of this. Keep in mind that there are essentially hundreds of ways to gain improper access to a system. The first are the ones that receive most media attention: that is, bugs, or "features," that allow an intruder to gain access to the system. In the early '90s, security reports of this nature were popping about in every system imaginable. This was not necessarily because the systems had become secure, but rather people began to look for holes. This was a good thing. Both operating system and application vendors became more security conscious. The result was more-secure systems.

This does not mean that there are no more holes. Rather, it means it is less likely that a novice hacker will be able to exploit them. To be able to exploit existing holes, you often need knowledge of the product that is as good as, or sometimes better, than the developers themselves.

The other way a hacker can gain access to a system is by someone giving them access. This does not need to be an administrator but rather can be any normal user. Once a hacker has gained access to the system, it is much easier to get even more access. Therefore, preventing that first access is *vital* to the security of your system. This is one place where thinking like a hacker is very useful.

One important aspect is understanding what the hacker is after. Some hackers will do it just for the fun of breaking into your system. After they looked around for awhile, maybe leave you a message, they will leave and bother someone else. In most cases, once you have frustrated the first few attempts, the hacker will move on.

However, if your system has something that the hacker wants, he probably will not stop until he gets it. Therefore, the question you need to ask is what information is on your system that somebody else would want. Note that what makes one company more successful then another is knowledge. That knowledge might be how to make a better product or the same product for less money. Therefore, if your competition has that same knowledge, they would be a threat to your livelihood. Even if the information was patented or protected in some other way, your competition may still find a way to exploit it.

Security Policy

A security *policy* is a set of decisions that collectively determines an organization's *posture* or attitude toward security. This not only includes what is and what is not acceptable behavior, it also defines what actions are taken when the policy is violated, what the responsibilities of each group of people are, and so forth. A network policy defines what is acceptable when using the Internet. These policies cover different areas but are very much intertwined.

Before you define a security policy, you must define your security posture. This is more-or-less decided by your company's overall attitude on security. If you believe that everyone should have access to everything and nothing will be limited, your security policy will be significantly different than if you want security above all, no matter how inconvenient it is for your users.

In order to have a *really* secure system, you need to have a security policy that defines exactly what security you want. It does no good to simply say that you want a secure system, without knowing exactly what that means. In order to do this, you should come up with both a security *statement* and a security *policy*. The security statement is a single line that defines the company's attitude on security in general. For example, your security statement might simply be that no access is permitted unless explicitly given. On the other hand, your security statement might be the opposite, whereby bald access is granted unless explicitly taken away. The security statement is then used as a guideline when developing your security policy.

It is logical that the level of security that you defined in the company's security statement should reflect the level of risk. That is, the greater the risk, the higher security you should have. Unfortunately, we are once again confronted with the old saying about the weakest link. Therefore, a high risk means that most, if not all, of your computer systems need to have a high level of security.

In general, you are defining what is acceptable behavior. It's often difficult to define what is considered "acceptable" behavior. Some companies give their employees the freedom to hang themselves; that is, they have complete access to the Internet, including e-mail, WWW, ftp, and so on. If the company discovers that the employees spend all their time downloading games and not working, the employees get a warning, a reprimand, and finally termination. On the other end of the scale, some companies say that a computer is for company business and will not be used at all for personal use, even if it means you can't get e-mail from your brother.

Without a well-documented computer usage policy, you could open yourself up to more than just attack from hackers. Alternately, the company is responsible for what the computers are used for and what is stored on them. There are many cases were computers have been used to store illegal software. For example, there are numerous cases of computers used to store parts of software. Can you, as the administrator, prove that you knew nothing about it?

One thing I feel should be in there, no matter what end you are on, is that you must clearly state that employees' activity on the Internet should present the "proper" image for the company. I had to put the word "proper" in quotes because this will obviously be different from company to company.

The first step in defining either your security or Internet policy is to define what is and is not permitted. Spell it out in *clear text* so that everyone knows what it means. To make things easier and perhaps the list smaller, you could simply define the "don'ts": Define specifically what is *not* permitted.

This could include the hours during which Internet activity is not allowed and the types of material that cannot be brought into the company (i.e., pornography, pirated software).

Also part of the security policy should be what protocols and programs you will allow. If you are only going to allow outbound connections, then the policy should state this. If inbound connections are okay, what protocols can be used? Are incoming ftp and http connections okay, but not incoming telnet? If so, this needs to be spelled out in the security policy. In addition, system administrators *can* configure this, so making it an obligation on their part should also be part of the security policy.

The policy should also define the system administrator's responsibility. There are bound to be a great many changes necessary on your system to make it conform to the security policy. By default, Windows NT is not very secure, so even with a minimalist security policy, you will need to make changes. These changes will need to be done by the system administrators. In addition, it is a good idea to make it the responsibility of the administrators to monitor the system to ensure that the security policy is being adhered to and the procedures in place are effective.

A key aspect of your security policy is your stance on passwords. If you have decided that passwords are to be of a specific length and cannot have specific contents (such as the user's first name or spouse's name), this needs to be spelled out.

Your security policy should also state that users must keep their passwords to themselves and must never write them down anywhere, including blotters, calendars, sticky notes, and especially in files on the computer. The hacker in The Cuckoo's Egg scanned e-mail files and found one in which the user told a coworker his password.

Have your company management sign a password security policy and make all employees sign it as well. This policy should specifically define what is unacceptable behavior when dealing with passwords. Make sure that the employees are aware of the consequences of violating this policy, such as letters of reprimand and even immediate termination. Users must be told that they will be held accountable for action taken by anyone using their account.

At first, termination might seem a little harsh for someone who gives his or her password to someone else in the same department, for example. However, there is no need to trade passwords. If that other person really needs access to the data, either the permissions on the file should be set or the file should be copied to a common area. If access to the account is necessary, that person's supervisor or someone else known to the system administrators should be called. The system administrators will either copy the file, change permissions, or change the password to something known (in accordance with the company password policy). This password will then be changed again when the account is no longer needed.

If you do detect an intruder, your company security policy should detail what to do. If you are monitoring his activity to see what other machines he is trying to break into, don't let him know you are there. If he is clever enough, he might have built in a backdoor, such as an account he was able to create himself or a share that he opened up the permissions on.

A security policy is something more than just a way to keep the users in line. It is also a way to help protect the company management as well as the company should a break-in occur.

Recently, there have been several stories in the press about CEOs of large corporations who have been sued by shareholders for mismanagement. In essence, the CEOs made stupid mistakes comparable to malpractice by a doctor. If a doctor can be sued for malpractice, why can't a CEO? Regardless of the outcome of the trial, it was ruled that a CEO can be sued for mismanagement. If proper security precautions or not taken on the computer system and it is broken into, could this be construed as mismanagement? This is obviously something for the courts to decide, but you need to ask yourself if it is worth the risk.

One thing to consider is perhaps assigning someone to be the company's security officer. This person at least drafts, if not defines, the company's security policy with regard to computer systems. This person needs to have the authority to implement the security policy as well as to decide whether or not the security policy can be overridden.

Depending on your security stance, I think the security officer should be able to override even the IT manager in the issues of security. It is often the case where the IT manager is expected to be a "jack of all trades." That is, he or she knows a little bit about the great many different things. On the other hand, it is the experts who are doing the day-to-day business. If this is the case in your company, it is possible that the IT manager does not have the necessary experience to judge the dangers resulting from a particular security-related decision.

I have worked with managers before who have had the attitude that even if the decision is wrong, their employees are obligated to follow it. Even though this might be acceptable when deciding between truly comparable software products, I believe the danger is too great when dealing with security issues. If you make the wrong decision when buying the particular program, the worst case is that you're out the money. On the other hand, if you make the wrong security-related decision, you may be out of business.

If the security officer does not have the authority to override the IT manager, the fact that the IT manager has overridden the security officer should be documented in writing and possibly sent to the company management. I feel that the security manager is *obligated* to report this to management, and it should even be made a requirement by including it in the security policy.

The goal is not to turn this into a power play but rather to protect the interests of the company (as well as protect the security officer from certain kinds of managers). Both the security manager and the IT manager are making the decisions based on what they think are in the best interest of the company. (At least we hope so.) Sometimes they have a difference of opinion (or hoping that it's not a power struggle).

If the existence of the security policy is not enough to curtail activities of your users, you can use threats. I don't mean holding a gun to the users' heads to force them to use good passwords and follow good security practices. Your security policy should state the consequences of giving out passwords or letting others gain access to your account. Users should be aware that they could be held legally responsible for anything done on the system with their account, especially if they are negligent.

The security policy for your IS department should contain things like:

- What defines "necessary access?"
- In what circumstances is particular access necessary?
- Who decides what access is necessary?
- In which cases should access furnishings be increased or decreased?
- Can a user lose access? If so, how?
- How can the user get access back once it is lost?
- How often are the access privileges reviewed?
- How often is the security policy reviewed?
- Who is authorized to request that a new user be created?
- How is this request reported to the system administrators?
- Is the creation of a new user, adding a user to a group, and similar changes documented in some kind of log file?
- Are users removed when the employee leaves the company, or are they just deactivated?

Security and Risks Analysis

Prior to developing your security policies, you will need to do both a security and a risk analysis. The security analysis is concerned with what protection mechanisms are already in place. The goal here is not to make a judgment, but rather to simply evaluate the current state of your security. As its name implies, the risk analysis evaluates the risk to those things you need to protect. This includes the likelihood that someone will want to gain access to the information or perhaps to destroy it, plus how easy it is to access the information and what the effects on the company would be if someone did gain access.

In some texts, you may see the security analysis as part of the risk analysis. I like to separate the two to keep one from influencing the other. If you are examining the risks at the same time you are evaluating your security, I have often seen people going overboard when the security is not quite adequate. By identifying the risk and then defining the necessary level of security, often just minor changes are necessary. In addition, people will some-

• • • • • • • • • • • • • • •

times misinterpret the extent of a security problem when they are also doing their risk analysis.

One of the very first steps is to figure out how great the threat is and how likely it is that someone could break in if they wanted to. That is, you evaluate your system to determine where the greatest threats are. If someone were to break into your system, what areas would provide the hacker the most useful information? What if the hacker were able to destroy that knowledge? That is, what would happen if the hacker were able to destroy your information? The hacker may not be able to walk away with 10GBs worth of data, but he may be able to destroy it. How easy it is to destroy information should also be part of your threat assessment.

Part of the threat assessment is determining the sensitive areas, both physically and on the file system. Where are the places that people shouldn't just wander through? Where are the areas where you want to know exactly who went there and when?

In addition, you also need to determine where your weaknesses are. Any system is only as strong as its weakest component. Therefore, your security system is only as secure as your least-secure components. You need to then evaluate the security on every component of your system.

One place that is often overlooked is insiders; that is, people who already have access to the system. One would hope that you can trust your employees. Unfortunately, experience has taught me that you only need one person whom you cannot trust in order to have a security problem. I worked in a company that experienced two of the greatest threats from insiders. In one case, we had a system administrator who intentionally caused system crashes. This resulted in several hours of system downtime. With hundreds of workers unable to work, the result was a loss of tens of thousands of dollars. In another case, we had an employee selling technical information to our competitor. We will never know what was lost in that case.

I often see backups overlooked during both the security analysis and the risk analysis. If all of your data are sitting on tapes, to which everyone has access, all of the security mechanisms on your computers are worthless. If fire destroys the backup tapes along with all of your computers, the damage is far more devastating than if you are infected by a virus.

When determining what is at risk, you are not just concerned with trade secrets getting into the hands of a competitor or a disgruntled employee destroying your database. Your concern is *anything* that can jeopardize the business success of your company. In terms of information management, this can show itself in a number of unexpected places.

In one company where I worked, we were very proud of the fact that we had ISO 9000 certicatation. In fact, we used this quite frequently in our marketing literature, and it was also used as a sales point in terms of ensuring the quality of our product. Although an ISO 9000 certificate does not necessarily ensure the quality product, it does indicate to the customer that you have taken certain steps and follow certain procedures.

One of the requirements was that the information, as well as the documentation describing the procedures, be protected so that it cannot be changed by just anybody. Therefore, the question arises as to what would happen to their ISO 9000 certification if it were discovered they had very little security and that this information could be changed with almost no effort at all? What would happen to the company's reputation if it became known that anyone could have free access to all of their data, including confidential customer information and so forth?

Many customers of ours placed a very high value on certification of this kind. Many questionnaires and discussions at trade shows indicated that customers chose our company over others who did not yet have their ISO 9000 certification. It is therefore likely that should the company lose its certification because of an insecure network, it will lose many customers.

Physical Security

One of the easiest and most-effective types of physical security is simply a locked door. This prevents the "crime of opportunity" from ever happening, such as someone who just walks away with pieces of equipment, or the whole machine, for that matter. The only thing that can prevent this kind of theft is more-elaborate security measures that are beyond the scope of this book. However, it is something to which you must give serious thought. Locking the door to the computer can also prevent people from breaking into the system. Anyone who has a set of installation disks or an emergency boot disk set can gain access to your system if they have access to the computer itself.

Another aspect of physical security is access to the machine itself. It may be impractical for someone to walk off with your computer. However, a knowledgeable user can gain access to your system if he or she has physical access. Once in, it doesn't matter what kind of security has been configured on the hard disk, because the only security the system knows is what it has been told by the floppy. You can create a boot floppy with Linux on it, for example, which can then read the NT system. Or, the hacker might simply install a new version of NT in a different directory.

The next issue is privacy. This can be the company's or individuals' privacy. You don't want unauthorized users to have access to payroll records, just as you don't want to have access to other employees' personal files.

Unfortunately, you will probably not be able to lock up all of your machines so that users only see the monitor. It is simply not practical and not really necessary. However, you do not want them to be randomly installing software on their system. Therefore, you need a mechanism to prevent them. The Windows NT resource kit provides a new service that can prevent accessing the floppy. The downside of this is when someone really wants to get access to the system, they could boot from a diskette. Even if you were using the NTFS, someone could boot a floppy with Linux and then have access to your system. The solution in this case is a floppy lock. Although someone who *really* wants to gain access to your system could replace the floppy with one without a lock, this does a good job of stopping most people.

The same thing basically applies to CD-ROMs. Should a CD-ROM be available, users can install software. If the hardware supports it, you can also boot from CD-ROMs. This can be a problem when the user really needs repeated access to the CD. However, there are solutions, which we discuss in Chapter 12 on sharing resources.

The old saying that a chain is only a strong as its weakest link definitely applies to computer security. It doesn't matter how secure all of the other aspects of the system are if there is one that allows easy access. One of the most commonly overlooked aspects is the physical security of the machine. All the security provided by the NTFS and other aspects of Windows NT are useless if someone can simply walk away with the computer. Even if the computer cannot be stolen, the security can be easily breached if someone can boot the system from a diskette.

At absolute minimum, the server should be kept in a locked room, and only a limited number of people should have access. This is not to say you have people whom you cannot trust, but rather the fewer people who have access, the fewer fingers there are to point. If a locked room is not possible, you may want to consider a cabinet that exposes only the keyboard, monitor, and mouse, but there is no access to the reset button or power switch. This helps to keep unauthorized users from rebooting the system into a different operating system that would give them uncontrolled access. It would be a fairly simple matter for someone to steal the hard disk or boot from a floppy disk and then access all of the data.

On some machines, you can configure the CMOS so that it will not boot from a floppy. In addition, on many systems you can set a "power on password," which prevents you from booting unless you input the correct password. Note that neither of these is foolproof, as they can be overridden. However, they require physical access to the insides of the systems. By making it extremely difficult to gain physical access to the system, you can discourage a large number of would-be hackers.

Changing Registry to Force Logging on to Do a Shutdown

To force users to logon before they shutdown the system, set the registry key as follows:

Hive: HKEY_LOCAL_MACHINE\SOFTWARE

Key\Microsoft\Windows NT\Current Version\Winlogon

Name: ShutdownWithoutLogon

Type: REG_RZ

Value: 0

On Windows NT workstations, you can shut down the machine without first logging on by clicking the Shutdown button in the logon window. Default is disabled on Server.

User Accounts and Passwords

If you write your password on a sticky note and stick it on your monitor, no operating system in the world can do anything about it. But what about cases in which you inadvertently give someone your password? This happens when users choose passwords that are easily guessed by someone trying to break in. Often users will choose passwords that are easy to remember, such as their license plate number or spouse's birthday. Password programs such l0phtcrack (see below) can run through a dictionary of over a million words in about an hour. Checking every combination of numbers and letters can be done within 24 hours. Adding a dozen or so punctuation marks takes a couple of weeks. It is no longer a question of *if*, but rather *when,* your password will be cracked.

Another comparison that works well is that of car keys. No one would think of leaving his or her car unlocked, let alone change the car so that an ignition key is no longer needed. It is just as inconvenient to have to use keys for a car as it is to use a password on a computer account. It's just a necessary evil.

In the company where I had cracked a large number of passwords, there was a large number of people who used their first names as their password. This was also the password they used to access our database. One afternoon our office in the United States reported that someone had changed the description on over 100 parts from American measurements to metric. Checking the database logs, we determined that one person had changed them all.

There were several problems with this. First, the database log showed a pattern that was consistent with someone in the administration. The factory has lunch from 12:00 to 12:40 and the administration from 12:20 to 1:00. The changes were made up to 12:19 and started again at 1:01. Second, on the day this was supposedly done, four people said that this user was not at his computer during the lunch break. Because his password was "common knowledge", any number of people could have logged in under his name and made the changes.

Because there was no company policy at the time telling people what they could or could not use for their password, there was nothing we could do in this case. It is therefore a good idea that correct passwords be made part of your company's computer security policy.

There is no way to make a computer completely secure other than to lock the room and turn the computer off. Systems can be made impregnable to the casual intruder as well as made more difficult for the experienced cracker. However, there are no guarantees.

There is an urban legend about the hacker who broke into a Windows NT system. His defense was that the logon screen said "Welcome. Please login." So he did. Because he used the guest user and simply tried a number of different passwords until he got in, he contended that he did not "break into" the system. Instead, he was invited to "Please login." Because the company could not demonstrate a reasonable attempt to keep unauthorized users out, that person was found not guilty.

Whether the story is true or not, you don't want to find yourself in a similar position. You need to take reasonable steps to keep unauthorized users out. One simple way is to tell them right at the logon screen that unauthorized access is prohibited. This is done by displaying a special notice when the person tries to logon.

Changing the Logon "Welcome" Message

To change the message users receive prior to logging on, set the two registry keys as follows:

Hive: HKEY_LOCAL_MACHINE\SOFTWARE

ey\Microsoft\Windows NT\Current Version\Winlogon

Name: LegalNoticeCaption

Type: REG_RZ

Value: What you want to appear in the windows title bar.

Name: LegalNoticeText

Type: REG_RZ

Value: What you want to appear in the text of the message.

What you define for the LegalNoticeText can be quite long. There is plenty of room to say a lot more than just "Unauthorized access is prohibited." You can be very specific about what type of access is authorized and what action will be taken should unauthorized access be suspected.

The more a would-be hacker has to guess, the harder it is for him to gain access to the system. One thing you can force users to guess is the name of the built-in administrator. This is done by simply renaming the account. Although it is possible to figure out the name of this account using certain tools available on the Internet, it does help to restrict the activities of the casual hacker. This is particularly important when your system is on the Internet, because such tools use NetBEUI, which is not used on the Internet, so there is no need to have it on any server connected to the Internet. By changing the name, the would-be intruder is forced to not only guess the password but also of the name of the account. In this case, you can change the name in the User Manager and don't need to make the change in the registry.

Another stumbling block that you can put in the way of would-be hackers is to hide the name of the last user who logged on to a particular workstation. Normally, Windows NT will remember the user name of the last user who logged in. This saves time for that user (2–3 seconds) the next time they want to logon in that they do not need to input their user name. If it is not displayed in the logon window, the would-be hacker does not know the name of the user who uses that workstation.

At first, this might seem like a rather mundane issue to address. After all, a hacker would need to gain physical access to the workstation in order to see the users name. Hopefully, your building is secure enough so that strangers cannot walk around freely. However, I think it is worth the slight inconvenience to your users for this added level of security. This is especially important if you have renamed the administrator accounts, and it was the administrator who last logged on to this machine. If someone were to notice that the administrator did not use their own account, it would be a safe guess that the account they used was that of the administrator. In addition, if your NT workstation is in some public area, hiding the user name of the last user is even more important.

Hiding the last user's name has an additional benefit that has nothing to do with security. Working on the help desk, I have received repeated calls from users who have locked themselves out of their account, because they did not notice the caps-lock was on. By forcing them to first input their user name, they will (hopefully) notice that they typed their user name all in caps. The inconvenience of having to input their user name is quickly compensated for by eliminating these kind of calls to the help desk.

Hiding the Last User's Name

To keep Windows from showing the name of the user who last logged on, change this registry key as follows:

Hive: HKEY_LOCAL_MACHINE\SOFTWARE

ey\Microsoft\Windows NT\Current Version\Winlogon

Name: DontDisplayLastUserName

Type: REG_RZ

Value: 1

Restricting Anonymous Access to Machines

To prevent anonymous access to machines, set this registry key as follows:

Hive: HKEY_LOCAL_MACHINE\SYSTEM

Key:\System\CurrentControlSet\Control\LSA

Name: Restrict Anonymous

Type: REG_DWORD

Value: 1

The problem is compounded by the fact that by default, anonymous users can list both domain users and the names of shares. This means that a would-be hacker need not look at each machine but can simply list all of the users at once. Service Pack 3 for Windows NT 4.0 provides a mechanism to restrict anonymous users from accessing this information.

One of the biggest shortcomings I feel Windows NT has is the inability to switch back and forth between users as easily as you can under UNIX. Because of this limitation, I find many administrators who make themselves members of the administrators or domain Admins group to avoid the inconvenience of logging off and then back on. Although this is not intrinsically a bad thing, it is fraught with danger. The default state is that the system administrator has essentially full control over the system as well as all of the files and directories. In many cases, this can lead to accidentally moving or even erasing files.

The simplest solution is to be careful. However, this is obviously easier said then done. I have experienced it myself where a flaky mouse has caused me to drag something to some other directory. If the directory is on another drive, there's usually enough time to see what happens. However, there have been occasions where I have not noticed it and suddenly the directory was missing. Fortunately, I can undo the move using the Windows Explorer. However, what if I don't notice the missing directory for several hours, after I've done a lot more work? I end up spending time either restoring the data or trying to track it down.

Because of this potential danger, I think you should give serious thought to not making all your administrators members of the administrators group. If they are constantly performing administrative duties, it probably makes sense to include them in the administrators group. However, if the administrators require that access less frequently (e.g., only when working on the hotline), then you might consider creating special accounts.

This issue is an obvious example of weighing security against convenience. If security has the highest priority, then separate accounts are more secure. However, if you are more concerned with convenience, then you should consider creating special accounts.

Being a systems administrator does not necessarily give a person "carte blanche" to do anything on the system. This is not to say someone will do something malicious, but accidents do happen. Therefore, you should give a great deal of thought to which administrators are given which privileges.

Windows NT is extremely flexible in how you assign the various permissions and privileges. There are already several predefined groups to perform limited administrative functions such as User Operator, Printer Operator, and so forth. I strongly recommend you consider using these groups for those administrators who do not need complete access to the system. In addition, you can use the Windows NT User Manager to assign administrators specific privileges. However, I think it is best to give all permissions and privileges to groups and then make the person doing the administration a member of that group, rather than making that user a member of the administrators group.

All of this should be part of your company's security policy. Although the company management may not be expected to go into the details of which administrator has access to what privileges, they can make company-wide statements about what levels of access are appropriate (access unless specifically denied vs. denial unless specifically granted). Then each of the individual departments, including system administration, has defined individual access based on the company policy.

Monitoring Accounts

User accounts should be monitored and inactive user accounts should either be removed or disabled. "Inactive" should be defined by the company's security policy (e.g., 3 months). Users should be contacted by telephone and told that they need to come in person to have their accounts reactivated. All accounts must have passwords on them. If possible, configure the system to disallow null passwords.

On Windows NT, the system will remember a given number of old passwords. This means that the user cannot keep using the same two passwords over and over again. Adding this to a minimum number of days before the password can be changed forces users to have better password security. How this is done is something we will get to in the chapter on administering user accounts.

Require that the person's supervisor or someone else known to the system administrators request new user accounts or make changes. You don't want someone calling up and saying that he or she is new in the accounting department and needs a new account. The request can be made via e-mail but confirmation of the request should be made over the phone in cases in which the supervisor's account was compromised. All accounts, as well as changes to groups and permissions, must be requested by the supervisors.

The administrator account should be the only shared account on the system. However, as I mentioned, I do not think it should be used. Only users who have a specific, *justifiable* need should be given administrator access. In addition, you should consider making people members of other groups (such as Account Operators or Printer Operators) to limit their power as well as the damage.

All guest accounts should be removed from the system or at least disabled. There is no need for a guest account. You should know in advance that someone will be using the system, and you can create an account for that person. This limits access to the system as well as provides a record of activity.

Monitor accounts that are no longer "active," because break-ins are more likely to be noticed. The hacker in The Cuckoo's Egg used an account from someone who was on an extended leave. Because Cliff Stoll was aware of this, he knew that whoever was using the account was doing so "improperly." One alternative would be to simply remove the account. When the real user returns, a new account can be generated. If the person leaves the company, the account should be disabled or removed.

Know who is on vacation and consider disabling that person's account. If that is not an option, occasionally checking the system to see whether one of these people is logged in might provide clues to a break-in. Using the "net user" command, you can see when was the last time the person logged in.

Many software products will create their own users. Be careful of these. Make sure you are aware of exactly what the purpose of those users is. If deleting them is not possible, make sure that they have limited access to the system. If there are guest accounts on your system that are not needed, delete them. You should also check the system at regular intervals to make sure no changes have been made that could compromise the system, such as an unexplained user in the Domain Admins group. Did you install the system? Do you know what accounts are necessary? Did the previous system administrator create any guest accounts?

Choose Good Passwords

In most cases, the first line of defense is the user name and password. All of the other safety precautions are essentially useless if a hacker gets hold of a valid user name and password.

Password attacks are perhaps the most common way of getting into a system, not bugs in the system. Studies have shown that unless the system stops "bad" passwords, password guessing will eventually succeed on at least one account, which is all that is needed. The hackers in The Cuckoo's Egg used the same techniques I did to crack passwords and gain access. As Stoll showed, known or assumed account names and guesses at passwords succeed amazingly often.

Password Guidelines

Don'ts:
- Don't use your login name in any form (as-is, reversed, capitalized, doubled, etc.).
- Don't use your first or last name in any form.
- Don't use your spouse's or child's name.
- Don't use other information easily obtained about you, including license plate numbers, telephone numbers, social security numbers, the brand of your automobile, the name of the street on which you live, etc.
- Don't use a password of all digits, all the same letter, or keyboard patterns like qwerty. This significantly decreases the search time for a cracker.

- Don't use a word contained in (English or foreign language) dictionaries, spelling lists, or other lists of words.

- Don't use a password shorter than seven characters.

- Don't use the same password on multiple machines.

- Don't use a password that has appeared in any published work as being a "good" password.

- Don't *ever* use your password again if it is discovered.

Do's:
- Do use a password with mixed-case alphabetic characters.

- Do use a password with nonalphabetic characters (e.g., digits or punctuation).

- Do use a password that is easy to remember so you don't have to write it down.

- Do use a password that you can type quickly without having to look at the keyboard. This makes it harder for someone to steal your password by watching over your shoulder.

- Do change your password often.

- Do choose a phrase and use the first letters of that phrase. You could also use a line from a song. For example, the first line of "Yellow Submarine" is "In the town where I was born," which would become Ittwiwb.

- Do use some nonsensical word like slewblue.

- Do combine words with some punctuation in the middle: rain;drain, lemon?curry.

By default, there's nothing in Windows NT 4.0 that forces users to choose specific kinds of passwords. However, Service Pack 2 and later included a password filter DLL (PASSFILT.DLL), which can be used to enforce stronger passwords. The primary benefit is that this DLL requires the user to choose a password that contains characters from the minimum of three of the following four classes:

- uppercase letters
- lowercase letters
- numbers
- nonalphanumeric characters, such as punctuation

Even if you have implemented the PASSWDFLT.DLL, consider running a password-cracking program at regular intervals. This will show you whether users are actually using good passwords or not and how successful the filter is. If you can crack a password, so can a hacker. If security really is an issue, you might want to consider writing a more complex scheme and replace the default PASSWDFLT.DLL. Although the password will eventually be cracked, your goal is to make it as difficult for the hacker as possible.

In addition, users are prohibited from choosing a password that contains their user name or any part of their full name, even if it fits the above criteria. The reason for this is to limit the success of dictionary attacks. Even with the functionality that l0phtcrack has of adding addition characters onto the end of the dictionary words, this criteria makes cracking passwords harder. Again, not impossible, as there is always the brute force approach.

Enabling the Password Filter

To enable the PASSFLT.DLL password filter, add this value to the registry key listed:

Hive: HKEY_LOCAL_MACHINE\SYSTEM

Key:\System\CurrentControlSet\Control\LSA

Name: Notification Packages

Type: REG_MULTI_SZ

Value: **Add** the string "PASSFILT", but do not remove the others.

One thing I need to point out is that to be effective, both of these attacks require access to the user database on the server. Either you have physical access to the SAM database file or you are able to dump the SAM database remotely. Both of these require administrator privileges. However, as we saw in previous sections, tricking the administrator into making this information available to you is a relatively simple process. In addition, the latest version of the l0phtcrack program can "sniff" the network and therefore does not need direct access to the SAM database.

All of these methods are fraught with danger. I have found that the more restrictive the passwords are, the more likely the user is to write them down. Most users try to be clever and write them on the back side of calendars or on a sticky note, stuck underneath their desk. However, I have known users who have put the sticky note directly on the monitor. There was no company policy preventing them from doing it, so they had no fear of a punitive action. The bottom line is the password policy needs to provide a reasonable amount of security without forcing the users to write down their password.

Another mechanism is implementing stricter password controls. Most of these are done in the User Manager. For example, you could limit the length of a valid password. That means after a specific period of time (for example, 6 weeks), the user is forced to pick a new password. You can also specify minimum password lengths or the minimum number of different passwords the user must choose before they are allowed to repeat one.

The Administrator Account

On a Windows NT system, the administrator can do most anything. Although it is possible to restrict the administrator's access to certain functions, a knowledgeable user with administrator privileges can overcome many of those restrictions. In many instances, you may have several people administering some aspect of the system, such as printers or the physical network. I myself have heard when someone says, "Well, he has administrator access. Why can't I?"

Access to the Administrator account should be limited for a couple of reasons. First, the more people with administrator access, the more people who have complete control over the system. This makes access control difficult.

Also, the more people who have root access, the more fingers get pointed (that is, the more blame is placed). I know from experience that people will deny having done something wrong. Often this results in a corrupt system, because everyone has the power to do everything, someone did something that somehow messed up the system, and no one will admit it. Sound familiar?

The fewer people who have administrator access, the fewer fingers must be pointed, and fewer people can pass the buck. Not that what they did was malicious; mistakes do happen. If there are fewer people with administrator access and something goes wrong, tracking down the cause is much easier.

Rather than giving several users the administrator password, some people think that it is safer to create several users who are all members of the Administrators group (or Domain Admins). Their belief is that because there are several login names, it's easier to keep track of things. Although you can configure auditing to keep track of who does what, you have not eliminated the problem of a person doing something by "accident," because they are not as familiar with the system as they should be and then everyone denies having done something.

My suggestion is that if several users need administrator powers, make it company policy that no one ever logs in as the administrator. Instead, each user should be given a normal account with normal user privileges and then their own administrator account to make auditing easier.

Once an intruder gains administrator or similar access, your entire system is compromised. It is therefore important not only to limit who has access but also to monitor the Administrator and other system accounts.

Another security precaution is to define "secure" workstations. These are the only workstations from which the administrator can login. In my opinion, it is best to only consider workstations that can be secured physically as "secure." That is, the Administrator account can only logon to workstations in locked rooms.

Setting Proper File Permission

Although this password protection stops most attempts to gain unauthorized access to the system, many security issues involve users who already have accounts. Unchecked, curious users could access payroll information and find out what their boss is paid. Corporate spies could steal company secrets. Disgruntled workers could wreak havoc by destroying data or slowing down the system.

Once logged in, Windows provides a number of methods to limit the access of "authorized" users. One way is in the form of file permissions. File permissions are one aspect of security with which most people are familiar with regard to computer security. On many systems, this is the only kind of security other than user accounts.

As we talked about earlier, each file has an owner (whether or not a user explicitly went out there and "claimed" ownership). It's a basic characteristic of each file that is imposed on them by the operating system. The owner of the file is stored, along with other information, in the inode table in the form of a number.

Normally, files are initially owned by the user who creates them. However, many circumstances could change the ownership. One obvious way is that the ownership is intentionally changed. Only users with the "Take Ownership" privilege can change its ownership. Unlike other systems, you cannot "transfer ownership" of a file to someone else. Although you can give another user the authority to take ownership, they must take it themselves. You cannot make them the owner yourself, as you can with UNIX.

Knowing the permissions should be is useful in detecting intruders or other improper activity. If the permissions on files (particularly programs) are changed, you should know why. This is especially important if the files are something the administrator uses often. It could be that the file itself has changed and is now a Trojan horse.

You should also check the write permissions on all system directories and files. If an intruder has write permission on a system directory, he can change log files or add his own version of system programs. While you're at it, check the ownership of system directories as well. It does little good if no one but the owner can write to a file, even though the owner is a normal user.

In principle, no one should have write permission to a user's home directory other than that user. In fact, there is little reason for them to have any other kind of access. If someone else has write permission, that person could create a Trojan horse program.

It might be useful to create a list that contains the permissions of various files and directories on your system. You can use the XCACLS.EXE program in the resource kit, along with perl (also in the resource kit) to create the file. Once you have your list, move it someplace away from that machine.

It should not be stored on the local machine. If a clever hacker gets into the machine and finds this list, what's to prevent him or her from changing it so it matches the modifications he or she made to your system?

As I mentioned previously, the default permissions for the system directories and files were designed for systems where security is not much of an issue. There are dozens, if not hundreds, of places where a hacker could change a file and trick an administrator into giving him or her administrator privileges. This is one very good reason why anything done on the workstations should be accomplished by a user with minimal privileges.

Necessary Changes to Access Permissions

Here are some changes you need to make to several system directories to bring security up to an acceptable level:

Directory	Permissions
\WINNT and all subdirectories	Administrator: Full Control
\WINNT\SYSTEM32\CONFIG	SYSTEM: Full Control
\WINNT\SYSTEM32\SPOOL	CREATOR OWNER: Full Control
	Everyone: Read
\WINNT\REPAIR	Administrator: Full Control
	Note that on older versions, everyone had read access, allowing them to access the user database, which was useful in a dictionary or brute force password attack.
\WINNT\COOKIES	Administrator: Full Control
\WINNT\FORMS	SYSTEM: Full Control
\WINNT\HISTORY	CREATOR OWNER: Full Control
\WINNT\OCCACHE	Everyone:
\WINNT\PROFILES	Special Directory Access: Read, write, execute
\WINNT\SENDTO	
\WINNT\Temporary Internet Files	Special File Access: None

Another thing you might want to consider is preventing users from changing file associations. The fact that any user can change the file associations applicable to everyone else creates a whole herd of Trojan horses. It is a simple matter to change an association so that double-clicking on a .TXT file, for example, starts a batch script that performs some nefarious function before starting the program it should have.

If you look in the file associations, there are hundreds of places where a hacker could make the association point somewhere else. Although this requires the administrator (or anyone) to logon to the system, the likelihood that they double-click on a file to start the associated application is extremely high. Hackers are nothing if not patient. This trick will eventually get them access.

Protecting the Network

If you provide access to the Internet or any network services, you should monitor these as well. Remember that threats do not need to come from outside. Disgruntled employees or someone who has been bribed by your competition can compromise security just as much as someone from outside. Good security does not mean pulling the plug on all network connections, but it does mean taking a few simple precautions.

Many of the texts I have read that discuss security suggest you remove the right to logon to the network from the administrators group and then specifically add it back for the individual users who are members of the administrators group. I have problems with this suggestion for a couple of reasons. First, I'm not a big fan of having the administrators do their day-to-day work with full authority of the administrators. I believe it is safer to have to separate accounts, one with systems administration authority and one without.

The next problem is actually a direct result of the first. If the system administrators have separate accounts, their administration accounts will need to be able to login across the network. I am not a big fan of giving the authorization to specific users; rather, I think it is better to give them to groups. Keep in mind you are giving the authorization to Joe Smith not because he is Joe Smith, but because he is an administrator. If, for whatever reason, Joe Smith no longer is an administrator, you would have to examine each of his privileges and authorizations to see if they were still applicable. Instead, you simply remove Joe from the appropriate groups and he automatically loses those authorizations.

One effective alternative would be to allow the administrators to login via the network, but to limit which machines they can login from. This can be done from the User Manager. However, as of this writing, you are limited to ten machines. In any event, my suggestion is that these machines be in restricted areas, to which few people have physical access.

Here we run into another problem. If work needs to get done on the workstation outside of this restrictive area, which requires administrator privileges, the administrator will not be able to login. The solution here is to separate functionality into different users or groups. For example, much of the configuration of the workstation can be done locally; that is, by logging in directly to the workstation and not into the domain or workgroup. Therefore, you need only login as the local administrator. Other activity, such as joining the domain, can be done through a specific account. In one company, we created an "installation administrator", who was given all of the authority necessary to install a workstation and bring it into the domain, but had none of the other privileges that normal administrators had. We go into more detail on this in the chapter on user and group management.

Automatic protections are also a good thing. I believe it should be part of the company's security policy that every workstation be configured with a password-protected screen saver that automatically starts should the workstation not be used for at most 15 minutes. There is the obvious inconvenience if someone is actually still working on their computer and is distracted for longer period of time, such as when taking a phone call. However, I feel that this is more than compensated for by the additional security that is automatically provided, should they forget to lock their workstation on their own. Trusting other computers is a double-edged sword, particularly if you do not have control over the other domain. You need to specify in your company's security policy just what kind of access is allowed. Maybe it's the extreme in which everyone trusts everyone else—maybe it's the extreme that no one trusts anyone. The middle ground would be to say that the database server trusts no one, although the database server is trusted by others. That way, if one machine is compromised, the database server is safe.

Keep in mind that the Windows NT domain model can be extremely intertwined. That is, it takes fairly little effort to give large numbers of users access to large numbers of systems. It is therefore important that you consider your security requirements when defining your domain model. For example, domains that contain very sensitive information should not trust any other domain.

You need to weigh convenience with security. I was able to crack the account of one system administrator, who was a member of the Domain Admins group. Therefore, once I had broken into his account, I basically had access to every NT machine in the company.

If you are setting up a system for the first time, you need to define your access policy before you hook up the machine to the rest of the network. Once on a network, where security *can* be broken, the new system is no longer secure.

Is access to your machine possible by modem? I had worked for one company for more than year before I found out that there was a modem on the system. It was connected to a terminal server that has its own password, so you actually needed two passwords to get into the system. However, this is important for every system administrator to know.

What are the characteristics of the modem and the port? Is hang-up forced when the user logs out? If the connection is broken, does the system log the user out? What are the permissions on the port? Can it be used by normal users to dial out? Are the answers to these questions in keeping with your company security policy? If RAS is running, is it set to call back?

It is a common tactic of hackers to check for numbers that are "around" the number of a particular company. For example, you might have the block of numbers 1200–1250. A hacker may be able to figure this out from the phone book or by getting the direct line to specific department (assuming they have one). By trying all the numbers within this block (other than the ones he already knows), a hacker can quickly find the modem. If possible, get modem numbers that are far away from the rest of the company's phone numbers.

For security reasons, you might want to consider twisted pair over thin wire. In essence, every machine on a thin wire segment is connected with every other. Each packet going by is subject to being captured and then analyzed. Although the password is encrypted, it is extremely easy to figure out where the password is and employ any number of password-cracking programs. Unlike cracking the SAM database, this does not require administrator privileges.

If you are running a twisted pair network, a potential hacker only has access to a limited number of machines, assuming the twisted pair hubs, routers, and so forth are physically secure. However, this requires you to have a secure hub. Although packets may reach machines for which they are not intended, the data segment of the IP packet is empty and therefore of no use to a would-be hacker.

Backups

Your system backups are an integral part of your security policy. Without them, you might as well not have any security policy at all. Not only are they useful when the system goes down, but they can be helpful in an investigation.

The backup policy is more than just deciding which files and directories should be backed up and when. The policy must consider what needs to be done to your system to restore it to a usable state. In addition, it should list what is done to protect the tapes after you have done your backup.

Deciding what to back up is also an important decision. However, you cannot just simply say you're going to back up everything, as this is probably not feasible for a number of reasons. You are likely to find that backing up everything requires too many tapes or too much time. However, there are alternatives that depend on the number of machines you have and what exactly you wish to back up.

One thing to consider is how long to keep your backups. If an intruder gains access to the system and does nothing for a month, do you have a clean backup from before the break-in? Do you have a copy of a clean system?

In one company I was in, we had five tapes for each machine, one for each day of the work week. We then got a tape loader that could hold enough for 2 weeks. However, each August the company shut down for 3 weeks. Several people from the IS department as well as some people in sales and customer service continued to work through the vacation. Therefore, regular backups were done. What would happen if someone came back from the 3-week vacation to find a file missing? There is no backup old enough to find the file!

In some cases, you can take advantage of the fact that hard disk prices have dropped dramatically. I have looked through many sources and have had extreme difficulty finding hard disks as small as a 3 GBs. For a workstation this could be 2–3 times the space needed for the operating system and applications, especially if all of the data are on the server. What do you do with the rest of the space?

In one company, we used this tremendous amount of free space to our advantage. In our smaller branch offices, where we had no server, data were backed up from one machine to another. This was done in the middle of the night, so there was no unnecessary load on the system. This was actually faster to recover files than using a tape, as you did not need to go hunting for the files you were looking for. Instead, you simply mapped a new drive letter to the shared directory containing your data files and copied the backup versions to your machine.

When dealing with a large amount of data, backing up to different machines quickly becomes impractical. You therefore need to come up with a different scheme. The problem becomes even more complex when you need to back up information from each of the workstations (such as configuration information).

This is one place where having standardized workstations comes in handy. If all of your workstations have the same configuration, there is normally no need to back them up. It may sound cold to simply make the user reconfigure everything, but this inconvenience needs to be weighed against the extra costs and administrative expense of backing up the data on each machine. In my experience of the amount of configuration most users do and the amount of times the machines requires a complete re-installation is so low, that it is not worth worrying about. If machines frequently require a re-installation, perhaps you should consider getting new machines. However, there are cases where you need to back up data on workstations.

Creating An Emergency Repair Disk

Run the command RDISK.EXE., which brings you to the window in Figure 6–1.

The button labeled "Update Repair Info" makes a copy of your registry settings, which can then be copied to the emergency repair disk. It is important that each time you make a significant change on your system, you update these files and make a new emergency repair disk.

The button labeled "Create Repair Disk" copies these registry files to a floppy. If you have a system that can no longer boot, you can start the installation process from the beginning, and NT will give you the option of recovering an existing system.

There are several backup schemes, each with its own advantages and disadvantages. The first is a full backup, and as its name implies, this is a backup of every file on your system. The primary advantage of this scheme is not needing to hunt for the right tape. Instead, you simply take the tape from the previous backup when you need to restore the file. The primary disadvantage of this method is the time it takes to do the backup as well as the time it takes to restore the files when you have the right tape. If you have a lot of

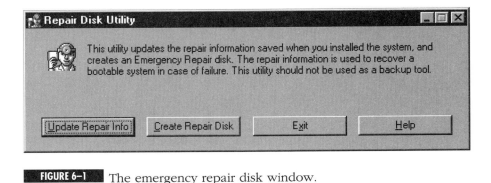

FIGURE 6–1   The emergency repair disk window.

data, it is possible that you can get through the backup at night. This means performance is diminished as people are waiting for the backup to complete.

The differential backup does a complete or master backup at regular intervals and then backs up all files that have changed since the last master. The master backup can be done over the weekend so that it is finished by Monday morning. This does not interfere with users but has the disadvantage of requiring at least two tapes to restore missing files.

An incremental backup does backups of various intensity. On a different day, you do various "levels" of backups. It starts with a master backup, which is done at regular intervals, such as on Friday, which is level 0. Wednesday, you do a level 2 backup. Monday, Tuesday, and Thursday, you do a level 3 backup. Each backup only gets those files that have changed since the last backup at a *lower* level. For example, the level 3 backup on Thursday gets all of the files that have changed since the level 2 on Wednesday. The level 2 on Wednesday gets all of the files that have changed since the level 0 on Friday.

The advantage of this scheme is the speed and reduced number of tapes necessary for the non-level 0 backups. However, I feel that the disadvantages rule this out. First, the scheme is more complicated. Granted, there are software products that will calculate which tapes you need, but there is still more administration effort required to manage this. Plus, you may need to access many more tapes.

Let's assume someone erased an entire directory on Wednesday morning. Because files were changed on Monday and Tuesday, you would need to get the full backup from Friday as well as the two tapes for Monday and Tuesday. If changes are made and backups are on the weekend, you would have to get those tapes as well. If you did a differential backup, you would need only the tapes for Friday and Tuesday.

In essence, you only need one extra tape in addition to the full backup, if you do a differential backup. Remember that you are trying to save time when restoring. The longer it takes to find the necessary tapes, the longer it takes to restore the data to get your users working again.

If you have multiple operating systems, you definitely need to consider how well the backup software deals with the different systems. The simplest solution is to get the same product for each operating system. However, this is not necessarily the best solution. There are a number of products available that run on one or the other operating system, but are still able to back up files on the other system. A client runs on each of the systems you're going to back up and copies the files to the central server. Even if you are just running Windows NT, you will find that the client-server solution can be a life saver if you have a lot of machines to back up.

Your company backup policy should not only address what machines are backed up and how often, it should also address who does the backup, where the tapes are stored, and even how long the tapes should be used before replacing them. This is part of the physical security of your backup tapes, which is, in turn, part of the security of your system. What good are backups if the tapes get lost, destroyed, or are no longer readable?

In addition, your backup policy should also contain comments regarding your disaster recovery procedures. For example, the policy might simply state that a disaster recovery plan will be developed and if it has been developed already, indicate where it is. Once the disaster recovery plan has been developed, the security plan needs to be changed. I feel it is much better to separate the contents and simply make reference to the others. That is, the backup policy refers to the emergency procedures and the emergency procedures refer to the backup policy. However, they do not contain any contents of the other. In this way, you decrease the likelihood that the two documents have conflicting information.

For "emergencies," a removable drive like my Syquest SyJet can be a life saver. Remember when I related the continual problems I had with the IBM hard drives? That taught me never to install an IBM hard drive again, but also taught me how valuable a removable drive is. I had a backup of my data, but the problem was in determining what is meant by "data." One thing that is often overlooked is something like the list of your favorite Web sites or the pages that you recently visited. I often visit a site, click through a number of pages without reading them and then get back to them when I am not on-line. If your email is also stored on the local machine, this can also be considered data.

The first time the IBM drive crashed on me, all of my email was on the local drive and the most recent backup was several weeks old. However, because I could still boot from a floppy, I was able to access the directory and copy all of my email, drivers specific for this machine, and everything else I needed to the Syquest drive. The nice thing is that the driver fits on the floppy, so I now include it with all of my emergency boot disks. If I need to pull something off quickly, I simply plug the Syquest drive onto the external SCSI port, boot from the floppy, and copy everything.

This also brings up another consideration. I have a single tape drive, but three computers. One is my server where the data are stored and where the tape drive is physically located. Initially, this made sense, as I really only needed to back up the data. Or so I thought. Over the last year, the failures of all of the IBM drives has cost me at least a week. I could reduce that time by backing up the system to tape and restoring it rather than reinstalling it.

However, my tape drive is not large enough to hold the operating system for all three of my computers. This increases the time necessary to do a backup. I need to switch tapes in the middle of the backup or deal with managing multiple backups and backup sessions.

This comes back to the issue of total cost of ownership. Obviously, getting hard disks that do not constantly crash on you would be the first logical step. The next step is to consider what is more costly: the time to switch backups, a larger tape drive, or the cost of tape drives for all the machines. In my case, the most logical choice was that the time needed to switch the tapes was less costly than the other alternatives. However, I have worked in companies where "data" on the local machines changed so rapidly, they needed to be backed up daily. (It required too much network bandwidth to store the application data on the network.) The best choice in this case was to buy a tape loader so that we could have multiple tapes, and the entire backup proceeded automatically.

System Auditing

Built into Windows NT is the concept of auditing. Because the operating system is controlling who has access, it can very well record who succeeded or even tried to gain access to a particular object. These "events" can then be viewed by the system administrator in the Event log. What is recorded and how large the log file can get are things that the system administrator can control.

Windows NT provides system auditing. This allows you to keep track of what actions are being done on your system. In most cases, you can get fairly detailed in what you monitor and your system can become full with audit logs.

What is audited is referred to as an event. An event can be anything from failed logins to successfully accessing a file. Normally, you have the ability to log events related to specific objects, such as files or directories or related to specific users. Some systems, including Windows NT, allow you to define multiple sets of audited events. For example, you can specify that failures by one group be recorded but successes by another group also be recorded.

Enabling Auditing

Much of the system activity is monitored by default; however, there is a lot of user activity that is not. To enable this, start the User Manager and select the Audit Option from the Policies menu. By default auditing is disabled, so click on the radio button labeled "Audit These Events," which brings you to Figure 6–2.

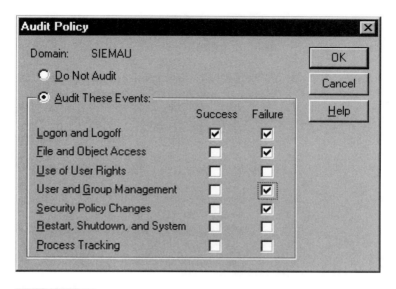

FIGURE 6–2   Audit policy window.

You can individually select whether to audit successes or failures for each of the events listed. Do not go wild and select everything, as your log files will fill up very rapidly.

Note that enabling auditing does not necessarily activate auditing for specific files or directories. This is done by changing the properties of the object itself. To do this, right-click the object and select "Properties" and then the Security tab. Clicking on the Auditing button brings you to Figure 6–3.

Click the "Add" button to select specific users or groups you wish to audit. Select a name and then click OK. If you select the special group "Everyone" then access by anyone will be audited. Once you have selected a user or group, click the name once and select the events that are to be audited. To set the options for a different user or group, select their name and then mark the options for them.

Sometimes the only way to see that your system is not secure is by catching someone doing something they shouldn't. This is where auditing comes in, and Windows NT allows you to monitor a wide range of activities on your system. However, you must decide on what you wish to audit before you start; otherwise, you may end up auditing too much, and you become overwhelmed by too much data.

In addition, auditing takes away system resources that could be used elsewhere. It takes time and, therefore, CPU cycles to identify an event that needs to be audited. It then takes more time to record the event. You may also end up taking a lot of hard disk space to record all of this information.

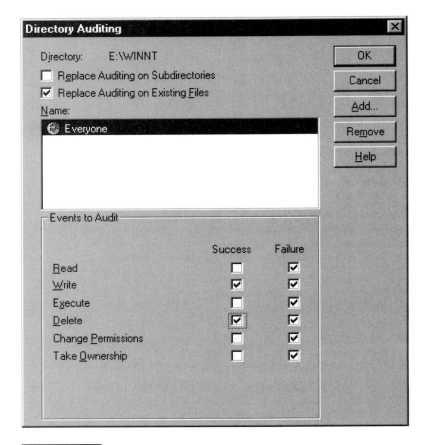

FIGURE 6–3   Auditing properties window.

Then there is the time spent going through the information looking for things of value.

Viewing Audited Events

Audited event is done through the Event Viewer, which is located in the Administrative Tools group. Select "Security" in the Log menu, which brings you to something like Figure 6–4.

By selecting the "Filter Events" option in the View menu, you can choose to look for specific events. You can filter by specific users, event ID, and several other things.

At an *absolute* minimum, you should audit *unsuccessful* login attempts. A single unsuccessful attempt may indicate that specific users have trouble using their fingers. However, repeated attempts by the same user may indicate someone is attempting to gain access to the system.

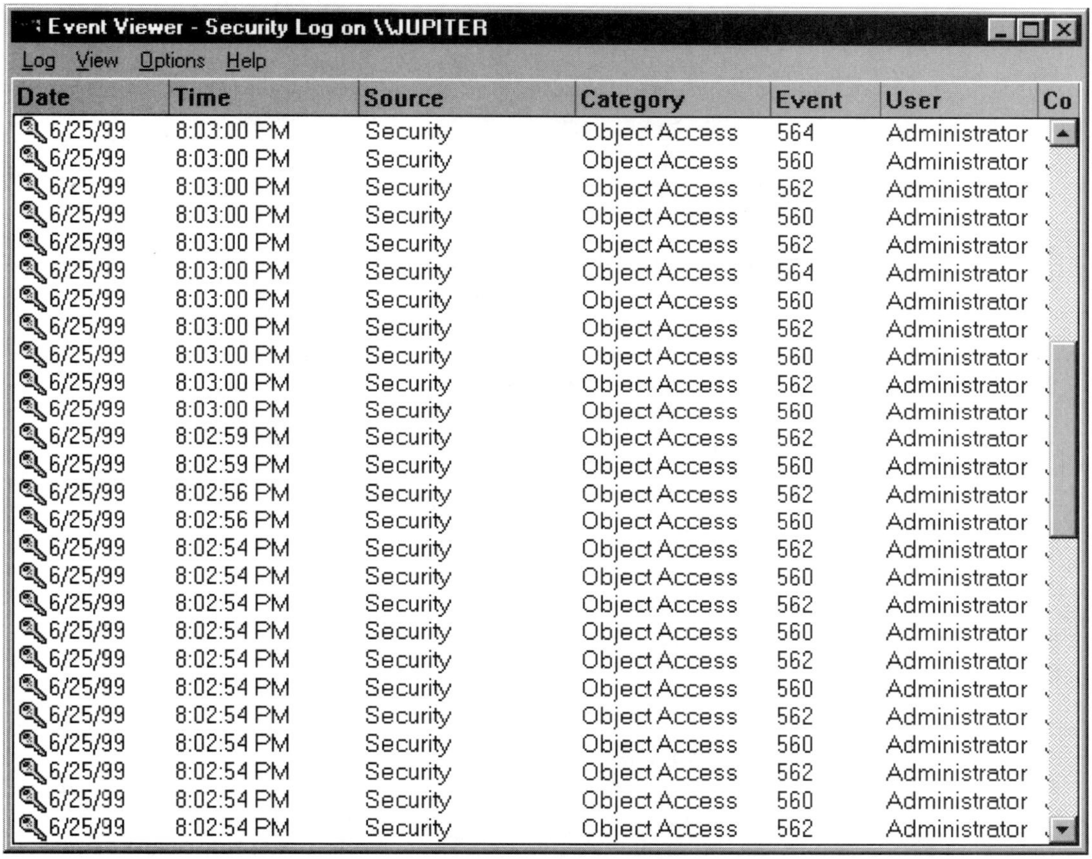

```
Event Viewer - Security Log on \\JUPITER                      _ □ ×
Log  View  Options  Help
Date       Time          Source     Category        Event  User           Co
6/25/99    8:03:00 PM    Security   Object Access   564    Administrator
6/25/99    8:03:00 PM    Security   Object Access   560    Administrator
6/25/99    8:03:00 PM    Security   Object Access   562    Administrator
6/25/99    8:03:00 PM    Security   Object Access   560    Administrator
6/25/99    8:03:00 PM    Security   Object Access   562    Administrator
6/25/99    8:03:00 PM    Security   Object Access   564    Administrator
6/25/99    8:03:00 PM    Security   Object Access   560    Administrator
6/25/99    8:03:00 PM    Security   Object Access   562    Administrator
6/25/99    8:03:00 PM    Security   Object Access   560    Administrator
6/25/99    8:03:00 PM    Security   Object Access   562    Administrator
6/25/99    8:03:00 PM    Security   Object Access   560    Administrator
6/25/99    8:02:59 PM    Security   Object Access   562    Administrator
6/25/99    8:02:59 PM    Security   Object Access   560    Administrator
6/25/99    8:02:56 PM    Security   Object Access   562    Administrator
6/25/99    8:02:56 PM    Security   Object Access   560    Administrator
6/25/99    8:02:54 PM    Security   Object Access   562    Administrator
6/25/99    8:02:54 PM    Security   Object Access   560    Administrator
6/25/99    8:02:54 PM    Security   Object Access   562    Administrator
6/25/99    8:02:54 PM    Security   Object Access   560    Administrator
6/25/99    8:02:54 PM    Security   Object Access   562    Administrator
6/25/99    8:02:54 PM    Security   Object Access   560    Administrator
6/25/99    8:02:54 PM    Security   Object Access   562    Administrator
6/25/99    8:02:54 PM    Security   Object Access   560    Administrator
6/25/99    8:02:54 PM    Security   Object Access   562    Administrator
6/25/99    8:02:54 PM    Security   Object Access   560    Administrator
6/25/99    8:02:54 PM    Security   Object Access   562    Administrator
```

FIGURE 6-4   The Event Viewer.

You might also want to consider auditing *successful* login attempts in order to identify cases where users are attempting to login at inappropriate times. Although you may have an employee who simply works odd hours, you might have someone trying to break into the system. You can prevent users from logging in during nonbusiness hours by making the appropriate entries in the User Manager. If you don't want to implement this, you should definitely consider enabling auditing.

Depending on how sensitive the data are on your file system, you may want to consider enabling auditing for specific files and directories. Note that for this sensitive data, it may not be enough to simply enable auditing of failed attempts. Just because a person is successful in accessing a particular file does not mean they *should* be accessing it. Successful access of sensitive files may mean you haven't thought out security well enough.

One thing you should consider auditing is the user and group management. If enabled, any change to the user database, such as creating new users or adding users to groups, are recorded. This also includes any time the user's password is changed. I have found this useful in several instances. First, if someone were to change the administrator's password, it would be recorded here. Second, if a user were added to the administrator's group, it would also be recorded.

I have also used it to keep track of other administrators who have not followed policies with regard to adding users to specific groups. We used the user groups to keep track of which users were authorized to use specific software. In some instances, a user would call certain administrators, who would simply add them to the group without informing anyone that a new license needed to be purchased. By auditing the changes, I was able to identify which administrators were doing this.

Auditing can often serve as a deterrent to inappropriate activity as well as identify securing violations. If users know that a certain action is being recorded, they will think twice before even attempting something they shouldn't.

One of the key aspects of auditing is that it must be able to uniquely identify the user in order to be effective. This is one reason why group accounts are not a good idea. You have no real record of who did what. Although you might be able to backtrack to find who was working and when, there is no real record.

The auditing logs are of little value if people can erase them, which is possible through the Event Viewer. Although an entry is made that the log has been erased, which itself cannot be erased, you lose the record of all previous events. Therefore, it is a good idea to save a copy of the log (also from the Event Viewer) at regular intervals and store this in a safe location, preferably on a different machine.

It may be a good idea to purge the logs after you make a copy of them. However, you should definitely make record of when you purged the logs so that you and other administrators know that this was expected and not the result of a hacker.

Remember a hacker is going to want to cover his tracks. This means removing evidence that a break-in occurred, or at least removing the proof. Therefore, a hacker may try to remove the logs through the Event Viewer or remove the file directly. This is normally the file: (%SYSTEMROOT%/SYstem32/config/SecEvent.Evt).

If you turn on logging, you may actually be defeating the purpose if you log too much information. If too many events are being recorded, you suffer from "information overload," and the real valuable information gets lost in the noise. The exception is when you think your system has been compromised. Here you should audit as much as possible, but monitor the logs regularly to make sure nothing gets lost.

Keep in mind that you can configure the system to limit the size of the log and what to do when the log gets full. If you tell the system to overwrite the log, a hacker could potentially create a large number of innocuous events to cover his tracks. If the log is not overwritten, a hacker could generate a large number of events to keep the system from recording any new ones.

Actually, this could be even worse. The system could be configured to shut itself down in the event of an audit failure. Personally, I feel that from a security perspective, shutting down the system is better than losing information. However, 500 users sitting idle as the system is rebooted might be worse than any damage caused by a hacker. In some cases, this is actually what the hacker is trying to do (e.g., denial of service attack). You must therefore weigh the consequences of each decision.

Because hard disks have dropped in price to the point where saving several gigabytes of logs would only cost $100, it is well worth it compared to not getting all of the information you need or having the system crash on you. I think you should set the size of the log as large as you can and tell the system to never overwrite the logs.

Configuring Event Logging

The event log is configured through the Event Viewer. Select the "Log Settings" entry from the Log menu. This brings you to Figure 6–5.

At the top, you see a list-box that has an entry for each of the three logs. This means, you can configure each of the logs separately. The maximum log size defines how large the file containing the logs can grow. As of this writing, the maximum size of the security audit log is 4GBs.

At the bottom of the window, you define what the system should do when it has reached the maximum size. You have a choice of overwriting entries as the system needs to, overwriting entries older than the specified number of days, or not overwriting at all.

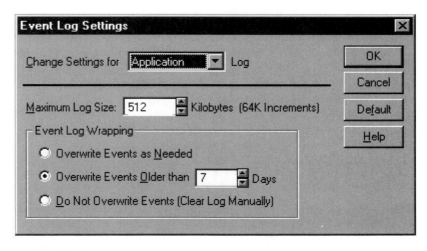

FIGURE 6–5   Event Log settings.

To force the system to halt when the log gets full or for some other reason it cannot generate an auditing log record, set this registry key to 1:

HKEY_LOCAL_MACHINE\System\CurrentControlSet\Control\Lsa\

CrashOnAuditFailure

Whether or not you suspect a hacker, what events you audit should be governed by your security policy. They should be set to identify potential hacking, while not overwhelming you with too much information.

Just because you have set the security policy, it does not necessarily mean that an event will be recorded. Although *system*-related events such as logons are recorded, object-related events, such as file or directory access, need to be specified for *each* object. This makes sense, as there are a lot of files on the system and each time one was accessed, an event would be generated. This would definitely result in information overload.

Therefore, you need to specify yourself what file objects are audited. This obviously depends on your system policy, and it is not necessarily a good idea to record access to all of the system files. The middle ground might be to set auditing for the system directories (everything under %SYS-TEMROOT%). However, you need to be careful, as your log will get full pretty fast. Therefore, you might only want to record access failures on the system directories, but perhaps *any* access to more-sensitive information.

As I mentioned earlier, permissions on the registry are just as important as on files and directories. Therefore, you should think about auditing events involving the system registry. Like files and directories, the registry is hierarchical, and permissions can be set at different levels of the hierarchy. In addition, you can also configure auditing at different levels and in different ways, just like for files and directories.

Note that it is not sufficient simply to change the permission on the registry editing program REGEDIT32.EXE so that normal users cannot run it. There are a number of programs that can change entries in the registry as well as the fact that you can run REGEDIT32.EXE on a remote machine. Although you are still limited to the same changes you can make locally, being able to make changes across the network makes it even more important to protect the registry itself.

Changing Users' Attitudes

Without the support of the company management, security will be inadequate at best. Demonstrating the loss in both productivity and company data as a result of security breaches is usually enough to convince management. However, users are generally a different matter. They are only concerned with the inconveniences brought about by higher security.

Another aspect is what is called "social engineering." There are many documented cases of intruders gaining access to systems by pretending to be legitimate users and getting the administrator to change their password or the reverse, pretending to be administrators getting users to change their passwords to specific values.

Users must know to never reset passwords to specific values based on email or even phone calls they have received. This would prevent a hacker from compromising the mail system and send a message to an unsuspecting user. Would your users be able to recognize mail if it didn't come from a real administrator? Do all your users recognize the voices of all your administrators? If the user gets a message to change his or her password to a specific password, it didn't come from an administrator.

If a user chooses an easily guessed password, it *will* be cracked using a dictionary attack. No question. Even if the hacker only has access to a small, low-powered PC, he or she can quickly crack the password. Many users believe that if a password is not a common word, it can't easily be broken. However, dozens of dictionary files spread out all over the Internet contain lists that are much longer. In addition, the words are not limited to just English anymore—there are dictionary files for several other languages as well. As I mentioned, I have a word list of almost 1.5 million words.

In his paper "Foiling the Cracker: A Survey of, and Improvement to, Password Security," Daniel Klein of Carnegie-Mellon University reported that during tests he conducted, 2.8% of all passwords were "guessed" within 15 minutes. He further states that on a machine with 50 accounts, at least one will be cracked within the first 2 minutes! Without user support, the number will be a lot higher.

As system administrator or IS manager, you *have* to educate your users. Explain the general need for the passwords and security. Make them aware of the real cases in which lax security had detrimental effects. Be sure that they know that the dangers are real.

One thing I found useful was making comparisons that the user understands. For example, compare the inconvenience of having a difficult password to the inconvenience when the system crashes. It might take 5 seconds longer a day to type in the correct password, but if the database is down for 2 hours, then the user could have typed his or her password 1,440 times. In other words, once a day for almost 4 years!

Whatever you decide is necessary, this should be defined in your company's security policy. Although your company has a security policy, you need to concentrate more on changing people's attitudes. Perhaps a violation of the policy leads to someone's termination, but does that recover the millions of dollars of research that was lost?

Keep Your Eyes Open

A perfect crime is more than one in which the perpetrator gets away clean. It is one where the crime is not even detected. If an intruder can access a system undetected, he is safe. Unlike stealing a TV, if you steal data, the original are still there. In many cases, you do not even know something was stolen.

Know your system. Know what kind of activity is normal for every hour of the day. Imagine it's late Friday night and you *know* no one is still working, though one computer is busily working on some process. Is it a job that someone started? Or is it a crack program that's going through a password file? This is how one system administrator was able to detect a person trying to crack passwords.

What processes are normal? If suddenly a new program appears on your system, and you are the only one who has access to a compiler or can install software, where did it come from? What services run on each system? If suddenly a new service starts, you might have a problem.

Excessive processes can result in a denial of service. That is, the system is so busy doing work for the hacking that it doesn't have time to do other things. Although you can configure the priority of processes, there is nothing on Windows NT to limit the number of processes a user can run. A hacker could bring the system to a standstill by running a large number of processes that overburden the system. If the hacker were to keep writing to the file system, you could run out of space, which might cause the system to stop. For example, if you have configured the system to shut down on all audit failures (that is, when the system cannot write the event to the auditing logs), filling up the file system could cause an audit failure, and the system would shutdown. Even if the system doesn't shutdown, cleaning up after this will cost a great deal of time and money.

One aspect of watching your system that can cause the most problems is what to do when you see that someone is hacking your system. Remember that in many places, the mere fact that someone has gained unauthorized access to your system means that that person has committed a crime. Like any criminal, he or she will want to cover his or her tracks. If you let the hacker know you have caught him or her, he or she might end up removing all the files on your hard disk and then disappear.

An important case was described in *The Cuckoo's Egg*, by Cliff Stoll. While observing "unexpected" access to the system, Cliff knew that the person was using commands that were inappropriate for that system. Although the hacker quickly learned which commands to use, Cliff was able to determine that this person was unfamiliar with the system. Because the person was using an account of someone who should have known better, Cliff was able to determine that it was not this person who was really using the system.

Hack Your System

One thing I find a very useful in determining the state of your security is to try to hack it yourself. There are a number of tools on the market that are designed to check the security of a Windows NT system. However, these only address the things the author knows about and only in a way they are told. I have found that trying to attack the system yourself can often show you the number of holes these tools miss. Even if you do not find any new holes, hacking your system teaches you a great deal about security.

Hopefully, you already have taken the first step in becoming a good hacker. That is, you are a fairly decent system administrator. If you do not know enough about the system to administer it, it is unlikely you'll be able to successfully attack it. Not only do you need to know what tools are available on the system, you also need to be able to determine if the system is well maintained and administered. If the system is not well administered, it is harder for the administrator to track down a hacker. The administrator will have troubled deciding whether or not the system's misbehavior is a result of his own mistakes or the hacker's. In addition, if the hacker knows how to administer the system, he will be able to do things to the system that will either confuse the administrator or make him or her spend a lot of time and effort to track down the hacker.

The Official Word

Several organizations and agencies deal with computer security issues. Perhaps the most widely know is the Computer Emergency Response Team (CERT) at Carnegie-Mellon University. They serve as a clearinghouse for known security problems for most common operating systems. They regularly issue CERT Advisories that detail the steps necessary to correct security problems without revealing too much about how to use the problem to break in. For details, check their Web site at *www.cert.org*.

Part of knowing the system is knowing what security holes already exist. One place to look is the latest security bulletins from CERT. These contain the brief descriptions of recently identified security problems and often the steps necessary to secure a system. In some cases, the way to secure the system is to obtain a patch from the vendor. Although these bulletins do not detail the steps necessary to exploit the specific weakness, the mere fact that weakness exists in the particular component is often enough for the hacker to figure out. Even if you cannot figure out how to exploit a specific hole, you can use the information from CERT to protect the system.

As computers became more widespread and those who wanted to gain unauthorized access became more devious, it became apparent that file protection alone was not enough. Because the U.S. government was steadily increasing the number of agencies that had computers, the level of system security needed to be increased as well.

The Rainbow Series

In 1985, the National Security Agency's National Computer Security Center (NCSC) created a set of computer security standards for the Defense Department, entitled *Trusted Computer Systems Evaluation Criteria*. This is commonly known as the "Orange Book," because it was published with an orange cover. (This is part of a series of documents by the DOD related to computer security, all with different colored covers.)

Within the Orange Book are four broad classes of security levels for computers:

- D: Minimal security
- C: Discretionary protection
- B: Mandatory protection
- A: Verified protection

The C class contains two sublevels, C1 and C2, C2 offering slightly more security than C1. Class B offers three sublevels: B1, B2, and B3.

Traditional PC-based operating systems, like DOS and Windows, fall within Class D. This minimal protection does not mean there is no security, just that it is not as high as the C class. You can buy add-on products to add passwords to your system or change the file attributes to prevent accidental erasure. There are even products available with which you can add passwords to DOS and Windows systems, but that's about it.

Class C systems include the features and functions to employ discretionary protection, which means that it is up to the system administrator's discretion to decide how much access people have. Class C1 systems offer enough security to let users keep their data private from other users and prevent them from being accidentally read or destroyed. Windows NT already provides this level of security in the form of user passwords and file permissions. Class C2 demands tighter login procedures, auditing of security-related events, and isolation of system resources.

Despite what Microsoft marketing wants you to believe, Windows NT 4.0 is not C2 certified at all, nor is it C2 "secure" out of the box. Windows NT 3.51 got a C2 certification, but only as long as it was not networked. A lot of good that does for a network operating system. In addition, Windows NT right out of the box does not protect the system from unauthorized access. As I previously mentioned, there are hundreds of places that a would-be hacker could plant a Trojan horse. These are not bugs, but rather intended behavior.

B-class systems implement mandatory protection; that is, the system administrator cannot turn it off if he or she likes. Class B1 systems have labeled protection, which means that security procedures and sensitivity labels (basically security classifications) are required for each file. Class B2 adds the requirement that the system must be able to account for every code in the system. This helps to prevent security holes such as Trojan horses.

Class B3 deals with the security of data access in terms of prevention of tampering and notification of security-relevant events.

The most secure class, Class A1, requires verified designs. Although they are functionally the same as B3 systems, A1 systems have also been formally defined as well as proven by tests.

For years, the Orange Book was seen as the bible for computer security. Often, people would see a system that followed the guidelines specified for a C2 level of trust and call the machine C2-"secure." This is a misnomer. The machine is trusted to provide a certain level of security, but it is not "secure."

The Common Criteria

Recently, groups in several countries have gotten together to update the guidelines defined by the Orange Book. They have developed the "Common Criteria," which is a standard for security criteria. These countries are Canada, France, Great Britain, the Netherlands, Germany, and the United States. Acceptance by these countries has made the Common Criteria (CC) more or less the de facto standard for information technology security worldwide.

Two of the more important basis documents for the Common Criteria is the Orange Book and the Information Technology Security Evaluation Criteria from the Commission of the European Community (ITSEC). However, the CC is not just a synopsis of other documents, but rather it is planned that the CC will replace these other documents.

Two key concepts in the CC are the protection profile and the security target. The protection profile is not product specific, but after being reviewed, it becomes part of the CC. It documents a particular IT-security problem and the appropriate solution. For this problem and solution, the requirements for specific product types can be developed.

Security targets enable protection profiles to be fit to a specific product; in other words, the product as a particular goal regarding security. With this, the security target forms the basis of the evaluation. A product evaluation determines whether a particular product has properly identified and addressed a particular IT-security problem.

The CC will be expanded as needed. The version planned as of this writing will contain requirements for cryptology. Cryptology solves problems of confidentiality, data integrity, and verification. The first version already addresses the issues of data protection and secure communication, even over open networks.

The evaluation process has several stages. First, a product manufacturer identifies an IT-security problem and decides to develop a solution and wants to have it evaluated. If a protection profile exists for this problem, the manufacturer can fit the profile to the product through the security profile.

If there is no security profile, a new one can be developed, and a standard can be established to measure similar products. However, a security target can be defined without reference to a protection profile.

First, the security target is evaluated according to the CC. Then the product itself is evaluated according to the security target. If the product passes the evaluation, it is given an Evaluation Assurance Level (EAL). The evaluation, which is conducted by an organization independent of the manufacturer, confirms that there are no obvious security errors. In the case of a higher EAL, the evaluation confirms that there are no hidden errors. Also, the evaluation confirms that there is user documentation.

One advantage that the CC brings is that it is flexible and provides a clear concept of security. Products that have been evaluated and certified by the CC will gain significance and acceptance. The costs resulting from the evaluation process will be compensated by the improvements to security as well as the increase in market demand for certified products. As of this writing, most of the protection profiles deal with network issues. However, because of its flexibility, the CC can be implemented in other areas.

For the current version of the CC, check out the National Institute of Standards and Technology's Web site at *http://csrc.nist.gov/nistpubs/cc/*.

Security and the Law

The laws governing computer break-ins differ from state to state and from country to country. Although there are now federal laws covering break-ins, they only apply to the United States. What about hackers who come in from other countries? Cliff Stoll can tell you horror stories of the problems he had.

One thing Stoll did was take very careful notes of the intruder's activities and keep print-outs of the hacker's activity on his system. What made this useful in court in many aspects is that he was very careful about how he handled the evidence.

There are several guidelines to follow if someone breaks into your system. The first thing is to contact CERT and your local law enforcement agency. Both will give you guidelines on what to do.

One thing that the law enforcement agency will do is to determine whether a crime has been committed. Although federal law says that the mere fact someone has gained unauthorized access to your system means that they have committed a crime, other issues may be involved, such as theft of trade secrets and loss in work.

Because of the federal laws involved, the FBI might have jurisdiction or at least want to be involved. However, I recommend contacting your local authorities first and let them determine whether the FBI should be involved. Additionally, the local authorities can provide you with information on how to proceed.

One thing that the law enforcement authorities will help you with is evidence collection. Maybe you know your system inside and out and have monitored the intruder's activities, but that does not mean what you have would be considered valid evidence in court. Your local authorities can tell you how to handle things properly.

If information has been stolen, you will want to find out what that information was. This is important in estimating the financial losses for unauthorized disclosure. As an extreme example, let's take a case in which an intruder steals plans for a new machine. You had planned to patent it, but because your system crashed, you are delayed. Although it would be foolish for a competitor to try and patent it itself, they could publicize your research to destroy your competitive advantage. Therefore, it would be much more difficult to obtain a patent yourself. The amount you lost in royalties are real damages.

If you decide to pursue the issue and press both civil and criminal charges, you have to be willing to make a commitment. The police (or whatever agency is involved) cannot do it alone. They need your help in terms of both time and resources. They need someone to show them the logs, identify the data that have been stolen, as well as identify any evidence found in the hands of the intruder. Even after the intruder is caught, you will still have to spend time to support the investigation, such as identifying data or appearing in court.

Unless you live in a large metropolitan area, there is a good chance that your local authorities may not understand the technical aspects of the crime. Basic concepts like data and networks are something they probably heard about, but understanding them is something else. There are just too many kinds of crimes for them to be experts in them all. Even if they have one computer crime a year, they just don't have the experience. Therefore, you may have to explain just what administrator access is and what the extent of the access/damage could be for someone with such privileges. In other areas in which crimes are reported regularly, there are special units that deal with these types of crimes.

Obviously, if you can't prove "who dunnit," there is no way to collect any compensation. That is why it is vital that the rules of evidence be followed. Although the police can give you specific guidelines, you should consider a few points while you are waiting for the police to arrive.

However, do not let this discourage you. In most places, there is a difference between criminal and civil charges. In a criminal case, the prosecution must prove its case beyond a reasonable doubt. In a civil case, the plaintiff must prove preponderance of evidence, which means that someone can be declared "not guilty" in a criminal trial but still be held liable in civil case. Look at the O.J. Simpson case as an example.

First, if the only evidence you have is based on on-line information such as files in the user's directory or email messages, you are on thin ice. Just as an intruder can steal files, he can also plant evidence. Though this kind of "evidence" might be sufficient to get a warrant to search the suspect's house, it might not be enough to prove the person's guilt.

It might be sufficient for you to use this information as grounds for termination of an employee. But you must also be careful. Is there a reasonable expectation of privacy when you send email or store files? If it is company policy that anything on the computers is company property, then you may have a case. I have worked for companies that have said email will not be read by anyone. There is a reasonable expectation of privacy, and the company could be sued if they looked through someone's email. Here again, talk to the law enforcement agencies.

Speed is also important when you are gathering evidence. Maybe an intruder has used one machine as a storage house for information that he or she has collected from other machines. Copy all the files and try to maintain the directory structure. This might be useful as evidence, because the likelihood that two people have the same directory structure is low (sort of like dental X-rays). If the intruder deletes all the files, your evidence is gone. There are repeated cases in which password files from other machines have been found along with password-cracking programs.

As I mentioned before, don't let the intruder know you are watching. The best (least bad?) thing he or she could do is simply disappear, maybe breaking out through some other hole that you don't know about. The worst that could happen is that the intruder reformats your hard disk in an effort to cover his or her tracks.

Another aspect of evidence is "chain of possession." This means that it can be proven in court where the evidence was the whole time. Who obtained it, who secured it, and who handed it to the police are all aspects of chain of possession. Once you have a piece of evidence, you should mark it with your initials and then seal it in a container so no one else can get access to it.

In The Cuckoo's Egg case, the logs of the hacker's activity proved to be a vital piece of evidence. Stoll was able to prove that certain actions on the system were made by hackers other than the one he was tracking. There were patterns to his behavior that Stoll recognized and could separate from those people who were just having a look around.

Although what I have just talked about provides the foundation for a security investigation, don't take it as gospel. Laws are different from state to state and from country to country. Talk to your law enforcement agencies now, before the first attack. Find out what services they can offer in case of a break-in. Most important, find out what the law is governing break-ins, rules of evidence, and especially privacy, because you don't want to lose the case and be sued yourself.

As you are aware, the laws in Germany are going to be different from those in the United States. Monitoring activity of specific users is much easier in the United States, even if the user is suspected of committing a crime. It is therefore important that you check with your law enforcement agencies about other issues, but also just how far you can monitor activity.

Another important aspect of computer security is the law. Most Western countries have enacted laws with regard to improper access to computer systems. That is, unauthorized access to a computer is illegal. For example, the U.S. Congress passed the Computer Fraud and Abuse Act in 1986. Among the things that this act defined as being illegal are knowingly accessing a computer without authorization or in excess of authorization.

There are two aspects of this to look at. First, just what is "unauthorized access?" Remember the case of the hacker that broke into a Windows NT system. He was caught but was found not guilty. The reason was that the logon screen said "Welcome, please login." In other words, he was invited to logon. His lawyers contended that because he was "invited," it was not unauthorized.

Fortunately, you can avoid this problem yourself. Windows NT provides the ability to display a warning message at logon that could indicate what is meant by "Authorized Access." For example, the message might simply state that use of the computer is limited to employees of your company as defined in the company's computer access policy. Therefore, someone who is not an employee of the company and who accesses the computer is guilty of unauthorized access. An employee who accesses the computer improperly is also guilty of unauthorized access.

The next part of this is jurisdiction. If the hacker is in another state or even another country, just who has jurisdiction is an important question. How often have different agencies decided that it was not within their jurisdiction? For example, the local police say that it is not their problem because the hacker is somewhere else. The police where the hacker is located say it is not their problem because the computers are physically outside of their jurisdiction. Therefore, to successfully prosecute you need the cooperation of multiple agencies. This is not always easy.

In addition, it is entirely likely that your company may not want to prosecute. I read about a financial institution that was broken into and the hacker did not steal anything, but rather threatened to make the lack of security public unless this financial institution paid him a large sum of money. In order to avoid the publicity and potential lack of business, this institution decided to pay. Even if your company is not being extorted, it may simply wish to avoid the negative publicity.

Right or wrong, this aspect should be decided upon at the very beginning. You should develop a reaction plan in case your system is compromised. That is, you should detail the steps to take if you detect an intruder. This may be just determining the extent of the attack and preventing further attacks. However, it can also include notifying local law enforcement agencies. In any event, it should be clearly stated whether or not such incidents are reported.

If you decide that intruders will be reported, you should get to know the local law enforcement agencies. In larger cities, there may be a special computer crime division. Not only should you know how to contact them in the event of an attack, it is also useful to get the know them beforehand. They can provide tips on what to do in the event of an attack.

Software

L0phtcrack

If you have a security policy in place that forces users to change passwords at regular intervals and are using the PASSFLT.DLL to prevent them from choosing easy-to-guess passwords, then a password-cracking tool may not be necessary. However, if you work in places like I have, where the management has a very lax attitude toward security (at least in practice), showing them how easy it is to crack passwords might help to change their attitude.

L0phtcrack from L0pht Heavy Industries is a fairly simple, yet powerful tool that helps you demonstrate how effective (or ineffective) your company's password policy is. Its functionality is based on the fact that the method used by Windows NT to encrypt passwords is well known, so it is very easy for someone to encrypt a word in the same way as Windows NT and compare this encrypted word with an encrypted password for the password database. As we discussed previously, this is how a dictionary attack works.

The interface is very easy to use (see Figure 6–6) and provides a real-time uptime of the passwords it finds. You also have a counter that tells you how much longer it has to go.

Another problem occurs when you are using the older LAN Manager encryption hash, which is necessary for non-Windows NT machines. This splits the 14 characters in half and encrypts each separately but in the same way. Therefore, you really only need to encrypt 7 characters instead of 14.

However, even having to encrypt the full 14 is no longer a problem. On my Pentium II/200 machine, I was able to crack all passwords in a 1.4-million word list of English, German, and French words in about 20 minutes. Using a brute force method (trying all combinations) I was done in less than 24 hours. Over a weekend, I got all combinations of numbers and letters.

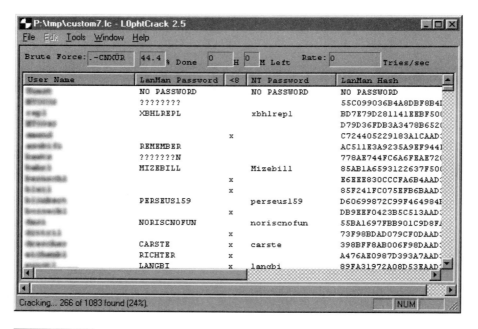

FIGURE 6–6   The l0phtcrack main window.

Trying all numbers, letters, and about 10 punctuation and other characters took me a couple of weeks. However, in the end I had cracked over 75% of the company, including most of the users in the administrators group, the Administrator account, many of the system accounts, department heads, and so forth. With the speed of newer machines, the alphanumeric passwords, which took me about a day, can take just 5.5 hours on a Pentium II/400.

Note that all alphanumeric characters and all symbols can be cracked within 480 hours or 20 days. It is no longer a question of *if* a password will be cracked but rather *when*. Using l0phtcrack, you can easily demonstrate that the passwords *will* be cracked. All you can do is make it harder for the hacker.

L0phtcrack has several features that help you crack the passwords. First, you can load an existing list of words, which are then encrypted and compared to the password database. Often, people will take such words and add a couple of digits (often numbers) to the end. This kept it from being cracked by the previous version. The latest version allows you to tack on a specific number of random characters, which slows down the process *a little*, but increases the number of passwords you can crack quickly.

In addition, being able to employ a brute force attack using alphanumeric characters, you can also define exactly the character set you want to use. This is especially helpful for me, because I work in Germany, and non-English characters are not normally thought of. However, with l0phtcrack, I can use any character I want. Even those not on the keyboard. For example, if you hold down the ALT key and type 0255, you get the letter ÿ). Although this is on neither the American nor German keyboard, it is accessible and can be used in a password. L0phtcrack allows you to input such characters into the list of those it will try.

Up to this point, I have been intentionally vague about how l0phtcrack gets access to the encrypted passwords in the first place. Well, if you are a system administrator, it is fairly easy to get a copy of the SAM database (where the passwords are kept). This might be useful in demonstrating how simple some people's passwords are but does not demonstrate the full scope of the problem.

One of the biggest problems is that right out of the box, Windows NT is lacking a great deal of security. As I mentioned previously, there are literally hundreds of places were a hacker could place a Trojan horse and eventually get administrator access to the system. However, this is not necessary, as the newest version of l0phtcrack will "sniff" the network looking for passwords.

Although Microsoft tries to insist that the NT passwords are safe across the network because they are sent encrypted, for programs like l0phtcrack, such statements are just marketing babble. Although it takes a little longer than with encrypted passwords, l0phtcrack *will* crack it. A couple of years ago, Microsoft claimed that cracking passwords like l0phtcrack does was purely "theoretical." This explains why l0pht has the slogan: Making the Theoretical Practical since 1992.

On the accompanying CD, you will find a 15-day version of l0phtcrack. This has all of the features but is limited to just 15 days. As of this writing, the full version costs $100 and is definitely worth the cost, even if just to show management that there is a problem.

Legato Networker

Although Legato is often not very intuitive to work with, it does provide an extremely powerful mechanism for backing up your systems. Here, one of the key words is "systems," as Networker shows its power when dealing with multiple systems. In all honesty, if you have just a couple of servers, you might be better off with something less powerful, such as the NT Backup program that comes with your machine.

On the other hand, if you are dealing with a large number of machines, then something like Networker is worth the time and effort of getting used to. Once you become familiar with the peculiarities (even quirks) of Networker, you will be pleased at how well you can manage your backups.

Figure 6–8 shows you the primary workspace for Legato Network. Here you define and configure the various aspects of the application. Because there are so many aspects to configure, it takes a little while to get used to where each option is configured. However, once you get the hang of it, it becomes an extremely useful tool.

Networker is a client-server system that allows you to have clients and servers on a wide range of different platforms. This does not mean, however, that the clients need to run on the same platforms as the servers. In one company where I worked, we had both UNIX and Windows NT versions of Legato. Because the UNIX machines were more powerful than the NT servers, we would back up a number of special NT Workstations from the UNIX machines. Although the UNIX servers had to back up more machines, they were better able to handle the load.

The Networker architecture allows you to have a single backup solution for all of the machines in your company. You are given a common front-end to the server regardless of what operating system the client uses. There you have a single access point, reducing the time needed to learn the program.

The client-server architecture provides additional security features. For example, it is possible to define which machines and which users can be used to administer the system. This is also one of the quirks I referred to earlier. You need to list all users that will administer the system and each machine on which they will logon. It is possible that a specific user can administer the system from everywhere except one specific machine. It is understandable that you need to have a high level of security when working with backups, but it is something you need to get used to.

One of the powerful aspects of Networker is that it is not just limited to single tape drives in terms of the media to which you can backup. In fact, you can configure the application to back up to any combination of devices

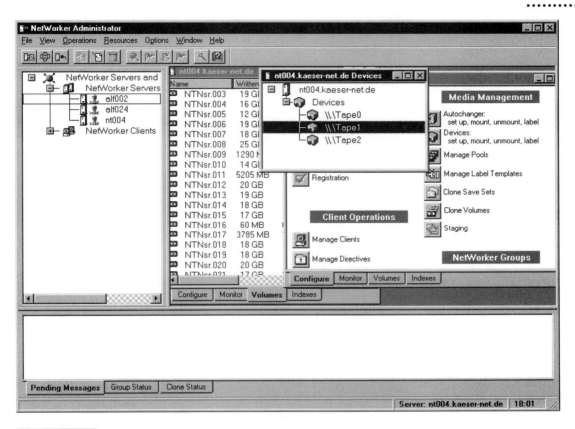

FIGURE 6–8   Networker main screen.

you have. For example, it would be possible to back up to optical drive, tape loaders, and even single drives, all within the same system.

Due to their very nature, tape loaders (also called autochangers) present their own set of issues. If you do a full backup every night and need multiple tapes, it might be worth considering getting a tape loader. If you just need additional tapes once a week for your full backups, you need to look at how expensive they are. However, in one company, our weekly full backup required seven tapes, even though the daily incremental backups fit on one tape. If we had done a differential every day (all the changes since the last full backup), it would have taken more than a single tape. This way, we filled the tape loader on Monday and simply removed the tape the next morning. On Friday, we again filled up the loader for the full backup on the weekend.

The process was made extremely easy by Networker. We not only could keep track of which tapes were in the loaders, but also how much space they took up. Although we never backed-up more than one day on a single tape, we could quickly tell whether the tape was empty or not. Because Legato kept track of where each file was, restoring from the previous backup meant we didn't have to go hunting for the tapes.

To keep track of where the files are, Networker maintains two indexes. One is for the client files and the other is for the media. In this way, you can quickly find out the tapes you need to restore. The Networker client interface provides you a browser to look for specific directories and files. If you need a version of the file older than the last backup, you can set the program to scan further back in time. Networker will then show you which tapes you need in order to restore the files from a specific date.

This ability can be extremely useful if unwanted changes have been made to a file and you discover this only after the backup. It is therefore necessary to have enough tapes to cover a number of backup cycles. Although there are no real rules as to how far back you go, some companies hold tapes for several years. This is easily done with Legato, where you designate a specific set of tapes for your quarterly backups (or however frequently you wish to save them).

Backups are managed by Legato in "save sets." These represent the data from a single client. Depending on what you need, this can be the entire system (including all partitions), single partitions, single directories, or even single files. Some databases require they be installed on a "raw" partition, which you can also back up using Networker. If the amount of data is large enough, you can break the backup across several save sets as to not overburden the client (e.g., if the backup would not be completely finished overnight).

In support of this, Networker can be configured to back up different save sets on different schedules. You can also group save sets together and then schedule the backup of the group. For example, in one company, all of the configuration information and data for a particular application was stored on the local drive. The directory containing this information was defined as a save set, the save sets for all of the applicable workstations were grouped together, and that group was backed up every night. The rest of these workstations were actually never backed-up because they were all a standard configuration. Only the user-specific configuration and data for this application needed to be backed up.

Backup information can be viewed in two different ways: by client or by media. When you view the backups by client, you can see what save sets have been defined for the client as well as a history of the backups. This is useful in quickly finding out the last time a particular directory (or file) was backed up. There is no need to hunt for the specific file, just look for the list of save sets for that client. Although I have personally not found a need for it, you can also look through the different tapes to see which save sets were written to it.

User and Group Management

There is more to user and group management than adding new users and putting them into groups. In order to be able to manage them efficiently, you need to have both policies and procedures in place. I have repeatedly encountered situations where group membership was repeated, groups were empty, a user had two accounts, although only used one, and many other problems that can be solved by developing an official policy.

Another aspect of this is the security. The reason why users and groups need to be created is for security reasons. If there was no need for security at all, everyone could log on to a single account. However, there are few cases where this is advisable. People have data that they wish to keep secret, certain departments have files that not everyone should have access to, plus dozens of other cases where access needs to be limited.

In this chapter, we are going to talk about the different aspects of user and group management, from creating the accounts, to setting the permissions on files and directories, to monitoring user activity on your system. In addition, we are going to look at some underlying issues that are important to help you manage users and groups efficiently.

·················

Windows NT Users and Groups

There are several predefined user groups, which allow you to spread out the responsibilities for administering your system among the different people without giving them complete access to the system. In the following section, we will be talking about these groups and some of the privileges they have. Because the goal of this book is not to cover all the details of administering a Windows NT system, there will be some aspects that we will not cover. You can find out the details by looking at the Microsoft documentation or any of the system administration books listed in the appendix.

Because the term "administrator" refers to a specific user account in Windows NT, in the following section I will use the term to refer to that specific account. However, in other sections of the book, I use the term administrator more loosely to describe anyone performing administrative tasks.

The Account Operators group is created only on Windows NT servers, which are configured as primary or backup domain controllers. This makes sense, because the function of this group is to administer users and group accounts within the domain. By default, no users are placed into this group. You might want to consider putting the people on your help desk into the account operators, as they will have the right to not only create and delete accounts but also to modify them, which means they can reset passwords.

At first glance, this might seem to be a large security hole, as you might think a member of the account operators group could simply place him or herself into the administrators group. Fortunately, the Windows NT designers already thought about this problem, and so account operators cannot change the groups that have higher security privileges, such as the administrators, server operators, and even the account operators group. In addition, the account operators cannot modify either the print operators or the backup operators groups.

The administrators group by default is the most powerful group. The group exists on all Windows NT workstations and servers, and members have all rights assigned to them by default, or they have the ability to grant themselves any rights they choose. One thing to keep in mind, however, is that members of the administrators group do not have access to all files by default. This is in contrast to the root user on Unix systems, who automatically has access to the files regardless of what the permissions are set at. However, members of the administrators group have the ability to take ownership of all files, and in doing so, they can change the permissions so that they then have access.

When creating users or groups, members of the administrators group also have complete access. That is, they can create a user and make it a member of any group they choose, unlike members of the account operators.

The backup operators group is intended for users who need to back up the system, hence the name. Because a person who is backing up the system needs access to all the files and directories, this can be a potential security hole. That is, regardless of what permissions are set at on a file or directory, a member of the backup operators group can read the file when doing a backup and write to the file when restoring it. It is therefore advisable that members of the backup operators group be as well trusted as are members of the administrators group.

The domain Admins group exists only on Windows NT servers, which is configured either as a primary or backup domain controller. This makes sense, as there is no domain to administer in other cases. The primary difference between the administrators group and the domain Admins group is that members of the domain Admins group usually have administration privileges on every machine in the domain. In contrast, members of the administrators group only have administration privileges on that one machine. By default, the administrator user on the domain controller is automatically made a member of the domain advance group.

Like the domain Admins group, the domain guests group is found only on the primary or backup domain controllers. As the name implies, members of this group have very limited access, very much like the guest account. By default, they only have permission to logon to the system and have no rights to read any files. As you might guess, the guest account on the domain controller is automatically made a member of the domain guests group.

The domain users group is found only on the primary or backup domain controllers. Although it does provide very little access, all members of the domain are made members of this group by default. This group is useful if you wish to give access to specific resources only to members of your domain.

Like the domain guests group, the guests group has a very limited functionality, but is only found on the server itself. For security reasons, members of this group are not authorized to log on directly into the server from the system console.

Power users are another special group in that they do not exist on the domain controller. This group exists only on Windows NT workstations and nondomain controller servers. In addition to the rights granted members of the users group, power users can create accounts and create and manage shares as well as configure printers. Additionally, they have some of the rights of the account operators group in that they can create both users and groups as well as manage the power users, users, and guests groups.

As its name implies, members of the print operators group can manage printers and print jobs for all users. However, this group is only found on the primary or backup domain controllers. By default, no users are members of this group.

The replicators group exists on all windows and systems, including workstations. Members of this group can replicate files between different Windows NT machines. In order to do so, members of this group need to be able to log on as a service. Because of this, membership to the replicate users group should be restricted.

The server operators group exists only on primary and backup domain controllers. In essence, members of this group can perform most of the administration functions necessary on the server. The most important exception to this is that members of this group are not authorized to make changes to the system security policies. In addition, members of this group cannot stop or start services. In essence, server operators have the same privileges as both print operators and backup operators. By default, no users are included in this group.

The users group contains all of the users on both Windows NT workstations and servers. Users in this group have very little default access.

In addition to the groups listed here, there are several system groups that are created automatically by the system but who do not show up in the User Manager. However, you can explicitly assign access rights to these groups.

Perhaps the most well-known and potentially dangerous of these groups is the everyone group. As its name implies, this group include everyone who is logged onto the system (locally, via the network, or using RAS). It is extremely important to understand that everyone really does mean everyone! This includes the system administrators as well as any user who decides to use this group to keep everyone else away from a particular directory. If the permissions on a file or directory are set so that everyone has no access, then everyone, *including* the system administrators and the owner of the file, have no access.

The creator/owner group is another common and extremely useful system. Like the everyone group, you cannot add or remove users from this group. When a file or directory is created, the members of this group are the users who created the file or directory and any subsequent user who might take ownership of it. It is useful in setting the permissions on a directory that is owned by one user so that any file created in that directory will be accessible by the user who created it.

The interactive group contains all the users who logged onto a Windows NT system locally. That is the logon on the console. However, this does not include users who log on across the network or those users who are started as a service. The network group contains all the users who connect across the network and logically does not contain members of the interactive group.

Creating Users and Groups

Proper management of users and groups starts with an effective security policy and continues on well after the users have started working on the system. A key aspect of this is to ensure that each user and group are created according to both the company security policy and common sense.

The program that administers both users and groups under Windows NT is the User Manager. Although the User Manager for the server has more functionality than the version for the workstation, the two versions function very much the same. Unless someone has moved it, the User Manager can be found in the programs menu under administrative tools.

What options you select as well as what values to input when creating users should be clearly spelled out in the company security policy. One of the things often overlooked is the comment field. This innocuous field can give a potential hacker valuable information, which can be used to more-specifically attack the system. For example, if the comment field indicates which users are system administrators or department heads, the would-be hacker might want to target these accounts specifically. Cracking an administrator's account would be like stealing the proverbial goose that lays the golden egg. Cracking a manager's account might give the hacker access to company secrets. Therefore, you might want to consider leaving the comment field blank.

Granted, this does lead to more administrative work when trying to determine what department the particular user works in. However, when I encounter the problem of needing to determine a user's department, I can look it up in the company's phone book. Here, again, we run into the battle of security versus convenience.

When you input a user's password, User Manager automatically marks the box labeled "user must change password at next logon." This happens both when the user is first created and later on, should the administrator need to change the user's password. I would suggest you leave it checked to force the users to change their password themselves. In addition, an administrator could force a user to change his or her password at any other time. For example, if a user's password becomes known, the administrator could force the user to change it. Some companies force all of their users to change their passwords at the same time, which can be done by selecting all of the accounts you wish to change and selecting the properties entry in the User menu as you could for a single user.

Creating Users

When you start the User Manager or User Manager for Domains, the first window is split in half with the individual users at the top and the groups at the bottom. To create a new user, select the "New User" entry from the User menu. This brings you to Figure 7–1.

- Username — The name that person uses to logon with

- Full Name — That person's real name

- Description — Details of that person, such as department and telephone number

- Password — That user's password

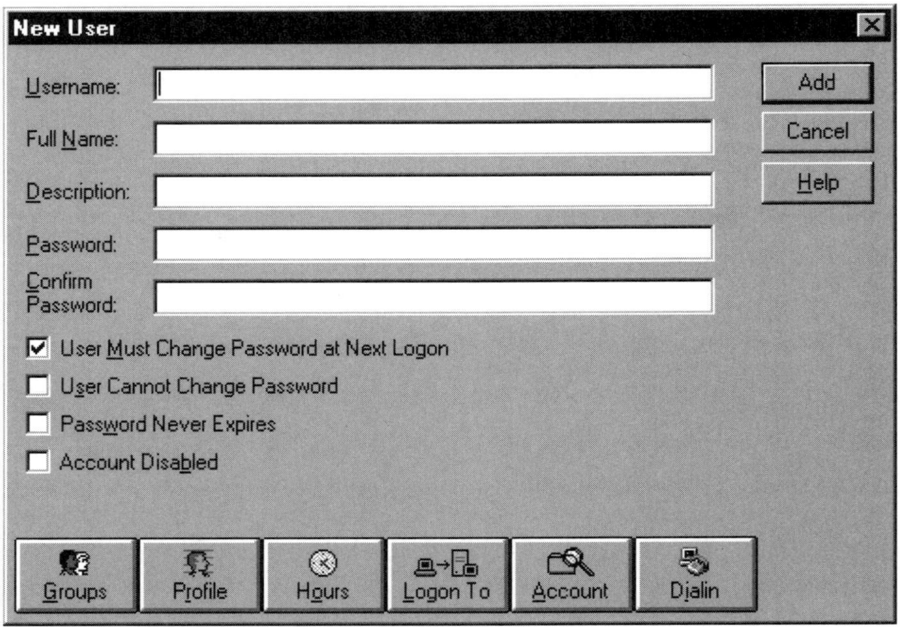

New User

Username:	[ ]
Full Name:	[ ]
Description:	[ ]
Password:	[ ]
Confirm Password:	[ ]

Add
Cancel
Help

☑ User Must Change Password at Next Logon
☐ User Cannot Change Password
☐ Password Never Expires
☐ Account Disabled

Groups   Profile   Hours   Logon To   Account   Dialin

FIGURE 7–1   The User Manager New User window.

In the middle of the window are four checkboxes. Their functions are pretty self-explanatory, details of which are in the text. At the bottom are six buttons, for various functions:

• Groups — Used to define the group which this user is a member of

• Profile — Used to manage the user's profile, logon script, and home directory

• Hours — Defines the times the user is allowed to logon

• Logon To — Defines the workstations to which this user can logon.

• Account — Defines when this account expires and what type of account it is (global or local)

• Dial-In — Used to configure this user's dial-in parameters, such as whether the user can dial in and whether the system will call him or her back.

The next check box, "User cannot change password," is useful in a couple of places. For example, system accounts that need to interact with other systems such as the replicator. Some companies use "group accounts" that are used by several different people. Therefore, no one in the group is allowed to change the password. Personally, I think group accounts should be avoided if at all possible. Keep in mind that Windows NT has no way of knowing who the real person is. Therefore, NT has no way of auditing who did what.

However, there may be cases in your company where group accounts may make sense; for example, in situations where multiple people need access to the machine and logging off then logging back on is inefficient. Giving each user his or her own workstation may not be cost effective. Therefore, a group account is the most logical solution. If this is the case, you must keep in mind the limitations you'll have in monitoring these accounts.

As its indicates, the check box "password never expires" overrides the account policy that specifies the maximum password age. Even if you "know" all of your users have good passwords, I recommend against ever using this option. The one exception might be the guest account, if you provide completely anonymous access your system. However, I am not a big fan of guest accounts, so I feel the password on *every* account should expire.

I want to emphasize my belief that this should apply to *every* account. This includes the administrators. Keep in mind that once you break into an administrator's account, you basically have free run of the system. Just because the person is an administrator, it does not mean he or she chooses good passwords. In one company where I worked, I ran a crack program on all our user databases, and the results were shocking! I found over 20 accounts that either had Domain Admins privileges or something almost as powerful. In some cases, the passwords could be found in any number of word lists available on the Internet, which meant the password could be cracked within a matter of a few minutes. Others consisted of real words or names with numbers tacked on the end. These were cracked within a day.

I think it is a good idea to set all passwords to expire every 6 weeks (42 days). This is short enough to be effective, but long enough so that users are not annoyed at having to change their passwords so often.

For me, the key motivation for a policy like this is security. A security-conscious administrator or manager will understand the need for such security measures. The ones that are not security conscious are most likely to be the ones who need to have their accounts monitored. The loss in productivity during the 20 seconds it takes for the manager to change his or her password is not even worth discussing in view of the damage that could be caused by someone who gains unauthorized access to the system. On the other hand, experience has shown me that once a person is shown just how easily passwords can be cracked, they are motivated themselves to choose a good password.

The check box "account disabled" prevents the user from logging on to the system. This can occur automatically should be user input too many incorrect passwords, or the administrator can do this manually. I think it is a good idea to disable all accounts immediately after you create them, unless the user will immediately begin using the account. I have worked in companies before where accounts were created well ahead of being needed. Because every new account was given the standard password, this meant there was an account on the system for several weeks to which everyone in the company knew the password.

Once the user has been created, the check box "account locked out" appears and is normally grayed out. An account is locked out when the user inputs an incorrect password too many times. The administrator unlocks the account by simply removing the check from the box. How many times the user can input an incorrect password is determined by the system's account policy.

When you create a new user, he or she is automatically put into the users or domain users group depending on whether or not the user is created on a domain controller. By clicking the button labeled "groups," you can assign the user to one or more additional groups. As we will get into more detail about shortly, group membership is an inefficient means of managing access to files and directories.

Personally, I think that every account should have expiration dates. This is especially true for the system administrators. I know many administrators who will insist they have a good password and therefore it does not need to be changed. However, you need to consider what happens if they are wrong? The danger to your system is quite considerable. (You can image the look on their faces when I proved to them I **could** figure their password!)

When confronted with the ease at which I was able to crack their passwords, many of the administrators replied that because the company did not take security seriously, there was no reason that *they* should. In my opinion, this attitude is justified. The company management needs to lead by example and needs to set clear guidelines on how all employees (not just the administrators) behave when it comes to security.

User Profiles and Logon Scripts

I have said before, and I will continue to say, that the best way to make your systems safe is to act like a hacker. A hacker is going to try to exploit existing holes, or force another user (preferably an administrator) to give them more rights than they normally have.

One security "trick" that was common when NT first came out was to rename the Administrator account. Although this is not a bad idea, it defeats the purpose if you rename it to something like "x87hnb." Unless every other user on the system has a similar name, it is obvious to a hacker that there's something special about this account.

In order to be effective, security needs the support of all of your users. The problem is that increased security often gives the impressions of lessening the functionality. Users need to be aware of the need for security but also need to be aware of what the consequences on the system can be without it.

I think it is a good idea to prevent users from accessing the floppy drive. This prevents them from introducing viruses into the system or bypassing security by booting another operating system (such as Linux). This is best done by inserting a floppy lock into the floppy drive. They only cost about $5 and are well worth the money. The floppy locked service can be installed from the Windows NT Resource Kit. However, this does not prevent users from booting the system using a different operating system.

The Windows NT user database provides an easy way to duplicate users. For example, a user "template" could be created for each department. This user would be a member of all the appropriate groups. When a new person comes into the department, this user template is copied, and the new user is a automatically a member of all the appropriate groups. What is not copied are things like the account name, full name, as well as security information like whether the account is locked. Therefore, you should lock the account to prevent someone from using it.

Under Windows NT, the user ID (UID) will normally not be used again. However, it can occur in Windows that users are created and there is a system crash. When the system is restored from backups, the most recently created users do not exist. However, there are files that have ACLs that contain security identifiers (SIDs) for these users. (This might also happen on additional partitions or when the filesystem is left intact and only the system itself is restored.) The next user that gets created may get the SID that gives them access to a file they shouldn't.

For example, the last users created in order are Chris, John, and Paul. They work for some time, creating files on a secondary file system. The system crashes and needs to be restored from backups. When these users are created, they are created in the order John, Paul, and Chris. It is not possible that John has access to the files created previously by Chris, Paul can access the files created by John, and Chris can access the files created by Paul. This is possible under other systems, such as UNIX; but it is much easier for the system administrator to see what UID the owner of a file has and force the new user created to have this particular UID. Therefore, the system administrator could force the system to give Chris, John, and Paul the same UIDs as they had before. Forcing a user to have a specific UID under Windows NT is extremely difficult (impossible in practical terms).

To prevent problems, the best thing on both systems is to disable the account rather than removing it. This gives you safety of not repeating UIDs, but also the ability to track ownership of files, even after a user has left the company.

The configuration options available in Windows NT that are related to users and security are very extensive. There are two ways of configuring what a user can do and how the environment is configured. The first is the User Manager, where all new users are created. Here you can define what groups each user belongs to, what logon script they should use, when they are authorized to log on, and so on.

One aspect that we use extensively is the logon script. In our logon scripts we run a number of checks to determine what software is running, what versions, and whether an update is necessary. In addition, we use the logon scripts to attach several drives to each computer so that everyone in the domain has the same set of drives, serving the same function. For example, all network-installed applications are on the P: drive, all data is on the R: drive, and we have a common location to exchange files, which is the Y: drive.

We also use the logon script to set a number of variables that the system can use. These are based on the location that a user is in, what domain, and so on.

Windows NT 4.0 took this one step further with the concept of the policies. With profiles, it was pretty much an all or nothing situation. If a user was given a particular profile, they had the same configuration as any other user with that profile. With policies, you can create different policies, which have much finer control over what can be done, and then assign users to that policy. However, you can then make changes to the policy for specific users without the need to create a new policy. In addition, you can assign entire groups to a policy.

Taking this one step further, the policy editor allows you to define policies for specific computers and not just for users or groups. The policy for the computer can define a wide range of aspects, such as shared printers and directories, remote access, and file system behavior (i.e., whether or not the system should create 8.3-DOS filenames for files with longer name).

When a user logs on to an NT computer, the system checks to see if there are any applicable policies for either the user, a group he is a member of, or the computer he is logging on from. If so, these policies are used to overwrite the entries in the system registry that would normally be used. If there are any system-wide policies that override those for users, they will have precedence.

For users, there are basically three levels of policies. If there is a policy for a specific user, then that policy will take precedence over one for a group that this user is a member of. If there is no user policy, the group policy takes effect. If there is no group policy, then the policy for the Default Users takes effect. If multiple groups are specific for which a user is a member, the priority is determined by the settings in the Group priority dialog box of the Policy Editor. Similarly, if there is no policy for a specific computer, the Default Computer profile is used.

Keep in mind that the policy comes from the user's domain and not from the computer's domain. Therefore, if you log on to a computer in one domain with an account from another, any differences in profiles can cause problems. The reason is that only the differences are overwritten. So if the domain with your account uses policies and you log on to a computer from a domain that does not, many of your settings will be retained by anyone who logs on after you do. The solution is to maintain a company-wide policy and ensure that all domains implement a similar structure.

Policy templates can be created that contain a base configuration. These can then be assigned to either users or computers.

One aspect of the user's profile that can be configured is the home directory. It is possible to configure this although you have not assigned a specific profile to that user. Essentially, under Windows NT, this means a specific directory that has certain applications will default. However, not all of them will. When you start a command prompt, this is the directory where you start.

The User Manager is also where you assign groups to the user. You can assign a user to any local or global group. The Microsoft documentation lists the maximum number of groups a user can be a member of as 1000. However, I have never tested it with this many.

Configuring Logon Scripts

The logon script can be defined for each user through the User Manager. Double-click on the user's name and click the bottom-marked profile. This brings you to the window in Figure 7–2. The first entry, User Profile Path, defines the directory where the profile is located. Profiles are used to not only define drive mappings but also other characteristics of the user's environment. We get into details of user profiles in this section on managing users and groups.

Note that this is just the name of the logon script. The path to the logon script is defined using the Server Manager. Select the appropriate server then click the button labeled "Replication." At the bottom of the window is the field labeled "Logon Script Path."

I have found that it is only necessary to create profiles in environments where you really need to restrict what users can configure. However, in most cases, this is not necessary, and I usually leave the user profile path blank. Instead, I simply include a logon script's name (the next field).

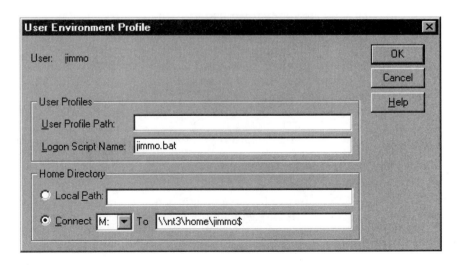

FIGURE 7–2   User profile properties.

Although you can have a different logon script for each user, I have found that it is easier to use the same logon scripts for each user. If necessary, the logon script can then start a separate script for each user. The primary script (the one that is the same for all users) does the configuration, which is the same for all users. For example, this is where the drive mapping to the company-wide data drive is accomplished.

In one company, we actually had three levels of logon scripts. The logon script defined in the user profile was the same for the whole company. A second script was then started based on the office in which the user was *currently* located. That is, the different script was started for each branch office regardless of which user was logging on. Finally, a third script was one that contained user-specific configuration. For example, this script often contained printer mappings. Normally, users print to the same printer. This was accomplished through this third script. Therefore, it was useful to define printer mappings through the law on scripts.

You might think that it would be easier to define the mappings through the local printer manager. However, such assignments are only valid for the local machine. In many cases, users might roll from one computer to another within a department depending on which was free. It would therefore be necessary to create these assignments on each machine. Instead, if the assignment was done in the logon script, it would not matter which machine was used; users would always get the right printer mapping. (When they were visiting a remote office, this would be a problem, however.)

This was also an advantage when machines were either upgraded or needed to be repaired. In general, we did not do upgrades per se (with the exception of service packs). Instead, we almost always did a fresh install, particularly on workstations. This meant that all configuration settings were lost. This also meant that we had to redo the drive mappings on all machines. Instead, if the drive and printer mappings were done to the logon scripts, they would automatically be redefined when the user logged on to the new machine.

Account Policies

Part of the user definition is the account policy. This is slightly different from what can be configured by the policy editor. Here you define such things as password aging (the maximum length of time a password can be used), minimum length, how many different passwords must be used before they can be repeated, and so on.

The user rights policy defines a wide range of functions that determine how users can interact with the system. Here you can define whether or not a user can log on to a local computer (such as the server), shutdown the system, load or unload drivers, and many more functions. Because user rights deal with specific system functions, they are different from permissions, which apply to specific resources like directories and files.

There are quite a number of ways that you can configure your system in terms of how often passwords can be changed, what they can be set to, and so forth. The purpose is to aid you to set a password policy that makes it more difficult for someone to guess or crack passwords, which should make your system more secure. However, one problem I often see is that making the policies too strict encourages users to write down their passwords, which ends up defeating the purpose. Which values users set will depend primarily on your company's security policy. However, there are things you need to consider in any event.

Setting User Password Policies

Setting user password policies is done through the User Manager. Select "Account Policy" and you are brought to Figure 7–3.

Maximum Password Age — Defines how long the password is valid before the user is *forced* to change it. Setting this low makes a brute force dictionary attack take *a lot* longer but may annoy users, as they need to choose a new password too often.

Minimum Password Length — Defines how long a password must be.

Password Uniqueness — Specifies how many different passwords the user must choose before he or she is allowed to reuse one. Setting the password uniqueness limits the usefulness of knowing a particular user's password. Your company security policy should dictate that if a user's password becomes known, the user is forbidden forever from using that password again.

Minimum Password Age — How long the user must wait to change his or her password. Set it for a week so users do not keep changing their password to get back to their "favorite."

Account lockout section — Determines whether or not incorrect passwords disable the account and for how long.

I have found that if you set the maximum password age to a low value (that is, users have to change their password more often) and set password uniqueness to a high value (that is, they must use a large number of different passwords before they can reuse one), users tend to forget their password. This means more administrative effort because you have to reset their password. Plus there is an increased likelihood the users will write down their password. Therefore, I think by setting the maximum of password age to 6 weeks (42 days) and password uniqueness to 5, you satisfy the need for security without annoying your users too much.

To keep your users from simply resetting their password until they get back to their favorite, you need to set a minimum password age to a reasonable value. I've seen some material recommend it simply be set to 1 day. However, I know users who have a morning ritual of changing their password every day until they get back their favorite. Therefore, I suggest setting

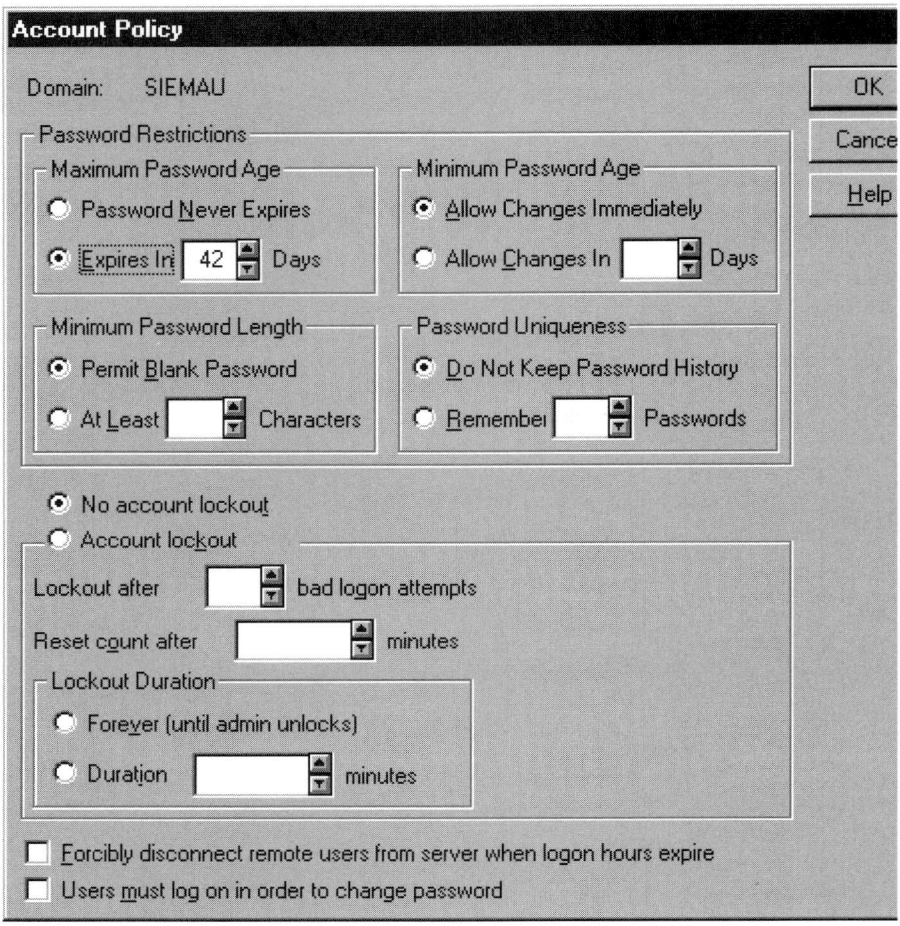

FIGURE 7–3 User Manager Account Policy.

this value to 7 days. I figured that after a week the user will become used to the new password and cannot be bothered to change back.

If you have any connections to your network from outside, you should always set the accounts to lock out for a couple of minutes. This is to prevent a hacker from using some automatic dialing method to get in. Keep in mind that this does not apply to the administrator account. Therefore, someone could try indefinitely to hack the administrator accounts, without the danger of the account being locked out. This means you need to keep close by on the security logs.

I think by setting the system to lock the user out after five unsuccessful attempts gives the user the chance to recognize they have the CAPS-LOCK on before the system locks them out. How long the account should be locked is a subject of a great deal of heavy debate. I have seen texts that recommended 45 minutes to an hour. Personally, I feel this is way *too* long. Above all, hackers are persistent. If they know that an account exists, and it probably has been easy to guess the password, they will keep trying.

Therefore, the value should be high enough to discourage the hacker, but not so high as to become an administrative burden. At 45 minutes, the users will call in to the help desk to unlock their accounts. If it is only 5 minutes, they are usually willing to wait.

Think about it for moment. One of the key issues in this book is that it is the job of the system administrator to configure the system in such a way that it is most efficient for the users. How efficient is the system if the user is unproductive for 45 minutes? Here again, we are caught in the eternal battle between security and convenience. Personally, I think 5 minutes is long enough to discourage a hacker, but short enough not to become an inconvenience. Once again, it depends on your company's security policy.

However, users must be made aware of what they need to do if they get locked out. I regularly receive calls from users who wish me to unlock their account. This is an unnecessary administrative burden. Therefore, it must be a requirement for the user to check the CAPS-LOCK and to wait the 5 minutes and try again.

On the other hand, I think the "Reset count after" value should be set fairly high. This is how many minutes the system has to wait before resetting the number of bad logon attempts back to zero. A clever hacker could create a program that checked a single password against all accounts before proceeding to the next password. If the system resets accounts after too short a period, the hacker's program may not be done with the first loop by the time this value has been reached. In effect, this parameter would have no significance. Therefore, setting this parameter to longer should not be a problem.

At the bottom of the Account Policy window is a check box labeled, "Forcibly disconnect remote users from server when logon hours expire." If your company allows access by specific users only at specific times, then you should consider this option. As its name implies, if the user is logged on at a time they should not be, the system will forcibly disconnect them. Some texts say this is a good idea during system backups. Personally, I disagree with this, because modern backup software is capable of dealing with files they cannot immediately accept (for example, when they are locked). Although users may experience some performance slowdown during the backup, I feel that it is less convenient than being forcibly removed from system. Finally, I think it is a good idea to require users to logon in order to change the password, which is the final option in the account policy.

One aspect of user and group management that I want to emphasize is the need for official policies with regard to making any changes that concern users and groups. This includes adding users to existing groups, creating new users and groups, and, particularly, making changes to the policies.

One important part of this is defining the policies and procedures for giving access to files or directories. In one company where I worked, there were no such policies. A user would call to the system administrators and say they needed access to a particular directory. The administrator would look to see what groups had access and then plop the user into some group that seemed fitting. The user thus had access to all of the other files and directories that group had.

The problem was that no check was made whether the user should have access in the first place. They called and we made the changes. First, this was (in my mind) a breach of security simply to have any user (sometimes unknown to the administrator) call and ask to be given access. Second, there was no real check to see what groups this user should be made a member of to gain access. A group was found that gave the user access to that directory, and he or she was added without regard to what other files and directories the person now had access to.

I feel the best solution is to have someone responsible for each directory or directory tree who defines who gets what access and what the permissions are. This person then has the final word as to whether someone else has access (assuming, of course, the company owner doesn't override it). In addition, each department should have a designated person who contacts the system administrators (or help desk) to request the necessary changes. In principle, there is nothing wrong with the contact person being granted blanket authority by the directory's owner to authorize someone else to have permission. However, there should be a "start of authority" for the directory and a person who contacts the system administrators (both might be the same person).

Setting Up User Rights and Privileges

Click on "User Rights" in the Policies menu of the User Manager, which brings you to Figure 7–4.

By default, all you see are the standard rights. By clicking the check box at the bottom of the window, you can also display the advanced rights. Assigning rights is done in the same way as for files and directories. That is, you select the object first (in this case, the specific right), and you select which user is given that right.

One right that you need to be extremely careful about is the ability to back up and restore files. This is because a user with this right has the ability to bypass system security and gain access to files, even if they normally would not have access. Having this right is a necessary evil, because otherwise there would be no way to back up that file. Therefore, you need to be careful about which users get this right and ensure it is absolutely necessary.

Also note that in order to be effective, virus software must also have the ability to read every file system. It is possible that your antivirus software requires it to have at least that right in order to access all of the files on a sys-

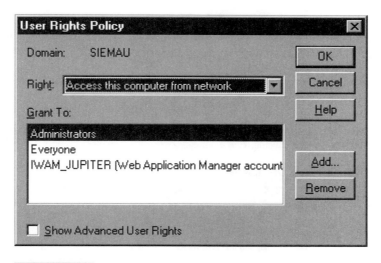

FIGURE 7–4 User Rights Policy windows.

tem. Here too, is necessary evil, so you need to keep an eye on what the virus software actually does.

All of the information that is available through the User Manager and much, much more is available to any user with the "net user" command. See the chapter on security for more details.

Creating Groups

Windows NT provides two kinds of groups, local and global. The best way to remember is to think about where each type of group is accessible. Local groups are only accessible within the domain in which they were created. Global groups are available from everywhere.

One of the key advantages (at least in my mind) is that local groups can *contain* global groups. The membership in each group is then transitive. That means if a user is a member of a global group that is included within a local group, that user is also a member of the local group.

Having groups within groups can be useful in many situations. A simple example of this would be when you have a number of different groups of users with different access on a particular directory. In one company, we had a lot of technical information that was available to everyone in the sales, customer service, and documentation departments, but only with read access. However, the department heads and group leaders in each department had write access. Two local groups were created, one with read access and the other with read and write access. The global groups from the different departments were then added to the respective groups. When a person left a department, got promoted, or for whatever reason was no longer in the global group, the membership in the local group was immediately changed.

Creating Groups

Creating Groups with the User Manager

Like users, groups are created with the User Manager. From the menu "Users," select either the New Local Group or New Global Group option depending on what you want to create. These appear in Figures 7–5 and 7–6, respectively.

In general, the fields for both are self-explanatory. One key difference is that with global groups, you see a list of members of that group as well as domain users, who are not members. Clicking the appropriate button adds or removes users. In the list of "Not Members," you will only see users and no groups, as a global group cannot contain other groups.

With local groups, you still see the list of members, but there is a button labeled "Add." This allows you to add user and groups from any domain (Figure 7–7). Select the user or group you wish to add and then select the "add" button. If you select a group, you can click the "Members" button to see a list of who is in that group.

Just as with users, you should have an official policy for creating and making changes to groups. In many environments, I think it is necessary to include even mundane things like documenting adding users to groups. Although this is recorded in the event logs, having it recorded often makes it easier to find.

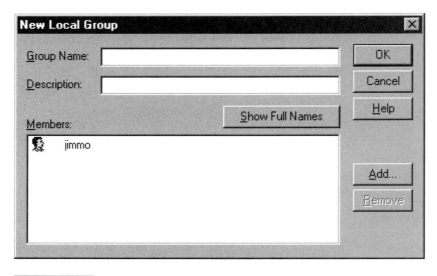

FIGURE 7–5   New Local Group window.

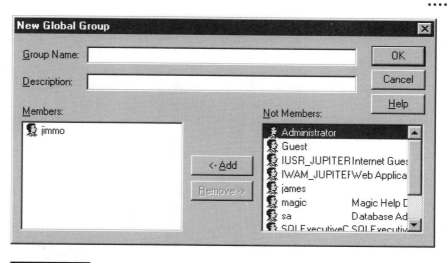

FIGURE 7-6 New Global Group window.

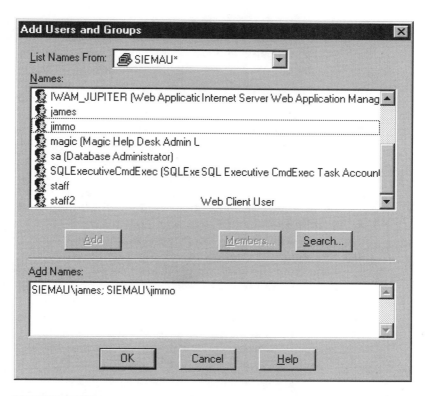

FIGURE 7-7 Add Users and groups to Local Groups.

. . . .

Permissions

It is a safe assumption that all computers in a network are doing some kind of work for users. In order to ensure that users do not have access to more information than they should or that users do not start processes which they shouldn't, there is a wide range of access permissions and authorizations that you can employ. In addition, we will also be discussing how the users and Windows NT domain fit together.

As in other operating systems, users gain access to the system by logging on. In order to be able to logon, a user account must be first created. A user account is not simply the user's name, but the entire environment that is created for that user. This includes such things as the user's home directory, the appearance of the user's desktop, which directory is connected to which drive letters, and so forth. If there is only one computer, all of this information is stored locally and exists only on that single computer. However, as we discussed, if there are multiple machines, it is possible to store and manage this information centrally, but have it available to the user anywhere in the network. Even if the computer that the user wishes to logon to has no previous knowledge of the user, the computer is able to get the user information from that central server (a domain controller) and allow the user to logon.

As with other operating systems, the user identifies him or herself by including the username and password. The Windows NT computer generates an SID, which is used to identify the user rather than the username. It is this SID that is used to determine what access a particular user has. In essence, the same principle applies whether the user logs on to the domain or directly into a workstation. One of the key differences is that if the user is created in the domain, he or she is able to logon to any computer in the domain. However, users created on a single machine can only logon to that one machine.

One thing I need to remind you of is the fact that the SID is a unique value. Therefore, when you remove and re-create a user, there is no way to give that user the same SID. This is a security mechanism to ensure that users are not given access unintentionally. Should a Windows NT machine crash and need to be reinstalled from scratch, you cannot simply recreate all of the users. This means, unlike operating systems such as Unix, you will need to reset the permissions on every single file and directory on your system. This is a strong motivation to ensure that you have good backups.

Another thing to note is that any case of domain controllers, the SID is dependent on the domain name. Should you ever need to merge domains, there is no simple mechanism to do this. Instead, you need to create all of the users by hand and then manually reset the permissions.

A common misconception is that permissions (as well as the user accounts) are valid both locally and in the domain. That is, a user created locally has access to files in the domain just because a computer is in the domain. In fact, the user information for the workstation is not shared with the domain. Therefore, no other machine in the domain is aware of the users created on the local workstation. Conversely, just because a user is in the domain, it does not mean they have permission to access resources on that computer.

I am a firm believer that there is very little reason to give a specific user access to common files and directories. Instead, permissions should be defined based on groups. One exception would be the files and directories in each user's home directory. However, these are not *common* files. Whenever you assign permissions based on the username, you may end up forgetting something. For example, a user in the personnel department has access to sensitive information. If he or she is transferred, there still might be files that are accessible because permissions were assigned to this user and not to the group "personnel." Although you can use the CACLS.EXE command to remove a particular user's permission on multiple files, there is still a possibility of missing something. If permissions are group based, you simply remove the user from that group and all is well.

As I mentioned previously, one advantage of Windows NT is the ability to have groups within groups. Windows NT has two different kinds of groups: local and global. As its name implies, local groups are local to a specific domain. Global groups reach out across the domain. This means that a local group can contain a global group, but a global group may not contain local groups. Note also that a local group cannot contain a local group from another domain.

These characteristics can be very useful in many different cases. In one company, we used group membership to define the access permissions to specific applications in order to help us manage the licensing. Although Microsoft itself stated that access permissions alone were not sufficient to guarantee adherence to the licensing conditions, we used group membership as an easy way to count how many licenses were in use. Because of this, a user can be given access to an application regardless of where he or she was in the company. That is, if they were given a license in their home office but were visiting another one, they could still use their applications.

In addition to having predefined permissions, Windows NT gives you the ability to set the permissions according to your needs. For example, you can give a user permission to write to a file but not to read.

In general, newly created files and directories take the permissions of their parent directory. This goes back to the concept of inheritance. Note that the permissions assigned to the special user, creator-owner are often unexpected for the inexperienced administrator. For example, let's assume that the permissions are set so that the creator-owner has full control over a particular directory, and everyone else only has read and write permissions. The owner of the directory is the user Joe. A new file is created in the directory by the user Mary. The user Joe attempts to assign new permissions to the file that Mary just created. He cannot because he only has read and write permissions on this file. This is because he is no longer the creator owner, as it was Mary who created the file.

Changing an Object's Permissions

Right-click a file or directory to bring up the context menu, and click the last entry, which is labeled "Properties." This allows you to configure various aspects of the object, including security, or, in the case of directories, whether or not the directory is shared. Click the Security tab and then Permissions button, you are shown a window similar to Figure 7–8.

At the top you see the name of the object (in this case, the path to the directory), the owner, and how any changes should be applied. The first allows us to make changes on subdirectories. Note that this is recursive, which means that any changes do not just apply to the subdirectories of this one, but on sub-sub-subdirectories, and so forth. The second entry allows us to change permissions on any files in the current directory.

The list in the center of the window lists the user groups that currently have access and what that access is. You can change access for an existing user by selecting the line for that user or group and using the listbox "Type of Access" to choose the type of access you want. As previously mentioned, there are several predefined types of permissions, but by selecting "Special Directory Permissions" or "Special File Permissions," you can define any combination you need.

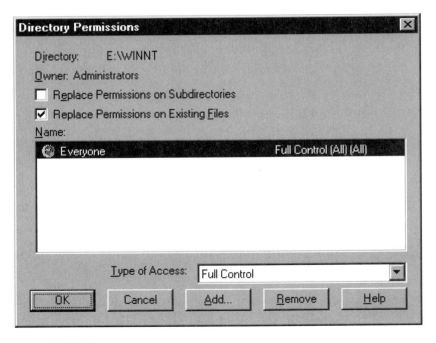

FIGURE 7–8 Directory Permissions dialog box.

Clicking the "Add" button, you can add groups and users to the list of those that have access. Here you can add both users and groups at the same time. However, you can only add one type of permission. For example, you cannot give Dave read permission and Paul read-write permission in the same pass. You must first give Dave read permission, then add Paul.

As I mentioned previously, a freshly installed NT machine is not very secure. There are literally hundreds of files that a hacker could use for a Trojan Horse to gain access to the system. In many cases, there are programs within the system directories that are either full control for everyone, or at least everyone has change permissions. This gives a potential hacker a field day!

Command Line Permission Changes—CALCS.EXE

Not every change is possible through Windows Explorer, such as the ability to *add* permissions. As of Windows NT 4.0, when you make a change to the permissions, you are actually resetting **all** of them. This is especially significant if you want to change permissions on all the files and subdirectories as their permissions get *reset*. In addition, you cannot make changes to groups of files.

The solution to this is the program CALCS.EXE. Not only can you add and remove *specific* permissions, but you can also do it recursively. Here is the general syntax:

CACLS <OBJECT> [/T] [/E] [/C] [/G user:perms] [/R user1 user2 user3 ...] [/P user1:perms user2:perms user3:perms ...] [//D user1 user2 user3 ...]

<OBJECT>	The file or directory where you want to set the new permissions.
/T	Changes the ACLs of the specified files with a directory or subdirectory
/E	Edits (changes, not replaces) the existing ACL.
/C	Continues even after getting an "access defined" error.
/G user:perms	Gives specified access permissions to specific user. Allowable permissions are R for read, C for change, and F for Full Control.
/R user	Removes the specified user from the ACL. This is used with the /E switch.
/P user:perms	Replaces the permissions for a specific user. Allowable permissions are as above.
/D	Denies access for the specific user.

If you specify the name of the file or directory with no other arguments, the current permissions are displayed.

Note that the CACLS.EXE program can be very dangerous. If a hacker can trick a user into executing something like a batch script, that script can call CACLS.EXE and make changes anywhere. This assumes the user has right to change the permissions on that file. Because everyone has the right to change the file associations, which would then be valid for the administrator the next time he or she logged on, a hacker can use any of the associated files to get the administrator to change the permissions.

The permissions to change do not only apply to executables such as .EXE, .COM, .BAT, and .CMD, but anything that contains executable code. Remember that all code is executed in the context of the user. Therefore if you can get someone to execute a .DLL or a control panel applet, you can get them to execute code that does what you want. Here are just some of the types to consider:

.EXE	Executable programs/applications
.COM	Commands
.BAT	Batch files
.CMD	Command files
.DRV	Drivers
.SYS	System files
.OCX	OLE Controls
.CPL	Control Panel applets
.MOD	Module files
.SCR	Screen savers

There are also a number of other files to watch. These don't execute code, but can force the user to execute specific code. For example, .INI files. There are a number of programs, even from Microsoft, that do not write everything in the registry. Should one of these contain references to a program, .DLL, or something else that is executed, it could be changed by a hacker if the file were writable.

This does not just apply to files, but also to the registry. If a normal user has the ability to change a registry entry that points to something executable, a hacker could make a change as well. Then there are the file associations. These are changeable by all users and are then applicable to all subsequent users, including the administrator. A hacker changes the default association to .TXT, .INI, .DOC, or whatever, and the next time an administrator logs on and double-clicks one of these files, the hacker becomes a Domain Admin.

System Management

The first question to ask yourself is, What is meant by the phrase "system management"? You can ask ten people and are likely to get ten different answers. The reason is not that some of them do not know what they are talking about, but rather system administration is such a broad topic that it is extremely difficult to define. Some might say it is to add users and do backups or monitor the file system and performance of the network. Although these are tasks of the system administrator, they do not define what "system management" is.

For me, the simplest way to define system administration is to define it in the broadest terms possible. That is, system administration is the steps you take to keep your system running as efficiently as possible. Now, that defines what system administration is but may not help the administrator do the administration. However, by being able to see it in these abstract terms, it is easy to know what belongs without having to explicitly list it.

On the other hand, I think that there are a number of aspects that need to be spelled out specifically. These are the issues that we are going to talk about in detail in this chapter.

A key part of the definition is "keep your system running." For me this is more that just rebooting the server when it crashes. It also means keeping the system safe. Therefore, the security and safety of your system are important aspects of system administration.

Although most of the issues we have talked about in other chapters could fall under the head of system administration, what we are going to talk about here is the issue involved with administering the system as a whole and not specific aspects.

Organization

Organize Functional Areas

One key aspect of system management is knowing your organization. Even if you identify the fact that you have no organization is a useful step. The first step is to group the objects that you manage in some way as to get an overview of what you have. Objects in this context can be physical objects such as servers and network cables, or can be abstract objects such as user groups and software licenses.

I am not a big supporter of the idea that there is a single organization that works for every company. In a number of sources, I have read where they talk about *the* organization to implement. In most cases, I have found that it did not apply to many companies I have worked for. For example, they make assumptions about the way the company itself is structured. They will talk about a company that has a decentralized organization, where each branch office is semi-independent. In other cases, they forget completely about the possibility that a company could have offices in other countries where not only the organization, but also the laws, are different.

Perhaps there is a single organization that is best. However, to implement in many companies would require a restructuring of the company itself. If this is impractical, any organization in the IT/IS department needs to reflect the company, not some ideal.

Therefore, it is impossible to define a system administration organization that is valid for every company. Added to this is the fact that companies are different sizes and in different businesses. For example, a 1000-person insurance company has a different system administration than a 1000-person manufacturing company does. There are obviously different computer needs in the different companies.

On the other hand, there is a set of constants that applies to every company, no matter how they are organized. It is these constants that you need to look at.

Figure 8–1 shows a table of different areas with a theoretical IT organization. Keep in mind that this is far from complete and is intended to give you an idea of what kinds of things need to be considered.

IS Infrastructure
  Hardware
    Facilities
    Servers
    Workstations
  Network
    Organization
    Hardware
    Cabling
  Systems management (management of systems)
Software
  Installation and configuration
  Licensing
User management
  Create of users and groups
  Security
  Help desk
Systems management
  Network protocols/monitoring
  Server configuration/monitoring
Administration
  Team Membership
  Knowledge management
  Absences
  Hiring
  Training
Projects
  Active projects
  Plans

FIGURE 8-1 Suggested organization.

Organize Teams

Many administration groups are not large enough to create teams in the conventional sense. This is because a team is typically thought of consisting of more than one person. The key is not necessarily to form groups of people, but rather to more clearly define responsibility.

Responsibilities need to be spelled out (i.e., published on your intranet, written down, etc.), so that everyone knows what is expected of them.

One thing I want to warn you about is using the list of responsibilities as an excuse *not* to do something. That is, don't pull out the list and say, "See, it's not my job." Use it to help assign work and, if applicable to your organization, provide a list of contacts that the users can communicate with.

The organization of your teams should be along the same lines as for your help desk (which we will talk about later). Some organizations have a help desk that is separate from the system administration. However, the problems that occur and the tasks that need to be done will generally be the same. For example, if a user calls in to the help desk with a network problem, there may be a single person who addresses the network problems. However, there is a separate group that actually fixes the problem.

One key difference between the system administration teams and the help desk teams is that the admin teams do not have direct contact with the end users. This happens when the help desk acts as filter between the users and the administrators. This is actually a good thing as it helps to weed out the simple problems, especially those caused by user error. However, I have worked in companies where users do have direct contact with the system administrators and the relationship worked out well. It all depends on your company.

In many cases, this is an important distinction. If you have two separate organizations (one for help desk and one for problem solving), you have the opportunity to pick and choose who is on which team. The help desk team has direct contact with the users and therefore requires much better communication and people skills than the other team. Because it is much harder to train the social/customer service aspects than the technical ones, it is vital to select people for the help desk who have the customer service skills from the beginning. (We get into more details about this in the chapter on the help desk.)

Within and *between* teams, communication is a vital aspect. In some companies, the teams are often completely separate organizations, with separate managers, separate budgets, and, as a result of all this, separate communications channels. I have seen it often where "knowledge is power" has become the guiding principles of each department. The managers wanted "power" over the others and therefore kept information (i.e., knowledge) to themselves. The result was that the end users suffered.

Even within the groups, information was kept secret. No one wanted to give up the information that they alone knew. This went from mundane things like useful "hidden" functions in different programs to significant events like the fact the PDC in a branch office was reinstalled and converted to a BDC for the company domain.

My belief is that sharing information must be made part of the job description. Failure to share information should reflect negatively on that person's evaluation (provided you evaluate them, and I suggest you do). Your goal is to support your users, not your ego.

Organize Your Network

You need to list all the different areas within your network. This applies to the physical areas of your network, such as different buildings, network segments, routers, cabling, and other physical components of your network. In addition, it also applies to the nonphysical aspects of your network, such as IP address ranges, subnets, DHCP scopes, as well as the other aspects of your network that are not represented by something tangible.

Part of this is a complete description of all of their characteristics. For example, in which room to the routers were the hubs located, the type of cabling you're using, what parts of the building are on different subnets, and so forth. This also applies to the nonphysical characteristics, such as subjects here that include information such as the subnet mask or which range of IP addresses are excluded in DHCP.

You need to find what to do in each case when the particular aspect of your network goes down. Again, this applies to both the physical and nonphysical aspects of your network; for example, what you do when a router goes down will be different from when DHCP cannot assign a particular IP address to a specific machine. All of this needs to be detailed within your SOP. This includes not only the procedures to undertake but also contact information such as name and address of your ISP.

If you are running different kinds of network protocols, such as TCP/IP or NetBEUI, you need to list which areas of your network use the different protocols. In addition, you need to list which areas use different physical networks, such as Ethernet, token ring, framed relay, such as FDDI.

Part of this is also describing what cards are in each machine. Although this belongs, to some extent, to asset management, it is an important aspect of network administration. For example, if just one machine has a 10-MB card and all the others have 100-MB cards, this machine will not be able to transfer at a rate of 100 MBs. Although this sounds like an obvious statement, I have worked in companies before where the MIS manager has failed to understand this. He had 10-MB cards in all machines but with a 100-MB card in the server. Therefore, the server could only communicate at 10 MBs, despite the fact it had a100-MB card.

Even if you have a small network, it might be worth considering breaking your network into smaller segments. There are some more reasons for this. One is the network performance. Obviously, this depends on how many hosts you have on a given segment, but it's a fact of networks that the more hosts you have, the greater the traffic. By reducing the number of hosts on a particular segment, you reduce the traffic; therefore, the greater the throughput you have.

Another aspect of this is the availability of your network. For example, if all of your machines are on one segment and that segment goes down, all of your machines go down. However, if you have multiple segments and one segment goes down, all of the other segments should remain unaffected. In addition, it is easier to troubleshoot, because you have fewer machines to look at.

There is also the security aspect. Most modern routers are capable of doing packet filtering. This can be done either by IP address, protocol, port number, or a combination of all of these. Therefore, you can restrict access to specific subnets. For example, you may want to split your bookkeeping department onto separate subnets. You can then prevent other workstations from accessing machines within these subnets.

Standard Operating Procedures

One important aspect of system administration I feel is extremely important is the standard operating procedure (SOP). I developed a love-hate relationship with the SOP during my time in the army but came to realize that it was a necessary evil. The SOP essentially defines what is to be done both on a recurring basis and when particular events occur. This makes sure everything gets done when it needs to.

I think it is necessary to make a distinction between the SOP and other documentation, such as troubleshooting guides. For example, a troubleshooting guide could list the standard procedures when a printer is no longer functioning properly. That is, it lists the steps necessary to get the printer back online. Although this is important information, it does not fall within the scope of the SOP. Instead, the SOP might say that the invoice printer must be up within 1 hour, but the boss's color printer needs to be fixed within 10 minutes. However, exactly what steps are taken are not listed.

Perhaps it might seem like this is redundant information. However, it is useful to have an overview or outline of the information in one central location. This can serve as a checklist or "cheat sheet" when a particular event occurs. The document containing the more-detailed information is then accessed separately, if necessary. For example, you need a quick reminder of all the daily activities, but once you have that reminder, you know the details.

On our company intranet, we had a list of daily activities for the "administrator of the day." Each was just a sentence or two, which provided a little kick in the backside to remind us what needed to get done. Each had a link to the documents, which provided more details about the particular task.

One question you might have is, what does the SOP for the administrators have to do with supporting users? Well, it goes back to my definition of what system management is. Your goal is to keep the system running efficiently. Although your secondary motivation is probably to keep your job, your primary motivation is to keep your users working. (At least we hope it is.)

A well-thought-out and easy-to-use SOP can help the users in a couple of ways. First, it helps define what levels of support they can expect. For example, the SOP defines maximum reaction times for specific events or what level of support will be provided. Therefore, the user knows how long the wait could be and what the administrators will do. Although much of this can be defined in a support level agreement (SLA) that you create between the administrators and the users, the SLA becomes part of your SOPs. (We go into more detail about the SLA in the chapter on setting up your help desk.)

Many people have an initial reaction that this does, indeed, mean duplicating effort. That is, the troubleshooting guide needs to be created and maintained as well as the SOP. However, I never said that they need to be separate documents; they just need to be accessed in separate ways. This is where something like the Standard Generalized Markup Language (SGML) would come in extremely handy. Your document could contain tags that label the information that should appear in the SOP. When you access the SOP (either online or by printing it), the parsing program just looks for the SOP tags. However, when you access the detailed instructions, the information in the SOP tags can be displayed along with the detail.

The SOP should not only contain mundane things, like how to react when a printer goes down, but also how to react in emergencies and other unusual circumstances. This includes:

- system crashes
- natural disasters
- power failures
- security breaches

In addition, I think it is a good idea to have a quick reference for all of the activities administrators perform, such as backups, adding users, and so on, as I described above.

Software Management

As you probably have noticed, each new version of Microsoft operating systems, as well as their applications, has required a more powerful computer, with more hard disk space. In fact, this generally applies to any application. The result is often that computers are no longer able to satisfy the requirements of both a new operating system and application. To reduce costs, many companies "hand-down" computers to users with less-demanding requirements. For example, this year's high-end graphical workstation may be next year's standard desktop. The computer is moved from the marketing department to the sales department, and the people in marketing get new machines.

Although this makes good business sense, what is often overlooked are the applications that exist on the machine. This occurs when there is a standard installation and then additional software (such as graphics applications) is added. Because the standard software is already on the machine, there is no need to reinstall. But what about the graphics software? Is it still on the machine? If so, you are obligated to pay a license fee for it. However, what often happens is that the software is simply installed on the new machine and the copy on the old machine is forgotten. If the company gets audited, this could cause a little embarrassment.

If there is no central license management, another possibility is that the old license is simply "forgotten." New machines are purchased so new versions of the software are necessary, right? Well, maybe you want the new version, but you don't necessarily need to buy a full version. Maybe you only need to buy an upgrade.

As a side note, some upgrades require that the previous version be installed on the system. You therefore need to make sure that you hang on to the old media, just in case.

Some companies allow individual departments to purchase their own software. Although there is nothing intrinsically wrong with this, it is fraught with problems. The more obvious problem is that the departments do not know what software the others have. This has two detrimental effects. First, you may be losing the opportunity for bulk purchase, such as a site license. Second, software that goes unused in one department may be useful in another. Even if the software is treated like other assets, it cannot be simply given by one department to another. Procedures can be developed whereby the transfer is easier.

However, centralized software management does have its own problems. For example, if the central agency also does the ordering, receiving, and distribution of the software, there will probably be unnecessary delays getting it to the users. There is, of course, the necessary time to order the software, do the processing when the software is received, and then distribute it to the users. I have seen it happen so often that the person doing the work at each stage ends up doing it "tomorrow." Even if "tomorrow" really does mean the next business day, it could be over a week lost, considering all of the steps involved.

In one company, we found that the best solution was to have a centralized approval authority. That is, each office was generally allowed to order software as necessary, but they had to first get approval from the headquarters. This usually meant at most a delay of a single day, as the license manager was required to respond by the next business day. However, because the only thing needed was to check to see if there were any applicable contracts to be able to get the software at a discount or any unused copies in the company, the response usually came the same day.

This was actually the same company that had all of the Windows for Workgroups (WfWG) licenses in the back of the warehouse. When a new office was opened up in South America, they bought used PCs with no operating systems. When they asked for approval to buy new licenses, the license manager simply packed up enough of the old WfWG licenses and sent them off. Had there been no centralized licensing, the WfWG licenses would still be sitting in the warehouse.

For me, assigning a person to be the license manager is one of the best ways to keep your software costs down. Policies can be defined for software use and having a license manager who knows what all of these policies are can save a great deal of hassle. For example, in one company where I worked as the license manager, I was repeatedly asked to install various software packages. Most of the requests were for CorelDraw, while they were working on a presentation or something similar. The company policy said that only people in Marketing were to use CorelDraw. Any exception had to be approved by their department head, who was not going to give it, just so they could use CorelDraw for just this single project.

There were actually two solutions to this problem, depending on the situation. In several cases, the drawing capability of Word Draw and PowerPoint was sufficient. This identified a problem in our training, as we did not show the user how much they could do with these tools. They ended up asking for tools that they really did not need. In other cases, where they *really* needed the functionality of CorelDraw, we arranged a time when they could work on the machines where CorelDraw was installed.

The only way that it was possible to do this was because of the company-wide policy that we had defined. The policy not only defined what groups were authorized to use what software, but dealt with essentially every aspect of software usage. This included everything from when updates were necessary to the company's attitude toward software piracy, and even to what constituted "acceptable usage." For example, I know some companies that rigidly say that all computers and the installed software are for company use *only*. Even during your lunch break, you are not allowed to use the computer for personal business. Other companies allow you to use the equipment during your breaks, and this is stated explicitly in the "acceptable usage policy."

Among the issues that you should address in your software policy are:

- Under which conditions are upgrades authorized?
- Which individuals or groups are authorized what software?
- Who is the approving authority for new software?
- How are licenses administered?
- Who determines or approves exceptions to these rules?
- What responsibilities do end users have?
- What responsibilities do the administrators and license manager have in regard to the end users?

When was the last time you tried to get out of a traffic ticket by claiming you "didn't know?" Just as with traffic laws, ignorance is no excuse with software licensing. Keep in mind that an end user could claim ignorance, saying that it is the job of the system administrator to keep track of licenses. This is true, especially if there are locks on the floppy drives and the user does not have Internet access. This might protect them from any legal action from the software vendor, but it would not necessarily protect them from the consequences within the company.

Each user should know what software they are allowed to use and *why* they are limited to just that set of software. In fact, they should be made aware of all aspects of the software policy. This includes the company's attitude on software piracy. You should therefore define *internal* software piracy as unauthorized use of *any* software. For example, a clever user might figure out a way to copy software from another user's machine or even use it across the network. Regardless of the fact that they were unauthorized, this could require the company to pay another license fee. This would then be a violation of the company's software policy.

In extreme cases, I believe that software piracy *should* lead to immediate termination in extreme cases. However, the problem is determining what the limits are. Obviously, someone who downloads a shareware program from the Internet and forgets to remove it should be treated differently than someone who is making copies for all of his friends and relatives of the commercial software you bought. However, what the limits are and what the consequences are should be clearly defined in your company policy.

If the person is using the software "just because" and has no real need for it, the company probably does not want to pay for it. However, the company may be forced to pay for it if audited (remember, some volume licensing agreements require you to "submit" to an audit). What should be done if an employee make thousands of copies of something? Termination? These copies would probably cost less than pirated software, so why shouldn't termination be a consequence?

For example, users who have grown used to MS Office have trouble, at first, with menus and toolbar buttons under StarOffice. Even the fact that StarOffice is a single unified application as compared to MS Office, being separate applications is often a little unnerving. However, once the user has worked with StarOffice for awhile, the benefits over MS Office become obvious, and the user is glad for the switch.

However, the key problem is the transition phase. Are the benefits that StarOffice has over MS Office worth the lost in productivity during this transition? Because most people use less than 20% of the functionality available in office packages, there is usually little in that 20% that one package offers that others do not. Therefore, it may not make sense to switch..

This is what the vendors are counting on. Once they have gotten you to buy 10, 100, or 1000 copies of their product, you are less likely to switch (assuming you don't hate their products and want to switch just to get away from them). When it comes time to update the software or upgrade to a new version, it is likely that you will stick with the same vendors. To help make this decision easier, most vendors have a number of licensing programs to choose from. Generically, these are referred to as volume licensing agreements (VLAs).

For the customer, a VLA has two key benefits. First is the price. You can often get a 50% discount or more on the software, depending on how many copies you buy. Second, procurement of the software is easier. You have a single contact for most (if not all) of the software. Some companies such as Merisel (www.merisel.com) even provide VLAs for several vendors. For example, if you select Corel for your basic office package and Adobe for graphics and desktop publishing applications, Merisel can provide you a VLA for both.

An additional aspect of the simplified procurement comes when it is time to upgrade the software. Even in the simplest case, where you simply buy the upgrade when you need it, you still have a single source as well as reduced costs. However, many companies offer very aggressive "maintenance" programs. That is, for a fee you get to upgrade to any new version that is released during the course of your maintenance contract.

This fee is significantly less than the normal upgrade price. The reason this is beneficial is those cases where you *expect* to be upgrading. If a new release is expected shortly and you need the current version now, you can save a little by purchasing a maintenance contract. However, I have seen it happen repeatedly that purchasing a maintenance contract locks the company into a particular vendor. They cannot change because they would lose money.

Here, too, the larger your company, the more options you have and the more flexible the terms can be. This is a matter of supply and demand. You are supplying money to the software vendor, and if they do not meet your demands, you simply go to another vendor. In most cases, these contracts are worked out on an individual (i.e., per company) basis. You can therefore have special requirement (i.e., demands) that the vendor has to meet.

For example, in one company they had a Microsoft Select contract covering all of their offices worldwide. There were several people that were constantly on the road to other offices. The problem was the language of the installed software. For example, someone who spoke only English needed to work on a document in the office in Bolivia, where they only had the Spanish version of Word.

The permissions *could* be set on the NT file system (NTFS) so that the only person who could use the English version was the one person visiting from the United States. In addition, the version on their PC in the United States could also be set so he was the only person who could run it. Therefore, using the NTFS permissions, the company ensured that the two copies could not be used at the same time as the user was either in the United States or Bolivia. However, this was not sufficient for Microsoft, and they required that the company pay a license fee for *every installed copy,* even if there was no possibility that it could be used. (Assuming, of course, that the NTFS can really prevent unauthorized access.)

The result was that the company went to a different vendor. Their attitude was that the company should pay licenses based on what was *used,* not based on what was *installed*. Although this was just a small fraction of the users in the company, they were not willing to pay for something that was not used. Instead, they turned to a company with a more customer-oriented licensing policy.

In addition to specific licensing issues, there are a number of other things that you should consider. For example, what the licensing terms are based on. For example, the Microsoft Select contract was based on a forecast. You promised to buy a certain number of licenses within a certain amount of time. If you didn't, you could be penalized and the contract stopped.

Paired with this is what kinds of licenses are counted toward your goals. If you bought a new PC that came pre-installed with Windows 98 and MS Office, you would hope that this would count toward your goal. Unfortunately, this was not the case for one company, and they ended up buying unnecessary licenses just to meet their goals.

You should consider any number of the available VLAs if you are planning the purchase of a large number of software products in the near future. This not only applies to cases where you are planning to change from one vendor to another, but also when you are planning an upgrade of your existing software. Depending on the vendor, you may be able to negotiate a reasonable VLA for the upgrades without having to buy new copies.

Even if you have an existing VLA, you might want to consider renegotiating the agreement or even switching to another company. Here I do not mean switching software vendors, but rather switching the company that provides you the VLA. As I mentioned, companies like Merisel provide VLA for many different vendors. If they have an agreement for all of the products you use and your current distributor does not, it might be a good reason to switch.

Classifying Software

Classifying your products is useful for several reasons. First, it lets you know exactly what you have. You not only know what types of programs you have but also what programs you have in each group. You may discover that you have programs that duplicate the work of other programs. Sometimes it is obvious, like multiple word processors, but sometimes the duplication is less obvious. For example, you may have an image processing program as well as Corel Draw, which contains Corel PhotoPaint. In many cases, this is sufficient and you can get rid of your image processing software. Granted, there are programs with more functionality than Corel PhotoPaint, and you may find it necessary to keep them.

This is also important from a licensing perspective. If you get rid of one or more type of software, there are few licenses and upgrades to pay for, and there is less administration cost to keep track of the different licenses. Even if you do decide to keep different programs, you know which products you need licenses for. In one company where I worked, several people brought in copies of software they used at home. In some cases, the users were just familiar with the other product and *wanted* to use it instead of the standard software. However, in other cases, the software was actually necessary. Official licenses were eventually purchased, but the company could have been in trouble if they had been audited by someone like the Business Software Alliance (BSA).

In terms of system administration, this is no different than what you did for your intranet. Although you were primarily concerned with the data format each application could support, your goal was to reduce the number of formats and therefore the tools you had to deal with. One difference is the programs that deal more with system administration and similar topics. That is, where the functionality is more important than the format. Here, too, you need to classify the programs to get a better overview of what you have.

Inventory

Another important aspect of system management is knowing just what your system consists of. This includes a complete inventory of all hardware and software. In one company I worked in, it was over a year before I knew that there was a modem connected to one of the terminal servers. No one else knew about it because the administrator who connected it originally had long since left the company. In the same company, there were several cases where we bought copies of software that we needed, thinking the copies we had were pirated.

If your company is small enough, you may already know this information. On the other hand, even medium-sized companies have too much equipment to be rolled to manage it without some kind of system. Exactly what kind of system you employ will depend on the size of your company as well as exactly what you're trying to accomplish. Even something as simple as a binder can be extremely effective. At the other end, there are a number of software products that can automate the process for you.

So exactly what do you need to look for when determining what is the best software for your needs? The best way into that question is to first look at all of the different characteristics that such software *could* have. The first characteristic to look at is the general behavior of the product. By this I mean whether the product is stand-alone or client/server. Stand-alone products actually come in two forms. First, there is simplest case were all data are input manually. This is more than just a preconfigured database.

It is also possible that a program is run on each machine, stores the data file, and is later retrieved for storage in the central database. This is different from a client/server, because with a true client/server product, the administrator does not need to actively collect the information.

In larger networks, automation of this collection can be an incredible time-saver. Depending on the scope of the software, you may be able to collect information on almost every aspect of the system. However, one needs to be extremely cautious with this kind of information. For example, in one company where we used Microsoft Systems Management Server (SMS), the information provided was often unreliable. The problem was simply that SMS's information was not as up-to-date as we would like it to have been.

However, this was a situation where we were in a Catch-22. We updated the information each time the system was started, but this often led to duplicate entries. For example, during the time when we were upgrading all or Windows for Workgroups machines to Windows NT, there were a large number of machines that appeared both as Windows for Workgroups and Windows NT machines. There was no way to uniquely identify the physical hardware, so machines would appear twice, once as Windows for Workgroups and a second time as Windows NT. We could have updated the information more frequently, but that would have meant some of the information would be outdated.

Getting into a VLA does not just mean signing the contract and buying the software. You must determine exactly what you need in *advance*. One company bought maintenance contracts for all of the machines in their inventory. The manager forgot to ask the administrators if all of the machines were in use. Unfortunately, 20 of them had recently been replaced with newer machines, and the old ones were still in the inventory. The result was several thousand dollars in unnecessary costs.

Knowing what you have also applies to the users. The same company bought an MS Office license for *every single* employee. Over one third of the employees never saw a PC and obviously never used any of the software. In some of the branch offices, more copies of MS Office were ordered than there were PCs, as many people shared a computer. Because Microsoft insists on a per-installation licensing, several of the licenses were unnecessary. This was all caused because the manager didn't know what the company already had.

It is therefore imperative that you know the difference between your PC count and employee count. I am sure that the software vendor will allow you to buy more than you have to, but you can avoid it by counting things correctly. Part of this is also knowing what software you have already purchased and *how*. As I mentioned, the Microsoft Select contract that one company had would not allow them to count licenses obtained with new PCs. If the same thing applies to your contract, what about licenses obtain from other sources? Maybe a new version has just been released and one of the big retailers like CompUSA has a sale on the older version. This might be cheaper than getting it through your contract. However, do software purchases like this count toward your totals? If not, you might be wasting money.

The result of miscalculation can have two negative effects. Obviously, if you don't count something you could have, you might end up buying more than you need to. In addition, if you can count certain software, you may be able to set a lower minimum purchase at the beginning. Even if you can't count the software toward the totals, you will probably be able to use it in determining how many new licenses to buy and how many to upgrade.

For example, assume that you have 1000 PCs in your company but only 500 copies of the Corel Office Suite. Because you want everyone to have a legitimate copy, you need to buy 500 new licenses. However, the 500 copies you have are already 2 years old and you want to upgrade them. You could therefore buy 500 upgrades, 500 new copies, plus 1000 maintenance. If, for example, 200 of the licenses that you bought were purchased from a vendor like Merisel without the actual software (i.e., just the licenses); you may be think you cannot count these (as there was no software). Therefore, you spend the money for 200 extra new copies when all you need to buy were upgrades.

On the other end, if your contract stipulates that these 200 are *not* counted toward your required purchase and you count them, you may be in for an unpleasant surprise. Most vendors will generally recognize that as an "honest" mistake and not take any legal action. However, you may be expected to still pay a penalty for not reaching your goal. That is, you expected to be able to count the 200 toward your goal, but the vendor did not allow it.

One very important aspect to be aware of is that most (if not all) of these VLAs have a clause saying that the company can audit you. This means, they *or their agent* can come into your company and make you prove that you have the correct number of licenses. The closer you are to being correct, the less likely it is that the vendor will sue you to recover damages. More than likely, you will just be given a specific deadline to get everything in order.

However, we come to the companies that employ "agents" to do the audit. For example, Microsoft is a member of the BSA, which has historically taken a less-friendly approach to "inaccuracies" in software licensing. I have worked for companies that have been reported to the BSA for having illegal copies of the software. Fortunately, in most countries, the BSA cannot just walk in and audit your company based on anonymous complaints (as these were).

On the other hand, imagine a recently fired system administrator who wants to get even and has "proof" that illegal software is being used. A friend of mine worked for a company that had such a case. Fortunately, they were able to correctly judge the behavior of this person and took the necessary steps. He was fired on a Friday and the BSA was closed until Monday. Therefore, the company spent all weekend getting dozens of copies of all of the software they needed. When the BSA did call, they were quickly invited to audit the company and found that every single piece of software was licensed correctly!

The question is: Do you want to go through the same thing yourself? Better yet, do you have someone who is *currently* working for you that wants to "get even?" In a case like this, you do not see it coming.

Part of the cost of licensing comes back to Total Cost of Ownership (TCO). That is, just how much the licenses will cost you in the end. It is nowhere near sufficient just to find the company that offers you the lowest cost per license. Experience has shown me that these are typical mail/Web-order companies that have essentially no after-sales support. Therefore, you have to go someplace else. On the other hand, companies like Merisel offer licenses and support as well as packages that include both. Here, you can end up getting a quantity discount as well. That is, you are buying more "products" from this company and therefore get a better deal.

The decision to go for combination agreements like this depends on your support organization. If you provide only "fire-fighting" support for your users, you are less likely to need this kind of agreement. For example, if a user can no longer print from MS Word, you spring into action. However, if the user is trying to import data from an Excel spreadsheet into Word, they are on their own. (Yes, I have worked for companies like this!) In this case, you might be better off by purchasing single-incident support calls.

If you do decide to go for one of these package deals, you should also address the technical competence of the reseller. Are they MCSE-certified for the Microsoft products or have similar certification from the other vendors?

The reseller should help you determine what your actual software count is. They should be able to provide you with guidelines on what to look for. Although not every type of license can be applied in every case, the reseller should still provide you with tips to help you count all the licenses correctly.

If you cannot give an accurate count of who uses what software, what versions are used, and where it is installed, there is a high probability that you are using pirated software. If you have a lot of people who surf the Internet, and you have no policy in place about loading software onto machines, the probability is even greater. Most commercial vendors may provide a demo version, which runs out after a specific length of time. However, most shareware vendors do not.

Shareware is a hot topic in terms of the legal aspects of licensing. There are too many people that believe shareware means "freeware" in that you can pay the licensing fee "if you want." Although this is the case with a lot of shareware, it is not the case everywhere. There are many products where you are "encouraged" to pay the listening fee for private use, but you are *required* to pay when used in a commercial environment, that is, if you use it in your business.

Without debating the moral aspects of pirating software, there is the simple fact that it is illegal. Title 18 of the U.S. Copyright Act provides severe penalties, including fines up to $100,000 and even jail sentences. Although it is unlikely that your company will get "raided" by law enforcement agencies, it is possible that you'd get reported by an unhappy employee. There are several organizations such as the BSA and the Software Publishers Association (SPA) as well as many vendors that provide piracy hotlines to report violations. The SPA reports that in 1994, they investigated almost 200 companies and recovered $14 million in lost revenue. Not only do you pay for the lost license fees but also for the administrative costs of prosecuting you!

Aside from just knowing how many copies of each software product you have, you need to understand the license agreements. Although the general idea is the same throughout, few license agreements are identical, even from the same vendor. For example, Microsoft originally had an "80–20" provision for MS Office. You used your copy of MS Office 80% of the time at work and 20% of the time at home. This meant that you could *legally* make a copy. However, this is no longer the case. On the other hand, both Star Division and Corel let you use their office suites at home. StarOffice goes so far as to let you use it at home for free *even if* you don't use it at work!

Perhaps the most important word in the preceding paragraph is "understand." That is, you should not only read your license agreements but *understand* them. For this you have to understand the various licensing types. In general, you can say that there are four types of licenses: per user, per machine, concurrent use, and site licenses.

One thing to keep in mind is that a per-user license is *not* the same thing as a per-machine license. For example, Corel products are licensed by user, whereas Microsoft are licenses per machine. Therefore, if a Microsoft product is installed, you still have to pay a license *even if* it is impossible for some users to access it. (I know I am beating this issue to death, but I don't want you to get burned like we did.)

If you have a product that is licensed for concurrent use, you pay for the maximum number of users that can use the product *at the same time*. Some products have a built-in mechanism to restrict the number to this maximum, whereas others work on the "honor system." That is, they warn you when you exceed the limit, but still allow everyone to use the software. This is a more gentle approach that gives you the opportunity to buy the licenses you need with no interruptions.

Upgrades

There are two primary ways of getting an upgrade: buying it when you need it or buying it in advance. Most end users only buy an upgrade when they need to or when the later version hits the streets. So, what's the point of buying it when you do not need it? Quite simple: You save money.

Many software vendors have different programs that make it easier for you to always have the most current version. These programs go by various names but all fall under the general heading of software maintenance. In essence, you pay a substantially lower price for the maintenance in advance than you would when the product actually becomes available.

If you are planning to upgrade your software, this is generally a good thing. However, it does lock you into the software of a particular vendor. Therefore, if you had MS Office, but needed the advanced features of the Corel WordPerfect Suite or Star Office, you'd either be out of luck or out of money. In addition, the full versions of other products are often cheaper than the MS Office upgrade, so you might not be out too much money.

• • • • • • • • • • • • • •

If you are a smaller company, you may not have the budget to buy all of the necessary licenses at once. Therefore, buying the licenses on credit can be extremely useful. For example, your company may decide to switch from a peer-to-peer Windows 95 network to a domain model running Windows NT on each machine. At the same time, you may decide to upgrade from MS Office 7.0 to MS Office 97. However, the costs of doing every machine at once may be prohibitive.

The obvious solution would be to buy licenses as you can afford to. However, this is not as simple as it sounds. I encountered a major problem with this approach in one company where I worked. We decided that the most effective procedure was to create a standard PC that included Windows NT and MS Office 97. Therefore, it was more efficient to install a machine with both components rather than first Windows NT and later Office 97. The problem was that we could not convert every machine at once. That meant that some people had Office 97 while some were still using Office 7.0.

In this regard, the biggest problem was the fact that Word 97 is not 100% compatible with older versions. Although we would store documents using the Office 95/Office 7 format, many users had trouble accessing the files. This also meant that documents stored in the native Word 97 format could not be read by Word 7.0. Therefore, we had to ensure that everyone who got the newer version of MS Office knew to save in the older format. This resulted in uncounted hours of work, as people forgot and others could not read documents. Although Word 97 can read the older versions, when saving as Word 7.0, for example, the first release actually saved it as rich text format (RTF). In addition, a large amount of the formatting was lost; for example, when saving numbered lists, they were converted to their text equivalence (i.e., the number 1 followed by a period). This meant that we lost this functionality in *hundreds* of documents. Unfortunately, there was not much we could do in this case, as we had to make the transition in several groups.

Even if you have a maintenance contract and you can install the software for free, it is not always a good idea to jump into an upgrade. The problems encountered with Office 97 are a prime example. There is also the issue of the time it may take to get used to the new version. A good strategy is to test the new version to see what the differences are and if you really want to implement it. If you do, you are already aware of what to train your users on to limit the time they need to get familiar with it.

I have worked for companies where they seemed to have an obsession with buying the latest version of software, even though they rarely used the software, let alone used all of the functions. Each time a new release was announced, they bought enough copies so everyone had the new version. There were also cases were some people actually did need the new version, but not everyone. However, the people that *didn't* get the upgrade couldn't stand the idea that someone else got the new version and they didn't. (Note that this contradicts the idea of having software standards. However, you should at least consider this side of things.)

In addition to the cost and time involved, you should know what effects the newer version of the product has on the operating system. As you probably know yourself, Microsoft is notorious for delivering operating system "enhancements" with their applications. Sometimes they announce this to you, whereas other times it simply is done as part of the "normal" installation. The result was that other applications no longer functioned correctly because DLLs were changed, and the new ones did not have the same functions. This meant upgrading those applications as well.

Also check to see what happens when you upgrade the operating system. I know there were several applications that specifically said they were for Windows NT 3.51 and would *not* run on NT 4.0. Plus there are many that only run on Windows 95/98 and not on Windows NT. Fortunately their installation routine would not let you install on Windows NT. However, what happens when you do an upgrade of the OS?

Even if the products allow you to install on either Windows 95/98 or Windows NT, the installation procedure (including what files are copied) may be different. Check this in advance, as you do not want to be unpleasantly surprised.

Prepackaged Licenses

What about cases where the licenses for a preinstalled package are not for the product you use in-house? For example, many computers are being delivered with MS Office preloaded. What if your company has decided on the advanced features that the Corel Office Suite or StarOffice provide as compared to MS Office? Selecting another vendor that does not come preinstalled may not be the best idea. Systems vendors are just that: vendors of systems.

Such vendors might not be inclined to provide you a system without MS Office for a couple of reasons. It is possible that their contract with Microsoft *forces* them to include MS Office on their systems, even if the customer wants something different. The vendor may have gotten a large discount on the MS Office licenses in exchange. Either they need to increase the price for everyone and not submit to Microsoft's demands, or they charge you extra for a different, albeit better, office suite.

If you cannot get the computer vendor to physically remove MS Office, you may get them to keep the end-use license agreement, (essentially keeping the license) and give you a rebate for the difference. (Note that there may be some difficult legal problems to overcome, as the computer vendor would still be giving you unlicensed software.)

Even if you cannot get the computer vendor to remove the license or give you a rebate, all is not lost. If you do decide to upgrade to the advanced features of something like the Corel Office Suite, Corel is willing to give you a special price. This is less than the cost of a full version. If the price of the competitive upgrade is $100 less than the full version, you have saved $10,000 when you buy 100 copies! Therefore, always check to see if there is an "upgrade" program from a competitor's product.

One of the first problems that cropped up with the Microsoft Select in one company where I worked contract was lack of communication, both between our various offices as well asbetween Microsoft and our company. Several of our branch offices were not aware of the contract and continued to buy software locally. Although it still counted toward the total number of licenses we needed to purchase, the software was more expensive than what we paid with the select contract.

Note that this was the case with the first contract we had. With the next one, things changed. We were no longer allowed to count original equipment manufacturer (OEM) licenses. For example, when we bought a new PC, any operating system license provided buy the computer vendor was not counted toward our total. It *was still* a valid license, and we could buy a maintenance contract for it. However, it did *not* count toward our totals. This was a problem, as it is often difficult to get new PCs *without* an OEM version of a Microsoft operating system.

The people in the headquarters were aware of the limitation, but not everyone in the branch offices. Some thought they had made a good deal by getting a license with the computer. However, it meant that we were close to not reaching our goals. Microsoft could prevent us from continuing the contract, *even though* we actually did buy enough licenses. It just wasn't the way they wanted.

We solved the problem by saying that all computer and software purchases had to be first approved by the headquarters. In many cases, we also did the ordering ourselves. I thought that this was like killing flies with a bazooka, as it meant substantially more administration work for us. However, it did keep us from buying licenses that were not counted.

One thing that might happen also is that the reseller won't let you buy maintenance contracts for licenses from other sources. There are no laws requiring that they do so, and this is common practice in other businesses. For example, if you buy a VCR from one store, you normally can't get an extended warranty package from other stores, even if they sell the exact same brand and model of VCR. Although you don't have the same technical considerations with software as you do with hardware, the distributor might put this kind of restriction in the contract.

Licenses can also be "lost" through older machines that are replaced or even reinstalled. For example, when new hardware is purchased, the older machine may just be put in a warehouse somewhere, given away, or sold. In many cases, only the hardware changes hands, but the license remains with the company. In one company where I worked, there was several bins in the back of a warehouse that contained hundreds of packages with diskettes and end user license agreements (EULAs) for WfWGs. The machines had been previously sold without software. When the machines were replaced, copies of the *full version* of Windows NT were purchased. However, these licenses *could* have been upgraded from WfWG instead of full versions.

Another place that you can be bitten is the client access license (CAL). This is a requirement of Microsoft that you not only pay for the server software, but also for every client that *could* access the server. This is a key point that ended up costing one company almost $30,000. They were running Windows NT 3.51 and had sufficient CALs for all of their workstations. For test purposes, they installed a single Windows NT 4.0 as a BDC and made a few shares available to the system administrators. Although they upgraded the CALs for the administrators from NT 3.51 to 4.0 (as they were the only ones who could access the machine), Microsoft said that this was not sufficient. They were told that because the *possibility* existed that users could access the server, an upgraded CAL was required. Even if not configured as a BDC so that it would not provide *any* services (BDC may provide logon services), the upgraded CAL was still required if the server was on the network.

Because testing had already begun on a number of applications and they were planning to eventually move to NT 4.0, the company decided they could not simply remove the NT 4.0 server and decided to pay for the licenses. Although they would have eventually paid the money, the fact that they were blindsided was annoying.

Another place that is often forgotten is the CALs that come with the servers. Although this generally is only a handful of licenses, that is several that you do not have to pay for. However, I have seen some resellers that offer a package deal of an *additional* 250 licenses when you buy the server software from them (often in conjunction with buying a complete system). Even if you do pay slightly more for the system with these 250 licenses, it *can* be cheaper than buying them separately. Also, some people forget that these are 250 *additional* licenses. If five licenses come with the NT server, they would actually be buying 255!

If you have a decent accounting department, you should be able to tell how much you are spending on software. However, you probably cannot use the same tools to determine whether you have purchased enough to comply with *each* vendor's licensing conditions. Some companies, like Corel, require you to pay for usage. That is, even though the computer is installed on every machine in the company, if the permissions are set so that not everyone can use it, you do not have to pay a license for every machine. On the other hand, Microsoft requires that you pay a license for every *installed* copy, whether it is used or not, *even if* their own NTFS would restrict access. If you are used to the Corel licensing policy and decide to switch to Microsoft (for example, to have a single source for all your software), you might find yourself in a difficult and expensive situation.

In one company, we found out about this the hard way. We had a standard PC that was copied each time a new machine was installed. This had the operating system and MS Office. To restrict access to MS Office, we placed the users into groups. As mentioned, per Microsoft, the NTFS security was not sufficient to ensure that the user could not gain access, and we were required to pay a license fee for each *installed* copy. Right or wrong, that was what Microsoft said. Because we felt that the administration of multiple workstation types was too great, we decided to pay the extra money for the few cases where the user did not use MS Office.

In our case, it amounted to several thousand dollars, but we felt that we would save it in the long run through reduced administration costs. However, your company might not be able to pay that kind of money, so you really need to be aware of what the licensing conditions are.

Software Monitoring

There are a number of tools on the market that can help you monitor your software to keep you legal as well as determine exactly what software you are using.

One of the simplest tools is built into the NT system. This is the "net group" command. In one company, access to specific software was determined by group membership. Although Microsoft said that this was not sufficient from a legal perspective in preventing unauthorized access, it did tell us how many people were using a particular application.

The net group Command

The syntax is:

net group <group_name> /domain

This will give you a list of the members of the group <group_name> from the domain controller. Note that you actually put the word "domain" and not the name of the domain. If you leave off the group name, you get a list of all groups within the domain. Using this command, you can also create new groups and add users. Although the list of group members comes out in three columns, you can still use it to get a count of how many users are in a specific group. If access to the application is controlled by group membership, you have the total number of users who can access the software. See the chapter on user and group administration for more details.

Using the "add" option, you can either create a new group or add users to an existing one. Using the "delete" option, you can remove users or groups.

The syntax here would be:

net group <group_name> <username> add /domain

or

net group <group_name> <username> delete /domain

Note that you can specify multiple user names on the same line.

It is relatively straightforward to create a perl script and access this information from your intranet server. Perl allows you to format and count the information, so you can find out quickly how many users are in each group. This can also be compared to the information in the SMS database, so we knew how many computers we had as well as with the license database, so we knew how many licenses we had. If we had more users in the group than licenses, we could easily order them.

Many of you may be asking why we did it this way, as there are a number of products that already do this for you automatically. Generically, these are referred to as asset management programs and perform wide-range but varying functions. Some products do just inventories of your systems looking for any application software. Basically, all of the commercial applications can be identified by looking at the executable itself. You can check this yourself by right-clicking the program and selecting the properties menu and then the version tab. This kind of software is useful to help you locate software that you may be unaware of.

The reason we did not introduce one of the existing software products is simply that the IT manager didn't have a clue. We could not convince him that it was necessary. Therefore, we spent uncounted hours managing much of the information by hand.

The next type is metering or monitoring software. These watch and report on usage of your software. The number and type of reports depends on the product. However, they generally report on what software you have, who is using it, and how often it is used. In addition, there are several products that can be used to distribute, install, and remove software on remote machines.

Depending on the size of your organization, you might want to consider software that addresses all three of these aspects. Obviously, identifying the software on your network is useful in determining what licenses you need. You could do it by hand, but this is not always practical. If you support a network of several thousand (even several hundred) PCs, you can find much better things to do with your time than look through every directory on every machine to find out what software exists.

A side benefit of getting an accurate inventory involves the year 2000 (Y2K) problem. Several monitoring products can also report to you on whether or not the software you have is Y2K compliant. Note that there is no practical way for the metering software to know this just by looking at your applications. Instead, it looks at a database of applications and reports the information it has. Therefore, it's possible that a vendor has reported its application as being Y2K compliant and is recorded thusly in the database, but in fact it is not compliant.

One thing to remember is that no product will be able to record the software you have on your shelves. Therefore, you will have to do a little work yourself to ensure the inventory is as accurate as possible. When conducting a physical inventory, you need to be careful with what you count.

Try to be as consistent as possible. Most companies provide a registration card with the software, which is then separated into two pieces, one you send to the vendor and the other you keep for your records. Both have the product serial number, which can be used as a "proof" of purchase. Microsoft provides an EULA, which is a pretty green certificate with a hologram on it. For them, this is the ultimate proof that you bought the software.

In some cases, you have neither the registration card, EULA, nor anything else that says you bought the software except the media. Even though Microsoft considers this valid, you still need to be careful. For example, the copy of Windows 95 that I first purchased was an update from Windows 3.1. To install it, I needed to prove that I had copy of another Microsoft product. Therefore, I had to keep my copy of Windows 3.1 if I ever wanted to reinstall Windows 95 (which I obviously had to do on a number of occasions). Plus, this was proof that I was even authorized to use the upgrade version.

In deciding on the software, there are a number of factors to look at. The first thing is its basic functioning; for example, whether it is client-server or everything is run from a central console. Usually, if it is run from a central console, all it does is inventory. That is because it is difficult, if not impossible, to monitor usage on remote machines. A local client can monitor and report any time a new application starts either into a local database (i.e., file) or report back to the server. In addition, there are also a few stand-alone products that simply write the information to a text file.

The fact that the inventory software simply writes the data to a text file may not be a bad thing. As telecommuting becomes more and more popular, there may be people within your company who have computers at home that are owned by the company. Even if the computer is owned by the user, often the software is purchased by the company. If not included in the inventory, they might be forgotten when calculating your volume discounts or when it comes time to upgrade.

This not only applies to computers at someone's home, but also to laptops. Laptops bring other problems with them. For example, some vendors allow a 80–20 rule. That is, you use the computer on your desk 80% of the time but are *not* expected to pay for an additional license for the laptop. However, this is not the case everywhere, so you should check in advance.

Regardless of whether the program is client-server or stand-alone, you need to ensure that it runs on every one of your machines (or at least enough of them to make it worthwhile). There are a number of them that only support Windows NT and Windows 95/98. However, this does you little good if you have Novell Server or OS/2 clients. Although other products will support the other systems, it is much better to get a tool that supports everything you have rather than getting multiple tools and trying to combine the results.

If a demo version of the software is available, I would suggest that you get it and test it for as long as possible. Because you will be risking great sums of money, you should even consider buying a copy if no demo is available (with the way the price of producing CDs has plunged, it is likely a demo is available). One thing you should specifically check is how accurately the software you know about is identified. You should flat-out skip any software that relies solely on the name of the program to identify it. In one company, we wrote a simple program to do just that but the users were smart enough and renamed pirated things like "winword.exe". This hid it from our search but not from commercial products that looked for characteristics other than the name. In this way, we could also identify those programs that actually did have the same name.

You should also check to see how detailed the reporting is. Although most products are more detailed, simply saying that it found MS Word is not enough. In this case, you need to know both the version number and the language, as the license price will be different.

This can also help identify several kinds of problems. For example, if you locate multiple copies of the same product on the same computers, something improper was done during the installation. Obviously, two copies of the same version is improper, but two different versions *might* be wrong as well. (I say "might," as we normally install the newest versions on the administrators' machines at first to test it and look for potential problems. However, we still need a copy of the older version.)

Some software requires that you input a serial number during the installation. Two copies on two different machines with the same serial number might be the result of an inattentive administrator. On the other hand, it might be the result of someone pirating software. If the inventory software can read entries like "This software is registered to…," it is even better, especially if the software is registered to another company!

Although less important, it is useful if you can record additional information with the data the inventory software records. For example, it would be nice if you could record location, asset tag number, or any other company-related information. Better still is when it records the information in a common format, such as a structured query language (SQL) server database, thereby making the information available to other applications.

The software should be capable of *searching* the hard disk for executable programs. Granted, the user may be able to hide the program by changing the extension so that it does not "look like" an executable. However, you will still be able to find the one where users are not trying to hide them. Plus, the fact that you did do a check *may* cover you legally should you be audited.

Part of this process is the reporting. Simply giving you a list could be accomplished with a perl script or Visual Basic program written in less than an hour. Instead, you want the program to be able to provide different kinds of reports depending on your needs. For example, if the product is client-server and collects from every machine in the company, can it produce a report listing all of the machines that have a particular software product installed? Can it report how many times the product is installed?

298 Chapter 8 ♦ System Management

At first this may sound like the same question. However, what about machines where the product is installed twice? If users are allowed to install their own software, one may think something is not installed and install it somewhere different. This may be reported as two installations, although there are multiple copies on a single machine, and you think you are short on licenses.

Another thing to check is to see if the inventory software can monitor how often an application is *started*. This is useful for two reasons. First, the software may be installed but never used. Why pay a license fee for unused software? Second, some products allow a network installation *even if* you do not have the necessary numbers of licenses. You may have products that appear to be installed only once but are actually installed multiple times.

Some products allow installation on a network drive. You could install it only on your master workstation, which is used to close all of the others. You can thus run the software from all of the workstations. The question is whether you are allowed to or not.

Part of this is whether or not the software runs over a remote access connection. Many software companies allow you to use a single copy at home and at work. (Microsoft does not!) If the inventory software will work across the remote access server (RAS), you need to make sure that the license at home can be identified correctly.

There are three primary criteria to determine whether or not you need a software inventory product:

- the number of machines you have
- the number of *different* products you have
- whether or not users can install their own software

These three criteria are very much interwoven. For example, 100 PCs with two different applications does not really need an inventory product, whereas 20 machines with 10 different applications probably do. Assume you were somewhere in the middle with 50 machines and four different applications, but not every machine had every application. If users were allowed to install their own software, an inventory program might be useful, as it is likely (if not probable) that there are people in your company who think, "He has it, so why can't I?" Even though they do not need a particular product, they install it anyway so that no one else has something they don't. An inventory program would show you that the software had been installed.

On the other hand, if users cannot install software (i.e., floppy locks have been installed), the administrator *should* know in advance what is installed on each machine. Therefore, with 50 machines and four different applications, there is less of a need for an inventory product.

Most modern inventory products work correctly with Windows NT, Windows 95, Windows 98, and even Windows 3.1. However, they may not have DOS clients. This obviously becomes an issue if you still have DOS clients. It may not be a problem if you only have a couple of DOS machines and are willing to do the inventory by hand. However, it should still be considered.

The ability to monitor as well as regulate software usage can be extremely effective in reducing TCO. First, by knowing who is using what software and when, you can make some informed decisions about whether certain software should be retained. For example, you might have purchased 10 licenses for CorelDraw, because every department manager insisted they had to have it. Despite the fact that CorelDraw is a very useful program, you discover that only three departments have used it within the last 6 months. The reason that they "had to" have it was that other departments had it. Although you may not be able to get your money back, you can probably save money by not purchasing the newest version for the people that don't really need it. The monitoring software pays for itself when you prove to the company president that certain departments never use the product and therefore do not "deserve" the latest version.

There are a couple of different ways that software licensing can be enforced. The more simplistic is when the administrator monitors where and when the software is being used. Some products will monitor themselves and have built-in mechanisms to limit the number of users or may simply report to the administrator when usage goes above the number of registered licenses.

Software Distribution

Many companies provide packages that not only do software metering but also software distribution. Such products allow you to manage the distribution of both new products and upgrades from a central location. In most cases, installation occurs automatically without intervention from the user, and the administrator is not required to go to each machine individually. The distribution and configuration of the software is handled from a central console, which allows easy standardization of the software as well as the configuration. Because the installation is done automatically, there is less chance that you have multiple releases of a particular software product.

In addition, because this is handled automatically, a large number of computers can be installed at the same time. This obviously causes a load on the network, especially when installing larger packages such as office suites. However, the time saved by not having to go to each machine individually more than compensates for that.

As you know, installing and updating your software can take a great deal of time. If you do it by hand, it will affect at least two people. First there is the system administrator who installs it, then there is the user on whose machine the software is being installed. Granted, the administrator could install the software on a machine somewhere else and then exchange the machines. However, this only works with standard configurations.

On the other hand, the time spent swapping out the computer might be far less than the user has to wait for a product to install. For example, the installation of MS Office might take 20 minutes, in which the user cannot work. However, if you are working with standard hardware configuration, it may be possible to simply swap out the computer and leave the monitor in place. This could be done in just a few minutes. Still, you need to calculate the time spent by the administrator to carry the computers back and forth from where they are installed.

One thing to look for is whether or not the installation software can also remove unwanted programs or perform other kinds of configuration on the system. For example, in one company, there was at least one user who was very clever in getting games smuggled onto the system. These spread quickly, and it was extremely difficult to track them down. If your software distribution product can recognize the games (i.e., by the name of the executable), you may be able to configure it to automatically remove these programs.

In Symphony, software monitoring and software distribution products can be used to save you a great deal of money. You first identify which programs are not being used on one machine and then reinstall them where they are needed, without leaving your desk.

Another aspect of this is the ability to detect changes on the system, such as the addition of new files. For example, a user may have renamed a game to something seemingly harmless, such as NOTEPAD.EXE, but there is no reason for it to exist anywhere other than the system directory. Therefore, if a copy were to appear somewhere else on the system and have a different size and date, it would at least be enough to make you question what the program really is.

Your distribution software should also allow you to set different criteria for the installation. For example, if the hard disk is smaller than 500 MBs or there is only 32 MBs of RAM, it does not do an installation. When evaluating a product, take a look to see how configurable this option is. Look at what criteria can be checked to see whether an installation should be done.

One of the most important features of distribution software is point-n-click. Technology is to the point that you no longer need to accept programs where input is only done through the keyboard. You should (must) be able to select computers to install from a list rather than having to input the name by hand. In addition, the software should be able to obtain a list of computer names by browsing the network and providing them for you automatically.

On the other hand, a purely point-n-click interface is not always a good thing. Anyone who has administered an NT system knows how cumbersome it is to have to administer multiple machines or users through the graphical user interface (GUI). In many cases, the easiest thing to do is to create a batch file that can do a number of things automatically. Hopefully, whatever software distribution product you decide on has some kind of scripting ability. It would be nice if there were command line options to perform certain tasks (perhaps reading a configuration file), but what would be much better would be a scripting language that you can use to automate your work.

Also important is the operating system on which the client runs. No two are alike in terms of which clients they support. Some support only versions of Windows, whereas others support DOS, and still others support OS/2 or Novell. Therefore, it is not only important to ensure that you have the correct server versions but also the correct clients. On the other hand, you need to evaluate the return on investment (ROI) for the product. If only 1% of your machines are not Windows (i.e., DOS or OS/2), insisting that there be a client for these systems may not be cost effective. You may find a better product that does not support one or the other and decide that the few remaining machines will be installed by hand.

You also need to determine how this will affect users. For example, in some cases, when Microsoft Systems Management Server (SMS) is installing software, the entire machine is essentially useless. That is, it is so busy that you cannot do any other work on it until the installation is complete. Even during the time it is checking to see if updates are warranted, there is not much you can do on the system. Granted, the system administrator does not need to intervene and SMS saves them work. However, the user is idle during this time. This is still much quicker that installing by hand, in any event, but it should be considered.

Paired with this is the bandwidth that the installation requires. If you are installing an office suite such as Corel, you can expect that over 100 MBs will be traveling across the line *for each user*. This not only affects the user on whose machine the software is being installed, but everyone else on that network segment. A number of products solve that problem by using data compression. The data are compressed by the server before being sent across the network and then decompressed by the client.

Another possibility is intermediate servers that store the data. For example, the package is copied to the BDC in your branch office, and the clients install it from there. The data only go across the slow WAN connection once.

Obviously the best time to install new software is when the user is not on the machine. Many companies require that you turn off your computers at night. Even though this is a good thing, it prevents you from doing automatic installs in the middle of the night. Although it is not always a good idea to leave your computer on overnight, the solution is to notify the user in advance to leave their computers on during the night, say for a couple of days until you have completed the installation.

If you have applications stored on the server that are accessed by multiple users, you need to look at the ability of the product to install to a different server. In principle, this is not much more work than for clients. However, obviously more users are affected. Here too you should look at the bandwidth of the connection. I worked in one company were the connection (56 K) was fine for normal activity, but the moment a remote software installation was started, everything came to a standstill.

Another important aspect is records of the installations. That is, does the software keep track of when each product was installed and what changes were made? If the installation fails, is this also recorded? Sometimes the installation fails for technical reasons, such as power failures or some system problems. In other cases, it might fail because a requirement component is missing. For example, Microsoft Internet Explorer (IE) 4.0 required SP3 be installed on Windows NT. If an installation of IE 4.0 fails because SP3 was not installed, this is also recorded.

This brings up the additional consideration of being able to define dependencies yourself as well as install multiple packages at once. Sometimes dependencies are not a requirement for any given package, but something that you define yourself. For example, you decide to install Adobe Acrobat Reader on all machines, but because it is already installed on the machine with Adobe Acrobat, there is no need to install it again. Perhaps you only want to install Adobe Photoshop on those machine that already have Adobe Illustrator. In each case, there is no requirement from the perspective of the product, but it is something that you define yourself.

Virus Protection

If you have just a handful of PCs, then single-station antivirus programs and Symantec will provide you the necessarily amount of protection. Even with Internet access from all machines, these products can protect you from viruses that you inadvertently download. There are a number of client-server solutions that allow management of the anti-virus software from a single workstation, but the cost is prohibitive. Installing single-seat copies by hand on a dozen or so machines is much cheaper than the thousands of dollars you will need to spend for client-server products.

Most of the newer single-seat products have two modes of operating: automatic and manual ("on-demand scanning"). On-demand scanning is what most people are familiar with, in that you start the software yourself and direct it to scan a particular drive (typically a floppy). If the software does automatic scanning, you can set and forget it. When the system boots, the software automatically scans your system. In most cases, when files are accessed from floppy or even the Internet, the scanning software cuts in and examines the file to ensure there are no viruses. Many can even check email attachments and compressed files (such as .ZIP or .ARJ).

I am a firm believer that we need to trust the user NOT to do anything stupid. Therefore, you might think it's okay that anyone can load files from floppies or CD onto their system. However, the problem is one of intent. Your users do not *intend* to do anything wrong. However, often their lack of experience, or even the fact they do not have the same mindset as the IT people, causes accidents to happen.

Personally, I think that if you can avoid accidents, you should. The solution is to have a single machine (or small number) where all files are loaded. The floppy drives should all have locks. Even if you use the Floppy Lock system service to prevent access by nonadministrators, users could accidentally leave an infected floppy in the drive. When the machine is rebooted, the virus can infect the system (e.g., the master boot record).

Obviously, a single machine that is used to load files means extra work for that person. However, most companies do not load files from floppies often enough to be concerned. I feel that the amount saved on not having to buy virus programs for every machine compensates for the extra work. However, you need to make that decision yourself. I know of cases, such as translation offices or typesetting companies, that actually do have a large number of floppies and email coming in as to make it necessary to give everyone direct access to a virus scanner. The difference is that these people are always conscious of the fact the information is coming from outside of the company.

The first anti-virus software products provided a single application that needed to be installed on each machine. With a handful of users, this was adequate. However, with larger companies, a unified anti-virus program is needed, and therefore tools are needed with centralized administration.

Even if the software vendor provides a networked client-server version of their software, they may also have single-seat licenses and may give you a quantity discount. However, the more files that are transferred between your system and others', and the more users you have doing it, the more you need to consider the client-server solution. Even if it does come out to be more expensive, you also need to consider the amount of time you save by centrally managing your PCs.

An extra variable comes into the equation when you exchange email. Here again, the more people you have doing it, the greater the need for a virus protection concept and therefore need virus protection software.

One problem with on-demand scanning is the sheer volume of data to which we are exposed. It becomes time consuming to scan every piece of email and every file entering the company. In addition, more and more companies are using self-made CD-ROMs in order to distribute large amounts of data. Therefore, large amounts of data need to be scanned here as well.

Even if the virus scan is performed automatically, some file types are often missed. For example, it is common with older virus scanners that they could not identify viruses in files with a compressed archive such as ZIP. Now, the ability to scan compressed archives or any type has become standard. In recent years, viruses have been created that hide themselves in macros of word processing programs, particularly MS Word. Many newer versions of anti-virus products have the ability to scan such documents for viruses as well.

Another problem with on-demand scanning is that should a virus find its way into your system, there can be a substantial delay until the scan is performed and the virus identified. Added to this is the substantial system degradation if the entire system is scanned.

Email brings its own set of problems. In general, email is not file oriented. Instead it is stored in a large database, such as in the case of MS Exchange or Lotus Notes. Many anti-virus products have special modules particularly designed to protect these email servers. Normally, they sit on top of the server and scan incoming packets even before they reach the email database.

In contrast to on-demand scanning there is on-access scanning, where the virus scanner sits on top of the operating system (normally as a service). Here it monitors behavior that is either caused by a virus or causes a virus to activate, such as accessing files or starting programs.

Typically, these kinds of virus scanners are installed on the workstation, where the activity is occurring. This reduces the load on the server as well as substantially increases the speed at which viruses are identified. In addition, because the virus is identified at the workstation, it is less likely to be transmitted to the server.

The key disadvantage here is that you will probably need a virus scanner license for each client. This is not as expensive as single-seat licenses for each client, but more expensive that a single license on the server. Even so, the cost is so low compared to the damages caused by a virus that it is definitely worth considering.

You also need to consider how current the virus scanner *stays*. Keep in mind that even if you get the scanner software the day it is sent to the stores, it is *already* outdated. This is simply because the scanner vendors cannot keep up with the virus developers. New viruses are released almost every day and it is impossible for the scanner vendor to keep current. They need time to identify the virus as well as develop the appropriate countermeasures.

To solve the problem of keeping customers updated, many vendors provide automatic update services, in which they send you updates at regular intervals. Although this saves you time, even if the updates come once a month, a new virus may be identified weeks before you get the update.

Many allow you to download the update directly from their servers. Often complete updates are limited to a specified time period (such as a year). However, some companies provide a "limited edition" which may only addresses a recently identified virus, such as the Melissa virus in early 1999.

If you are hit by a virus, the damage caused can be more than just time wasted disinfecting your system. In some cases, you cannot simply disinfect your machine. Often, the damage is permanent, in that it cannot be repaired. For example, a virus that overwrites the boot information on your hard disk or a file that was changed, but not yet backed up. In the first case, the system must be reinstalled. In the second case, work needs to be repeated. In both cases, time (and therefore money) is lost.

If a virus is identified on a workstation, you need to be sure that it has been disinfected before you can continue working on it. I feel that the safest thing is to completely disconnect it from the network while you are cleaning up to make sure you do not inadvertently spread the virus to other machines.

Another consideration is viruses that have worked their way into files that are seldom used. Although it is not likely (but possible) that the virus targets unused files, on-access virus scanning will not identify them. Therefore, a manual (on-demand) scan is useful to identify such "sleeping" viruses. In addition, some virus scanners can work in conjunction with your backup software to catch these files when they are saved to tape.

A polymorphic virus is one that changes itself as it infects each system. Such virus programs are more difficult to track down as they do not have one specific signature. The code is so written that with each iteration, something new comes out. However, changing its own code is a characteristic that few programs share with viruses. Therefore, finding a program that does this means there is a high probability it is a virus.

One important consideration is the distribution of the virus software. If you get a single-seat product you may be stuck with installing it on each machine by hand, unless it can be installed with distribution software like SMS. However, many client-server products provide their own distribution mechanism that overcome the problems with SMS.

Also look into what mechanisms the product has for sending messages. If you start a scan manually, the program will certainly pop up a message. This is also true for on-access scanners when they detect a virus. One problem lies with the users who simply click away system messages without reading them. Although you may have configured the software to disinfect automatically, you really should be made aware whenever a virus is detected.

You also have the additional problem for products that run on the server (i.e., during backups) that there is often no one at the console, particular if the backup is done in the middle of the night. Therefore, you need to have a mechanism for identifying events that you are not immediately aware of. This is where a good log comes into plan. Most virus scanners have a log of some kind, even the single-seat products. However, you need to make sure to check how you access the information. If it is stored in a proprietary format on the workstation, you may need to physically go to the machine to look at the log.

Another key feature is whether it supports all of your operating systems. Even though the newer ones will support Windows 95, 98, and probably Windows NT workstations, they may not have a server product. Conditions on the server are different from the workstation, especially considering you have many more people working, more files are open, and so forth. If you have an Alpha-based version of Windows NT, you need to look into whether this is supported or not. Some are limited to just Intel.

If the software can be installed remotely with its own tool, it can also be administered and configured remotely. This is especially important if you have a large number of workstations and even more so if some of them are in remote locations. Look into the aspects of how they can be configured.

- Can workstations be grouped together for more efficient administration?
- Can you change characteristics for all the clients at once, groups, or only individually?
- To what extent can you define the actions to be taken (always disinfect, disinfect only specific kinds of viruses, etc.)?
- Can you change when messages are generated (always report, report only when the virus cannot be removed, etc.)?
- To what extent can you define the reporting (pop-ups to a specific group, only log entries, etc.)?
- To what extent can you define what the scanner does when it detects a virus (blocks activity, automatically disinfects, etc.)?
- Can you schedule scans? To what extent?
- Can you scan specific types of files? How many different types?
- To what extent can you define what files to scan (all files, only those that have been changed since the last scan, etc.)?
- To what extent can you define when to scan on access (always, only when reading, etc.)?
- To what extent can you prevent users from changing the settings?

You should also investigate the behavior of the scanner including the accuracy of the scan. For example:

- How frequently does the product generate false alarms (report an infection when there isn't any)?
- How effective is the scanner? Does it miss any infections?
- What effect does the scan have on the performance of the system? Can users continue to work?

Detecting, preventing, and curing computer viruses is basically the same as for human viruses. That is, it never 100% accurate. Even if you ignore the fact that new viruses are appearing every day, it is impossible for any program to be accurate all of the time. The biggest problem is the fact that there or already tens of thousands of computer viruses, each with its own behavior that needs to be identified. In many cases, the virus is a polymorphic virus. Therefore, your virus scanner might be able to identify one form of the virus but what about the other forms that it can change itself into?

To be able to solve this problem anti-virus developers implement a set of heuristics to identify different viruses. A heuristic is simply a plan or procedure to follow to solve a particular problem. The most common example is that of a traveling salesmen who needs to visit 20 different cities. If San Francisco, Denver, and New York were three of these cities, it would be quicker, and probably more efficient, to visit the cities in this order. Traveling from San Francisco to New York and then back to Denver would cause the salesman to repeat part of the trip. To plan his trip, the salesman might simply take a map of the United States and try to have the fewest occurrences of overlapping paths. Theoretically, he could spend many weeks and eventually come up with the optimal solution, where no path is repeated in the total distance that's the shortest. The question is whether or not he's willing to wait weeks to get his answer.

The same thing applies to virus scanners. It may be possible to check for every type of virus in every combination, but the question is how long would it take? It would essentially mean checking every byte on your hard disk in a number of different combinations. This could actually take weeks to complete a single scan of your system.

The simplest and most common heuristic in terms of virus scanning is simply to look for known characteristics. In virus terms these characteristics are referred to as "signatures." The signature is essentially nothing more than a sequence of bytes somewhere in a program or file that appears in a particular known virus. In most cases, this sequence of bytes will be unique to the virus and usually represents a small percentage of the size of the virus. For example, the virus might be several hundreds or thousands of bytes, whereas the virus signature is only a dozen or so bytes. Using this technique, an antivirus program can quickly see if a program contains the signature. However, it cannot determine with 100% accuracy whether or not it contains that particular virus.

One problem with checking the virus signature is that it only identifies those viruses that have been previously reported. A new virus with a different signature will not show up in this search. Like checking for fingerprints, you check for those virus signatures that you have on file. Sometimes a criminal will be missed, and sometimes an innocent person may be identified as having been at the scene of a crime. In the same vein, viruses may be missed, and sometimes unaffected programs may be reported as having the virus.

Another heuristic that virus scanners use is also comparable to the heuristic used in police work. Here, the virus scanner looks at the behavior of a particular program. For example, most programs should not be writing directly to the master boot block of the hard disk. So if the virus scanner identifies a program that does write to the master boot block, it may report that this program contains a virus. As you might expect, this is not completely accurate. This would be comparable to observing someone entering a bank wearing sunglasses and a long jacket, who moves around very nervously. This does not mean the person is going to rob the bank. However, it is a good indicator.

When scanning, an anti-virus program will examine the overall structure of the program to scanning, look at the logic, instructions, and any data within the program, and several other attributes. Based on what it finds, it will make an assessment of the likelihood that this program contains a virus. However, as you expect, this could cause you to miss an infected program or wrongly identify a program as containing the virus. Despite this, most virus scanners have an accuracy of 70–80% in the detection of new and therefore unknown viruses.

One of the most significant characteristics that virus-scanning programs look for is the behavior of certain kinds of viruses. For example, as previously mentioned, most programs do not write to the master boot block of the hard disk. Therefore, finding a program that does would subject to it more detailed scrutiny.

Another thing a virus scanner does is to look at those places where viruses are most likely to occur. You're most likely to find a virus that attaches itself either to the beginning or the end of the program. Considering that most programs are hundreds of thousands if not millions of bytes, restricting your search to the beginning or the end can save considerable amounts of time. Granted, this will not catch every virus, but it does get enough to make this an effective method.

Another behavior that might be an indicator of a virus is writing directly to .COM or .EXE files. There is generally no legitimate reason why a program would want to change the insides of another program. Overwriting it is one thing, but changing the program itself is generally not done. Therefore, if a program were to do that, it would most likely be a virus.

One of the simplest ways to detect viruses is to detect changes in the "external" characteristics of programs. For example, a virus scanner will create the database of all the programs on your system, recording such information as the size, last modification date, and read-only attributes. Granted there are a large number of viruses that can trick the system into thinking that what the system sees, is. However, many do not. It is therefore an extremely efficient way of identifying changes to the files on your system.

The problem with all of these techniques is that they are static. Checking the signature or behavior of potential viruses all requires that some previous knowledge be stored within the virus scanner or at least that it has access to that information. The problem with this approach is that new viruses are developed almost daily, no signature is available, and their behavior may not fit into something that was previously recorded.

On the other hand, this is the simplest form of virus scanner, and there is very little programming required. It is therefore possible to get very inexpensive virus-scanning software that does nothing more than scan for signatures.

Slightly more complex is a heuristics scanner that does not rely just on a catalog of signatures and behavior. This is not enough, as the signature might be a coincidence or the behavior is mistaken for something malicious. Instead, the scanner will load the program into a virtual computer, which makes the possible virus think it is on a real computer.

While the virus goes about its business, it will eventually need to call the operating system to do the dirty work of infecting another file or another system. What it does at this point will tell the scanner what its real intentions are.

In addition to virus signatures and heuristics, a virus program should offer you complete protection of your system. That is, from the time you turn it on until it shuts down. One important aspect if you are running Windows 95/98 is a DOS component that starts before the operating system is loaded. It is possible that you can have a virus infect a program that is started in your AUTOEXEC.BAT program that runs before any Windows-based anti-virus software.

Most virus products offer several different protection levels. You can obviously start the program by hand to scan as you need to. Others can scan the system at regular intervals as well as when the system is booted or even shutdown. Some will start automatically each time a program is launched.

Management Tools

When computer systems consisted of a bunch of serial terminals connected to a central computer, system administration was a lot easier. When a user's "workstation" went down, there were a very limited number of causes. Either the user kicked out the plug, or there was a hardware problem. With the advent of desktop computers and desktop workstations, the system administrator not only has to administer the server but all of the clients as well. Added to all of the active components in the network, the different operating systems and applications, system administration has really become a full-time job for many people.

One of the major problems of system administration in today's networks is that despite the fact that all of the components are communicating with one another, it is often difficult for the administrator to "listen in" on the communication to keep track of what is going on or to directly communicate with each component. If communication is even possible, each will have its own language that the administrator will need to learn. For example, monitoring and configuring a 3COM router is different from monitoring and configuring your NT server.

Fortunately, in the last few years, a number of tools and concepts have been developed that address these issues. The key aspects of any system administration tool is to make the monitoring, administration, and maintenance of machines as uncomplicated and cost effective as possible. What this means in terms of what work is automated (or should be automated), what functionality the administration tool requires, and what is "nice to have," will differ from company to company. However, there are a number of general classes of features that are common to all administration products:

- Network management
- Security
- Event management
- Configuration management

- Performance monitoring and management
- Storage management
- Help desk

In a nutshell, the company help desk is the place where users go to get problems solved. Because I feel it is so important to the effective operation of the system as a whole, I have decided to treat the help desk differently and go into much more detail about it later on.

Among the functionality one can find under network management is the able to recognize and work with all of the common network protocols. Here, I am not just referring to the "standard" protocols, such as TCP/IP, NetBEUI, and IPX/SPX, but some of the lesser known ones like DLC. Part of this is the ability to monitor the statistics of the various protocols.

Recognizing the protocols is not enough; the products should also be able to gather statistics on them. That is how many packets have been sent, where they come from, where they are headed, and so forth.

There are two classes of management tools to look at. Each has its own set of benefits and shortcomings. The first is the more common class, especially for people who read the more popular computer magazines such as BYTE and Windows NT magazines. These are utilities and programs that are installed on a single PC. Although there are a number of vendors that provide applications for specific tasks, the two most successful companies in this area are NAI (formerly McAfee and several other companies) and Symantec, both of which provide a wide range of administration and management tools.

The next class is the enterprise suite. In general, these have a different scope than the individual products. One could say that such products provide many of the same functions, but for the system as a whole. For example, there are often network-monitoring tools, virus programs, and so forth.

A number of tools are necessary to effectively manage your system. These include those tools that one normally considers part of system administration (e.g., User Manager, Server Manager), but also includes a number of additional tools.

In this context, I refer to "tool" as anything that an administrator uses to more efficiently manage and monitor the system. For example, one of the most important tools is the "knowledge database" or "knowledge base". This is the collected information of all system administrators, both past and present, as well as information obtained from other sources. For example, part of the "knowledge base" is the Microsoft TechNet CD and from third parties such as MicroHouse and Knowledge Brokers.

Internally, your knowledge base does not necessarily have to have a defined structure. The key aspect is accessibility. Granted, a common structure makes accessing the information easier. However, I would be willing to trade a common structure for more content. I know a number of companies that have spent so much time building a specific structure that they quickly lost interest in converting what documents they have to the new format.

One of the key differences you will find between the individual solutions, such as those from Symantec, and one of the larger, enterprise products, such as from Network Associates, is the integration with existing tools. In general, the single PC products store data in their own proprietary format. Even if it is in a common format, there is little need, if any, to share the information among multiple machines.

When you have one of the enterprise products, they are normally based on some common standard. More often than not, they run on a relational database, such as SQL Server. Although there are some products that store information in an Access or Paradox database, this is becoming less and less common.

Another key difference is the connectivity with other applications. For example, if a system management product runs on the same system as a help desk product, there may be ways to share information. If both access an SQL database, this is generally no problem. Even if the connections are not built-in by default, it is a simple matter to connect them. For example, with some of the help desk products you can easily create a new form that displays the information from a table created by the system management product. It may also be possible that the system management product can create a new entry in the help desk table. This means that you can automatically create trouble tickets/problem reports from the system management tool.

Even if this functionality is not available (e.g., when the two products use different databases), there may be a certain level of indirect communication. For example, it is advisable to get a system management tool that can automatically send email messages when certain events occur. Most of the better help desk tools can monitor incoming email and generate problem reports based on this mail. Therefore, when an event occurs, the system management tool sends a message to the help desk to generate the problem report.

One characteristics that these two types of products have in common is their configurability. At least, the better ones do. Configurability is an important aspect, especially with the enterprise tools. Not every system is identical, and it is useful to be able to define what is monitored and what events should be reported.

For example, both types of programs generally have a component that monitors hard disk space. One of the single-PC products had the default level set to check every hour and report when the free space dropped below 10%. Because PCs do not change that often, monitoring once an hour might be too much. In addition, if your PC has 2GBs, 10% free space means that you have 200 MBs free. This is far too much to be concerned with. Fortunately, the program allows you to change the interval in which it checks the file system, plus it allows you to change the threshold values. For example, I could set it to 1%, which meant 20 MBs. In addition, some programs will allow you to change what is being monitored, such as the free space in percentage or the free space in MBs.

Although there are tools that address each one of these areas (distribution, inventory, and metering), it would be much more effective if you have a single tool that does all three. However, I need to emphasize that this is not always the best solution. For example, if you have a very specific set of applications that specific users have with little or no deviation, there may be less of a need for a metering tool, particularly if users cannot install their own software. You already know who uses what and why. A distribution product would be useful to install upgrades, etc., and an inventory product would help to find improper software (i.e., illegal). However, who uses what software is difficult to determine in larger organizations, when users can install their own software or when users move around a lot.

If you determine that you do not need all of the available functions, then you may be better off purchasing a product with just the functionality you need. However, you may also find yourself in the classic case where the "economies of scale" come into play. That is, it becomes cheaper to buy more things at once. In this case, it means that buying a product with everything in it is cheaper than buying the components individually.

For the long term, buying such an "all-in-one" product may be beneficial for other reasons. For example, one thing you can be sure of is that the information is compatible. That is, the information from each component is stored in a format that can be read by the others. For example, your distribution package writes into the inventory database every time that it installs something.

Even if you decided not to buy the entire package, look to see if the product is modular. That is, you decide to implement the distribution component now, but may add the inventory product later. Is this even possible? If so, is it a matter of simply installing the new component or do you have to reinstall the entire package?

Another very useful example is the ability to distribute software based on existing inventory or other criteria. For example, when you want to install Adobe Acrobat Reader, the inventory software identifies which machines have Acrobat and does not install the reader. When the software is installed, it will need a license. It is therefore a useful functionality when the distribution package can automatically make an entry in the license database.

Another important criterion is that reporting is done from several directions. For example, can you list on what machine a particular package is installed (i.e., to count the number of licenses). and can you list what packages are installed on a particular machine (i.e., to determine if it has a "standard" installation)? Both of these are useful, but not always available.

What format the information is stored in is important in determining its compatibility with other applications. For example, Network Associates stores the information in a Microsoft SQL Server databank, which means it is accessible from a large number of other applications, including Web pages. If the format is proprietary, you may find yourself stuck with the product with no possibility to move to another product.

This is important functionality when you set up your help desk. Unless you end up buying one of the low-end, single-user help desk products, you are likely to find that the help desk package stores the information in an SQL database. In some cases, you have choice of which database, and this choice usually includes MS SQL Server. Some help desk products store their information in an Access database (.MDB), which can be accessed using open database connectivity (ODBC). Therefore, you may not be able to connect the two products directly, but you could easily create a common interface (i.e., a Visual Basic program of an HTML page on your intranet).

Some third-party inventory and licensing product are compatible with SMS. That is, they can either read from or write to the SMS database. This means you can easily add to SMS's functionality by adding the third party licensing program. However, certain functionality for managing licenses (such as software metering) is included in SMS 2.0.

One important thing to look for is to see how well this management software integrates with your help desk product, assuming, of course, that you have one. Therefore, I recommend that you avoid any management software that stores information in the proprietary format. There are a large number of products that store the information in an SQL database. With many products, you even have the choice of which SQL product you want to use. Unfortunately, MS SMS is not one of them, as it requires Microsoft SQL Server. On the other hand, there are the large number of help desk products that support Microsoft SQL Server, such as Network Associates Magic Total Service Desk. Therefore, MS SQL Server may be the right choice.

There are actually two reasons why your management software and help desk software should be integrated like this. First, if a user calls into your hotline, you can quickly determine exactly what hardware and software configuration they have. That is, your help desk software contains a record for each machine, which is linked to the appropriate entry in your management database. If each user is assigned a specific machine, there may be a link from that user to the assigned machine and then to the appropriate record in the systems management database. When the user calls into the help desk, the support person has immediate access to that information.

The other reason why your management software and help desk software should be integrated is that many system management products can generate their own problem reports. For example, the management software may notice that a hard disk is becoming very full. It then generates a problem report in the help desk database. In addition, many products not only allow for automatic creation of problem reports, but also allow for manual reports as well.

Another important thing to look for is how well the system management software integrates with your other applications. Some products allow you to launch other applications from within the management software. For example, the management software may report a hard disk is becoming full and allows you to launch the Microsoft Explorer so that you can check the files on that system yourself. Some allow you to link to files or applications. That is, a data record within the database may be a link to a file that can contain more-detailed information about the problem or maybe information on how it resolves the problem.

One thing I would like to warn you about is the danger of going overboard with management tools. You can really save enough time and effort by employing a product to make the expense cost effective. Many people go overboard and look for a tool that will essentially monitor or even administer every aspect of their system. There are two reasons why this is not always a good idea. First, I worked in places where they spent months looking for the "perfect" product. However, much of the monitoring and administration could have been done by other tools. Rather than being satisfied with one tool that did 80% of the work, they spent months looking for a product that addressed that last 20%.

Here I'm not referring to calendar months, but rather to person-months. The calendar time was well over a year. In that year, the person responsible for the project spent countless hours on the Internet looking at product descriptions, reading brochures, and arranging for demo copies of the products to be sent to his office. The demo copies then had to be installed, tested, and evaluated. Basically, every product was missing one or more features that the MIS manager deemed as being vital for system management. Most of the administrators did not feel this way, but the MIS manager had his own opinions on this. In the end, more time was spent searching for the perfect product than could have ever possibly been saved by using those features. However, because the MIS manage never did any of the work and never asked anyone, he obviously knew better.

Therefore, it is important that you define at the outset what aspect of the system really needs to be monitored and what functionality would simply be "nice to have."

If your company is small enough you may already know this information. On the other hand, even medium-sized companies have too much equipment to be rolled to manage it without some kind of system. Exactly what kind of system you employ will depend on the size of your company as well as exactly what you're trying to accomplish. Even something as simple as a notebook can be extremely effective. At the other end, there are a number of software products that can automate the process for you.

System Management Software

Norton Crash Guard

Norton Crash Guard is a product that is designed to monitor your system to look for and eliminate potential problems. It is targeted for both home and business users who wish to eliminate the frequent and annoying crashes and system freezes when running Windows 95. The diagnostic and reporting facilities that it provides allow more-experienced users and system administrators to identify the exact cause of the problems. Depending on how it is configured, many of these problems can be solved automatically, without user intervention. This is very useful for people with less experience. The package consists of a number of components, each of which can be configured and run separately.

The deluxe version of Norton Crash Guard has an enhancement to live update called Live Update Pro. This will download and install the updates to other software, which will minimize the possibility of crashes and other problems caused by incompatible versions.

The system check component performs scans of memory, the hard disk, the Windows Registry, shortcuts, disk space, disk fragmentation, as well as the necessary information to create a "rescue disk." When the scan is finished, not only are the problems and errors displayed, the system check will also provide suggestions and how to correct them. In many cases, system check winning changes for you. It is also possible to correct all of and identify problems at once. However, this requires that you simply accept the solutions suggested by Crash Guard. Although I have yet to disagree with the suggested solution, it is something that you need to be aware of.

If this is not to your liking, you can automatically correct a subset of the identified problems, or none. Instead, you can click on each problem individually and either correct the problem by hand or have Crash Guard do it for you automatically.

One problem I had is not really the fault of Crash Guard, but rather of the deinstallation program of a number of applications. One of the things that the System Check module checks is file associations. Many applications (typically Microsoft) insist their program become the default association for specific file types and make the change without asking you first. Should you decide to remove that program later, the association is not returned to its original state. When you run System Check, it will report that the application belonging to this particular association is no longer present on your system.

Supplemental to the System Check component is Auto Check. As its name implies, it automatically monitors your system and displays the status information using the Windows taskbar. By default, Auto Check runs several times a day, running the checks you previously defined and, as you expect, correcting or reporting the problems it uncovers. Auto Check will also report on problems that it cannot fix automatically and therefore require user intervention. There are some cases in which the problem is so serious that the user should be notified, whether the problem is fixed automatically or not.

The Crash Guard component can be a lifesaver, particularly if you are like me and do a lot of work during the time between automatic saves in whatever program you're working on. Although I have set many of my programs to automatically save every 10 minutes, even losing that much work can be extremely annoying. In essence, Crash Guard monitors your system for things that are likely to cause the system to crash. In other words, it guards your system against crashes and therefore helps prevent data loss.

Supplemental to this is the anti-freeze component. As its name implies, anti-freeze is used to get things moving again when applications "freeze up." Although this does not work in every case, it has been a lifesaver on a few occasions. Instead of having to resort to pressing Ctrl+Alt+Del and either ending the task or shutting down the system completely, anti-freeze gave the application a little "kick" to get it unstuck. In addition, anti-freeze can be added to the Ctrl+Alt+Del menu, which is extremely useful if the application no longer reacts to either the keyboard or the mouse.

For those of you who make frequent changes to your system, the Norton rescue component will come in handy. This creates an emergency boot floppy that contains a copy of the systemstart files, CMOS data, partition information, and much more.

Rather than simply stopping at problem solving, the Crash Guard package takes this one step further. I am a firm believer that the more you know about your system, the better able you are to support it. It seems that Symantec has applied the same principle to Crash Guard. To this end, the System Guide component displays basic information about your system, including your hardware, such as the processor speed, controllers, memory, hard disk space, and many other things. Added to this are other tools to help you learn more about computers in general. For example, there is an online glossary containing a large number of computer terms. In addition, there are a number of videos that explain how to do a wide range of tasks on your computer and Windows 95.

To further protect your system, CrashGuard comes with a simplified version of Norton AntiVirus, which it refers to as the "starter edition." As with the other components, AntiVirus as SE will run automatically as part of our check or as needed by the user.

However, should you have the full version of Norton AntiVirus, it will be completely integrated with CrashGuard. You will therefore be able to scan your computer but also find files you obtained from the Internet, such as email attachments. Norton AntiVirus has an auto-protect feature that runs constantly to check your system looking for a wide range of viruses.

A system that is well maintained is less likely to crash than one that's left to its own. Unfortunately, it is almost impossible to monitor the Windows 95 system to the point where it never crashes. Therefore, implementing one of the numerous tools available to automatically monitor the system can be a real lifesaver. Addressing this issue Symantec paraphrases one of Microsoft's advertising slogans and asks, "How much work will you lose today?"

The hard drive integrity scan examines the file allocation table of all the hard disks on your system. It can automatically correct problems such as crossing files and lost clusters. This can increase overall stability of your programs and your system, as both of these can cause application hangs or even cause the system to crash.

The Shortcuts Scan can determine if all shortcuts on your system are still valid. This includes MS-DOS program information files (PIF), Internet shortcuts (.URL), and Windows 95 shortcuts (.LNK). Obviously, your system cannot operate properly if referenced files do not exist. Therefore, checking the shortcuts at regular intervals ensures your system's running position is possible.

Another scan performed checks how much free space you have on your hard disks. The performance of your server or workstation may suffer unless there is enough free space. How little space is available before it is reported is something that you can configure yourself. By default, the system will report less than 10% or less than 25 MBs. This is an important difference depending on the size of your hard disk. Although it is possible, you'll be hard pressed to find people running with a hard disk that is only 250 MBs. That is, where 25 MBs means 10% of the hard disk. New computers are typically being delivered with at least 4 GBs. At least, that's the way it is as of this writing. In all likelihood, by the time this book gets to press, 4 GBs may be considered small. Ten percent of this is 400 MBs. This is actually bigger than the first WfWG machines that I administered. If you're concerned with the amount of free space, 400 MBs is quite a lot. Therefore, if your disk is this size, you might want consider only reporting its space that's less than 1%. On the other hand, no real harm is done by reporting too often; it could just be an inconvenience.

One problem that can occur if you have little free hard disk space is disk fragmentation. Here, parts of the file are spread out all over the partition. The more places the system has to look for the different pieces, the longer it will take to load the file. Depending on how many pieces, or fragments, a particular file has, how far apart they are on the hard disk, and the speed of accessing your hard disk, fragmentation can cause significant loss in performance. CrashGuard provides a hard disk optimization scan, which will combine the fragments on the hard disk into contiguous files. The thing to note is that while the system is optimizing, or defragmenting, your system you cannot do much else. Therefore, you should either start this when you go off for lunch or have it run automatically overnight.

The rescue information scan simply verifies that the rescue disk information is up to date. Each time you create a rescue disk, CrashGuard makes a record of this. If you have made significant changes to your system, it is a good idea to update your rescue disk.

For me, a very useful feature is CrashGuard's ability to keep track of the problems it encounters. Among the things that the records is the date and time an application crashed or froze, what types of problems CrashGuard detected, and how it solved them, how severe the problems were, and even which Windows modules, such as DLLs, caused the system to crash or freeze. In addition, CrashGuard also reports on which module it was that identified and/or corrected the problem. By keeping of record of which programs "misbehaved," you could possibly identify some underlying problems in a particular application.

One thing to consider when looking at any product designed to prevent crashes where the system hangs is the amount of resources it takes up itself. On one machine, I installed so many system management tools, anti-virus programs, optimizers, and so forth, that unrecoverable system problems occurred more frequently.

Norton AntiVirus

One of the first anti-virus products to gain international fame and popularity, Norton continues its tradition of providing excellent anti-virus software with version 5.0.

Norton AntiVirus can be considered at the top end in terms of functionality for the non–server-based anti-virus products. It naturally provides protection using standard signature recognition, as well as both static and dynamic heuristics. The latest signature files can be downloaded from Symantec as you need them, and the product even warns you at regular intervals that the virus files are out of date, giving you the opportunity to use the Live Update feature to download them from the Symantec Web site.

One of Symantec's biggest selling points is the Symantec Antivirus Research Center (SARC), which investigates new viruses and preventive measures as well as develops new methodologies to combat unknown viruses that existing heuristics cannot detect.

Most recently, SARC developed the "Bloodhound" technology, which claims to detect 80% of all new and unknown executable viruses. I emphasize the word "executable," as SARC has also developed a variation of Bloodhound specifically designed to look for macro viruses. In addition to just executable and macro viruses, the Bloodhound technology also works in detecting other dangerous code, such as Java applets, ActiveX controls, and Trojan horses.

The basics behind the Bloodhound technology are that it implements both artificial intelligence and expert systems to help identify unknown viruses. The artificial intelligence portion analyzes the suspect program looking for the portions of the code that comprise the logic of the virus. That is, what portions of the virus make the decisions. For example, a virus might only infect programs of a particular size or only those with a particular timestamp. Once the logic areas of the program have been identified, Bloodhound will poke and prod the virus to get it to jump, thinking that it has found the necessary criteria to be activated. Because the Bloodhound technology examines every logic area of the program, it is capable of detecting more viruses than simply running the virus inside of a virtual machine.

However, having the virus jump is not enough. Having certain logic in the program does not necessarily mean that it is a virus. Bloodhound uses an expert system to make intelligent guesses about a program. An expert system is a system of rules and decisions based on these rules. Although it can never be 100% accurate, expert systems are used in many fields other than just finding viruses and are very highly sought after. Even though the expert system really only guesses, the success rate is extremely high.

One area that expert systems have been extremely successful is in fraud cases. Credit card companies use expert systems to identify unusual buying patterns, which often indicates a stolen card. For example, the card is rarely used for several years, then suddenly thousands of dollars are being spent. I once got a call from one of my credit card companies after a purchase had been made on the other side of the country from where I was.

Another example is insurance fraud. Doctors who have sudden increases in business near the time when quarterly claims are due tend to raise a red flag for the insurance companies. I read of one company where the expert system they used saved the company several million dollars in claims in 6 months including a doctor who did surgery on herself (the patient used her maiden name).

One of the new features is something Symantec calls Quarantine. What this does is to copy (that is, isolate) possibility infected files until you are able to deal with them. This not only ensures that other files on your system stay safe, it prevents you from accidentally giving access to them to someone who is not protected by an anti-virus package.

Symantec has also improved on their Live Update by configuring Norton AntiVirus so that it only downloads the most current signature and update information. In previous versions (and still with many other anti-virus products), there is a single file containing all of the changes since the most recent release. If you update your system repeatedly, you end up getting the same information more than once.

The "Scan and Deliver" wizard is an additional tool to help identify unknown viruses. Infected files are first place in the Quarantine to protect the rest of your system. The wizard then helps you to send the files to the SARC for analysis. Should it turn out to be a new virus, you are sent new virus definitions. Quarantine keeps track of all files you have sent to the quarantine area as well as those that you have sent to SARC for analysis.

Norton AntiVirus is also "Internet aware" in that you can configure various options to protect yourself while surfing. You can now configure the program to monitor files you download from the Internet as well as email. In addition, Norton AntiVirus will protect you against other malicious code that you might find in other places, such as ActiveX controls and Java applets.

Figure 8–2 shows the main screen. Here you select the drives you want to scan as well as whether you want to enable "Auto-Protect," which does several protection-related tasks in the background to ensure the integrity of your system. In the center of the screen is an indicator showing you what the date of your virus definitions file is, so you know whether you should get an update or not. In addition, you have access from here to the Quarantine, scan logs, Live Update and the most current list of viruses.

Clicking the Options button brings you to Figure 8–3. As you can see by the register tabs, there are a number of different areas that you can configure.

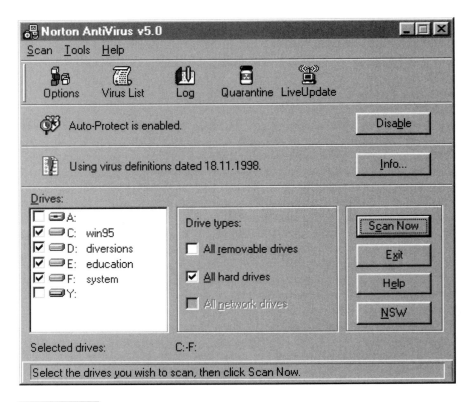

FIGURE 8–2   Norton AntiVirus 5.0 main screen.

The start location is the scanner itself. Here you define what areas of the system to scan, what kinds of files, and what the system should do if it finds a virus.

At the bottom is a button labeled "Heuristics." This is used to configure the sensitivity of the Bloodhound technology as it scans your system. The higher the sensitivity, the more thorough Bloodhound is in detecting viruses. Keep in mind, however, that this means it will take longer to scan your system.

In addition to defining what areas to scan and what kind of files, you can also tell Norton AntiVirus which files and subdirectories to exclude. By default, the primary Microsoft Office applications are included (even though none were on my system). This is because they exhibit "virus-like" behavior by making unexpected changes to your system without asking and other behavior characteristics of a virus. In addition, you can exclude programs from generating warning messages when they exhibit other "virus-like" behavior, such as low-level formatting a hard disk, writing to boot records, and writing to program files.

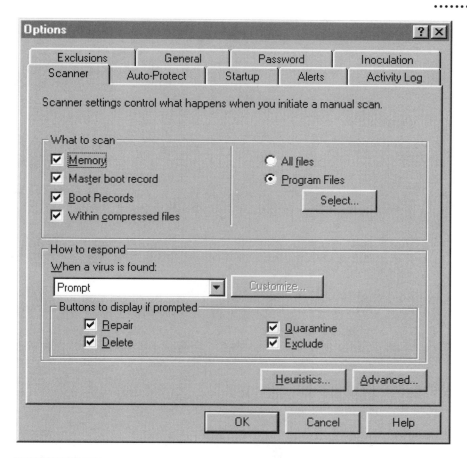

FIGURE 8–3 Norton AntiVirus 5.0 configuration options.

How Norton AntiVirus behaves with Auto-Protect enabled is configured using the "Auto-Protect" tab (where else?). You can tell the system to automatically scan the system each time it is started as well as when other basic operations are performed, such as running a program copying, moving, and even opening a file; as well as creating or downloading a file. When a virus is detected, the option is also as varied. For example, you can do anything from prompting the user, denying access, automatically copying the file to the Quarantine and even shutting down the computer. A bit harsh if it reports a false positive whenever you started MS Word. However, it's your choice.

In other software I have seen, the anti-virus options could be password protected. That means that only the person with the password can change any of the options. However, this was generally all or nothing. That is, either the configuration was blocked or it wasn't. Norton AntiVirus allows you to password-protect different aspects of the virus protection. For example, a user may be able to change the exclusion list, but not the Auto-Protect settings.

Norton AntiVirus also has several options regarding the scanning, which you can log. In addition, you can define the maximum size of the log as well as the location of the logfile, which you can then access from the main screen.

Symantec also provides both a server and firewall version of the Norton AntiVirus software. The server version is installed on a Windows NT server and can be used to automatically distribute the client to Windows NT workstations. A distribution utility is provided to allow you to manage the distribution in that you can not only start the distribution from a central console, but also keep track of which systems have been updated and which have not.

In essence, you have the same basic functionality as with the standalone version, including the Bloodhound technology and the various levels of configuration. In addition, alerts can be sent to a central SNMP server or to specific users via email (SMTP).

Norton Utilities

Norton Utilities has been long recognized as a leader in workstation administration tools. In fact, if you look at the marketing literature of other similar products, you will see that in most every case, the product will compare itself with Norton Utilities.

Norton Utilities is a palette of services and programs that helps the user to identify and correct a wide range of Windows problems. In many cases, Norton Utilities can be configured so that problems can be corrected immediately, as soon as they are identified.

Perhaps the central program to the Norton Utilities is the Norton System Doctor. This monitors various aspects of your system, including system resource usage, disk free space, a disk fragmentation, virus scan, who, and many other aspects of your system. Figure 8–4 shows you the Norton System Doctor window. The System Doctor also shows you the status of your virus definition files.

The program can be configured to automatically fix specific problems as well as report to the user when these problems are occurring. The messages that appear are usually sufficient for even the most novice user to understand what is happening. Unfortunately, not every user will be able to decide what to do. Even so, System Doctor will step the user through each part of the process to correct the problem, including starting the appropriate application from the Norton Utilities palette.

The sensors that are displayed can be configured to appear in several different ways. For example, you can choose to display the information as a dial (like in Figure 8–4), a bar, a digital counter, or a histogram, which shows the behavior over time.

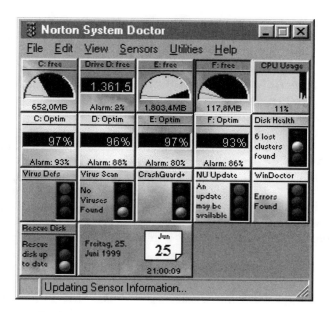

FIGURE 8-4   Norton System Doctor.

Alarms can be defined, which alert the user to various events. What the thresholds are to alert the user are different for different kinds of activity, but can also be different within a specific category. For example, your main one to know is when there are 100 MBs free on your system partition, but you can wait until there are only 50 MBs free on the other drives.

System Doctor works together with the CrashGuard by monitoring system resources. If system resources get too low, this is reported to the user.

One of the newest additions to be palette of tools is Norton WinDoctor. As its name implies, WinDoctor scans your system looking for existing problems which are specifically Windows related. Norton System Doctor looks for system-related problems. For example, fragmentation on your hard disk is a problem whether you are running Windows or not; that is the responsibility of System Doctor. However, registry problems are Windows specific and are handled by WinDoctor.

Problems are grouped according to their cause or which area of the system they affect. For example, registry problems are grouped together, missing shortcuts are grouped together and unused DLLs are grouped together. This allows the user to correct all problems of each single type at the same time, rather than having to select each specific problem individually.

For example, it will scan your registry looking for entries that are either problematic or "orphaned." Orphaned entries are those that referred to some component that is no longer on the system. For example, this occurs when you delete an application simply by removing its directory, rather than using the uninstall function. Obviously, simply removing the directory does not remove the registry entries.

Figure 8–5 shows you the Norton WinDoctor main window. On the left side are the various categories of problems and on the right are the specific problems. In this example, two problems were caused by moving a directory from one drive to another. When you double click on the entry, you are give different choices on a course of action depending on what the problems is. In this case, you could delete the shortcut, rename it, or change the properties so it points to the right place.

Norton Utilities has an integrated version of Norton CrashGuard, which as we discussed previously, is designed to prevent applications from crashing while at the same time has the ability to "unfreeze" applications that have gotten hung up.

Norton SpeedStart, as its name implies, is designed to speed up starting of applications. It works in the background and applies to every application and therefore requires no configuration. If you are already running Windows 98, the same technology is built-in.

All of these tools and gadgets are worthless if you cannot boot your system. Norton Utilities provides the ability to create eight "rescue" disks, which-copy all of your DOS startup files (CONFIG.SYS, AUTOEXEC.BAT) as well as CMOS and partition information stored on the floppy. In addition, several

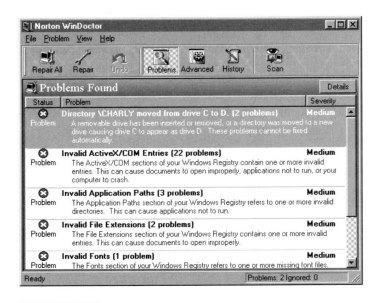

FIGURE 8–5 Norton WinDoctor.

DOS basic utilities are copied to disk, which help you discover and solve the problem.

By default, a couple dozen files and programs will be copied to your rescue disk. So many in fact that it is not correct to call it "a" rescue disk. Instead, you end up getting three disks that contain the necessary files to recover your system. Fortunately, you can select which files are copied as well as add new ones to the list.

There is one thing to complain about and that is there does not appear to be any way to automatically back up the registry. Although the Registry Editor will do that for you, Symantec did not seem to think that it was part of the necessary information needed to recover your system. There have been several cases where I had to reinstall my system because the registry was trashed and I did not have a valid backup.

A Rescue Recovery Wizard is provided to guide you through the necessary steps to be able to recover your system. In addition, the recovery Wizard is able to boot a full copy of Windows either from a ZIP or a JAZ drive. You can therefore save a complete copy of your system and use it to recover should you not be able to boot from the hard disk.

Norton Utilities also provide a "lite" version of Norton AntiVirus. Although it provides the same level of protection, it does not have all of the features.

Speed Disk is a tool that strives to increase the performance of your hard disk. Over time, your disk will become fragmented, as parts of files are spread out all over the disk. If the system has to go hunting for each of the parts, it takes longer to load applications and access data.

Speed Disk also optimizes your system by moving in frequently-used files and directories to the beginning of the desk. This decreases the access time considerably, because the heads do not need to move as far. In addition, files that are less frequently used are moved to the end of the disk. If files are frequently modified, they are actually placed ahead of all the free space on the disk to decrease access time even further.

In support of the Speed Disk is the Space Wizard, which is used to identify infrequently used files as well as duplicates of files. In many cases, the duplicate files are not needed and Space Wizard gives the user the choice of compressing, deleting, or moving the duplicates to free up space on the hard disk.

As its name implies, the Norton Disk Doctor is used to detect and solve a wide range of problems on your disk drives. You can use Disk Doctor not only on your hard disks but also on your floppies should they become damaged.

Norton Utilities also has two tools for managing the system registry. The Norton Registry Editor is used to access the registry directly, allowing users to examine as well as add, modified, or delete registry information. It is also used to troubleshoot registry configuration settings as well as create a backup copy of the registry. The Norton Registry Tracker does just that: It tracks changes to the registry. This allows the users to restore the registry to the state it was in before specific changes were made.

Norton Protection is a supplement to the Windows recycle bin. Whereas the recycle bin protects you if you intentionally delete a file, Norton Protection protects against overwritten files as well as files that are deleted from within an application, even a DOS window.

The Unerase Wizard guides the user through the process of recovering erased files. As long as the data has not been overwritten, the Unerase Wizard should be able to recover the file. However, even if some portion has been overwritten, the Unerase Wizard can help you recover as much as possible.

Supporting the entire recovery process is built into this utility. It takes a "snapshot" of different aspects of your system. This increases the likelihood of a full recovery from a system crash as well as cases where you accidentally delete files or directories. Norton System Doctor monitors the image files, ensuring they are updated as needed.

Norton CleanSweep

The goal of Norton CleanSweep is to "sweep" your system clean of unneeded programs and files. If you are familiar with Quarterdeck's product Clean-Sweep, you may be slightly confused as to why Norton has come out with a product of the same name with the same functionality. This is quite simply because Symantec purchased Quarterdeck in early 1999 and CleanSweep was the only Quarterdeck product that remained essentially unchanged.

Although Norton Utilities can remove certain kinds of unused files, CleanSweep helps clean up a wider range of files and in places the Norton Utilities does not look. For example, as you browse the Internet, you collect a number of cookies, ActiveX control, and other files that you do not need to hang on to.

You can configure CleanSweep to monitor your system and remove files automatically. However, because we do not live in a perfect word, CleanSweep provides two mechanisms to protect you from deleting too much. The SafetySweep features back up all files before they are deleted. In essence, this is the same as the undelete feature, but the files are protected and will not be overwritten until you remove them by hand. In addition, when SafetySweep is on, users can only select to remove files that Clean-Sweep has deemed completely safe to remove.

CleanSweep Safe is another feature that allows you to protect specific kinds of files. If either you or CleanSweep removes one of these files, it is stored in the safe until you delete it by hand.

One interesting feature is that CleanSweep uses color-coded "safety levels." These warn users prior to making irreversible changes. The colors green, yellow, and red indicate increasing levels of "danger," with red being "too dangerous to remove."

CleanSweep monitors the system during the installation of applications and records what changes were made to the system. When you deinstall the application, CleanSweep monitors deinstallation to ensure that all of the components have been properly removed. Rather than rescanning your system, CleanSweep knows what changes are made and ensures they are undone.

CleanSweep is careful not to undo changes that other components may need. This is accomplished using an application "knowledge base." This is a database of a large number of existing applications containing information about the changes each application makes. This provides CleanSweep with the necessary information to ensure all unused components are removed, but not too much.

WRQ Express Meter

As we discussed previously, being able to accurately identify the software you are using can not only save you money, but can also save you from any legal troubles. Not only do you need to know what is being used, you need to know who is using it. Having an accurate and easy to use monitoring software is a key part of this.

Regardless of where your software is physically located, it will be accurately identified by Express Meter. Although there are only clients available for the Microsoft operating systems, it does not matter to Express Meter where the software lies. Therefore, if you need the extra performance and are therefore connected to another kind of file server, such as Novell NetWare or UNIX, Express Meter can identify it.

Although having a metering product that you can rely on to accurately measure software usage is a great first step, there is more to it. All such software can do is deliver numbers. That is, there is no real information. It is up to you to make the decision about what these numbers mean. However, it doesn't have to be.

Express Meter can be configured to monitor software in groups, which are typically sold in bundles or suites. For example, if you had MS Word, MS Excel and MS PowerPoint, Express Meter could be told to monitor these as the MS Office bundle. It can then make recommendations about what could or should be purchased as suites and what as individual products.

A key aspect is the amount of time spent collecting and processing the information to accurately manage the licenses. I worked in one company where there were so many offices and software packages that license management was almost a full-time job. The primary reason is that it was all done by hand. Although we used SMS to count the machines, SMS is not very good at identifying software which is used, only what is installed.

I know from experience how time-consuming it can be when you have to collect the information by hand. Therefore, the automation that Express Meter provides is especially welcome. Once the client is installed, it monitors software used and collects it in a database, which can then be analyzed as necessary.

One thing to be aware of is that something like Express Meter won't give you the right answers if you don't wait long enough. One of the first things is to analyze your usage patterns. For example, users may not use PowerPoint much until the end of the quarter when reports are due. Therefore, you won't see much PowerPoint usage if you analyze the information after collecting it for just a month.

Express Meter does more than just collect usage information. First, it allows you to specify how many licenses you have purchased for each product. You can also include the price you paid, so Express Meter can provide information on how much the licenses are costing you. This is done through the "Savings Meter," which tells you how often you go over your license limit, how much new licenses would cost, and so forth.

Express Meter can not only monitor who has access to particular software, but can regulate it as well. For example, if you have a limited number of licenses for a particular software product, you can configure Express Meter to prevent additional users from using the software until an existing user exits the applications. However, if you want, you could simply warn the user by telling he/she the license limit has been exceeded (or you can do nothing at all).

What do you do if there are several people waiting for an application? Simple, you create a waiting list for the product. That means the user who has been waiting the longest gets access first. Part of this is the ability to warn current users that others are waiting, particularly if the application has been idle for awhile. It is also possible to force users out of the application that have been idle longer than the adjustable time limit.

How the information is presented to you is as important as what information is collected. Express Meter has a large library of predefined reports to allow you to see the information from different views.

More than likely, you are not going to want to monitor everything. For example, NOTEPAD.EXE comes with Windows NT, so you know that if the operating system is licensed, the program is licensed as well. Express Meter allows you to specify what applications are monitored. In addition, you can tell Express Meter that it should only monitor applications that are launched locally, only those launched from a network server, or both.

Unfortunately for the system administrator, computer software does not remain static. Therefore, Express Meter will not always be able to identify every product. In many cases, it will be able to read information from the program binary to determine to what application it belongs. However, this is not always possible, so Express Meter allows you to add entries by hand and WRQ provides updates of the software database.

One extremely important thing to note is that the information collected by Express Meter is accepted by the Software Publishers Association (SPA) for its license audits. If you have a volume license agreement, you may be contractually obligated to submit to auditing by someone of the vendor's choosing. This may not be the SPA, but a separate organization, which will normally accept the SPA's determination of the validity of information provided by metering software. Therefore, the auditing agency would then accept the information provided by Express Meter.

WRQ Express 2000

Paired with Express Meter is Express 2000. As its name implies, Express 2000 is a monitoring package that checks your system for potential as well as existing year 2000 (Y2K) problems. Like Express Meter, Express 2000 will inventory your software and report on what software is installed and if there are any known Y2K problems.

Express 2000 has an added benefit of giving you an inventory of what software is installed, including the version number, which helps you identify out-of-date software. It can also identify PCs that have BIOSes that are not Y2K compliant.

To help you plan your Y2K strategy, Express 2000 can be used to prioritize your applications in terms of addressing any known problems. It monitors application usage of a period, which you define yourself. The monitoring reports tells you how many people access each program, how often, as well as how long they use it. You can then see the usage patterns of each application, which helps you prioritize which problems should be addressed first. You can store this information in the Express 2000 database and indicate the status of each product. For example, applications can be marked "waiting for vendor" if you have ask for a Y2K compliance statement.

By adding Express Meter, you have complete control over your Y2K problem. Not only can you monitor applications and identify Y2K problems, but you can specify what should be done. For example, you can configure Express meter to prevent users from running non–Y2K-compliant software until it is updated.

Executive Software's Diskeeper

Microsoft marketing would have you believe that the NTFS is so well designed that fragmentation is not a problem. Although there are some mechanisms built in to limit the problem, you cannot completely eliminate it without sacrificing performance in other areas. When the NTFS writes a file, it will often leave space at the end of the file so the file can grow. This saves time over writing the file completely to a new, larger location. If the space between this file and the next file becomes too small, the NTFS either has to move the file completely (which takes time) or put the end of the file somewhere else, which causes fragmentation. On the average, fragmentation starts becoming a concern after the disk is about 50% full. However, once the disk reaches 80% full, fragmentation becomes a problem.

You could prevent fragmentation by always storing the file where it can remain contiguous. However, this means you would often have to move large portions of the file to new locations. This would not only cancel the performance gain achieved by having an unfragmented disk, it actually takes more time and is a greater burden on the system.

So what can you do? It seems to be a Catch-22. Either you lose performance by fragmentation or you lose it by preventing it. Well, that's true, but nothing has been said yet about correcting the problem once it has occurred. That is, defragmenting the disk. The solution lies in a defragmenting software like Diskeeper.

There are many defragmenting tools available for DOS and Windows 3.x/95/98, which I talked about for some of the other products I discussed. What makes Diskeeper unique is that it runs on both the Windows NT workstation and server. This is an extremely important difference, because of the complexities of the NTFS over the FAT file system.

What Diskeeper does is to read the Master File Table (MFT) one file after another. Each file is checked individually to see if moving it will make the free space more contiguous. Contrast this to a system whereby files are moved to fill in gaps on the file system in order to create a large free space at the beginning of the file system. The files are then moved back into the free space. This has the advantage of potentially reducing the fragmentation more. However, it takes more time and suffers from the law of diminishing returns. (Is the performance gain really worth that extra work? Typically, no.)

Note that the files are not actually moved, but rather copied. Provided the file has not been opened for exclusive use, Diskeeper makes a contiguous copy somewhere else on the disk. When the copying is completed, Diskeeper makes a bit-by-bit check to ensure the files are identical. When the copy has been verified, Diskeeper changes the pointers in the MFT so it will now point to the new copy and the space it previously occupied is freed.

An interesting aspect is that this is done at the file system level. Diskeeper does not open the file when it makes the copy as with other applications. In addition, this is task that does the defragmenting at a low priority so as to limit the effects on your system as much as possible. Because the files are not copied in the traditional sense, and the change in the pointers is made at the file system level, this method is extremely safe, even if you lost power. The original file is still intact until after the "transfer" is made and could be restored in the unlikely case where the system went down at the exact moment the new pointer was being written. Once Diskeeper is sure the new copy is in place, it frees up the space previously occupied.

There are a couple of aspects of Diskeeper's behavior that are confusing to the uninitiated. First, Diskeeper does not completely remove fragmentation. For the most part, it is simply a matter of diminishing returns. Second, there are cases when Diskeeper cannot access the file; for example, when it is opened for exclusive access. One common example is the Windows NT paging file. However, there are two solutions. First, create a large, permanent paging file when the system is first installed. That way the file is created contiguously. Second, you can temporarily move the paging file to another partition.

Steps to Create a Contiguous Paging File

- Start the system applet in the control panel.

- Select virtual memory.

- Create a paging file on a different drive with the same size.

- Set the maximum and minimum on the first drive both to zero.

- Reboot the system so the new paging file is used.

- Run your defragmentation software.

- Redo steps 1–4 to recreate the paging file on the first drive.

- Reboot to activate the paging file on the original partition.

One trick is to make the maximum and minimum size of the paging file the same value. This ensures that the paging file does not change size and therefore does not become fragmented.

PowerDesk

On the one hand, it is difficult to justify something like Mijenix's in a business setting. At first glance, it appears to be a full-featured "toy." There are a lot of things that are "nice to have," but a direct benefit that can be converted into dollars is not easy to see.

However, time is money. If users can work more efficiently, there will be a cost saving (if not easily identifiable). This is one of the key issues behind something like PowerDesk.

PowerDesk is actually composed of two components, the PowerDesk proper, which is an excellent replacement for the Windows Explorer, and a toolbar, which provides more than just a quick starter for your applications. Together they are an extremely useful addition to your system.

Figure 8–6 shows you the PowerDesk. As you can see, it has the same basic appearance as the Windows Explorer. At the top are the menus and toolbars and the bottom are the windows displaying your drives and directories (left pane) and the files and directories (right pane). The way files and directories are presented in the file pane is the same as for Windows Explorer, in that you can have icons, a list, and detailed list and sort the files based on any of the standard criteria.

However, there are a couple of nice differences. First, you can sort by the file's extension. Windows Explorer sorts them by the type of file it is, which is not necessarily the same as the file extension. DLLs are "application extensions," which sorts them next to the files ending in .EXE, which are applications.

The second difference is the ability to show multiple directories without the need to open up a second copy of PowerDesk. Another time when you

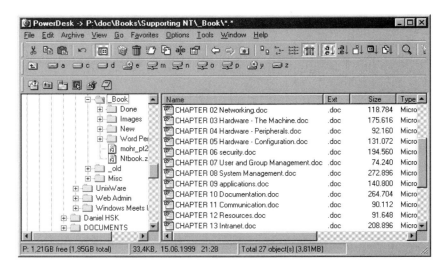

FIGURE 8–6   Mijenix PowerDesk.

do not need an additional copy is when copying or moving large numbers of files. With Windows Explorer, you can open a second window while the first is busy copying the files. The difference with PowerDesk is that the copy (or move) runs as a distinct process and therefore separates itself from the original PowerDesk process. You can then continue as needed. Also, should Windows hiccup and the PowerDesk process gets killed, the copy will still continue.

Like your typical Web browser, PowerDesk also has a list of favorites. These can be programs, files, or anything else you can save on the file system. Entries in your favorite list are stored as links in a directory (i.e., C:\PowerDesk\Favorites), which allows you to configure a large number of favorites at once.

One difference is the very bottom toolbar, which is not found with the Windows Explorer. PowerDesk refers to this as the "launch bar" as it is used to launch applications. You can drag an icon or a file onto the launch bar and the appropriate icon will appear. You can also add buttons by hand or edit existing ones. In general, you can configure the same kinds of parameters as you can with an icon on your desktop. Also like icons on your desktop, you can also drag directory icons onto the launch bar, which immediately displays the directory in the file pane. However, here you can specify different icons for different folders.

PowerDesk expands on the functionality of the Windows Explorer in a couple of different areas. The first is the sheer number of functions that are possible from within PowerDesk. First, all of the functionality is available from a menu at the top of the PowerDesk window. This is in contrast to Windows Explorer where certain functions are only available from the context menu and therefore only available in Microsoft-defined contexts. For example, you can only format a floppy by right-clicking the A: drive in Windows Explorer, which you may have to scroll up to find. With PowerDesk you just need to select the appropriate entry in the Tools menu.

The same thing applies to things like access to the control panel, a command prompt (DOS) Window, recycle bin, adding/removing programs, creating a rescue disk, and so forth. Yes, these things are already available on your system. The thing is that they are scattered all over the place. Here, they are all in one place and you do not need to waste time looking for the things you need.

Time will also be saved with functionality that the Windows Explorer does not have. For example, the context menu for directories (which you get by clicking an open area in the file pane) is very limited at what you can do. You can create new files of specific types, arrange the icons, and look at the directories properties, but not much else. With PowerDesk you can do all of that, plus move to different directories and drives, access your favorites list, select and deselect specific files (also using a filter), plus move back and forth through the directories you have visited. Yes, some of these are available elsewhere and some may not be absolutely necessary. However, if this functionality saves you just 15 minutes a day, that's about 5 hours per month!

The Tools menu also contains some other interesting features. In addition to the disk functions, such as formatting and copying, you can also erase disks, create a rescue disk, as well as map network drives. In addition, you can both compare and synchronize the contents of directories, which is something that I waited on for a long time.

Built into the PowerDesk is a file viewer. By clicking on the magnifying glass on the right end of the toolbar, the viewer pane is opened up. Clicking on a file will display different things depending on what kind of file it is. For example, text files as simply displayed without any changes; for executables and DLLs, you are shown technical details of the program; JPEG and GIF are converted and displayed as images.

One of the nifty things is that PowerDesk does not assume it is the only such application a person has ever used. Therefore, you can configure the keyboard hotkeys to be the same as either Norton Command, X-Tree Gold, or the standard PowerDesk configuration.

Another nice thing is the ability to jump back to the directory you were just in, even if it is on a different drive. PowerDesk keeps track of where you have been, so like the Forward and Back buttons of your browser, you can move back and forth between the directories you have visited.

PowerDesk is provided with several supplemental tools that are very useful. The most significant one is the PowerDesk Toolbar. This is a separate application, which provide a toolbar with a wide range of functions. When first started, the PowerDesk Toolbar starts the Toolbar Wizard to ask you about the basic configuration of the toolbar. You have the option to create a floating toolbar, one that is locked to the edge of the window or is part of the system tray. I prefer the locked variant, as it is too small as part of the system tray and gets in the way when it's floating (or I can't find it at all).

Figure 8–7 shows you the PowerDesk Toolbar, which I have configured on my system. From left to right are a configurable clock, QuickLaunch icons, and system monitor indicators. This is what I have configured, but there are several more functions provided.

During the initialization process, the PowerDesk Toolbar loads the folders from your Start Menu, giving you immediate access to all of the applications, as well as the other junk that ends up in these folders. Personally, I do not use this feature, as all of my applications are loaded on the PowerDesk Toolbar as QuickLaunch icons.

Another function is "MultiView." Here you can define a number of virtual windows, in which you can start different applications. By either clicking the appropriate icon in the toolbar or by configuring a hotkey, you can move back and forth between the windows. If you need to switch between fairly regularly, using the hotkey is much more efficient (in my opinion) than clicking the appropriate icon on the Windows taskbar.

Another function I do not use is the ability to configure multiple clocks. Why would this be important? Well, assume you have an office in a different location that is in a different time zone. If it's 1 or 2 hours, you can usually do the math in you head. However, I have found that the greater the time difference, the "nicer" it is to have the clock in front of you.

Three other functions, which I do not use are the print manager, command line window, and the system control. I don't have that many printers that I need to manager. Because I usually issue a lot of commands when I am at the command line, a single command does not have the functionality I need. The system control is used to restart or shutdown Windows as well as log you off. This is a functionality I hopefully need only once a day and the only time I used it was by accident, and my system shut down before my eyes.

On the other hand, one function that I have grown to rely on is the system monitor. I have several configured, which monitor CPU time, memory, and system resources. I do not know how many times I have *not* become frustrated when Windows 95 seems to hang. I see that status indicator for the CPU is constantly close to 99% and at least it is changing. I know the system is really doing something, and it is just a matter of time before things are back to normal.

FIGURE 8–7 The PowerDesk Toolbar.

Previously, I might have become impatient and rebooted the system. However, this would not have necessarily solved my problem. There are some applications that occasionally take up all the CPU time; for example, indexing functions for certain word processing packages. If I reboot the system, the indexing is not completed so it needs to start up again.

I have also found the system monitors useful when I begin to run out of memory or system resources. The system may be reacting slowly, I look at the system monitor and know that I need to shut down some applications before my memory problem becomes critical.

Another tool provided is the size manager. This gives you a graphic overview of the space taken up on each of your drives. There are several different ways of viewing the information, such as whether sizes are reported in bytes, kilobytes, blocks, and so forth. You can also see how much space files are actually taking up as compared to just getting a sum of their sizes.

PowerDesk also provides an enhanced file finder. In my opinion, it would be better to call it "advanced" in view of all of the features it has. Obviously, it has the same functionality as the "find files or directories" program in Windows. One addition is the ability to find files by attributes as well as the file association.

In addition, the search criteria are more advanced than what Windows provides. Instead of looking for sizes greater than or less than, you can search for files in a specific size range or even files that are not within that size range. You can also check for files that are close to a specific size (within 25% or 50%). Instead of looking for files that were modified or created within a specific period, you can select specifically created, modified, or accessed.

However, I think the most powerful aspect is the ability to save the search results. The Windows finder will only save the search criteria (which PowerDesk does, as well). However, there is no way in Windows to save the list of files you find. PowerDesk can.

Mijenix also provides ZipMagic. As its name implies, this is a package of tools that allows you to not only create but also manage your ZIP files and other archives. Perhaps the most significant aspect is that ZipMagic is actually a supplement to the operating system. As such, it can display compressed archives as directories, giving you direct access to the individual files. You can copy these files in and out of the archive as well as starting applications by double-clicking a file. Because the decompression occurs at the operating system level, all other programs see the archives as directories, as well.

Note that this does not apply to just files using the ZIP compression method. Instead, ZipMagic supports all of the common archiving methods, whether compressed or not. As of this writing, ZipMagic supports the following formats:

- ARC
- ARK
- ARJCAB

- DWC
- GZ
- LHA/LZH
- PAK
- RAR
- TAR
- TAR
- Z
- ZOO

As well as the common email attachment formats:

- UUencode
- XXencode
- MIME/64
- BinHex

ZipMagic also provides plug-ins for Netscape Navigator, Microsoft Internet Explorer, as well as several common email packages. When downloading files from the Internet, you can have ZipMagic decompress them automatically.

One problem may crop up when doing backups. If the backup program were to see the files as directories, it would save the individual files and not the archive as a unit. ZipMagic solves that problem by allowing you to specify the drive where archives should be seen as files or you can turn off ZipMagic at times when the backup is running. You can also tell ZipMagic which applications will always see archives as files.

Taking this one step further is Mijenix's product FreeSpace. Like Zip-Magic, FreeSpace is an operating system supplement or enhancement, and therefore activities are significantly faster than separate applications. Using its own Dynamic File System Enhancement, FreeSpace performs the compression and decompression on the fly, with no real noticeable performance loss.

A key feature of FreeSpace is that you can chose which files and directories will be compressed. Other programs, like Windows' DriveSpace, require you compress entire drives. Compressing files or directories becomes as easy as other file operations. When you right-click a file or directory, there is an entry in the context menu to compress the selected object.

A FreeSpace "analyzer" is also provided for you to monitor various aspects of your drives, such as how much free space is available, how many clusters are free, and so forth. Many file activities are also available here, such as moving and copying files, as well as compression and decompression functions.

Fix-It 99

In the beginning of 1999, Mijenix entered the world of system utilities with Fix-It 99. For a first effort, they did an excellent job. In fact, despite being the first version, this is a fantastic product. Everything is in a single package, unlike other products that have the functionality spread out over several different products and different interfaces, which all have a different apperance. This common interface makes learning how to use Fix-It 99 a lot easier than many products.

Fix-It has integrated all of the tools that other companies sell separately. For example, some vendors will sell you one product that detects and repairs problems in the system and then another one that removes unused files. Fix-It, on the other hand, provides both of these functions within a single product.

Figure 8–8 shows you the "Disks and Files" portion of the product. On the left side, you see the domain of functional areas of the product. On the right side, you see the specific programs for that area. Each one of these is actually a button that starts the necessary function. Note that a separate program doesn't get launched, but rather it all remains within the single Fix-It window. That means that the appearance remains consistent.

If you are familiar with the functionality and behavior of system utilities in general, I find useful to be able to configure the various aspects from a

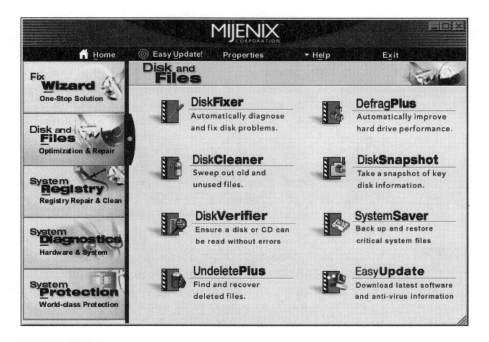

FIGURE 8–8   Fix-It 99 disk and file utilities.

central location rather than having to bounce around all over the program. Fix-It has addressed this issue. At the top of the main window is a properties button, which when clicked allows you to configure the behavior and characteristic of the entire product.

The FixWizard is a function that allows you to diagnose and correct problems all over your system. Rather than having to start each function individually (which means starting separate programs with some packages), Fix-It can be configured to run through the entire suite at once.

Fix-It not only improves the interface, it has improved on many of the technologies. For example, IntelliCluster is a component that monitors your system and keeps track of the programs you run, how often you run them, as well as which files each program uses, including the data files, DLLs, and so forth.

When you tell Fix-It to begin defragmenting your disk, the DefragPlus component uses this information to organize the files on your disk. Therefore, the hard disk heads do not need to travel as far and as a result access is quicker.

DefragPlus speeds up access even further by consolidating frequently accessed files and storing them in the same general area on the hard disk. DefragPlus actually groups files into two categories: frequently accessed and frequently modified. Each of these groups is given a separate "zone" on the hard disk, and files that fall into this category are stored in that zone.

This makes sense, because frequently modified files should be accessed quickly. However, you need to provide room for them to grow. Therefore, the frequently modified file zone is located next to the free space on the disk so it can use that free space without becoming fragmented too quickly. You have the ability to configure what Fix-It considers frequently accessed and frequently modified. The default in both cases is 30 days. That is, files not accessed for the last 30 days are not considered frequently accessed.

Fix-It also has a function to check the Y2K compliance. Although this checks a wide range of issues, it is limited to just your real-time clock, but BIOS, and Windows itself. It does not check applications.

The System Explorer provides you information about the current state of your system. As with other packages, the System Explorer will show you what drivers are installed, outputs the content of various configuration files, what drives you have (including network drives) and how full they are, and many other things.

One very nice thing is that the System Explorer will show you which programs are running. Several other programs will show you which programs are running, but only the ones that you see in the task manager. There are quite a few programs and system tasks that are not displayed in the task manager. As a result, they are not displayed by many different tools.

However, this is not limited to just which programs are running and how much memory they are using, but every other thing you can conceive of. You are shown which modules are being accessed, how much stack and heap is being used, which threads of the program are being run, and so forth. All of this information can be saved to file or printed as a report.

For the most part, all of this functionality is available in other products. Some companies provide the functionality in several different packages, but it is available. Perhaps the most impressive aspect (in my opinion) is WinCustomizer. WinCustomizer allows you to customize a great many aspects of your system. A great many are accessible from other programs, but it is very nice to see all of them in one place.

However, there are a number that I have not been able to figure out how to do except by making changes to the registry. One place is the logo that Windows displays while it is starting up and shutting down. For example, I'm not interested in knowing I should wait while the system is shutting down. I notice. All I am interested in is knowing right now to turn my computer off. It is nice to be able to disable the shutdown logo and I would swear the system now takes less time to shutdown than it did before. If you like having notices, but don't like what they say, you can challenge which bitmap is displayed at each point.

There are a number of things that I can only refer to as "neat." For example, I can turn off the annoying habit of Windows of adding "shortcut to" to all-new shortcuts. I am not really interested in the fact it is a shortcut, but rather I want access to the file.

There are also several "security" features. For example, you can get Fix-It to remove all of the "histories" the system keeps track of, such as in Internet Explorer, the "Run" menu, "Find Files," and so forth. If you want, you can also get Fix-It to log your own network automatically. (Not something I would recommend all the time.)

As with other system utilities, Fix-It allows you to schedule the various tasks. Here you configure exactly what is run and when.

As a side note, Fix-It did not reinvent the wheel in a lot of cases. Instead, it uses programs that are already provided by Windows. For example, Fix-It does not provide a registry editor, but rather uses the one from Windows. Whether you find this as being good or bad will depend on how happy you are with the standard Windows tool. Personally, I would rather see them providing functionality that is not available rather than repackaging existing functionality under a different name.

What'sUp Gold

What'sUp Gold from Ipswitch is a very easy-to-use network monitoring tool. It supports all the common Windows NT network protocols, such as TCP/IP, NetBEUI, and IPX/SPX. In addition to being able to monitor the status of your network, What'sUp Gold gives you a visual display of your entire network or any network segment. Status of a specific note can be displayed based on any number of criteria, particularly which services are running on that node.

What'sUp Gold can be configured to obtain the necessary information in several different ways, depending on what information is needed. For example, when you first start, What'sUp Gold needs to be made aware of what nodes exist in your network. Loading the host information is perhaps the most direct approach and is accomplished relatively quickly. However, you can also configure "auto discover" mode, which will go out and explore your network on its own.

Once the information about your network is loaded into What'sUp Gold, you can change the layout (the appearance), as well as the symbols used for each node. Figure 8–9 shows you a portion of a network displayed with What'sUp Gold. The key word is "portion" as it is possible that your network is too large to fit onto a single map.

Although you could try and squeeze everything together, it quickly becomes unreadable. Therefore it is useful to break the network into segments. What segments you choose and how you break up the network is up to you. You could have different physical segments on different maps or you could

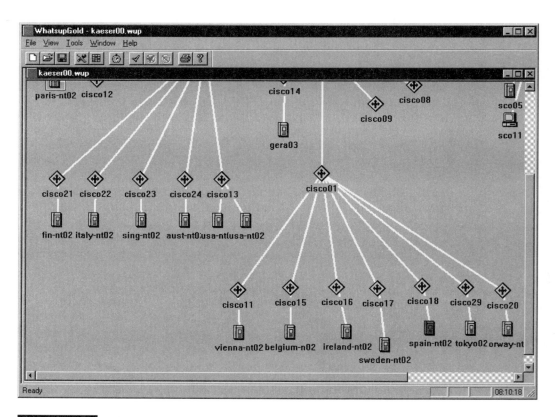

FIGURE 8–9 What'sUp Gold Main Screen.

separate them by IP subnet. Therefore, it is completely scalable from small, flat networks to large enterprise networks with various segments and subnets.

To accurately depict your network, you will need more than just identifiable dots on your map. Therefore, What'sUp Gold provides symbols to represent each node.

What'sUp Gold not only monitors basic connectivity, but also a wide range of standard protocols, as well as several user-definable protocols. Among the protocols monitored are:

- HTTP
- SMTP
- SNMP
- POP3
- IMAP4
- FTP
- Telnet

What'sUp Gold has two operating modes. First, you can start it like any other program and have complete interactive access to all of the features. Second, it can be run as a Windows NT service, which means it can be automatically started when the computer boots. In addition, because you are not opening the maps and the associated graphics, it requires much fewer system resources.

Should a node be inaccessible through any of the define protocols, you have your choice of methods to send a message indicating a problem. For example, you can simply send an audible warning by beeping or playing a WAV file. Or you can have a visual warning by sending a pop-up. In addition, What'sUp Gold can be configured to send messages through a pager, beeper, or email. If that is not enough, you have the ability to start any arbitrary program.

Depending on the method you choose to send the message, you have a wide range of variables to choose from that can automatically be inserted. You define the basic text that contains these variables and when the message is sent, the variables are replaced with the appropriate values. Among the variables you can use are:

- a = IP address or hardware address
- d = date (yy.mm.dd)
- h = Hostname
- n = Display name
- S = status (such as "timed out," "did not respond")
- t = time (hh:mm:ss)

You can also send messages based on whether a node has gone down or come back up. This keeps you from running around trying to solve a problem that no longer exists.

One useful function is the ability to define relationships or dependencies between different nodes. You can tell What'sUp Gold only to check a specific node, if another one is reachable. For example, it makes little sense to check the accessibility of the server in a branch office when you cannot even reach the router there. It is also possible to check certain nodes only when other nodes are down.

It is also useful to be able to define specific time periods when to check connectivity to specific nodes. Keep in mind that the more you monitor, the greater the load on your network just for the monitoring activities. Therefore, you might not want to check specific nodes when you do not need to. For example, there may be no need to check the connectivity to a branch office during times when they are not working.

What'sUp Gold provides a range of standard graphical tools that are either not available on Windows NT or only in a command-line version. For example, ping, traceroute, and nslookup are all available as graphical tools. In addition, What'sUp Gold supports other protocols, such as LDAP and Windows networking. (This shows you all Windows machines and the available shares.) There is also a scan function that searches a particular IP range looking for machines. Here, you have a choice of seeing whether a machine is simply "reachable" or whether it is running any number of common services. In addition, you can also tell it to scan a range of ports. This can then be automatically imported into a map, if you want.

One tool that I found extremely interesting is simple network management protocol (SNMP) to examine the SNMP values of any node. You can select any element of the management information base (MIB) to look at or you can select an entire subtree. There is also a graphic component that allows you to monitor values as they change.

Another tool allows you to monitor the throughput on a particular segment. Here you have a choice of how many packets to send, maximum size of the packets, which node to check, and so forth. A random number of bytes is sent up to the maximum size and packet count. For each packet, the tool displays how many bytes were sent and received, the response time, and the throughput. In addition, an average is displayed.

What'sUp Gold is also Internet capable in that you can monitor your network from any Web browser. In general, this provides the exact same information you can access from the What'sUp Gold console.

Mind Manager

Checklists, flowcharts, outlines are all useful tools depending on what you are trying to accomplish. However, in many cases, they do not provide the necessary "view of the task," which you are trying to accomplish. The main problem with these applications that provide information in these formats is that they are structured. That is not to say that structure is bad. In fact, the applications are created because these formats *are* structured. In other words, they do exactly what they are supposed to.

One of the key aspects is the fact that many issues that you deal with in supporting users are not as structured as what you can depict using checklists, flowcharts, and outlines. Perhaps you might want to force some kind of order and structure onto it by sorting it alphabetically. However, in many cases, this is an artificial structure because what letter of the alphabet a particular topic begins with will be different in different languages. However, the organization doesn't change.

A good example of this problem is the subject of this book. Take a topic like "Users." The German word is "Benutzer," so they are situated at different ends of the lists. However, the importance of the topic has remained unchanged. You could try to create your own order regardless of what letters are used in what language. However, you run into the problem of setting the order. What should be higher on the list: users or hardware? Should network management come before or after the help desk?

The bottom line is that often there is no order that is the "correct" one. Therefore, you need a system that can depict the topics regardless of some artificial order or priority. A common tool is simply to scratch a diagram on a piece of paper. However, as we already discussed, this has its own set of problems.

MindJet, LLC has come to the rescue with their Mind Manager product. This is based on the technique of "mind mapping" method developed by Tony Buzan. As its name implies, the main concept is the graphical representation or "mapping" of concepts and ideas, regardless of any conceived order or priority. As I mentioned, this order is often artificial and does not really apply to the topic.

Figure 8–10 shows you a *portion* of a relatively complex map. It consists of a central idea, in this case the various "views" of the IT department. Branching off from this central idea are the various subjects, which often have branches of their own. At the top of the window, you see the toolbars for various functions. At the bottom are (left to right) the symbol gallery, the note window, and the overview window. The overview window shows you the whole map and what portion of the map is currently being displayed. These three can be turned on and off as you need.

This map depicts some of the ideas involved with supporting users. The branch labeled "IT Infrastructure" lists different subjects concerning the framework of the IT organization. The branch labeled "Help Desk" list topics related to the help desk. The branch labeled "Net/sys Mgmnt" has the information necessary to aid in network and system management.

Each of these topics has several subtopics, which may, in turn, have subtopics of their own. In any IT organization, security is part of the infrastructure, but it is also part of the network and system management. There-

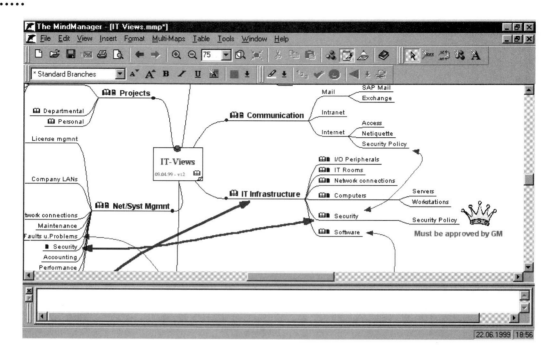

FIGURE 8-10   Mind Manager main window.

fore, the relationship between these two is shown on the map. The same thing applies to the problems in system management and the help desk. When problems occur in the system, information is passed to the help desk, so there is a relationship there as well.

These relationships are linked to the topic and are not simply symbols laid on top of the map. If you move a branch, the relationship lines follow the branch. In addition, you can change the way the lines flow to make the map more readable, such as not having lines running through the middle of some text. How these lines are depicted is also configurable. You can change the color, thickness, and whether the lines are solid, dashed, etc.

Often you cannot depict everything on the map. For example, the central topic may be so complex and so detailed that your map becomes too large to work with. Although you can configure Mind Manager to display just specific levels, the map may still grow too large. To solve this, Mind Manager allows you to link maps. That is, you have a separate map containing the details of a subtopic (or perhaps a different topic), and you create a link from one of the branches. When you double-click on the branch, Mind Manager loads the other map.

An important thing to note is that linked maps are not just ones that you load by clicking a topic header. The text in a branch you see in the top-level map becomes the text for the main topic in the linked map. This is so far linked that when you change the text in the top-level map, it also changes in the linked map.

When you load a new map, either by clicking a link or opening it from the file menu, it does *not* replace the existing map. Instead, all of the maps you have loaded are still available. In the tool bar are two arrows, which you can use to move back and forth between the loaded maps. In addition, you can choose a specific map from the list in the "Window" menu.

It is also possible that you want to include details about a topic. Although you can include "free text" directly on the map, writing several paragraphs for each topic would probably make the map unreadable. Mind Manager actually solves this problem in two ways. The first is notes that you include in your map. At the bottom center of Figure 8–11 you see a window containing your notes. Although the text in this case is relatively short, you can include quite a bit of text. The existence of notes is indicated with a book icon in front of the topic's name.

In many cases, you need more text than is really practical. In addition, you may need to link the topic to some other kind of data such as a spreadsheet or an external document. This is no problem, as you can link the topic to another map *as well as* to an external file. This file can be a word processing document, spreadsheet, even an URL to a Web side. In fact, you can link to basically any kind of external file, such as a program and even automatically give arguments to that program when it starts. A link is indicated by an icon in front of the topic's name.

One of the most power aspects is the ability to point-n-click and drag-n-drop while working on a map. Double-clicking on a open area of the map creates a new main branch at that location. Branches nearby are scooted out of the way to give you more room for the new branch. If you right-click an existing branch, you can insert a new subtopic.

Rearranging the map is just as easy as creating new branches. You can drag the branches to new locations, just as you would drag in any other application. If you drag a topic onto an existing branch, it is removed from the first topic, and it will become a new branch of the other topic. It is also possible to copy topics from one branch to another using standard Windows cut-and-paste shortcuts.

Mind Manager provides a number of functions for both inputting information into your maps as well as outputting the information from maps. I intentionally did not use the terms "import" and "export," as it is more than just a conversion of the information from one format to another.

As I mentioned previously, you can link maps together and then click on the branch to load the other map. The biggest question is how to get the information into that other map. Perhaps the most obvious approach is to open a new map, cut the branch off from the first map and then paste it into the new map. Although this works, there is a much simpler way.

You can select a branch and then export it and automatically create a new map. The top-level branch of the new map remains as a branch of the original map, and a link to the new map is created automatically.

Transferring the information to another map is not the only way you can output your map. Mind Manager has the ability to create an outline of your map, which you can save either as text or RTF. Branches become the heading and subheadings of your outline, and the notes are added to the outline just after the respective header.

When first developing this book, I created a mind map of the topics I wished to discuss. I included notes for many of the topics. I then exported the map and had a working outline for the book that I could easily import into my word processor (being that the outline was in RTF). This then became the framework for this book.

In addition, you can export your map as a task list or simply listing the notes for each topic. The entire map itself can also be exported as a GIF file.

Mind Manager has also kept up with technology and is Internet aware. As I mentioned previously, you can create links to URLs from branches. However, you can also export the entire map as HTML pages. Any notes you have for a branch are written to the page. The subbranches can then become links to new pages. On the new page are the notes for that page, with a list to its subbranches.

You can also export the pages with a Java applet. This applet displays the files similar to the way the Windows Explorer does (see Figure 8–11). In each case, you can define what Mind Manager does with linked maps as well as how many levels should be exported.

This is actually how I created the framework for the IT department's intranet in one company. Using a map similar to Figure 8–11, I created a number of linked maps based on the various IT views. I then exported them to HTML pages. When I was done, the structure was there, and I just needed to fill in the pages with content.

Mind Manager provides a wide range of options to choose from to define how the finished Web pages appear. Nine standard templates are provided, which you can alter to suit your needs. The templates describe the color scheme used for the pages, background image, separation lines, footnotes, company logo, and which URL should be loaded when you click on its many other aspects.

You can also change the order in which Mind Manager creates the outline or Web page. By default, the main topics appear in the order they are on the map, starting at the top and going clockwise around the map. However, you can maintain the layout of your map and still change the order in which the topics are exported. (i.e., putting them in alphabetical or chronological order).

Mind Manager also support Object Linking and Embedding (OLE). It is therefore possible to insert a Mind Manager map into a different document

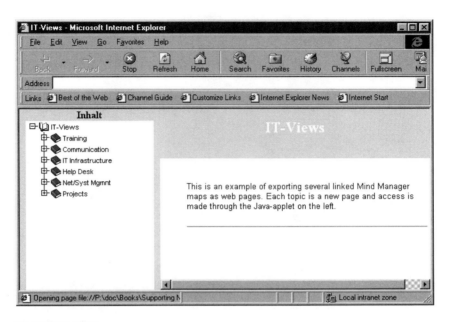

FIGURE 8-11   Mind Manager Java Explorer applet.

(such as an MS Word file). Clicking on the map then loads it. Mind Manager also registers itself with Windows so that it will appear as one of the OLE objects that you can load directly from the other applications, without having to use the clipboard.

There are also a number of different ways that information can be brought *into* Mind Manager. Maps can be imported, as they can be exported. You can either import an unrelated map or you select a node containing a linked map, and the system will import it. Mind Manager will then ask you if it should remove the file containing that map. You can also cut-and-paste lists from other applications, which will create the necessary nodes.

Mind Manager can be more than just a collection of lines. There are a number of symbols that you can insert anywhere on your map for any number of functions, such as calling attention to specific headers, indicating the priority of various entries, and so forth. In addition, you can format the appearance of Mind Manager in a wide variety of ways, including the shape and color of the lines, text formats to use for the branches, and so forth.

Mind Manager also servers as a groupware product. You can set a Mind Manager conference in which you can not only chat with other participants, you can also make changes to existing maps, which the other participants can see. A nifty little function is the ability to "raise your hand" so that other participants see that you wish to say something. A protocol of the conversation is automatically generated and saved as an HTML page.

Applications

Finding the Right Applications

There is more to choosing the right application than finding the one that has the most features. The first question you need to ask is whether or not the application has all the features you need. It's possible that one application has more features, but one of the features that's missing is something that you cannot do without. For example, assume that you have a large number of documents that use SGML. This is a standard feature of WordPerfect, which you must pay extra for if you have MS Word.

Like hardware, buying the least expensive software is not always our best choice. Even if the software doesn't have all of the *desired* features, what you save on the price you may make up with other costs. For example, applications from the same vendor usually have the same interface. Therefore, it is much easier to learn new applications from a vendor that you are already familiar with. Being familiar with the interface, the application is easier to use.

In addition, the benefits of a single software vendor are basically the same as a single hardware vendor. You have one contact for support, one place to look for updates for patches, and one place to look for upgrades. As with hardware, if you have one supplier for your software, you are more likely to get a quantity discount.

I have worked for companies that were nothing less than zombies when it came to software upgrades. That is, every time the new version of the software came out, they had to upgrade. Rarely, if ever, did the newest version have any features that they required. Instead, MIS managers believed that they always had to have the most recent version. Having their own MIS manager, you can guess that they were not small companies. There were close to 1000 users that had to be upgraded to newest version. Not only was there the cost of the new software, but also the time spent to install software. Because not all 1000 users could be converted at once, there was usually the transition, where some people were using the new version and others were using the old version. As is the case with MS Word, older versions cannot read the new format. Therefore, we received uncounted calls from users complaining that they could not read certain documents. The reason was simply the users had the old version, but the files stored were in the new version.

Even if your company has some kind of maintenance contract that allows you to upgrade to the newest version, you should consider the related costs of upgrading to the newest version. This includes the time and effort to install the software but also lost productivity as users become accustomed to the new version. I'm hard-pressed to think of any application that does not require a certain "acclimation." To this I mean only a few days, but it could be several weeks. During this time, users are not as productive as they were prior to the introduction of the new software.

Management of the software updates and upgrades is an important aspect of this. Here, I refer to *updates* as patches or bug fixes that do not change the release number or version number of the software (or may just change a minor number). Upgrades, on the other hand, are complete version changes of the software. Each has its own particular problems that need to be addressed. In most cases, updates are free. At least, the vendor does not charge money for them. Keep in mind that this does not make them "free." You still have to spend time, and therefore money, in order to install them. Therefore, a good question to ask is whether or not you need the updates. Obviously, if it is a security-related fix, you should always install. What about updates that fix or add functionality? The simplest way to decide whether you should install the update is to decide whether or not you need this new functionality. If you don't, there may be no reason to install the update.

In general, the same thing will apply to upgrades. However, an upgrade usually costs money. Once again, even if you do have a maintenance contract that allows you to install upgrades for free, "free" is just what you pay the vendor. You must also consider the administration costs.

When deciding on the software product, you should determine how long the vendor will support a given release. As previously discussed, this will depend entirely on the vendor, and there is no industry standard. However, you can expect a vendor to support at least two previous versions. I have never experienced a case where a vendor did not support the last two versions. A part of this is the vendor's update and upgrade policy. If an update consists solely of bug fixes, in most cases you do not have to pay for it. On the other hand, if the update also includes new functionality, some vendors will charge for it. It would be worthwhile to find out what the company's update policy is prior to your investing a lot of money in the product.

Another thing to find out is how the company reacts to bugs in their product. I have yet to find a company that will not provide a patch for free should the product have some major fault that prevents functioning properly. On the other hand, the question remains as to what is proper functionality. You may think that the product does not behave correctly, but the vendor thinks that it does. Therefore, you should be realistic in your expectations. You really need to consider whether it is a bug or a feature that you think is missing. You should not expect that the vendor provide you an upgrade to move you to the next version because it is missing a feature you think it should have.

This is not as farfetched as it may seem. I worked in tech support for one operating system vendor and received a call from a customer complaining about the email program. This was at a time where email programs did not have any of the "word processing" capabilities that they do today. Instead, this had a very simple line editor. Although word processing programs did exist that did automatic line wrapping, the email editor did not. Instead, you were expected to press return at the end of each line. The customer failed to do this and lost parts of his messages.

He expected the email editor to behave like a word processing program. We expect a customer to press enter at the end of each line. He expected us to fix this "bug" and kept calling back almost every week to find out when the patch would be available. It was our contention that he was not using the program correctly. Because there was a very simple way to avoid this problem, he was unrealistic to expect a high priority to fix this "bug." (I still don't believe that was a "bug.")

Another aspect of updating your applications is understanding what happens to your system when the product is updated. Hopefully, if the application has any configuration files, the new versions will not simply override them. Although this is becoming somewhat less likely, I have encountered some products that explicitly tell you to copy the configuration files into a safe location prior to the upgrade and then copy them back once you're done. On the other hand, how many actually read the documentation prior to doing installation?

Even if the configuration files are not overwritten, you need to be concerned with what the installation does. Microsoft is notorious for overriding existing DLLs when installing their products. Only when the existing DLLs are newer than the ones being installed or are in a different language will Microsoft products even question whether the DLLs should be replaced. Part of this is due to the fact that Microsoft more than other vendors tends to copy

DLLs into the SYSTEM or SYSTEM32 directories. Other vendors tend to keep DLLs in the applications directories. Because DLLs (and sometimes other files) are blindly overwritten, I have lost track of how many times programs have ceased to work correctly after the installation of a new version of some other product. Therefore, it is vital that you know the effects the installation will have prior to upgrading every machine in the company.

To help you with this, a good thing to have is a test machine or set of test machines on which you can install new versions of applications. Not only should you test to ensure that all other applications work correctly, but it may be useful to determine what, if any, system files are changed as a result of this installation. One tool to do this is RealHelp from Quarterdeck Corporation. When installed, RealHelp will monitor and record changes to the system that are made when you install other software products. It can also be configured to back up the few deleted overwritten files. If necessary, you can completely undo the installation of that software product using the built-in features.

Even without the ability to undo the installation, seeing what changes were made can be very useful. For example, you can use it to determine if a specific DLL had been replaced. I have encountered situations where a DLL was replaced by the new version in one piece of software, and the older versions of the software no longer worked. It was easier to identify the problem because I could quickly find out which DLLs had been changed and in what program.

Within the next year to a couple of years, it's likely that you will want to upgrade your Windows 95 machines to Windows 98 (or perhaps Windows NT). It is imperative that you test the behavior of your existing software on these new operating systems. Despite what Microsoft marketing says to the contrary, not all programs that run on Windows 95 will run on Windows 98 or Windows NT. Although the likelihood that a Windows 95 program will run on Windows 98 is quite high, I have encountered many Windows 95 programs that specifically state that they will not run on Windows NT. In several cases I even tested this out, and it was no surprise to find out that they did, in fact, not work.

With this in mind, it would be very useful for you to test the behavior of existing software on any new operating system prior to deploying it to your end users. I am a big fan of test machines on which system administrators can test the necessary configurations. In one company where I worked, the test machine was simply the one that the system administrators used on databases. This gave them the opportunity to test new configurations without having to leave their desks. On the other hand, your systems administrators may not be able to do this, for example, if they cannot afford to have their computer down for any extended length of time. If this is the case, I would recommend that you would have at least one additional machine to test new configurations on.

One thing I need to stress with regard to these test machines is that they must have a standard configuration. If the test machines have larger hard disks or more memory or more powerful video cards, it is often not a valid test of how the software will behave for most of the users. We learned this the hard way in one company where the systems administrators' machines were also test machines. Each of the administrators' machines had twice as much RAM as the machines most end users had. The result was that applications would often function correctly for the systems administrators but not for the end users. Therefore, test machines should be configured like any other test environment. That is, the environment should be controlled and reproducible.

Let's jump back for a moment to that section on workstation configuration. As we discussed, you may find it necessary to have different workstations for different types of work. Therefore, you may find yourself needing to test the new software on multiple configurations. This is an important aspect of testing the new software, because the different workstations may behave differently. For example, if your graphics workstations have a lot of memory, then a new version may perform better than on other machines. On the other hand, if the graphics application is running and you try to start the new software, you may find that the new software performs *worse* than on other machines. Both of these situations need to be tested.

One aspect of upgrading that is often overlooked is the amount of time it will take to upgrade to new version. If you use automatic distribution software, such as Microsoft System Management Server (SMS), you can generally save yourself the time needed to go to each machine and install the new version of the software. However, you need to be aware of how long the installation will take so that the end users will be prepared. For example, you may want to send out an email message to all users prior to the upgrade telling them that the upgrade will occur and approximately how long it will take. If you don't do this, the user may get rather impatient and think that the machine has become frozen. He could then reboot the machine, forcing the installation to start from the beginning. The worst case is that the system is in an inconsistent state, and either the software needs to be completely uninstalled and then reinstalled, or it may be the case that the entire machine may need to be reinstalled.

In any event, I think you should plan for the worst case scenario. That is, cases where an installation takes the greatest amount of time. You probably won't take everything into consideration. However, I usually plan for installations to take twice as long as they normally do. If everything goes successfully, you can go do something else. However, if you run into problems, you can use that extra time you planned on.

This is especially important to client/server applications when you're installing the server side. It may be necessary in such cases to reboot the server (or reboot the server several times, as in the case of Microsoft applications), and you need to consider what effect this has on your users. It is totally beneficial in such cases to plan to do the installation on the weekend or after normal business hours. However, don't forget about your users in other offices. I'm speaking from experience where, say, administrators may forget about these people, especially, if they have little interaction with people in the branch offices. I worked in companies where administrators were often oblivious to the fact that there were other offices; as a result, they often did things without regard to the effect it had on the other offices.

Software Licensing

Licensing your software becomes less of an issue if you have two copies installed on each machine. However, it may not go away. If you have local copies of your software, it may be necessary to purchase a license for each copy. However, if you have installed a network version of the software, it may not be necessary to purchase the license for everyone in the company or for every machine. Many software products have a built-in mechanism to determine how many users are authorized to use the software. If you exceed that amount, you may get one message to that effect or the software may just not work.

Some software does not have a built-in mechanism and leaves it up to the system administrator to ensure that the number of licenses is not exceeded. This was the case with older versions of MS Office. MS Office had a network installation to install it on the server, but there was no mechanism to restrict the number of users. The solution to this problem was actually quite easy. It required the use of both local and global user groups. If you remember from our discussion of user and group management, local groups are valid only for a particular domain but can contain the global groups. Access to a particular program was given to a local group. For example, we had a local group that defined access to MS Word. We then created a global group that listed all of the users who were authorized to use MS Word. This group was then made a member of the local MS Word group.

This might seem a roundabout way of defining access, but there was a certain method to our madness. By defining access to the file based on the local group, we could include global groups from other domains. In our case, other domains were other branch offices. We could then include the MS Word group from all of our branch offices in the local MS Word group and therefore give all users access to MS Word no matter which office they were currently working in.

Vendor Programs

A site license is essentially one that covers the whole company. You are licensed for any number of copies you have. Normally, site licenses are in the *thousands* of copies, so it is not always the best choice. However, the key word here is "site." Some licenses list a site as a physical location. Therefore, you need one site license for your office in the United States and another one for your office in Botswana. Some vendors have enterprise licenses that are valid for the *entire* company, even if offices are in different physical locations. A vendor may also have a site license *and* an enterprise license. If the office in Botswana only has ten people, you may not want to pay the extra money for the enterprise license. Instead, you get a site license for the United States and individual licenses for Botswana.

No one licensing scheme is the best for every company. The simplest scheme is when you purchase one license for each computer. Even if no one uses a particular software package on a specific computer, purchasing a license for it makes administration simpler nevertheless, because you know that 50 PCs equals 50 operating system *and* 50 application licenses. You do not need to spend time counting who uses what software. On the other hand, if the difference is too dramatic, it might be worth it to you to count and only buy what is really needed.

Shared- or concurrent-use licenses are a good choice when you know that not everyone will be using the software at the same time. You buy just enough licenses to cover the *maximum* at any one time. However, problems arise when the maximum is reached. For example, if the software has a hard limit and does not let any more users on, you lose productivity as well as get a number of complaints from people asking why they cannot use the application. Even if they have been informed about the number of licenses and how the system works, you know yourself that there is nothing more important than the work of the person calling, demanding that you fix something. In the same light, their work is so important that *they* need the priority when it comes to licensing.

Often, comments like that are annoying, but they can also be true. You might have some people or whole departments that need "immediate" access to certain software. A number of software products that support concurrent users have the ability to "reserve" licenses for specific individuals. This is really only necessary when the software has a hard limit but is useful for ensuring that those people who *really* need the software have access.

Even if the software has a soft limit on the number of licenses (that is, it simply reports that the maximum number has been exceeded), you can run into problems. Just because the software allows you to use more copies, you are still obligated to pay. There is nothing stopping you from installing Corel-DRAW on every machine, although you have only paid for a single license, and there is nothing in this software to stop you. However, you are still obligated to pay. Software with soft limits on the licenses are the same way. Therefore, you need to closely monitor them to ensure compliance with the license agreement. This means more administrative work, which increases total cost of ownership (TCO) of the software. If the effort is great enough, it *might* be simpler to just buy licenses for everyone at the start.

Buying more concurrent licenses than necessary can also be a problem, at least financially. If the software supports soft limits, I would recommend buying *fewer* than you expect to use. That way you can see just how many are needed. However, you need to monitor usage *very* carefully. On the other hand, monitoring it can also provide useful information.

For example, you buy 10 licenses but discover that there are 15 people who are using it at once. You then decide to buy five more licenses. As it turns out, the extra five people only use the software occasionally, and you just looked at the maximum usage, *not* the average. As it turns out, the average is only eight users. In fact, the number of users is pretty consistent at eight except for the end of the quarter when reports are due. You could leave the floating licenses at 10, but develop a schedule so that people are not stepping on each other.

Site or enterprise licenses can reduce the administrative costs, but they can also increase your software costs unnecessarily. For example, your company might decide to go for a site license at the 1000-seat level, because you are expected to grow from the current 900 seats to over 1000 within the next year. By purchasing the software licenses now, you make all of your current PCs compliant, plus you don't need to worry about the machines that you buy in the next year.

Well, what would happen if next year, you had another economic crisis like the one that happened in Asia in the spring of 1998. You end up closing the offices in Kuala Lumpur, Bangkok, and Hanoi instead of opening up new offices in Bombay, Jakarta, and Manila. The result is you drop from 900 to 700 employees, but you still have the enterprise license calculated for the *growth* to 1000 employees. Because you got a 25% discount on the software, you paid the price of 750 licenses for the 1000. Now you end up paying more than had you bought individual licenses.

Granted, you cannot always foresee financial crises like the one is Asia, and it is a good thing to plan for the future and expect that your company will do well. However, as with other aspects of your business, you need to at least look at the effects of a wrong decision with regard to licensing.

If, in the previous example, you get a 50% discount instead of just 25% (which is entirely possible), even at 700 users, the cost per license is *still* cheaper. Therefore, it would be worth being taken advantage of, because no one really expects to drop from 900 users to less than 500 if their company is doing well.

Another thing to look at is how lenient the vendor is in terms of miscalculating your usage. For example, you buy a site license for 1000 users for each of three of your offices and four site licenses of 500 for another three offices. For the rest of your offices, you buy smaller bundles or even individual licenses. You then have a sudden boom in business, and you now have over 5000 employees worldwide, which is the minimum for the smallest level enterprise license. The price per license for this contract would be less than for the others (administration would also be less), and you would even compensate for the individual licenses you had purchased. The question is, is the reseller willing (or even able) to change the contract?

Often the reseller is bound to the conditions set forth by the software vendor, particularly if it has been several months since the contract was signed. Therefore, it would be in your interest to determine *at the beginning* what changes (if any) are possible. Also investigate what the consequences are of making the wrong decision.

Another aspect of leniency is how much over the limit you can go before you are expected to pay for more licenses. If you buy a site license for 10,000 users, I think it is pretty ludicrous to expect you to buy licenses for even the next 100 users. That is just 1% of the total, and certainly the vendor can overlook this. The question is, will they? This is something that you should ask before you sign the contracts.

A variant of this scheme offers reductions in prices *above* a certain level. You agree to purchase *at least* a specific number of licenses and with that comes a discount on the price. In many cases, you simply agree to buy the agreed on number of licenses within a specific time period. *All* licenses from that vendor (or maybe just that product) are bought at the agreed-on discount. If you don't reach your goal, you may have to pay a penalty, but if you go above it, you do not lose in that some licenses are actually bought individually.

You will probably be hard-pressed to find any software vendor willing to give you "volume discounts" for anything less than ten copies (although resellers might). However, once you begin to deal with quantities of this size and larger, you will quickly see just how much you really can save. One of the important reasons (in my experience) has little to do with the belief that the more you buy, the cheaper it should be. Instead, there is a certain behavior that applies to software. That is, once you get used to the way particular software behaves, you are less likely to accept the behavior of another product as being "correct."

Part of this is knowing what programs the software vendor offers and which are more applicable to your company. You might consider doing a little research on your own to find out what programs are available. You should even go to the extent of making a preliminary determination of what program would be best for your company. If the reseller does not even mention other programs, you might want to look elsewhere. If they suggest a different program than the one you looked at, you should ask them why.

Also, you should determine how well the reseller knows the vendors' programs. Let's look back at the example of the 200 software licenses obtained from a different reseller. If this reseller says you *cannot* count these when you really can, you might buy more licenses than necessary. If the resellers say that you *can* count them, but you cannot, you may end up paying a large penalty.

As I mentioned, you cannot simply count the PCs and users to determine how many licenses you need. Not everyone may need a license, and you may be planning to upgrade the whole company really soon. Both of these are factors that will come into play during the "cost modeling." Here, you (or the reseller) develop *several* models of licensing based on traditional volume license agreements (VLAs) as well as the enterprise license agreements. Each model needs to not only determine the cost of the software itself but also the administration costs.

For example, an enterprise license where you pay per PC might be more cost-effective than one that is paid per user, even though you have more PCs than users. This kind of situation often occurs when not every person uses every software product. However, you could simply say that each PC has a standard installation (such as Windows NT and Corel Office Suite), even though some users do not use Quattro Pro.

Assume that you have 100 users. With normal licensing, it might be cheaper to buy just 50 Corel Office Suite licenses and 50 WordPerfect licenses. However, with an enterprise contract, there is a greater requirement for you to demonstrate your compliance. As a result, with the extra administration of keeping track of who uses Quattro and who doesn't, it might be easier to simply say *everyone* uses Quattro and buy licenses accordingly. This can really be an issue if you buy licenses in blocks and then later discover that you need just a few more licenses.

Enterprise-wide licenses generally mean less administration. You make fewer purchases, report less often, and often have more leeway in terms of many licenses you can have "missing." The reduction in administration as a result of this generally means you save time. Time is money. This means that you could end up paying more for licenses up front, but the TCO is lower.

If at all possible, try to negotiate the contract to avoid such phrases as "the customer will ensure compliance with licensing requirement *to the best of their ability*." The problem with phrases like this is that the reseller or even the software vendor determines what is *"to the best of their ability."* You may think you have done everything necessary, but the vendor may have other ideas. For example, one company that used Microsoft's SMS to count the number of PCs found out the hard way from Microsoft itself that this was not a sufficient tool to count the number of operating systems in use, as SMS often reports machines doubled. Instead, each PC had to be counted *by hand*.

Another thing you need to be careful about is blanket contracts that cover "all PCs" in the company. For example, you get a special deal on upgrades if you upgrade *every* machine in the company. However, when you agree to this, you forget about the 50 old PCs at the back of the warehouse that are still on your books. Although they are not technically scheduled to be upgraded, the contract requires that you buy an upgrade for them.

This might come down to your relationship with the reseller or vendor. If they want to stick to the letter of the contract, they could force you to buy unneeded licenses. Granted, you may want to switch resellers, but you may also have lost a great deal of money.

Another thing to look carefully at is software bundles versus "pay as you go." There are two aspects to this. First, there is what most people think about when they buy a software "bundle." For example, buying the Corel Office Suite is less expensive than buying WordPerfect, Quattro Pro, and Corel Central as individual products. Often the price difference between a single product and a bundle is not worth arguing over if you use at least two of the products, *even if* most people are not likely to use every component. Some resellers will go a step further and bundle other products. For example, Corel has bundles that include CorelDRAW or Corel Ventura. This may not be a wise decision for everyone in the company but worth looking at for those people that need it. It decreases the initial cost of the software and often the cost of maintenance as well.

Finance Programs

How you actually pay for the software is another key consideration, particularly if you need to purchase a large number of licenses up front. In some cases, you may end up paying a large chunk of money up front. Checking into finance options can be very beneficial. Like any product you buy on credit, you can expect to pay a certain amount of interest. However, you avoid the huge lump sum that might be necessary in the beginning.

The bottom line to this story is that a financing option with the reseller allowed us to install the products as we could *technically*, not when we could afford it. This helped us to complete the migration a lot quicker than would have been otherwise possible. Therefore, we were able to minimize the "damage" caused by the bugs in Office 97.

Vendor Services

The services provided by the reseller should continue beyond the actual purchase. For example, if you have made a major purchase and have agreed to payment over an extended period, procedures should be in place to have the reseller bill you well in advance of the deadline. If yours is like many companies, it may take several weeks to make the payments, even though this is an on-going cost.

Another area that you should look to the reseller for guidance is the on-going monitoring of the program. Hopefully, you work for a growing company, and new people are getting hired. They will obviously need new licenses. The question is how to automate this task. Although you could make it a matter of policy that the personnel/human resources department automatically informs IS of all new hires, this may be impractical in some companies. Perhaps the reseller has either ideas or tools to facilitate this.

Another key aspect of getting the right software is getting it at the right price. There is more to this than shopping around at the various computer superstores or looking at dozens of Web sites looking for the cheapest price, one aspect that is frequently overlooked is the various licensing programs that software vendors offer. These are overlooked for two reasons. First, some companies are not aware of them. Second, companies think they only apply to large-scale purchases of hundreds or even thousands of licenses.

The truth of the matter is that although the license will cost you less money if you are applying thousands at a time, you can still save a great deal with just a dozen or so licenses. In addition to the savings you get for quantity purchases, you normally don't buy a mixed media such as CDs or books. Instead, what you are buying is simply the "right to copy." As the name implies, you are buying the right to install the software on multiple computers. Because the vendor does not need to produce anything, it has less costs and passes the savings on to you.

Although the number of licenses you are required to purchase, the cost, and the related support will differ from company to company, the basic concepts are the same. Therefore, I am only going to talk about the licensing programs of one company but mention characteristics that are different from other vendors.

The vendor that I'm going to talk about is Corel Corporation, developers of the Corel Office Suite, CorelDRAW, Corel Ventura, and many other products. The Corel License Program (CLP) is a wide-ranging program, covering all of Corel's products, and can be fit to any size company.

At the low end of the scale is CLP choice. This is intended for smaller companies and departments, which require a small number of licenses. The key aspect of CLP choice is that there is a low minimum purchase (only three licenses), which makes it ideal for the vast majority of companies.

Another advantage of CLP choice is that, unlike other licensing contracts, there is no signed agreement. Instead, you simply purchase a single copy of the prepackaged software from anywhere and submit a CLP choice order form, requesting the number of licenses you need. Corel then sends you an official license certificate, which lists the number of copies of each product you are authorized to install.

The CLP choice program is also extremely flexible. It is based on concurrent use and not necessarily the number of installed copies. Unlike the Microsoft Select contract, which requires you to pay for every installed copy, regardless of whether it is in use or not, with CLP choice you only pay for the software you actually use. That is, you pay for the maximum number of copies that are "in use" at any time. In this context, "in use" means that any portion of the software is in RAM. Therefore, you could not have WordPerfect running on one computer and Quattro Pro running on another computer and consider them a single license of the WordPerfect suite.

This concurrent use of policy expands beyond the office. Therefore, you can have a single license installed on your desktop machine, a machine at home, and a laptop, provided there is no way that more than one copy can be in use at any time. Corel refers to this as "24-Hour Licensing." That is, the user is licensed 24 hours a day, no matter where he or she is working.

A common problem is that companies may not be able to have every machine at the same license version at the same time. There may be technical reasons, such as machines that cannot be upgraded as well as administrative issues of not having the time to upgrade all of the machines. With the CLP this is not a problem. When you purchase a license, you are licensing the previous versions at no extra cost. It is even possible to have local versions of the software installed on the same computer at the same time, provided they are not all in memory at the same time. This "backward compatibility" allows you to license your software properly and still allows you to upgrade the software when you can.

CLP Universal is another of Corel's licensing programs. It provides the same general features of CLP choice, such as concurrent usage, home and laptop usage, backward compatibility, and so forth. In addition, you have classic service technical support at no additional charge as well as the ability to obtain free upgrades and savings on premium service technical support.

Another key difference is that CLP Universal has multiple discount levels, whereas CLP choice provides the same level of discount no matter how many additional copies of the software you purchase. With CLP Universal, the more you buy the more you save. Once you reach a particular savings level, it stays in effect for the next year, because the discount level is cumulative. On the other hand, Microsoft Select requires a specific number of licenses for each contract period in order to be eligible to continue.

In addition, unlike CLP choice, with CLP Universal you are required to purchase a minimum of 500 "points" in either licenses or maintenance contracts. Note that the 500 points does not necessarily mean you have to buy 500 copies of any given software product. Instead, different products have different point values. For example, a new upgrade or maintenance license for the Corel Office Suite has a point value of two, whereas WordPerfect has a point value of one.

You can help reduce the total cost of ownership of your software by purchasing maintenance contracts. These allow you to upgrade to the newest version of the product for free during the lifetime of your maintenance contract. You can therefore budget your licensing costs while still having access to the most current technology. CLP Universal also offers free email and Classic Service support with the contract.

CLP Freedom provides licensing throughout your company. Like CLP choice, you sign a contract, but in this case you purchase software for your entire company. This means you can add users without the extra administrative burden of reporting users and purchasing new licenses. Note that CLP Freedom does not just apply to those in multinational corporations. It is possible to qualify for this program with only 100 employees or workstations. If you reach your goal and wish to extend the contract for another year, Corel offers an additional 20% discount.

CLP Freedom also provides electronic support (i.e., email) as well as Classic Service free with the contracts. You can also earn support at the higher levels based on the number of licenses you purchase. For example, 10 licenses give you a free Priority call, 100 licenses give you a free Premium call. (We'll go into the details of the various support options shortly.)

What kind of support is available is another important thing to look at. Support can range from no support at all to simple installation support provided for free to consultant services, where a representative of the vendor comes and gives you on-site support.

How much each type of support costs and what it entails will differ from company to company. However, like licensing, there are some basic concepts that apply to all companies.

One of the first things to look at it is what services are provided for free. One of the most useful free sources is an on-line knowledge base, which you can use to search for solutions to specific problems. Although Microsoft was one of the last major companies to provide this service for free, it does have a very extensive library, which not only deals with pure Microsoft issues, but how Microsoft products interact with those from other vendors.

Having access to the same knowledge base as the support engineers can save you a great deal of time and money. When trying to find solutions to specific problems, I always look for an on-line database and almost always find the answer. If you can find the answer in the knowledge base yourself, there is no need for you to pay to have a support analyst look for the answer for you.

However, just because a company has an on-line database, it does not necessarily mean you have access to it. Basically, all major software vendors provide access for free, but you may still find some that only provide access for registered users or those with a valid support contract.

Another source of free support is newsgroups and mailing lists. Although there may be newsgroups for the product, you need to see how closely tied they are to the company. If the company sponsors the newsgroup, there will likely be some representative of the company (support staff or engineer) who monitors the group and will contribute solutions and other information. Although you don't get any "hand-holding" (or at least it is rare), you do have access to the same level of expertise that you get with fee-based support. You may just have to wait a little longer.

Next up is the length of the free call-in support and for what products it is valid. Free support varies extensively from company to company, with some actually providing free call-in support for the duration of the product. Before you decide on a product, check the kind of free support you get. If you are implementing a new product or are switching vendors, you will likely need a lot of support at the beginning. If you have to pay for it, it increases the total cost of ownership of that product.

Also check to see how the free support applies to volume licensing programs. You may not be entitled to anything extra, although some products include support as well. If you can get a discount on fee-based support because you have a volume-licensing contract, it may be worth considering to actually pay for support.

Pay-per-incident support is where you pay for each "call." The word "call" is included in quotes because the definition of what a call is varies from company to company. In some cases, the call ends when you hang up, even if you do not have a valid solution. In other cases, a call may go on for several sessions. That is, the support analyst gives you something to try and you call back later if that solution does not work.

Sometime vendors provide "call packs." These are pay-per-incident calls, but you purchase a number of calls at once. If you expect to be calling in repeatedly, but a limited number of times, this is a viable alternative as it is cheaper than single calls.

However, you need to be careful. There are often limitations with call packs. In some cases, you are expected to use up all of your calls within a specific time period. If you do not, all the unused calls simply become invalid.

Parallel to the pay-per-incident is the pay-per-minute. This is almost exclusively a 900 number where the cost is charged to your phone bill. Personally, I say stay away from these unless you are absolutely sure that you can get an answer quicker than a per-incident call. The problem is that if you end up with an analyst who is unfamiliar with the problem, they may end up wasting your time and costing you money. Trying to prove that the time was wasted by the analyst is hard to prove.

On the other hand, most companies have already identified this problem. It is my experience that in most cases, analysts on pay-per-incident or per-minute support lines are able to solve problems more effectively. Also, most of the companies I have dealt with do not charge for calls if it turns out to be a bug.

Some companies also provide unlimited support. That is, you have an unlimited number of calls for the duration of your contract. This is often very expensive and is generally only useful when you have a large number of users or machines. On the other hand, there are a number of third-party support providers that can support the full range of products you use. If you find a support provider that allows unlimited calls on any product you have, you might be better off than having individual contracts.

Keep in mind that what "unlimited" means will be different from company to company and maybe even product to product. You may be able to get an unlimited number of calls, but the support itself may be limited. For example, at the lower end of the spectrum, the support analyst probably will not walk you through the steps to perform a particular task, particularly one that is detailed in the manual.

On the other hand, many companies provide support contracts that will walk you through, hold your hand, and basically do much of the work themselves. Keep in mind that these are expensive. Something on the order of $50,000 per year is not unexpected. Considering how much you would pay for an additional system administrator whose job it was to look through manuals, knowledge bases, and so forth looking for the right answer, you are probably getting away cheap. When I worked in support, there were many companies who gladly paid this amount. We (vendor support) should be the ones spending the time looking through the manuals, knowledge bases, and so forth looking for the right answer. The companies knew exactly what they wanted.

At the high end of the spectrum are consultant services. This is much more than technical support. Instead, the vendor gives you advice, guidance, or anything else you might need to implement their software. This may also include visits to your site.

Another thing to consider is the times you are allowed to call in for support. Support contracts at the lower end of the scale normally do not have a 24 × 7 schedule. That is, you can only call in during normal business hours. I have encountered some companies with completely free phone support, which only allowed calls 2 hours a day. Granted, this was a specialty application, and once you got it running, there was generally no need to call in for support.

Also involved here is the response time. As we will discuss in more detail in the section on help desks, what "response time" means can be interpreted in many different ways. With some companies, the moment you are in a queue waiting to talk to a support analyst, they have "responded" to the call. In any event, with contracts at the lower end of the spectrum, you can expect to wait longer to talk to an analyst.

Corel Corporation provides support at basically every level that we discussed so far. They have an extensive knowledge base, covering all of the products as well as on-site consultant services and everything in between.

Premium Service is the highest level and is intended for medium to large companies that need a more personalized level of support. One thing to note, which many also apply to other companies, is that Premium Service is only available for the Corel Office products and not for their graphics or desktop publishing applications.

Within Premium Service, there are actually five levels of support, and you do not necessarily get unlimited calls with each level. In addition, not all levels have 24 × 7 support nor do all levels have an Service Account Manager, who manages your contract and serves as your contact within Corel. You will also find that the number of people within your company who are authorized to submit support requests differs among the different levels.

The next level down is Priority Service. Although you can still get 24 × 7 support, this kind of support normally does not provide the same level of personalized service you get with the Premium service. Here you have a choice of pay-per-incident or pay-per-minute (as we discussed earlier). Note that Corel is fairly clear about what they mean by "incident." Sometimes, problems require several phone calls, but are still considered a single incident. However, multiple questions or problems within a single call are considered multiple incidents.

Classic Support for Corel Business Applications is a support service that is free to all registered users of any of the Corel business applications (which excludes the graphic and desktop publishing applications.) Unlike the fee-based support, Classic Support is only available 6:30 AM to 5:30 PM Mountain Time, Monday through Friday. In addition, you can generally expect that the support you will get will be professional, but it probably won't be at the depth as the fee-based programs (i.e., no hand-holding).

Corel also provides a separate email support program called "Answer-Perfect." This is less expensive than other options and is a good alternative if you can wait for a response.

The Y2K Problem

As I write this, the new millennium is rapidly approaching. You may be reading this after the new millennium already arrived. This does not mean that all of the problems associated with the year 2000 (Y2K) are behind you. In fact, many may not have yet cropped up. I think it unlikely that even the most junior system administrator would not know about the Y2K problem. However, for the sake of being complete, I will give you a quick overview of what this problem is all about.

It all began in the early days of computers. At that time, memory was extremely expensive. That is, you may have paid hundreds if not thousands of dollars per KB of RAM. Therefore, progress was intense on saving space. In a lot of applications, the year was stored simply as two digits. That is, the century (19) was left off and only the last two digits were stored. This worked well for some time. However, many applications will no longer function after the year 2000. This is quite simply because calculations based on the year will no longer work.

Let's take a part of an application that calculates a user's age. Assume that the user was born in 1961. The birth year is therefore stored simply as 61. In 1999, the program calculates the user to be 38 years old. That is, 99 − 61 = 38. In the year 2000, the calculation is 00 − 61 = −61. That is, the user is now −61 years old. In the year 2026, the user will be 65 and eligible for retirement. However, 26 − 61 = −35. Because the calculated age is less than 65, the computer thinks the person is not yet eligible for retirement.

Although this is a very simplistic example, it has been demonstrated that unless it is corrected, this kind of problem will occur. Also keep in mind that the Y2K problem is not limited to just software. There are already many known hardware problems that have been demonstrated. For example, many older BIOS will not be able to work properly after the new millennium. There are uncounted pieces of hardware that have built-in controllers where dates are stored as just two digits.

Many pieces of equipment have built-in safety mechanisms that keep track of the time since the last maintenance was done. If maintenance is not performed often enough, the equipment will simply shut itself off. Imagine being in an elevator on New Year's Eve at midnight 2000. The controller in the elevator suddenly determines that the last maintenance was almost a hundred years ago and decides to shut itself off rather than endanger the passengers.

Many administrators are under the misconception that this problem only applies to older software or is limited to applications. Believe it or not, Windows NT 4.0 with Service Pack 3 did not address all of the problems surrounding Y2K. For example, the user manager does not properly recognize the fact that the year 2000 is a leap year. We all know that any year that is divisible by 4 is a leap year. Most people know that years that are divisible by 100 are *not* a leap year. However, there are a lot of people, including programmers at Microsoft, that are not aware of the fact that a year that is divisible by 400 *is* a leap year. Therefore, the year 2000 is a leap year. This fact is not reflected in the user manager. This can easily be tested by setting the expiration date for an account to February 29, 2000. You will receive an error message saying that February 29 does not exist in that year.

Although this may seem like a trivial example, the question still remains open as to where else the Microsoft programmers made this kind of *very* simple mistake. What will happen on February 29, 2000? Will all accounts suddenly expire? Will all passwords suddenly become invalid? Will replication work correctly? Will your at jobs work correctly? If you are relying on at for your backups, it is entirely possible that your backup will not get done on February 29, 2000. You need to find out what else will cease to function or at least cease to function properly as a result of Y2K.

The fact that Y2K will cause many year calculations to become invalid and the fact that it is a leap year are not the only problems involved. Programmers took a large number of different approaches to solving programming problems. Therefore, it is impossible to say exactly where all of the problems will appear. There are a number of common places that you can look to verify whether or not your system is ready for the next millennium.

It is recommended that you define an individual or even a team of people who are responsible for what could turn out to be *your* "Y2K problem." In addition to determining whether or not your computer systems are Y2K-compliant, they can also serve as a contact and when you're approached by other companies. Believe me, this will happen! Companies are already examining their suppliers and other business partners to see if they are Y2K ready. I know of some companies that have switched vendors, because the one they had had not even begun to address the Y2K problem.

One thing that you should definitely take a look at in regard to the Y2K problem is the product Express Meter from WRQ, Inc. As its name implies, Express Meter can be used to "meter" your software, in that it maintains a record of what software is used and by whom. The product is able to scan your system to see what software you have installed.

When it does this, it can compare this list to an internal database and generate a report on the Y2K compliance of your software. Keep in mind, however, that such a report can never be absolute. Although it can tell you what software you have that is not compliant, you can never be 100% sure when something is reported as being compliant. In many cases, the information is provided by the vendor. As we all know, vendors have a tendency to not want to show their products in a bad light. As a result, they may report a product as being Y2K compliant when it is, in fact, not compliant. For example, I asked one Microsoft representative if Windows 2000 would be Y2K compliant. He replied that Windows NT 4.0 already was Y2K compliant. However, he appeared genuinely surprised when I showed him that Windows NT 4.0 was *not* Y2K compliant by demonstrating the problem in the user manager.

The question is therefore: "What does Y2K compliance *really* mean?" This is something you will probably have to decide for yourself. Once you have made this determination for your company, you can evaluate how each product complies with *your* standard.

Office Suites

Corel WordPerfect Suite

The Corel WordPerfect Suite is comparable to other office suites, such as MS Office, in that it is composed of the same applications, such as a word processor, spreadsheet, presentation product, and a handful of other tools. However, for the most part, this is where the similarities stop. In my experience, the Corel WordPerfect suite is far more full-featured than MS Office and addresses issues. Although, these are generally "little things," there are so many that add up to a product that is more logically organized.

Although this applies to all products of the MS Office suite, I will be concentrating on MS Word in the following section, for a couple of reasons. First, MS Word is Microsoft's flagship application and should be representative of the features available in the suite as a whole. Second, in my experience the other applications actually are much less configurable.

Once place that WordPerfect excels (no pun intended) is the extent to which you can configure it. Granted, you can configure menus, toolbars, keyboard, and so forth, like you can with MS Office. However, there are certain aspects of MS Word in particular that are either configurable by drilling down through a half dozen menus and pop-up windows. With the WordPerfect Suite they are configurable right where you see them.

One thing that has always bothered me was the status bar at the bottom of the main window. Although it is a nice feature to be able to click on one of the indicators at the bottom of the screen and have it change the behavior (WordPerfect can do this as well), what has been sorely missed (in my mind) is the ability to configure the status bar. Well, at least this is an inability of MS Word, as the functionality is readily available in WordPerfect. So much so that

WordPerfect does not call this simply a "status" bar but the "application" bar, as it is used to view as well as configure various aspects of your application.

Ironically, the behavior of the Application Bar is extremely similar to the way the Windows 95/98 taskbar works. On the left are open documents (instead of running tasks). Tools and utilities are on the right. What's really ironic is that Microsoft did not have the foresight to include this functionality in their own product.

Note that this is not simply moving the configuration options from the toolbars at the top down to the bottom of the window. Instead, you have access to many features not available from the normal toolbars. Among the things you can display are the normal status aspects like typeover/insert, page number, position, current printer (which is not done in MS Word), and so forth. However, you also can display, the date and time, current font, SGML document type and element, and keyboard.

Keyboard? Well, that was my reaction at first. Keyboard behavior is not necessarily tied to a particular template or your normal.dot as it is with MS Word. Instead, you have access to any number of keyboards, which you can activate by double-clicking on the keyboard icon in the application bar.

Another aspect is the intelligent behavior of the WordPerfect toolbars. For example, one of the default toolbars is the Property Bar, comparable to the format toolbar in MS Word. Because there are different things you can do with the formatting of a table, as compared to normal text, I would think that you would have different options for the formatting. Well, WordPerfect thinks the same way and changes the Property Bar in accordance with the object that is currently being worked on.

The way WordPerfect handles the pull-down list of fonts is so logical you wonder why no one did it before. How often have you looked at the list of fonts that MS Word provides and asked yourself the difference between Kaufmann BD and Kaufmann BD BT or some other fonts? WordPerfect provides a preview mode, so that you can see what the fonts will look like.

One thing with MS Word that I found annoying is that the paragraph alignment (left, right, blocked) has always been three separate buttons on the toolbar. Instead, WordPerfect has them on a drop-down menu, the appearance of which is dependent on the alignment of the currently selected paragraph. I know of no one who changes alignment so often that they need all of them immediately accessible like in MS Word. Instead, you have the toolbar cluttered and the buttons taking away space from other things.

Another annoyance is what MS Word does with the toolbar button for creating tables. When you click on the button, you drag the mouse to create a table of the necessary size. As you do, squares expand out. Those squares are huge! There is no need for them to be that big. As a result, there is not enough space on the screen to get a table that is very wide or very long. With WordPerfect, the squares are large enough to be useful, without taking up too much space.

If you are an *almost* touch typist like me, you make many mistakes repeatedly, such as "teh" for "the" or "wehn" for "when." The ability to correct these kinds of mistakes was a welcome addition to MS Word. However, WordPerfect took this one step further. Keep in mind that although there are a number of such cases already input for you by Microsoft, the list must be created by hand. What WordPerfect did was to link the functionality into the dictionary. Therefore, even if the word is not in the list and it can determine there is only one possibility, WordPerfect will make the correction (assuming you have so configured it).

Added to this, WordPerfect also has a "Grammar-As-You-Go" feature. This makes automatic changes, when grammatical mistakes are discovered.

One thing that took getting used to (and I am glad I did) was what WordPerfect does with formatting. WordPerfect gives you much finer control over which formatting codes you have access to (and therefore can remove). When I first started working with WordPerfect, I might have accidentally removed the tag to end a particular format. Suddenly, everything from the start tag to the end of the file took on those properties. It was a fairly simply matter to "force" the formatting like MS Word. However, that meant a larger file because of the superfluous tags and potential problems later on.

WordPerfect allows you to look at the "source code" of the file (Reveal Codes), somewhat like looking at the HTML code of a Web page. You can split the screen so that you see the formatted text in one half and the text and formatting codes in the other half. This includes fonts, colors, emphasizes, URLs, indentation, margins, and any other aspect you can think of. It is then very easy to see exactly how the document is being formatted. Not only can you see it, you can edit either window.

For most users, this is more of a toy than a feature. However, most users are used to forcing the formatting, like MS Word does. However, format is not the same as content. In an environment where you are very concerned with content, such as when using SGML, XML, and so forth, you need to able to mark the text according to its content, not give it some arbitrary appearance. In fact, most users *want* to mark the content but have grown accustomed to forcing the formatting. You mark a word in italics to emphasize it, not just because you like italics.

WordPerfect has complete support for SGML in the ability to both edit SGML documents and create our own document type definitions (DTDs) using tools that are provided by default. In contrast, as of this writing, MS Word only supports it as an add-on product. Microsoft has announced support for XML in Office 2000, but it is highly unlikely that support is for the complete SGML standard.

With the exception of the visual DTD editor and DTD compiler, all SGML components are integrated directly into WordPerfect. Therefore, there is no need to access an external application.

Normally, DTDs are stored as ASCII files. However, this can be extremely inefficient if you need to check complex syntax rules, particularly if you have a large DTD. Therefore, WordPerfect compiles the DTD into "logic files," which are nothing more than the binary representation of the DTD. This makes accessing the information much more efficient.

Another key advantage that the entire WordPerfect Suite offers over MS Office is the integration with Netscape Communicator. If you are already using MS Exchange, then you ought to stick with MS Office, due to the tight integration. However, if you need the advanced features of Netscape Communicator, particularly the advanced features of a UNIX-based email server, you can use any package.

Integration of your office suite and email package is no longer a "nice-to-have." It is a necessity. Therefore, you should really consider how well they integrate with existing products before choosing one. Personally, I do not like to be tied down to any single vendor; therefore I like Netscape Communicator, despite having the more advanced features.

Another aspect is support. Reports by the International Data Corporation indicated that even as late as 1997, three quarters of U.S. corporations were still using Windows 3.1. Although the number is less today, there are still a large number of companies that have not, cannot, and should not upgrade their system. The costs involved are much too great. If the older systems are still creating documents efficiently, why upgrade, other than to feed someone's bank account? In addition, Microsoft usually stops support products after two subsequent releases are shipped. Therefore, support for Word 2.0 and most of the older DOS versions stopped being supported when MS Word 97 shipped. Therefore, in order to get support, customers are forced to upgrade. Corel is still supporting older versions of WordPerfect.

The commonality of features and the overall look and feel across the applications in the WordPerfect Suite are other key features. Despite claims of some people that it is hard to tell when you switch applications, the similarity is truly amazing. Once you have gotten used to one, switching is a breeze.

Another thing that is often missed is the total value of ownership (TVO). This is where the features that a product offers come in. The more you can get out of a product, the more value it is to you. For example, if you use only those features on MS Word that are available in WordPad, the value of owning MS Word is low. In addition, if you need SGML support or any of the advanced features of WordPerfect, which MS Word does not have, the value of MS Word is low as well.

Another component of the WordPerfect Suite is CorelVersions. This is basically a revision control system that extends beyond just WordPerfect. In fact, all components of the CorelVersions can take advantage of the features. Although you can save any number of previous copies, the default is 10, which is generally enough for most business. You can also compress previous versions to save space. You check in and check out the documents and can compare specific versions with any other one.

Even the file dialog box has been enhanced (Figure 9–1). This has become almost a miniapplication, giving you much easier access to file-related

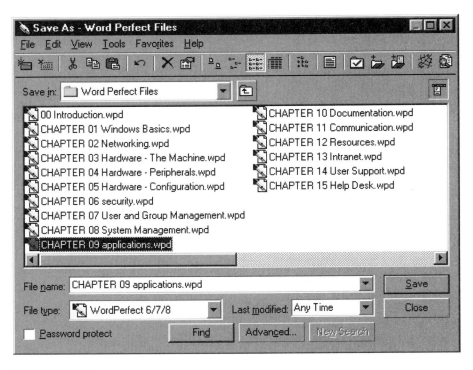

FIGURE 9–1   The WordPerfect file dialog.

functions and features. In addition, the search functionality has been improved as well, giving you much better control.

The WordPerfect Suite also comes with a number of supplemental applications to enhance your productivity. As a communication tool, WordPerfect includes a full version of Netscape Communicator. Some people may believe there is less integration than between MS Office and MS Exchange. However, I have yet to find any limitations, and the advanced features Netscape Communicator provides certainly outweigh an occasional inconvenience, if there are any.

By default, Netscape Communicator supports the Internet standard email format. Using Exchange, you need to make special modifications, thus increasing the TCO of the product.

Coupled with Netscape Communicator is CorelCentral. This is basically a person information manager, which includes a network-capable calendar, address book, card catalog, activity log, and so forth. Admittedly, there are a few features that CorelCentral does not have that MS Exchange does. For example, there is no automatic logging of the files that you have used recently. Although I can use the search function in the open file dialog of any of the applications, the MS Exchange journal is much faster.

In addition to the Internet email standard, both the Corel and Netscape products support the Lightweight Directory Access Protocol (LDAP), something that Microsoft is only now beginning to embrace. Support of this standard allows these products to share calendars and address books across the network. Because this is an open standard, unlike MS Exchange, you can share information across a wide variety of applications, even across multiple platforms.

The "QuickCell" feature of Quattro Pro is also fairly interesting. You can drag a cell onto the Application Bar and watch how its value changes as you make other changes to your table. One way this is extremely useful is testing values and observing their effects on that cell. Something like this is necessary when you are working with large amounts of data, and bouncing back and forth would be a tremendous waste of time.

Quattro Pro also helps in other ways when working with large amounts of data. First, there is the QuickFilter function. This allows you to easily filter out specific information you are looking for by telling Quattro Pro what it should or shouldn't display. In addition, you have up to three levels of search criteria, with a wide range of conditions on which you can base the filter.

Another filter mechanism is the ability to "outline" groups of data. Here, you group rows and columns, enabling or disabling the display of these cells as you need to. In this way, for example, you can hide the details or display key elements such as totals or summaries.

Quattro Pro also has a couple of features, which it lists under the heading of "auditing." These tools perform "watchdog" operations to ensure the validity of your data. For example, you can effortlessly trace dependent cells and calculations to ensure you are getting the results you expect.

Additionally, Quattro Pro supports the same kind of Property Bars that WordPerfect supports. Here, too, the Property Bar takes on a different form depending on what you have selected. Therefore, you are presented only the tools that are applicable and are not distracted by erroneous buttons.

One neat feature is the ability to add comments or QuickTips to individual cells. When you stop the mouse over the cell, a tiny window pops up showing you the comment. In essence, this is nothing more than what many applications (including those in the WordPerfect Suite) already do with buttons on the toolbars. These provide explanations of the cells, helping to make the table self-documenting. In addition, you can also put the equations the cells contain into the comment, so there is no need to click on the cells to see where it gets its value.

Like WordPerfect, Quattro Pro is designed for integration with other applications. It contains a larger number of filters to import and export data, including the ability to export the tables directly into HTML. Plus you can add hyperlinks in your tables that link to other tables as well as to pages on the Web.

Another output enhancement is the ability to specify exactly how many pages to print. I don't know how many times I have fought with the margins on other spreadsheet applications in order to keep the last column or two from being on a page by themselves.

Corel Presentations is, as its name implies, the presentation component of the Corel WordPerfect Office Suite. Like the other components, Corel Presentations was specially designed to take advantage of Intel's MMX technology. This helps to optimize memory usage and avoid the annoying system crashes common with other large applications on Windows 95. In addition, transitions and displaying graphics are much faster, so your viewers don't have to wait.

One feature that I was especially glad to see is called "Custom Audiences." Here, you can save multiple versions of the same presentation within the same file. This supports the whole idea of having a single source with multiple outputs. Here you specify what slides belong to what presentation and then chose the set you want to display. This could be useful when you have a technical presentation and need to "water it down" for management. The ease at which you can switch is aided by the ability to give these sets long, descriptive names.

Like the other applications, Corel Presentations provides a wide range of filters allowing you to import information from a larger number of sources. In addition, you have the same Internet publishing functionality.

In the package are a handful of added applications, such as Corel PhotoHouse, which is an image manipulation and processing tool. Although not as powerful as Adobe Photoshop, it does provide a wide range of tools and is extremely useful for most business applications.

In support of the ability of the other Corel applications to export their files to HTML, Corel also provides Corel Barista. In essence, you can use any graphics, formatting, or fonts in your document and have it faithfully recreated on your Web pages. This allows your documents to go beyond the limitations of standard HTML. This includes multimedia elements. As an added bonus, Corel Barista also behaves like a printer driver. Therefore, all you need to do to create your Web page is choose the Barista printer.

One limitation of many spreadsheet programs is the lack of advanced reporting features. Spreadsheets let you organize your data or, as in the case of Quattro Pro, filter your views of the data to see specific details. You can generate graphs of the data and even analyze trends. However, much of the work is done manually, and there is no reporting functionality as you get with database programs. This is where the Corel Data Modeling Desktop comes in.

As its name implies, the Data Modeling Desktop is used for data modeling. Reports can be generated by simply dragging row and columns from Quattro Pro (or other applications) onto the modeling desktop. Once there, you can "experiment" with the position and appearance of the labels to get the format you need. Doing so also manipulates the data to provide the resulting information you need. The Data Modeling Desktop also supports dynamic data exchange (DDE), allowing it to communicate with other DDE applications (including Quattro Pro) as both a server and a client.

Corel's DataBase Publisher is another data access tool, which allows you to query a wide range of data sources, such as Paradox, dBase, MS Access, MS SQL Server, and most any other database that supports SQL. Note that even in this content the word "query" takes on the same meaning as in other SQL contexts. That is, you cannot only read data, but also write it and make other changes to your databases. One place I find tools like this is when I am developing my intranet pages. I work on my queries here to make sure I am getting them right before I port them to the intranet pages. This saves me a lot of time in debugging as the response I get here is much quicker and the messages are much clearer.

StarOffice

Comparing StarOffice from StarDivision to MS Office does not do StarOffice justice. Regardless of the limitations of MS Office, it is still a collection of individual products. Each time you load one of these applications, they run in their own separate memory space. In contrast, StarOffice is a single application, with each type of document (text, spreadsheet, Web page) all accessible through a single interface.

StarOffice separates itself from MS Office in a couple of other ways. First, the pricing is much more attractive. As of this writing, a full version of StarOffice is cheaper than an upgrade version of MS Office. In addition, whereas Microsoft no longer allows you to use MS Office at home if you use it at work, StarDivision lets you use StarOffice at home even if you do not use StarOffice at work.

Another major advantage is when you have a mixed Unix–NT environment. StarOffice runs on most major versions of Unix. In addition, there is an application server version that allows you to run StarOffice on the rest. Therefore, all of your users have access to the same application regardless of which operating system they use.

For people who are used to MS Office, StarOffice is full of pleasant surprises. In many cases, they are small things. However, when you think about them, you ask yourself why they weren't implemented in other products. For example, one major aspect is the integration of all the functionality into a single interface. With MS Office you have basically double overhead if you were to load Word and Excel, for example. That is, all of the menu, toolbars, and everything else Windows needs to carry around with it to manage applications is in memory twice. This is one of the primary reasons why Windows applications appear to run out of memory while saying you have a lot free. This is because you are not running out of memory, per se, but rather system resources. StarOffice solves that problem by having everything in a single interface.

With StarOffice 3.1, there were a number of separate applications, just like MS Office. The primary applications were StarWriter, StarCalc, StarChart, StarDraw, StarImage, and Starmath.

In contrast to the changes in MS Office 7.0, StarOffice 4.0 was more than just new functions, bug fixes, and has similar improvements. Instead, StarOffice 4.0 was essentially a completely new product, which integrated all of the components at the same time adding almost all of the additional functionality one needs in a true office suite.

The fact that StarOffice is a single application should not be underestimated. In addition to saving resources, you also save time. How often does it take you to load each of the MS Office applications? Once StarOffice is loaded, you basically have full access to all of its functionality. StarOffice doesn't require a moment to adjust itself when switching from one document type to another. This is simply because the menus, toolbars, and so forth are different depending on what kind of document you're accessing. However, this is hardly noticeable, and at any rate it is substantially faster than having to load one of the MS Office applications from scratch.

One of the StarOffice's marketing slogans is "Do Everything in One Place." With version 5.0 this is even more true. In addition to your standard office applications, StarOffice 5.0 can also replace your standard Windows desktop (Figure 9–2). Here you have the same basic functionality as the Windows desktop.

StarOffice is Internet aware more than just being able to insert URLs into documents. This applies not only to documents on the Internet but also on your company's intranet. That is, you can create links to documents on the

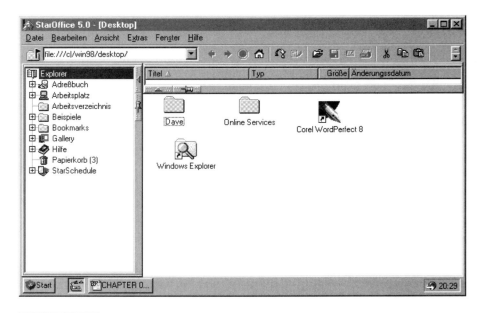

FIGURE 9–2 StarOffice desktop.

file system, just like you can with most modern office products. In addition, if it is supported by your server, you can load Web documents, change them, and save them back to the server.

Another aspect of the integration is that you have access to the exact same ends in every program. For example, it has always annoyed me that spelling dictionary is different among the various Microsoft applications. That is, I could add a word to the dictionary in one program and I knew it would not be available in the other applications. This meant I had to repeat the work if I wanted the same entries.

The concepts of network computing are another aspect of StarOffice. In addition to being able to the edit documents on the Internet, linked document will automatically be recognized as such. For example, if you insert a URL, StarOffice will format it accordingly. From then on, clicking on it will start your browser; for example, this applies to email as well as documents on the file system. Part of this is the fact that documents loaded from the file system are done by using the FILE Internet protocol. If you want, you can input a different protocol such as HTTP or FTP. Therefore, the functionality is always the same regardless of where the document exists.

Unlike MS Office, StarOffice has email as the integrated component. That is, no external application is started for you to either send or receive email. This makes integration easier and saves you a great deal of time. In addition, StarOffice supports all of the Internet email standards, such as SMTP, IMAP4, POP3, and LDAP.

StarWriter, the word processing component of StarOffice, includes an HTML mode, allowing you to create your own Web sites, without the need of starting any external applications. Although this functionality is available in other word processors, StarWriter takes this one step further and allows you to create HTML frames. This means that the individual documents written to the frames are not treated individually, but rather you have everything as it would appear in a browser.

An image map editor is also provided, which allows you to create "hot spots" in graphics. These are images on Web pages, when you click on them, different pages are loaded depending on where you click. You have your choice of different shapes such as rectangles, ellipses, polygons, and even free-hand polygons. Depending on your Web server, you can save these image maps directly in the HTML file (as a client-side image map) or on the server (as a CERN and NCSA map).

Interactive pages can also be created. This means that StarWriter allows you to create forms and test them directly in StarOffice. StarOffice also supports Java, Javascript, as well as Netscape plug-ins.

For me, the most dramatic and perhaps awe-inspiring feature of StarOffice is the ability to recover from a crash. I first have to say that when using StarOffice, the application crashes much less frequently than in MS Office. Although I have never had the Unix version crash on me, I have had problems with the Windows version. Whereas MS Office might force me to *reboot* a couple times a day on Windows 95, I am surprised when I have to simply *restart* StarOffice more than once a week.

Another key aspect is what happens when StarOffice is forced to shutdown as a result of some Windows problem. I get a friendly message from StarOffice (but not always from MS Office) indicating that it cannot continue and that all of my changes have been saved. When I restart StarOffice, all of my changes have, in fact, been saved. At first, I wasn't entirely sure whether everything was there. However, when the application crashed on subsequent occasions, I made careful record of what my last change was. Sure enough, when I restarted StarOffice (not reboot Windows), everything to the last input character was still there. How many times has an MS Office application given up the ghost and you lost half an hour of work?

As I mentioned briefly, StarOffice can also take over the functionality of your desktop. The entire workspace is called StarDesktop and it tries to take on the appearance of your normal desktop as well as give you access to everything you normally have from your desktop. In essence, anything that you can lay on the standard Windows desktop, you can put on the StarDesktop. This includes the ability to link to applications, files, directories, and even documents on the Internet.

StarDesktop also provides a status line, which is similar to the taskbar in Windows 95/98/NT. Here you see the open documents as well as running applications. Unlike MS Office you do not have to hunt for the open documents. A mouse click on that document or application and you are immediately switched to it.

Another place where you see how well the components are integrated is when you need to access elements that are generally considered a part of a different application. For example, it is not unreasonable to expect that you need to insert a table into a text document. Although this is entirely possible in MS Word, the table functionality is extremely limited. To overcome this limitation, you have to insert an Excel table into your document. This means you have to bring extra components with you.

However, this is not the case with StarOffice. All of the functions are always available to you, without the extra overhead. In addition, the auto identification function automatically recognizes headings, numbers, text, and so forth and formats the contents accordingly. In addition, once you have defined the default formatting of your numbers (such as for currency, number of decimal places, and so forth) this formatting is applied to all of the different components. You'll never again have the problem with a formatting being different between the word processor and the spreadsheet (unless, of course, you wanted it).

StarOffice also takes auto-correction one step further. We are all used to the auto correction where "teh" is automatically corrected as "the." With StarOffice, this auto-correction also applies to phrases. For example, "iti s" is correct as "it is." It is also possible to define where rules are not applied. For example, it is common for word processors to "correct" to capitals at the beginning of a word. However, "PCs" as the plural of "PC" is spelled correctly.

It is also expected (at least in my mind) that any sentence preceded and followed by an empty line is a heading. StarOffice recognizes this and uses the proper heading format. StarOffice can also correct for cases where the author is used to working with simple text editors. For example, *bold* and _underlined_ are common formatting tricks. StarOffice recognizes these and automatically changes them to bold and underlined.

StarOffice is built on a concept of systematic and interrelated templates. This is similar in concept to the cascading style sheets found in HTML documents. Changes at one level can be made to ripple down to all subsequent levels, unless that particular style has already been defined at one of the lower levels. For example, assume you have defined a style to be twice the size of what the standard size is. If you were to increase the standard from 10 to 12 point, the other style would increase from 20 to 24 point.

It is possible to make separate (i.e., noncontiguous) text areas and apply the same formatting to each. It is also possible to link this function with the search-and-replace function. For example, you could find the company name everywhere it appears in the document and replace it with a link to the Web site.

The search function is further improved with the ability to look for "similar" words. It's possible that you misspelled a word somewhere in the document. A traditional search won't find it unless you first do a spell check. StarOffice can be configured so that it will find a word even if characters have been switched, new ones added, or some are missing.

The StarOffice is also supplied with a scripting/macro language called StarBasic, which is very similar to BASIC. Even as early as StarOffice 4.0, you are provided with a complete development environment rather than a simple text editor. This also included the characteristic of displaying different components in different colors. For example, keywords such as if, then, so, and, and so forth are blue. Comments are gray. Expressions such as variables or function names are green. This functionality was then taken over by subsequent versions of MS Office and their Visual Basic applications.

As with other macro languages, the simplest way to create a macro is to record specific actions, which can then be played back later. However, you can edit these macros as well as create your own from scratch. It is also possible to store functions and some routines into libraries, which are then accessible to every other macro.

The spreadsheet component is called StarCalc and provides a number of mechanisms to include data in individual cells. Logically, you can input the values directly. Also, as with StarWriter, StarCalc has an auto-complete function. That means, the program offers a possible completion to a value or word you have started. All you need to do is simply hit the Enter Key for it to complete the word. This applies not only to values such as words and numbers, but also to formulas.

The second possibility for inputting data is a selection that you reach through the context menu (using the right mouse button). This will offer you a selection of all of the different values that appear anywhere in the same column. You simply click on that value and it is input into the field. In addition, as with other spreadsheet programs, StarCalc will expand lists of members or values automatically. For example, if the first two cells are the numbers 1 and 2, StarCalc can fill in the following cells with 3, 4, 5, and so on. Most of this is available with spreadsheet programs.

StarCalc also supports expansion of predefined lists, for example, days of the week or months. One impressive aspect of StarCalc is the ability to use "natural language" in your formulas. Let's assume, for example, you have a table where the rows have the names of the months and columns have the names of cities. You could create a formula that simply says January San Francisco + February San Francisco + March San Francisco to get the results of the first quarter in that city. Alternatively, you could say January San Francisco + January Los Angeles + January New York to give you the totals for those three cities.

StarCalc also has something called a "Scenario Mode." Here you create a number of "what if" conditions and observe how the values in the tables change.

The presentation component of StarOffice is called StarImpress. As with the other components, this is integrated into the StarOffice desktop and is not a server application. In addition, it has the same basic features as the other components, such as an "auto pilot" to create new documents as well as documents templates, spell checker, auto correction, auto formatting of headings, and the ability to change references to URLs to real hyperlinks.

As with other presentation packages, you have the ability to present your document with all of the standard features such as animation, fading in and out, and so forth. With StarImpress, it is also possible to have the presentation running in one window and still have access to your desktop.

As an extension, StarImpress offers what it calls "live mode." During a running presentation, you can make changes without having to start the presentation from the beginning or click through to find the right spot. You have access to all of the normal editing functions that you would normally. In addition, because of the tight integration between the various components, you can include such things as tables, make changes to their values, and watch how the values changed on-screen. Together with the scenario mode of Star-Calc, you have a very powerful presentation tool.

As with the other modules, StarImpress works with a linked template structure. That is, changes to one template can have a ripple effect to all linked templates. StarImpress not only allows you to create templates for your presentations but also for the graphics. Because graphics are elements that can be placed into any kind of documents, the graphics templates you create are available from anywhere.

The kinds of graphics that you can create with StarImpress are truly impressive. Although not yet up to the level of more-complex graphics applications, such as CorelDraw, you are provided with intermediate levels of functionality. Not only do you have the same basic functions you have with other tools, you have the ability to convert any kind of objects including text objects into polygons, curves, and even 3-D objects. There are a number of 3-D objects that are already created for you, and it is a simple matter of converting a text object, into graphics objects. These objects can be changed in a wide variety of ways, such as changing the size, orientation, as well as the direction, strength, and color of the light source. When you're finished with your drawings, they can be exported into common formats such as GIF or JPEG, allowing you to publish them on the Internet.

StarImage is described as being a "classical drawing program." Its purpose is to create and manipulate simple drawings. It is closer to a bitmap editor than it is to a true graphics program like CorelDraw. However, it can import and export a wide range of common graphics formats.

StarChart is a diagramming module, which can take data from a wide range of sources. Under the heading of "visualize your data," StarChart offers a wide range of ways to display your data. Plus both 2-D and 3-D charts are available. An AutoUpdate is included, so even if the data source has changed, your chart will still be accurate.

StarBase is the built-in database for StarOffice. When you create a database, you can create it as a dBase database, straight text file, or connect to an existing database using ODBC. Several AutoPilots are provided to help you create tables, forms, reports, and queries.

Documentation

Documentation with respect to supporting users takes many different forms. This includes not only the documentation that you create about your information systems; it also includes documentation that came with the hardware and software products that you implement. Each has its own unique set of characteristics, but one of the key aspects is making it available to the users.

Categorize Your Documents

The very first step in getting your documentation in line is to analyze what you have in order to determine what type of documents are being used. Here, we are not referring to MS Word as being different from MS Excel, but rather offer letters as being different from order confirmation letters, for example. Each contains similar information, but they are not identical.

I think it is very useful to classify documents based on their functionality. You can tell that this idea is not new by the fact that all common word processing programs come with a set of predefined templates. In many cases, these templates contain suggested text for a particular document but at the very least contain common formatting

380

elements. It is very simple to take these templates as a base and to create your own as needed. This ensures a great deal of standardization between documents. Having these templates not only ensures a common appearance as seen by the customer, but it also serves as an aid in administering the system.

Most file systems that I have seen have a general format; however, there is no detailed structure. For example, in one company we had a directory on the server called PROGRAMS that contained the program directories and DATA that contained the data. Each was shared and all workstations were connected to these directories with the same drive letter (i.e., E: for programs and F: for data).

Although this was a noble effort, there was nothing set up for what the structure looked like underneath these directories nor was there anything in place that prevents administrators from putting programs in the DATA directory. There were several cases where data already existed, and a program update was simply loaded into the same directory as the data "to make things easier." Data was also stored in the PROGRAMS directory so that it was "closer" to the program. In addition, the structure of each drive was unorganized. At first, some people might think that programs cannot be organized. However, with a little thought, we discovered they could be.

To solve this problem, we began to organize the products by functionality. For example, there were a number of tools that only the administrators should or needed to have access to. These were all moved to a directory called System, along with the drivers and other files we needed to administer the system. We set the permissions on the directory so that normal users could not even see the contents of this directory.

The main goal of all this is efficient access to the files. It is a waste of time and therefore money if you have to hunt for what you need. By classifying or categorizing your documents, it is much easier to organize them on the file system. This makes finding them much easier.

A secondary goal is easier administration. A disorganized file system means that it is likely that some directories and documents are either superfluous or exist in another form somewhere else. The result is often multiple groups with the same functionality that could be combined. You may also find there are groups with overlapping functionality that can actually be combined.

Up to this point, we have been talking about documentation and documents as general concepts. The reason is that a document needs to be thought of as more than just a word processing file, which is usually what most people think of. It is more useful to think of a document as anything that contains information. This can be a word processing document, such as from MS Word, but it can also be an Excel spreadsheet, and Access database, a CorelDraw image, and in many contexts, even programs can (and should) be treated as documents.

You should consider these different file types all as documents for the various ways in which you access the information. In general, documents are accessed with the program that created them. However, using various "connectivity" protocols, such as Dynamic Data Exchange (DDE), Object-Oriented Database Connectivity (ODBC), and even object linking and embedding (OLE), you can use different programs to access the information.

Note also that often the tool that you use to access or even create a particular document may not necessarily be the correct one. The key word here is "correct" and not "best." For example, in one company, we purchased several copies of a flow chart software to create flowcharts for our documentation. However, we discovered that the WordDraw component of MS Word created diagrams that were sufficient. If the diagrams were much larger than what we needed, WordDraw might not have been enough. However, for our modest needs, it worked out. We could therefore eliminate the flow-charting program for our inventory, which saved money on updates as well as on training and support.

Information needs to be organized in the way that the user sees it, not as the IS/IT sees it or expects it to be. For example, IS/IT may see the information as grouped according to the program used to access it. For example, they may be directories labeled "Excel Data," "Word Documents," and so on. In these directories, there may be no additional structure, which makes finding the right document difficult at best. (Believe me, I have seen companies that sort information like this.)

On the other hand, from the users' perspective, documents are grouped by department or process. Because the users are the ones that will be accessing this information more often, they need to be the ones that the organization is designed to fit.

Document Standards

There is more to writing documentation than simply putting words onto paper. However, there are many companies where I would be happy if they even did that much. If the information is written down, even in a nonstandard format, it is usually better than no documentation at all. (The exception is when it takes too much time to figure out what is being said.)

Despite the varying contents, you will find that most documents have the same basic structure. Obviously, documents of a particular type (e.g., project proposals, datasheets) will have a common structure. However, there are a number of elements that are common to all data types.

Each document, regardless of type will have a body. This is where the information is. Most will have some kind of "front matter," which often contains a table of contents, introduction, list of figures, and so on. Each of these elements has a common structure as well. The body often consists of sections and subsections, each with a heading, body, and possibly its own front matter.

It is usually the case that each type of element has its own format, but that format is consistent through the document. For example, a level-1 heading on page 42 looks the same as a level-2 heading on page 6. Figure captions have the same style, and these styles are generally consistent, even between documents. I have worked in companies where there was a standard for formatting within different kinds of documents, but the process to reach that standard was not defined.

Let's take as an example the level-2 heading and assume that it has been defined as 12 point, bold, italic. One key aspect is that there is normally a "standard" text style that is changed so that it is 12 point, bold, and italic. Therefore, someone could make the text "standard" and simply change the characteristics so that it fits the description of the level-2 heading. In other words, it "looks" like the level-2 heading. Some people may take a level-1 heading and change the characteristics accordingly.

When the standard changes (for example, it moves to a different medium), every single heading needs to be changed individually. That is, any place that is a level-2 heading within the document needs to be changed by hand.

Some people attempt to solve the problem by using document templates in which particular styles (such as the level-2 heading) have defined characteristics. When the style is changed, they only need to change it once, and it is valid for every case where that style is used. What about the 63 other people that do not use document templates and styles?

The obvious solution is to require that everyone uses the company's templates. However, the standard formats that are used in these templates may not be used by some users. For example, in one company, we did have a number of templates. However, these defined the general format of the document. Although there were specific styles defined, many people still used their own method. The reason: Nothing was done/said when the predefined styles were not used.

The solution to that problem is to require management not to accept documents that do not fulfill the requirements. Imagine the reaction of a young, energetic employee who works all week to get the report in on time but is told it is not done yet because it does not follow the company policy. You would not think twice about reprimanding an employee about not following policy in terms of working hours, dress code, or a dozen other things. Why can't this same thing apply to document standards? It can. The fact that the employee has to spend all weekend redoing the document to meet company standards is good motivation to get it right the next time.

Some people may think that I am going overboard with this. After all, one person not following the procedure on one document is no big deal. However, I know from experience (and you probably know yourself) that this is not limited to one person and one document. In addition, the more often any single document gets changed, the more acute the problem becomes. Although, I am not suggesting that you convert all existing documents to the appropriate standards, I am suggesting that you at least start with the new documents.

Naming Your Documents

File names should also adhere to a predefined convention. There should be something within the file name to describe what kind of document it is as well as the contents. What the convention is is often a matter of personal preference. However, the convention must be consistent throughout the company.

For example, assume you have a customer named Dickson and Blinn, Inc. Have a directory SALES, which is the domain of the sales department. Underneath is a subdirectory called customers followed by another subdirectory Dickson-Blinn. All of the sales information is in a directory with the company name and broken into projects. You might have a letter that contains the initial offer, which you have named, "Letter First Offer 980720.doc." You can tell by the name what kind of document type it is (a letter), what is about (first offer), and the date it was created. If you had sent a fax instead, the document might be named, "Fax First Offer 980720.doc."

Because Windows NT (as well as Windows 95/98) supports long file names, you could name the file something like "Dickson-Blinn Letter First Offer 980720.doc." After a while, the file names may get incredibly long, so you might want to come up with some abbreviations. However, this scheme allows you to immediately identify the document without having to open it first.

I usually like to include the date as part of the name of several reasons. First, if the document is copied or sent via email, the original date can get lost. If it's in the name, I know when it was created. I really don't care what the file system thinks the date is, which is not often the date the file was created. Second, I can completely ignore the date column in the Windows Explorer as I already have the date in the document name.

Note the order of the date. In this example, I used YYMMDD. In my opinion this is the best format because it automatically sorts the files chronological. First all of the documents from a specific group (company, type of document, content) are located together. Within that set are all the documents from a specific year, then month, finally those on a specific day. If you used something like DDMMYY, you would still need to sort things using the file date, which may not be accurate.

Document Formats

Defining a standard document format is beneficial to both the administrators and the users. Users a not frustrated by getting a document that they cannot read, nor do they need to become familiar with all of the programs needed. Administrators do not need to manage all of the different formats and applications, plus management of the licenses is much easier.

Perhaps the most effective format when providing information on the Internet or Intranet is HTML. Provided you don't do anything fancy, any browser will be able to read your pages. You run into problems, however, when you are providing larger documents. Although, the same problems apply to customers, in this case I am specifically talking about your users, such as service or sales people that are on the road a lot.

The first solution is to provide them in their native formats, which the user can the processes. Although you might expect most people to have an MS Word compatible word processor, not everyone has one that can read Word 97 documents. If they are employees, you could ensure that each has the most current version of the application to make sure there are no compatibility problems. However, you also need to consider the applications that they may not need.

This is brings up the intrinsic problem of always upgrading to the latest and greatest. In general, older versions cannot read files created with new versions. If they can, there is a lot of information that is lost. This problem accounted for several calls a day during the time we converted to Windows NT and MS Office 97. Nothing was said to the users about the different formats, so new those with MS Office 97 were saving them in the default format, which made the files unreadable by those with the older system.

Terminology Standards

Even with a minimum on standardization, you will save yourself a great deal of work, beyond just the issues of changes to the formatting. However, this requires standardization of more than just the formatting, but the contents as well. This is useful in several places. One necessary place is in translation of the documents. If your business only sells products in the United States, it is unlikely that you have offices in other countries. Therefore translation is less of an issue.

However, if you have either offices or customers in non-English-speaking countries, standardization will ease the translation. This comes from standardizing what phrases are used to mean certain things. For example, in one company within one document there were references to a "deficiency report," "notice of deficiency," and an "error notice." All three meant the same thing. Using different phrases like this makes it harder to understand what is meant in just one language. Plus, it makes it harder for the translator to find the right phrase. In addition, using the same words in English means you can more easily come up with a 1:1 translation.

Sometimes (not always) different phrases within the same document can be understood correctly. However, when different phrases are used in different documents, it is much harder to determine whether the writers mean the same thing or not. We found that in an extremely large number of cases that different words were used, and the users were uncertain what was meant.

If the word or phrase comes from another source, use that phrase unless you already have a predefined phrase within your company. If this is the case and the other sources will be referred to (such as a software user's manual), always make a reference to the differing phases. My suggestion is that if you are providing a description of the software (e.g., specifics on how to use it in your business) you should use the words and phrases in the program. However, if you are providing a more general document (e.g., an implementation plan) that is not necessarily intended for the users of the product, use your own term and a reference to the other as needed.

In general, the same thing applies to abbreviation. Standard abbreviations should obviously be used. If your company has their own set of abbreviations, they either need to be defined the first time they are used or you need a glossary of abbreviations. Remember that an abbreviation may be "common knowledge," but only for the people who have worked in the company for several years. I have worked in places where such abbreviations were used (unexplained) in documentation intended for new hires. How are they expected to know what the abbreviation means?

We found it useful to create a company-wide dictionary. Originally, this was an Excel table with one column for each language. The disadvantage was that the translators (or whoever wanted to use it) had to first start Excel. Because this was the only reason that Excel was being used by many of these people, there was also the issue of unnecessary Excel licenses. Eventually, this was converted to a simple text file and accessed via a perl script on our Intranet server.

An extension of this is a company glossary. An explanation is provided along with the phrase so that users can be assured that they have the correct phrase. In most cases, this is only necessary in a production environment where the sheer number of similar terms makes finding the correct one a challenge. However, a company glossary can also be useful for new employees.

The reason why the document had three different phrases is that the writer wanted it to be more colorful and thought using different words sounded better. This works for a novel and may work for a book like this one. However, for a list of instructions it only leads to confusion. Standardizing phraseology means that the meaning is clear (hopefully) and the writer does not waste time searching for a "fitting" expression.

Choosing a standard format is also important for the reader. Recognizing special elements is easy when there is a constant format. In many cases, that actual text can be skipped and just the appearance is looked at.

In addition, there are a number of recognized standards organizations such as ANSI, NIST, ISO, and so forth. If they have a standard that applies to your business, then that's what you need to use. Another standard to consider is the application you use. Prior to implementing a new application, you might have used a specific term within your company. However, the application uses its own phrase for the exact same thing. If your documentation describes this, then you need to make a reference to the fact that there is a difference there. This does not mean your documentation must use the same term as the application, but rather the documentation needs to refer to the fact that the application uses a different one.

Whatever standard you choose, whether an internal one or from an outside agency, make the list of words, phrases and abbreviations available to everyone in the company. A perfect place is the company Intranet. With very little programming, you can provide the information both alphabetically and with a search function.

Templates

Templates are an excellent way of encouraging if not forcing users to adher to standards. Although you cannot stand behind everyone to make sure they use the templates or the formatting styles within the template, the templates provide an easy way for the user to apply styles. Because it actually is less work for them, they have a good reason to use them and not format things by hand.

As we talked about a moment ago, if you classify your documents, you can define a single template for each type of document. The template will then contain the appropriate formatting styles. This won't "force" people to use the standard formats. However, it makes it easier for them so there is less resistance as well as it is more likely that use will follow the standard.

Even the template and the names of individual styles within the template should be standardized. For example, if you company is named Acme, Inc., the name of your company fax template could be named acme_fax. It is then obvious from the name the scope and its function. The style acme_fax_ heading used to define the style of the fax heading.

Headings are a point where you need to pay attention. You need to make a decision whether there is a separate style for each heading or not. If you decided that the fax heading will be different than the one in a letter, then it makes sense to use different style names, so you know what you are referring to. However, just because the styles are identical, does not mean they should have the same name. Instead, you could still create new headings that are simply copies of each other.

It is also useful to define a stated set of style names that can be used in almost all of your documents. This makes changing them later much easier if you need to. Having templates and a specific set of styles gives all of your documents a common appearance. This actually makes finding the information within the document much easier.

Choosing What to Document

Documenting the right things is just as important as documenting the first place. Although you can go to extremes, I think there are a lot of things that should be documented, but are not. Always keep in mind that if you failed to document, now the information is probably lost. Even if you do remember to write it down a week later, you have probably forgotten some of the details. Often, having parts is as bad as having nothing

What things get documented need to be as much a part of the standard as the format and styles. In many cases, such as ISO certification, you are obligated to document certain aspects of your company, its business and processes. However, there are certainly a number of things not required by ISO (or whomever) that you should document.

For example, although organizing and running meetings might fall into a category of communication, it is a good idea that these meetings be documented. Part of this is decided in advance, like who will be taking notes at the meeting and where the minutes will be stored when the meeting is over. I'm a strong believer of taking minutes at these meetings, but there is no need to force the minutes on people instead by storing them in a common location people on access to them if they want.

Once again, no matter what you decide to document, it needs to be part of the company standard. The standard should say what needs to be documented, how, and where it is eventually stored.

Documentation Content

You can spend all of the time in the world deciding what should be documented, writing it down and then publishing on paper or on your Intranet. However, if the content is unusable, you have wasted your time. Providing useful content is not just a matter of putting words onto paper. There are several key aspects that you need to address in order to make the document worth the reader's time.

Know Your Audience

The very first step in writing anything is knowing for whom you are writing. Without a clear idea of who your audience is, all the other parts are simply "going through motions."

For example, if you do not know who your audience is, how can you be sure the information is understandable? It may be understandable to you, but not to your audience. After all, who is your audience? How can you make the information accessible, when you do not know what information the audience needs? Who cares if what you say is accurate, when the people reading it do not care about what you are telling them?

By knowing who your audience is, you can address those topics that are important and of interest to them. Let's take, as an example, a status report for a project you are working on. If the report is for other departments working with you, they may be interested in just knowing how far along the project is. If the report is for the finance people, they may only be interested in how well you are keeping within budget or how much has already been spent. If it's for management, they may be interested in both.

Next, you need to understand why your audience is reading what you are writing. The answer many might give is that they are required to (e.g., a company report, textbook). That is just a superficial answer, as there is some motivation behind the person who is "making" them read it. What is in your writing that makes someone else read it?

If people choose the topic themselves, they more than likely have an interest in that subject. For example, this book is about Windows NT, and it says so on the cover. I know someone who buys this book has a specific interest in learning about Windows NT. Therefore, I addressed those issues that were important for learning about Windows NT. I could have spent a great deal of time talking about operating system theory and programming, but neither is essential for learning about Windows NT. I spent only enough time on those topics to provide the appropriate background.

Whether or not you are writing user documentation, you need to know the level you are writing for. If intended for the beginner, the internal workings of the application may be too deep. If for an advanced user, "getting started" sections might be too boring.

By understanding who your audience is, you can then go directly to those issues that are important. In addition, you can present the information in a way and at the level the audience can understand. By talking about what interests and is important to your audience, as well as writing at the level they need, you are addressing their needs.

For example, as I mentioned in the introduction, this book is intended for system administrators and managers. I also said that this was not a book on using Windows NT, but rather I said that it was specifically intended to help support users who are running Windows NT. Therefore, it would be inappropriate for me to go into detail about using the File Manager. I might talk about a specific aspect and how it could be used, but the nuts and bolts would generally be inappropriate for this book.

One problem that we often encountered was what appeared to be an attempt by the author to "impress" the reader. For example, long words were frequently chosen, where a more simple term would apply. Complicated sentence structure was used, which often required the reader to read the sentence or paragraph several times in order to understand it. I distinctly remember a sentence in one company that was eight lines long. It was loaded with conjunctions and parentheses and almost useless because it was so hard to understand.

Organize

Your goal in any writing is to pass information. If your audience cannot get at the information that you are providing, then you have failed in your task as a writer. By organizing your document effectively, your audience can quickly access the information it needs.

How you organize your material will depend on the subject matter, who your audience is, as well as the information that you are trying to impart. For example, consider a major project in a big company. A report describing the financial status (expenditures, cost overruns, etc.) will have a different organization than a report describing the status of each portion of the project. Both have the same audience and subject (the status of the project), but the information you want to impart is different. A software manual for a graphics package intended for people just wanting to "play" with the software will have a different organization than one written for graphic artists or advanced users. Same subject and information, but different audiences.

The key is to allow quick access to the information. This does not necessarily mean the reader should be able to quickly find a specific piece of information, but rather that the reader is able to quickly grasp the overall information.

Let's use the graphics software again as an example. The information you are trying to impart is how to use the product, not how to draw a circle. Therefore, your organization should be based on using the entire product and not on specific functions. One approach would be to have chapters based on general functionality, such as creating basic shapes, combining shapes, or working with colors and shading.

One approach is to take the menu headings and use them as chapter or section headings for the documentation. There was some logic in grouping the menus the way you did, so organizing the documentation the same way makes sense. For example, you have a section on editing the drawing and another on working with colors, as Edit and Color are two of your menus. Alternatively, you could group the tasks into more slightly abstract terms. For example, creating shapes requires the use of both the Edit and Color menus.

In other kinds of documentation, the process is the same. If you are preparing a status report on a major project, you may want to break down the information according to each of the groups (departments) involved in the project. If the project is composed of component projects, then you could organize your document according to these smaller projects.

One thing that I always find annoying is when a writer has to digress to make the subject understandable. This is usually the case when a certain amount of background knowledge is necessary. For example, in our software manual example, you may be talking about working with colors and need to mention the different types of color representation, such as RGB (red-green-blue).

Although this is useful (and maybe necessary) information, having it in the middle of the discussion on using the appropriate controls in the program may throw people off. If this is something a particular reader knows, he or she has to wade through the material to find what is interesting.

There are two ways around this. First, include a section at the beginning of the chapter or section that provides the background. Alternatively, you can include sidebars that provide the necessary information. Which way you do it is a matter of choice and varies with the type of document. For example, in technical manuals, I prefer to have the sidebar. However, with report-type documents, I prefer to have the background information at the beginning. Regardless of what way you choose, be consistent throughout the document. If background information is described in a sidebar in one chapter, do not make it the introduction to the next one.

If you are writing a manual, then you will probably have some examples of how to do certain things. Although you should include examples in your descriptions, you need to be sure that they are appropriate and properly placed. Background information or an overview does not need instructions, but a reference might. If your document is task oriented (such as a user manual), then the document will be based on instructions.

The best documents, whether reports or for training, are a combination of reference and instruction. Instruction is more than just learning a new fact, like the fact that the project is overbudget. However, if the report mentions the reason is because of the cost of implementing a new material that has a better cost/weight ratio, the audience has learned about this new material. Conversely, if you have a training manual, you want the audience to be able to complete certain steps. However, you want a certain amount of reference, so that they don't have to reread everything to get at a piece of information they are missing.

Make the Information Accessible

What good is a document or other piece of information if the reader cannot find it. Here, I am not talking about physically finding the document in the file system, but rather finding a specific piece of information within the document. This might be caused by insufficient "navigational aides" within the document. For example, I have found a number of documents where the index is not much more than a repeat of the table of contents. The table of contents was also vague in terms of what is in each chapter.

If you are providing documentation for your users, there is no need to be "cute" with chapter titles. You must be clear about what each section means. The most effective thing is to simply state what the chapter or section is about. For example "Livening Up Your Document" might be a nice chapter for a book, but the same information in a user manual might be "Adding Graphics."

Graphics are also a very useful tool in any document. I am a firm believer that a picture is worth a thousand words. If you have a graphical representation of something, this provides the audience with quick information. Even if this is a repeat of the text, often having the graphic there emphasizes and even clarifies the topic.

In general, I consider anything that is not in paragraph format to be a graphic. This includes lists of instructions, bullet lists, drawings, pictures, etc. Each serves a particular function, and where they are applied depends on the information being presented.

If you are writing some user documentation, then it is likely that there are tasks that the user will need to accomplish, such as drawing a circle or changing the color. It is much more useful to detail the steps in a list, rather than just an abstract description or instructions in paragraph format. This makes getting at the information easier. First, finding it in the text is easier. Second, the reader can more quickly see what he or she needs to do the task.

One mistake I commonly see is that only the steps are listed, but not the reaction by the program. For example, when changing the color of a drawing, you might click on a menu, which then brings up a window where you select the color. If you simply say to click on the menu and then select the color, the reader may not have a problem when the new window appears. However, if an error occurs and the new window does not appear (like when you did not select an object), the reader may be looking for a new menu entry. If any errors could occur at a particular step, these should also be mentioned.

Consider breaking down long lists of steps into smaller groups. If the list is too long, the reader may become intimidated and may skip over important information. Rarely do I find procedures that require more than a dozen steps. If it requires more, the procedure is usually composed of multiple tasks. For example, let's say you want to create a three-dimensional (3-D) object that casts a shadow on the background. First, you have to create the 3-D object and then create the shadow. These are actually two processes. In the section on creating the shadow, you could have a reference to the section on creating the 3-D object and thereby save steps.

Bullet lists are useful for introductions and references. As you see, each one of the pages in this guide has a bullet list. This not only gives you specifics about the topic, but is also a quick reminder of what you just read.

Drawings, photos, screen shots, and similar graphics depict images that cannot be described efficiently in a text format. For example, you know what the color input screen looks like, because there is a screen shot, and you can see exactly where the fields are and what they are labeled. Your boss can see the ratio of expenditure to budget in each area, because you included a chart. (Make sure that the screen shots match the product!!)

No matter what kind of graphic you have, make sure that there is a "call-out" (a reference in the text). It may be obvious from the caption or the graphic itself. However, having the call-out makes the reader aware that there is more information to be had.

Be consistent throughout the document. If you use photos in some places and drawings in others, the document may look unorganized. However, it will depend on the material. Use consistent phrases in lists. For example, having entries like "Changing Colors" and "Creating Basic Shapes" looks better than "Changing Colors" and "How to Create Basic Shapes." In the first example, you are using verbs ending in "-ing," but there is no consistency in the second example.

Part of accessing the information is having the user relate to it. If there is no personal context for the reader, it is more difficult to find the information useful. For example, in my first two books, I was describing how to use a particular computer operating system. Each was filled with experiences from customers I had as well as my own experience. The reader could then relate to the issue or problem, saying something similar to: "I know what that's like."

Even in a business report, you can create context. For example, by describing the problems you are having with one project as being similar to those on another project, the reader has a better understanding of the issue (assuming they know about the other project).

Making the information accessible in your document is more than just the content alone. Even the layout plays an important role. Having page after page of nothing but text can be intimidating. Screen shots of how the program reacts is good for manuals, whereas graphs and diagrams are good for reports. Additionally, white space helps the reader access the information. By "opening up" your document, you make it easier for the audience to find a particular piece of information. It is easier to separate components of the document, so the reader can spot the particular passage much quicker.

I am a big fan of having a good index. Perhaps it is not fitting in a status report, but user manuals and similar documentation require it. The alternative is that the reader must search through the table of contents looking for a section that may answer the question.

Three things I do when creating indexes. First, I create an entry for each labeled section (i.e., a section with a heading). This makes finding key topics easier. Supplementing this is permuting the heading to provide more index references. For example, there might be a heading "Creating Circles." I would have an entry for "circle, creating" as well as "creating circles." (Maybe there is an index heading of creating, with a subheading of "circles.")

Next, I try to think of other ways of describing the same thing. For example, the section might be on creating circles, but there is also an index entry for "drawing circles." Finally, any new term defined gets it own index entry. I also like to include a glossary of these terms, with index entries pointing to the glossary as well.

I have also found that headings are a very useful tool for a couple of reasons. First, it helps break up the document and appears less intimidating. Second, if a reader is scanning through the document, looking for something, a heading tells them what the section is about, without having them read anything in the section. This also tells them what is important in the document.

One thing that I get really annoyed about is the lack of chapter numbers, especially when there are references to them. For example, one section might indicate that you can get more details about a particular subject in Chapter 6 (with no title). However, the chapters are not numbered, so you cannot simply flip though until you find that chapter. You have to look in the table of contents to see where Chapter 6 begins.

Make the Information Understandable

To some extent, using the correct level of "jargon" and speaking in plain English go hand-in-hand. You need to use words that your audience will understand. If your audience is so loaded down with technical terms that they cannot understand the meaning of the sentence, you lose. If you have sentences that go on and on and on, your audience will forget the first part of the sentence when they get to the end.

When I was in the army, I was assigned to a liaison office that translated reports for various German government agencies. There were two offices that had an on-going competition to see who could produce the most complicated text. German technical documents are notorious for being long-winded, but these two offices took it even further. At one point, it became so bad that other German agencies simply filed the reports without reading them, as they were too complicated even for other Germans. That's not a good way for your reader to get the information.

Because you are trying to convey information, the language you need (words, grammar, etc.) needs to be as simple and as clear as necessary. I emphasize the word "necessary" because you should not make it a simple as possible. It is possible to write a financial report so that a ten-year-old can understand it, but your boss may not appreciate it.

You have to be careful to select the correct level. This applies to the complexity of the document as well as the amount of jargon. If you try to use words that are too simple, then they are probably not the words that your audience will find in other contexts. If they are new to the material and read your document, when they read something else and the terms are different, they will become confused. This is one of the big tradeoffs.

One comment that I heard most often about my first book was that the reader did not get a feeling that I was a teacher in a classroom or the all-powerful guru. Instead, they said that they felt that I was carrying on a conversation with them. I often used humorous anecdotes to describe the problem and solution. This also helped to put the reader at ease. My goal was not to impress people with how much I knew about the subject. Instead, I was trying to share my knowledge with them.

In support of the stories, I used plenty of examples. I described the product using real-world situations to which the reader could relate. Often, I brought up cases where I misunderstood something while I was learning the product. This further put the reader at ease, because they realized that everyone has to start at the beginning, plus there was an example that applied to something that someone really did with the product.

The use of examples also helps to put the document in the proper perspective. Without knowing what the document relates to, the audience has a hard time understanding the specifics. With manuals that provide step-by-step instructions, that would mean providing the audience with the processes leading up to these steps or a reason for following these steps. Perhaps you would give a scenario in which this procedure would be followed.

One suggestion is to use the traditional rule of thumb: Tell them what you are going to say, say it, then tell them what you said. This is one rule that I find myself breaking a lot, because it does not always work. Often the title of a chapter or section tells them what the chapter is about, so you have already told them what you are going to say. Also, it leaves a bad taste in my mouth when things are "forced." For example, saying "In this chapter you will learn ..." or "In this chapter you learned. . . ." Some people insist on having these kinds of sections, but I find them annoying. You want an introduction and a review, but do not restate the obvious. Here, again, you have to make a tradeoff.

Another thing that annoys me is inconsistent terminology. I see this a lot when documents are written by multiple authors. This goes back to having a standard list of terminology that is to be used in your documentation, particularly if the authors have different backgrounds or are emphasizing different aspects (e.g., an accountant and an engineer writing a project status report). Words are constantly being introduced into our technological society, and it is often hard to keep track of what word has a new meaning. Sometimes you will describe a situation using several words, only to find that there is a new, single word that means the same thing.

Because this is often unavoidable, you can do a certain amount of "damage control" by at least being consistent within the document itself. Obviously, if there are already terms to describe what you are talking about, you must use them. Otherwise, you damage your credibility, because your audience may get the impression that you do not know what you are talking about. However, if there are no special terms (yet), using the same terms consistently means your audience will know what you are talking about from one chapter to the next (at least within your document).

Even if you are not working on the document with someone else, creating a style sheet is a good idea. When I do my writing, I have a particular style sheet for each type of document. This makes it easier to change things. For example, I had a formatting type called "command" that I used when the text included a command line or the output of a command. Originally, it used the Times New Roman font. However, I later changed it to Courier. Aside from being easy to change, the audience knew that whenever they saw something in Times New Roman (and later Courier), they knew it was a command or the output. Even if your word processor cannot handle styles like this, creating a list of styles helps your document be consistent.

Be Correct

You might think that it goes without saying that you should tell the truth. However, truth is not necessarily an absolute. Some software companies make no mention of bugs and quietly correct them in new releases. Others provide a list of known bugs with their product. Even if they call them "limitations," you are not caught off-guard when you come across them. Maybe the circumstances that cause the program to freeze are very rare, but you help your credibility by telling your audience about it in advance. This is a tradeoff with being positive. For example, it would be better to say that this combination of actions causes program instability than telling them never to do those steps.

I remember the announcement by a vendor of antivirus software that it had discovered the first virus for the Linux operating system. The announcement on their Web page went on to say that this virus did not affect other operating systems. This demonstrates two issues with regard to the "truth." The first is that the vendor did not "discover" the virus. It was reported to them by a Linux user, who knew someone who worked there. Second, because the source code is available for the virus, it can easily be converted to run on any of the other operating systems (if it has not already).

There were many more "irregularities" in the press release, which did not help the company's credibility. There were also several technical mistakes in the document. As a result, many people who discussed this issue on the Internet lost their trust in the company because of these "untruthful" statements and technical mistakes.

Obviously, this applies to documents sent to customers, but many people do not apply the same standard to internal documents or information. In one company, the people responsible for supporting office products simply stated that a certain functionality had been removed, disabled, or whatever. In fact, the functionality was still there; they just did not want to support it. When users found out about it, they lost their trust in the applications group.

Being accurate is just as important as being truthful. If you list steps on how to do something that are incorrect, the document is not serving its purpose. In fact, any piece of information that is incorrect decreases the value of the document. Therefore, reviewing your documentation and comparing it to the "facts" (e.g., menus in the software, actual financial state of the project) is essential for your documentation. Once the validity of one part of the document is questioned, the rest becomes suspect.

One thing that I have found quite often is documents that are filled with half-truths. These are the most dangerous types of "misinformation" that you can include in a document. When I was in the Army, I taught classes on resistance to interrogation. One common approach to interrogation was to convince the prisoner that you were the "good guys," and therefore helping you was the moral thing to do. This was quite often accomplished by using half-truths. If the prisoner (or anyone else for that matter) knew that half of what was said was the truth, a logical extension of that truth is considered to be true as well.

For example, an emotionless description of communism often convinces people that capitalist countries were the bad guys. This happened frequently during the Korean War. However, the North Korean captors failed to show the other half of the fact that real communism was not practiced and that North Korea was an oligarchy. The result was that many American prisoners believed what the North Koreans said.

For a prisoner who has no way of verifying the other half, this approach can be effective for an interrogator. However, if your audience can find out the validity of the other half, you end up destroying your credibility (like the antivirus company). In addition, the audience now knows that one half is untrue and therefore questions the other half. This is a complete reversal of the original intent.

One way of avoiding the half-truths is to be as specific as possible. For example, the statement that German drivers are better than American drivers because there are fewer accidents per capita in German is a half-truth. If we assume that the mark of a better driver is fewer accidents, then this statement seems to be true. However, when you compare the number of accidents per 100,000 miles driven, you find that there are fewer in the United States. The reason that Americans have more accidents is that they simply drive more. The more you drive, the greater the chance you have of getting into an accident.

Part of the problem with the previous example was that I was not being as accurate as I could be. The statement "German drivers are better than American drivers" is an opinion based on a specific set of facts. By specifically saying how many accidents per capita and how many per 100,000 miles, the audience can make up their own mind. By stating my opinion, I have generalized the information to a point where it is almost useless.

Even in manuals that list step-by-step procedures, I see a lot of generalization. Words like "easy" and "difficult" are relative and rarely add anything to the text. Easy as compared to what? Difficult for whom? State the problem or task and then how to solve it. If there are any caveats (i.e., things to watch out for), include them. Describing a task and then saying the next task is more complex or more time-consuming than the first is not subjective like "easy" and "difficult" are.

Often writers will tell you to look in another chapter of the manual for details on a particular subject. Most of the time, they give you the chapter number, but less often do they say what section. Depending on the program you are using to write your documentation, you may not have the option to reference specific pages. However, you can reference the section. Even doing this by hand increases the value of the documents by making it easier to find the information.

Documentation Management

The documentation process does not necessarily end once the writer has completed his or her work. There are undoubtedly many documents in your company that are used again and again. It is entirely possible that 6 months after they are first created, some of the information is no longer valid. Therefore, these documents need to be brought up-to-date. In addition, you may not want to publish a document just because the writer thinks he or she is finished. Instead, the document needs to be reviewed first. What this review can do is not only to ensure the accuracy as well as make sure that the right things are being said.

Part of the documentation management is ensuring the accuracy of that information. Granted, a technical review of all documents should be done when the document is created, but companies often forget to review documents after they are created. In some cases, out-dated information can lead to more problems than can no information. Therefore, all documents should be reviewed at regular intervals to determine if the information is still valid.

A key part of this is not to review all documents at the same time. That is, it does not make sense to do a complete review of your documents every 6 months. Rather, the documents should be reviewed individually. To this end, each document should have a specific review date or period assigned to it. For example, a document with a 6-month review period should be reviewed every 6 months. That is, all documents created in March with a 6-month review period should be reviewed in September, whereas all documents created in April with a 6-month review period should be reviewed in October. However, all documents created in March with a 3-month review period should be reviewed in June.

What time periods you define will depend on your organization and the documentation itself. For example, if you have a large company with several administrators, you may have something like a bulletin board, where the information is valid just for a single day. In smaller companies, where accounting is also the administrator, the shortest-term documents have a longevity of 3 months.

Regardless of the longevity, you need to define a person who is responsible for the document. This person will regularly review the document as well as be the contact person in case an error is discovered or the document needs to be changed for some other reason. Reviewer and contact can also be different people. For example, in one company, it was part of the responsibility of the administrator of the day to review the documents. Documents did not expire every day, but when they did, the AD was responsible to check them.

Keep in mind that documents should be changed whenever necessary and not just on their review dates. If you know that a document is outdated, it must be changed as quickly as possible. Here again, invalid information is often worse than no information. In one company, we had an administrator who installed a new tape loader on the weekend prior to going on vacation. On Monday, no one knew how to set up the backup properly. It took several hours to find the documentation and figure out how to use the new loader with the backup software. This taught us that the documentation should be written before the changes are made.

Who does the review will depend on your organization. In some cases, documents are reviewed by their creators. They are responsible for monitoring their own documents. This is best suited for organizations where each person is responsible for a particular set of documents. However, in companies where anyone could create a document for any area, a central documentation management is better.

The information about who is responsible, longevity, subject area, and so forth can be stored in a couple of ways. In some cases, it is useful to have this information available directly in the document. That is, when the document is displayed, this information is immediately available to you. Alternatively, you can take advantage of the application to store this information. For example, there are a number of different properties that you can set for MS Word documents.

There is a predefined set of information such as the title, author, and even keywords that you can define for each document. You can then search for specific values to these properties. In addition, newer versions of MS Word allow you to create your own properties, which you can then search for. You could then create a property called "expiration" and then search for all documents that expire during the current month. You could also assign an owner to the document, who is then responsible for its contents. Regardless of what system you implement, you need to have a way of easily identifying the person responsible for the file as well as the expiration date.

Change management is also an important aspect of the documentation. This does not mean just the ability to backtrack the documentation to see the changes. It also means the process of making changes in the first place. I recommend against allowing just anyone to make changes to the documentation. Someone should be assigned as a kind of approving authority before the changed versions are published. In fact, documents should be approved before they are published the first time.

Even with things like troubleshooting guides and other "nonofficial" documents, keeping track of the changes is a good idea. The current version of the more common wordprocessing programs allows you to do this automatically. For example, in Corel WordPerfect there is a built-in revision control system. Here you can keep track of what changes were made, by whom, and when. You also have the ability to compare documents.

Corel actually takes this one step further with their Corel Versions. Not only do you have the same version control capabilities as with other word processing applications, Corel Versions can be applied to any document type. In addition, Corel Versions also allows you to archive as well as manage previous versions of documents. With this you can retrieve, view, and compare any version you have archived.

In addition, there are a number of external programs that you can use, depending on the document format. For example, straight text, such as HTML, can be administered with programs that were originally designed for source code control. For example, Microsoft's Visual Source Safe and the Revision Control System (RCS), which is provided standard on many UNIX systems and is available as freeware from many sources on the Internet.

Part of the revision control needs to be including the dates of the changes, when the documents were approved and published, as well as who approved them. In one company, we had a very well-developed program for documenting company procedures, as were required for our ISO 9000 certification. Using this standard as our base, it was very easy to implement similar standards for our other documentation.

Graphics

A picture is worth a thousand words. So it makes sense to include pictures on your intranet site, in your documentation, and most anywhere else you are trying to pass along information to your users. To accomplish this efficiently, there are a number of things that you need to consider above and beyond what kinds of things you want to take pictures of or whether or not the pictures are in color or black and white.

One of the first things is the resolution of the image. Many people want to have the clearest picture possible. The higher the resolution, the more pixels (dots) there are in the image and the more detail you see. This generally means that the higher the resolution, the clearer the image. This means that people will want high resolutions on the intranet server to get the clearest possible picture.

However, the problem is most computer monitors can only get about 75 dots per inch (dpi). Therefore, if you display a picture, you will not be able to see any difference. This means that it does not make sense to have images that have a higher resolution.

Well, it actually means that it does not make sense to have images that have a higher resolution if you are only going to display them on screen. However, if you are going to print them as well, you will need to have multiple resolutions. Typically, you will need three resolutions: one for on-screen display (75 dpi), one for print in newspaper (150 dpi), and one for other kinds of print, which you can also use to magnify if you want to just show a specific portion of the image with a larger size (up to 2400 dpi). Alternatively, you could have a fourth group of higher resolutions (e.g., 300 dpi) in addition to the 150-dpi images.

For your printed documents, as well as those you publish on your intranet site, you are going to need a number of different graphics. Depending on the medium, you might even need the graphics in different formats. For example, for printed media, you may want the images in TIFF format but need them in GIF or JPEG when publishing the document on your intranet.

To access the images they need to be organized. You will need to organize by both the image characteristics (size, color or b/w resolution) as well as subject. My recommendation is that you organize the image first by characteristics and then by content. This is because you will use specific characteristics depending on what you are working on. However, the subjects will be different.

For example, if you are working on your intranet, you will need images that are 75 dpi. You only need to look in the directory for the 75-dpi images and not the 300-dpi images, for example. The sorting is done by function and not by content.

What if there are some 300-dpi images you want to include? Well, my recommendation is to have three copies of all of the images. Tools are available to do batch conversions of images, so you could start the conversion when you go home at night and have it finished when you come in the next morning.

You could then establish a policy that all images are scanned or created with fairly high resolutions and then scaled down to fit the other categories. Granted, there may be a number of images that will never make it onto your Web site and, therefore, do not need to be reduced. However, with the available tools, making the conversion is extremely simple, especially if you do it in batch mode (i.e., once a week).

Once you have grouped the images per resolution, you run into a tough decision. Some people break it down at this point between black and white and color images, then by subject. Others break it down first by subject and then by black and white and color. Here, too, the decision needs to be made based on what you are working on. If you are working on a brochure, then you will probably only have color images. If you are working on a manual, then you probably have just the images of a particular product. You can't have both.

Well, actually you can. You need to have a physical structure, because that's what Windows NT wants on the file system. However, this is not necessarily what Windows Explorer needs to see. As I said, my recommendation is to break it down by characteristics first, then by content. Therefore, after resolution comes color and then content. You might also want to consider the physical size of the image as a separate characteristic, or that might be included along with resolution.

The marketing people are probably the group that is going to be using the most diverse range of images. Therefore, they are the ones who need to find things more quickly. For this reason, I suggest sorting first by characteristic and then by content. The marketing person would then be working in a single directory tree (i.e., based on the resolution).

For the others, you could create directories containing shortcuts. For example, the technical publications department needs images of all the products broken down by category. These directories contain shortcuts to the actual directories where the files reside.

The next big issue is, "What is the subject of each of the images?" Many of the images date back when you were running under Windows 3.1, so name them things like CBHN0992.JPG. This is not too easy to figure out what the name is.

You need to come up with a naming convention that describes the images as best as possible without making the name overly long. In one company, we had names that were based on the location in the file system and therefore the characteristics. For example, the file 75_2X4B_BLDG_0399_6.JPG was a 75-dpi image, with a 2 x 4-cm physical size, black and white, depicting a building, taking in March 1999, and was the sixth image of that type. (No, the pictures were not Y2K compliant.)

Granted, you could make the names longer like this:

```
75_2X4B_FRN_HQ_BLD_SHOWING_FOUNTAIN_0399_6.JPG
```

Although this gives you more information, it still does not explain everything about what the picture is. Keep in mind the old saying that a picture is worth a thousand words. Therefore, to name an image that accurately describes the picture, you would need to have a name that was a thousand words long, which is impossible with the NTFS.

The solution is to open up every image and look at it to see what it really contains. However, even with just a dozen or so pictures, this becomes a very tiresome task. Even making the names longer to contain more information and a better description, you still cannot get those thousand words you need to really describe the picture.

What you need is a method by which you can simply scan the pictures without having to load any extra programs. There are a number of programs on the market that provide you a "thumbnail" view of the images. Thumbnails are smaller versions of the image, which obviously do not have the same resolution, but are much smaller and give you a better idea of what the image contains.

This also helps solve the issue of whether to convert the images to different resolutions or not. Granted, the level of automation provided by many tools makes the actual conversion less of an issue. However, you need to consider the disk space. I know from experience that users often just see the size of single files. Because each is relatively small, they assume that they do not take up much space. However, 1000 images that are each 100 KBs in size means that you have taken up 100 MBs of your file system. Considering that images suitable for printed media can be well over 10 MBs *each*, you quickly get into the gigabyte range. In one company, our image archive of 4500 images was over 9 GBs *before* we considered converting them to different resolutions.

The basic principle with programs that make thumbnails is that you scan in a directory and the program creates the thumbnails. These are then displayed with a window of the program. A double click on the thumbnail then loads the correct images.

There are some programs that make a thumbnail image that is stored in an extra file. That means, for each image, you have two files to deal with. On the other hand, the program scans the directory for the thumbnails as it loads. Therefore, if you copy a file and its thumbnail into a different directory, the thumbnail is automatically displayed.

An alternative is to store the thumbnails in a single file. This has the advantage that all of the files are stored together. In addition, the programs that I know of where you store the thumbnails together have the advantage of allowing you to store more information about the images, such as keywords, resolutions, and so forth. In essence, they give you a database of your images that you can search.

Another aspect of this is how you generate the images. This is different from the manipulation. Hard copy images are generated using a camera. Today, cameras exist that store the images electronically (e.g., digital camera). They can then transfer the images directly to a PC.

Digital cameras are not only useful for images you place on the intranet or in published documents, but are useful for the system administrator. One useful place for digital cameras is documenting the inside of your wiring cabinets. You can take a picture of the inside, which you can then label to indicate the various pieces of equipment. When you come back 6 months later, you know automatically what is what. Another possibility is when you have remote offices. When the wiring cabinet is set up, you take a picture, label it, and store the image on the network. If someone needs to do remote troubleshooting, all they need to do is call up the image. Taking this one step further, anything could be photographed and then sent across the network to aid in troubleshooting (i.e., the inside of a remote computer).

Another useful place for digital images is user documentation and troubleshooting guides. For example, most printers come with a handbook, but you cannot expect a user to wade through the book to find answers, especially if they are not spelled out exactly. Instead, you create a troubleshooting guide with known problems and step-by-step solutions. These refer to the pictures that you took with the digital camera and include in the documentation. The same set of problem and solutions is available to everyone in the network at a fraction of the costs of printed copies (especially if you have a large company).

You also need to consider just how the images are made available. With MS Word, you can either embed the images into the document or link the image into the document. Embedding means that the image becomes part of the document. That means, when you copy the document, the image goes with it. The downside is that it increases the size of the document. I have had two-page Word files that were 5 MBs in size, because huge graphics were embedded.

When images are links, they do not become a part of the file. Instead, each time the file is loaded, the image is loaded separately. This has two advantages. First, the size of the file is much smaller. Second, you can change the image, and the change will be automatically reflected the next time the file is opened. The disadvantage is that you have to keep track of multiple files.

Keep in mind that documents you make available on your intranet or the Internet (i.e., the Web pages) are already multiple files. By splitting them into separate files when dealing with Word documents, you maintain a similar structure.

However, you need to keep in mind that the image you display on the Web may not necessarily be the same image that you have in your printed documentation. Although the subject of the image is the same, the resolution will probably be different. In addition, there may be no need to use color images for hard copy documentation. Making the images black and white (actually grayscale) does not necessarily mean that the images are smaller. If you use 256 colors, you need 1 byte per pixel. If you use 256 levels of gray, you still need 1 byte per pixel. However, you don't need a color printer to print them out.

Depending on the printer, you may not be able to tell the difference between a color image and a grayscale image, as the printer will select the proper grayscale for a given color. Note also that for things like user documentation (i.e., troubleshooting guides), there is probably no need to use color images for the on-line documents. Although you are using 8-bit gray scale, you are using the same image as what you print. This makes management a little easier.

How "text" documents are presented/made available is another important consideration. If you are using MS Word, you can generally leave them in the Word native format. Both Microsoft Internet Explorer and Netscape Navigator in the current versions can display MS Word documents directly in the browser, so there is no need to convert them if the documents are only to be used internally. However, if you decide to present the same information on the Internet, you will need to consider the fact that many people will not have a browser that supports this.

There are actually three solutions to this problem. First, the documents can be converted to standard HTML so that they are accessible for all browsers. Essentially all word processors (at least the more common ones) can now save files as HTML. This requires the document creator to be sure the documents are saved in the proper format. You can also convert the document to the Adobe PDF format. This requires them to get a copy of the Adobe Acrobat reader, which is available for free. Here, too, you have the problem of ensuring that the files are converted properly.

Alternatively, you can store the files in their native format and have the user download the file itself. This is a problem when the user does not have the necessary program to view the file.

One thing that is commonly left out is references within the text to the image. In many cases, the reference is completely left out and the reader has to work at trying to match the text with the picture. Sometimes there is a reference to the graphic simply as "see the following image" or "as indicated in the image above." When the content is changed, often the flow of the text changes and the images come before the text instead of after. Therefore, we made it part of the standard that all graphics, tables, and so forth be numbered and all cross-references were specific to the numbering. This meant that we could move the graphics and still have the proper references.

Another important aspect of this is to use the cross-reference function in whatever word processor you are using. I would be hard pressed to find a product that does not allow you to insert cross-references (at least in the current version). With this, you can insert new graphics, tables, whatever, and let the program do the numbering for you. I have worked in places where the references were included by hand, and when a new graphic was added, a dozen others had to be renumbered.

This emphasizes the value of using the built-in functionality of the program. I mentioned the issue of headings and using styles to mark headings. Here, you are using the functionality of the program, which allows you to define different styles. Numbering graphics and using cross-references are other examples. It needs to be clear in the documentation what aspects of the program functionality the writer must use.

As with other aspects of the documentation, you need to define a standard for graphics. This applies to pictures as well as graphics created with drawing programs such as CorelDRAW or Adobe Illustrator. The first thing to define is the format itself. Although you can save your graphics from either of these programs into a form that the other can read, you often lose something in translation. Therefore, I feel it is better to stick with a single application and use its native format. Most word processing applications can import either and you can save as GIF or JPEG when publishing to your intranet.

In general, the same thing applies to pictures. However, you need a format that can be used by the largest number of applications, which is usually either GIF or JPEG. I have seen older, legacy applications that support neither, so you may end up having to use TIFF for an internal user, but GIF or JPEG on the intranet.

This is actually not too bad. Because you are not dealing with objects, as you are with graphics programs like CorelDRAW and Adobe Illustrator, you tend not to lose any information when converting from one format to another. In any event, whatever format you decide on, you should standardize this throughout the company.

In my experience, there are a great many occasions when a list simply cannot give me all of the information I need. A list might contain a description of all of the characteristics of different components, but it is extremely hard for a list to show you the interactions between the components, Often it is more useful to see a visual representation of something. Two of the most common examples are flow chart and organization diagrams. Without the ability to display them graphically, an organizational diagram begins to sound like something out of the Old Testament. (The management begot the sales department which begot the West Coast sales department which begot the branch offices in Los Angeles, San Francisco, and Seattle.)

You certainly need to diagram something during planning, development, troubleshooting, or just to get your thoughts straight. Doing it on paper has the advantage of not restricting you to any specific format. Drawing the diagram in a software application usually makes it easier to read, and it is less likely to get lost. In addition, having a software program allows you to capture the image for possible publication on your company's intranet.

Like every other branch of computer software, there has been an explosion in the last few years of software products that are used for diagramming, modeling, and a number of other things related to existing structures and even random ideas into easier-to-use graphical form.

I think there are two questions you need to ask yourself before you even start looking for a product. The first is, "What am I going to diagram?" There are so many tools on the market, and not everyone is suited to drawing every kind of diagram. You could use a general drawing tool, such as CorelDRAW or Adobe Illustrator or even within the drawing module of something like WordPerfect. All of these have the double advantage of being software products and being fairly "free form."

However, one major disadvantage of these is the fact that they are "free form." In many cases, the exact shape you need is not available, so you have to end up drawing it from scratch. Sometimes the drawings do not come out right, which makes it look almost unprofessional and even unclear as to what you really mean. For your own notes, you may not need anything more complicated, and you can figure out what your own scratches mean. You need a tool to quickly diagram your ideas and where the functionality provided is sufficient.

In other cases, you may need the "real" symbols as they are going to be "published" in some way, say on your company's intranet. You would then definitely need something that looks better. On the other hand, even when I am writing notes for myself, I often first sketch them out on paper. However, by the time I get done, there are lines all over the place, things have been crossed out, and I cannot see the forest for the trees. Therefore, I usually want something that is easier to read.

The most direct solution to this problem is by creating a template in WordPerfect that contains all of the necessary symbols. In one company, we had several diagram types (i.e., flow chart, organizational diagrams, room and building layout, etc.) for which we created templates. Even though few of each kind of diagram were ever created and or ever published on the Internet, the quality of these drawings was fairly good and sufficient for our needs.

The next big question to ask is, "How often are you going to create such diagrams?" The more often you create diagrams, the more you will want a tool that helps in the creations. Using a template, we had to constantly cut and paste the different symbols. With a large number of diagrams or diagrams with a large number of different symbols, this kind of thing becomes very time consuming.

If you buy a tool that is specifically designed to draw a particular kind of diagram, then it will mostly have the ability to insert the necessary symbols using different mouse actions or key combinations. This will also apply to all of the lines used to connect the various components. For example, with a flow chart, you have a number of arrows indicating the flow of activity. Flow chart programs will allow you to connect two elements of the diagrams and automatically insert the proper arrow. You can then move the components and the arrows will follow, something which is not available with every drawing program.

However, depending on the size of your company and the kind of products you produce, you will need a larger number of different graphics. There are often graphics in commercial products that you have not even thought about. When you come across that particular graphic, you either need to make do with what you have or create a new one.

The basic functionality of other types of drawing programs needs to be part of your diagramming tool. For example, you must be able to:

- Insert the various elements using drag-n-drop.
- Format the elements using the mouse, toolbar/menu, or the keyboard.
- Change colors, fonts, and sizes.
- Open multiple windows.
- Rotate, flip, and change the stacking order.
- Add predrawn symbols or mouse or keyboard actions.

This is obviously not a complete list. The best thing is to think about the basic functionality you have in a drawing program. Most of your basic needs should be included in any good diagramming tool.

An important aspect is the ability to work with different formats. First is the issue of important different formats. Look to see what formats your other programs can generate and then see which of these can be accessed by your diagramming tool. Most will be able to handle the standard format types like, GIF, JPEG, TIFF, BMP, and so forth. However, if you are using special programs like CAD applications, you may not be able to use the native format of the CAD application. Instead, you would need to export it from the CAD application into a more common format and then import it into the diagramming tool.

Also see if the diagramming tool supports OLE. If this is the case, then you may not need to worry about the format. Using OLE, you can insert most any kind of object. If the diagramming tool does support OLE, see how well it integrates with the other product. For example, once you have inserted the object, can you start the original application by simply double-clicking on the object?

The most recent versions of drawing software should be "Internet aware" to some extent. At the very minimum, the program should be able to export the file into either JPEG or GIF, and some programs allow you to export the page directly as HTML. Typically, the graphic itself is exported to JPEG and GIF and dropped into the middle of an HTML page. However, there are a number of drawing tools that allow you to multiple pages within a single "drawing." When exported, they become individual HTML pages with hyperlinks between them.

....

SGML

Why SGML?

Before we talk about what Standard Generalized Markup Language (SGML) is, let's talk about why it is needed. Take a moment here and consider how you currently create and manage documents. If yours is like many companies, most internal documents are created and stored using one of the commercially available word processing programs, such as WordPerfect or StarOffice. Documentation for your products might be produced using tools more-suited to this task, such as Adobe FrameMaker.

If you have an international company, you run into problems with the difference in languages. I know of several companies that have established English as their "official" language, even though they are not American companies. This makes sense in that English is probably the language that you will find spoken in most of the countries where you have offices. Spanish might also be a consideration if you have a strong presence in South America. In one company I worked at, we even made the language of all of the NT servers English to make administration easier.

Instructions on how to perform routine tasks, such as process orders, may be best accomplished in the local language. If procedures are the same in every office, then it makes sense to have a common set of documentation. Even if the language is different, the content can be the same. Managing this is a lot easier than you would think.

Although having all of your documentation on-line makes for easy access, there are many cases where having a hard copy is more useful. For example, a technician who is in a remote office and working on the wiring in the communication cabinet might be better served by having the documentation in his hand. However, if this same information is available on-line, then it must be identical information. The content of the information remains constant; only the manner in which it is presented will be different for the different media types.

One of the most common and obvious problems is that a lot of the documentation that people write is made up of the same blocks of text. Particularly with product documentation, it is common to find as much as 95% or more of the text to be identical between the various models or versions of the product. Companies long ago discovered that it was not practical in such cases to keep separate versions of the documentation for each product. Instead, blocks of text are stored separately and inserted as needed. In some cases, the differences are so minor that there is just a single document, which simply makes reference to the various models.

Unfortunately, this is not always possible. There are many cases where portions of the documents are repeated, but there are enough differences that each model requires a separate document. The documentation producers then have the added task of managing all of the various components. Fortunately, the tools available on the market allow you to quickly combine the parts that are needed to create the complete document.

Although this solves some of the problems, there are many others that need to be addressed. For example, it might be that in the portions of the document that are different, they are still 95% identical. The only difference is the technical information. If something other than the technical information were to change, every single document would need to be changed accordingly. The solution here is to create text blocks in ever-smaller sizes so that you can simply insert those that are consistent and edit the ones that change.

The problem with this is that the more pieces you have, the more time you spend managing the text blocks. However, you have not solved all of the problems, because even at the paragraph or sentence level there is a lot of repetition.

You might have a sentence that says, "The model LVL-4711 requires a minimum of 1 liter of the coolant MB-34F." This single sentence appears in the user's manual, safety instructions, and spare parts list, all of which are separate documents. Added to this, the coolant designation is dependent on the model number. Therefore, this sentence appears in the documentation for every single product, but 90% of the text is the same. If the coolant were to change (such as new environmental regulations), it might need to be changed for every single document or at least for every applicable text block.

Although this is a fairly simple example, it does demonstrate the problems every company encounters. If just a single piece of information changes, dozens of documents need to be changed, all just because a single phrase changed.

Let's look at offer letters you send to your customers. They all have the same basic format. There is a page or two that outlines the basic information, such as your name and the customer's name. There might be general information about the product. There might also be some legalese about the offer not being valid after 90 days or something. Buried within all of that is just a single page that contains the technical information. I worked in a company that sold several dozen products, each with a number of variations. Each had its own offer letter "template," which was copied and changed as needed. In addition, because we were an international company, we had each of these templates in various languages. Although the text was at least 90% identical, there were hundreds of documents that had to be managed.

When the wording changed, each document needed to be loaded, the correct position found, and changed. Then it had to be translated. When the technical information changed, each of the translated versions needed to be changed as well.

Let's look at a different kind of problem. Assume you go looking for a book at amazon.com. You input some keywords, and some program goes looking for information in a database. It comes up with ten possible titles, each with the same pieces of information (title, author, etc.) and then displayed in a consistent fashion. If you printed out each of the pages, you might think that each existed as a separate entity on the server. However, this is only appearance, because there is a program that reads the database and presents it in a fashion that is pleasing to the eye.

Now instead of a book title, let's think about the model. Instead of the author, let's think about the coolant. Instead of a page on the Web, let's think about a page in a manual. On both pages, the general layout is the same, regardless of the contents. All that changes is specific pieces of information depending on what you are looking for. Change the title and the author changes. Change the model and the coolant changes. However, the appearance on the page and all of the other remains the same.

What Is SGML?

So what is SGML anyway? To explain it, let's talk about something you already know. I chose the analogy of a Web page for two reasons. First, you can see how easy and common it is to present information where just a small fraction of the content changes. Second, if you are already familiar with the Web, then you have experienced the power of SGML.

The language of the Web, Hypertext Markup Language (HTML), is just an implement of SGML. HTML is not directly concerned with how the page appears on your monitor; that's the job of your browser. All HTML does is to mark a certain line as being a level-1 heading, for example. How the browser displays that line is dependent on the browser and how you have it configured. Often, the way the page is presented in Internet Explorer and Netscape Navigator is completely different. However, the information that each browser receives is identical. That is, the Web page is the same in both cases.

HTML consists of a number of tags, which identify certain kinds of information, such as the headings, emphasized text, table rows, and, of course, links to other pages. HTML has developed to the point where you can include different text at various points in the text, depending on a set of dynamic criteria. This is how active server pages work.

Bringing this back to the technical manuals, we could create tags that identify the text representing the model and coolant. If you look at the page for the LVL-4711, the active server page inserts the model number, coolant designation, and other characteristics at the appropriate locations on the page. If we replace the browser with a word processor, it would be possible to edit the surrounding text, leaving the tags that load the data. The next time we printed the document for any of the 100 different products we have, the new text is present, although it was changed just once. This is what SGML is all about.

Up until recently, there had not been much change in the way printed documents were created. They were basically static. Even in cases where text blocks were used, the contents of each block was static. Web pages have changed so the information presented varies, although 99% of the text remains unchanged. In essence, SGML takes common data processing techniques and brings them to printed media, just as HTML has done it for the Web.

Keep in mind that SGML is not a genie in a bottle. It will not solve all of your problems overnight. It will take a lot of work to get a system in place. However, once in place, it can save you a great deal of both time and money. Rather than turning this into a book just on SGML, I would like to point you to two great books: *$GML: The Billion Dollars Secret,* by Chet Ensign (Prentice Hall) and *Industrial Strength SGML* by Truly Donovan (Prentice Hall). The first describes a number of case studies of companies who have implemented SGML and have saved money. The second goes into the technical aspects of SGML and what it can do for you.

One of the most important aspects of SGML is that the format is not proprietary. In fact, you are the one who defines a specific implementation of it, just as HTML and the newer XML are implementations. Added to this is the fact that the information is stored in text files. You do not have the common problem of differing formats, such as you have when trying to read MS Word files in WordPerfect, just as your browser needs to know how to display each of the elements. In addition, it would be extremely simple to take an SGML file and run it through a script that converts the SGML tags into HTML for display on a Web page.

One of the first questions to ask yourself is whether SGML is right for you. If you have a lot of existing documents, you need to convert them all in order to implement SGML. In other cases, you can convert as you go, leaving the older documents in their existing format.

In my mind, the two biggest factors are how many different formats and media you will need to provide for the documents and how frequently the documents will change. The more different media types you need, the greater the likelihood you will need to use different formats. For example, if you provide printed, Web, and CD-ROM copies of the documents, you will have three different processes to create the final results. Another aspect of the format is how structured your documents are. The more common the structure, the better suited it is for SGML.

How frequently the document changes is a matter of both how many documents you have as well as how often any given document changes. Ten documents that change everyday is equivalent to 50 document that change once a week. Not only that, you need to consider how much is changed and how uniform the changes are. Let's take the offer letters as an example. In each case, once the document is created, it is not changed again. Even if there is a new offer, a new document is created. The changes are uniform and therefore extremely easy to implement using SGML.

Also keep in mind that SGML is not limited to just defining the appearance of the document; it can also be used to control the content (in fact, content is more to the point of what SGML is). For example, there might be a "hidden" field in a document (i.e., one that is not printed), which contains a customer class, which determines the discount a customer gets. The list price is loaded into the document, but the actual price is calculated before it is displayed.

The fact that SGML documents are stored as ASCII text is not something to be taken lightly. In many cases it can be much smaller than the equivalent word processing file. For example, if you mark a heading in MS Word to be 14 point bold, MS Word needs to know that it is both 14 point and bold. In other words, it needs to save two pieces of information. SGML is only concerned with content, so there is a single piece of information, such as the HTML tag <H1> to indicate a level-1 heading. Even if MS Word marks the line as a heading, it still must carry around with it the extra information to describe what formatting that heading has. Again, SGML is not concerned with formatting.

Second, it is accessible from essentially any program that can edit text. Although you need a little time to get used to the tags embedded in the text, you can use a simple text editor such as NOTEPAD.EXE if need be. In addition, you can access the text as well as the tags from any program that can read a text file. This allows mass searches and replacements in hundreds of documents in just a matter of minutes without having to load each into a word processor.

Imagine that your company moves. You now have to change every document to reflect the new address. A perl script, for example, could scan the directory tree and automatically replace everything marked as an address.

Because SGML is concerned with content, you save a lot of time for employees who try to "force" a particular appearance. I know many who manually add extra spaces at the beginning of a line to get a hanging indent or to block justify the text. All you need to do is define a paragraph to have a particular type and let the application display it correctly. The nice thing is that if the application does not understand the tag, it simply ignores it. Try it in an HTML page by putting some random characters into a pair of angle brackets.

As you may know from HTML, there are a number of tags that are not displayed but that still contain information for the browser. As you would expect, this can apply to any implementation of SGML. For example, there are HTML tags indicating where the <HEAD> and <BODY> of the document are. You could label a section of text as <INTRO>. This could have a special formatting when printed, but you could also extract that intro into a separate document or display it through a search engine on your Web site.

HTML uses META tags to contain certain pieces of information. I have used it on intranet sites to contain information such as the author and expiration date of a particular document.

Because I have been using HTML as an example all along, you may be wondering why you shouldn't save everything as HTML. If you are only concerned with publishing small documents, then it might be acceptable. However, HTML has a limited set of markup tags. Although this limitation has been removed somewhat with dynamic HTML and cascading style sheets, you cannot create your own truly unique codes. In addition, you cannot cre-

....

ate structures with your documents or force a particular appearance. For example, HTML is happy having a level-4 heading immediately following a level-1 heading.

In addition, HTML is for formatting, not for content. Active Server Pages (ASPs) and related technologies can be used to include content dynamically: You are stuck with whatever server product you have (such as IIS). Because SGML is an open standard, you can access the content from anywhere, including ASPs. If you decide to change technologies or the technologies change on you, you do not have to change your documents.

Although SGML was a well-kept secret of the publishing business for many years, it is no longer restricted to the publishing business or to the internal documentation departments of large corporations. It is currently being used by Grolier to manage the almost 30,000 pages of their encyclopedia. Exxon uses it for its engineering specifications. Sybase uses it for their database documentation.

However, SGML is not limited to large corporations. This fact has been recognized by several software companies who have begun providing SGML support in their products. One of the most notable is the Corel WordPerfect Suite. The reason it is notable is because Corel provides the SGML support as a "matter of fact." Other vendors, such as Microsoft, charge extra for the SGML support. However, Corel provides it as part of the base package.

Central to SGML is the Document Type Definition (DTD). This contains "definitions" for the various elements as well the "rules" that a particular document must adhere to. The DTD describes things, such as which elements (tags) are used, in what order they must appear, attributes they may have, and so forth. An application that understands SGML uses the information in the DTD to display the information as it sees fit. That is why the appearance of a Web page in MS Internet Explorer is different from the same page displayed in Netscape Navigator. Remember that SGML, and therefore HTML, is concerned with content and not with appearance.

Note that it is not necessary that all documents of a particular type share all of the components. A DTD can be broken down into pieces so that some portions are shared and others are not.

Converting Existing Documentation

If your documentation is all kept in binders, it is not as easily accessible as when it is all on-line. Although it is fairly easy to make all new documentation accessible on-line, you undoubtedly have a large number of documents that only exist in their hard copy form. How do you make these accessible on-line? Better yet, should you make them accessible?

There is always a tradeoff between the ease of access and the work necessary to convert the documents. For example, you might consider using links within MS Word documents to other documents in your intranet. Not every document will have a link, but you could have thousands or tens of thousands of documents that could contain links. This makes accessing the documents even easier, but the question to ask is whether it is worth the effort to make the conversion.

One thing to consider is how often the document will be accessed. Obviously, documents that are archived and may never be looked at again do not need to have links in them or be on-line at all. On the other hand, a document that is accessed once a day may need to be on-line, especially if it is accessed by 100 people each day.

Before you begin any big conversion project, you need to consider whether the time and effort you will save in the future outweighs the effort you make now. We have found it useful to do the conversion is two phases. Certain documents that are accessed daily were processed at the beginning of the project. This was a relatively small number of documents (a few hundred) that were actually the entry points into the systems. That is, these documents were usually the first ones loaded. Other documents were processed as they were encountered.

Another thing to consider is the existing documentation. The question to ask yourself is whether the documentation should be converted for use on-line or just left as hard copy. The most significant questions to answer are how many documents you have, how often you need to access them, and to what extent they are related.

The answer to the first question is pretty obvious. If you have tens of thousands of pages, you might better leave them in hard copy. On the other hand, there are a number of excellent scanners that scan as fast as do many printers. Assuming a slow 10 pages per minute, it would only take about two business days to scan them all in. If all you are interested in is the text and that the quality is decent, you can expect to have a recognition rate higher than 99%. That means a couple of incorrect characters per paragraph.

One thing to pay attention to is the ability by many of the better scanning products to identify "sets" of pages. That is, they can number the pages for you automatically as they are being scanned in, or in some cases, stored in separated files under similar names (e.g., report1.txt for page 1, report2.txt for page 2, and so on). This allows you to automatically create a rough organization of the pages as you are scanning them in.

If all you are storing is text, you would be amazed at just how little space is used. For example, assuming that an average page has 3000 characters on it (which is quite a bit), you could get over 200,000 pages on a single CD-ROM! This includes the space necessary for the directory entries.

Obviously, just copying them all onto a CD-ROM is not the ultimate solution if you need to refer to the documents regularly. You need some method of managing the pages. This is very easily and quickly done with something like the Microsoft Index server or the Netscape Catalog Server. Although it might take awhile to generate the index initially, once this is done, you can do full-text searches on all of the documents.

Several years ago when we began the intranet project in one company, we were stuck on the question of a common format. That is, every document made available needed to be in the exact same format. The most commonly available format was HTML. We therefore had plans to convert all of our documentation to HTML. Considering that most MS Office applications already had the ability to save in HTML format, that seemed like a logical choice.

What we overlooked was the mass of documents that already existed. Each one had to be converted to HTML to make the project useful. Even if we limited the project to "live" documents (those that changed or were accessed often), the number was overwhelming. We did a search of the file system for the MS Word documents that were changed within the last 6 months and came up with over 10,000 documents (the maximum the Windows NT search mechanism could find). This did not account for the documents that were older than 6 months that were still accessed regularly.

There was no way we could either convert all of them or select the right ones to convert. We had no defined structure within the file system, so it was nearly impossible to tell which documents were "one-offs" (i.e., created and then forgotten) and which were regularly used. We came to the realization that it did not make sense to convert just the newer documents, but rather it was better to convert them as groups. That is, documents in a specific area would be left alone and therefore accessed with MS Word. Documents in other areas could be converted. The question was, what documents in what areas?

This uncertainty actually turned out to be a lifesaver for us. In the meantime, both Microsoft and Netscape added the ability to view Word documents directly within the Web browser. We could leave the documents as MS Word and only convert or create the documents in HTML as necessary. In essence, only those documents that involved a great deal of interactivity (i.e., ASPs, daily messages) where created as HMTL. The rest were left in their native format.

Optical Character Recognition

Because you can directly convert the time savings into money in the bank, it is often difficult to justify converting documents to electronic versions on a large scale. I have worked in companies whose basement was full of binders containing all of the old invoices, bills of lading, faxes, and so forth. Occasionally, a customer would call in who had not done business with us for several years. To get information about his account and previous purchases, someone would have to go find it in the basement. This process usually took about 15 minutes; this would happen at most two times a month. Converting all of the files to electronic versions would have taken at least 6 months if not a year. It was definitely not worth the time.

On the other hand, I worked for a consulting firm whose client was the German government agency whose responsibility it was to resolve property disputes after the reunification of Germany. After World War II, the East German government confiscated a lot of property and gave it to other people. In other cases, the owners had fled during the war and could no longer lay claim to the property because of East German law. When the reunification occurred, many people began laying claim to property that their grandparents, parents, or even themselves owned prior to the war.

Somebody had to wade through all of the documents to find out who were the rightful owners of a vast number of properties. There were many cases in which someone was the legal owner, but other people had been living in the house for decades. It was not right to simply give the property to one person or the other, so the German government needed a way to decide who got the property and who got monetary compensation. They created a special government office, whose sole responsibility it was to regulate these property issues.

When a dispute arose, it was not realistic to expect a clerk would go digging through the piles of documents. Something of this scope needed to be made much more efficient. So the solution in this case was to scan in all of the documents and make them all immediately accessible to everyone.

Doing so has been a big job for three important reasons. First, there were literally millions of pages of documents that needed to be sorted through. There were birth records, marriage certificates, death certificates, wills, and other documents used to demonstrate who was the rightful heir to the original owner. There were deeds, sales contracts, bank records, and many other documents that showed how the property changed hands over the years. Each one needed to be accessible, or the entire system was useless. It would take months just to scan in the documents.

The next big problem was storing and accessing the documents. Where I worked, there were three big boxes, each about the size of a refrigerator. Inside were 144 CD-ROMs, each of which could be accessed within seconds. In addition, each CD-ROM was double-sided. This was a tremendous amount of information; the programs that accessed the documents needed to be accessed fairly quickly and had to keep track of the millions of cross-references that were made between different documents.

More than likely, your company will be somewhere in the middle. You are likely to have documents that are so rarely used that it is not worth the time to convert them. However, you will probably find a great many documents that should be converted.

To convert the documents, you need a scanner with the appropriate software. What software is appropriate depends on the documents and how you want to access them. In some cases, it may be sufficient (or even necessary) to simply scan the documents and store them as images. In the case of the German agency, they need to see the document in its original form, so they essentially needed an on-line picture.

In other cases, you will want to be able to process the information further. In one company where I worked, we needed to scan in all of the trouble-shooting guides, handbooks, and so forth for all of our older products, because we promised our customers we would provide spare parts for 15 years. Customers would frequently call in with questions about these products, and the only place the information was stored was in binders. Because the older stuff was in binders, the information for the newer machines were also printed out and stored in binders.

When we started up our intranet project, customer service wanted their information on-line as well. The newer stuff was no problem, but we needed to scan in the older stuff. To simplify the process, customer service wanted the ability to change much of the hard copy information. This requires the use of software that does optical character recognition (OCR) to convert what the scanner sees as an image into the letters and numbers that are used by a word processing program or database.

OCR is relatively old technology and because of that it is a mature technology. This means that in a great many cases, documents can be scanned, processed by the OCR software, and stored into text files without human intervention. In other words, documents are stored automatically into electronic versions. How quickly this is done depends on how fast your scanner is and how fast your computer is on which the OCR software is running. However, you could start the process and return later after the scanning has completed.

Just because no human is processing the documents does not mean it is full of mistakes. If the OCR software had just a 90% recognition rate, there would be a mistake approximately in every other word (assuming an average of five characters per word). In most cases, a human reader will still be able to understand the remainder of the text and be able to figure out what the meaning is. If the software has a 95% recognition rate, one word in four would have a mistake. At 99%, one word in 20 would have a mistake or approximately every other sentence.

Actually, that is a pretty high failure rate. I have worked with some recognition software that had less than three or four character errors on a single page. That gives a recognition rate of about 99.9%. Even if you have "only" 99%, it is an acceptable rate if all you are doing is using the documents for reference. In addition, some recognition products have built-in tools to check spelling as well as to mark the character that it either does not recognize or is unsure of. Depending on the importance of the document, you could do another scan with the spell checker. (I have yet to find a case where the character was not correctly recognized, but it still yielded a real word.)

Basically, all of the available OCR software on the market today will boast at least 99% accuracy. Even if the vendor says such a high rate is only guaranteed with "laser printer quality documents," I am impressed. Added to that is the fact that most mistakes by OCR software will make it up creating words that do not exist and would therefore be caught by the spell checker of any good word processing program. When a document is completed, there may be no mistakes at all.

However, all these numbers are based on the page being almost full of text. If what you are scanning is a short letter, the OCR software has fewer letters to recognize, so the absolute number of mistakes is low, and the document may not need to be processed any further. In fact, you may be completely satisfied with the quality in every case and not even bother with a spell checker.

In fact, you can be happy with 99% accuracy, but you do not need to be "stuck" with it. The most well-known OCR software is OmniPage from the Caere Corporation. I am usually disappointed when I get recognition as low as 99%. Remember that 99% recognition means an error every other sentence. With the latest version of OmniPage, I rarely find more than single mistake in each paragraph, if that many.

Another key aspect is how well the product behaves with different text layouts. Not everything you are going to scan will be in the regular formats you find in any book. What if the document you're scanning consists of multiple columns or has a number of pictures and graphics. This was a problem with older OCR software, which might read the columns as single lines or tried to detect some text in the middle of the picture. In such cases, it is extremely useful to be able to tell the software which areas to look at and which to not, as well as in what order.

The very first OCR products that allowed you to define the areas that were to be processed usually only allowed you to accept or reject specific blocks. It took awhile before products developed to the point where you could define the areas yourself. However, new products have the ability to select those areas to recognize and even in which order. You are first presented with a picture of this scanned document (a preview), you select areas of the page you wish to scan with a box, and can change the size of the box as needed.

You're likely to find that a large number of documents you want to scan will have the same format. For example, they are all invoices, which were all printed on your company's letterhead. All of the information (such as the return address, customer information, details of the products involved) is located on the same place on each page. In addition, there is a lot of information that you do not need. Therefore, you have a large number of documents which you want to scan and then recognize the exact same area of the page. It is bothersome to have to mark out the scanner area each time.

Fortunately, you don't have to. Repeating formats is a common occurrence; therefore, the software should be able to recognize the fact that the layout is the same. This is accomplished using a "zone template." As its name implies, it is a template of which zones of the document you want to have recognized. Before you process the image, you load the zone template to be applied, and the system will automatically be set to recognize just those zones.

You'll also likely encounter text in regularly shaped blocks, often flowing around a picture or some other graphic. Some OCR software will only allow you to choose rectangular-shaped areas to recognize. This means you end up getting portions of the graphics into the scan area. Although this increases the number of errors slightly, you can avoid that problem by looking for OCR software that allows you to create blocks of irregular shapes.

Another "must-have" feature is the ability to edit the documents as they are being processed. Long gone are the days when the process image was stored into a text file, which you then had to edit afterward. Instead, modern OCR software gives you the ability to see the original document image and edit the text. This is extremely useful, because the human brain is much better at recognizing characters from their contact then a computer is.

In some cases, you can also process the document interactively. This means that every time the program finds text that it cannot recognize, you are given the opportunity to input the correct text. The OCR software should have a built-in spell checker and therefore be able make reasonable guesses about what the word could/should be.

Another common function is the ability to load existing images. This is extremely useful for things like fax software, which cannot always be connected directly to your OCR software. The fax software more than likely has the ability to save the fax into a TIFF file, which you can then load into the OCR software. Or, if you have thousands of documents to scan, it might be simpler to scan them all and then process all of the documents together, rather than scan one and then process it.

In addition to images on your pages, see how well the program deals with tables. The program should have no problem recognizing the text in tables. However, it should be able to maintain the structure of the tables. That is, the software should be able to recognize when text is part of a single cell and not try to merge text together into a single line. Depending on the application and the OCR software, you might be able to completely retain the table structure so that it is actually seen as a table object.

Desktop Publishing Software

Adobe PageMaker

It would be fairly safe to call Adobe PageMaker the great-grandfather of desktop publishing. First available in 1985, it was one of the first professional-level tools that was capable of creating high-quality, complex electronic versions of publications, which could then be transferred easily to print.

As with recent releases of all of their products, Adobe has striven to provide a common interface among all of its products, such as in Adobe PageMaker (Figure 10–1). The appearance is the same, so you do not have to readjust each time you switch applications, plus Adobe has standardized the behavior of the keyboard shortcuts, created common, standardized menus, and ensured that the functionality of tabbed palettes is the same across applications.

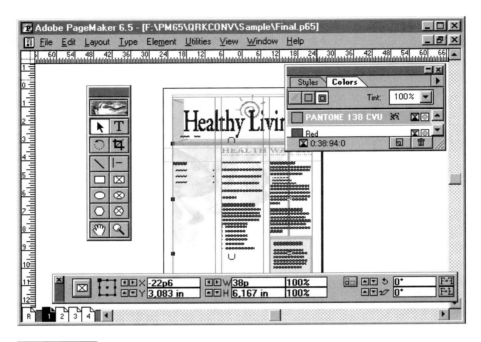

FIGURE 10–1   Adobe PageMaker work space.

One common functionality that is available on all newer Adobe products is the idea of layers. As with Photoshop and Illustrator, a layer is a set of graphics elements, which can be treated as a single object and stacked with other layers in different orders. Using this concept, it is much easier to make global changes.

One key aspect of this is that the layers are document wide. That is, they do not just apply to the current page, but to every page in the document. Like Photoshop and Illustrator, the layers can be "turned off" so that their content (or the effects they generate) are not visible.

In addition to normal graphics design, layers are extremely useful when creating documents that have the same visual appearance but the content is different. An example would be brochures that you want to create in different languages. You would create a layout, which would be common among all of the brochures, then create the actual text for each language. By turning off the other layers, all that is displayed is the text for a single language.

This could also be extended to product manuals, which have the same basic content. Granted, this is not the best solution when you have huge documents, with thousands of pages, composed of thousands of different text elements. That is where a product like Adobe FrameMaker would come in. However, PageMaker would be a useful tool on a smaller scale, especially if your documents have a lot of graphical elements.

The latest version of PageMaker includes enhanced features that aid in adjusting existing text and graphic elements when you change the document's master page. The master page contains formatting and other information that needs to be applied globally. By changing the master page just once, you can change the layout of the entire document.

However, that's part of the problem. When you change the layout on one page, it can have repercussions on pages elsewhere in the document. Margins no longer fit right, text does not flow correctly around graphics, and many other problems. PageMaker addresses this issue by including a built-in logic, which examines the changes and existing formatting, then makes the necessary changes on every page. Not that the same change is made on every page, but rather each change is made with respect to the elements and formatting already on that page.

PageMaker also has enhancements to their grid manager. The grid manager is a plug-in designed to assist the user in lining up the various elements of the page. For example, if the document has a columnar format, column guides can be created to help you line up the column. Such grids can also be applied to the master page, thus making them available to all pages.

Although the idea of grid lines to help align elements is nothing new, PageMaker has taken this to the next logical step, by giving you the ability to copy guides from one page to another as well as to save the guides to be used in other documents.

Also new is the introduction of both layout (graphics) and text frames. You can therefore design the layout without regard to the text content. In addition, you can write the text without regard to the layout. Once both components are ready, they can be merged into the final page. However, if you want, you can still design the text and graphics at the same time.

PageMaker is not a graphics development tool but rather a page layout application. Therefore, your graphics elements will need to be created elsewhere and then imported into PageMaker. Using other Adobe applications, such as Illustrator, makes the integration much easier. In other cases, you need to export the graphic into a common format, such as TIFF or embedded postscript (EPS) files. As a result, you lose your ability to do any changes at all to that graphic (perhaps with the exception of changing the size). However, you can import Illustrator graphics directly and still retain some of the ability to make changes.

This interaction among Adobe applications goes in both directions. That is, elements from Illustrator or Photoshop can be dragged from that application and dropped into PageMaker. PageMaker elements can be dragged and dropped into those applications as well. This includes Adobe PageMill, simplifying the creation of your Web pages.

PageMaker has also addressed the changes that have been made in the computer world over the past few years by including support for both Internet and intranet applications. For example, PageMaker comes with a hyperlinks palette. This allows you to both insert and verify links to pages on the Internet or on your company's intranet.

Once the pages are complete, they can be exported as both HTML and PDF, thus maintaining the exact same appearance. Obviously, the links to Web sites are retained when exporting the pages. When exporting to the Web, you have a choice of either JPEG or GIF formats, regardless of what format the graphics were in originally when they were imported into Page-Maker. A copy of Acrobat Distiller is provided with PageMaker, allowing you to create the PDF files.

Adobe FrameMaker

For companies with large numbers of documents to distribute with dozens or even hundreds of pages, Adobe FrameMaker provides an excellent work environment. Rather than being a tool just for hard-copy publications, FrameMaker has followed the lead of other Adobe products and adapted itself to the changing computer world, allowing easy on-line publication of information. Information can be exported easily into standard formats, such as HTML and PDF, allowing exchange of information across multiple locations, with varying technologies. Despite the fact this version has a slightly different look-and-feel than other Adobe applications (See Figure 10–2), it is very intuitive and easy-to-use.

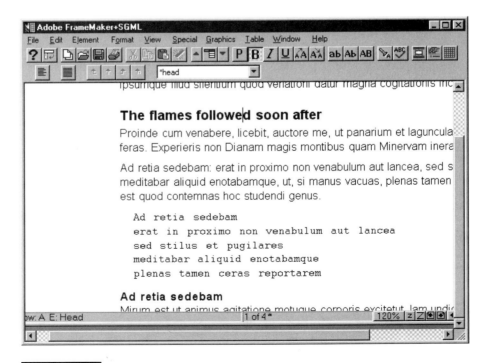

FIGURE 10–2 FrameMaker main window.

In addition, the basic design of FrameMaker documents allows for a common structure among multiple documents. The most obvious implementation for this function is the ability to have a common layout for all of your product documentation. However, you provide documents for multiple locations by not only switching content for different products, but also for different languages.

FrameMaker takes this one step further by allowing you to create multiple versions of the same document. For example, I have worked in companies that had multiple versions of product manuals, technical data sheets, and so forth. There was one set for the sales and customer service departments, another for our distributors and resellers, and another for the end customers.

It was not that we were trying to hide things. However, neither the resellers nor the customers needed certain technical information. In the past, some would use this information to get to the other side of the sticker labeled "No user-serviceable parts." The result was that they would void their warranty and would blame us for their woes. We then removed those parts of the document, so customers would not even think about doing something they shouldn't.

With a product like FrameMaker, this is not a problem. Portions of the document could be labeled "For Internal Use Only" and never make it into the copies provide to the resellers and customers.

All of this is based on the "condition text" feature of FrameMaker. As its name implies, you set certain text as conditional, and whether or not it will be included depends on the conditions you define. What text you want to make conditional and how much is conditional are up to you. In addition, you can define your own condition indicators, such as different colors or strikethrough to indicate conditional text. You can also set the condition and then hide the text that does not apply to that condition. Use of the conditional tags helps keep documents with a common base consistent as well as saves you administrative overhead and disk space.

Another key issue is that large-scale documents are rarely worked on by only one person. Instead, there is usually a team of developers. FrameMaker simplifies the work and increases the productivity of groups with several features that aid in collaborative work.

In support of this is a powerful cross-referencing functionality. The functionality of many word processing programs either disappears or becomes extremely limited when you begin working with a large number of documents. However, with FrameMaker you not only can reference specific sections, heading, or pages, but you can also make sport cross-references to specific words or phrases, even across documents. If you convert the documents to HTML or PDF, these cross-references become hyperlinks.

Multiple documents can also be grouped into books, although they do not represent a book in the conventional sense. A book is simply a convenient way to manage documents with related content. Each book can have its own properties, which you can change all at once, as needed, or you can change properties within the individual documents.

One common problem is the existence of multiple copies of specific documents. Although revision/version control systems should prevent this, companies often do not put them into place until after the first time they run into problems. FrameMaker helps ease the pain by providing a very extensive documentation comparison and reporting tool.

After the documents are compared, you have a choice of either creating a composite document or simply a summary of what the differences are. The summary report is a separate document that lists all of the differences and how often they occur.

The composite report identifies the changes used in conditional text and change bars. As previously mentioned, conditional text is where different text is displayed based on specific conditions. Change bars are indicators within the text showing where changes have been made.

FrameMaker has two additional features that make it an excellent tool for companies with large documentation projects. First, it supports the industry standard Open Document Management API (ODMA), which allows you to connect FrameMaker to a document management system (DMS), such as Documentum and Filenet. ODMA gives FrameMaker common revision control functionality, such as check-in and check-out as well as a search function within a DMS.

In addition, in the FrameMaker+SGML there is built-in support for SGML. This does not mean you need to be familiar with SMGL to use it. Instead, the functionality is completely transparent. When you load the document, FrameMaker+SGML reads the DTD and allows you to edit the document as you would in any WYSIWYG editor. When you are done and save the document, it is saved as SGML. However, if you want, you can work in either SGML mode or WYSIWYG mode.

Both FrameMaker and FrameMaker+SGML have the ability to export their documents to your intranet as standard HTML. In addition, starting with version 5.5.6, there is full support for the Extensible Markup Language (XML), which is a subset of SGML. Many products, including Microsoft Internet Explorer 5.0 are already XML capable, which gives users easier access to databases and other sources of information.

Corel VENTURA Publishing

As its name implies, Corel VENTURA is a desktop publishing application. Even before the acquisition of VENTURA by Corel, VENTURA Publishing was the standard by which all desktop publishing (DTP) products were judged. In fact, VENTURA was the first true DTP application for the PC. Corel has kept that tradition alive by enhancing and improving the product to meet the demands of today's businesses. It combines text, graphics, and many other elements into books, magazines, Web pages, or any other kind of document.

One of the key aspects of documentation today is that it goes beyond simple reports. Modern word processors like Corel WordPerfect have the features that DTP packages had a few years ago. In order to meet a company's needs, DTP products grew as well. Today, DTP products such as Corel VENTURA have become more than just fancy editors; they must manage your documents as well. In addition, having a single source for multiple documents is a must in today's publishing world, which is one area where Corel VENTURA will not leave you short.

As with CorelDRAW, Corel VENTURA can output or publish to many different destinations. For example, in addition to printing to paper, it can export to HTML, print to postscript files, and using Corel Barista (also provided on the CorelDRAW CD-ROM) to export to Java, which can then be used on any system.

Corel VENTURA comes with several additional tools to help you develop high-quality, professional documents. First and foremost is a complete version of Corel WordPerfect. This is a complete version of the stand-alone product. Therefore, it also contains the Corel SCRIPT Editor, Corel SCRIPT Dialog Editor, Corel Versions, and the Corel DataBase Publisher. On the graphics side, there is Corel PHOTO-PAINT, CorelSCAN, CorelCAPTURE, and Corel Barista.

In my opinion, Corel VENTURA is a very intuitive user interface (Figure 10–3). As I have mentioned repeatedly, the ease of learning an application is

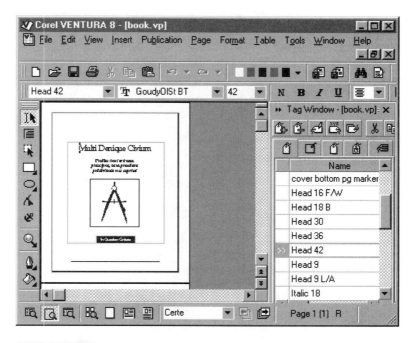

FIGURE 10–3   Corel VENTURA Publishing main window.

important to keep total cost of ownership (TCO) down, and an intuitive interface is necessary to make learning the application easier.

Version 8 of Corel VENTURA has unified the interface with the other Corel design applications like CorelDRAW (Figure 10–4). As you can see from the two interfaces, they have the same "look and feel." As we discussed earlier, this constant interface makes switching from one application to another much easier, so you can learn the new product faster and be more proficient. In addition, buttons and other controls have the "flat" appearance of many newer application. In my mind, this makes the application less "noisy" compared with the 3-D look of many Microsoft applications.

As with Corel WordPerfect, Corel VENTURA supports the Corel scripting language. The increases your proficiency by allowing you to redo takes automatically, without having to do them by hand. In addition, like WordPerfect, the interface is completely customizable, so you add or modify menus, toolbars, keyboard behavior, as well as the overall appearance.

Another key feature (actually set of features) is how well VENTURA supports work groups. It is common that larger documents are worked on by

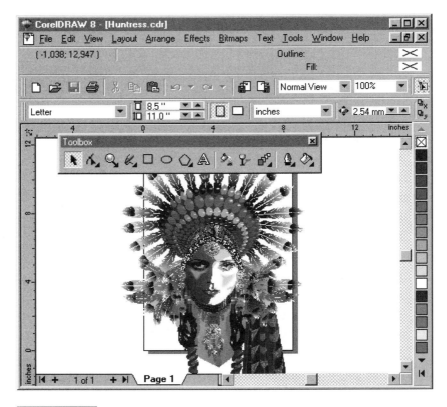

FIGURE 10–4 CorelDRAW.

different people. One way VENTURA supports this is in the consistency in which you can apply style tags. These style tags can be stored in stylesheets, which can either be internal to a document, imported from another document, or stored within libraries. It is therefore not necessary to know where the style sheet comes from, but you still have access.

This is useful when you have a set of documents within your organization and you wish them to have a common appearance. This is different from templates, as templates relate to a specific kind of document. Templates can contain these style sheets, however.

Another feature is the ability to create linked text for any file contained within your document. When you select this text for "Export on Save" each time the document is saved, the new version of the text is saved into the appropriate file. This file can then be edited by some other application. When you reload the document into VENTURA, the changes made in the other application appear there. This is extremely useful when the content creators are not the same people who do the actual layout. Another place that this can be useful is in documents with differing contents, such as multiple languages.

Another useful feature is relative paths for linked or external files. This overcomes an annoying "feature" of many Microsoft applications, whereby the path to the file is given by the universal naming convention (UNC) name. If you were to move a who directory tree to different machines (such as a printer or other service bureau).

The Lock Page Tag option is also useful in environments where different users are working on a single document. This option locks the page tag so that it cannot be moved or changed accidentally.

Movement through your document is made a lot easier by the use of the VENTURA Navigator (lower right corner of Figure 10–3). Here you have access to all of the document components, such as subdocuments, table of contents, index, scripts, cross-references, and so forth.

Coupled with this is the tag window. This gives you quick access to all of the tags, which can be applied to text, text frames, and pages. When tags are assigned to an object, the tag name appears in the property bar, so you know which tag is being applied to a specific object. All related tags can be updated from the property bar or you can easily create derived tags.

As with CorelDraw, Corel VENTURA has a Prepare for Service Bureau Wizard. This helps you through the process of preparing your documents to be sent to a "service bureau," like a printer or typesetter. Among other things, this ensures all link files are together.

Aside from just the look-and-feel, the menu structure of VENTURA is consistent with the other Corel products. Granted, there are features and functions that are only available in one of the other products (which is why they are sold separately). However, the general menu structure is the same, and common elements are in the same place. This is one of pet peeves with many Microsoft products, in that you often hunt for a specific feature.

Because you are likely to have many different sources being combined into a single document, integration is a key aspect. Therefore, it is not surprising that VENTURA can important a wide range of file types. This is not just limited to other Corel formats but to all common graphics and document formats, from word processors to CAD applications and so forth. In addition, many of these formats can be opened as if they were VENTURA documents without the need to first import them. This means that all of the original formatting is maintained.

As with the other Corel products, VENTURA is fully aware. In addition to being able to create links to objects on the Internet, you have a wide range of features to export your documents into HTML. There are also a number of different options that allow you to export your document using frames and then to configure the exported frame. In addition, you can format the appearance of the exported graphics.

Version 8 of Corel VENTURA also has support for cascading style sheets. This ensures proper positioning of the graphics as well as maintaining the formatting of your document. What really impressed me was VENTURA's support for image maps. When you place a graphic in an HTML document, you have the option of creating an image map using the graphic so that certain areas are clickable and load other documents (i.e., URLs).

In addition, you can define different protocols for different objects within your document. For example, you cannot only use HTTP, but FTP and mailto, as well. As with any other link in the World Wide Web, you can link to HTML documents, images, or any other document you normally could.

Interoperability goes beyond just importing and exporting files. Corel VENTURA has the ability to create tables from many different database sources. The gives your VENTURA documents a very dynamic character and ensures that the information is always up-to-date. In addition, there is basically the same set of formatting options that are available with static tables. If necessary, this information does not need to be in a table in the traditional sense, but can take on most any form.

Another key aspect is that like Corel WordPerfect, Corel VENTURA is SGML capable right out of the box. In support of this, VENTURA also comes with Corel Visual DTD, which enables you to easily create your own DTD files.

Graphics Software

CorelDRAW

CorelDRAW is a vector-based graphics development tool (much more than a simply drawing program). Whereas Adobe Photoshop is the standard by which all other photo manipulation tools are judged, CorelDRAW is the standard for graphics development tools. With version 9 (the latest as of this writing), Corel continues to add more and more functionality.

Particularly in the area of graphics products, it would be commercial suicide for a company to be completely dependent on its own proprietary format. Instead, vendors need to support an incredibly wide range of graphics formats. In addition, the days in which graphics programs operate independently of other applications are long gone. Instead, integration with other applications, even from other vendors, is a must. Typical environments include both graphics and text from multiple sources, combined into a single document. With OLE, it is fairly easy to embed an object, but there are a number of changes you can make.

Corel has addressed these issues by improving the integration with other applications, enabling you to include and process many different graphics formats. This includes Adobe Photoshop PSD files, and the layers will be preserved so that they can be manipulated individually in either CorelDRAW or Corel PHOTO-PAINT.

As we previously discussed, the time spent learning how to use an application is included in the TCO. Therefore, it is useful to have a common interface. This is what Corel did with CorelDRAW and Corel PHOTO-PAINT. Once you get familiar with one interface, you basically have immediate access to the same function in the other application. In addition, the interface is basically unchanged between the Windows and Power Mac versions.

The CorelDRAW product is more than just a graphics development tool; it's an entire package of tools. The main application is CorelDRAW, supported by Corel PHOTO-PAINT. CorelTRACE is a utility that will convert bitmap images to vector images, thus allowing manipulation of each object individually. CorelTEXTURE, as its name implies, helps you develop textures for your graphics. CorelCAPTURE is a screen capture tool, which allows you to save actions on the screen as animation files.

CorelDRAW also provides a number of development tools to more efficiently create graphics by allowing automation of repeated tasks. There is complete support for Microsoft's VisualBASIC for applications, allowing you to integrate Corel graphics with the Microsoft Office products. In addition, the CorelDRAW suite supports Corel's own CorelSCRIPT and includes the CorelSCRIPT editor, which can be used to add commands that you cannot automatically record.

Corel allows increases efficiency by helping you manage your graphic documents more easily. CorelDRAW 9 comes with the Canto Cumulus Desktop 4.0. This is touted as a "digital asset management tool," which can organize all sorts of different kinds of graphics formats. These are then stored in a browseable catalog in which the graphics objects are indexed, making finding as well as accessing the images much easier.

A common stumbling block in many graphical applications is color. Although everyone knows what colors are and can recognize a large number of them, how they are defined and represented in a computer is not always obvious. In addition, depending on what project you are working on, you generally need a specific subset of the available colors. It is extremely cumbersome to have to deal with 16 million (or more) colors at once.

To solve this problem, colors are often grouped into palettes. As with a painter's palette, palettes in a computer program are simply collections of colors. Although you could have a mixture of colors with different characteristics, generally palettes all have similar characteristics. A painter could have multiple palettes, setting each one aside before starting to use the next one.

With a computer, this should not be a problem, as you simply click from one palette to the next. However, this has not always been possible. Although many products have allowed you to access or even create multiple palettes, it was generally only possible to use a single palette at any given time. With CorelDRAW 9, you can have multiple palettes open and access them at any time. This gives you much more flexibility and convenience when developing your graphics. In addition to being able to define your own, CorelDRAW provides a range of predefined palettes. You can also drag from the palette onto an object to assign that specific color.

Obviously, having the image on-screen is not always sufficient. You need to be able to output it. To this end, CorelDRAW has a wide range of output and printing features. One new feature is the ability to publish directly to Adobe PDF files. This ensures that the output is as close to the on-screen version as possible. In addition, once exported, users can navigate the document, just like they would any other PDF file, including bookmarks within your PDF documents. You have different output options, including PDF for the Web or document distribution. Hyperlinks can also be included that open up new Web pages or jump to specific locations within your PDF document. Creating the PDF files has also been simplified by allowing you to create a PDF "style," which you can assign to documents without having to recreate them each time.

Here, too, is management of the document easier. Both CorelDRAW and Corel PHOTO-PAINT allow you to create "job tickets" for documents being sent to printing companies. Although the technology has not yet been standardized among different vendors, many details of the print job can be easily transmitted using this mechanism. In addition to technical details about the document, you can include setup as well as binding instructions within the ticket.

Output enhancements also include printing. CorelDRAW 9 has a "miniature preview" window, which allows you to immediately see the changes without the need to start the "print preview" by hand. This window also has tools to zoom, so you can view a larger image. Added to this is something Corel calls "preflight warnings," which is basically important information or warnings about your print jobs. When you print a file, the print engine analyzes the jobs and provides this information via the preflight tab. Plus, the new print engine allows you to print multiple documents, which will be printed as a single print job. If the elements are small enough, you can also choose to print them all on a single page.

In support of this Corel has its Prepare for Service Bureau Wizard. Here you can automatically gather all of the files associated with a particular document, including any linked images. This also includes the ability to automatically create a PDF file that serves as a proof of the document, so the service bureau (i.e., the printer) can see what the document should look like.

Another neat tool is CorelDRAW's Link Manager. This manages all links within your documents, including links to local files and URLs on the Internet. It will also provide information about the status of the links, such when the destination document is no longer valid. This can be extremely useful if you are sending a large number of linked files to a printer and want to make sure all of the files are available.

In version 9, there are a number of new and enhanced tools. One is an improved "connector tool." This makes it easier to connect objects, such as in a flow chart or organizational chart. Like other products, when you move one object, the lines and their orientations are changed accordingly. Another is improvement to how Corel handles contours. By reducing the number of nodes ("corners") in a contour, it is easier to change, export, and print. One addition I am fond of is the ability to view the exact position and size of the object in the property bar, without the need to specifically access that object's properties.

New is the natural media tool, which behaves like "natural" tools such as pencils, brushes, and so forth. You can configure a tool to provide "strokes" of various widths and styles. In addition, you can change the behavior of the tool based on how one might really use it. For example, putting more pressure on a brush results in a different appearance. The natural media tool reflects this.

CorelDRAW 9 enhances the ability to create "drop shadows," which are objects that appear to be shadows of other objects. You can change the shadow's direction from the object, vanishing point, color, opacity, and how much the edges "feather."

It is not surprising that CorelDRAW 9 also has some advanced Internet features. For example, it is possible to export a document and the text to map specific styles using Cascading Style Sheets (CSS). This makes for a better conversion to HTML pages and allows the text to be edited once it has been exported. In other applications, the text becomes part of the image and therefore can no longer be edited.

Should a document contain multiple copies of a single bitmap image, this image will only be exported once, and all references in the page will point to that single bit map. If you have links in your documents to other sites, you can preview these by right-clicking the linked object. You can also then load the target page into your browser.

Adobe Illustrator

Sometimes you need to create your own graphics and not just manipulate images. Even if you are not a graphic artist, there is a wide range of applications where you need to create your own graphics. In some cases, the drawing programs accompanying many word processing applications will satisfy your needs. However, I have found that these have limited functionality, and even those tasks it can accomplish can be cumbersome.

This is where something like Adobe Illustrator comes in. Illustrator is Adobe's graphic design tool and can be used for things as simple as organizational diagrams and flow charts to extremely complicated graphics for illustrating your products.

Its interface (Figure 10–5) is essentially identical with that for Photoshop and PageMaker (see Figure 10–1), which makes switching back and forth between the applications extremely easy. As you can see, all of the toolbar and property boxes float on the desktop, which means you can move them around your work area and enclose the object you are currently working on.

Adobe Illustrator is a full "Windows logo compliant" application, which means it completely supports OLE. This means Adobe Illustrator allows you to insert objects from a wide range of applications, including text developed with Adobe ImageReady, PageMaker, and many other word processing applications. This also means you can include Illustrator graphics in the other applications. In both cases, you simply double-click on the object to start the appropriate application.

In addition, Adobe Illustrator supports a wide range of other formats, many from other companies, including CorelDRAW, AutoCAD, and the Mi-

FIGURE 10–5 Adobe Illustrator main window.

crosoft Office family. You can also export your graphics into all of the common formats, such as the JPEG, GIF, TIFF, BMP, and, of course, Adobe Photoshop and PDF. You can also open and then edit EPS files, which can be created by most graphics programs. Even if Illustrator cannot directly edit a specific program format, it can still access the files, if the application can save it as EPS.

One important feature included with version 8.0 is the ability to include Adobe Photoshop images without having to "flatten" them. When the Adobe Photoshop image is flattened, the layers (See above.) are merged to create a single image. It is now possible to import Photoshop images and still have access to all of the different layers.

One of the highlighted features is what is called a "bounding box." This is used to define a rectangular area covered by a particular object. In many other applications, as well as previous versions of Illustrator, an object was the following by its borders. This is especially useful when your object is composed of a number of lines with little or no definable borders. I think this is a much easier and, in fact, more intuitive way of changing the size of objects rather than dragging them around by their borders.

Another highlighted feature is the pencil tool, which Adobe describes as "almost like sketching with the real pencil." Although the validity of this statement really depends on how well you can work with a mouse, the pencil tool helps you to draw graphics that are very close to what you can get with a pencil. Assuming you have an existing object, by using the pencil tool, you can easily change the shade without having to click on the object and do it by hand.

New to Adobe Illustrator 8.0 is the ability to record macros or actions just as you can with Adobe Photoshop. Here, too, you record an action once and it immediately becomes available with the click of a mouse.

Adobe Premiere

A picture is worth a thousand words, and videos are worth a thousand pictures.

One shortcoming I have always found with either books or on-line help is that they can tell me what the steps are, but they cannot show me. Training videos and CD-ROMs can often show me, but it takes time to find the right spot I want to watch. In addition, the problem I have is often not listed on the training video. Added to that, you are probably going to have topics for which there are no premade videos or CD-ROMs. The only solution is to create them yourself.

That simple-sounding statement is a lot simpler to say than to put into practice. You probably don't have any full-time video producers on your staff, and creating videos at the level of commercial training products takes time and money. However, the key question is, how much time and how much money are you willing to invest?

One key factor is that technology has advanced and prices have dropped to the point where video development tools have almost become consumer goods. For just a few hundred dollars you can get products that would have cost you thousands a few years ago. Now you can have all of the features and functionality you need.

The first step is obtaining a video camera. Although going into the detail of that is beyond the scope of this book, I would like to make a couple of comments. First, always remember the total cost of doing something. If you already have a video camera for other purposes, there is generally no issue with using it to create training videos. If not, find one that is very easy to use compared with having a lot of fancy gadgets. You probably won't win an Oscar for your training videos, so you are more interested in getting them on tape than having any artistic value.

One place a video can be extremely useful is in hardware training, such as replacing cards in computers, changing toner cartridges, and so forth. These can then be converted into AVI or other digital formats and made available on your company's intranet. Therefore, the camera needs to get in close enough to be able to see what is going on.

As a warning, I would like to say that making videos like this takes practice. Your first few attempts are not likely to be ready for prime time. However, the tapes can be recorded over, and it usually only takes a few tries before you get the hang of things.

The next issue is the software. You are going to make mistakes, or you will need to have some kind of text detailing specific aspects, such as warnings or notes to the viewer. Therefore, you will need easy-to-use software, which can not only edit, but also add captions. In some cases, a few effects make the videos entertaining enough to not be boring.

One such product is Adobe Premiere. One of the key aspects of Adobe Premiere is that version 5.1 (the latest as of this writing) was designed to resemble a professional editing bay (Figure 10–6). Here, you have access to all of the editing tools you have in a professional video editor. On the top left-hand side is the project window, which lists the various source videos. On the top, right-hand side is the monitor window. At the bottom are the time lines with various video and audio tracks. As the video is being displayed, a marker moves across the time line indicating exactly where on the time line you are currently located.

Once a clip (sound or video) has been imported, you can simply drag the clips onto the timeline where you want to insert them, and you have a "rough cut" of your video. Trimming is then accomplished in the monitor window by simply marking the segments you want to remove (or keep). When a segment is removed, there will be a gap in the video. To close this gap, all you need to do is slide one or the other video along the time line. If you way, you can also insert still, which will be displayed for a specified amount of time.

Your original videos are displayed in the source window, where you have precise control of which portion you want to mark and include in your

FIGURE 10–6 Adobe Premiere editing window.

target video. You can then insert them anywhere on the time line, even to overlay (not necessarily overwrite) existing clips. At any point, you can display the edited clips in the program window and at any speed.

Adobe Premiere also has some advanced features to help you place titles and captions on the screen. More than likely, many of the features Premiere has are more than you will need to create simply training videos. However, you do have the full range of options to control fonts, sizes, orientation, scrolling, and so forth. Text can also be made transparent to not interfere with the images.

Although sound is probably less important with training clips displayed on your intranet, videos created for more formal training generally have some kind of sound. I have worked in companies where the training videos were created by placing a video camera at the back of the classroom and filming the class. This was extremely useful for review or for those who could not attend the classes. The problem often is that the sound quality is not always the best. Premiere addresses this issue by giving you a wide range of options to filter and enhance the audio. This makes sure all of the information in the class is available on the video.

Despite the fact that Adobe Premiere is used for a completely different kind of work, it has the same general "feel" as other Adobe applications, although the "look" is slightly different. Editing tools and other windows can be docked to a particular spot or float free on the screen, so they are accessible when you need them.

If you have offices in different countries, you can still use Adobe Premiere to create the videos. The three major televisions are supported: the American standard, NTSC, PAL (used by most of the rest of the world), and SECAM (used mainly by France and many East European countries).

If you plan to create videos as well as other graphics work, you should look into the Adobe Dynamic Media Collection. This is a collection of several of Adobe's graphics products: Premiere, After Effects, Photoshop, and Illustrator. If you need all of these products, you can save a fair bit of money by buying this as a bundle. Because they all have the same Adobe interface, switching from one to another is easy.

ThumbsPlus

With the latest version of their product ThumbsPlus (4.0), Cerious software has bridged the final gap between a simple image viewer and database. Previous versions already allowed you to store descriptions and keywords for files within a database file used by ThumbsPlus. It was possible to configure several of these databases, so you could sort your files as needed without having the database file grow too large.

The current version has taken this one step further in that they provide you connectivity using ODBC. You can therefore store all of your picture information within a "real" database and still have access to all of the information.

Figure 10–7 shows you the primary workspace of ThumbsPlus. At the top, you see a customizable menu and a toolbar. Although the toolbar does not have the look and feel of most Windows applications, it is very intuitive.

On the left side, you see the directory structure of your system. You will see different icons for the different types of drives you have. That is, local drives look different from CD-ROMs, which look different from network drives. The icon for each drive is also color-coded to indicate whether the drive contains thumbnails.

When you double-click on a drive, the directories are displayed. Clicking on a directory expands it as it does in Windows Explorer. Here, too, the directories are color-coded depending on whether or not it contains thumbnails. In addition, the color is different if the directories subdirectories that contain thumbnails, the subdirectories contain thumbnails, but the directory itself does not, or if the directory contains thumbnail, but the subdirectories do not.

On the right are the thumbnails. Any file that does not have a thumbnail is still displayed. Underneath the thumbnail (or where the thumbnail would

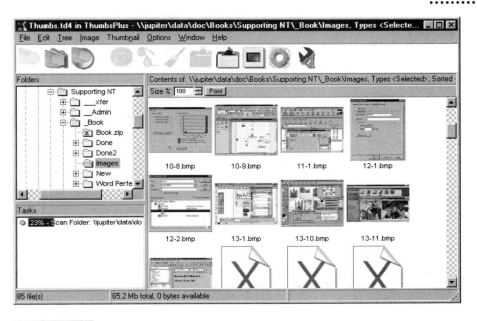

FIGURE 10–7   ThumbsPlus work space.

go) is various information about the file, which is configurable. Typically, I have just the thumbnail (which can also be disabled), file name, and the size. However, you can also include the resolution, date, and images dimensions.

Basically all of the standard file functions are available from within ThumbsPlus. That is, you can copy, move, delete and rename files as well as create and remove directories. One really nifty functionality is the ability to automatically copy or move files that would overwrite others with the same name but only if they are either newer or are identical (which you can define yourself).

ThumbsPlus can keep track of previous work in several ways. For example, all of your thumbnails are stored in the database, even if the drive containing the pictures is not available. You can still see the thumbnails and other information, even if you cannot access the original files. The drives are then indicated with different symbols when they are off-line (not available). You can also configure ThumbsPlus to keep track of what database you used last as well as what directory you were in.

If you have a large archive of files, you way want to consider compressing the images into ZIP files to save space. As we talked about in the section on file systems, clustering causes you to lose space at the end of the last cluster of each file. By compressing a large number of files, you lose only the space at the end of the compressed archive and not at the end of every single file. In addition, I compress images when I write them to CD-ROM, as it makes the writing process go a lot faster.

This is not a problem for ThumbsPlus, as you can configure it to treat ZIP files as if they were directories. They then appear in the left-hand side, and when you click on them, they open up as if they were normal directories, and you then have access to the files.

ThumbsPlus not only has support for dozens of different formats in addition to ZIP files, it can convert back and forth between most of them. You can basically change every aspect of the file, including file type, size, resolution, and the number of colors used. In addition, there is a wide range of filters that you can use during the conversion process.

The batch processing can continue in the background while you are working on other tasks, even when using another copy of ThumbsPlus. Although I have noticed a slight slowdown in system performance while converting large numbers of files, it's not too bad.

Making changes to the images is not just limited to batch mode. Most of the changes you can make in batch mode can also be done manually. You have a large number of filters to use that can (among other things) sharpen or soften the image. You can also rotate or flip the image, change the colors, as well as automatically crop it to remove any border.

There are a number of input and output options that you can use. Being an image management and processing system, it is not surprising that ThumbsPlus can also scan images directly using the TWAIN API of Windows. You also have the ability to scan images in batch mode (Multiple TWAIN Acquire), and ThumbsPlus will automatically change the file name for each picture. If you stop and continue later, the program remembers the last file name used and continues from there.

Of course, you can print images from within ThumbsPlus, but you can also create "contact sheets." Like the contact sheets made for real photographs, these are simply single images that contain thumbnails of a number of other images. How many images appear on a contact sheet, how large they are, and how they are laid out is all configurable. There are also a large number of other configuration options for the contact sheets, such as background, borders, fonts, headings, and footers, as well as what other information is displayed with the image.

This can also be automated, so you can select a large number of images and have them all made into contact sheets. If you have more images that can fit on a single contact sheet, ThumbsPlus will split them across as many sheets as are necessary.

In keeping with the growth of the Internet, ThumbsPlus can also export files into Web pages. In essence, this is similar to contact sheets. However, as one would expect, each image is then a link to the full-sized version. If you have more than one page, appropriate links are created to allow you to move back and forth between the pages.

If you need to distribute your images, ThumbsPlus also comes in a development kit version. Normally, the locations of files stored within the database is dependent on the volume name of the drive where they are stored. However, even using the same drive letters and volume name for a writable CD-ROM, you still cannot get the database to behave correctly with self-written CD-ROMs.

Actually, this is intentional. This is the same with any product that provides development versions. Run-time licenses are separate from the development version. However, I think that you should seriously consider getting the development version if you distribute large numbers of files. You can then provide a licensed copy of ThumbsPlus to use with the database on the CD-ROM, which is essentially what you are paying for when you purchase the development kit.

ThumbsPlus is available in a shareware version from many sources, including the accompanying CD-ROM. Once the evaluation period is over, you are reminded of this fact each time you start or stop the program. You can therefore continue to use it, but I seriously recommend you buy it. If you have a larger number of images to manage, it is an invaluable tool.

When you do decide to purchase it, ThumbsPlus has a wide range of options from single-user licenses to larger site licenses. There are also a concurrent-use and unlimited-user enterprise licenses.

Visio

Visio produces a whole series of products for developing diagrams. Calling the Visio products simple drawing programs would not be fair to them. It is much safer to call the Visio products information modeling or information development tools, as they not only help you to draw your models and diagrams, but can help you automate the process as well as develop applications using information you collected using the Visio tools.

Each product is intended for a different kind of customer. In many cases, you want to be able to create simple flow charts or organizational diagrams. In other cases, you need to design complex models and the basic functionality.

The product is called Visio Standard. It provides an incredibly long list of predefined graphics types with the associated symbols. The graphics are broken into several key groups, such as Business, Database, Flow Chart, Internet, Maps, Network, and Software. Each of these groups consists of a handful of specific diagram types, some of which are more than your typical graphic or diagram. In addition, Over 1,300 symbols are provided for you for each of the diagram types.

For example, in the Business group, you can create layouts of an office, including all of the associated equipment, such as desks, doors, PCs, power outlets, and phone jacks. There is a calendar template, which you can use create to create calendars (what else?). You input the date and the calendar is created for you.

A common graphic type is an organizational chart. This is something that Visio can obviously do. However, I was amazed at how easily you can create the charts, especially compared with programs such as Microsoft's Organization Chart program. Drag-and-drop is naturally available, and it is amazingly easy to create relationships. In additions, some groupings and relationships are not possible with other tools. In addition, Visio can create the organization chart directly from personnel information stored in your database.

Each entry can be linked to other documents and even exported to the Web. A click on the entry and you get a complete job description as well as any other information you need. Because pages can be linked, you can create a "drill-down" through your company, starting with the company management and working your way to each department, section, and then individual employee. This functionality does not just apply to the organization charts. Instead, you can export and link any of the available document types.

One very nice feature is the ability to export these diagrams and charts into basically all of the standard formats. Windows BMP, GIF, JPEG, TIFF, EPS, and HTML are just a few of the more common formats that are supported. Plus, there are an equal number of data types that you can import into Visio, including ActiveX controls, Lotus Notes data, as well as any other object that supports OLE.

In addition, if you don't want to use any of the predefined drawing types, you can create your own in a "free-form" mode. This behaves like most any other drawing tool.

In addition to the standard diagrams that you are able to depict with other products, Visio Professional provides you the functionality to develop database models, network process, workflow diagrams, and so on. However, keep in mind that it is much more than a drawing tool. It is an aid for development and management of your information architecture.

At the upper end of the scale is Visio Enterprise. It is intended to fill most of the information modeling needs of any size company. Although it might be appear to be a bit too overwhelming for smaller companies, properly implemented it can save you well more than the price of the product in lost productivity, repeating work, and not failing to develop the most efficient systems possible.

Visio Enterprise is broken into three main functional areas in additional to more traditional diagrams like flow charts. The first is network design and documentation. I intentionally chose the word documentation, because I often find that companies have insufficient knowledge of their network. They may know the network IP addresses or where the hubs are, but many need to sit down and count the routers, physical segments, and so forth.

Visio Enterprise addresses the problem of documenting your network by providing several tools to collect and manage the information about your network. Figure 10–8 shows you the "auto discovery" mode of Visio Enter-

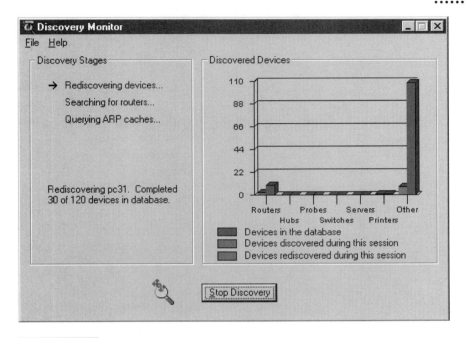

FIGURE 10–8   Visio Auto Discovery.

prise. You can scan your network for all available network devices, which are then laid out automatically (Figure 10–9). As Visio is scanning your network, you can monitor the progress. Although this may seem like a pretty mundane function, it is really necessary when you have a large network. Depending on how many networks and how many devices you have, the scanning process could take several hours.

You can speed up the process by only selecting the connecting devices, such as routers and hubs. This gives you good graphical overview of the general structure of your network without having to wait until every device is loaded. Once you have the basic structure, more important nodes (such as the servers) can be added extremely easily using basic drag-n-drop.

The next functional area is database modeling. Unless prepackaged products are implemented, I have found that many companies do not plan their databases in much detail. One person needs a table to manage hardware, so he/she creates something in MS Excel. Another person needs something to manage the software licenses, so he/she creates something in MS Access. As time passes, they discover some component is missing, so they might add a new table and possibly create a relation between the two tables. Soon there are a dozen tables, often with repeated information.

The more types of information managed, the more duplication of effort. In addition, such databases are quite often inefficient for the task at hand.

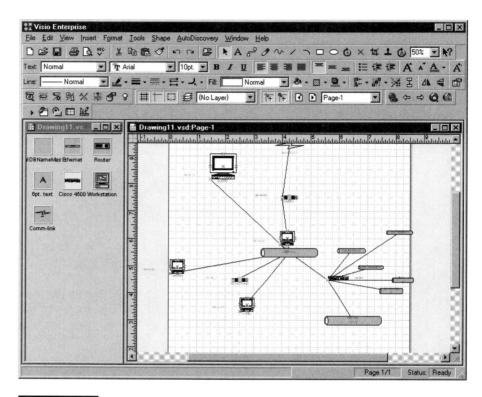

FIGURE 10–9 Visio Network View.

Visio Enterprise allows you to design and redesign databases based on all of the leading database vendors (plus any other that supports ODBC). You can also synchronize your database models with the actual databases to ensure that you are continuously up-to-date.

For me, one of the most exciting functions is the ability to reverse-engineer a database. Here, Visio Enterprise will read all of the tables from a given database source (such as MS SQL Server, MS Access, Oracle, and Informix) and generate a model of that database. By dragging the tables from the list provide onto the work space, Visio Enterprise will generate a visual representation of that model.

I used this feature to get an overview of how our SMS database (MS SQL Server) was designed. Although I could get the information I wanted using the SMS console directly, I could not see how this information was stored. Aside from satisfying my curiosity, I wanted to be able to display a lot of this information from Web pages and combine it with our software license database. Having the visual representation provided by Visio Enterprise, I was able to save myself a great deal of time by not having to hunt down the information I wanted.

Once you have your database model on the screen, you can make changes to the database structure, reorganize tables, change indexes, field names, and so forth. When you have finished making the changes, Visio provides a Wizard so you can the migrate (export) those changes back into the database extremely easily.

Visio also provides support for changing or editing the "code" of the database. For example, you can use Visio to make change to or even create stored procedures, views, and triggers.

In support of this are two very useful functions. First, you can continually synchronize your database with the model that Visio generates. That is, even after you migrate the changes back into the database, you can make changes to the model and then later update the new changes.

Second, Visio provides a "three-way" compare. Here, you can compare the database, the original model, and the updated version all at once. This lets you verify changes and ensure they are correct and complete. In addition, this feature will show you changes to the database that do not exist in your extracted model and allows you to selectively apply those changes to your model.

Visio Enterprise has a unique tool called the "Verbalizer," which provides you the details of a particular database object. Objects can be any table, view, or relationship in your database. Figure 10–10 shows the output of the Verbalizer for a table in an SMS database.

Visio takes into account that no one is perfect and can check your database model for errors prior to migrating it. Visio checks the model for logical (structural) errors and when as errors specific to the database you are using. You also have a choice of doing the check automatically as the model is migrated, or you can do it by hand whenever you want.

Often, seeing the visual representation is not enough. Instead, you would like to see a description of the database. For this, Visio provides three basic report types: statistical, table, and types. A statistical report lists (as its name implies) statistical information about your database. The table report shows how the tables in the logical model will appear in the physical report. A types report provides information about the various data types in your database, including built-in and user-defined types.

Visio also supports the Unified Modeling Language (UML), which is used as an aid for software development. In this way, you can layout the logical structure of your applications before you write your fist line of code. Visio supports almost two dozen software design methodologies, including Windows 95 and 98 user interfaces.

One interesting feature deals with the fact that often elements of your application may not appear in any diagram. For this, Visio provides a "UML navigator," which allows you to navigate through all of the objects within your model, including objects, classes, components, and even states.

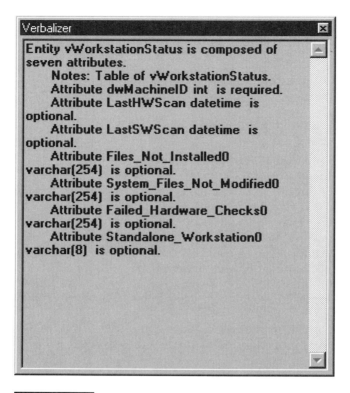

FIGURE 10-10 Visio Verbalizer.

Scanners and Scanner Software

Having a good OCR software product is of little value if there is no way to get the text into your computer to be able to process it. There are a number of fax products on the market today that allow you to store the image rather than printing it out, so you could fax the pages to yourself, but that is often too cumbersome, and you often do not get the quality necessary to do OCR. It's fine to read the image on screen, but the recognition rate can be extremely low.

The best solution is to get a scanner. Prices of good-quality scanners have dropped to the point where is they have almost become a commodity, as compared to a luxury as they several years ago. The amount of time saved by not having to search through walls full of binders or having to retype documents is far more than the cost of a scanner.

Scanners are also useful for converting images into electronic files, which can then be processed further. Although new images can be created using a digital camera, what about the existing ones? Particularly, if you have historical images (the first headquarters building or products that are no longer produced) there is no way to recreate the image. All you have is the print (possibly a negative). To get it into the system, you have to scan it.

This has the added advantage of giving you the ability to process the images. If all you have is a 30-year-old print, it is possible that it is faded, scratched, or has other damage that makes it not the perfect picture for publication. Many photo-processing tools, such as Adobe Photoshop, can take out a great many defects and restore the image to a point that most people won't be able to tell that it was ever less than perfect.

As with printers, one of the key characteristics of a scanner is the resolution, which is measured in dpi. With a printer, the resolution determines the level of detail you can show on the printout. With a scanner, the resolution determines the detail that you can recognize and store. In both cases, the greater the resolution, the more memory that's needed.

There are actually two types of resolution: optical and interpolated. Optical is often referred to as the "true" resolution of your scanner as this is the level of detail that the scanner can really see. Interpolated resolution can be thought of as "software enhanced." Typically, software resolution is double that of the optical resolution and is useful for scanning in things like line art or large images.

The resolution you choose will depend completely on what you want to do with the image and not necessarily how big the original is. If the image you are scanning will be used on your Web site or somewhere else on-line as is, you can get the necessary solution scanning at just 100 dpi or even 75 dpi. This is simply because your monitor cannot handle a higher resolution. Even if you are going to print out the image on a laser or inkjet printer, you generally do not need much more; typically, about 300 dpi.

As we talked about in the section on hardware (Chapter 5), the color you see on the screen is a combination of the three basic colors: red, green, and blue. You will hear these are referred to as "channels," such as the red channel. Many software products like Adobe Photoshop also talk about color channels.

How many bits are used for each channel determines how many colors you can display. The lowest level is just a single bit, without regard to channels. This gives you a black-and-white image, as the bit is either set (white) or no (black). However, using a technique called halftones, you can arrange the black and white dots in such as a way as to give the illusion of grayscale.

Using 8 bits, you can get a total of 256 colors (2^8 = 256). Today, you will typically find that 8 bits is used to define the number of shades of gray, as 256 colors is far too few for normal use with color images. This is referred to as 8-bit grayscale. Note that 256 shades of gray is actually more than the human eye can differentiate.

With 24-bit color, there are 8 bits per each of the red, green and blue channels. This means that you can use a total of 256 shades for each of the three colors for a total of approximately 16.7 million colors and is referred to as True Color or photo-realistic color. Note here too that 16.7 million colors are more than the human eye can see. The next level up is 36-bit color, which is composed of three 12-bit color channels. This provides over 68 billion colors.

Coupled with this is the term dynamic range, which is the ability of the scanner to recognize a range of tonal values. Take an image of a tree casting a shadow onto a building with different colors. Each surface can either be fully illuminated, in its own shadow, in the shadow of something plus illuminated by reflected light, and so forth. The "real" color of the surface remains constant, but in the image there are fine gradations or tones in the color. The more bits the scanner uses for color, the greater the dynamic range. Therefore, a 36-bit scanner has a higher dynamic range than a 24-bit scanner.

Why if the human eye cannot even recognized 16 million colors, why even bother with 68 billion? Well, computer software can recognize that many. It is useful in many cases to be able to process that many to get the necessary levels of color in order to get the proper color shading.

Because it is often necessary to use higher resolutions and a greater number of colors, you need to be careful that you have both enough hard disk space and RAM. One common misconception is that doubling the resolution doubles the size of the image. Just remember that you are actually doubling it in two directions. Therefore, doubling the resolution gives you an image that is four times as large. As you increase the resolution and number of possible colors, the size of the image can grow to incredibly large.

Let's take a 5" x 7" photograph that we want to scan using 24-bit color and a resolution of 75 dpi, which is useful for on-screen display. When stored on disk, they would have a size of approximately 577 KBs. If you increased the resolution to 2400 dpi, the file would be about 590 MBs. An 8.5" x 11" photo at this resolution and color depth would be about 1.5 GBs.

To get the proper output of a scanned image to your printer or any other output device, you need to calibrate the color. Often what the scanner sees is not what is shown on the monitor or what is printed. By calibrating your various devices, you ensure that each reproduces the color in the same way. Microtek scanners use an exclusive technology called Dynamic Color Rendition, which helps ensure that the scanner reproduces the image as closely as possible. This helps to eliminate time-consuming postscanning processing necessary with some other scanners. In addition, you can calibrate the Microtek scanners, as you need to ensure that colors continue to be recognized accurately.

When selecting a scanner, look at what tools it provides. The most important one is the actual scanning tool.

Many scanner vendors make the most recent version of the scanning software available on their Web site. Even if you do not have a scanner yet, this will give you a good overview of what the scanner is capable of doing and what features the software provides.

Microtek scanners provide a program called the ScanWizard (Figure 10–11). It provides a wide range of functions to enhance the quality and ac-

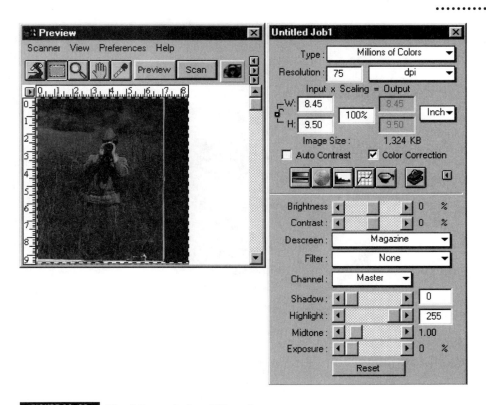

FIGURE 10-11   The Microtek ScanWizard.

curacy of your images. Not only can you adjust the colors, but also brightness, contrast, and many other common characteristics of the images.

Another tool that Microtek provides is their ScanSuite (Figure 10–12). This has a number of tools for scanning images (as compared to processing the scanned image, although it can do this to some extent).What more is there to scanning images than converting it to a file or loading it directly into an application? Well, a lot.

First, rather than sending the scanned image to an application such as Adobe Photoshop, why not send it directly to a specific printer? You have certainly done this before but never looked at it in the same way. You have some document of which you need a duplicate. You lay it on a sheet of glass, press a button, and it copies the duplicate.

We know this better as "making a photocopy" or simply "copying" the original. The only difference is that the Microtek ScanSuite runs the copy through your PC, while at the same time saving you the extra expensive of a copy machine. Granted this is a bit cumbersome with large numbers of originals or copies, but it can save you a great deal if you just occasionally make copies.

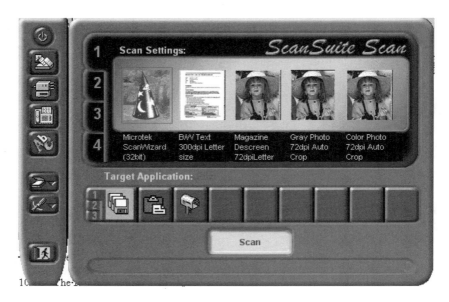

FIGURE 10–12 The Microtek ScanSuite.

What if instead of sending the image directly to a printer driver like an laser printer, you send it to a fax machine? This can be a fax modem or a printer that serves as a fax. For example, in addition to my Microtek Scan-Maker 636, I have a Brother MFC-9500, which is a multifunction center. Although the Brother MFC-9500 has the ability to scan document (it needs to, as it is a fax as well), it can only scan loose sheets, not books or magazines (assuming I don't want to tear out the pages). Using my Microtek scanner in conjunction with the Brother MFC, I can scan in another, make copies or faxes, with very little room taken up on my desk.

The Microtek ScanSuite has a wide range of options to define what the input source is. For example, you have a wide range of paper sizes, including both American and European standards, envelopes, index cards, as well as a user-defined setting for uncommon paper formats.

The Microtek scanners are fully TWAIN compliant, which means you have access to the scanner from a wide range of software products. For example, when using Adobe Photoshop or even Corel WordPerfect, you can scan the image directly into the application, without the need to first store it on the hard disk and then load it into the application.

When you first access the scanner using the TWAIN driver, the Scan-Wizard is activated to do the actual scanning. You therefore have access to all of the image-enhancement functions you normally do. One of the key aspects of the ScanWizard is what Microtek calls "Advanced Image Enhancement." In addition to being able to make a wide range of changes easily, all of the changes are displayed immediately. Therefore, you do not need to first save the file before you see the results.

The ScanWizard allows you to adjust the brightness, contrast, and exposure. Each refers to a different aspect of the amount of light in your image. Brightness determines how many shades you get, whereas contrast is the intensity of those shades. The overall light is defined by the exposure, and by changing it, you can bring out more detail in the image. These terms have the same definition in photography.

Coupled with this are the shadows and highlights. These let you select what are the darkest and lightest values on your image, respectively. With a limited number of colors or grayscale, changing these values can help to bring out more detail. The ScanWizard can be used to adjust these as well. In addition, different aspects of the color, including the tint, can be adjusted.

Often the image you are scanning has specific characteristics that require special treatment. For example, if you are scanning from a magazine, the resulting image will be different than scanning it from a photograph using the exact same configuration on your scanner. Therefore, you need to be able to adjust the scanner to compensate. The ScanWizard does just that. It provides a number of different descreening masks, which automatically compensate for the effects of different media.

Sometimes the image itself is too light or too dark. The ScanWizard has an automatic contrast control, which you can enable to automatically adjust for extremes in contrast. Coupled with this is the "curve tool," which is used to modify the middle ranges of gray (as compared to the extremes). This is called the gamma. Using this tool, you can adjust the middle ranges of gray without changing either the shadows or highlights,

Aside from being able to make real-time changes to your images, the ScanWizard saves time by allowing you to scan several images at once, even if the originals are completely different media. For example, you might have text, a color image, and a grayscale image. By defining each "job" in advance, you can scan them one right after the other, without having to restart the scanning process. It is even possible to take a single image and break it into several jobs, which are then stored as separate files.

Microtek offers a wide range of scanner products for the casual user to high-end graphics professional, who have the greatest demands in scanner performance. Depending on the scanner, you will find parallel, SCSI, or USB connections. Using a technology called Zero Reflection Technology, the Microtek scanner improves image quality by reducing the amount of light reflected off the image.

At the bottom end of the scale is the SlimLine C3. As its name implies, this is very thin (1.7") and lightweight (7.7 lb). Although it has a 36-bit color depth, it only has a resolution of 300 × 600 dpi, which is probably too low for professional scanning applications. Using the Enhanced Parallel Port (EPP), you can connect both the scanner and a printer to a single port. What makes the C3 so small is Contact Image Sensor, which allows direct contact between the image and the image sensor. This is in contrast to other scanners that use the Charged-Couple Device and a mirror to scan the image.

Ideal for more active home users or small businesses is the Microtek ScanMaker V636, which I use. This has an optical resolution of 600 × 1200 dpi, which can be interpolated up to 9600 × 9600 dpi. To improve performance, I chose the SCSI interface, although the V636 can also be obtained with an EPP connector.

Microtek also provides corporate scanners, which have greater performance than these models. For example, the ScanMaker 4 has an 600 × 1200-dpi optical resolution with a 36-bit color depth. It has two scan beds, allowing you to scan photos and prints in the upper bed, then films and other transparent media in the lower bed. It uses a Microtek patented process called Emulsion Direct Imaging Technology (EDIT), which allows for direct contact with the media without the problems when there is a piece of glass between the image and the scanner.

The ScanMaker X6EL has a 36-bit color depth and a legal-sized scan bed. An optical resolution of 600 × 1200 dpi makes a good choice for most typical business applications. Performance is increased through the use of an Adaptec PCI SCSI host adapter, which is included. Also included is an adapter to scan 35-mm slides.

The ScanMaker 6400XL has a tabloid-size scan bed, with a resolution of only 400 × 800 dpi (6400 x 6400 dpi interpolated). This allows you to scan in much larger originals, as well as 10 3.5" × 5" standard photographs in a single pass.

Graphic professionals are also satisfied with the Microtek line. The ScanMaker 5 is a high-end version of the ScanMaker 4, including the dual scan beds. However, it has a legal-sized bed and an optical resolution is increased to 1000 x 2000 dpi.

The ScanMaker 9600XL is the high-end version of the ScanMaker 6400XL. Optical resolution is increased to 600 × 1200 dpi (9600 dpi interpolated). The scan bed is also tabloid-sized. Included with it is a Transparency Media Adapter for scanning transparencies and film.

Depending on the scanner, Microtek also provides a lite edition of Caere's OmniPage OCR software. Although this does not have the same features as OmniPage Professional, it is useful for home users as well as small businesses with a limited amount of scanning. You will also find a copy of Caere's PageKeeper document management software. To be able to process the scanned images, there is also a copy of Adobe PhotoDeluxe. Low-end scanners include the Ulead PhotoImpact imaging software but neither of the Caere products.

Another one of Microtek's products is called the "ImageDeck," which is a stand-alone scanning device. By "stand-alone" I mean that it operates completely independent of a computer. It has an Iomega "built-in" 100-MB drive and a 3.5" floppy to store the scanned images. The heart of the unit is a 26-

bit, 600 × 600-dpi scanner and includes a parallel port. This means it can also serve as a copier.

With no computer software running it, the ImageDeck operates completely by push button. In addition to defining the scanning options, such as resolution, color, or black and white, and image or text, you can also format the floppy.

As with the printers, I did not want to turn this into a Microtek product catalog. Although I use a Microtek scanner and find it extremely easy to use, and it produces excellent results, my goal was simply to provide you an overview of the solutions that Microtek offers.

OmniPage Pro

Figure 10–13 shows the primary work space for OmniPage Pro 9.0. The left-hand frame shows you all of the pages you have scanned for the current document. In the center is an enlarged version of the current document with the zones that have been identified. On the right is the text editor where you can proofread and edit the recognized text. In this of each of these frames is adjustable, allowing means that the view you need.

Just above reason three frames internal bar used to control and the flow of the OCR process. Which button you can press and therefore which action you can start is dependent on which step of the scanning process you are

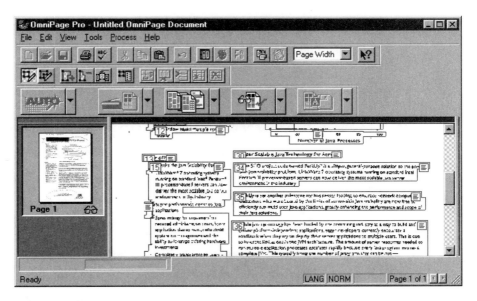

FIGURE 10–13 OmniPage main work space.

currently at. For example, if you have not yet scanned in the document, then the button to process and proofread is grayed out. Under each button is a drop-down menu listing the various choices you have at each step. For example, instead of scanning an image, you can load an existing image. Instead of recognizing text in a single column to the you could recognize that in multiple columns or any makes format including images.

The order in which the text is inserted into the document does not necessarily mean conveying based on the original ordering of the pages. You can click on one of the thumbnail images of the pages and dragg it to a location where you want the text to appear in the resulting file.

OmniPage has several settings that help it deal with existing applications. For example, applications are made "OCR Aware" from within Omni-Page by "registering" them. A new entry, "Acquire Text," appears in that application's File menu that you use to scan the document directly into the application. If the application understands rich text format (RTF), you can save much of the formatting as well.

The new menu entry, "Acquire Text Settings," allows you to configure the OCR behavior for that application. This includes things like automatically straightening the page, recognizing the page layout (multiple columns, images, etc.), defining the language, and recognizing the zone automatically, all of which are possible from OmniPage directly.

OmniPage does a very interesting thing. Text that it does not recognize is marked in green in the editor window. When you double-click on it, that portion of the image is displayed so you can verify the text and make the necessary changes by hand.

OmniPage also does a good job when working with forms. First is that, like all other documents, recognition goes extremely fast. A normal letter takes about 30 seconds to scan, and processing depends on the document and what you want recognized. About 2 minutes! Second, you can define scan templates that OmniPage uses on subsequent documents. Here you define each of the areas to scan and in what order. Each time you load a new document with this format, you can tell OmniPage to use the template.

PageKeeper

So what do you do with all of the documents you have scanned in? In fact, what do you do with all of your documents to begin with?

For small to medium businesses and even for personal use, Caere provides the solution in the form of their product PageKeeper. You can take existing documents and import them into PageKeeper, or you can scan documents directly. Once the document has been added, you can group them into different categories and store the groups for easier access.

At first, this appears to be simply another way of storing files, similar to the way the file system works. However, the power of PageKeeper lies in the tools it provides. The simplest example is the ability to store thumbnails of the document. Even before you open it, you have a general idea of what kind of file it is.

Files are imported into PageKeeper, which simply keeps track of the physical of the file and does not make a separate copy or move the file. Instead, PageKeeper simply creates a thumbnail of the document and stores the necessary information.

You can also clip files together to form convenient units to manage your files. When clipped together, you can treat the files as a single unit and do with it everything you could with single files. For example, let's assume you were storing the monthly status reports from each of your branch offices. They consist of word processing documents containing things like the report proper, spreadsheets with sales information, and maybe pictures of damaged products. You could then clip all of these documents together and then store it as a unit.

In addition, if you wanted to, you could print out all of the files stored within a clipped group. Because faxing is just another way of printing a file, it is not surprising that you can fax clipped groups as well as single files. Taking this one step further, you can also send the groups as an attachment to email.

If need be, you can also clip together already clipped groups of files, which can then be treated as a unit. At the end of the year, you could clip together all of the status reports from your branch offices. The downside is that if you ever unclip them, the individual files are separated and not the previously clipped groups. However, you can remove individual documents from the group.

One interesting function was that during the installation PageKeeper scanned my system for applications that would most likely want to be linked up with PageKeeper. It found MS Word, Corel WordPerfect, both my browsers (MS Internet Explorer and Netscape), along with several other applications. PageKeeper keeps track of which application would be used to access a particular document. Double-clicking on the icon starts the associated application, or you can load the document using a different application by simply clicking another one on the toolbar.

Figure 10–14 shows the primary work space of PageKeeper. This behaves very much like Windows Explorer. On the left side of the window, you see the hierarchical structure of your files and folders. On the right side are the details of the directory you are currently in. Like the Explorer, you can list the files in four different ways (detailed list, list, small icons, and large icons), as you can see in the right half of the window. As with Explorer, you can click on any of the headings to sort the directory list.

Files are added in several different ways. You can add files from the file system either through the context menu (or File menu) by clicking the entry "New Document from Disk." This allows you to include single files or small groups of files. (There is a limit to the number of files this method will allow.) Second, you can drag-and-drop them from Explorer. This is a much

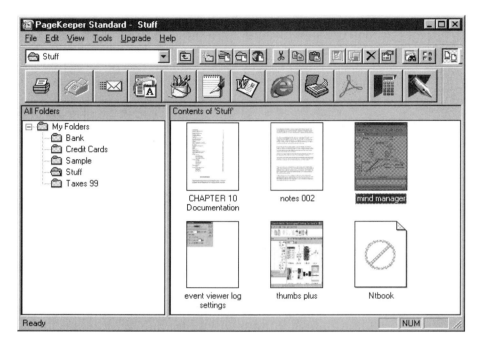

FIGURE 10-14   Caere PageKeeper main screen.

more efficient method if you have a lot of files you want to import. However, each file that you import with this method needs to be read to create the index. It might take a long time to load in and process all of the files. If you copy a large number of files, PageKeeper will not be able to process them all at once, so it will create a number of jobs that are processed as the system gets around to them.

In addition, you can download a page from the Web. This is a bit cumbersome to use, as you are expected to input the URL and cannot search for a specific page.

The last way I found to be "nifty," because it is so straightforward and so simple, is one many people do not think about. This is creating a shortcut to PageKeeper and putting it in the Send To directory. You can then send a file to PageKeeper by selecting the "Send To" entry from the context menu in Explorer. This allows you to register files into PageKeeper as you continue to do your work. As you come across files you would like to manage with Page-Keeper, you click a menu and the file is in.

As you would expect, being a Caere product, PageKeeper can also directly scan in documents. In addition, if you had a large number of documents and a scanner with an automatic document feed (ADF), you could scan them all at once into PageKeeper.

In addition to storing thumbnails of the different documents, Page-Keeper stores a number of different pieces of information about the file as well as creates an index. There is no need for you to create a list of keywords.

When you go looking for information, PageKeeper helps in the process by accessing the index it created as pages are added to the

PageKeeper includes support for more than 40 of the most common file formats. This does not just include word processing formats but image and spreadsheet formats as well. Among the formats PageKeeper supports are:

- Adobe Portable Document Format (PDF) and Photoshop (*.psd)
- GIF, JPEG, TIFF, and BMP
- MS Word, MS Excel, and MS Write
- Ami-Pro and Lotus 1–2–3
- Corel WordPerfect and QuattroPro
- ASCII, ANSI Standard text, RTF, Character Separated Value (CSV), and HTML.

One handy feature is the ability to add annotations to the document. In general, this is the same basic functionality as what is provided by Adobe Acrobat. You add notes to the document as necessary and even use the contents of the notes as search criteria to find the document later.

FolderWatch is a method by which PageKeeper monitors the folders on your file system and manages the contents for you. Rather than loading files by hand into PageKeeper, FolderWatch will automatically add the document based on criteria you define any time you save, move, or copy a file into one of the predefined directories. Any time existing documents are changed, the thumbnail is changed accordingly. If the target file is moved, FolderWatch keeps track of this as well, so you do not need to update the index manually.

SmartFolders helps you manage your documents further by automatically grouping related documents. You define "filing parameters," such as file type or date, keywords, or phrases, and any new documents that meet those criteria are automatically filed in the correct directory.

OmniForms

One type of document that presents a great number of problems is forms. You probably have dozens of different forms within your company. In some cases, they are off-the-shelf forms (such as for phone messages). In other cases, they are printed specifically for your company (such as vacation requests). OmniForm provides you with a mechanism that not only loads the form into the system, but fills it out electronically and automatically loads that information into a database.

Forms can be scanned in using the same OCR engine that other Caere products use. Using a newer version of the Logical Forms Recognition technology, OmniForm does an outstanding job of maintaining the "look and feel" of the original form. However, you are not required to load all of your forms from other sources. Instead, OmniForm comes with a forms editor, which enables you to create new forms more easily.

If you already have forms on-line, you can import them into OmniForm by starting the application and printing to the OmniForm printer that is automatically set-up when you first install OmniForm. This starts up the OmniForm application, so you can make changes as needed.

When data is input into a form, it is stored in a flat-file database, which means it can be imported into any current database application. However, using ODBC, OmniForm can communicate directly with a wide range of database applications, such as MS Access, MS Excel, MS SQL Server, and Paradox.

When you scan in a form, you have various levels of configurability you can choose from. For example, you can tell OmniForm that you wish full control over the design and layout of the form or that you wish to maintain as much of the original's appearance as possible.

Figure 10–15 shows you the OmniForm designer. As you see, it has the same general appearance as most any other Windows application. At the top are the functions one would find in other programs, such as character formatting options, file operations, printing, and copying. On the left side is the Drawing Toolbar, which is used to create the elements in your form, including what type of form element it is (text box, radio button, etc.). On the right side is the Arrange Toolbar, which is used to arrange and line up the ele-

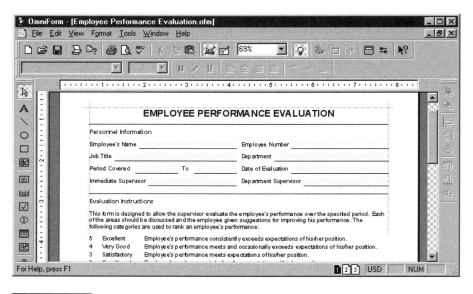

FIGURE 10–15 OmniForm Designer.

ments on the form, such as aligning elements along a column or changing the layout of the elements.

When designing the form, you can specify the characteristics and behavior of each of the form elements. For example, if you provide a list of choices in a drop-down menu, you can specify whether additional options maybe input by hand or the user must select an option from the list. It would also be possible to define fields as being required.

You obviously need some method to "fill out" the form. This can be done either from within OmniForm or with the supplemental product Omni-Form Filler. You can also save the form as RTF so that others can share the form. However, this does not have the database connectivity you have directly with OmniForm or OmniForm Filler. However, you can save the form as a mailable executable, which you can send to someone who fills out the form and returns it to you. Finally, OmniForm supports PDF, so you can send the file to users of the Adobe Acrobat reader.

There are many cases where certain fields will be filled with specific information, depending on the values in previous fields. If you have already input something similar, the "Type-Ahead" functionality will automatically fill in the rest of the field for you.

Other functionalities include:

- typical form elements, such as check boxes, text fields, plus elements only available on-line like drop-down menus
- validation of input information
- links to other forms or even Web sites
- embedding OLE objects into the form

An interesting feature is the ability to generate unique serial numbers. Each time a new record is created, OmniForm automatically increments the serial number by the number you configured.

OmniPage Web

Taking this one step further, OmniForm Internet Publisher allows you to publish the form on a Web server. The Internet Publisher has all of the functionality of OmniForm, such as the ability to scan in forms or create them from scratch, plus support for HTML and PDF formats, all in the same work.

OmniPage Web is essentially the fusion between scanning software and a Web development application. You can scan in large numbers of documents, and OmniPage Web will produce a structured Web site within just a few minutes. Using newer technologies, such as cascading style sheets (CSS) and frames, you get the appearance you want fairly automatically.

Because nothing is perfect, OmniPage Web provides a design tool to allow you to change the pages after they are scanned in. However, Omni-Page Web is not an authoring tool. That is, it does not have any of the advanced features that tools like PageMill or NetObjects Fusion provide. Instead, OmniPage Web is a supplement to these kinds of products, serving as the bridge between on-line documents and the Web.

As it is based on the standard OmniPage OCR engine, OmniPage Web provides the same basic scanning functionality of the other Caere products, such as defining zones for your documents. In addition, OmniPage Web uses Caere's nonproprietary Logical Structure Recognition technology (LSR), which is used to create the structure of your Web site based on the structure of the documents you scan in. LSR examines both the formatting and language of the page and make determinations about the objects in the text, such as headings, tables, and captions. In addition, it automatically links in cross-references (such as "see page 45") and hyperlinks.

When you save your documents, you have three choices. First, you can tell OmniPage Web to export the document as a series of Web pages, based on the structure defined during the LSR phase. Second, you can save the pages but immediately launch your browser. Finally, you can save the documents in the OmniPage Web format and defer exporting them, so you can work on the pages later.

Pages are created either at the heading levels that you define or at the start of a new file. You can also configure OmniPage Web to insert a link on the page that leads to an image of the original document. When the image is created, you can define the resolution, whether it is color or black and white, and a number of other options.

When exporting as HTML, there are a number of options you can use that define the layout of your pages. For example, you can configure OmniPage Web to export the pages using "plain" HTML. That is, pages are generated using none of the advanced features possible, thus making the browser viewable in most browsers.

If you want to use other features, there are those you can use to define the layout of your pages. For example, if you tell OmniPage Web not to export using plain HTML, it can automatically generate a navigation toolbar, which then appears at the top or bottom of the page. Several icons are provided for you, or you can provide your own. Other elements can be also aded automatically when the page is created. Common elements, such as a page "signature" or copyright information

Using the headings it finds in the document, OmniPage Web will create a global table of contents. As you would expect, each entry is a link to the appropriate page. Prior to exporting, you can tell OmniPage Web exactly which heading levels it should use for the table of contents. In addition, if pages contain multiple headings, you can create a "local" table of contents for that page. These are then links to the appropriate location on the page.

OmniPage Web also supports cascading style sheets. You can therefore define different styles for different components, which will then be valid for every page using that style sheet. OmniPage Web also provides 20 predefined "themes" for your pages, which provide an easy choice in a wide range of applications.

When completed, OmniPage Web has generated a series of interlinked Web pages that you could simply drop into an existing site. Because site management and development of new pages is not a function of OmniPage Web, you can easily import the pages into any of the more common Web development products, such as Adobe PageMill and NetObjects Fusion.

Communication

Unless you do all of your business from a central location, you're going to need to communicate with your users, and the users are going to need to communicate with you or with the system. The longer users are away from the office and the farther away they are, the greater the need to have an efficient communications system. Perhaps the most obvious approach is a mobile phone. However, this requires that both parties are in a position to talk at the same time. Particularly when time zones are involved, this is not always easy.

Another problem is that your contact person may not always know the answer to a specific question or know where to get specific information. This means one or the other of you will need to call back after the information has been dug up. Again you have the problem of finding a time when you both can talk.

You could solve this problem with answering machines, but that has a limitation in that generally one person leaves a message for one person. There are few ways that several people can communicate with one another. Information typically flows very slowly from place to place when using methods like this.

However, using computers, information can be created and changed at an incredibly fast rate. Whereas it used to take weeks or even months before something like a price list would reach salespeople in the field, today changes can be made and the information become immediately accessible.

Unfortunately, that is not always true. The information may have been changed, but it is not immediately accessible. This is because the salesperson in the field does not have immediate access to the information. In fact, in many cases it is not until the person returns to the office (which may be several days later) before the information is actually received. This defeats the purpose and benefit of being able to create and chang information so quickly.

I recently read an article on Knowledge Management that said the thing that makes one company more successful than another is knowledge. You might know how to make a better product or know how to make the product for less money. You might know the right customers or the right sales approach to sell your products. However, it all comes down to knowing something the other companies don't. Remember that knowledge is power.

One thing to keep in mind is that knowledge is basically useless unless is it shared. That means you must pass the knowledge from one person to another, which means you have to communicate.

Communication is a vital aspect of the IT department. This is not just communication between the IT department and the rest of the company, but also between the members of the IT department and between people in different departments. Unfortunately, I find often that communication is lacking. The company might use the fastest servers with the best network monitoring tools and the most detailed help desk product. However, if they cannot communicate, most of the tools they have are not put to the best possible use.

In many cases, I've found communication is essentially nonexistent. Each person has his or her own basic area of responsibility. When changes are made—events occur, or someone hears something—the person makes no effort to inform others. This wastes a great deal of time. For example, when one administrator expects a certain configuration and finds out it has been changed, he or she must track down exactly what that change was and why it was changed. Time is also wasted when problems arise and one administrator needs to rediscover the solution someone else found 2 weeks earlier. The same kind of thing applies to other departments.

Communication is not just limited to online applications, such as email or groupware. It is better to think of communication as the relaying of information from one person to another, regardless of the medium. Your intranet is another example, but this also includes forms of 1:1 communication other than email. There are cases where email or even the intranet is inefficient, such as when you need to transmit a large amount of data. In such cases, email is efficient, provided time is not a great factor.

In cases where you wish to send pictures, graphics, and other things directly in the document to visually enhance the text, email becomes a problem. Although all modern email readers allow you to send any kind of file via email, this is not always sufficient in that the graphics and other nontext do not appear in the correct context. That is, things are often sent in several files, and it is up to the recipient to make the necessary associations.

The most obvious solution is to combine the text and graphics into a format that can be sent as a single unit. For example, you could create and MS Word document and embed the graphics into that document. The problem with this is that it requires the recipients be able to read MS Word files. Even if they do have MS Word, they may have an earlier version, which means you have to convert the file prior to sending it.

But what about people who don't have MS Word? Many people require the advanced features provided by WordPerfect or StarOffice, and although these products can read and send MS Word formats, often some of the formatting is lost in the conversion. Depending on what was lost, it can make reading the documents difficult.

The solution to this problem may be to save the file in a universally accessible format, such as RTF. However, RTF cannot do everything the other formats can, and so you still end up losing some of the formatting. The solution to this is to provide the document in a way that you can also provide a mechanism to display the file. This is the concept behind "digital documents."

Digital documents are fine for smaller quantities of information but really are not efficient when you start getting into multiple megabytes sizes. Although email is useful when time is a factor, you need a different medium for larger quantities of information, where time is less important. Theoretically, you could copy everything onto a small hard disk and send it using a courier service or even the mail. This has several problems, not the least of which is installing the hard disk at the other end or compatibility problems with the hardware. (We'll go into more detail about digital documents in the chapter on sharing resources.)

One solution is a removable drive such as one from SyQuest. Sizes of the disks range from a few hundred megabytes to a few gigabytes. Byte for byte, they are more expensive then hard disks, but the advantages they have cannot be overlooked. First, all you need to do is ship the media without the drive itself. This is simpler and faster than sending the entire hard disk, and the only prerequisite is that they have the same SyQuest drive on the remote end.

If large amounts of data are transferred regularly, this is not a bad idea, particularly if the information is changed on the receiving end before it is sent back. The simplicity lies in the fact that SyQuest drives appear as regular hard disks. You drag-and-drop files, access them through your favorite word processor, and everything else you do with files.

The problem with removable drives becomes apparent if you are sharing data among multiple sites. If each site needs the data but can wait until the others are finished, a removable drive might be effective. However, you may have the added cost of needing a drive at each site. This problem becomes even more acute if the data are never changed. A good example would be parts lists or technical manuals that are only changed at the head-quarters.

A solution to this problem is a medium that is inexpensive but still allows distribution of large amounts of information. For this purpose we purchased a CD-ROM writer. The cost of writeable CDs has dropped to the point where they cost just a little more than diskettes but can hold hundred of times more data.

Communications Tools

Which communication tool you select depends on the communication methods you implement. The more means of communication you have, the greater the need to have a single tool to access all of these methods. One communication method that is often overlooked in these cases is your company intranet. We will go into more detail about the intranet later, but you must also consider the ability to access Web pages from your communications tool.

The most common all-in-one communications tool is possibly Netscape Communicator. Netscape is well known for its Navigator Web browser. However, the Communicator not only includes the Web browser, but basically every other kind of communications tool, including email, Internet news, and online conferencing. In essence, all of the components of Netscape Communicator have the same look and feel, which makes moving from one to the other extremely easy.

Although you have different interfaces, it is still considered a single application. Each component is intertwined with the others. For example, if you are reading an email message with a reference to a particular Web page or newsgroup, clicking on the entry will start the appropriate component. In addition, you have access to the configuration options for every component from anywhere.

StarOffice from StarDivision is another all-in-one tool; like Netscape Communicator, all communications methods are accessible through a single product. StarOffice takes this one step further by not only providing a common look and feel, but providing everything in a single program. StarOffice has the motto of "Do everything in one place." All the functionality is available through a single interface, so there is no delay switching from one application to another.

StarOffice takes this one step further by not only providing a communications tool, but also everything else one needs in an office. This includes word processing, spreadsheets, drawing, presentations, a database, and even an Web page development tool. Note that this not a watered-down version of these products, like you might find in Microsoft Works. Instead, StarOffice is comparable to, and in many respects more powerful than, MS Office (for less money).

What is needed in this case is that only updates the files that have changed. One such product is Symantec's Mobile Update product. Mobile Update is composed of two components: one on the server and one on the client. The server component is responsible for monitoring the information to be published and keeping track of the changes. At user-defined intervals (as well as manually), the server checks the files for any change. Based on the configuration, the files are sent or the user is simply notified of the change.

The client portion manages the distribution process by having the user "subscribe" to the information he or she needs. Part of the subscription is exactly what files are checked, at what intervals the server should checked, and whether the user is to be notified or files should be sent.

When the user subscribes, the Mobile Update server takes what Symantec calls a "digital snapshot" of the file. The file is then broken down into logical segments, which the server then uses to determine if changes have occurred. If a segment has changed, only that segment is packaged and sent and not the entire file. To further speed the process, the packaged segments (called the Update) are then compressed before being sent.

The packages are then sent via email, so the users do not need to make any special connection to the headquarters or anywhere else. They just need to check in their inbox as they normally do. The document is sent as an attachment, so all the user needs to do is to open that attachment, and the Mobile Update agent will process the change automatically. The change packet is uncompressed, the segments are identified, and the old ones are replaced with those from the update package. In addition to having the user specify what files to subscribe to, you can use the "invite" feature of Mobile Update to make users aware of new files as well as automatically have them subscribe to the file or directory. Like the Mobile Update packages themselves, the invitations are sent via email, and the user opens the attachment to launch the Mobile Update agent and either accept or reject the invitation. The response is returned to the server, and with acceptance the complete file is sent the first time and then only the changes after that.

Communication Standards

The most obvious reason for lack of communication is that the company does not provide the necessary tools. However, that's not always it. I have worked in places before which had the means to communicate, but they were simply not used. For example, they had mail and groupware, such as Microsoft Exchange. However, most administrators felt that using such tools was a waste of time. They knew where the information was that *they* needed and felt no obligation to store it in a central location. The problems stemmed from the fact that communication was not a *requirement* defined by the company management or at least by the department head. In order to communicate efficiently, administrators need to have tools, but management needs to ensure they are used.

One company where I worked went to an extreme with this. In several departments where communication was deemed vital to the day-to-day operation, notifying others of changes, including your schedule in the department's calendar, were defined as requirements for the job. You either used the tools or you went somewhere else. Repeated failures to use them could be grounds for termination.

On the surface this may sound very harsh. However, the time spent by one person putting in the information is minor compared with the amount of time spent by others when the information is not kept up-to-date.

The simplest solution is providing your users with email. Although this may seem too obvious, I worked for a company that even as late as mid-1999 did not have an effective email system. Although a system was used in and by the headquarters as well as by all offices that were directly connected, there were a large number of salespeople and branch office managers who had no email access when on the road. In many cases, the branch managers would authorize their sales force to establish accounts through online service providers such as CompuServe. However, they still could not communicate with the headquarters.

Even if your company has an effective email system, you need to be careful to ensure that the users do not suffer from information overload. That is, you do not give in to the habit of sending all of your users and list streams of even, which they do not have time to read and therefore simply delete. If this happens, you run the risk of important information not being seen because of the information overload.

This is the result of the desire to get away from the "push" mentality, in that companies are providing the same kind of information on their company intranet. This information is still made available to remote users through a number of different means. However, people get the information they need ("pull") when they need it and not when someone thinks they should have it. Many companies provide access to the information on the company's intranet as well as through normal Internet connections.

One misconception many IT managers have is that pushing information is a bad thing. The pendulum has swung completely away from "pushing" information to users. Granted, many people do suffer from information overload and much valuable information is lost. However, this not a problem with the technology but rather with how it is used.

Recently, the push technology that users are trying to get away from has actually become more popular in support of remote users. When the process of pushing information is automated and the information pushed is urgent, the user has specially requested it, or the sender *knows* the user needs the information, pushing information is a valuable tool.

If your email system allows it, you might consider restricting the size of messages that are sent as well as restricting the size of users in-boxes. This is necessary for two reasons. First, you are likely to have a number of users who will save their email and never delete things. (I am one of those.) Uncontrolled, you can fill up the file system as well as burst the limits of your email system. For example, MS Exchange has a limit of 16 GBs. Believe it or not, during the Clinton impeachment trial, several organizations, including the U.S. Congress, reached this limit and were unable to send email until they freed up some space.

Another problem is preventing denial-of-service attacks. A person with nefarious intentions could overload your system by sending huge messages. This would overload your file system as well as the bandwidth of your Internet connection. Not every attack can be prevented, but you can limit the extent.

As with documentation, I feel there should be a communications standard. Not only should this standard define that communications must take place, it should also define various circumstances that should generate different kinds of communications. For example, a vacation should generate an entry in the department calendar, a server crash in the branch office should generate an entry in the help desk and an email to the other administrators or a posting on an electronic whiteboard. Although you can go overboard with this kind of thing, is important the standard list those things that require notifying the other administrators or specific users.

This standardization also applies to responding to messages. You should therefore set guidelines as to when and how quickly people need to respond to messages. It takes only a few seconds to simple say "No, you cannot attend the seminar," and it saves the sender the time to track everyone down and force a response out of them.

Part of this requires a certain amount of retraining of your users. People are social animals and I have found there is often a tendency to go on and on about the kids, the vacation to Hawaii, the latest Star Wars movie, and other things. Save this kind of thing for your lunch break. Keep the communication on track and efficient. Although this kind of thing may not be appropriate for a written communications standard, it is appropriate for any training you give.

Being able to use email or any other communication tool efficiently does not mean you simply give your users an email reader and set out the necessary accounts. They need to know how to use it properly. This does not mean just knowing which buttons to press, but rather the methods, procedures, and even etiquette of using email. This has become such an important aspect of the Internet that it is more commonly referred to as "netiquette."

One of the most important aspects of netiquette is based on the fact that using the Internet is not free. Somebody, somewhere, whether it is yourself or your company, has to pay an Internet service provider for the connection to the Internet. In addition, if you have a dial-up connection to the Internet, you have to pay for each phone call. In some places, like Germany, local calls are not free. Therefore, it costs real money each time users download their email.

Even for those people who do not have to pay for their local calls, there is an issue of time. This also applies to internal email. If you receive dozens of messages about subjects that are unimportant to you, you have to spend the time to delete them. Some people may assert that this is not a big deal as it only takes the few seconds for each message. However, most people do not appreciate being *forced* to spend time even if it is just a few seconds.

There is also the issue of the *combined* time spent. If you get 10 of these kinds of messages a day, each taking 30 seconds to identify as being unimportant, you waste 5 minutes a day. If you have 100 employees, that's a total of 8 hours a day or the equivalent of a single day's work for one person. Could your company afford to pay someone whose sole task was just to delete unwanted and unnecessary email?

There are two solutions to this. First, only send messages to those people who you *know* want the information. There are cases where it is not easy to tell or it is likely that the person "may" want the information. To solve this problem, the thing to do is not to send all of the information, but rather a pointer to where the information lies. (Assuming you're sending large pieces of information.) This tells the recipient what the information is about and allows him or her to get the details if necessary. This saves them the time of reading even the beginning of the material to see if they really want it. (Plus it saves space on the file system.)

It is a convention, not a rule or standard, that you only send email on the Internet to people who want that information. Unsolicited commercial email, also referred to as *spam*, is frowned on in the Internet community. Although the messages you send may not be commercial in nature, they are often unsolicited and often unwanted. The result in many cases is that you simply annoy people. However, many ISPs have policies that allow them to cancel your service without notice if you become a nuisance to the Internet community.

Another aspect is that you are representing your company. Although you may not be officially speaking for your company, people often have their company address in their signature block. Even without this, the company name (or at least the domain name) is listed in the return address. If you send messages to people who do not want the material, you may end up putting the company in a bad light.

Messaging Standards

Without a language that both sides understand, communication is impossible. Although the "language" that computers use is generally referred to as a protocol, the basic principle is the same. That is, unless computers use the same protocol, they will not be able to communicate with one another.

Among humans, the language bringing you the widest range of possibilities is English. Although relatively few countries and only a small percentage of the world's population speak English, no matter where you go you are likely to find someone who does speak it. Therefore, if you were to choose a language to use in communications, it would probably be English. In the computer world, it is best to choose a protocol that gives you the widest range of possibilities. Because the Internet has grown to become the world largest communication forum, it seems logical to choose protocols that allow you to participate in these forums.

What this means is that it is in your best interest to choose the protocols that are used on the Internet. If not, you need some kind of "translator" if you wish to communicate with your customers, suppliers, business partners, and anyone else on the Internet. The problem with any kind of translation is that it may be 100% accurate, but time is lost in doing the translation.

There are a number of communication or messaging products that use their own proprietary protocols. In many cases, they only provide conductivity with the Internet standards through the use of add-on products. It may be that you only need to install the add-on, but it may also be that you have to go out and buy. Some vendors provide an "enterprise" version of the messaging products, which includes this "connector." However, this version is much more expensive than the one with just the proprietary protocol, so you still end up paying for it.

In addition to the greater cost, there is more administrative overhead. Obviously, if you have different protocols, both need to be configured and administered. You end up actually having a third thing to configure if you want the protocols to be able to communicate with one another. For example, if your messaging product uses a proprietary protocol and you wish to connect to the Internet, you have to first install and configure that messaging product. Next you have to configure the connection and related protocols to exchange information with the Internet. Finally, you need to configure the system so that the proprietary protocol is converted to the Internet protocol and vice versa.

Keep in mind that the proprietary messaging systems have their own addressing scheme, which is different from the scheme used on the Internet. Therefore, each time you add a user to the system you have to configure the user's address for both the proprietary system and the Internet. Essentially, double the work.

Also note that it is not only you who has to do more work, but your computer as well. It takes processing power to make the translation to and from the proprietary protocols. This is one reason why Microsoft recommends a separate machine for MS Exchange so that it does not interfere with file and print operations.

Of all of the Internet messaging protocols, the most important one to support is the Simple Mail Transport Protocol (SMTP). Without this, you can say a product does not support Internet mail. Although it is possible to exchange email across the Internet without using SMTP, if you choose a product that does not support it, you are basically cutting yourself off from the vast majority of users around the world.

Another important protocol is the Post Office Protocol Version 3 (POP3). Here, incoming messages are stored on a server and the users download them when they want to. This requires extra effort on the part of the users to actually go out and pick up their mail, but it is very beneficial in environments where users do not have continuous access to the server, such as those who travel frequently.

A new protocol is the Internet Message Access Protocol Version 4 (IMAP4). It provides a similar mechanism to POP3's in that mail is stored on the messaging server and users download the messages as needed. One of the key aspects is the ability to synchronize the messages between the client and server. With IMAP4 you can download all or just a portion of the messages and still leave the messages on the server, or, if you want, you can remove them from the server. In addition, the system must be able to prevent you from losing documents as well as from getting them more than once. Therefore, it must be able to synchronize the messages on the server with what you have already downloaded.

Supporting standards does not just apply to those concerned with transferring the mail messages. There are a number of security-related standards that need to be supported for your messaging server to have a truly open architecture. One important standard is the Secure Sockets Layer (SSL). Many people are already familiar with SSL as a means of security when transmitting Web pages. However, many newer messaging servers currently support SLL for transmitting email between the client and server. This is of particular interest for dial-up connections or other cases where there is a greater risk of eavesdropping.

Another standard is authenticated SMTP. This is a slight modification of standard SMTP, whereby the user must first authenticated himself or herself to the server before sending a message. This prevents unauthorized users from using your server to distribute spam or for some other reason hide the actual source of the message. Coupled with it is Secure MIME (S/MIME), which encrypts the mail message just as it would a Web page.

Users should not always need to enter a username and password in order to authenticated themselves. This is where users certificates (X.509) are useful. Users log on once and thereby obtain a certificate. This certificate is then accepted as authentication on this and other servers.

Calendar Standards

Because standards for calendar and scheduling (C&S) applications are still being debated, you'll find very few products (if any) that can communicate with the products from other vendors. Therefore, it is not necessarily a wise decision to allow users to choose their own C&S applications. Otherwise, it will be impossible to share information or, at the very least, users will need to manually copy entries from one application to the other.

A key aspect of this is that users on one system cannot communicate with others using another system. That is, there is no way to schedule joint events other than calling or sending email to the other user to find out when they are available. In fact, even if the products are from the same vendor, it is possible that users cannot communicate with one another. Many of the available products are completely stand-alone, with no interaction between users at all.

Implementing a C&S application that allows you to communicate among users is just half of the solution. The key is an application based (at least in part) on existing standards. For example, it makes sense that communication is accomplished using standard Internet email protocols (such as SMTP, POP3, or IMAP4) rather than some proprietary email system that is incompatible with the rest of the world. Applications based on the Lightweight Directory Access Protocol (LDAP) can exchange directory information with other systems.

The Internet Engineering Task Force (IETF), which is one of the driving forces behind Internet standards, is currently working on standards for C&S applications. One key aspect of these standards is calendaring data interchange, including the ability to drag calendaring information from one application and drop it into another. This not only means between different calendaring applications, but also between different applications of any kind. For example, you could drag the syllabus from a training course onto your calendar application. People can look at the calendar and see what is scheduled, then click the link to the syllabus to get the details.

Interoperability is also one of the design goals for the IETF. This means that C&S applications, which support the IETF standard, will be able to communicate with one another. For example, a resource has been defined by one C&S application, but you use another to schedule it. This also extends to the ability to "invite" users to meetings who use a different application, something that is not possible unless you rely entirely on email.

Taking this one step further, access to the C&S information will be standardized using a set of protocols. This means that you could have a server from one vendor but use a client from another. In essence, this is how current email standards, such as SMTP, IMAP4, and POP3, work.

To be fully interoperable, any C&S standard must work with existing directory and messaging standards. This means that the standard needs to support LDAP to find user information and needs to support (at a minimum) SMTP for the users to communicate. Netscape, for example, already supports these, so there is time spent waiting for them to adopt existing standards.

One pseudo-standard that is already in place was developed by Versit. This includes the vCard and vCalendar information that you may have found included with email sent across the Internet. Several vendors, including Netscape and Lotus, already support the vCard and vCalendar standards. Netscape, which hosted the original IETF C&S meeting, has already announced support for the final C&S standard when it is published by the IETF.

Communication Software

Netscape Calendar Server

Although an intranet has a good start with the Netscape FastTrack server, it is still missing a couple of pieces that can substantially expand its usefulness. One of the things it is missing is a calendar server. This provides a centralized location for all of your calendaring and scheduling activities throughout the company. If you have ever tried to organize a meeting with people from several different departments, you know how useful calendaring services can be. Having this information available to everyone allows you to more efficiently coordinate activities, reserve conference rooms, and all of the other activities of any company.

One of the major problems that many scheduling programs have is that they are completely user oriented. By that I mean there is no mechanism in place to schedule resources. In any company, there are always resources to be scheduled, such as conference rooms, company cars, video cameras, and so forth. If your scheduling application or mean deals with people, it is only doing half of the job.

One solution to this problem is the Netscape Calendar Server. Because the server is based on Internet standards and not on proprietary protocols, users can access calendar information at any time from anywhere. It also provides direct access to email, so you can "invite" other users to meetings.

The Netscape Calendar Server has native support LDAP. This allows system administrators to centrally manage users, groups, resources, and the applicable contact information. This information can then be shared with any other LDAP-capable application.

One key aspect of the Netscape Calendar Server is its scalability. Even if you are a small company or department, you can reap the benefits of using the Netscape Calendar Server. However, a single calendar server can support thousands of users money single server. The architecture of the calendar server is such that larger organizations can install it on multiple machines and shared information between the various servers. You could even do this on a smaller scale if you needed individual servers in each department, for example. It is also possible to have multiple servers spread out all over the world, because the Netscape Calendar Server automatically takes into account time zones and daylight savings time differences. This has a means your advantage over replication or message-based servers, because time zone differences are often not considered.

The Netscape Calendar Server as the added advantage of being able to schedule events in as close to real time as possible. Granted, there will always be delays due to network traffic and computer-related issues. However, you have essentially instant access to the company no matter where it is in the world. Once an entry has been many, it is accessible to every other user in the company. Again, this has advantages over message- and replication-based systems because of their inherent time delays. Since the scheduled events are only stored once, you will never have a case where entries conflict with one another.

In all likelihood, there will be times when you cannot or do not make changes to the calendar yourself. For example, this is often the task of a secretary. The Netscape Calendar Server allows you to designate others who can modify your calendar, including scheduling meetings, making notes, and assigning tasks.

Assigning the permissions is extremely easy for both your representative (designee) and events. An event or other calendar entry can be defined as confidential, personal, normal, or public. Confidential information for example, is something not even your designee can see.

When working in a group it is important to know when you can schedule a meeting. The Netscape Calendar Server can search for a schedule time among several different users. In addition, there is a group view that allows you to look at multiple calendars side by side.

Netscape Calendar Server is more than just an enterprise-level scheduling program. It also allows you to keep track of tasks you are currently working on. Each task can be assigned a number of different priority levels. These can either be 1–9 or A–Z. This gives you much more flexibility than other similar tools that will he view low, are normal, and high priority. In addition, you have the ability to include starting and due dates and times, reminders, percentage completed, and, of course, a description of the task. It is even possible to add attachments (external documents) to these tasks.

Administration can also be done by the users. For example, users can create their own groups, which can also be shared with other users. Users can also create their own resources and define the access permissions as they see fit. If necessary, users can also define which days are holidays, which is important when you have servers in multiple locations in different countries.

Administration is simplified further through a Web interface. Unlike other products that have one interface to configure the Web server and another to configure the scheduler, Netscape products are managed through a single interface, and a calendar server is no exception. In addition, there are a number of command line utilities, which allow the administrator to perform routine tasks from the command line.

Netscape Collabra Server

There are two important shortcomings with email. First, it is "push" technology. That is, the sender pushes the information to the recipient whether he or she wants it or not. Second, it is generally a 1-to-1 or 1-to-many communication method. Internet news, in contrast, is many-to-many, and you read those messages you want to.

Internet mailing lists also provide the many-to-many in domain communication of newsgroups. The problem is that every recipient gets a copy of the message. That means if you have 100 employees and each subscribes to the same newsgroup, there will be 100 copies of that message on your server. With newsgroups, however, there is just a single copy (provided users do not download the messages by hand).

One of the key aspects of network newsgroups is that they are "threaded." This means you can keep track of who posted what message, who replied to that message, who replied to the replies, and so forth. Messages have a unique ID, so it is even possible to track messages between different severs.

Network newsgroups do not just spring into being. They need to be created and managed. Netscape Collabra Server is designed explicitly for this task. It provides an easy-to-use interface, which allows you to set up, administer, and manage any number of discussion groups. Because it is based on the Internet standard Network News Transfer Protocol (NNTP), Netscape Collabra Server can be used to manage internal network newsgroups and newsgroups that you replicate to the Internet.

Replication of newsgroups can also be done between branch offices and different companies on an extranet. The SSL ensures the data remain safe, even when transmitted across the Internet. As you might guess (or at least hope), Netscape Collabra Server can easily be configured to replicate any or none of the groups on any given server. The replication itself is selective in that only new messages are replicated to different servers. If necessary, it is also possible to create redundant servers with full replication in case one fails.

Part of the management task is something that is referred to as "moderating." In many cases, it is not desirable that just anyone can post to a particular newsgroup. Instead, you wish to filter the messages to ensure they are appropriate for the group. For example, it may not be desirable to have someone post a "for sale" notice onto the newsgroup listing of coming company events. Netscape Collabra Server provides an extremely simple interface to allow the newsgroup moderator to accept or reject messages as needed.

An added advantage is the ability to assign the various administration functions to different users and remove some of the burden from the system administrators. This model may include the ability to create the newsgroups themselves but also to perform moderation functions.

Netscape further simplifies the administration by creating a single point of administration. As with the other Netscape servers, the administration of Collabra is done through a Web browser and therefore can even be done remotely across the Internet. In addition, the interface is uniform across platforms, which basically means the administrator does not need to about the underlying operating system, just what he or she needs to know to be able to configure Collabra.

Access to the Collabra newsgroups is done through any NNTP-compliant client. This means that your server can run on one platform and the clients on another. In addition to supporting the Internet news standard NNTP, Netscape Collabra Server also supports LDAP, which allows you to share a common directory structure among the other Netscape servers. System administrators, therefore, have just a single database where they manage users, groups, and shared data.

Netscape Collabra Server also supports rich content, which means you can include HTML tags along with multimedia, such as audio, video, and still pictures. Since it supports HTML, you can also include links using any of the knee standard protocols such as HTTP, FTP, MAILTO, FILE, and even NEWS. This means you can link from one newsgroup to another with no problem.

In addition, Netscape Collabra Server provides a number of tools for extracting information from newsgroups. First, you have the ability to create what are called "virtual discussion groups." In essence, this is a customizable view of specific topics across multiple newsgroups. This means you get access to just the information you're looking for without being overwhelmed by information overload. Netscape also provides an API to the Collabra Server, which allows you to write programs that can act on the posted messages.

One key aspect to keep in mind is that newsgroups are not just there to provide a forum to sell your old lounge chair or to discuss the latest episode of Stargate. Instead, newsgroups provide an extremely effective collaboration tool. You have the possibility of conducting "virtual meetings," which are not restricted to specific times and locations. You can exchange ideas and even make decisions without the need to gather everyone to meet at the same place at the same time.

One place in which newsgroups and particularly Netscape Collabra Server have been employed successfully is for project management. As you can imagine, it can significantly reduce the time spent on organizing, conducting, and attending meetings, while still allowing each member to contribute his or her ideas. In addition, you automatically have the minutes of your virtual meeting, because newsgroup messages remain on-line even after you have read them.

Another advantage of newsgroups is the ability to clearly express your thoughts before you post the message. Obviously, this is not a requirement, as many people still post messages without thinking. However, when I post messages to newsgroups, I am a lot more careful of the way I formulate things to ensure there is as little misunderstanding as possible. Part of this is to help avoid arguments where one person insists another person said something, who denies ever having said it. With newsgroups, you can demonstrate quite clearly what it is the other person "said."

Many companies provide newsgroups as an open forum to discuss problems or grievances with the company management. Company executives take part in the discussion to get a better understanding of the attitudes and

· · · · · · · · · · · · · · ·

feelings of the employees, but also to explain decisions that are often not accepted by the masses.

Because you can have references from your intranet pages to specific newsgroups or from news messages to specific Web pages, your newsgroups become an integral part of your intranet. Using something like Netscape Communicator, users have a single interface to all forms of messaging. In addition, administration of the various media is also accomplished from a single interface.

For those of you who have already used groupware products, such as Microsoft Exchange, you'll probably see that much of the functionality of Netscape Collabra Server added to the other Netscape servers is identical. Although this is true from the users' perspective, what the administrator sees is entirely different. The most dramatic aspect is the fact that Netscape Collabra Server is based on established Internet standards, whereas Microsoft Exchange is entirely proprietary. That is, once you choose Microsoft Exchange you're locked in, and you do not have your choice of clients.

Netscape Messaging Server

Netscape Messaging Server is more than simply an email server. Although its primary function is the management and distribution of email, it can also be used to manage information submitted through HTML forms. That is, it manages a wide range of "messages."

As with the other Netscape server products, the Netscape Messaging Server is based on Internet standards rather than proprietary protocols. For example, it fully supports SMTP, IMAP4, and POP3. In addition, user name lookup can be provided either by the Network Information System (NIS, previously known as Yellow Pages) or LDAP.

The Netscape Messaging Server also has a number of security features built-in. For example, it fully supports SSL 3.0, allowing for secure remote administration as well as client communication. You also have a choice of either 56-bit or 128-bit encryption between the client and server.

It also supports authenticated SMTP, which prevents unauthorized message transmissions. To access the server, you need to provide a user name and password. This is particularly useful on the Internet to prevent your server from becoming a relay point for unsolicited commercial email (spam).

There is also support for IMAP4 over SSL, which fully encrypts the messages between server and client. Here, too, you have a choice of either 56-bit or 128-bit encryption.

An additional security mechanisms is available for attachments. Some email systems encrypt the message, but the attachment is only encoded using the MIME encoding mechanism. There it is still possible to get access to the information in the attachment. The Netscape Messaging Server supports secure MIME (S/MIME), which also encrypts any attachments.

As I mentioned, the Netscape Messaging Server supports LDAP. This means you can have a centralized user and group database for all of your messaging systems.

By supporting Internet email standards, you give your users free choice of clients. This basically allows for seamless integration with existing email clients and continued support for new ones. This means you are not forced into any proprietary messaging technology, which naturally locks you in with a particular vendor.

A key aspect is the support for IMAP4. This allows users to download all or part of the messages from the server. This is extremely useful in cases where the user has a slow connection to the server (e.g., through modem) and cannot take the time to download all of the messages. The user can then select just the messages he or she wants to view. These are then downloaded to allow the user to view them off-line. Users also have a choice of removing the messages from the server or leaving them there for later. When the client read connect to the server, the IMAP4 protocol will synchronize the two.

Large organizations have certainly encountered the problem of locating and identifying users. When you can the need to locate users across many different companies, the task basically becomes impossible for people to handle on their own. The solution is a kind of computerized directory that can provide the information fast and efficiently.

Unfortunately, it's not as simple as that. It's unreasonable to expect a centralized organization to handle all of the information for every company. It is hard enough for some companies to handle this task for themselves, let alone for other companies. Therefore, it is necessary to have a mechanism whereby information can be exchanged between companies. This is the basic concept behind LDAP.

Many of you may already be familiar with either the X.500 Directory Access Protocol (DAP). LDAP is a subset of DAP, which requires less processing power and can therefore run on PCs and lower end workstations. In addition, it uses the TCP/IP stack rather than the Open Systems Interconnection (OSI) stack, which means it can go access the Internet. LDAP is also a simpler protocol, which less work for the client. The result is an LDAP server is less expensive and easier to configure than a server running the full X.500 implementation.

Version 3 of the LDAP standard has a couple of very interesting additions. The first is referred to as "intelligent referrals." Here, a query is named to one server, which it then refers to other servers and so on until a response is returned. In essence, this is similar to the way DNS works. From the users' perspective, it appears as if there is a single directory scattered all over the Internet containing millions of entries.

LDAP is also extensible. It is therefore possible for applications to create their own data, which are stored on the directory server. This could be used to store application-specific information, such as configuration information or personal preferences.

....

Netscape Directory Server

Obviously, LDAP is little good if you do not have a server to manage information. This is the goal of the Netscape Directory Server. Although it would be less useful in medium-to large-size businesses, it would be safe to say that the power of the Netscape Directory Server used overkill for smaller organizations.

The current version (as of this writing) is version 4.0, which can handle over 50 million entries on a single server. Throughput is also exceptionally high, attaining 5000 queries *per second*. The Netscape Directory Server demonstrated almost linear scalability with multiple CPUs. This means that two CPUs provides twice the performance, three CPUs three times, and so forth. Typically, applications do not scale linearly.

The Netscape Directory Server fits well into the Netscape administration scheme. The Netscape console provides a single point of administration for all of your Netscape servers. As with the other servers, you can delegate work on the server, workstation, and even task level on the directory server and thereby reduce the administrative burden on the system administrators. In addition, unlike other Windows-based applications, every administrative operation on the Netscape Directory Server has eight command-line equivalents. This you can include administrative tasks and scripts to automate your activity.

Because it supports LDAP, the Netscape Directory Server is not bound to any proprietary protocol. This is taken one step further in that you can use any database to store the directory information. This means you can access directory information from almost any application without the need to directly access the directory server.

The support for LDAP means the Netscape Directory Server is extensible. One example would be the ability to set an expiration date on an account. Once that day arrives, the information for the account is no longer considered valid. You can also define are sent which then perform certain actions. In addition, entries can be automatically set based on other values. For example, all users in a specific department might have the same fax number.

The Netscape Directory Server is more than a simple lookup of information; it also can provide authentication using the extensible simple authentication and security layer (SASL). This allows the Netscape Directory Server to work with other authentication systems such as Kerebos. LDAP applications can also authenticate the user using the Windows and key user names and passwords.

Because it is LDAP compliance, the Netscape Directory Server provides LDAP services over SSL. In addition, it supports X.509 certificates for both the servers and the client. The system can also be configured to prevent particular users from performing certain tasks as well as giving specific users a certain level of administrative control. This could be control over an entire directory tree, a specific entry, and individual attributes of entry. For example, you can configure the server so that everyone can see each other's email address, but only people within the same department are allowed to see the users' pager numbers.

One of the key advantages that the Netscape Directory Server has over Microsoft's Active Directory is that the Netscape Directory Server is already available. Microsoft has announced support for the Active Directory in Windows 2000 and therefore does not support previous releases. On the other hand, the Netscape Directory server already supports Windows NT, 3.51 and 4.0, as well as a number of different Unix versions. This means that the Netscape Directory Server is a major were, well-tested product, unlike the Active Directory, which will be Microsoft's first attempt.

Another aspect is the extensibility of the Netscape Directory Server. According to Microsoft's own marketing literature, Active Directory has a much more closed architecture. More than likely, it will only run on Microsoft's own database (SQLServer), and it does not have the ability to define business rules.

Norton Mobile Essentials

If you are like me, you have a ritual that you go through each time you are going on a business trip. You check and recheck your modem to make sure it works, you copy the files you will need onto your laptop, as well as many other things to ensure you can work on what you need to and when you need to.

However, most of this ritual has become unnecessary due to products like Norton Mobile Essentials. As its name implies, Mobile Essentials is a suite of products that help you or your users work more efficiently, before and while you are on the road. There are several functions to help you prepare for your trip as well as a number that help you work and even diagnose problems once you are at your destination.

To start with, you have the "Before You Go" utility. As its name implies, this is used while you are still making preparations for your trip. Its primary function is to automate all of the tasks that you used before you walked out the door.

This is more than just copying files to a particular directory to copy onto your laptop. Instead, it performs a wide range of necessary tasks, such as checking your system to make sure it is working correctly, identifying any additional equipment you may need, and backing up the files you will need.

The System Check is the component that, as its name implies, checks your system. Three components are provided by default, but you can start any component as you need to. The Connection Doctor checks your modem to ensure that it is working properly. The disk is checked for problems by the same Disk Doctor that you find in Norton Utilities. In addition, there is a copy of Norton AntiVirus that makes sure the system is clean before you leave.

SpeedSave is the component that creates backups of your files. Depending on how you configure it, the files can be saved from your desktop machine to either disk or directly to your laptop. In addition, you can also copy files *from* your laptop in case it gets lost or stolen, so you at least have a copy of the data.

To back up your files, you first create a "backup profile." You could have a number of different profiles depending on where you're going, how long you need to be gone, what work needs to get done, and so forth. The profile contains a list of all of the files that you need to save and then copies them to the desired location prior to your departure.

The Destination feature is used to gather the necessary information about your destination, allowing you to get additional equipment if needed. You select the country where you are headed, and Mobile Essentials tells you things like what kind of power is used and what the power-adapter plugs look like, as well as what phone connections you will need.

Finally, the Checklist feature provides a number of checklists (what else?), which help you gather additional information you need prior to traveling. This can include anything you think necessary, such as equipment you need to take with you, tasks to perform prior to departure, hotel and car rental information, phone number of on-line services (i.e., CompuServe), credit card company emergency contact information, and so forth. Like the backup profiles, you can have a number of different checklists based on destination, work you will be doing, or any other criteria.

The location Controller is a tool that helps you adjust your laptop to the new location once you have arrived. Here you will need to set up the dialing parameters, such as how to get a long distance connection and the country code for the United States (or wherever you are based). In addition, many other things need to get changed, such as the default printer, network logons, setting the clock to the local time, and so forth.

All of this takes a great deal of time. However, you can prepare most of it in advance and automatically adjust your system once you arrive. As with the other aspects, you can create a number of different location settings.

Norton pcAnywhere

Symantec's pcAnywhere is best described as a communications tool that allows its users to communicate with remote PCs as well as transfer files and synchronize folders between two machines. The two machines can be connected using any standard method, including telephone, normal network connections, as well as parallel and serial cables. The only condition is that both machines run the pcAnywhere software.

The most important thing to keep in mind is that the pcAnywhere software is more than just a terminal program for Windows. Instead, when the modem connected, it is as if you're actually working on the remote computer.

In addition, you can control the remote machine even if someone is currently working on it. However, the prerequisite is that they let you.

This function is an excellent tool for users on the road as well as for your help desk. Users can be shown the necessary steps to perform desk different functions, even though the help desk might be on the other side of the world. Users on the road could access their desktop machines and even start programs as if they were logged on locally.

You can also use pcAnywhere to transfer files between two machines. You have a choice of either doing this automatically each time you logon, or you can do it manually as needed. One important aspect of this is that directories can be synchronized to ensure both sides have the most recent version of particular files.

Figure 11–1 shows the connection and configuration screen for pcAnywhere. You select whether your machine will act as a host or if you want to remotely control another machine. In addition, you can also select to have your computer serve as a pcAnywhere gateway. This allows multiple machines to share communications devices. In addition, the gateway provides both dial-in and dial-out services.

One of the most amazing things about the connection is that it is fairly close to real time. Unfortunately, communication between the two machines

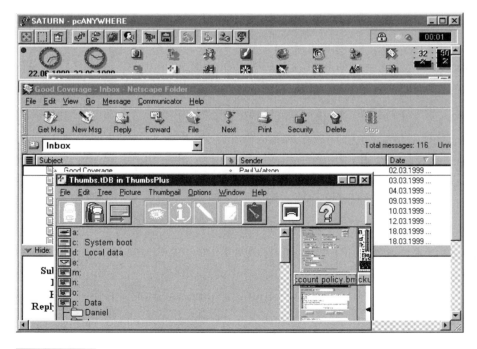

FIGURE 11-1 pcAnywhere connection window.

does take a certain amount of time. Therefore, there is a delay between the time you do something locally, it is actually done on the remote machine, and the time you see the results on your monitor. Despite this, the process is very fast, especially when considering the alternative would be to either have nothing at all or actually go to that remote site.

If a user is currently working on a machine you connect to, they will still be able to work on the machine. However, any time you input something on the keyboard for moved amounts, it will end up on the remote machine, which might tend to get away of the user doing network. However, this can be a good faint, particularly in a help desk environment where you are watching the steps a particular user is taking before the certain action, so you can see where they are actually making the mistakes. If you want, you can also "lock" the remote keyboard, so the user *cannot* input anything.

There are a number of useful tools that you have access to during your session. pcAnywhere Chat is used to communicate with the person on the remote end. This has a slightly different behavior than the standard WINChat. First, the text is not transmitted until you press the Enter key. Second, the complete dialog is written to a single window. This allows you to save the complete transcript of your communication.

AutoXfer is a utility that automatically transfers files to and from the remote machine. The files you wish to transfer and a number of other options can be stored in a file and used repeatedly. Files can be compressed prior to transfer, thus speeding up the transmission. In addition, AutoXfer has a "crash recovery" option, which will take up where it left off if the connection is broken for some reason. You can also select to have all downloaded files be automatically checked for viruses.

You also have access to the clipboard on both systema and can transfer it in either direction. That is, you can transfer the local clipboard to the remote machine or transfer the remote clipboard to your machine.

If you regularly perform tasks on a remote system, it would be nice to be able to automate those tasks. To do so, pcAnywhere provides a well-equipped scripting language. Essentially, all functions that are normally available can be accessed using a script. You can then automate any task, such as starting specific applications or even transferring files in the middle of the to avoid unnecessary burden under network.

Although the script must be written within add or their that can save ASCII files, the script is actually compiled before it is executed. This increases the speed of execution even more than what is possible by inputting the command manually.

Basically, the scripting language is as complex as that of many other communications tools. That is, not only can you send text, but you can also wait for particular output from the other side. In addition, you have complete access to all of the functions you would normally have when making a pcAnywhere connection.

You can also create scripts by putting pcAnywhere into "learn mode"; it will then record all of your actions and save them into a script file. Should you need to, the script file can be edited or simply run as is.

Dragon NaturallySpeaking

NaturallySpeaking from Dragon Systems, Inc. is a product that for some people borders on being a "toy." In essence, NaturallySpeaking is a voice recognition product that (as you might guess) converts your voice to text. The version provided with WordPerfect works only within WordPerfect. However, the professional edition will work with any product, including Windows itself.

This last point needs a little bit of explaining. By working with Windows itself, I mean you can dictate commands, which are then transmitted to the operating system. For example, I issue the command "Start WordPerfect" and Dragon NaturallySpeaking will automatically start WordPerfect for me. I say "Check Email" and Dragon NaturallySpeaking will check mail on my email server.

I am thoroughly convinced that this product is definitely worth much more than its price in terms of increased productivity. Using Dragon NaturallySpeaking, I find that I not only produce more material in a give time, I produce it much more efficiently.

Commands are not limited to simply starting specific applications. Instead, NaturallySpeaking can be used to access menus, input text into message boxes, and even move the mouse. You can even combine command and keystrokes into scripts. For example, I have a command to open a file in a specific directory. The opened dialog box is displayed, it switches it to the necessary drive, then switches to the appropriate directory. I can then issue commands to open specific files. I also have a command that opens the last file I worked on.

All of these commands, and any other you can think of, can be accessed from any application. In addition, you can create your own commands to be basically anything. Essentially, all keys and key combinations are available for you to create personalized commands.

In addition, there is a wide range of internal commands that you can use for your personalized commands. This goes beyond simply typing in combinations of keys. In fact, there is an entire scripting language, which includes programming constructs such as if-then statements. You can define new commands to apply globally or to specific applications as well as parts of applications (like the Open file dialog window).

The way to justify something like Dragon NaturallySpeaking is to consider the saying, "time is money." You need to consider how much productivity to increase like employing a product like this. How often do you have people in your organization who dictate messages into a tape recorder, then hand the tape off to a secretary who listens to the tape and types in a message?

The most obvious benefit is that you no longer need the secretary to type in the message. However, this is not the only benefit. You could eliminate the need for a secretary by having a person type his or her own message. Unfortunately, that does not save the greatest consumer of time, which is actually typing in the text. This is where Dragon NaturallySpeaking really shows its worth.

Imagine a manager or anyone else dictating a text into a recorder and having that message be immediately input into the electronic document. You do not need to spend the time spinning the tape back and forth, repeating passages to get exactly the content you want. Instead, you simply tell Dragon NaturallySpeaking to delete or override certain passages with the new text you dictate. No time is wasted waiting for the mechanics of the tape recorder to get you to the place you want to be.

In addition, Dragon NaturallySpeaking is capable of formatting your document at your command. Therefore, the person dictating the text does not need to break off the flow of what they're dictating to change the format. It is simple as saying "set font bold" or "set font size 14" to change your document.

To me, the most dramatic benefit is a result of the fact that people can normally talk a lot faster than they can type. Therefore, it is obviously a lot quicker to dictate something and then to type it. I have noted that when I use Dragon NaturallySpeaking I can usually work two to three times faster than when typing by hand, and sometimes more. In addition, I don't need to worry about spell checking because Dragon NaturallySpeaking does it for me.

Dragon NaturallySpeaking helps me correct problems in a couple of other ways. For example, if I want to delete something I had just said, I simply say "scratch that" or "undo that" and text will be deleted. I can also search for specific text, which I can then replace. This is in addition to the ability to use the standard search-and-replace function by voice command.

Because you are dictating, and you can do other things with your hands. Take this book as an example. If I am describing a product or a particular function within Windows NT, I can be working on the product on one machine, while dictating a description of that product on another machine. I don't need to stop working in order to write description.

Taking this one step further, you can be doing other things than just working on the computer. On many occasions I have used Dragon NaturallySpeaking to dictate material, while at the same time I was cleaning my office or sorting out bills. There were times when I had to stop dictating for a moment or two, because what I was doing at that very moment required my full attention. However, no time was wasted starting back to work as I simply began talking again.

You can also configure the program for multiple users. When you first start, you are given a list of users who have been configured for the system. You can also choose among different sets a vocabulary. For example, you might have a set of words that just applies to standard business correspondence and then another set for technical documents.

This is useful as I have found many cases where words are so close together that it is hard to tell them apart when speaking at a normal speed. Humans have an understanding of what is being said and almost immediately identify the correct word. The computer cannot and must, therefore, go purely by how the word sounds. By having multiple vocabularies, the program has to search less for the appropriate phrase.

Dragon NaturallySpeaking can also learn new words in a couple of ways. When you first install the product, you are asked to read text aloud for approximately 15 minutes. Because the system knows what words should have been dictated, it can analyze your voice and matches it to the words in the text. This results in a fairly good recognition rate, usually over 95%. This means that there will be a couple of words in each paragraph that are incorrectly recognized.

Unfortunately, recognition is not 100%. To solve this problem, Dragon NaturallySpeaking can be trained as you work. If a phrase is not recognized correctly, you simply say "Spell that" and you can type in the correct phrase. Taking this one step further, you can also start a special training module that allows you to input words and phrases by hand.

Dragon NaturallySpeaking will also scan in documents looking for words that are not in its vocabulary. These are then added to the list of words it knows, making recognition much easier.

Dragon Systems has several products, ranging from those that work with just word processors to the Professional version, which work anywhere. There are also specialty products that are especially designed for medical or legal texts.

In addition, Dragon Systems provides a specially designed recorder (NaturallyMobile), which you can take anywhere to dictate your text. This is then connected to your computer, and you can convert the dictated document to text. Because it is being read by Dragon NaturallySpeaking, you can use all of the commands you normally do. In addition, the transcription from NaturallyMobile works faster than normal speech.

Shared Resources

Shared resources are perhaps the single most important aspect of the computer network. It makes little sense to connect two computers unless they will be communicating and somehow. In the ancient history of computers, resources were "shared" in that when you could make a remote connection to another computer and run programs or access files.

Today, shared resources go a way beyond this. In a Windows environment, sharing resources includes providing access to the programs, files, printers, and even individual pieces of data buried deep within a database. In order to access these resources as efficiently as possible, you must use a proper tool and an appropriate organization. Without a proper tool, users may not even be able to use the resource. Within improper organization, users may never find what they're looking for.

I have worked in companies before where their network sprung out of the ground and grew to the point where it was no longer manageable and to some extent no longer useful. In such cases, an expedient means of accessing resources was implemented (the incorrect tool), and the resource was put in a location that was "convenient" for the creator, but for no one else (inappropriate organization).

For example, the company phone list was maintained in an Excel spreadsheet. Although the layout of Excel is useful when your information in consists of rows and columns as the company phone book was, no calculations were made on the data. Another table was used to maintain a record of the assets that were assigned to each person. Still another table was used to maintain information about the hardware and software in the company. Each of the use tables was related to the other in some way. However, no relation was defined to limitations of people's knowledge of Excel. In this case, the better solution would have probably been an MS Access database.

In the same company, there was a single directory on the server that was used to store "data." This directory was then shared, and each user connected to this share used the same drive letter. This meant everyone simply *knew* where to look find data. At least, that was the theory. In practice, things were not so easy. For example, there was another drive that was used to store programs. One administrator might think that the data belonged with the program and therefore store the data on the program drive. Another administrator might think that the programs belong with the data and therefore would store the programs on the data drive. In addition, the organization of both the program and data drives was far from optimal.

Neither choosing the right tools nor developing an appropriate organization is an easy task. One might think that selecting the right tool is simply a matter of seeing which data formats you have been using and the selecting a tool that can access those formats. The problem is that you may end up with dozens of different formats and therefore dozens of different tools to the access these formats. The more tools you have, the more tools you need to administer and most likely to more you'll have to pay in license fees. By limiting your organization to just a handful of formats, you can save yourself a great deal of both time and money.

The organization you select for your company's hard disk is, in my opinion, less important than the fact that it should organize the data somehow. Many companies organize the data based on department. Others may organize the data based on function. Either is valid, but you must stick to this organization. It does little good to have a good organization on paper but that your file system paints a completely different picture.

Because it is easier to select the right tools than the right organization, let's begin with the tools. In this context, a tool is any program that you use to access files of data. In general, we can simply call them programs. This could be large packages such as the Corel Office Suite, or they could be something as simple as a Delphi program that you have developed yourself to access an SQL database.

One of the key aspects of this is limiting the number of programs. As I mentioned, this decreases the amount of administration as well as decreases your licensing fees. The difficult part is deciding exactly what programs you need. The mistake that most people make is that they choose a program to access a particular format of information. For example, they have information stored in an MS Access database. Therefore, they believe that Access is a *required* program.

However, the information could just as easily be transferred to an SQL database and MS Access could be gotten rid of. Granted, MS Access does have some advantages over an SQL database, but for simplicity's sake, it may be useful to get rid of MS Access. On the other hand, for simplicity's sake it may be better to get rid of the SQL database. Either choice is valid. Another alternative would be to store the information in an MS Access database and read the information from Web pages.

To be able to determine which programs are necessary, I have found it very useful to create a table of both programs and formats. You can also list all of the programs that you currently use at the top of your list and the all of the formats that you use within your company along the side. You fill out the table by simply making an X if a program supports a particular format.

This table gives you in visual overview how many different programs support any given format. There are two things to look for here. First, look specifically for those formats that are supported by a single program. This does not mean that having this program is a requirement. It's possible that you have some legacy application that just happens to be in this format. Therefore, it could make sense to convert the data to some other format. In any event, formats that are supported by just one program are a special case and need to be treated specially.

For example, I worked in one company where they had an Open Access database used to administer and manage the company cars. This was a DOS version of Open Access and was kept around simply because no one had bothered to convert the data to a more commonly used format. In this case, no extra licensees were required because the software was never updated. However, there was a great deal of administration required each time the operating system was updated. We had to ensure that the program ran correctly on the new operating system. Although we had other database products in-house, such as MS Access and MS SQL Server, no one ever bothered to port the database.

Organizing Your Data

If you have a directory structure that is like in most companies, it probably grew up over time and was not planned. The result is a hodge-podge of directories, which is often than difficult to navigate. Although it is likely that you'll increase the efficiency of your users by changing the structure (it is easier to find things), there is likely to be a great deal of resistance, because people have grown accustomed to the structure and know where to look for certain things, even if the structure is not logical.

Fortunately, when a company first starts an intranet project, they usually have identified problems with the existing structure. Therefore, the structure on the Internet tends to be slightly more organized. Even so, there is no one structure that can be absolutely defined as being "correct." Instead, it will depend on your company, and in some cases, personal preference.

For example, one of the standard schemes for organizing information is based on each department. That is, you have a sales department, so you have a sales directory. You have a marketing department, so you have a marketing directory. It may be that your directories are organized by function. Sales is a function within the company, but the sales subdirectory does not belong specifically to the sales department, but can contains information that is maintained by both sales and marketing.

How you organize your data will be an important factor in how easily your users can access that information. One of the most common stumbling blocks that people seem to still have is the misconception that the information must be organized hierarchically. This status from the fact that until fairly recently, all file systems under Windows had to reorganize like that. The alternative is to organize your data as a Web. Each node of the Web represents the particular piece or set of information, and the connections between the nodes represent either processes or flow of information.

For me, the biggest drawback to the hierarchical system is that someone, somewhere, had to decide on a particular structure. Often, how that person looked at the data was not the same way as the people using the data. For example, the common way of organizing data on your file system is to create a set of directories for each department. However, the action that a particular user is performing at any given time is not necessarily related to his or her specific department. For example, the sales department may get a call from a customer wishing some technical information on your product. At that moment, the person in sales is not necessarily involved in the "sale" of the product, but rather is more concerned with the technical aspects of the product.

In one company where I worked, the solution to this kind of problem was to have copies of the technical information stored underneath the directories for the sales department. There were the obvious problems of outdated information as well as the administration effort involved in copying the files from place to place. However, there is also the fact that this represented a great deal of information and therefore needlessly filled up a huge chunk of the hard disk.

The most obvious solution is to put all of the technical information into a single directory on the server, which is then shared to the workstations. This quickly becomes impractical if you have dozens of different kinds of information that need to be shared between departments. The solution was the introduction to Windows of something that had been around in Unix for a decade: *symbolic links* or *shortcuts*.

In essence, the shortcuts file does not contain data but rather contains locations of another file. This has two very significant advantages. First, shortcuts can be used to point to directories. That means the technical departments can still maintain all of the technical information, but a shortcut can exist underneath the sales directories that points to this information. Second, shortcuts do not needed to exist on the same hard disk or even the same system as the files that they are pointing to. Although shortcuts can contain the path in terms of drive letter and directories, this requires that a given share be mounted to the same drive letter all the time. Instead, shortcuts can be used to point to the Universal Naming Convention (UNC) named a share and therefore can be accessed, whether the drive is connected or not.

By using shortcuts, each department, or individual for that matter, can create the virtual structure that makes the most sense for them. This structure is designed based on the way they work and the way they look for information and not on a way some administrator decides it should be. For example, your sales department may have a subdirectory for customer projects. These in turn contain subdirectories detailing the various components that the customer purchased; underneath these are shortcuts to the technical directories containing the technical specifications of the product they purchased. The technical information physically resides in a subdirectory managed by your technical department. Customer service may have a subdirectory containing tips and tricks and how to troubleshoot problems. These then might also contain links to the technical information of the products.

In this way, you can create a structure that is much more dynamic. That is, your users can create shortcuts to the files and directories that they access regularly and thereby speed up the search time. One user may organize the shortcuts by department or another organizes them by function.

The sales directory may contain a subdirectory for each branch office, which in turn contains the sales reports for each quarter. The company sales manager could create a directory for each quarter, which contains links to the sales reports of the various offices. Each branch office is interested in the sales report for their office; therefore, they create a "view" just for their office. The sales manager is interested in the information for a specific quarter and therefore creates a view that shows the reports per quarter.

When setting up these directories, it is important to consider the access permissions. Therefore, I feel that the data should exist physically in a directory that is the responsibility of the department *creating* the information. For example, because the branch offices are generating their status reports, the physical files should reside under the subdirectories for those offices. Therefore, the sales manager would be the one creating the shortcut to the files. I feel that this scheme is much easier to manage the security for: It is the people who are generating the information who most likely need the most access.

In the previous example, you might give the sales manager read access to the directory, whereas each branch office might have full control. Otherwise, you will need to set permissions on a number of individual files, which increases the likelihood of errors.

One thing that you are liable to encounter is the contradiction between a common structure and flexibility. Not every department needs the exact same structure. However, the structures can be organized so that accessing information is easier. For example, you might have a set of subdirectories that is common to each department, such as a subdirectory containing administration information, such as the departmental organization, standard operating procedures, contact information, and so forth. Another directory may contain reference information. For example, in the sales department you might have data sheets for the various products. In the personnel department, the reference information might be employment laws. Although the content of each directory would be different between departments, the structure would remain fairly consistent.

It is imperative that all offices and all departments match this structure as closely as possible. I have found that it is possible to have the first two levels consistent throughout the company. Then, subsequent directories can be dependent on the respective department. This is unavoidable and expected. However, "forcing" this structure on users encourages them to maintain the structure on their own (i.e., making copies).

I have found that an aid to both administration and information access is to limit the number of entries at each level. That is, you should limit the number of subdirectories to between 10 and 15. This gives you enough flexibility, and at the same time you're not overloaded with too much information. I've seen directories that contain so many subdirectories that you have to page down three or four times to see all of the entries. This is far too many. Limiting the number of entries to between 10 and 15, you see everything on the screen at the same time.

Experience has shown that this probably won't apply to individual files. That is, you'll probably end up with many more files in a given directory. This is okay provided you don't go overboard. You should still limit the number of files in a subdirectory to make the information more accessible. One or two screens should be sufficient. If you have any more, I have found that there is always a way of grouping files in creating new subdirectories.

When mapping drive letters to share two directories, you have the option of reconnecting that drive letter the next time you log in. However, this is only valid for that user on that one machine. You need to find a way to map drive letters that are consistent for all users and all machines. We accomplish this through the logon scripts.

Sharing resources means providing access to them. This does not just mean giving them the proper permissions, but it also means making the information easily accessible. In one company, almost all shared data was stored on a single drive. The single subdirectory on the server shared and connected all workstations by using the same drive letter. In principle, this is a good thing. However, that one directory contained so many subdirectories that you quickly lost track of where a particular piece of information was.

The organization (not just reorganization) of this information took well over a year and resulted in countless phone calls to the system administrators, looking for the right directory. The problem was not the fact that we be organized data, but rather the data were unorganized to begin with. Users were used to the unorganized structure of the directories and could therefore find what they were looking for. However, once the reorganization was completed and everyone got used to it, users commented on how easy it was to find the information they were looking for. A great deal of time could have been saved if the directories had been organized to begin with.

How you organize shared data will not only depend on your company's organization, but also on how data *flows* within your company. For example, consider the two departments: marketing and sales. In general, they were close together. However, there will be information that is not shared between these two departments. Therefore, you might end up having three separate directories, one for each of the departments and one shared. The structure allows you to set access permissions on the directory based on the department. For example, only the sales department has access to the sales directory, but both sales and marketing have access to the shared directory.

Experience has shown me that there is not one single structure that is valid for every company or even for every department in the same company. In fact, I have found that often *different* structures can be valid within the *same* company. For me, the most important thing is the fact that you have some kind of structure that is easy to identify. By this, I mean that you do not have to spend too much time explaining to users what the structure is; instead, the structure is fairly self-explanatory. A simple example would be to create directories for each department and label them accordingly. For example, you might have directories named sales, marketing, purchasing, human resources, and so forth. It is then obvious from the names which department the directory is intended for.

However, organizing information by departments is not always the perfect solution. In some cases, you may want to organize the information geographically, that is, by the physical location of the people accessing the information. You might also organize your data by products. Then again, you may find that a combination of any of these may be the perfect solution. For example the top-level directories are organized by department. The subdirectories underneath the top-level directories are then organized by function.

Easy access to information is the primary goal of organizing your data. However, you have a side benefit of easier administration. Experience has shown me that the more disorganized your data is, the more different groups you'll have to administer. The reason is simply that it is extremely difficult to identify which groups are necessary. You end up with quite a few orphan groups, that is, groups that are no longer being used. In addition, you'll probably end up with a number of duplicate groups. By this I mean groups that serve the exact same purpose. For example, in one company, both the sales and marketing directories contained subdirectories that were shared by the other department. However, there were two groups created to allow access to the two subdirectories. This was unnecessary, as the two directories served the exact same function: A directory and a group were redundant.

Perhaps the most difficult obstacle for many people to overcome is the dependency on a *hierarchical* structure. We have grown used to hierarchy that is forced on us by computer file systems, with directories containing subdirectories, and so on. This is supported by the fact that most companies are organized hierarchically. Many people believe that this is the way information *must* be structured. However, the World Wide Web has shown us differently. In addition, people do not necessarily think hierarchically. Instead, our thoughts are intertwined, like in a net—or like a web.

When information is organized hierarchically, you generally search for information through what is called "drill-down." That is, you drill deeper and deeper into the information until you find which were looking for. You start with a more general subject and select more and more detailed topics until you find the piece you want. An example of this would be the table of contents in a book. The book has a general subject and each chapter covers specific subjects. Within each chapter, there are some headings that cover subjects in even more detail.

On the other hand, when you look for something in an index, you are basically doing a keyword search. Granted, the organization of the index is also hierarchical, but you are looking for information on specific keywords.

Both of these search methods have their own advantages depending on what kind of information you were looking for. If you look at the Web search engines, such as Yahoo, you'll see that they use both drill-down and keyword search.

If you look at the data *flow* within your company, you will probably discover that it is not hierarchical. Although there is certain information that always starts at the top and flows down, information generally flows in every direction.

I have had the most success in organizing data when I get rid of the preconception that information *must* be stored hierarchically. Instead, I organize data like a web. That is, I provide multiple entry points into the structure and multiple paths to the same information. This is not as difficult as it sounds. The key comes in organizing the data. Instead of organizing it on the hierarchy of your administration, you organize it on the flow of data. The data flow is represented in the web by the different paths and the information itself but those places where the paths crossed.

I usually begin with a typical organizational chart of the company. I then draw lines to indicate the flow of data. Within a short time, a web develops. This is your information web or information network.

The problem you now have is that file systems are hierarchical. You do have a limitation in that files must be stored in directories that are subdirectories of other directories and so forth. However, you can take advantage of one of the features of both newer versions of Windows by creating shortcuts between directories. As we discussed in Chapter 1—Windows Basics, shortcuts are nothing more than pointers to other locations on the file system. The other location can either be a single file or an entire directory. In this way, you can essentially have two paths to the same information.

Still, using shortcuts on the file system allows you to create a web structure and therefore make access to the information easier. However, you need to be aware of this limitation of shortcuts.

One thing that I would like to emphasize is that no matter what structure you decide on, you should remain consistent. That is, you should have the same or very similar structure in all of your branch offices. This not only makes accessing the information easier, but also makes the administration easier.

In terms of access, someone transferred to or simply visiting a branch office does not need to go hunting for the information. Instead, the structure is the same as he or she is used to. In the same light, administrators do not need to first examine the file system to determine its structure; instead, they immediately know what it is.

For example, in one company where I worked, all data were stored in a single directory, that directory was shared, and each user mapped this directory to the same drive letter. In fact, the directory existed on the same partition on every server. For example, it might have been a subdirectory of the D: drive. This was the same on *every* server. We used a number of scripts to clean up temporary files and even to do our backups. The same scripts could be used on every machine in the company with essentially no changes. This was only possible because the structure was identical.

Sharing Directories

Microsoft Windows uses the term *share* to refer to the process by which directories on one machine are made available to other machines as well as refers to these directories themselves. Although there are a number of directories that are shared by default, these are mostly system directories or drives. In general, the directories most users typically access are the ones that are explicitly shared either by the system administrator or by other users.

When you share a directory, you can specify the maximum number of users that access the share at any given time. This is confusing because "maximum allowed" does not mean "unlimited." It means the maximum allowed for the machine you are on. For example, if you're using an Windows NT workstation, you can have at most ten simultaneous connections. If five users are already using other directories, the maximum allowed for this new directory would just be five. If ten users were accessing other directories, no one could access this directory.

Permissions on the share can also be confusing. Always remember the permissions you set here apply to the share and *not* to the underlying directory. Although this is a subtle distinction, it is an important one. When determining access, the system first looks at the permissions on the share, and then it looks at the permissions on the directory. This means that if a user does not have access to the share, it does not matter what access they have to the underlined directory; the system will deny them access to the share.

It is also important to note that as of this writing, the default permissions on all shares is to allow full control for *everyone*. I have mixed feelings about this. Although it bothers me from a security standpoint, I have rarely changed it. Instead, I simply accept this fact and rely on the permissions of the underlying directories. Only in cases where I need to ensure that the directory is safe do I change permissions on the share.

Sharing Directories

Right-click the directory name. Select "Sharing" or "Properties" then select the "Sharing" tab. In both cases, you are brought to the window shown in Figure 12–1.

By default, the option "Not shared" is selected and all of the other options are disabled. Select the "Shared as" option and define values for the remaining entries as needed. The "Share Name" field defines the name used to access of this directory on the network and when browsing.

The User Limit box allows you to specify the maximum number of users who can access the share at one time. By default, the option "maximum allowed" is selected.

The "Permissions" button is used to set access permissions for this *share*. These are not the permissions on the directory itself.

The last button is labeled "New Share." This allows you to share a given directory using more than one name. For example, partitions are shared by default using their respective drive letter. You can then share them under a different name.

As I mentioned above, in one company, we configured all of the drives using the logon scripts, using the "net use" command. In this way, we automatically mapped shares to the same drive letters during logon all of the time for all users. This was originally started when we had Windows for Workgroups and it was easier just to continue the practice.

I would recommend that you always delete the drive mapping prior to connecting it in the logon scripts. This ensures that the drive letter is mapped to the correct share. If the drive letter were mapped to a different share, you would get an error message to that effect, and the correct drive mapping would not occur.

Mapping Drive Letters

1. From the Windows Explorer

Select the "Map Network drive" entry in the tools menu of the Windows Explorer or can the appropriate button on the Windows Explorer toolbar. Both of these bring you to the window shown in Figure 12–2.

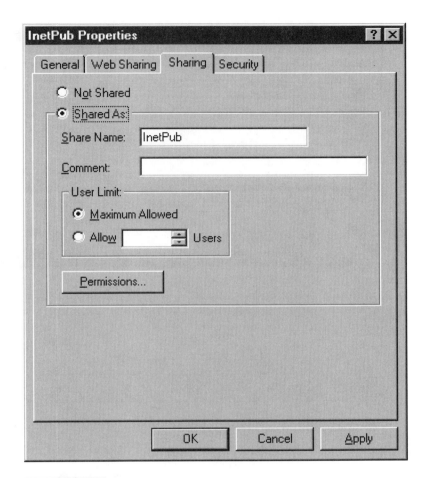

FIGURE 12–1   Properties for shared directory.

The Drive field is simply a list of all the drive letters on your system. Should a drive letter already be mapped, you see the name of the share along with the drive letter.

The Path is the UNC name of the share. The UNC has the following format:

```
\\computername\sharename
```

The computer name is the NetBIOS name of the computer, defined when the system was installed. The share name is the name of one of the shares on the computer.

2. From the command line:

There are different options for the command "net use." For example: net use g: \\nt5\data

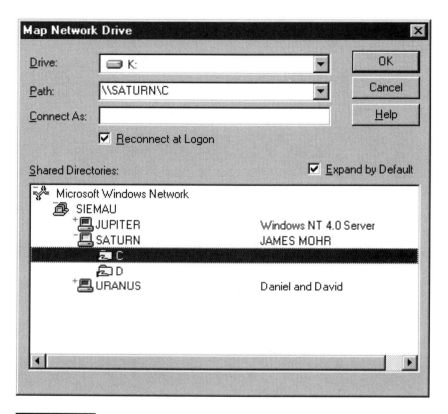

FIGURE 12–2 Map drive window.

Note that under "User Limit" you can specify the maximum number of users that can connect to the share at once. This can be done to reduce the load on a particular server or network segment. Some people use this to restrict access to software with a limited number of licenses. All I can say is "Be careful." This might not be sufficient. For example, I was told by the person managing our Select contract at Microsoft that file and share permissions were *not* a sufficient mechanism to ensure adherence to the license agreement. This makes sense, because as we talk about in Chapter 6—Security, there are a number of ways of bypassing NT security.

Clicking the Permissions button brings up a window similar to the one used to change file and directory permissions. This allows you to set the permissions on the share and *not* on the underlying directory. This serves as an additional shield against unwanted access. Note that the default permissions on shares is to allow FULL CONTROL for everyone. Therefore, you either need to change this or ensure that the directory permissions are set to the way you need.

I think it is a good idea to have a policy in place that defines exactly what the permissions should be set to. This includes the permissions on the shares as well as the underlying directories, what shares are created by on each machine, which shares are *removed* by default, and so forth. Create a checklist of what needs to be done in order to ensure everything is done and done as it should be.

Removing Shares

Shares can be removed in three ways:

- By using Windows Explorer by clicking on the "Sharing" entry in the context menu or the Properties entry in the File menu. Click on the tab "Sharing" and the click the radio button "Not Shared."

- From the Server Manager by selecting the entry, "Shared Directories" in the Computer menu. Select the share you want to delete. then press "Remove."

- Use the "net use"; for example: net use g: /d

Shares can also be created using the Server Manager by selecting the name of the computer then by selecting the entry, "Shared directories" in the Computer menu. You are first shown the lists of shared directories on that machine. Click the "Add" button to add a new share or the "Permissions" button to change the permissions on an existing share.

There are a couple of things to note when creating and removing shares. First, shares can only be created or changed by the administrators or server operators (also power users on workstations). Removing a directory does not remove the share. If a directory with the same name is created later, it will be shared with the same name and permissions as the previous directory.

It is often not a good idea to let users even know about the existence of specific shares. By giving the share a name with a trailing dollar-sign ($), it will be hidden from the Windows browser. However, it is still accessible if the permissions allow access. This has two advantages. First, if you share all of the users home directories, they never really need to be accessed, except when that user logs on. By adding the dollar sign, they don't clutter up the browser. Second, if users don't know the shares exist, they probably won't be curious and try to access them.

You can set the permissions on shared printers, just as you can on shared directories. This might sound like a superfluous function, but it has come in handy to me on a number of occasions. For example, our marketing department has an expensive, photo-quality color printer. When people first found out about it, they went wild and started printing all sorts of useless things. You could tell the users not to print there, but the only way of ensuring that they do not is to set the permissions so they can't, even if they wanted to.

Another occasion when this is useful is when you want to restrict users to specific printers, such as those closest to their desk or in their own department. I have had users who end up printing in other departments because they do not want to wait for other print jobs to be finished. Sometimes the other printer does not have the right kind of paper, which ends up being a waste of everyone's time and paper.

Since a printer is a different kind of resource than a directory, the permissions are slightly different. There are the two standard permission types: Full Control and No Access, which have the same meaning as with files and directories. The Print permission is just that. Specified users have the right to print to that printer. By default, everyone has the right to print to any shared printer.

The Manage permissions allows a user to manage the print jobs on the printer. This includes starting and stopping the printer and print jobs, deleting the print jobs, and changing the priority. Users have the right to manage their own print jobs, as they are the Creator-Owner of that object (the print job). Note that being able to manage a printer does not necessarily mean you have the right to print there.

There is a special group, "Print Operators," that are given the rights to manage all printers by default (they are given Full Control). In addition, both Server Operators and Administrators are also given Full Control by default.

Depending on what it is you are printing, there is also a potential security problem with the printing process. All print jobs are spooled to the hard disk. This means that for a brief period, there is a file on the hard disk containing the contents of the print job. If someone has access to the spool directory (normally %SYSTEMROOT%/SYSTEM32/SPOOL), they could theoretically have access to the information in the document. Because users need to be able to access the directory in order to print, you might consider giving users their own printer attached to the local machine if there is a security issue.

Format Standards

Making the resources available is not just an issue of sticking it somewhere in your network and configuring a new share. Obviously, users need the tools to be able to access this information. In Chapter 10—Documentation, we talk about document standards. Having such standards makes creating, managing, and accessing the document and the information may include much easier.

One thing to consider is the physical format of the files on the hard disk. This can be done using DOC, rich text format (RTF), HTML, and so forth. In this context, even databases are considered formats. The more formats you have, the harder it will be to develop effective standards and more likely you'll need more tools to access the information. More tools means more administration and more cost. Not only is there the cost in terms of time to administer all of the different tools, but someone has to pay for them in the first place.

In deciding on a format, you need to consider where the information will be used and what the information will be used for. Information that is used by a large number of people often has a different format than information used by smaller groups or individuals does.

Consider how the information is currently used and currently accessed. Just because that's the way you have been doing it for years does not make it right. The prime example is creating tables and performing calculations in MS Word. Another example would be writing letters in MS Excel. It can be done, but it is not the most efficient method.

In the one company, having information in the OpenAccess format meant that only OpenAccess could read the data. This did not mean that OpenAccess was an indispensable program. Instead, since there was only one program that could access this type of file, there was only one program that actually used this type of file. Therefore, it was worthwhile for us to look at ways in which we could replace that database.

However, this is not always the case. For example, you will often find that your company uses a particular file format, and you have no other choice but to use the application that created those files. For example, it is very common for CAD applications to write in the format that only they understand. Although other programs may be able to display the files, they will normally not be able to change them. Therefore, unless you want to convert all of your technical drawings to another format, you'll have to continue using your current CAD program.

At the other end of the scale is the need to look at the formats that are supported by the greatest number of different applications. It would then make sense to consider using one of these formats as your standard. For example, all modern word processors will support RTF. Although RTF does have some limitations, it does provide the common format. When the other hand, most word processing programs will support at least the MS Word 6.00 or 7.0 format. In one company where I worked, the standard was MS Word 7.0, as a number of our branch offices were still using MS Office for Windows 95, although the headquarters already migrated to MS Office 97. In addition, all modern word processing programs support HTML, which could also be used as your standard format.

The eventual goal is to be able to get rid of programs that you do not *really* need. You define a standard for your company in terms of what file formats you use and select the smallest set of programs that supports these formats. All of the other programs can easily be done away with.

This is obviously an overgeneralization. You'll find in many cases that a program that you might consider getting rid of has certain functionality that you really need. You might end up increasing the set of programs you use to include support for all of the formats you need as well as specific functionality. This is acceptable, provided the functionality is something that you really need.

Classify Information

In order to choose the right tool, you need to know what kind of information you have. Knowing what kind of information you have allows you to group that information into categories that allow you to reduce the number of tools that you are working with. Experience has shown me that companies often have a lot of redundant tools, that is, more than one tool that does the same job.

Redundant tools mean extra cost in several areas. First, you have to pay for the different software. Then come the updates. Users often don't want to work with a product that is several years old, especially when they see the features of the new version (even if they won't use these features). Depending on your organization, managers in other departments may insist that you get the latest version.

Then there is the issue of compatibility. Many products, like StarOffice, WordPerfect, will allow you to import a wide range of formats. These are inserted as objects into the document. However, it is not always the case that the format is supported. There is a standard set of formats that each program supports (for example, RTF for documents and TIFF for images); however, it may mean that you have to convert to another format before you can import it into another program.

Although the issue of different formats may never be completely resolved, you can reduce the number of formats by reducing the number of programs that you work with. To do that, you have to know what programs you need. To do that, you need to know what kind of information you are working with.

In order to know what kind of information you are working with, you need to classify it. The first step is not to start grouping the types of information but to first describe each type of information you have. When that is done, you will begin to see patterns that you can use to group the information. Each group is then accessed using a single program.

One thing I need to point out is the fact that the classification of your data will not be a simple procedure. Even in small companies, it will take several days or even weeks to classify all types. Sitting down and listing everything that comes to mind will only get you about half of what you have. You might get more, depending on how familiar you are with what *everyone* in your company does and how they work. However, you can rest assured that something will be missing.

In one company, the first thing we did was to list all of the programs and applications we already had. This did two things. First, it gave us an overview of what kind of information was being processed (text documents, databases, graphics, etc.). Plus, it also began to show us how much duplication there was.

The next step was to get a list from all the departments of what kinds of information they work with and what they currently use to access them. Despite what one IT manager said to me, the people who know how someone works is not the IT manager, but rather the people actually doing the work. Perhaps they cannot classify the information in terms of IT characteristics, but they can describe it sufficiently that a classification is possible.

You now have two lists, one with the current tools and one with a description of the information. You can take the second list and begin to classify the information. During this stage of the classification process, do not make the association between the information and the application being used yet. Experience has shown that this tends to influence the classification process. ("We have always accessed this information through our word processor, so that *must* be the right way to access it.")

The list on page 503 shows the basic classification types. I have talked with people who have commented that this does not reflect all types. However, I have found that although not all types are listed specifically, combinations of these types will yield anything that is missing.

Because this is not a book on information engineering, I am not going to go through this process step-by-step. Instead, I am going to address the basic issues.

Once you have completed the list of data types and programs, you can begin comparing the two. First take the list of data types and begin listing out what characteristics it has. List only one quality from each of the different groups. It is probable that you will end up with data types that, for example, have a longevity between medium and long. This is okay at the start. You will see later that you will not have one program for each of the different types of information. Instead, there will be programs that cover a range of data types. Therefore, it is expected that some of these areas will overlap.

The next step is to take the list of programs and list what data types the program *could* be used for. Here, you will find that certain programs can be used for several different types of data. The key here is not to list the data types that you are currently using the programs for, but rather the types that the program *could* be used for.

We found that the best solution was to do this in two steps. First, we created a table listing all the applications and what data types they supported based *only* on access type, longevity, scope, and size. We did not include the type of information it was, such as whether the data was a description or a procedure, as it is the other characteristics that are generally more useful in determining what programs can or should be used to access them.

For example, in one company we had a lot of flow charts for our ISO 9000 documentation that were created with a flow-charting program. We therefore listed flow charts as a data type that the flow chart program supported. We listed this type under MS Word and CorelDRAW, as both of these programs *could* be used to create flow charts.

When we completed the work, we discovered that the only thing the flow-chart program was used for was to create flow charts. In addition, the flow charts were not very complicated. Therefore, either WordDRAW within MS Word or CorelDRAW could be used to create flow charts. We then decided the quality of flow charts created by either of the other programs was adequate for the ISO documentation. We then stopped using the flow-chart program, which saved us money on updates and meant fewer programs to support.

Once this list is completed, the next step is to find all of the data types that are supported by just one program. First, look to see if you have misclassified something. That is, you have two different data types that are essentially the same, but one of them is only supported by a single product. Often this comes from being too specific when classifying the data types. For example, you might say, "MS Access database with customer information" and "Oracle database with product information."

In this case, it is possible to combine these two. By simply calling them databases, without saying what programs are used, you could then consider replacing MS Access with Oracle.

The next step is to sort the programs you have in order of the number of different data types they support, with the programs supporting the most data types at the top of the list. At the bottom of the list, you will find the programs that support just a few data types, sometimes only one. The next question to ask is whether there is another program that *adequately* supports these data types.

The key word here is "adequately." For example, the Windows Paint-Brush program could be used to create flow charts. However, it would be difficult to use and probably cause more work than it would save. WordPad in Windows 95 and Windows NT could be used to create documents. However, it is missing many of the advanced features that we needed. When we determined that a program did not *adequately* support a particular data type, that data type was crossed off the list for that program.

Next, look at all the programs that support only a single data type. Look at any other program that *adequately* supports this data type. If there is another program that *adequately* supports this data type, then the first program could be removed from the list and therefore from your company.

One thing to be careful about is two programs that both support one a single type of program. For example, we ended up with two programs that the only data they supported were "technical drawings." We ended up having to keep both because one was used for 3-D modeling and the other was used for drafting. The problem was not the method we were using, but rather that we had not accurately described the data types. This is one reason why it is vitally important that each department come up with a list of data types and not the IT department. This is a good example of where you often get caught between having a list that is too detailed and one that is not detailed enough.

At this point things become more difficult. You will find that there are several data types that are supported by several different programs. The question is which programs should you use for what data types. The first thing to consider is which of these programs supports the *largest* number of data types. For example, if one application supports five data types, two of these might be the only types supported by another program, which you could then get rid of.

The biggest problem arises when you have several products that all support many different data types. It may not be possible to simply remove a program from your list. You may have to try several different combinations of programs to find one combination that will cover all data types, although this is not always the best solution. Again, I need to emphasize that you are looking for programs that *adequately* support the data types.

One important thing to look at is the possibility that one data type could be converted to another. For example, we had a company telephone book that was accessed through a Web browser. However, the administration of the data was done through an MS Access database. This database was listed as one data type, which meant that we had to keep MS Access. After discussing the situation with the person who administered the information, we all agreed that it could easily be converted to a spreadsheet program. This actually made administering it easier because of the filtering and sorting functions within the spreadsheet. Once we got rid of this data type (converted it), we could get rid of the one application that supported that data type.

Classifying Information

Information Type

Description: current state of an object: where it is, what it is connected to, what is it used for, who is responsible (e.g., building plans, network layout, description of company domains)

Procedures: description how a specific process flows and with what means, tools, or equipment (e.g., how to request vacation, how to order a part)

Work Instructions: step-by-step instructions how to perform a certain action/function (e.g., filling out vacation request forms, correcting entries in the procurement software)

Program: an executable program. (e.g., winword.exe, notepad.exe)

Data: a document (also a file) that does not provide any information on its own, but must be evaluated or loaded into a **program**

Access Type

Static: information that is used mainly as a reference (e.g., **descriptions, procedures, programs**)

Dynamic: information that changes fairly regularly (e.g., log files, processes in memory, total number of customers orders for that day)

Interactive: information that is search for or is changed by the users (e.g., problem-solution database, company telephone book, spare parts orders)

Use

Workgroup: information that is shared between coworkers

Workflow: information that is used as part of a process

Longevity

Short: information that is either continually changed or only valid for a short time (e.g., log-files, e-mail, stock prices)

Medium: information that can measure its longevity in weeks or months (e.g., projects, vacation requests, potential sales contacts)

Long: information that can measure its longevity in years (e.g., organization diagrams, building plans)

Scope

Global: (entire organization) information that is valid for the entire organization, regardless of location (e.g., organizational diagram)

Branch office: information that is valid only for a specific office (e.g., building plans)

Interdepartmental: information that is used by more than one department, but not for the entire company (e.g., sales and customer service, press and marketing)

Department: information that is valid only for a single department or should only be accessed by a single department

Personal: information that is only relevant to a specific person, but still should be available to others (e.g., project status, appointments)

Private: information that is only relevant to a specific person and should *not* be accessible by others

Size

Small: a few sentences or paragraphs (e.g., problem-solutions)

Medium: several paragraphs or pages

Large: many pages

················

Sharing Other Resources

CD-ROMs

Often overlooked when discussing shared resources are the resources that are not connected to the computer or are not stored directly on the server. One common example is the CD-ROM. There are the great many programs currently available that require repeated or even constant access to the CD-ROM. Even if a single user needs access, you still need to make a decision about where to put the drive. Giving your users their own CD-ROM drive basically allows them to install any software they choose to. On the other hand, putting the software on the network may degrade performance noticeably.

If you need to make the information available to a large number of users, there are a couple of alternatives. The simplest and most direct is to load it into a CD-ROM drive that is attached to the server. This starts becoming a problem after you have added your second or third drive. Quite possibly you're simply running out of space in the computer case.

The first solution to this problem is an external CD-ROM tower. This solution is very cost effective if you have a number of older CD-ROM drives lying around that you can use for those CDs for which access time is less of an issue. Obviously, you can put in faster drives if speed is an issue. However, in many cases, even something as slow as 4X speed can be used, provided not too many people need access to information spread out over the CD.

One problem with connecting the CD-ROM to the server is that the server performance may be degraded due to constant access to the CDs. The solution is a CD-ROM server. This is not necessarily a separate machine, whose sole function it is to provide access to the CD-ROM drives. Instead, CD-ROM servers are actually a network interface that typically have an Ethernet connection and a SCSI interface, which then connect to the actual CD-ROM drives.

Internally, they have their own operating system and can provide access to the CD-ROMs via SMB or NFS, which allows you to access the same CDs from Unix machines. Interestingly enough, you can use both protocols at the same time. That is, one group of machines can be accessing the CD via SMB, while another is accessing the CDs via NFS. There are also some on the market that provide management functions via HTTP, which means you can administer the server with any Web browser.

In smaller offices, I think several CD-ROM drives in an external case attached to your server is probably sufficient. Only when you start noticing degraded performance should you consider moving the drives someplace else.

Another possibility is a CD changer. Here you can load a handful of CD-ROMs into the changer, but only one can be read at any given time. The operating system keeps track of which CD is loaded into which slot of the changer and loads them as needed. This is obviously not as fast as having separate drives for each CD, but it does save on space and money.

One of the key aspects you need to consider is the system performance resulting from the resources being accessed. It may happen that accessing the CD is comparatively fast, but all other network performance suffers as a result. Therefore, you need to give some serious consideration to location of such devices in your network, how many people need to access them, how often they will be accessing them, and so forth.

Documents

Regardless of the format you choose to use, you will eventually run into problems, because the documents will get larger and larger. Therefore, finding an efficient means of distributing the documents will become increasingly difficult. Simple documents with little or no graphics can easily sit on a single diskette. However, you'll probably get to the point someday with a document that can no longer fit on a single diskette. Also, if you have a large number of documents, putting them all on diskette can be inconvenient.

Modern technology provides quite a few alternatives for distributing documents. Each has its own advantages and disadvantages, depending on the situation. You may find that there is no single solution that you can use in every case. Therefore, you should take a look at all of them to see which one is the most useful in your circumstances.

The two key questions to ask yourself is how much data you're going to transfer and whether you're going to be providing this information to people in other companies. The answers to these will help you determine which solution is best.

Potentially, you might consider moving large documents across the Internet. This is extremely useful if the information needs to be sent very quickly. However, you cannot always expect that the recipient has an Internet connection that has the necessary bandwidth. Also, there is the issue of how much other traffic there is on the same line. To decide whether or not this is a viable solution, you need to know how much information you need to transfer as well as who is the recipient. If the recipient is someone else in your own company, hopefully you know what kind of connection may have. You can therefore judge whether or not that connection has the necessary bandwidth.

On the other hand, if the information is going to another company, you'll probably have to do a little research to find out if their connection can handle the load. Remember, a network connection is only as fast as its slowest link. Therefore, if the recipient only has a 14.4-Mbps modem, whereas you have a T1 connection, the fastest the data can be transferred is 14.4 Mbps. Also remember that the longer the connection is up, the more susceptible it is to interference. Although with recent technological advances, this is becoming less and less of a problem, I cannot even begin to count how many transfers I've had to restart because I lost the connection. And you also need to keep in mind the fact that not everyone lives in high-tech areas such as the United States, Western Europe, or Japan. There are places that are still working with ten-year old communications technologies, which means the likelihood of interference is far greater.

Unless the information is extremely time critical, I would recommend that you avoid this method unless the documents are under 1 MB in size. Documents of this size can be transferred quickly and do not overburden the network, and there is less chance of interference or that you will lose the connection. However, what do you do about the documents that are time sensitive, and all of them are larger than that 1-MB limit?

To answer that question, I will relate to you a story about what happened in one company where I worked. We got repeated calls from one of our branch offices indicating that the network connection to the headquarters was basically useless. The routers that we used allowed us to display the transfer statistics. This showed us that, in fact, the line was exceeding the guaranteed bandwidth. Something was going across the line and taking up all the bandwidth. We then noticed that the traffic was coming from the head-quarters going to the branch office. After a little detective work, we found that are marketing department was sending 30-MB MS PowerPoint documents to the branch office for translation. Since this was something that had to be done, we needed a solution.

In this case, the documents were not time sensitive, but far exceeded the 1-MB limit. Even using something like Mijenix Zipmagic, we could still not compress the file smaller then about 20 MB. That meant that copying it onto diskettes was impractical. One administrator came up with the idea of automatically copying documents like this between the offices in the middle of the night. Users would copy their files into a sort of "outbox" destined for a particular office bandwidth in the transfer data time that it would not interfere with the users.

Because this scheme turned out to be extremely useful, I felt it required a little more exploration. We created a universally accessible directory that contained two subdirectories. One subdirectory was for outbound files, and the second was for inbound files. Each of these subdirectories had a subdirectory for each of the branch offices. For example, the outbox would have a subdirectory labeled Singapore for files heading toward the office in Singapore. If a user in the United States wanted to send a file to Singapore, they would then copy it into the Singapore directory. The next day, the people in Singapore would look in the U.S. subdirectory of their inbound directory and find the file.

After working with the system for several weeks, we made some modifications to the system. Every 15 minutes the directories were scanned. If a file was less than the 100 KB, it was transferred immediately. Every two hours the directories were scanned, and all files less than 1 MB were transferred. All other files were copied in middle of the night.

You may be asking the question, "Whose night?" That is a good question, because when the people in the United States are working, it is the middle of the night in Singapore. This was not an easy question to answer. However, since most of the traffic was between the headquarters and the branch office, it was decided that the transfer work be done in the middle of the night for the office *sending* the information. Fortunately, only a small number of offices were working during what was the middle of the night at the headquarters. Therefore, they were very rarely affected by data transfers from the headquarters, since transfers between branch offices were pretty rare.

But what about larger amounts of data or cases when you don't have a network connection to that office? This is often the case when you are providing large amounts of information to salespeople who are constantly on the road. Although they may have a laptop with a modem and therefore could connect to a computer at the headquarters using something like RAS, it is generally not cost effective to transfer large amounts of data in this way. To solve this problem, we actually used two solutions.

The first solution was to buy our own CD writer. With them costing just a couple hundred dollars, a CD writer is a very efficient and cost-effective means of transferring large amounts of data. Depending on the amount of information we're writing, a CD can be prepared and written in under half an hour. In this way, we can distribute hundreds of megabytes of information for just a few dollars. All of the newer CD writers that I have seen have the capability of storing files using long file names—this is a function that should not be overlooked. Being able to name your files something obvious can save you a lot of time. Therefore, it is worthwhile to find CD-creation software that can do this well.

We primarily use CDs in cases where the data flow is in just one direction, that is, if the headquarters is sending large amounts of data to the branch offices. However, if the data goes back in for, we use the different solution. In such cases we use removable drives, such as those from SyQuest The size of the SyQuest drives range from a couple hundred megabytes to over 2 GB. By the time this book goes to press, they may be even more.

In one company we used the 230-Mbps SyQuest EZFlyer to transfer data between our office and the typesetters who did all of our printing work. Since the easy EZFlyer works just like any other disk drive, files were transferred to inform the drive within a matter of minutes. The files could then be sent to the type centers processed and easily returned to us for approval. Because of the size, it was impractical to do this using diskettes, because the data were changed so often it did not make sense to burn the CD every time. A removable drive was a perfect solution.

At home, I actually have two SyQuest drives. First, I have a 230-Mbps SyQuest EZFlyer. I use this primarily when I travel, when I need to have access to large amounts of data. Because the version I now to works off of the parallel ports, I can easily connect to my laptop or to my desktop machines with no problem. I can then transfer all of the data between them within just a few minutes. In addition, I also use this drive when transferring data between my home machine and my machine at work. The fact that it is connected via a parallel port has the additional advantage of not requiring a SCSI host adapter on both machines. Therefore, no matter where I go, I can always find a parallel port. I always have the driver disks with me and can quickly install it on any machine, thereby making the drive accessible within just a few minutes. However, I would strongly recommend never doing this on a server, as the performance impact is significant.

The other SyQuest drive I use is the SyJet 1.5-GB drive. Obviously, this would be a good solution if you are regularly transferring more than 230 MB worth of data. Because I personally never need a drive larger than 230 MB, I do not use the SyJet for this purpose. Instead, I actually use it at home for backing up my data. It is much more convenient and much quicker than using a tape drive. All of the files that I consider data (my books, articles, e-mail) are stored in just a couple of directories. I select these directories and simply drag them onto the removable disk drive and my backup is done within five minutes. SyQuest also provides software to automate this process.

Backing up data in this way not only has the advantage of time and convenience, but all of the SyQuest drives are seen as any other drive. That is, with the appropriate driver, they can be read from any machine. The advantage of the SyJet drive I have is that it is plug-and-play on almost any system. Whether I am using Windows 95, Windows NT, or even Unix, I simply connect the drive to the SCSI bus and can instantly access files.

In many companies, doing backups on a removable drive like the SyJet is impractical. More than likely, you'll want to backup more data than can fit on the desk. Therefore, you would need multiple drives. However, for smaller companies with limited amounts of data, a removable drive is not only a good way of sharing information, but it is also an efficient means of backing up the data.

On a company intranet, you are generally certain which formats your users can read. However, this is not always the case if the same document needs to be available on the Internet. To do this, you need to have a commonly accessible format, which is what HTML is all about. However, HTML does have shortcomings, particularly when the information is read offline or needs complex formatting that HTML cannot handle.

You may also find yourself in the situation where information needs to be shared with people.

The solution to this problem is to create what are referred to as "digital documents." These are not bitmaps images of the original document, but rather components are stored as objects in a readily accessible format. Because they are not bitmaps, the files can be much smaller and can be enlarged interviewing program as needed without any significant loss of quality.

You should not look on digital documents simply as paper documents in electronic form. Although they appear as printed documents when you first look at them, there is significantly more that you can do with them. Digital documents use the existing technology in such a way that you can add comments or notes directly into the document and even go so far as to mark specific passages.

An advantage of such documents is that the viewing program can be run on a wide range of operating systems. For example, it is often possible to create the documents on a Windows machine and read them later on a Unix workstation or Macintosh. Therefore, you need to make sure the user has the appropriate viewer and not whether the document is in the appropriate format.

Even if you've only been using computers for a short time, you have more than likely have encountered a document that was created with Adobe Acrobat. There are an incredible number of companies that provide Acrobat documents on Web sites and just as many that provide Adobe documents with their software as part of the online documentation.

The key behind Adobe Acrobat is the portable document format (PDF). In essence, you print to the Adobe printer, which then in turn creates the PDF file, which can be read from the Acrobat Reader. The reader is available for all versions of Windows, Macintosh, and most common Unix versions, including Linux. This makes it the perfect tool for distributing documents on the Internet.

Because Acrobat works like a normal printer driver, the original if format elements are not lost when the digital document is created. In essence, the digital document looks identical to the original document. The finished PDF document can be processed further and that links, forms, notes, and even video are added.

As I mentioned, digital documents like PDF are not pictures or bitmaps, and even with the best possible compression methods, the file would be much too large. In addition, processing the document after it was created (such as to add links) would be basically impossible. Instead, PDF is a "page description language," which is similar to PostScript. Areas are defined, and their contents are described.

An interesting characteristic of PDF is that it is extensible. It has a modular architecture so that additional modules can be added at any time. As a result, media formats that do not yet exist can be added later with no problems.

Even though the elements are treated as objects, PDF documents are still compressed to a certain degree to make the document as small as possible. However, a compression normally means a loss of data. The PDF format tries to reduce the data loss as much as possible, while at the same time trying to make the document as small as possible. In order to do this, different compression methods are used for the different kind of objects in the PDF file. For example, compression mechanisms used for text are not good for pictures and vice versa. In addition, the compression methods for black and white pictures are different for color pictures. It is also possible to choose which compression methods are used, if you're more concerned with size as compared to quality, for example.

Once the document is created, you can navigate through it in several different ways too. However, which methods are available are actually dependent on the document's creator. For example, you can create a table of contents that is used to jump to specific points in a document. You can also create an overview, which shows thumbnails of each page.

Adobe Acrobat is actually composed of five different products: Distiller, Exchange, Catalog, Writer, and Capture. Distiller is used to "distill" the PDF from a document produced by another application. There is also a "Distiller Assistant," which helps you through this entire process.

Intranet

....

One thing that has increased in popularity substantially within the last couple of years is the company intranet. Originally an intranet was simply an internal version of the World Wide Web. That is, information was made available to users using HTTP almost exclusively. This was not an internal version of the Internet, as common Internet applications and/or calls such as telnet and FTP were not in use. Recently, more and more companies are applying not only Internet technologies but also the technologies that had been reserved solely for internal use such as the Windows NT file system.

Why an Intranet?

The reasons for creating a company intranet are essentially the same as for creating a company Internet site: efficient distribution of information. Although you may not have an Internet site, you should definitely consider the advantages of a company intranet. Perhaps the two most important aspects are efficiency and cost.

Access to Information

Having the company's information in a central location makes access quicker, as your employees do not need to go looking for it. Even keeping the information in a set of binders next to the department secretary is much less efficient than having the computer do the work for you. First, you take advantage of the speed that the computer can search (assuming a search mechanism is included). Next, the information is stored in a *single* location for the whole company (or perhaps just the department). Depending your policy, changes can be immediately available to everyone. (How often have you had one department working based on one set of standards and another working based on another, outdated set?)

In addition to the efficiency, having the information in a single location saves the company money. There is no need to print out 20 copies for each of the different departments. Plus, you do not waste time distributing them. (There is also the environmental advantage of not wasting all that paper). The people managing this information do not need to update the 20 copies, but rather make changes at a single location.

This changes the mode of communication from "push" to "pull." With hard copy memos and so forth, the information is "pushed" into someone's in-box. With an intranet, each employee has to go "pull" the information for themselves. This has advantages other than just saving paper. Users can now access information when they need it, not just when it is handed to them. How often have you received a memo in your in-box that you decide to read "later"? That "later" never comes and you lose the memo. With an intranet, you pull the memo when you have time to read it, and it doesn't get lost.

Another aspect of the efficiency of an intranet is distribution of information. Everyone in the company who has access to a computer has access to the information. You will no longer hear an employee say they did not know something (provided they have a computer). Obviously this will only work if they look, so they should be required to read specific areas of the intranet at regular intervals and therefore cannot claim ignorance. Whether this central location is a set of Web pages or a company internal newsgroup, everyone has access.

However, you should keep in mind the people who do not have access to a computer. If you are a manufacturer, the people running the machines often do not use a computer (at least not in the same way people in the administration departments do). Therefore, you need a way of providing the information. How this is done is beyond the scope of this book, and we will continue to just address those people who do have a computer.

The efficiency in distributing the information is supplemented by the speed at which the data are accessed. Here we are not talking about the processing power of the CPU or the bandwidth of the network. The issue is using the computer to do our work for us. Whether that work is the steps

Chapter 13 ◆ Intranet

necessary to connect across the network or to search a directory tree for a specific file.

Another key advantage is the interaction that an intranet can offer. This does not just mean you can give search criteria and have the server search for information. This is how the search engines like Yahoo! or AltaVista work. Instead, you can also add information to the system through. For example, you could have a Web browser interface to your customer database. When a new customer calls, you input information into a form on a Web page, which then transfers the information to your database.

As with the Internet, an intranet does not need to consist of a single server containing all of the company's information. Instead, you can have information spread out all over the company. Each office or even each department could have its own server. This has several advantages. First, if one server goes down, only a single office or single department is affected. Second, performance on one server does not affect performance on another. You may have one department that needs a larger, faster server, such as your technical department. They have more information to access and therefore need a more powerful server. However, the purchasing department may not have much internal information and requires a smaller server. As the requirement of a specific department change, the changes to the server affect only that department.

Perhaps the most significant aspect of the intranet is the ability to access essentially all information from single interface: your Web browser. The current versions of both Microsoft Internet Explorer and Netscape Navigator allow you to view a wide range of file formats directly in your browser. For example, you no longer need to start MS Word to view a Word document; instead, it can be displayed directly in your browser. In addition, using languages like JavaScript and VBScript you can easily access any number of data sources including MS SQL Server, MS Access, MS Excel, or any other format for which there is an open database connectivity (ODBC) driver.

Like with data on your file system, it is important to decide which tools you will use to access data in your intranet. In many cases, the best solution is to leave the information in its original format, such as MS Word or MS Excel. In other cases, converting the files to HTML might be more useful. In still other cases, the most effective means of accessing the data is to access it using ODBC or some other method.

For example, in one company the internal telephone book consisted of the MS Excel spreadsheet. Approximately once a month, the phone book was printed out on two sheets of paper (front and back) and copied several hundred times for all the people within the company administration. Eventually I wrote the Visual Basic program that parsed this information so that it no longer needed to be printed out, but that still meant that an extra program was needed to access the data. When we created our company intranet, repetitive something made the MS Excel file available for the Web browser. However, this was just as static as the printed copy and was essentially a step backward compared with Visual Basic program, which allowed the search for specific names and even telephone numbers.

Because an ODBC driver is available for MS Excel, it was a very simple matter to design a Web page containing VBScript that accessed to the information in the phone book. This was a step up from the MS Excel file, in that there was no need for a hard copy of the information that could be searched. It was a step up from the Visual Basic program because it reduced the number of different programs the users as well as the administrators had the deal with.

Leaving the company telephone book in an MS Excel file did not offer us all of the advantages of storing it in the true database like MS Access. However, we need the conscious decision to sacrifice the benefits that MS Access would bring for the speed of getting this information into the intranet as quickly as possible. Eventually, the company phone book as well as all of the other MS Excel files were ported to MS SQL Server. This was simply because of the number of tables, data, and relationships we soon had in our data.

One thing I would like the point out is that although leaving the information in MS Excel files is okay, especially for smaller organizations, it needs to be a *conscious* decision. By designing that, you do not do what we did and leave it in MS Excel in order to quickly get your intranet running but then you later forget to port your database. If your intention is to eventually port the data, you should set a time frame to do so. For example, you might have a time line of 6 months to get your intranet running. It is then reasonable to expect that at the end of 12 months, all MS Excel files have been converted to MS Access or even to MS SQL Server.

One of the considerations that we had was the fact that much of this information already existed within the company's primary application: SAP. It was not feasible at that time for number of reasons to access all of the data directly in SAP. At least this was the case at the beginning of our Internet project. Our goal was eventually to change the Web pages so that data accessed SAP directly.

At first, this sounds like we did a lot of double work. In fact, we did! We expected this and even planned for it. We went beyond the immediate issue of getting the information into the intranet and passed the issue of accessing the information from within SAP. What we've looked at was how the information was currently being handled. Different departments required the information in different formats. As a result, it was copied out of SAP by one department into a particular format, passed to another department to be put into a different format, and passed again. In many cases, the information was processed three or four times so that every person and department had the information in the format that they needed. We came to the conclusion that the most effective way to use our resources was to limit the amount of processing. The necessary information could be obtained from SAP using standard reports. Rather than printing it out, it can be exported to a text file, which in turm with importing to a database such as MS SQL Server.

Once the information was in SQL Server, it could be accessed them Web pages. Each department was able to display the information in the way it needed. A year later, when we were finally able to connect to SAP directly, the Web pages and respective layouts were already in place. All that was needed was to change a few lines of code to access SAP rather than SQL Server. What we gained was a whole year of access to this information without the need to process it repeatedly.

Being able to make this decision required that we know two important aspects of our system. First, we knew how data were being processed within the company and knew the benefits we could gain by implementing the particular solution to. I often see companies make the mistake of not knowing exactly how particular pieces of information are used. Therefore, they assume that one format is better than another. In addition, I often see companies overlook the fact that it is not always necessary to jump to that final, all-encompassing solution. Instead, they can move slowly toward their goal in slow, easy-to-manage steps.

One thing that we encounter in developing our intranet was something that is common to many companies that an intranet is unexplored territory. In many cases, there is a severe lack of know-how in developing the intranet. Here I am not just referring to those aspects that are specific to intranets, but rather to Internet technology in general. For example, it's likely that the administrators know how to develop simple Web pages. The question is whether or not they are able to access databases from these Web pages or how interactive they can make them. During the early stages of all our intranet development we were forced to learn a great deal about Internet technologies.

There was a conscious decision on our part not to overburden ourselves. There were countless resources detailing how to access things like MS Excel files and MS Access databases from within Web pages. However, information about accessing SAP from Web pages was extremely limited. We were not in a position nor were we willing to pay the extraordinarily high consulting fees that SAP demanded for this kind of service. In addition, developing the SAP interface at the same time we were learning about the Internet technologies would have meant we were spreading ourselves much too thin.

Intranet as Groupware

The intranet can also take over other functions within your company, such a "groupware." Previously, groupware functionality was limited to separate programs such as Lotus Notes and MS Exchange. In essence, the groupware product is designed not only to provide e-mail, but to provide a complete messaging and "cooperation" solution. Such products allowed users to send private messages to each other, store information in shared folders, and participate in discussion groups, all from a single interface. The goal of it is efficient cooperation between individuals, workgroups, departments, and even the entire company.

Within each organization there are three types of communication, based on the number of people who are participating. With traditional e-mail, you have a 1:1 relationship. That is, one person sends the message and another person receives it. Although e-mail can be sent to multiple recipients, the basic relationship is still 1:1. Other technologies such as Microsoft's proprietary Winchat or the Unix standard talk are two more examples of this 1:1 relationship.

Traditional information distribution within a company is usually 1 to many or 1:N. That is, the information is sent by one person and received by many. Finally, we have many to many or M:N relationship. Here, any number of users can produce the information, and there can be any number of recipients. The most well-known communication method in this class is the Internet newsgroup.

In the right context and the appropriate information, each of these communication types has its place. The important thing is to realize which type to use in which circumstance. For example, personal or personnel issues with your boss are probably best served with a communication method better suited for a 1:1 relationship such as e-mail. The company's Christmas holiday work schedule would be more suited for a 1:N method, such as posting it on the company's bulletin or intranet server.

To some extent, each one of these methods can be integrated into your intranet interface. Netscape has integrated all of the common Internet communications technologies into its Netscape Communicator product. Although there is a separate application for each communication method, the overall "look and feel" of the various components is consistent. Products such as StarOffice have all of the functionality integrated into a single interface. StarOffice also integrates all of the other business applications into the single interface. That is, through the one interface, you not only have access to your communications tools, but also to your word processor, spreadsheet, presentation, and roaring programs, Web browser, and you even have the ability to start external applications. StarOffice truly lives up to its claim of "doing everything in one place."

Traditionally, Internet newsgroups have been used for "conversation" rather than for true business processes. However, this is not the limitation of the technology but rather how it has been implemented. Using newsgroups with some other kind of similar groupware, a great deal of "collaborative" work can be accomplished efficiently. There is no longer the need to hold regular meetings to inform all of the participants of the status and for each member of the team to provide some kind of report to the others. Instead, status reports and similar information can be stored in a central location to be retrieved when it is convenient. Once again we see the shift from pushing the information town during the meeting to pulling it from the intranet when you need it.

Most groupware or newsgroup products have the added advantage that you can include links to other documents inside your messages. It is therefore possible that your "status report" consists of just a few lines with a brief summary of the status and has links to other documents with much more detailed information. How often have you gone into staff meetings where someone gave a status report and handed around copies of a 20-page document that most people were not interested in? Most of the copies ended up in either the trash or a drawer somewhere, which wastes time for both the producer of the information and the recipients. The intranet technology makes this no longer necessary.

A side benefit of holding your staff meetings on-line like this is there is an automatic record of what has been said. You no longer have to designate someone to take minutes, and you don't have to worry that something important will be forgotten. I have been to a number of meetings where something important was discussed but never made it into the minutes.

Unlike in traditional staff meetings, you have now control over when or even if a particular user accesses the information. This is one of the primary concepts within the intranet. That is, users become more responsible for obtaining the information themselves. As I mentioned previously, with the push technology comes "blame." With the pull technology comes responsibility.

Keep in mind that this requires a dramatic change in the overall company attitude. Without changing this book to one on management styles, I will simply say that if the company has an overall attitude toward finding blame rather than giving responsibility, the intranet is not going to change. Instead, the change in attitude by the company enables the intranet to succeed.

Another activity that can be switched over to the intranet is coordination. That is, coordination of different projects, individual work, and so forth. Everything from the initial concept through the planning and implementation can be made public and available through the intranet. Everyone has access to all of the information of all the faces of the project, which allows them to make comments or suggestions as the project proceeds.

Here too, employees can no longer say, "I didn't know." In one company where I worked, it wasn't until the engineers arrived and began tearing holes in the walls that half of the IT department knew that we were switching from thin wire to twisted pair.

Although you can develop a fairly complex system using just Web pages with a handful of links, you do not fully realize the potential force of the intranet until you implement or at least look at a program specifically designed for group activities. There is, of course, MS Exchange, but there are a number of other outstanding tools that take this one step further. The two most common are Lotus Domino and Netscape Collabra Server. In the case of Netscape and Lotus, they have integrated the groupware functionality into the Web browser. The Web browser becomes the groupware client, which parses all of the information onto the server. Just like other groupware products, the server is responsible for maintaining the logic in the information itself within its database. The client is responsible for providing the access.

When implementing a product such as Lotus Domino or Netscape Collabra, several important aspects of the intranet become clearer. For example, the groupware functions are taken over by a server that can display all of the information from a central interface This further reduces the number of interfaces users have to the data. As we discussed, this reduces or even eliminates the time necessary for the users to become familiar with the new program. They can concentrate on the work rather than on learning new technologies.

An offshoot of this is the ability to make this information available to people outside of the company. Not all information should be made available, but there is a great deal that not only could be provided but *should* be provided to partners and customers. This is not limited to simple discussions among your employees, but also to discussions among your customers. For example, there are a number of companies that have created Internet newsgroups specifically for their products. Customers help each other than the newsgroup is usually monitored by some group within the company.

Intranet Basics

As I mentioned previously, the concept of the intranet has developed to being more than just providing Web pages. Using all the technologies available to the Internet, you can increase efficiency as well as communication within your company. In fact, a well-designed intranet can mirror the entire communications infrastructure within your company. That is, all of the different processes that distribute and access information can be accomplished using your intranet.

Where to Start

An obviously important aspect for the success of your intranet is a careful planning of both the structure and the tools you choose to use. As you imagine, an intranet will be put to its greatest use if it is implemented company wide. One problem is that it is not always possible to include the entire company at one time. Even if you have a relatively small company, you might be better off by implementing the project in pieces.

How big the pieces are, and what information these pieces encompass, depends on your company. You may decide to implement a subset of the information but include every department. On the other hand, it is also reasonable to start with a single department and include as much information is possible. Each approach has its advantages and disadvantages.

By including a subset of the information, you expose the capabilities of the intranet to a larger group of people. The disadvantage is that you're not likely to realize the full potential of the intranet due to the limited amount of information you're making available. Usually, the information that is made available is relatively simple, perhaps mundane, information like the company phone directory, announcements, plans, and other information that takes little effort to display and usually has no relationship to the information.

By this I am not saying there are no links in place, but rather each page could be seen as an individual unit. For example, the company telephone book may simply parse the text file to search for the necessary information. However, on the page describing the company's Christmas party contact information, the information for the organizer is put in by hand, not from the company phone book. This means that should the person change offices and their telephone number, the Christmas party page needs to be changed as well.

Unfortunately, this is the nature of the beast. You want to get out as much information as possible and convince as many people as possible of the value of the intranet. Granted, the previous example could be corrected fairly simply, but it serves to demonstrate what things might be left out.

On the other hand, if you are concentrating all of the information to a single department, the relationship between the various pieces of information comes to the forefront. Your goal here is to represent the data flow within that department as best as possible. Therefore, you'll probably be more concentrated on the relationship between the various pieces of information than just individual pieces of information. As a result, the links between the various data sources become more important. Again, the disadvantage is that fewer people will be able to see the value of the intranet.

Personally, I prefer to the latter approach. First, you have the widest range of data types. The tendency with a company-wide project is to start off only with static information. If you are restricting yourself to specific departments, you have static as well as dynamic information. In this context, dynamic information is essentially anything that could change from one visit to the next: product prices, for example. In order to be able to access the various types of information, you need to develop the necessary skills. With static information, all you really need to know how to do is design and save pages as HTML. You do not even need to learn the details of HTML, as there are many products available that will do all the work for you.

On the other hand, by reading more dynamic pages, you will not only need to become familiar with HTML but also with a scripting language such as a VBScript or JavaScript. In addition, you need to learn about the interactions between such scripts and your various information sources. Therefore, you'll probably be required to become familiar with ODBC to allow you to incorporate various data sources in your pages.

In one company where I worked, we chose the sales department for our pilot project. We did this for a couple of reasons. First, the sales department had information from and for almost every other department in the company. In addition, much of the information they used they created themselves. Added to this was the requirement that the information also be available to the sales force when outside of the company. This required that we become familiar with random-access storage (RAS) and other technologies that allowed our users to gain access to the information from remote sites. The bottom line was that the sales department provided us with the biggest challenge and afforded us the opportunity to learn the most about the available technology. We were then able to decide which technology would best suit our needs, and we then implemented that technology in other departments.

In essence, the sales department became a guinea pig. Fortunately, we had people in the department who immediately realized the value of an intranet and provided their complete support. When this pilot project was finished, the IT department had the necessary knowledge and experience to implement the project company wide. In addition, we had a working model that we could present to the other departments. Finally, we had the support and backing of everyone in sales who had nothing but good things to say about the intranet. In my opinion, these last two points are perhaps the most dramatic for implementing a pilot project within a single department rather then trying to include all of the departments at once.

Keep in mind that implementation of an intranet requires users to change both the way they work and their attitudes. Neither is easy. By having an entire department supporting the change as well as helping the others adjust to a change, you have a greater chance for success. On the other hand, by implementing the project company-wide you are more likely to run into opposition. If there are enough people who fail to see the value of an intranet because of the limited scope in which you implemented it, you'll have a harder time making the projects a success.

On the other hand, you can take this one step further. That is, implement a company-wide intranet at the same level I described for an individual department. This is possible but may actually take years to implement depending on the size of your company. However, this method does have the advantage of forcing you to look at all data sources and relationships that once. As result, it is easier to integrate the different pieces and prevent duplication of effort.

For example, if your company is like many, specific pieces of information are handed from one department to the next to be molded into a format that the new department can use. They hand the information off to another department that processes the information further. A company-wide intranet project can more easily identify the information that is passed from department to department and therefore can either simplify the handoff or be eliminated altogether. For example, each of the different departments may need the information in a slightly different format. However, it is all being drawn from a single source. By implementing the intranet for just a single department, you will probably need to simply accept the fact that certain information will be passed from department to department. I feel that this is an acceptable procedure provided you are conscious of that choice.

The effort you will need to put into your intranet project is dependent on your current situation. Not only does the knowledge base play while role but also the existing infrastructure. The more you need to redesign the infrastructure, the longer it's going to take before you have an effective intranet.

However, let's first look at the knowledge you have within your company. If you are to implement the intranet using standard Web browsers and other applications, you'll have to have TCP/IP in your network. TCP/IP is the de facto standard on the Internet, and therefore all Internet applications run on top of TCP/IP. The problem is that many smaller companies have implemented networks using NetBEUI and as a result have more work because of the need to convert or at least implement TCP/IP.

If your company does not have the experience working with TCP/IP, the migration or implementation of a TCP/IP network will be a long process. I have found that companies that do not have experience with other Internet standards such as HTML have a much harder time as well. As I mentioned, there are a number of tools available on the market that will create your Web pages for you. However, to go beyond what these tools offer or to troubleshoot your pages, you need at least a basic understanding of HTML. Granted, there are many more things to consider, but this should give you an idea of the benefit of previous experience.

Another advantage that the pilot project will bring you is the ability to "verify" your structure and the chosen technology. Perhaps the specific technology works fine for the few small tests to two-run but begins to break down as soon as a handful of users begin to access. For example, we had a number of MS Excel files that we wanted to make available on the intranet. We had simply displayed the Excel files in the browser, but that did not allow us to search the file. Instead, we created a VBScript that allowed us to search the Excel file directly. It wasn't until we implemented the intranet that we discovered the server could not parse the file at the same time it was being edited through Excel. We therefore converted a great number of Excel files into access databases. In addition to giving us more functionality, this allowed us a much better concurrent use. Had we implemented the solution with Excel throughout the company, we would have had a lot more work to do.

Forming Your Team

Creating an intranet is not a one-person show, unless that's all there is in your business. You need people from all over your company to be part of it. The two most obvious are management and your technical people, so we will get to them first. However, since the process of providing your product from start to end involves the entire company, the entire company should be represented in the development of your intranet site.

Since it is management that will be giving you the money to complete this project, they need to be convinced that an intranet is a good idea. This was a major problem in one company I worked in, because the owner wanted a hard copy of everything. He was not a big fan of a paperless office, because what he saw on a computer screen was not real to him. It wasn't real until he saw it on a piece of paper. In fact, he never had a computer installed in his office.

The result was that anything that took away his hard copies was something to be avoided. We therefore had to develop an intranet concept that allowed easy printouts of the information. This meant more work, as we ended up doing things twice in some cases to make printing easier.

The owner's son was less of a problem, but still was not to the point that he felt comfortable with on-line information. In order to get his support, we developed a test intranet that contained just a small fraction of the information that would eventually be on the completed intranet. However, there was enough there to show him the potential of an intranet.

One of the key aspects that we addressed in our test intranet was ease of access to important information. We took examples of where communication was lacking in the company and showed how easy it became with an intranet. This dealt not only with internal information but also information from customers and suppliers as well as information we needed to pass back to them. Information was easier to access, which saved time. Saving time meant saving money.

One thing that management wanted to see was savings. Like every company owner, he always talked about saving money. However, saving money was *not* something we talked about. The reason is that setting up the intranet would take time and in some cases would require extra money (i.e., to buy new servers or software). By showing management how much time could be saved, they were able to see themselves how much money could be saved *in the long run*.

Your IT/IS department is responsible for the technology. They need to know not only the technology you will implement, but what is else is currently available, what direction the industry is taking, and so forth. In order to implement an effective intranet you not only have to take advantage of the technology you have but also look to see what technologies are available that you should implement.

Along with the technologies are the standards. If your IT/IS department is not up-to-date, you might waste time and money in something that is either incompatible with other systems or outdated soon. You should also keep track of pending standards or suggested standards in case they actually get implemented.

Hopefully, the IT/IS department knows what technology hardware exists in the company, but they also are the people who should determine what needs to get purchased. This also applies to the software. One important thing that the IT/IS department should do is to help determine what must be obtained and what would be "nice to have." Here again, each department knows its job best. However, the IT/IS department can demonstrate the advantages and disadvantages of the technology.

One responsibility of the technical staff that I often see ignored is training. You shouldn't use the "sink-or-swim" philosophy by throwing new technology at your users and expect them to use it efficiently. One company I work in had people using their word processing program to do spreadsheet calculations and were keeping a database in their spreadsheet. This was the fault of the MIS department for not teaching them how to use the technology.

Your technical people won't necessarily write up the HTML code any more than they will write up orders using the word processor. However, they are responsible to train the people who do use it. Define someone who is responsible for the training and the training materials. However, creating the interface between the on-line ordering system and the database would be something your technical staff would be responsible for.

The marketing department is responsible for developing the overall marketing strategy and managing the marketing programs. In general, they would also be responsible for the overall design of the *Internet* Web site. They might decide what image of the company they want to present. This probably includes actually writing the text that will appear on many of the pages. Since market research is part of their responsibility, they will need to work closely with the technical staff to decide what questions are asked in the surveys and how the information is to be stored and processed.

You need to ensure that the information that is made available to customers is also made available to employees. If you provide customers with technical information on your products that employees cannot access, your employees run into trouble when trying to answer questions from customers. Since the marketing department needs to design the information for the customers, they should also be involved in the development of the intranet.

Depending on your organization, this may also include sales. Customer service helps define what services can/should be provided via the Internet to your customers. This might include tech support. If so, customer service might help define how the support will be handled, what levels of support are offered, and so on. Once again, information available to the customers should also be available on the intranet.

Sales needs to define what information should be monitored to aid in the sales efforts. Since your sales force knows the kind of questions that customers ask prior to making a purchase, this kind of information can be made available on the Web.

Webmaster

If you surf the Web, you will often see a "Webmaster" link. The Webmaster is the person who has overall responsibility for the Web. When you click on the link, you can send email to the Webmaster. Just like a postmaster, a Webmaster does not need to be a real user, but someone should monitor the account for incoming messages. Within your intranet, this could be the person responsible for the specific page and not the intranet as a whole. On the other hand, it might be easier to have an "intranet coordinator" who determines the central contact for all issues regarding the intranet.

Part of the aspect of ownership is who provides the information. Some companies will say that since the IT is organizing it, they are responsible for providing all of the information. However, remember, as I mentioned before, only the people actually doing the work know what information they need. Therefore, at the very least, they should provide the information to the IT. Maybe it is the IT that puts it into the correct format. However, the individual departments must provide the information.

Depending on the size of your organization, you could make a person in each department responsible for their own content. This may not require giving each department its own server, but it does require giving full control of at least one directory to this person. This person is required to follow the company standards, but maintaining and managing their part of the intranet is their job. This takes a lot of the burden off of the central IT and helps ensure that the correct information is provided.

Developing Your Intranet

The very first thing to do before you start configuring your intranet is to establish your goals. You need to specify what you want to accomplish. Remember that these goals, like any business goals, need to be realistic. What kind of information do you want to provide? Who should have access to what information? You may spend days getting the right combination of fonts and colors for a magazine ad, why should you spend less time on your intranet?

It is only after you develop the groundwork for your intranet, such as what information you want to provide and what departments are responsible for what information, do you being to design the actual layout.

The development of your intranet needs to be looked at from two different perspectives: the technology and the application. Part of the technological aspect can be thought of simply as the communication, that is, how the information gets from one place to another. The geographical separation between servers, users, and different offices plays a key role in how you develop your intranet. For example, if all of your users are within a single building, all connected the Ethernet, you are less concerned with bandwidth than if you have a number of remote offices connected from a dial-up line. This might force you to be more concerned with bandwidth issues, as you are not going to get the same performance.

Perhaps the simplest solution to this problem is to create multiple intranet servers. That is, in each location to which you have limited bandwidth you can set out a new server. Content can then be replicated in order to ensure that the information is as current as possible.

The larger the company, the greater the likelihood that you are going to have individual servers for each department. It is also possible that you'll have individual workgroup servers. This helps to spread below the across multiple machines in terms of both computer performance and administrative effort. In companies that have a decentralized IT organization, this is extremely effective in keeping any one department from becoming overburdened.

One thing I need to warn you about is the necessity of maintaining standards, even if the server is maintained by different departments. First, it makes long-term administration much easier. The an administrator from one department can easily administer the server from a different department. Second, maintaining a common structure allows you to more easily integrate the two servers.

Remember, this is a web, not a tree. You have to learn to stop thinking hierarchically. If you come from a DOS or Windows environment, this is often difficult. Other examples of links would be product literature that can point to both sales and the technical manuals. Technical manuals can point back to both of them and also to tech support. The concept of links applies to links to files and directories on a file system as well as links on a Web page. Both work best if they are a web, not a tree.

Also, it is important too that during the planning stage you organize and manage what links you will have. In other words, you should design the way the different components fit together during the planning rather than simply have the structure develop dynamically. Map out where the links are coming from and where they are going.

You should also keep a written record of it. This helps later when updating the site. Some Web development products will keep track of your links and report if any are missing, even if you have pages that no others link to.

Building an intranet is a bit different from building an Internet site in terms of how soon you can go "live." Normally you should wait until you have a fairly complete site before you go onto the Internet. However, you can start up your intranet piece by piece. In any event, I would recommend that the information you provide at the beginning be useful. You could provide with very little effort a company phone directory, the menu for the cantina, a list of upcoming events in the company, and maybe a list of job openings. All of this is useful information, and it does not take a long time to develop.

On the other hand, I would really recommend waiting until you have much more designed and developed. One option is to have servers in each department, and the department decides when its Web is ready to be accessed by others.

Understanding your users has several aspects. The first is how they will access information and use the intranet. If they are hungry for information, they might end up using the intranet more than expected. This could overload the bandwidth of your network or your server. If you are unable to improve the performance of either the network or server, you need to reduce the amount of information that is downloaded. This means fewer graphics, for example.

Another issue is how many people will be accessing each page. General company information will be accessed by everyone. However, this does not mean that they will be accessing it every day. On the other hand, there may be some information that is accessed by a larger number of people at the same time.

You also need to consider the experience your users have with the concepts of an intranet. There may be people in your company that have never been on the Internet. There are also people who are old hats at it. The more people with Internet experience, the more complicated you can make your intranet. You can develop a group of users who can help the less-experienced users.

Also, if the users have a lot of on-line experience, they are used to having to wait for things to download from the Internet. Since your intranet will probably be faster than the Internet, you *could* have more graphics and even multimedia. However, this needs to be weighed against the bandwidth of the network.

What if your users are used to having all of their data on the local hard disk? If so, even the time waiting to load something across an intranet will be slow by comparison. This also needs to be considered in deciding what kind of information can be presented. In general, consider both the experience of your users as well as the current network.

Establish Ownership

Ownership with regard to a Web site has two aspects: First, you need to establish who in your company has the overall say as to the way the site is designed. What information is presented? Marketing? MIS? Management? This decision must be made by your company. Not me. I say keep MIS out of it. I will tell you what technology is available, but it is up to the individual departments or management to decide how to use it.

In your company different people could decide different things. Maybe company management decides the overall format as this more or less defines the company image. Marketing and sales then determine the content. You want a single format/style throughout your intranet. Maybe the page background for tech support is different from that of sales. However, the "feel" needs to be the same. Navigation needs to be the same, so sales decides that MIS should create a "toolbar" that works on every page, for example.

Grouping the information according to its scope or who is responsible to create it is a good way of building the framework for the security that you want to implement. For example, by defining a data object as "belonging" to the human resources department (that is, *not* interdepartmental), you can limit access to just members of the personnel department. File system permissions can be set to limit access to larger files and you can also set up permissions on your Web pages.

This is one place where Netscape's FastTrack Server can also be useful. In addition to the wide range of security options, the FastTrack Server allows you to create *virtual* domains. In essence, a virtual domain is where several domains all exist on the same server. These could be different domains within the same company or domains for completely different entities. For an intranet, this would mean that you could have a separate virtual domain for each department. The would simplify the administration since the FastTrack Server allows you to configure each virtual domain individually. You no longer need to keep track of what directories are accessed by what department. Instead, you can keep track of the individual servers.

For example, assume there were servers for three departments named www.finance.jimmo.com, www.sales.jimmo.com, and www.hr.jimmo.com. We might then assume that the finance and HR servers were sensitive and that a high-level of security was required. It might be that the finance server is accessible only by members of the finance department, but there is *some* information on the HR server that should be accessible by everyone. The directories containing that information could then be made secure.

Determining who will access the information helps you make two kinds of decisions. First, you know how to present it. For example, a problem solution database that will be accessed by everyone needs to be more detailed than one accessed by your IT department. If just for the IT department, it probably needs to be less interactive, as the specialists probably need just a quick reference.

Content ownership doesn't have to be for the whole site. You could/should have different branches with different ownership. One branch we had was for the technical documentation. We had the entire set of technical documents for all of our products on-line. This was the responsibility of our technical publications (Techpubs) department, not MIS or marketing. However, the branches on company history and "What's New" were the responsibility of marketing.

When you are defining the content ownership, you also need to define what the procedures are. You have defined a standard for content and image; you must also define a standard for procedures. Should everyone/anyone have the right to simply overwrite a page with a newer version? Can you be sure that they checked to ensure all the links are correct? Is it better to have an inbox where pages are placed and one person-department responsible to put them where they belong?

We now get to the aspect of "legal ownership." This is especially important when you outsource the creation of your pages. If you pay someone to create a program for you, you should have the rights to the source code as well as the finish product. The same applies to an Internet Web site or your Intranet. If you pay someone to develop the pages, then everything about them should be yours. I have seen Web pages where the "responsibility" for the content belonged to the company for whom the site was developed, but the advertising agency had the copyright on the pages.

Think about consultants. I have seen sites for companies that are very impressive and contain a lot of information. However, the copyright is held by the designer! If you pay for it, you should keep the copyright. This is extremely important if you put up company information such as technical data. One could imagine a persuasive lawyer telling a jury that the Web page says the information is copyrighted by the consultant, and because the company didn't object for three months, it actually is the property of the consultant. Even if the lawyer isn't persuasive enough, you will spend lots of money defending your rights to your own property. You must make it clear from the beginning! Therefore, each page should have a statement saying that you have the copyright. For more details on all this, see the section on consultants.

Standards

As we discussed in the last chapter, one of the first and most significant problems that you're going to encounter is the different formats you have spread throughout your company. This time we're going to expand our definition so that format not only refers to the format of the data, such as MS Word, HTML, RTF, and so forth, but also how the data are stored physically. For example, data on your file system are stored in a different format than data in a database are.

The fact that you have different data set formats increases the difficulty you could have in both accessing and exchanging the data. The more different formats you have, the more difficult it is to access the information you need. One primary reason for this is what I refer to as "media switches." Not only is there time lost in making this switch to the different format; there will also be a certain loss of efficiency, because these two media are not accessed the same way. For example, you might have customer information stored within your company database (e.g., SAP), but when the customer calls with a technical problem you first look in the database for the product they have, then look in some hard copy manuals for the technical specifications on that product.

Another issue is the fact that different media types are likely to have different states. For example, hard copy tends to be more outdated than information you have on-line. Information that has been written to a CD-ROM, for example, is often even more out-of-date. Finally, information that is obtained from outside your company, such as your customers, or sent to printers for inclusion in a brochure, is the most out-of-date of all. Therefore, one of the key goals in any intranet project is ensuring that the information is as up-to-date as possible.

One thing I developed for one company was a style guide. Here, I defined not only what elements should be common on each page but also defined some of the content. For example, part of what we made available on-line to employees were solutions to common computer problems. The information that was required included who this problem affected (user, administrators, just people in the production halls), what area this problem affected (network printers LaserJet), and who was responsible for the page (i.e., if errors were found or the procedure changed). This ensured us that pages would not be orphaned and end up out-of-date.

Here, too, we defined what standards we would use on our Web site. At the time, HTML 3.0 was not yet finalized, so we decided to use elements available only in HTML 2.0 to ensure that most of the visitors could use the pages. When 3.2 was finalized, we switched the standard. When HTML 4.0 came out, we started using the new features it provided.

One thing we were careful with was browser independence. When we first started the intranet, we had several branch offices that were using Internet Explorer (IE) 3.0, although the headquarters and most of the other offices already had IE 4.0. We were therefore careful to use only those elements supported by IE 3.0 on the pages that were used by other offices. However, there were many pages that used the more advanced features.

Despite the fact that you will be providing information from a wider range of sources, your *primary* file format on your intranet will most likely be HTML. Web development tools such as Adobe PageMaker allow you to create very complicated pages without the needed to understand anything about HTML. For me, this is like driving the car without knowing how it works. Many people do it, but they run into trouble if things do not work exactly as they expected. Even if the development tool you select does exactly what you expect, I have often found that when subtle changes are needed to be made, they can only be done by editing the HTML code directly. Therefore, it might be worthwhile to become familiar with HTML.

Newer versions of the more popular Web browsers are capable of displaying MS Word and MS Excel documents directly in the browser. Although you can define the standard browser on your intranet, this is not always possible for the extranet and not at all possible for the Internet. Therefore, the information that you make available must be in some common format. Obviously, if the person accessing the data has a Web browser, he or she can read HTML. This makes HTML a good choice for distributing information outside of your organization. However, it does have limitations in terms of exactly how that information is presented.

If you were to provide information as an MS Word or WordPerfect document, you have much better control over the appearance than simply using HTML. However, this requires that the user also have MS Word or WordPerfect. The solution is to put the information into a format that is accessible no matter what word processing program the user might have. This does not means storing the data as a text file or RTF but rather something along the lines of the Adobe portable document format (PDF).

Push Versus Pull

The old method of distributing information (push) can also be thought of as "information just in case." That is information that is often sent to people "just in case" they might need it. This is the reason my manager in one company had over 1000 mail messages in his inbox and 800 of them were unread. There were so many people in the company that sent him messages "just in case." Unfortunately, what happens in many cases, and happens in a lot of companies, is that among the unread messages was some important information. Like so many managers, mine suffered from "information overload."

As we discussed, the solution is simply the "pull" method of distributing information. This is also referred to as "information on demand." The user goes out and gets the information as he or she needs it and not when it is pushed into his or her mailbox.

Another key benefit of the switch from push to pull is the time saved in distributing the information. I know so many companies that will print out different documents even though it is available online and distribut it to hundreds of people. You waste time printing the document. You waste time distributing the document. You waste the paper necessary for those hundreds of copies, plus, there is always the chance that you will forget someone.

During the course of one intranet project, I came to the realization that the push method was important in certain contexts. In general, information that applies to everyone in the company or everyone within the department "could" be pushed. However, this is not "just-in-case" information, but rather information that everyone should or must have. In our case, we had changes to the components of products that we sold. That it is, a product consisted of 10–20 different pieces. It might happen that our engineering department decided that the maintenance set for a particular machine would have 12 O-rings instead of just 10. This information had to be made available, not only to the people bundling the packages, but also to the salespeople who needed to know exactly what they were selling.

It was decided that this information was so important that was not just enough to expect people to go look for it. Instead, they were informed of the change. However, we realized it was not necessary to inform them of the details of the change but simply that a change occurred. Therefore, any time a change was made in one of the packages, all of our sales personnel got an email message informing them they needed to look at specific pages on the intranet. One suggestion was to announce all of the changes on a specific page. However, this required that each user look at that page at regular intervals. It was common that our outside sales force would not look on the intranet for days at a time. However, they would read their email daily. When they got the message, they would then look for the appropriate information on the intranet.

As with the intranet as a whole, this switch from the push to pull method of information exchange brings with it a couple of changes in the processes within a company. In one company where I worked, a common excuse was "No one told me about it." Often, other people in the company considered the information "common knowledge." However, there was never a message on the bulletin board, and no one sent out any such message. Therefore, people could claim that they didn't know. In this case, " blame" was put on the person responsible for informing them.

With the introduction of the intranet, the users become responsible for getting the information themselves. If the information is readily available on the intranet, there is no longer the excuse "I didn't know about it." The "information-on-demand" paradigm as well as the intranet as a whole will only become successful once the company has changed its attitude from blame to responsibility.

Security

The problems that you encounter with an intranet may not be on the same scale as for an Internet site, but the principles are the same. One issue that many of my colleagues overlook is security. Although the danger of malicious acts is hopefully low, there is always the danger of the curious employee getting hold of information that they shouldn't. (Come on, wouldn't you like to know what the company president earns?)

One thing to keep in mind is that you already have a situation that leads to the most security problems: physical access to the system. Once a hacker is on the system, further attacks are much easier. On the other hand, these are your employees and *should* be trusted. Perhaps you should consider more monitoring than more security. One employee getting fired because they tried to get access to information they shouldn't is a good deterrent for the others.

Windows NT comes with built-in security features that you can use to restrict access. Even when you provide information via Web pages, you may want to restrict access to specific pages. Even if you do not implement the advanced security features like encryption or certificates available with a commercial server like the Netscape Enterprise Server, you can provide an effective security system.

Normally, even if everyone in your company has access to some information on the intranet, there will be some areas that need to be restricted. This restriction can be accomplished in many different ways, depending on what program is used to access the information. If the information is in data files, you can use the normal file permissions to limit access.

Because you have already classified your information, it is much easier to decide what restrictions are necessary. In general, each specific type of information will be accessed by one group with one application.

Another reason for restricting access is the physical location as well as the method used to access the information. A salesman in one company wanted a remote connection to the server to be able to download information when he was at a customer's office. This is a reasonable request; however, the information he wanted was that famous 30-MB PowerPoint presentation! On the other hand, this PowerPoint presentation should be made available to others within the company.

The structure of your intranet is dependent on your organization. If your company operates where all the information comes from the top and each person simply follows instructions, then your intranet should be built in a similar way. That is, you should have a centralized intranet. If you are organized into workgroups that work semi-independently, you should have a more spread-out intranet.

One thing you need to consider when providing information to remote locations is the security of that connection. Many of you have a leased line, whereby you have a 24-hour connection between the two offices; you should still consider how secure that connection is. Remember that any system is only as strong as its weakest component. In your security system that weakest component could be the connection you have to your branch offices. Although your local phone company, oral or whoever it is that is providing into connection, usually guarantees you the certain amount of security, you need to weigh the risk against the likelihood of compromise.

When transferring data across the Internet, the problem becomes much more acute. Once the data leave your office, you essentially have no way of controlling where they go before they get to their final destination. Although you can follow the path of your packets using the trace route command, you personally have little or no control over the route. You have no way of knowing who has access to the intermediate nodes. It is entirely possible that your competition has bribed some technician at one of the intermediary locations to give him access to your transmissions. This means he has complete access to all the data being exchanged between two offices.

The solution to this problem is what is referred to as a Virtual Private Network (VPN). The key to a VPN is that in contrast to a really private network across a leased line, a VPN runs across the Internet. It is a virtual network in the sense that it does not really exist as a separate network. It is private in that no outsiders can communicate with the machines on the VPN. The security on the VPN is accomplished by what is referred to as "tunneling."

Creating Your Pages

Another aspect that is often overlooked is a change in the creation process. Logically, if information will no longer be provided in MS Word documents, for example, but rather as HTML pages, your users are going to require training on how to create the Web pages. Also, if each department will be responsible for administering their own labs or servers, someone within the department will need to be trained on how to do this.

Even the process of creating the information will need to be changed. When using the push method, oftentimes the information is formatted in such a way as to facilitate the distribution. For example, in one company, the boss's secretary spent a great deal of time and effort ensuring that the company telephone book was in nice neat columns, because it was going to be printed out and distributed to everyone in the company. Each time new employees joined the company or someone left, the phone book had to be reworked to ensure that it was organized properly by department and that there were no orphan entries (for example, the last entry from one department was alone at the top of the next page).

••••••••••••••••

The reason that this had to be done (other than that the boss wanted it) was that people were keyed on the distribution of the information and not on its contents. For most people, half of the company phone book was wasted space. For example, people in the paint shop never called the sales or export departments. Even if people in a specific department called people in another, they usually had specific contacts, so they needed to know one or two phone numbers out of maybe 20. With the introduction of an online phone book, they still had access to every phone number and every person in company. However, they could search specifically for the entry they needed. No one had to worry about the format, because once it was programmed on the Web, the format came out right every time.

An obvious side effect of this was that the secretary no longer needed to spend time formatting and distributing the information. Instead, she was concerned with the content of the information.

Also keep in mind that information is useless if you can't find it. Along the same lines, an intranet that provides all of the company information is worthless if people can't find that information. You need to make it easy for them.

There are several ways to make accessing the information easy. The simplest way is a menu system You don't need any special graphics, just a few lines of text with the appropriate links. Menus are perhaps the most common way of navigating through an intranet. This is incredibly easy to create just by using links to new pages. In fact, if you have a list of key parts of your site, you can create a menu simply by turning them into links.

There are a couple of menu types that you can use. If you use just a top-level menu, then each entry points to just a few key pages. If you have top- and middle-level menus, each key area has its own menu pointing to pages that are even more detailed. You could expand this even further so that there is a menu at every level.

One nice modification that you can make is to turn your menu into a "toolbar." This can then be put on every page to make navigation through the site very easy. The simplest way is to have small images as your hot spots. The problem with this is the way the images might look with different viewers or different resolutions. For example, you might develop them to appear in a straight line across the top of the screen. If you suddenly have a lower resolution, the images get spread across multiple lines.

Another nice effect is to create a single image that looks like the toolbar. You also have to be careful about different resolutions, but you don't have to worry about images getting split up. Each part of the image is a link to a different page. The way this is accomplished is by using the image maps

There are a couple of ways to do toolbars just like menus. You can have a single toolbar that is the same on every page, such as:

Company—Personnel—Technical—Customer Server—What's New

or you could have different ones on different pages. One way is like many companies do, where one of the buttons is "disabled." This is the button for the page that you are currently viewing. This is accomplished by having a different graphic for the button that is "disabled."

In one company, we used frames. The left-hand frame was a menu that changed depending on what page was being viewed. The menu "folded out" like Windows Explorer as you went deeper into the intranet. This gave you an immediate reference as to where in the intranet you were.

Another way is instead of a menus expanding out, you have the toolbar. For example, on the homepage:

Company—Personnel—Technical—Customer Server—What's New

On the Personnel page you have:

Personnel Actions—Current Openings—Cantina Menu

On the Personnel Actions page you have:

Vacation Request—Pay Inquiry—Insurance Claims

Another alternative is to have a toolbar at the top of page related to the page you are currently on, such as our example above. At the bottom of each page is a toolbar that's the same on each page (i.e., a table of contents). Or you could have the opposite, where the table of contents is on the top and the specific toolbar is on the bottom.

In one company we created pages consisting of three frames. The top frame was a toolbar that was the same for every page in the company. For example, there was a link to the company's telephone directory, calendar of events, news, and so forth

On the left was a menu that changed depending on the page you were viewing. For example, if you were on the HR department's homepage, the menu would contain the key areas within the HR department. One menu entry might be labeled "Benefits." Clicking brings you to a page where the menu lists all of the various benefits. Clicking one of this entries brings you to the page describing that particular benefit.

Your pages should be designed to look good on *all* of the monitors you have in the company. I have seen cases where the people developing the pages have nice 20″ monitors. However, many of the end users had 17″ or even 15″ monitors. The result was that the pages looked good for the developers but were useless for the end users.

One of the problems that occurs is that fonts often are too small. On a 20″ monitor, they fine, but not on a 17." Also, a problem is the amount of information on the screen. If you have to scroll more than once or twice, the page is too large. However, on a 20″ monitor, you can get more information before you have to scroll. The developer scrolls once, but the end user scrolls three or four times.

You should also check to see how the pages look and if they work correctly in both Netscape Navigator and IE. Both have their own editions of the HTML standard, which may make the look odd if displayed in the other browser. Note also that Microsoft has its own version of JavaScript, called JScript. JavaScript was developed by Netscape, which therefore set the standard. However, Microsoft made changes to JScript, which made it nonstandard and therefore presents compatibility problems.

Although you can standardize on one browser internally, you do not lose much, if you forego the features that are only available in one or the other browser. Thus, intranet pages can be provided on the Internet with no conversion.

An index on your Web site works the same as an index in a book. If you don't know the exact location of the information you need, you can search for it using specific words or phrases. A full-text search works in a similar way, but an index is something that is not generated dynamically. Therefore, it may not catch pages that have been added in the last couple of hours or so.

If you build an index, which is then made available to your visitors, you don't have to watch for things like capitalization, tense, singular/plural, and so on. You decide what entries will be made available. However, this does not take full advantage of what the system can provide you. Indices can be created dynamically with a perl script in which you search for the text that the user inputs. If a page is found containing this information, you can dynamically create a Web page that points to this information. How complex you want to get is entirely up to you. The advantage is that whenever a new page is added, you don't need to change the index.

Another advantage is from the visitor's point of view. A site with a dynamic index is an active site. The site is reacting for input from the visitor and doesn't just sit there. The visitor has control over what the site does.

If you do decide to use a dynamic search, I suggest including a list of words to ignore. These are words that will more than likely appear on every page. These shouldn't be searched for. Examples of such words are: *is, are, and, the, or, not.*

Although it makes programming more complicated, consider having a radio button that switches between Boolean AND and OR. There are some sites that have very complicated search mechanisms, such as "*a* AND *b* NOT *c*."

Another way of improving the user friendliness is to parse the input and specifically look for *and, or,* and *not.* This allows the user to input somewhat complicated statements. However, it does require a little bit of programming on your part.

Fortunately, you do not need to do all of the work yourself. Products like Netscape Catalog Server can create the index for you.

Web Development Tools

There was a time not too long ago when a Web master's primary tools were a simple text editor and a Web browser to view the pages he or she had just created. Times have changed. There is a wide range of programs to help you create exciting Web pages with fantastic graphics. Even the process of creating the simplest of pages is as simple as point-and-click and drag-and-drop.

However, effectively managing a Web site is more than just creating good-looking pages. The keyword here is "manage." With a handful of pages, you might be able to manage them simply by using Windows Explorer and movingthe files around to where you need them. When you start getting into hundreds or even just dozens of pages, you need something that can take over some of the administrative tasks for you. Fortunately, there are several very good products designed to do just that.

To be honest, it is unfair to look at these products simply in terms of how well they manage your pages or let you edit HTML code. Instead, it would be far better to think of these products as "development environments." Not only can you manage the organization of your Web site, you can also design your pages using the same interface.

As with any product type, there is a difference in what features are provided and even how they implement the features they share. Despite this, there is a set of features that any package should provide, and without them you should look elsewhere.

One common feature is the ability to publish your pages onto a different machine. Here, pages are developed on one machine and then copied by the software to the server that actually makes them available to everyone else. Although this functionality is extremely useful when your development machines are not physically connected to your Web server (e.g., in cases where the Web server is provided by another company), it still has its advantages for the company intranet.

Although it seems to be an almost universal feature, take a look to see to what extent you can configure the default appearance and other characteristics of your pages. Any development environment you select should allow you to the define the default color for the text, background, and the links. Note that the user could force the browser to display these things in different colors. However, you should be able to define the default.

In many cases, you want to have a specific background image on each page. Therefore, you should check to see whether this is configurable or not. That is, can you make the change once and have it immediately valid for all pages.

Another, almost mundane, point is the ability to the far in the default file extension to use when saving your Web pages. By convention, Windows machines use .htm, whereas Unix machines use .html. If you already have Unix servers or decide you need the extra performance, it may be simpler to use the Unix convention.

Another reason why you might want to define the extension as being .html is if you are using other tools to develop as well. Many programs, such as MS Word, allow you to save files in HTML format. The default extension used by MS Word is .html, even though the default extension used by MS FrontPage is .htm. Although this might seem too trivial an issue to concern yourself with, I feel that it reduces the amount of administrative work if you maintain a common naming scheme.

Check to see how well the product deals with more complex Web page elements, such as forms, tables, and frames. Most of the development tools can create these elements in preview mode (as compared to HTML mode). However, there is a great deal of difference in terms of how easy it is to edit or change the existing elements. In some cases, I've founded easier to directly edit the HTML code rather than using the built-in functions. This is fine for me, because I am fairly familiar with HTML. However, if you are not familiar with it, this becomes a burden.

Take a good look at how well the product allows you to edit form elements. You should not only be able to create the elements, but you should also be able to name each element and set values. One of the most difficult elements to get right is the selection list. Here, you have a number of options that appear in a pop-up menu. The biggest question to ask yourself is whether or not you can edit the list directly. Some programs allow you to edit the list on screen in the form. Others require that you call out a special function of the editor. One program I found actually allows you to do it either way. Of course, you can always edit the HTML code directly. All are valid possibilities and are useful depending on your preference.

If you are creating a table, it is useful if you can specify the size of the table when it is created. This can be done either by importing the rows and columns into a pop-up window or by clicking on the button in the toolbar and dragging the mouse until you get the correct size. This is the same way most word processing programs allow you to create tables. However, I have seen some programs where you simply get a default size (e.g., 2 x 2), and you need to add rows or columns later on. How easily you can change the size later on is another important issue.

Also, check to see how well the program behaves with tables within tables. It should be fairly straightforward to put cell and insert a new table. However, I have seen some programs that end up becoming completely confusing.

I feel this is an important issue because I often use tables to maintain a consistent layout for my forms. There is nothing in the HTML specification that says you cannot have a table within a form or a form within a table (although FrontPage does its best to stop you). There have been cases where I wanted multiple forms within a single table. Not every product allows you to do this. Although you could use a standard text edit to "force" the correct behavior, this is not the point of having a graphical user interface (GUI) editor. Therefore, if you want to use a GUI, look to see how well it does what *you* want.

I've noticed a difference in behavior in terms of how programs react when formatting several elements at once. In my opinion, the program should not make any assumptions about what you had intended but should format the way you tell it. For example, if you mark a bullet list and change the text to bold, the program should start bold at the top of the text and iend it at the bottom of the text. Some programs end up formatting each element individually. Therefore, when you add a new line, it ends up with the default format and not the boldface you wanted.

Paired with this is how the program reacts to mistakes in the HTML code. Sometimes I am much quicker editing the HTML code directly. On occasion, I have forgotten closing quotes or a greater-than (>) to close off a tag, and when I saved the file, FrontPage decided for me what should be done. The result was everything after the missing character was treated just the opposite of the way it should be. For example, everything that was inside of quotes was now considered part of the tags or text, the greater-than and less-than symbols were replaced by their HTML equivalents (> = > < = <). The worst part of this was that the undo button did not work, and since I just saved the file, all of these *forced* changes were in the saved file!!! In many cases, it was much easier to start from scratch rather than trying to fix the damage. Shortcomings like this can really increase the total cost of ownership for this product if you have to spend hours repeating work.

Another required feature is the ability of the program to manage links between pages. This functionality actually consists of three parts. First, the program must be able to show you some graphic representation of the links on your site. Getting a list of all the pages on the site, such as what you might get using Windows Explorer, is very useful. However, you need to be able to see the relationship between the pages on your site. This is extremely useful in analyzing the different ways a visitor navigates through your site.

Keep in mind that great many thought processes are not linear. That is, they do not always flow from one concept to the next. This is what brainstorming is all about. You basically let your mind flow.

Another important aspect is that people tend to think in a different order, with different thoughts branching off from a single idea. As a result, there are often many paths to reach a single idea or solution. This is how the Internet works. How often have you started off looking for information on one specific topic and have ended up somewhere completely different. It is quite likely that someone else had a different starting point but still ended up at the same page you did.

In essence, this is how an intranet should work as well. There are many paths to the same page. For example, let's assume you want to find the document describing how to troubleshoot printer problems. One user might start off on the hardware page, moving to the printer page, and finally to the page with troubleshooting tips for printers. Another user might start off on the help desk page, moving to the troubleshooting page and finally to the page listing troubleshooting tips for printers. Both of these users ended up at the same page, although they took separate paths to get there.

If your Web site development software provides a graphical look at how your pages are linked together, it is easy to see if you overlooked any one of these paths. In addition, this functionality is also useful for finding pages that are not accessed from anywhere else or for finding pages that point to the wrong place.

The next thing you should look at is the software's ability to verify links. This is especially useful if you have links to other sites. When you verify these links, the software checks to see if all of these resources are accessible. It is also owned important that the software or report the status code return by the remote system. For example, it is important to know whether the remote you are on is simply not found, there is a permission problem, or any one of the various messages possible.

It is also important to see what the software does when you move a page. When you move a page, you do not want to deal with the hassle of making sure all of the links are changed accordingly. Instead, this is something you should expect the software to do for you. However, you should check to make sure this is not done automatically, but rather you are given the option whether this action should be carried out.

When selecting your tools, there are a number of criteria that you need to consider. Features and functionality are just a part of it. However, there are several basic concepts that you need to look at.

For both Internet and intranet applications, one of the key aspects is the speed at which applications can be developed as well as modified. The software market still allows companies like Microsoft to deliver products two years or longer after they are first announced. However, because of the ever-changing environment of the Internet and an intranet, companies cannot wait that long.

This is where rapid application development comes into play. Developers do not want to nor do they need to spend the time reinventing the wheel. That is, there are a great many functions that are common to many different applications, and with minor modifications, code from one application can be moved to another.

Being able to develop applications more quickly, developers become more productive. Rather than spending all the time on mundane things like designing the user interface, they can spend their time expanding the functionality of the program. This rapid development often comes from programs with an integrated development environment (IDE), visual interfaces to the code, the ability to modularize the code (reuse code segments), and the ability to program with little programming experience (e.g., with server-based scripting). All of these speed up the development process, making the developer more productive.

Performance of the application is also another important factor. Even if the application can be developed quickly, it does little good if it takes longer to access needed information than it did with previous methods. Performance can be increased with the right programming techniques, but relatively speaking, most of the performance increase comes from the server. Not only is the hardware an important issue but also how well the server is configured.

For example, caching frequently used pages or load sharing across multiple servers are two common ways the server software affects performance.

Paired with performance is reliability. A down server on your intranet may just mean annoyed users. However, if the users have grown accustomed to using the intranet to access information, they may have trouble returning to their old methods (if they can do it at all). A nonfunctioning Internet site is tantamount to a "Closed" sign on your front door. If pages are defective (i.e., they contain dead-end links), users may think your products are defective as well. A good Web development package or server needs to ensure that the site remains up and is not "broken."

Next is the issue of scalability. This week the intranet server might be providing pages for just the sales department, but next week it's the whole company. Although this kind of growth can be planned for, you have less control over what happens on theInternet. You might suddenly have a tenfold increase in the number of visitors. So, the question arises of whether the products you have selected can provide that level of service.

Pair with scalability is extensibility. That is how you can expand the system to meet different needs. This is not an issue of meeting more of the *same* needs but rather *different* needs. How can you change or adapt the system to address issues that come up as the system develops? Users may want a different way of accessing information or have it presented in different formats depending on what options they choose. Managers want integration of information from your old legacy systems. Can the product(s) you implement address these issues?

Then there is the issue of security. Hopefully, your managers are security conscious, so they will want to have security features. Unfortunately, it is not easy to simply transfer your existing security procedures to an intranet. The lines between what is private for specific departments and what can be shared becomes harder to define the more different sources you have. Even if all of your information is in one place (e.g., a database), you have to have mechanisms in place so that people do not gain inappropriate access to the system.

From the developers' standpoint, one of the key aspects is ease of use. Not only does the development environment (i.e., the actual development application) need to be efficient, but the method of accessing the information must be simple. For example, you might have an HTML editor that is extremely easy to use, but you need to code all of the script by hand that accesses your database.

One major exception to this is FrontPage. In typical Microsoft fashion, FrontPage saves configuration in its own format, which makes it incompatible with everything else. The result is that in many cases, pages developed with FrontPage often only work with the Microsoft server. Once you choose Front-Page, you are basically stuck with it, unless you want to rewrite all of your pages. My suggestion is you stick with an editor that can save the pages as normal ASCII, such as Adobe PageMill. This makes them usable on every version of Windows, UNIX and most every other operating system.

You might consider having two Web sites, especially if your intranet is linked to the Internet. That is, there are parts of the intranet that are also accessed from the Internet. One Web siteis for development, and the other is live. Changes are first made to the development Web site before they go live. Consider also using a revision control system (RCS) for your Web pages.

Most people I know who use RCS, use it for program source code management, but it can easily be used for HTML source as well. There are versions that run under Windows NT, such as the version from MKS as well as noncommercial versions.

Be sure to establish test procedures for your intranet. With test procedures coupled with the development procedures, you can easily avoid those problems when your site looks "broken." A broken Web site implies a broken product. One thing to consider is who is going to do the tests. Just like all the other aspects of your Web development, you have to define who is responsible for the testing and who does the actual testing.

You also need to decide what gets tested. What gets tested will depend on your company and your intranet. Most definitely you need to test all of the aspects of the site that you defined as being a requirement. For example, if you have decided that a toolbar is required on each page, is it? Do all the links work? You could create a perl script (part of the Windows NT Resource Kit) that searches through the pages for IMG SRC = entries, HREF = entries, and so forth and looks for the links and ensures they are there. If not, an error is displayed. However, there are some products out there that will test the integrity of your Web site for you.

You need to have someone (maybe several people) test every page and every link, at least for those parts going onto the Internet. I don't know how many times I have been annoyed by clicking on a link and getting an error message saying the link did not exist. Often the reason that the link does not exist is a simple spelling mistake. For example, all the pages on the Web site end in .html, but one ends in .htm. Changing the URL corrects the problem, but that should be the job of the developer. On the intranet, this is less critical, but still should be considered.

I also suggest you check the source for each page and look for spelling errors. Many HTML editors, such as Adobe PageMill, have built-in spell checkers. If you develop your pages in StarOffice or WordPerfect, they already have a built-in spell checker.

Test it and test it again. Test boundary conditions in your forms (0,1, and infinity). Can you move freely and easily? Do the links bring you where you expect and then back again? Are the forms behaving correctly? What happens when someone puts in garbage? Have someone not involved in the development test it. Have marketing test the techpubs pages and techpubs test the marketing pages. Look for anything that is bothersome, cumbersome, or just plain annoying. If either department created something that bothers someone internally, you can bet that there are customers who will be bothered.

Adobe PageMill

PageMill is Adobe's easy-to-use contribution to the Web development market. For the most part, both the interface and the functionality are very intuitive, especially if you are new to Web development.

If you are used to working in directly with HTML code, PageMill takes awhile to get used to. This stems from the fact that I have become accustomed to marking text and in selecting the appropriate HTML tag from a list box. When I first began working with PageMill, I was taken aback by the fact the list box did not contain the HTML tags but rather a description of what that tag does. For example, there is no entry for a level-1 heading (<H1>). Instead, this is represented in the list box by the words "largest heading."

However, this makes perfect sense. Whether I'm a beginner or expert Web author, I am not really interested in what tag is used to make the largest heading. Instead, I want the ability to mark something and then format it as the largest heading. To then mark something as a level-2 heading (<H2>), I select "larger heading." This then applies to all of the other headings as well.

Figure 13–1 shows the PageMill workspace. In this view, we see three separate work areas. On the left is the site overview, which shows you the files and directories on your site, both with potential errors and files with links to other sites.

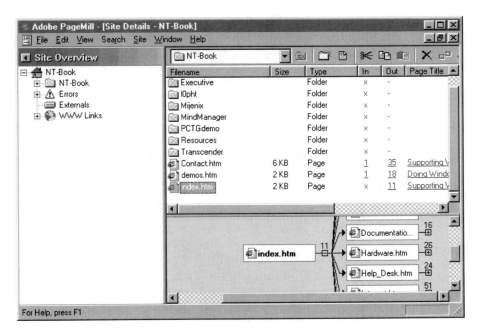

FIGURE 13–1   The Adobe PageMill workspace.

The right side of the work area is broken down into two windows. The top part shows you the site details. Here you can see the title of the page, the date it was last modified, as well as whether the file is referenced by another page or and has links to somewhere else. Not having links to other pages is not much of a problem. However, if a page is not referenced, the only way to access it is to explicitly input the URL. In essence, the site-detail window functions like Windows Explorer. That is, you can sort the files and directories using various criteria. For example, you can sort by modification date in order to see which files have been changed most recently.

Figure 13–2 shows you the details window in PageMill. When you click on a page, you see displayed in the lower half which pages to this foreign as well as the pages to which this one points. Immediately next to the page is a small square that may contain a plus sign. You click the plus sign to expand out the links. If the links are already expanded, there is a minus sign instead. You will also see a number there that indicates how many links there are to or from this page. By double-clicking any of these pages, it is immediately loaded into the editor.

PageMill gives you the ability to define specific programs to view both your Web pages and graphics that you might have included on the page. This is useful if you want to see how your page might look into different browser. You can configure PageMill to allow you to switch to any number of browsers. Although PageMill does have a built-in preview mode, it cannot display the same way every browser can. Loading the page directly into the

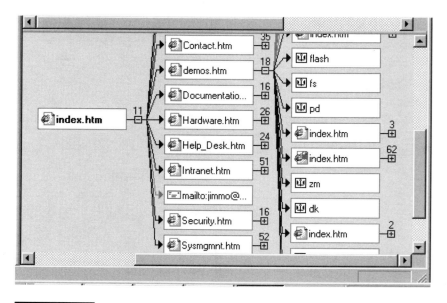

FIGURE 13-2   The Adobe PageMill Details window.

browser lets you see exactly how it will be displayed and not just some approximation.

If you are developing an intranet, then you are likely to have a number of pages that are linked to many others; for example, to the company's new page or menu in the cantina. Being able to quickly access any one of these links is a handy feature. PageMill addresses this issue in a couple of ways. First, it provides you with something it calls the "paste board." As its name implies, links are pasted onto the link board, which can then be quickly inserted into the page you are working on.

The next way to access the frequently used links is when they are stored in the Netscape Navigator bookmarks list or in the Microsoft IE favorites list. You can open up the Netscape bookmark.htm file or open up the "Organize Favorites" window in IE and then drag it onto the page you are currently editing. It is also possible to store the links on a single Web page, load this with PageMill, and drag them onto the page you are editing.

PageMill provides a useful tool called the attribute inspector." Not only can it "inspect" the elements on your page, it can change them as well. Using the attribute inspector, you can define characteristics of your page, such as the background color or background image, default text color, line colors, and so forth. In addition, if the page you are currently editing has form elements, the attribute inspector can configure these, including naming them and setting their values. If you have frames on your page, these can be configured from the attribute inspector as well.

Another useful feature is the ability to define aliases for your directories. This is extremely useful if you are developing on one machine, but the files are actually published on another machine. When editing, you want to see how the pages will appear, including graphics or other elements you insert. These may reside on a different drive in the local system, for example, when multiple developers need access to the same files. PageMill has no way of knowing where to look on the Web server for these files. Therefore, you can define an alias so that way when the files are uploaded, the paths are changed accordingly.

You can also load images or other objects directly into different applications. For example, you can configure PageMill to load GIFS or JPEG files into your favorite image processing software. I have Photoshop on my machine, which PageMill recognized during the installation and configured as the application I would switch to when I wanted to edit my graphics.

Sometimes when you are editing a Web page, it is useful to be able to edit graphics or other objects you're embedding in your page. PageMill allows you to do this in a couple different ways. First, you can drag the object onto the application you want to use to an added. Second, you can't explicitly configure PageMill to start specific applications. You then mark the object you wish to edit then select the appropriate application from the "switch to" menu.

As an added benefit, PageMill comes with the lite version of Adobe Photoshop. Although it does not have all of the features of the standard version, it is sufficient for many companies who simply need an easy-to-use tool to manipulate images. The most obvious thing it is missing is the ability to work with layers. This is a powerful feature, but it may not be worth the extra expense for sites with a limited scope.

Despite this fact, I use PageMill as my primary Web development tool. It does have one annoying weakness, and that is you cannot create templates like you can with most word processing programs. Although you can specify defaults for the pages, such as the background image or text color, you cannot specify any particular content. For example, in one company we used cascading style sheets as well as a JavaScript, which built up a frame set a single page.

To overcome this limitation, you can simply create a separate directory containing a number of files with the characteristics you need. You can then copy the files from this directory to where you need them and then edit the files accordingly.

Active-X and Java are two ways of making your Web pages behave more like applications. If you plan to use either one, you need to see to what extent they are supported by your development software. Although the software is not likely to prevent you from including either one, some products do not support them in bitter preview mode. This means you need the ability to load the page into a "real" browser.

HomeSite

HomeSite is a Web development product from Allaire, developers of Cold-Fusion (which we will get to shortly). This is a full-featured product that might actually be overwhelming to the uninitiated. Despite its easy-to-use interface, businesses that do little Web development and just publish simple, noninteractive pages might be better served with a less-powerful product. However, for the professional Web designer or larger companies that are actually building Web-based applications, HomeSite can be a very useful tool.

A key aspect of HomeSite is that it is not just intended for single developers. Instead, it fully group aware application. This includes the ability to create projects, on which several different people are working at any time. In addition to grouping the files together as a unit, a project is useful to make global changes, such as formatting or even terminology used on the page. In addition, entire projects and not just the individual pages can be exported to the Web server as a unit.

One important aspect of working in groups is ensuring that people don't step on each other's toes. That is, two people do not work on the same page at the same time and possibly undo each other's changes. This is one of the basic principles of source code control (SCC) or revision control. SCC is nothing new. It has been around for many years, used most commonly in programming environments. However, because of the need to maintain the same kind of control over other kinds of documents, SCC systems are in place in other areas. These are more likely referred to as RCSs. However, since HomeSite is used to work with HTML source code, the term SSC is used.

HomeSite is not provided with its own SCC system. Instead, it relies on the functionality of something like Microsoft's Visual Source Safe. HomeSite uses standard SCC commands to check out the files for editing, check in the files so others can use them, as well as view version information (e.g., date of the most recent version).

Figure 13–3 shows you the workspace of HomeSite. Like PageMill, this is a single application where you can see both the structure of the site and the pages in the same interface. At the top are the menus and toolbars common for each module of the program, along with the QuickBar, which contains buttons for both formatting and configuration. On the left side is the resources area with the site viewer, file list, and resources tab. On the right side is the editor, with tabs for all of the open documents at the bottom of the editor window.

Resources in the context of HomeSite require a little explanation. At the bottom left-hand side of the workspace are several tabs, which give you access to different resources. For example, your site is composed of directories and files, with a particular structure. These are resources and are viewed in the resources area of the HomeSite window. Projects are resources, and you can view project information here as well.

One annoying thing is that you are required to have a copy of MS Explorer 4.0 to view the files in *design* mode. Even if the pages do not contain

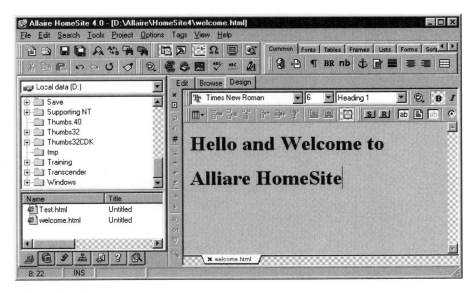

FIGURE 13–3   HomeSite workspace.

anything special that IE4.0 provides, you are still required to have a copy. Without it, you are forced to edit the HTML code by hand.

Color-coded editing is provided by the editor in the same fashion as otherIDEs, such as Borland's Delphi. Different elements have different colors, which help them stand out and are more easily identified. For example, context text is black and tags are blue.

After developing with a number of other products, I find that HomeSite is loaded with many tools and toys that make development much easier. One of the aspects that I found nifty was how HomeSite generates new pages. In may HTML editors, a new page is empty, that is, there are no tags in there are all. When HomeSite creates a new page, it provides the basics tags for you (<HTML>, <HEAD>, <TITLE>, and <BODY>). This helps ensure all of the elements are there and in the proper location.

Taking from other IDEs, HomeSite allows you to find the matching tag in tag pairs. This comes in handy in many different cases. For example, if you have a lot of objects within objects (tables within forms, tables within tables, etc.), being able to find the matching tag saves you the time of hunting back and forth through the page.

Another nifty thing is what HomeSite does with the on-line help. Instead of it being a separate application or having to start WinHelp, the HomeSite help pages are loaded directly into the application as if they were HTML documents stored as part of a project. In fact, that is exactly what they are. The help files are stored as a collection of HTML pages, with images, cascading style sheets, and everything else that is part of a Web site. It is also possible to display the help content in a separate frame of the HomeSite window. You can finally see the application and the help file at the same time!

Search and Replace has taken on a whole new feel with HomeSite. With most other Web development products you have the ability to search for specific strings. With HomeSite you can create fairly complex search and replacement patterns. This is because HomeSite uses the regular expression used in many UNIX tools.

HomeSite can save small code segments, called snippets. The basic premise is that there are portions of pages, scripts, and so forth that repeat from page to page (e.g., navigation bars). If enough code is repeated, it might be easier to copy the page and remove what you don't need. In other cases, you go looking for the page with the code you want and then cut and paste what you need. Instead, HomeSite saves these code segments and gives you immediate access to them from any page. Snippets can then be shared among all of the developers.

People rarely work in the exact same fashion as others. However, computer programs have traditionally been designed to work in a single manner. There are often slight differences in how people work that makes the behavior of certain programs a "problem" and not a "feature." To address this issue, more and more application programs are configurable. The most common way this shows itself is the ability to configure menus or toolbars.

Like many applications, such as WordPerfect, HomeSite allows you to configure the appearance and behavior of the application. For example, you can add buttons to existing toolbars or even create new ones. In addition, you can change the behavior of the keyboard, so different key combinations insert code or snippets, change formatting, and all of the other functionality available from menus and toolbars.

HomeSite has taken the configuration almost to the same level as the more-powerful word processing applications, such as WordPerfect. Using the Visual Tool Markup Language (VTML), which is also available in Alliare's ColdFusion Studio, you have the equivalent of a macro language.

The Tag Property inspector provides two useful functions. First, you can view the page in terms of the HTML structure, that is, you see where each of the different sections are (head, body) as well as all of the tags. Clicking on the tag moves the cursor to that location in the editor window and displays all the attributes that tag can use.

Take a look in Figure 13–4. Here, the cursor is sitting within the table data tag (<TD>). In the window at the lower left is a list of the attributes that you can use within the <TD> tag. Any attribute that already has a value (e.g., WIDTH and VALIGN) is already loaded with these values. If you insert a value into one of these attributes, the tag is changed accordingly in the editor window. Note also that the attributes are sorted by functionality and that there is a minus sign in front of each group. Clicking on the minus sign closes that section, just as it does in Windows Explorer. This is very useful if there are more attributes than will fit in the window and you only need access to a few of them.

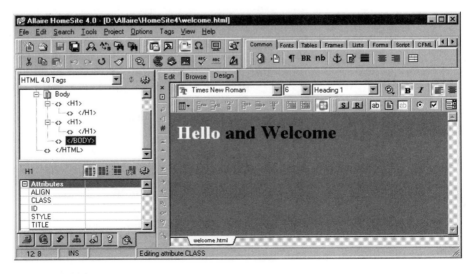

FIGURE 13–4   HomeSite Tag Inspector.

One advantage of HomeSite over other products like Microsoft Front-Page is that the program does not do things for you unless you tell it. For example, as I mentioned before, FrontPage will change the entire structure of your page if you make a mistake (e.g., leaving off a quote). This often results in the page becoming useless, and you either restore it from backups or start over. Instead, HomeSite will validate the page, displaying the mistakes it finds without making your page unusable.

Many products on the market have "wizards" that ask a series of questions and then perform some task (e.g., creating a new page) based on the input to the Wizard. HomeSite takes this one step further by allowing you to create templates for the Wizards. As the Wizard runs, it identifies places in the template that requires input. Pages are then generated based on the template and your input.

ColdFusion

ColdFusion takes Web development one step further. Four basic components make the entire ColdFusion suite: ColdFusion Server, ColdFusion Studio, ColdFusion Administrator, and ColdFusion Extensions. Note that the ColdFusion Administrator is part of the server package and the ColdFusion Extensions are an integral part of the entire ColdFusion methodology and therefore part of both the Server and the Studio products.

The server product is an additional layer that works alongside your Web server. Requests for pages are initially handled by your Web server, and depending on the page, are passed along to the ColdFusion server for additional processing.

The idea behind ColdFusion stems from things that have occurred on the Web in the last few years. When it first started out, the Web was providing static information. Computer graphics interface (CGI) enhanced this functionality to allow interaction with database or other information on the server. It has now come to the point where Web-based applications are just as powerful and just as complex as traditional applications are with their own separate interface.

One of the key differences between traditional and Web-based applications is the structure imposed by the technology. Traditional applications tend to be closed units, where interface and functionality are enclosed within a single package. Even client-server applications tend to be enclosed within a package, essentially creating a single object on the system.

Web-based applications have to address the fact that for the most part, the Web is broken into three distinct layers. The user interface layer (i.e., the browser) is a separate entity from the functional layer. This is due to the fact that there are generally no guarantees that a particular user interface will be used. Not only do people use different browsers, but they are used on different operating systems. The developer cannot (or should not) expect specific behavior. Therefore, the user interface needs to be as generic as possible.

The application logic is separate from the user interface layer. What is used usually depends on the server being used. MIIS might use Active Server Pages. Apache might use CGI, Netscape might use LiveWire. In essence, the program runs on the server, hidden from the user interface. Therefore, it is irrelevant what that user interface is.

Finally, the application logic layer retrieves data from the data storage layer. There is a wide range of sources that can be accessed in many different ways. For the most part, the behavior of the application (i.e., the application logic layer) is independent of the data source and to some extent how the data are retrieved. This may be a few lines of code that actually access the data source, but the processing (logic) generally depends on the data and not the way they were retrieved.

As a result of this separation and the needs of businesses, a new era of applications has arrived. Existing applications are being moved to the server and accessed using Web technologies; in essence, a return to the days of the mainframe where most of the processing was done on a central machine. However, today's client has a greater ability to display the information in different ways and to some extent process the information further. In addition, this allows for immediate upgrades and other changes to the system, while still providing the interface independence the browser does.

New applications are being added to a company's palette. On-line stores, customer server and tech support, sales force automation, collaboration (groupware), and many other applications are springing up. With the implantation of a company intranet, the number of possible applications increases even further.

ColdFusion is a rapid application development (RAD) tool that strives to provide easy development for all three layers of Web-based applications. IDE provides the tools for creating the pages that the user interface (browser) will load.

One key aspect of ColdFusion is the Cold Fusion Markup Language (CFML). This is more than server-side scripting language like VBScript but requires less programming experience. It has a similar format to HTML and XML, which makes learning it much easier. The experienced programmer will especially appreciate the increased productivity as a result of the easy access to data sources and simple integration with the Web server. The server itself processes the CFML and does the actual database access.

The functionality is similar to Active Server Pages, Service Side Includes, or any other server-based technology that can create dynamic Web pages. However, ColdFusion is not limited to a single interface but can access the underlying functionality of the Web server using various protocols, such as ISAPI (Microsoft) and NSAPI (Netscape). Based on the CFML tags it finds, ColdFusion can interact with many different aspects of the server including the file system, databases, SMTP (email), and even other applications. ColdFusion generates the pages, which are then passed back to the client's browser.

ColdFusion addresses the requirements for an enterprise-level server in many ways. First, for those familiar with HomeSite, the ColdFusion IDE is essentially identical. Figure 13–5 shows the workspace for the ColdFusion Studio. The appearance is almost identical to that of HomeSite (Figure 13–3). It is only after close examination that you notice the difference. For example, you will notice more tabs in the QuickBar, which are specific to CFML and database access. In the lower left corner is an additional toolbar, which is used during development of your ColdFusion applications (e.g., debugging, breakpoints, and watching variables).

As with HomeSite, ColdFusion uses visual tools to develop the pages. The same kind of visual tools are used by ColdFusion create the interface to your data sources so that developers do not need to be bothered with the Applications can therefore be developed much more quickly and efficiently. As a result, the productivity of your developers increases.

Along with the ColdFusion Studio is a single-user copy of the ColdFusion Server. This allows your developers to work on their projects and still have interactive access to the database. Once the development is completed, the pages can then be easily replicated to the server.

Like HomeSite, ColdFusion Studio has a Wizard that helps you get started creating your site. With the ColdFusion Studio, the Wizard leads you through the steps necessary to create applications and not just simple pages.

The ColdFusion server has built-in support for server clusters. Multiple ColdFusion servers communicate with each, ensuring that the load is bal-

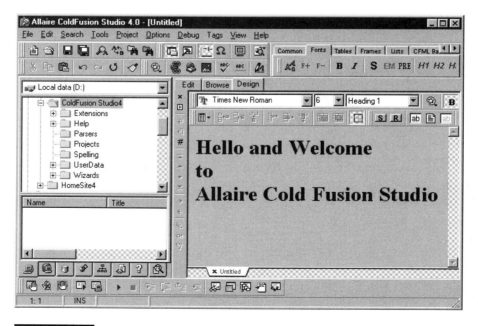

FIGURE 13–5 The ColdFusion IDE.

anced and ensuring automatic failover should one of the servers in the cluster fail. This not only increases the reliability of the server, but also the performance, as no single server becomes over burdened. Performance is increased further by first compiling the CMFL templates and the caching them for quicker execution and then quicker access. The server can also be configured to cache the generated pages and only update them at regular intervals. This is useful in decreasing the access time on pages, which you know to be fairly static.

ColdFusion is extremely scalable as a result of several of its features. First, ColdFusion was developed to be able to take full advantage of systems with multiple CPUs. Because of its multithreaded architecture, it is well suited for such environments. The clustering capabilities allow you to expand the number of servers in your system as the load increases. Plus, the caching the ColdFusion server does mean that it can immediately take advantage of any increase in RAM.

In addition to integration with databases, ColdFusion provides access to a large number of other applications, protocols, and data sources. As I previously mentioned, ColdFusion can directly access files on the file system as well as POP3 servers. Plus, ColdFusion integrates with other standard protocols, such as XML, LDAP, COM, and CORBA. There are also a number of third-party supplements that provide access to even more applications, such as SAP.

This integration also means that ColdFusion is extensible. You can expand your system to access most of the data sources and communications methods in your system. ColdFusion also provides an API to give you access through C and C++. Plus, CFML is extensible, allowing you to create new tags as you need them.

The security of the server and the information is a key aspect of ColdFusion. Authentication of users is integrated with the server allowing you to use the same users as your on Windows NT domain. Because ColdFusion also supports LDAP, it can seamlessly integrate into the directory structure announced for Windows 2000. In addition, ColdFusion can also use the native authentication provided by the underlying Web server. Once authenticated, ColdFusion uses a "rules engine" that determines exactly what objects a user can access.

Should you have multiple Web servers on a single machine, ColdFusion is able to differentiate them, providing different kinds of access according to your needs. This goes one step further in that multiple applications can exist on the same server but also have different security.

NetObjects Fusion

I think it is safe to say that NetObjects Fusion belongs to the next generation of HTML editors. It is more than just an editor in that it can be used to manage your site. It can therefore be classified as a complete Web development environment.

It seems as if one of the central goals of Fusion is to make as much of the design process as automatic as possible. You are provided with a range of options that automatically generate pages or at the very least set the default configuration options. For example, dozens of different styles are provided that have default characteristics, such as the background, buttons, and colors.

In my opinion, it has the same "feel" as many graphic development tools, such as Adobe's Photoshop, although it does not have the same "look." On the top is the toolbar with access to the more general functions or "views" of Fusion, such as site management, page editing, styles, assets, and publishing.

In essence, the toolbar at the top is where you plan and design, or as NetObjects calls it, "architect" your site. That is, you define the general layout of the pages as well as the structure of the site as a whole.

A nice feature is that the menus change based on which view you are in. With some products, menus and menu entries as simply grayed out when that function is not applicable to the current screen. I find this annoying, because you are often not sure if the reason the function is grayed out is because it is not available or you have misconfigured something. In addition, if the menus for all of the functions are always displayed, you have to wade through them looking for what you need.

Figure 13–6 shows the primary editing window of Fusion. This is the Page View. On the left side are the toolbars (here with all of the toolbars dis-

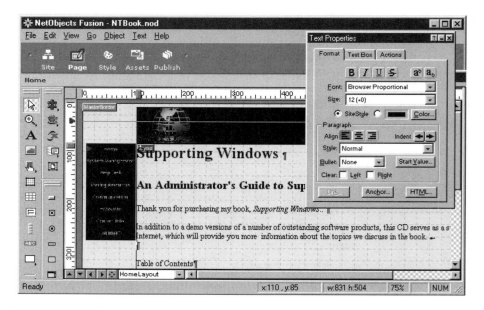

FIGURE 13–6   NetObjects Fusion editing window.

played). In this example, they are docked to the left side, but you can remove them so they are floating or dock them to a different edge of the window.

In the center is the primary workspace or layout space. You also see a floating properties window. This allows you to change the properties for whatever object you select. That is, if you select text on a page, you can change the text properties and the properties window changes accordingly. If you click on an image, you can change the properties for the image and the property window changes again.

Surrounding the actual workspace are the MasterBorders. his is used when you want to define objects that should exist on each page, such as banner, navigation bars, and footers. Changing them once changes them for the whole site. You can also associate the configuration with layout templates, making them available to other sites as well. You also have a choice of how the content of the MasterBorder is to be displayed. Either it becomes a part of the site, or you can choose to have the elements separated and displayed in frames.

As with other editors and development tools, Fusion allows you to edit your pages in several different modes. Figure 13–6 shows the standard design or layout mode. This is the default mode. You also have a text mode, which is useful when your pages have less graphical content than the default. You can also edit the HTML code directly.

Admittedly, I was initially not very pleased with the way Fusion allows you to edit the HTML code. Rather than switching to a completely new window, you get a window that pops up. Editing in this window seems to be more cumbersome than with other HTML editors. However, the reason I had to use the HTML editors of other products (e.g., FrontPage) is that they often cannot create the desired behavior in their graphics modes. Therefore, the *only* way to do this with FrontPage is to edit the page in HTML mode.

However, if you really do not like this way of editing your HTML code, Fusion doesn't stop you from using a different HTML editor and then importing it. Many Web development products let you import pages. That's how they can allow you to develop on an existing site without having to redo every page. However, the difference with Fusion is that you have the ability to import just the body, that is, the content of the page, or the head as well. In addition, you can either replace the head of the current file with the head from the imported page, or you append the head of the imported page to the current one.

Fusion is fully integrated with dynamic HTML (DHTML), but it does have problems with other dynamic objects, such as Service Side Includes. However, it provides a DHTML "builder" that makes it fairly easy to integrate DHTML and thus makes your site more interesting.

The Styles View displays a list of style templates available to you. Each has a number of characteristics that you can change. In addition, you can copy existing styles and change them to suit your needs, or you can create completely new styles. If your site has a style already assigned to it, you can change the style and all of the characteristics will be applied automatically.

The Site View shows you the layout of your site. You have your choice of a graphical or outline view. The graphical view is similar to an organizational chart and gives you an overview of how the pages on your site are linked together. The outline view is like Windows Explorer, which gives you a different perspective on your site.

If you select an existing page in either view and insert a new page, it will be added as a child of that page. However, no links have been set. You can edit this page all you want, but nothing will link to it. This is not necessarily a bad thing. You can design the layout of your site without regard to what links actually exist.

Once you have the layout, you can add content and links to the pages as you develop the site. Double-clicking on a page in the Site View loads that page into the editor. Note that there may not be a link to the page at this point. Instead, you will need to go to another page and add the link by hand.

One useful feature is the ability to set the status of a page as either "done" or "not done." This is useful when managing large sites and helps you publish those pages that actually should be published.

Another view is for "assets." What some products refer to as "resources" Fusion refers to as assets. The Assets View is a central management location for all of the assets on your systems. In essence, assets for the "environment" of your site and pages. Figure 13–7 shows you a list of all of the files that are used by the site. The column headings show you the characteristics of the files such as what type of file editors, whether reducing use or not, and its location on the file system. As with other applications, clicking on the column names will sort the entries based on that criteria.

The tabs at the top allow you to access the different kind of assets that are available. Files are, as the name implies, the files that the pages on your

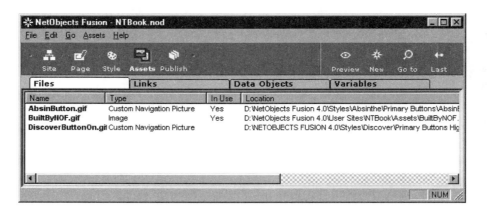

FIGURE 13–7   NetObjects Fusion file assets.

site access. These are not the pages that make up the site but are rather accessed by your pages.

The links assets are a list of internal and external links in your site. An internal link is simply a link that points to another page within your site. An external link is one that points outside of your site.

The DataObject assets are any database references your site makes. Fusion supports a number of database file formats (e.g., Access, Paradox, FoxPro, Dbase, and Excel) in addition to any database that you can access using ODBC.

The Variables assets are just that: variables. For sites that are still in development, this is an extremely valuable asset. You can use a variable to take the place of specific text and then replace that text with the "real" value when you go on-line. For example, assume you are developing pages for a new product that has not been named yet. You know all the functionality, but the marketing people are still fighting over what it should be called. No problem; you keep developing the site using the variable and replace every occurrence when you are ready.

Figure 13–8 shows you the "publish" window. This shows you the publish view of your site. The left-hand window shows you the directory structure of your site. Here you can select directory used or entire trees that you want to be published. The right-hand window is a list of files in the selected directory. Here you select individual files to publish. Here you also see the information about when a particular file was last published.

If you want, you can publish the entire site or all of the files that have changed since the last time you published. It is also possible to publish all of the files into a single directory although they have a specific directory structure on your machine. If you want, you can also publish just a specific kind of file, such as just the graphics.

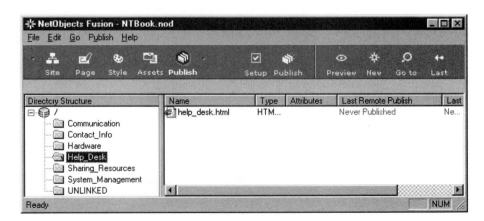

FIGURE 13–8 The NetObjects Fusion publishing window.

The publishing features of Fusion go one step further and give you much finer control over how the pages are published to the Web server than many other products. First, you can publish to multiple servers, each with its own configuration. You can choose whether the server directory structure should mimic the structure you used when developing, whether the directory structure should be "flat," and so forth.

Fusion also allows for "incremental publish." This means you can publish only those pages that have changed since the last time you updated your site. This saves me a lot of time tracking down which pages have been changed or unnecessarily copying pages that haven't changed. You can also tell Fusion to delete pages that are no longer being used on the server. Since I am limited in the amount of space I have, I find this functionality extremely useful.

One key feature is that the export is completely server independent. Unlike Microsoft FrontPage, you do not need special extensions on the server to take advantage of Fusion'spublishing features. You can use Fusion with any server, even with MIIS.

Once interesting thing is that when you develop a site, Fusion will create a navigation bar with buttons for you. These are actually GIF files that are generated for you with the text for each section (or page). The background of each button is based on the style you selected (more on those in a moment).

One nice feature is what NetObjects calls "Everywhere HTML." For those of you who have had to develop sites for multiple browser types, you know how much of a pain it can be. Although there is a standard HTML, each browser has a number of often-conflicting extensions that add to the power of HTML but make developing browser-independent sites a nightmare. Using the "Everywhere HTML" features, you can generate HTML pages that work across different HTML standards (2.x–4x) as well as DHTML, which works across different browsers. Since older HTML standards did not have DHTML, you can also generate standard HTML code for the segments that would normally be DHTML.

One of the newest features is the integration of Fusion and Web application servers such as ColdFusion. Using a number of different Wizards, you can connect to a variety of data sources without having to program the interface yourself.

NetObjects ScriptBuilder

In my opinion, one of the biggest shortcomings of Web development tools is the inability to efficiently develop scripts. Although many tools allow you to edit your scripts, necessary features such as testing and debugging are missing. Another problem arises when you start developing on multiple platforms. If you have Web servers on both Windows NT and UNIX, you will probably have several different kinds of scripts. JavaScript for client-side scripts, Active

Server Pages and VBScript for server-side applications on Windows NT machines, and CGI perl scripts on your UNIX machines, all make for a complex development environment.

The NetObjects ScriptBuilder addresses both of these issues and many more. It is the first Web development tool specifically designed to be platform independent, which allows you to develop scripts regardless of what server you are running on. In addition, ScriptBuilder is intended primarily for building your scripts and therefore is not cluttered with things used only to design pages. Therefore, it is the perfect tool regardless of what product you use to develop your pages, and it works seamlessly with NetObjectsFusion, Allaire HomeSite, Microsoft FrontPage, Adobe PageMill, and many more.

One of the most important things to note is that NetObjects Script-Builder is a very complex tool. Although it can greatly simplify development of your scripts, it does require a certain amount of previous experience with the languages and features you develop with.

Figure 13–9 shows you the primary editing window. As you can see, it has the same look and feel as other IDEs available for Windows. At the top you have the menus and toolbars. This gives you quick access to the various scripting elements. In addition, since it designed as an aid to Web page development, you have access to all of the standard HTML elements.

On the left you have several tabs to show you not only the structure of you pages but also provide you quick access to a long list of prebuilt scripts, including VBScript, JavaScript, Netscape LiveWire, LotusDomino, and perl. Plus, there are a number of drop-in components, like clock, calendars, form

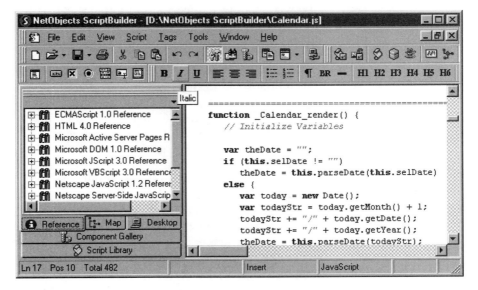

FIGURE 13–9   NetObjects ScriptBuilder.

elements, and so forth. There is even a complete reference library for the various scripting languages as well as HTML, Active Server Pages, and DCOM.

On the right you see the primary editing window. Since you are editing scripts and not developing the graphical appearance of the page, you edit the code directly. Unfortunately, you cannot see it with a black-and-white photo, but the different elements are color coded as they are in most other IDEs, such as MS Visual InterDev. This makes recognizing the elements, and therefore development, easier.

NetObjects describes the ScriptBuilder editor as being "smart" in that it adapts itself to whatever language you are developing in, including HTML. In addition, all of the features available with scripting languages, such as color-coded syntax, is also available with HTML. This helps makes it a great tool for editing HTML code, although there are few components that you can add automatically like you can with other HTML editors.

One of my favorite features is the script library. As I mentioned earlier, this contains a larger number of predefined scripts for a wide range of functions and languages. These scripts data a modular or object approach, even though the language is not specifically designed for that. You can expand the library by adding your own code segments as well as download new additions from the ScriptBuilder Web site.

NetObjects Authoring Server Suite

A limitation of many HTML editors and other Web development tools is that they are generally designed for a single developer. That is, there is limited interaction between the developers of your intranet site. The result is that work is often duplicated or often not done at all, little communication between developers, and a site that obviously looks like there was no unified effort. This is all compounded by the fact that with an intranet, you have many more contributors than with your typical Internet site.

You can limit some of the problems by requiring the developers to use specific templates or to follow rules in developing their pages. However, at best this generally can only lead to a more uniform appearance. The inefficiencies in developing pages are still present. Pages need to be efficiently produced and the IT department needs to ensure the overall integrity of the site, ensuring that links lead to the correct pages, there are no orphaned pages, access permissions are correct, and so forth.

Unfortunately, in a multiuser environment, many of the available Web development tools are not useful as they do not have the necessary functionality. NetObjects has addressed these problems with its Authoring Server Suite. This is not just a network-aware or multiuser version of Fusion. Instead, it is a suite in that there are a number of different components that go into the product, starting with the server itself. This is the "control center" of the site and manages content as well as access by the various developers. All information, including the content itself is stored in an SQL database. However, this fact is generally transparent to the developers. The server also keeps track of the changes, enabling you to publish just the pages that have changed.

The Server Administrator is used to manage the development teams as well as the Web sites. That is, you can manager multiple sites with multiple development teams. Management of the development teams includes creating users and assigning rights. These rights range from simple page publications to complete site administration. Site management includes the ability to create and remove sites as well as keepi track of their publishing status. In addition, you can manage the sites and teams from any machine, provided you have the necessary permissions.

To develop the pages, you have the TeamFusion Client, which is much more than Fusion. It includes a revision control system, where you check in and check out the pages you are working on. This ensures that multiple users are not working on the same page at the same time and therefore undo each other's changes.

The Content Contributor Client is a Java applet that allows users to contribute new content without the need for any development skills at all. In that it is a Java applet, you can add content from any browser. The key here is that most everyone in the company should be capable of providing content on some level but who is not responsible for managing or developing any aspect of the site, including the appearance pages. Therefore, all they are responsible for is content, which the Content Contributor allows them to provide.

Graphics Tools

On the one hand, the purpose of an intranet is to provide information and not to entertain your users. However, I have found that an intranet needs to be "pleasing to the eye" in order for it to be effective. In my experience, most administrators could not care less about how the intranet looks. However, this is not the same for the average user. That's why most sites on the Internet spend a great deal of time to make their sites entertaining as well as informative.

In addition, "a picture is worth a thousand words." I have found this especially true for people working with topics with which they are unfamiliar. The primary example is most users who are trying to do something new on their computer. Reading descriptions along with graphics or pictures makes it a lot easier for the novice user to understand the topic at hand. Therefore, it is useful to have screen shots of applications as well as photographs or other graphics.

One of the big questions to ask yourself is, How complicated do I want the graphics to be? The more complicated the graphics, for more likely you need a more powerful tool. The more powerful tool means more expense.

This needs to be weighed with the benefit you will get from being able to develop more-complex images.

A complex image does not necessarily mean in a thousand different objects in dozens of different colors. Instead, complexity is a characteristic of how the different components relate to each other. For example, a simple bitmap is not complex at all simply because there are no objects. Every single point in the image is independent of all the others. If necessary, you could change the color or even erase any point without having an effect on any of the other points. However, this becomes a major disadvantage when you *want* to change all of the other images.

There are a number of products available on the market that allow you to create graphics that are extremely complex as well as interrelated. Here, changing the characteristics (e.g., size or shape) can have an effect on many others. It is also possible to group objects together, process them as a single unit, and then dissolve the grouping so that the elements can be managed individually.

Another aspect is the extent to which you can manipulate these objects. Rotating, flipping, cropping, resizing, and so forth are basic functions that you will find in any product. However, being able to change the overall appearance of the image (e.g., making it look like a painting or drawing) is not available in every product. Although functions like these have limited value on the company intranet, they often help to make your Internet site more aesthetically pleasing. Remember, you don't want to buy a cheaper product now just for your intranet only to find that you are missing some needed function when you start moving information to the Internet.

So, what does all this have to do with an intranet? Well, it has to do with how complex you want your graphics to be. This can be anything from organizational diagrams to schematics of your network structure to details of how your key database application is designed. Although it is possible to develop any one of these using the tools built-in to many word processors, you eventually run to limitations. You eventually get to a point where you need the advanced features of separate graphics applications.

Another thing to consider is what to do with photographs. Cropping, resizing, and so forth are common to all photo manipulation tools. However, you should investigate how easy it is to perform a given function. For example, I have found some programs that will not allow you to cut out a portion of an image and then change its size. The only way to do it is insert the portion you cut out into a brand-new image, change its size, cut out what you need, and paste it back into the original image.

Adobe Photoshop

Adobe Photoshop is almost synonymous with photo manipulation and processing. If you are planning to do anything more than simple cut-and-paste you should take a look at Photoshop. Adobe's Web development tool

PageMill already comes with a copy of the lite version of Photoshop. Implementing something as powerful as Photoshop on an intranet might be overkill. However, much of the information you will provide for the intranet will eventually wander to the company's Internet site. Therefore, you will need a tool that can provide the level of quality that Photoshop can.

Another consideration is the ability to create exciting graphics that can be used in printed literature as well as on the Internet. I think it is better to spend a little extra now rather than buy an cheaper product now and have to deal with compatibility issues later on. You can create a single image and use it on your intranet, the Internet, and in published documents. Perhaps you will need to change the resolution of the image for one medium or the other. However, Photoshop makes this a snap.

One of the most dramatic features of Photoshop is its built-in integration with the other Adobe products. First, it is extremely easy to move objects from one program to another. There is no need to worry about compatibility issues because of the built-in integration. Granted, it is possible to create an image in Photoshop in a format that applications have difficulty with. However, there are a great number of filters built-in that simplify importing and exporting objects. As I mentioned previously in the section on Web development products, it is very simple to switch back and forth between PageMill and Photoshop while developing your intranet.

Second, the interface that Photoshop provides is essentially unchanged from all the other Adobe products (see Figure 13–10). Therefore, it is extremely easy to switch back from if you do not mean to spend time getting used to the different interface. Although they are still separate products, you can create graphics and Adobe Illustrator, prepare photographs in Photoshop and import them both into PageMaker. Since the basic concepts of the interface are identical between these three products, it is almost secondary that they are sold individually. (However, Adobe does provide them all the single graphics bundle.)

At first this might seem like a minor point. However, you must remember to consider the total cost of owning a product. It is possible to find products that are less expensive than Photoshop. Regardless of the fact they are going to have less functionality, you (or your users) will need to spend time learning the new interface. Even after they become familiar with each product, there is naturally a certain amount of time needed to mentally switch between applications. For example, how often do we expect to find a particular function on the menu because that's the way it is in another application? If it is not where you look first, you have wasted time. Having essentially identical interfaces, as is the case with the Adobe products, there is no time lost when moving from one application to another.

Have you ever taken a photograph that you wanted to use in a brochure or on the Internet only to the find the color was off or it needed some other change? This usually forces you to retake the picture. Photoshop saves you a lot of that hassle. The image can be scanned (even directly from

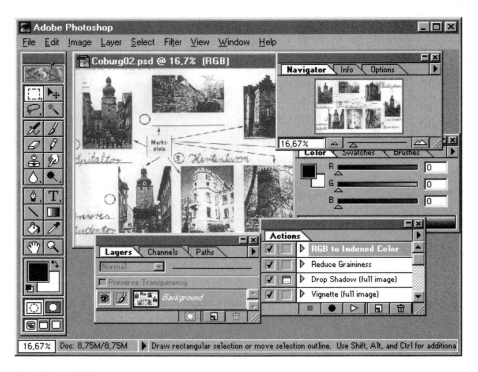

FIGURE 13-10 Adobe Photoshop main screen.

Photoshop), loaded into Photoshop, and processed as necessary. I have used this myself on prints made from old negatives and restored the image to a point where you could not tell there was ever a problem with the negative.

A great deal of Photoshop's power (at least in my mind) comes from its ability to work with layers. As its name implies, a layer is a set of objects or even just characteristics that can be laid one atop the other. Layers do not necessarily completely cover the layers underneath but rather can be specific objects. You can apply changes to layers as well as change the order in which they appear.

One implementation would be to have text in different languages in different layers. You then disable all of the language layers except for the one you want. This allows you to have all the languages you need but just one file.

Of course, you can use Photoshop to cut-and-paste different objects. One feature of Photoshop that I've used repeatedly is to define the size and shape of the area which I want to copy somewhere else in the image to use it as a template for the part I actually want to the copy. For example, assume you have a picture of a house and you wish to insert different objects into the window frames. Because the picture is taken at an angle, the windows are not perfect rectangles, so cutting out the right-sized image is not easy. Instead, you outline the region of the window and use this as a template for the object you wish to insert. This ensures inserted objects fit the frame exactly.

The actions palette is a way for you to automate repeated tasks. In essence, this is nothing more than the macros you have grown accustomed to in word processing or spreadsheet applications. As with these other applications you simply record the series of steps that should repeated, and they become immediately available with just a single click of the mouse. In addition, Photoshop comes with dozens of predefined macros.

Adobe PhotoDeluxe

If you are doing just a simple processing of your images it might be hard to justify the expense for Photoshop. However, if you want a really professional-looking site bidder was an obligation to get it. The alternative is Adobe PhotoDeluxe Business Edition.

One shortcoming is the limited number of graphics formats it supports compared with Photoshop's. Although the more common formats are supported, it is still limited compared with Photoshop. You should check out the Adobe Web site before purchasing either one if you think this might be a problem.

Another drawback is the interface to PhotoDeluxe is *not* the same as for the other Adobe products. However, I actually like the interface. It is very easy to learn and to use. Plus, it does not have the almost "clinical" feel that many other products have. Although you can do quite a lot with it, PhotoDeluxe not a tool for the professional. However, it is ideal for the small business or individual who needs to quickly clean-up or process images either for publication on the company intranet or in a printed publication. For the novice who is doing just simple graphics manipulation it is ideal.

As you can see from Figure 13–11, the workspace is completely different from Photoshop's (Figure 13–10). On the left side of the window are several menu options that bring you back and forth between the main areas of the product. At the top of the work area are different tabs, depending on which area you are currently in. Selecting a tab presents you with the options for that specific function.

One complaint I have had with many programs is "information overload." There are so many menus with so many different options it is often hard to find the function you are looking for. PhotoDeluxe addresses that problem by allowing you to switch between a long and short form of the menus. For the beginner the short menu helps keep them from being overwhelmed, whereas the long menu is useful for the more-experienced user.

One very nice feature is the ability to import images from external sources, such as scanners, digital cameras, or video cameras. If you have branch offices you need to support or provide support over an intranet, then I highly recommend a digital camera. After a few months, you've saved your-

FIGURE 13-11 The workspace of Adobe PhotoDeluxe.

self the time and effort of taking pictures the old-fashioned way and then scanning them in. In addition, PhotoDeluxe can download the images from an Internet photo service if you have an Internet connection.

PhotoDeluxe has a built-in database, which it refers to as a "photo organizer." This gives you the ability to sort and store your pictures according to topic. If you need to work on an image in the organizer, you simply drag the icon out onto the workspace.

Another thing that really impressed me was the handbook. I am a stickler for documentation. If you have bad documentation, users will waste time when looking for answers. The PhotoDeluxe handbook is far from complete, but the way it presents the material is exceptional. It covers both the "getting started" topics and a few of the essential details in a manner that is easy for the novice to understand. The words and phrases used to describe different topics might not be the one that professionals use, but they are understandable to everyone. This makes it perfect for the casual business user who does not have the technical background to wade through more-complex manuals.

Intranet Servers

One thing that we found was that the Web server itself (both hardware and software) is actually one of the least significant aspects of your intranet, especially in terms of administration effort. Once the server is installed and you have defined your structure, there is very little you need to do. Much more important is the content itself as well as how to content a structured. Added to this is the maintenance of the information. That is, it is much more important that the server content be up-to-date than it is from server software (not accounting for bugs, of course).

Like the Web development tools, choosing the right server is a matter of what you need more than what you want. The single most important aspect is what kind of information (i.e., services) you are going to provide. If you are a small company that will only be providing a handful of pages to keep employees up-to-date on current events or providing easy reference to a handful of documents, performance is less an issue than if you will be processing on-line orders for dozens of customers at any given moment. Also, the more static the information, the less performance is required from both the hardware and the HTTP server.

If you are providing information from a databank, then means to access that database needs to be considered as well. How large the database is and how much information will be provided to the customer both are issues that you need to address. If it takes too long to return the requested information, the visitor might get tired of waiting and move on. You have failed in your task of providing information and service to your customer.

Another aspect is security. Others can provide Secure Sockets Layer (SSL) support, certificates, and other security features. Obviously, if the Web server will be connected to your internal network you should see how well each server integrates into your firewall concepts (i.e., proxy servers).

If you plan to have servers on both UNIX and NT, I recommend not using MIIS. Although it provided with the NT Server (at least in version 4.0), it is not necessarily free. Aside from the fact that it is less configurable than the Netscape FastTrack Server and far less configurable than the Apache Server, it only runs on the Windows NT Server, not the Workstation. This would mean that each organization that has an intranet server (e.g., what a branch office or department would need) its own server, something that few companies can provide.

Since it only runs on Windows NT, there is no version for UNIX. This means that if you decide to have intranet servers on both Windows and UNIX, you would need a different server for each platform. Since this is not necessary, you end up having more administration work and gain nothing. In addition, since NT runs only on Intel x86 and DEC Alpha processors, you are extremely limited in your choices of hardware.

On the other hand, if your intranet servers will only be on your Windows NT machines, then you should still consider MIIS. Despite its shortcomings, it does provide a common interface if you are only running NT servers. Compared with any of the Netscape servers, it does have an addition advantage that once you have the NT server, you do not need to spend anymore on the intranet server.

However, just because you do not need to spend any more money on the server does not mean implementing MIIS will not cost you any more money. If the NT server is only providing Internet-type services like HTTP,

FTP, and so forth, you do not need any extra licenses. However, if you plan to use the NT server to provide file *or* print services, a client license is needed for every machine that connects to it.

Be *very* careful here. If you upgraded your Windows NT 3.51 server to Windows NT 4.0, you need to upgrade the client licenses as well. This is because the client license is for accessing a particular version of the server, not just to be able to access any NT server. In one company, we upgraded a single server to 4.0, and we were told that we had to upgrade more than 700 client licenses. Even though we could set permissions so that certain machines couldn't access the server (i.e., those in branch offices), they were still on the same network and therefore could *potentially* access the server. This meant they needed an updated client license.

Hardware is another area where you need to be careful with the MIIS. Remember that you cannot shut off the Windows NT GUI. It takes a lot of memory to manage all the windows plus whatever it needs for other tasks. Without anything running other than what Windows starts by default, I have found that over 30 MBs of *physical* memory is used up. This is pretty close to the 32 MBs that Microsoft says is a minimum for MIIS. Therefore, a more realistic minimum is 48 or 64 MBs. Once you start adding Microsoft Exchange to the server, you need to double or even triple this figure.

On the other hand, memory is the last place that you should try to save money, especially if there are a larger number of pages that are going to be accessed repeatedly. These pages can be held in memory as long as possible. The more memory, the longer the pages remain and the less often they need to reread from the hard disk. Even if you are running just 64 MBs, doubling it to 128 MBs will only cost a few hundred dollars and can make a big difference in performance.

You should not try to save money on the hard disk either. Get a drive that gives you plenty of room for growth. Although 1GB seems like a lot, the difference between it and 2 GBs is no longer discussed. If you are running on an NT server, you might consider getting yourself at least four drives. This allows you to create a RAID 5 array, which increases the speed and gives you redundancy if one drive should fail. Although you can get RAID support for most UNIX dialects, it is often a supplemental product. An alternative would be a hardware solution, so it doesn't matter what operating system is running.

I would recommend that you split the work load across multiple servers if you can. There is obviously the performance issue, but there is also the issue of availability. If you have all of your servers on one machine and it goes down, users cannot start applications, get their email, access the intranet, and so on.

This is a very compelling reason to implement something like Linux for your intranet and email servers. You can install them on a less-powerful machine, since you do not need to be running a GUI, so you save money there. Also, because there is no GUI needed, you save money on RAM. Because the operating system, HTTP, and email servers are all free, you save even more money. The last time I checked, more than 10% of all Internet servers were running Linux. This shows that it is a stable operating system.

Going through the installation of the various Microsoft servers is beyond the scope of this book. However, there are a few issues that I would like to address. The first is the choice of services that you want to provide. Remember that you do not have the same access to configuration information on Windows that you do under UNIX. It is therefore not as easy to tell that your system is secure. Considering how inattentive Microsoft was with the security of files and directories for the operating systems itself as well as already-detected holes in the MIIS, you should be *extremely* careful with the services you provide.

When installing the MIIS, one default is the Gopher service. This is fine for the Internet, but it is unlikely that you will need it for an intranet. In addition, FTP is activated by default. Although this could be useful, you can provide the same file services without it. Therefore, I would recommend disabling *both* of these.

You have two ways of configuring the services once they are installed. The first is the traditional Microsoft GUI and the other is through a Web browser. I would recommend installing the Web browser option (HTML) at the very least. This reduces the number of interfaces you have to the system. (Note that if you are used to working with the Netscape HTML interface, you will find the Microsoft GUI very lacking in most areas.)

The next issue is another sign that Microsoft is not very security conscious. The default location for the MIIS files is %SYSTEMROOT%\system32. Considering the default security on that directory allows EVERYONE more control than is safe, placing an Internet server here is not a wise decision. Change it!

The safest thing is to place it on a completely different drive. In previous versions of the MIIS, users could simply add ../ to the URL (to go to the parent directory) and get "above" the root directory of the HTTP server. On their first try to correct this, Microsoft only fixed a single ../ but allowed ../../ to move up two levels. If this were on your system drive, you could potentially open up your system for everyone.

Apache

The Apache server was first developed in 1995 and was *originally* based on the NCSA HTTP daemon (version 1.3 at the time). Since then it has been completely rewritten and the functionality it provides makes it comparable to any commercial Web server and better in many respects. In fact, there are a large number of functions that are possible with the Apache server that others do not have. Because of its features, functionality, and most important, performance, the Apache server has grown to become the most widely used HTTP server on the Internet.

At first glance, the most compelling reason for using the Apache server is its price: free. The Apache server is distributed under the GNU public license, and therefore you can install it to your heart's content. That is, you can install it on every machine in your company without having to pay for licenses for every machine. The key word here is "every." Aside from being available in source code and therefore portable to every platform, it has already been compiled for a wide range of systems. Like Netscape, it doesn't matter what platform you are running on; you can use the Apache server.

If the price tag and availability are not enough, consider what the Apache server can do. The first thing to look at is that you do have the source code. No matter what function is missing, you can add it yourself. In addition, the source code comes already with a wide range of options. For example, many of the defaults can be changed with simple definitions during the compilation of the source.

One of the strengths of the Apache server is that it is modular. You can change the functionality by adding or removing modules that are provided or create your own modules. An application program interface (API) is also provided, which the modules use to access the basic functions of the server. In addition, this API is used so that modules can communicate with one another. These modules include everything from basic configuration information to how the servers handle CGI script, image maps, authorizations, and so on. In fact, there are several dozen modules that you can choose from.

Although the Apache server does not have the pretty graphic interface, it can be configured in ways that most other servers only dream about. In the section on configuring your Linux system, I will go into some details about configuring the Apache server.

Netscape Servers

Netscape servers have a very compelling advantage over those from Microsoft for mixed networks: They run on both UNIX *and* Windows. An additional advantage is that in contrast to the MIIS, the Netscape servers will run on the Windows workstations.

As with the Microsoft servers, Netscape provides a wide range of choices. The Fast-Track Server's an excellent low-end server. It provides all of the basic functionality with less cost and less administrative overhead. In addition, it is more configurable than the MIIS. It is available for most dialects of UNIX, including Linux and both Windows NT Workstation and Server. This makes it an excellent choice for a personal or even Netscape (?) Enterprise Server regardless of what operating system is running on the desktop.

At the other end of the spectrum is the Netscape Enterprise Server, which is really designed for the Enterprise. Among its features is the ability to publish directly to the server from your client. Its search engine is built-in and not a supplemental product like Microsoft Index Server. Also impressive is its built-in version control system.

During the installation process of the Netscape Enterprise Server, you will have the chance to install support for the lightweight directory access protocol (LDAP). LDAP has a number of advantages, as user and group information does not need to be stored on the same server. You could have a central server that provides all of this information to the various department servers.

One of the other servers that Netscape provides is the Calendar Server. Combined with Netscape Calendar, the server provides the expected workgroup calendar functionality, such as recording appointments, scheduling meetings, and so on. In addition, you can keep track of telephone calls, memory, and other office information. All information is updated in real-time so that it is immediately available. The Calendar Server is also integrated with SMTP to enable you to notify others and be notified through email of specific events (e.g., planned meetings).

Despite the fact that the Netscape Enterprise Server built in an indexing functionality, it is not as extensive as those for the Microsoft Index Server. To compensate for this, Netscape provides the Catalog Server. Like the MS Index Server, the Netscape Catalog Server can automatically build an index of resources on your intranet. The information is indexed and classified according to user-defined rules. The advantage is that this information can then be provided in either summary or full-text form, making searching much easier.

The Directory Server is used as a central location to administer information about the users of your intranet. It can provide information such as names, phone numbers, email addresses, and other important information. Since the server can handle up to one million and several tens of thousands of requests per hour, it is likely that it can handle the needs of your company.

There are other advantages to the Directory Server. Because all of the Netscape servers are integrated, when a user is removed from the Directory Server, all the others are aware of the change. In addition to access to documents being removed, the user's mailbox is also removed as well as access to any newsgroups.

Netscape's Certificate Server is an extra added level of security. This is a way that users can authenticate themselves with a greater level of assurance than with simple passwords. In addition, the Netscape Certificate Server also works with email, so the messages can be encrypted and digitally "signed," which not only helps ensure the privacy of the data, but also authenticates the message.

In addition, the Certificate Server helps authenticate across multiple servers. There is no need to have user names and passwords for all servers. Instead, each server queries the Certificate Server for authentication.

The Netscape Messaging Server is the Netscape counterpart of Microsoft Exchange. Built into the Messaging Server is support for all of the major messaging protocols including SMTP, MIME, POP3, IMAP, as well as LDAP, SNMP, and SLL.

Netscape FastTrack Server

Netscape FastTrack Server has the advantage that it will run on most any platform. I have installed it under Windows NT, Linux, and a couple other Unix dialects, and the administration is identical. Therefore, it is ideal as an intranet in server environment, where you need to provide resources from different platforms. Having the same server on multiple machines decreases the administration considerably.

Among the characteristics of the server are a graphical interface (using HTML), as L. 3.0, administration of remote machines, support for virtual domain, and complete copy of the most recent version of Netscape Communicator. This gives you a fairly powerful HTML editor.

Not only is the configuration based on HTML but the installation is as well. As with many other programs, there is a kind of installation loader, which then loads Netscape Navigator to do the actual installation. Why develop an additional tool, which is based on nonproprietary standards, when you can use existing, well-established standards?

The FastTrack Server installation serves an additional purpose in that it provides good examples of what you can do with HTML and a Web browser. Not only thing you see nice examples on HTML and CTI scripts, but most of the interface is provided through JavaScript.

The FastTrack Server actually consists of at least two servers. First, there is administration server, which is used to administer the entire system, that is, it is used to configure the others Web servers, start and stop them, and perform all of the other administration tasks. Although you could stop with just the administration server, it does little good, because you're not providing any resources. Therefore you need at least one additional Web server, which is the server providing resources. Note that this is the server that users seeing from the outside. Whether "outside" means different departments in your company or people on the Internet is up to you. However, what you're configuring here is a virtual server.

Even during installation you can begin to configure it as your first Web server. Here you define the server name and the document root directory for the first server. Once the installation is complete, Netscape Navigator is started to test your Web server and see if it can make the connection.

As you can see in Figure 13–12, the configuration page is split into three frames. In the top frame you have domain areas, such as "system settings," "axis control," and so forth. When you press these buttons, the appropriate menu will appear in the left frames. The main frame in the lower right is where you configure the individual options.

An extremely useful advantage from the configuration through HTML pages is the ability to create the pages dynamically. That means, what you can configure on any page is dependent on what has already been configured and therefore changes over time and between servers. For example, if you define a file, which should be displayed if an error occurs, this appears

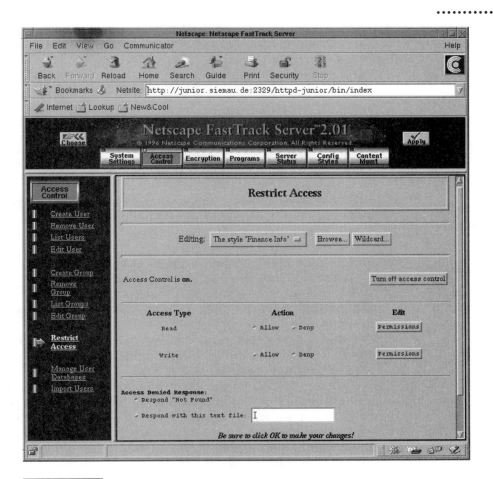

FIGURE 13-12   The FastTrack Server main configuration page.

on the "systems settings" configuration page. If no error page has been defined, no such entry appears, as there is no need to display it. However, the rest of the page is the same.

The system settings are basically the same entries that one finds in the httpd.conf on other servers (e.g., Apache). Here you define the basic characteristics and behavior of the server itself. For example, you define the main directory for the server (server root), the names of the log files, directories, and so forth. In addition, aspects of the network such as the server name and port number are defined here as well.

The entire configuration of the FastTrack Server is done with a specific, predefined user. By default this is the system administrator, but you can change it to suit your needs. This user does not have to be one that exists on a system, but one that remains internal to the FastTrack Server.

You can also configure access to the resources provided by the Web server. For example, you can specify that will mean certain users have access to certain directories or even individual files. It is also possible to limit access to specific computers; or the reverse, you can deny access to specific computers. It might be that you do not want any computers from unsecured locations in the warehouse to be able to access your intranet server or even just specific directories. It is also possible to defined "exceptions." That is, access is granted or indicted to a specific list with the exception of users or groups in another list.

Your users and user groups are completely separate from Windows NT. At first, this seems to be more work. Actually it is, because you need to create the users twice. However, it is a question of security. The FastTrack Server can separate Web page access from access over the file system. It is also possible to have no couple user databases. For example, you could have one set of users for each of your virtual servers. This helps ensure users do not have access information they shouldn't. This has the additional advantage of being able to easily move the server to a new machine without having to recreate the users from scratch.

Keep in mind that you do not need to create a large number of users by hand. Instead, you can import the text file containing list of users and have the FastTrack Server add them all at once.

For me, as an administrator, one of the key advantages of the FastTrack Server is that all of the configuration information is stored in text files. I've never been a big fan of the system registry and felt it was like swatting flies with an atom bomb. Granted you need to be familiar with the application to know where it stores its configuration files, but you need to know how the registry is laid out in order to find the specific entries.

In my experience, you can find the configuration files and specific entries much faster than you can with the Windows registry. In addition, I find individual files much easier to make global changes as well as to copy the configuration from one server to another or one machine to another. In addition, the configuration files are separated by a server, so it is much easier to find what configuration goes with which server.

One extremely useful feature is the ability to create configuration styles or templates. As with the templates in other products, bees it defined appearance of your Web pages as well as a general behavior. For example, you can define a configuration style that defines the standard settings for log files and access permissions. Styles can then be a starring to specific directories without the need to explicitly change the settings on that directory.

Another useful feature is the ability to create footers for your pages. This isn't anything more than the specific text, which you want to appear on each page without having to edit each page individually. In addition, you can include various pieces of information in the footer such as the date the page was last changed.

Being able to the far to access permissions for specific directories is only one part of the problem. You need to be able to determine how effective your security measures are. The FastTrack server provides the ability to log all events on the server and to view these events through your Web browser. To help you manage the log files, the FastTrack server can be configured to archive the log files at regular intervals, for example, once a week. That way, if nothing special has occurred, you need not wade through all of the log entries to find something you're looking for. However, you still have the logs if you need to come back and look at them later.

Netscape Enterprise Server

A step up from the FastTrack Server is the Netscape Enterprise Server. Whereas the goal of the FastTrack Server is to get your Web server off and running quickly, the Netscape Enterprise Server provides much more functionality. This is not to say it is difficult to use. However, it will take longer to become familiar with all of the various aspects, as there is, quite simply, more to learn.

Although it is not entirely accurate to simply call the FastTrack Server an "application," it might be an effective label if you also consider calling the Netscape Enterprise Server a "system service." The difference is that the Netscape Enterprise Server provides full support for symmetric multiprocessing (mobile CPUs) and the used of kernel threads. Adding a highly efficient algorithm to optimize catching, the Netscape Enterprise Server provides the power the enterprise needs.

In addition to providing Web services, the Netscape Enterprise Server provides an integrated copy of the Netscape Directory Server. This means you have a central location to manage your user information. Like the other Netscape servers, the Enterprise Server provides the same administration console, allowing you to manage all of the servers from a single location.

There is also support for the simple network management protocol (SNMP). This means you can integrate the Netscape Enterprise Server with a number of the common management tools, such as HP OpenView, IBM/Tivoli Tivoli Management Environment (TME), and Computer Associates (CA) Unicenter.

Enhanced reliability is provided in a couple of ways. First, there are actually several servers running on a machine at any given time. If a Web application were to fail, only a single server would be affected, and all of the others would be able to continue on as before. It is also possible to configure multiple machines running the Netscape Enterprise Server into a cluster. The administration console allows you to manage the various aspects of the cluster. This includes the ability to manage them as a single unit as well as individually. Here too, administrative tasks can be delegated to different users at different levels.

Using the LiveWire database service, which is included with the Netscape Enterprise Server, you have direct access to a wide range of commercial databases. This enables you to easily provide dynamic content for your Web pages.

Netscape SuiteSpot

Netscape's SuiteSpot takes the Web server to its highest level. SuiteSpot provides all of the tools you need to run a powerful, efficient Web server, whether it be on the Internet, intranet, or a combination of both. It starts off with the Netscape Enterprise Server to provide the basic Web services. This is followed by the Netscape Messaging Server, Calendar Server, and Collabra, which provide the communication media for your users. These are all wrapped together with the Netscape Directory Server.

For businesses that need even more power, Netscape provides a professional addition of Suite Spot. This includes the Netscape Mission Control Desktop, which enables administrators to centrally manage both client preferences and the distribution of software to the clients. There is also a copy of the Netscape Compass Server, which is an automated "search and discovery" engine, which searches both your intranet and the Internet. These documents are then catalogued, providing your users quick access.

Netscape SuiteSpot Pro also provides two products to help increase the security of your system. First is the Netscape Certificate Server, which enables you to issue, starring, and manage public key certificates. In essence, certificates allow one company to "vouch" for the identity of someone else. For example, a central server within your company is trusted by your business partners. Users from other servers can still access information on your partners' server because they have been given a certificate that says they are to be trusted.

Supporting Users

There is a lot more to supporting users than simply answering their questions and handling calls into the hotline. Hopefully, by now this has become obvious considering all of the different issues we have addressed so far. In this chapter, we're going to discuss those issues that are directly related to supporting users, particularly as it relates to your help desk, hotline, or whatever you might call it.

Here, I am not talking about the solutions to specific problems or how to use specific programs. Instead, I am talking about the processes and framework that support all of that. There is actually a lot more to this than meets the eye. Whether you have an official help desk or just someone who answers questions for other people, the framework and procedures need to be organized. Poor organization is just as bad as not having the right answer.

Solving Problems

Solving problems does not necessarily mean that end users calls a system administrator who then gives them an answer or solves the problem for them. There are many cases where users cannot solve the problem; either they do not have the appropriate knowledge or appropriate tools. However, oftentimes users have their hands held through solutions, as it is either easier for the administrator to do it, or the users feels like they are not able to solve it themselves.

Both of these situations are detrimental in the long run. Users must be in a position to solve their own problems as much as possible. If you hold their hand or do it yourself, they will need to call back the next time it happens.

What solving problems really means is providing the user the information necessary to solve the problem. A minor difference may have major consequences. For example, if a user calls with a question, the answer to which is available from some other source, that is not efficient use of your resources. Instead, the user should be aware of what the other sources are. For example, users should be made aware of the on-line help functions of the various software products as well as how to use them properly. I have worked in companies where users were afraid to use the on-line help, because they had never been told how. This is not efficient use of your resources. When you train them to use the software, you *must* train them to use the on-line help is well.

Unfortunately, not all problems can be solved using the on-line help. However, there are a number of problems that the users can solve themselves. For example, users may need access to a shared directory that they usually do not use. It is therefore necessary for them to make a new network connection. The users need to know how to map a network drive. Obviously, if they don't know, they need to know where to look. Although this is something provided in the on-line help for Windows, it is a common enough problem that it should be made more readily available. For example, you could make it available on your company's intranet.

Expecting Problems

After a long holiday or vacation (Christmas, for example), you may find a lot of users have forgotten the password or that it is expired. Many European countries have a long summer vacation that could be as long as three weeks. I have experienced cases where a large number of users return from the summer vacation and have forgotten their password. In other cases, they still remember their password; however, it has an expired during the vacation. Remember that Windows NT provides a mechanism to limit the length of time a password is valid. If the user does not change the password soon enough, the account will be disabled. I have experienced this for a lot of users after long vacations.

To prevent a flood of calls from users requesting that their password be reset, it may be beneficial to take preventive measures. There are two approaches that you can take. One is to reset each account about a week before the vacation, forcing the user to change the password at the next login. This ensures that the password will not expire when the user is on vacation.

The other solution is, in my opinion, much more effective. This is user training. This means training the users to think up passwords that are easy to remember. However, not ones that are easy to guess (a Catch-22). In addition, this also means training your users how to change the password on their own, so they will be able to change password themselves prior to going on vacation. Obviously, this is not going to solve every problem. However, it can help to reduce the number of calls to your hotline.

One very important aspect of this is documenting the complaint procedures. That is, the users need to know what they can do if they are not satisfied with the solutions or help they get. Customer satisfaction is obviously an important aspect in any case or you are paying for support. However, it is often ignored when dealing with internal help desks. For many, this is a fatal error.

Remember that your job as an administrator is to provide the users the means of working as efficiently as possible. Users cannot work efficiently if they do not get answers to their problems. If users are not getting answers to their problems, then there is likely to be a problem with the help desk procedures. By providing users a way to submit complaints or any other kind of feedback, you can more-quickly identify problem areas and then find solutions for them.

Troubleshooting

Being able to find the cause of a problem is just as important as being able to solve that problem. Once again, this may sound like an obvious statement. But, finding the cause of a problem is often the more difficult task. I spent four years working in tech support for a major software vendor. If I were to estimate how much time was spent looking for the problem compared to how much time the spent solving the problem, I would say that least 75% of the time was spent *looking* for the problem.

Unless you have encountered the same problem or a very similar problem before, there is no set way to find out what the problem is. I think the easiest way to describe troubleshooting is to compare it to Taoism. Taoism is not something that can be "taught." It must simply be "experienced." The same applies to troubleshooting.

However, there is a set of basic steps that you can follow no matter what the problem is. The first I got from the Sherlock Holmes' movie "The Seven Percent Solution." In it, Holmes made the statement that you need to eliminate the impossible, and what ever remained, regardless of how probable, must be the truth. The key here is eliminating the impossible. That is, eliminate everything you know that *cannot* be the problem.

For example, assume that users are having trouble connecting to network resources. You eliminate the network as a problem by trying to connect from the workstation to the server (for example, with ping). However, this is not always as easy as it sounds.

When solving problems, you do not always deal with them on a first come, first served basis. You must set priorities! Priorities should be defined well in advance so that both the users and the system administrators know what the priorities are. Priorities range from things that must be dealt with immediately to things that are simple suggestions.

One thing I found very useful is to create a troubleshooting toolkit. This does not necessarily mean to carrier box of things around to use. Instead, it means quick access to those things the most useful in solving problems. For example, there are a number of diagnostic tools, such as Micro 2000's Troubleshoot or Windsor Technologies #1 TuffTEST, both of which are very useful in detecting hardware problems.

Another part of this toolkit and is a set of drivers for all the hardware that we use. This is one reason why you should limit the vendors that should have. Obviously, the more vendors you have, the more different drivers you need. By limiting the number of vendors, you minimize the number of drivers that you deal with.

I found it useful to copy all of the drivers into a single directory and then write to a CD that contains all of these drivers. This CD can then be taken with you when you need to go to a branch office. You therefore don't need to worry if the people at the remote office lost the drivers' disk. Even if you have a network connection between the two offices, having the drivers on CD saves the time needed to download the driver. In addition, you are in a real bind if the you are missing the driver needed to create the network

Documentation for the hardware you have is also an important aspect of this, although you cannot be expected to carry copies of every single configuration manual that you have. You might think about copying the pages that show the layout of the card as well as the jumper settings. I have found that this is sufficient as most of the documentation addresses basic configuration issues that are the same for every kind of hardware.

One thing to consider is to define specific titles data responsible for specific areas within your IT organization. For example, the security officer develops the security-related policies for the company and ensures that they are implemented correctly. The software manager is responsible for managing software licenses. In addition, he or she orders new software, updates, and may even decide who gets what software. The hardware manager, for example, decides who gets what hardware. He or she also sets and develops policies for the hardware use.

Obviously, the number of managers you have and what areas they are responsible for will depend on your company, that one person will be responsible for administering everything. However, if you have 10 and administrators, it might be useful to define the responsibilities in this way. In essence, each one is responsible for developing the policies related to his or her area of responsibility. This is not to say that they are the ones to define policy. Instead, and fees are the before that develop the policies and standards and submit them to the company management for approval. It's possible that in your company, management does not how not be experienced to be able to develop effective policies and standards. Therefore, it is imperative that the other members of the department develop these policies. Hopefully, you work in a company where management listens to suggestions and ideas of the employees.

Branch Offices

Supporting branch offices has its own unique set of problems. You are less likely to see these kind of problems if the branch office is in another town 50 miles away. However, I have worked for companies that have branch offices all over the world. That is, at any time of the day at least one of the branch offices was working. They need to be supported. What kind of support they would get was an important management decision. We did not have the staff to be able to provide 24-hour support. However, this was not necessary, as most problems were not that urgent. Problems that were urgent normally could not be solved over the telephone. Instead, the needed to be solved by someone locally; in most cases, this was provided by a local consultant.

You obviously need to weigh the costs of providing 24-hour support with the need of providing that support. It is obviously not always possible to provide 24-hour support, and it is not always necessary. What support is provided and when will of course depend on your company. However, you must publish this information for your users. That is, the people in the branch office must know when they can expect to have support and when not. You may also consider publishing the home telephone numbers of your system administrators to be used in emergencies.

Another aspect of this is the language. In this company English was not the language used at the headquarters. This often presented problems when the branch office spoke just the local language and English. It was therefore necessary to ensure that people working on the help desk spoke English sufficiently well to provide the necessary support.

Then there is the language of the applications they use. Microsoft provides both the operating systems and applications in all of the world's major languages. It is therefore possible to provide a local version of the software and, in most cases, the applications as well. The question you should ask yourself is whether or not this is desirable. For example, in one company it was decided that the Scandinavian countries would get the English version instead of the local version. The people in the Scandinavian countries spoke English well enough to be able to use the software and it was easier for the administrators to solve problems, especially over the telephone. There was no need to translate menu entries from the local language into English and thereby create misunderstandings. Instead, both the support people at the headquarters and in the branch offices were using the exact same software.

Supporting users in branch offices has other issues than just the language and time zones. One of the key questions commonly left unanswered is, exactly what are the limitations of the support. Here, again, I'm not saying the two need to have limitations. However, any limitations that you do have must be spelled out to your users. For example, users in branch offices were provided with the exact same support as those in headquarters with the exception of network troubleshooting. That meant that if users in a branch office noticed the connection to the headquarters was down, they were responsible for determining where the break was.

We actually decided on this rule for two reasons. First, many of the branch offices were in different time zones. As a result, there may not be someone in the headquarters at the hour they are working and noticed the problem. Instead of calling someone at home in the middle of the night, who would then have to troubleshoot the problem, they were given a checklist of things to look for. Based on this checklist, they were to call their local ISP, telephone company, or whoever was responsible.

The next thing that should be defined is a contact person. This includes the contact person within the headquarters as well as a contact person within the branch office. In some cases, you may allow anyone in the branch office to contact anyone in headquarters. However, this may not be an effective solution. For example, in one company we had dozens of branch offices. Although we had recorded information about the hardware and software configurations in these branch offices, we found it much more efficient if one or two people took responsibility for those offices. It was therefore easier for them to answer questions, plus you developed a better working relationship.

The person responsible for the branch office served as a focal point for basically all contact with headquarters. This not only included reporting problems but also for making requests for new software and so forth. By defining someone with primary responsibility for each branch office, we found that people were less likely to pass the buck saying that was not their job. In essence, there was an administrator who was responsible to see that all the needs of the branch office were met.

Parallel to this is defining a contact person within the branch office. Assuming you want to limit the number of people making requests of the headquarters, you need to assign someone this task. Employees at both the headquarters and the branch office should be made aware of who the contact people are and what the contact procedures are. For example, if someone in the branch office needs a new software product, he or she will make the request of the local contact person who then contacts headquarters. Normally, the contact person in the branch office will be someone who is capable of evaluating the request before passing it along to the headquarters. It might be that the user could make do with other software that is already available.

Without a system like this in place, where anyone in the branch office can contact anyone in the headquarters, experience has shown me that you'll probably end up with duplicate requests. For example of branch offices needs a high-end graphics program such a score old raw. Two people in the branch office make the request of two people in headquarters. Two copies are purchased although only one was needed.

This example obviously assumes that software requests are processed through the headquarters. It is less likely you'll run into this problem when your organization is decentralized and branch offices are allowed to make their own purchases. Whether this is a good idea or not goes beyond the current discussion. In any event, I think it is a good idea to limit the number of people who can make requests of this nature.

Another important question to ask is how you're going to communicate with the branch offices. The telephone and fax machines are the traditional methods of communicating with people in other locations. However, this is not always efficient when transferring information. For example, it is not efficient to transfer a document via fax that needs to be edited at the remote location and returned to the headquarters.

In the section on sharing resources, we discussed various ways of making information available to branch offices. We briefly touched on connections via a modem for the Internet. However, the issues do not stop there. The question is not simply whether or not you should connect via a dial-up or the Internet, router what the details of that connection are. For example, is a 24-hour connection a requirement? Twenty-four-hour connections across leased lines are generally more expensive than connections made on demand. However, if you have a lot of traffic then on-demand connection may be impractical. The time you save in not having to make the connection every time offsets the added cost of the leased line.

It may also be that a 24-hour connection is a requirement. For example, in one company where I worked we were using SAP. Although users were presented with a graphical interface on their computers in the branch offices, all work was actually done on the servers at the headquarters. Therefore, a connection was required any time someone needed to do something was SAP. It was not efficient to initiate a connection every time someone needed to work on SAP. Instead, it was decided that the connection with the lowest total cost of ownership was a 24-hour leased line.

In other offices that did not use SAP, all that was needed was a simple dial-up connection to the Internet. This was not used to connect to the headquarters, but rather simply to send email. For these offices, on the few occasions where we needed to transfer files, they were simply included as attachments to the email. This provided a fairly efficient, low-cost means of communication and data transfer. This also provided the offices with the ability to communicate with their customers, which was not possible if all there was the leased line between offices.

Resources in branch offices bring with them a whole new aspect of support. There is not just the issue of distance, but oftentimes users in the branch office may be in a different time zone and may even speak a different language. You are therefore confronted with issues like staffing longer hours, higher phone bills, and increased administrative costs of managing your software in several different languages.

In this section on users and groups, we discussed developing a user and group concept that helps in the management process; for example, creating user groups that not only indicate the function but also the location. This is less of an issue if each location has its own domain. However, separate domains mean extra work, which is not always necessary.

Within a single domain, self-identifying groups are much easier to manage and to track down problems. For example, assume a user in Singapore is having trouble accessing the directory containing sales information. You know that only the Singapore sales group (SI_sales) has access. You can quickly check that group to see if the user is a member. With a group named such as this, you do not need to know in advance what the name of the group is, as you can easily figure it out.

In a situation where users and resources are managed centrally, someone in the branch office should be specifically assigned the task of notifying the headquarters when new users are created. Most likely, the headquarters will be informed as soon as that user needs access to the network. However, experience has shown me that waiting to the last minute usually means that no thought is given to what access this user really needs. The result is they end up getting more access than they should "just in case."

Part of having someone specifically assigned the task of notifying the headquarters should be procedures to follow when new employees are hired. Specifically, this means things like deciding on a user name, what groups the user should be put into, what software the user needs access to, and so forth. If these things are defined in advance, it should generally take only a few minutes rather than repeating the work when it does not get done right the first time.

I would like to point out here that a good commercial help desk product can be extremely useful in this case to automate much of the work. An email message could be sent to a predefined user, who is actually a mailbox is connected to help desk. The help desk software reads the message, evaluates the request to create a new user, puts in a request for new software, and could even create the new user account. Granted, this last part could be a potential security hole, but the user could be created and immediately disabled, whereby it would need to be activated manually. In any event, a number of things could be automated to reduce the work and potential errors.

If you are supporting users in other countries, providing them with the necessary software does not necessarily mean providing it to them in their native language. In one company where I worked, all server software was in English. Almost all of the workstation software was in the local language, but we did have a few offices where this was not the case. For example, all of our offices in Taiwan and in the People's Republic of China had English software, because our primary financial application did not work with the Chinese version of Windows. In addition, our office in Sweden also wanted the newest version to help simplify support when problems arose. Since everyone there are ready spoke English very well, this was not a problem. When they needed for support, there was not the problem of translating menus or messages into English, which often was not sufficient for the support analyst to figure out what the English equivalent was.

A corollary to this is the communication between the branch office and the support staff. In this case, I am not necessarily referring to the meaning of communication but rather the language. Even if the people in the branch office speak the same language as the people at the headquarters, it may not always be that easy to understand each other (assuming that one or the other is speaking a foreign language). Therefore, the less you need to guess about what is on the screen, the better.

Depending on how many branch offices you have and how frequently people go to those offices, I have found it extremely useful to make readily available maps to the offices, detailed written instructions how to get there, and a photograph or photographs of the building. A map is useful in orienting the person, but it does not replace the necessary instructions to avoid mistakes. It has happened to me on the numerous occasions that I have missed turnoffs because of missing or inadequate signs on the road. The description avoids this problem. In addition, in some cities where I've been, it seemed like it was almost random whether or not there were addresses on the buildings. Therefore, a photograph was useful.

If you need to do any hardware support across the phone for these branch offices, I think a digital camera is a very worthwhile investment. You can take pictures of the inside of the server, workstations, communications cabinets, and so forth and store them on the server back at the headquarters. Using a graphics manipulation tool such as Adobe Photoshop or Corel-DRAW, you can add arrows, labels, and notes to the photographs so that someone trying to diagnose a problem across the phone can see what the user sees.

Documentation

Documentation of both the hardware and software that is present in the branch office is, in my opinion, more important in documenting those at the headquarters. Even if the headquarters has several thousand users, it may be a simple matter of minutes to physically checkout the machine. On the other hand, the only way to check the branch office is to send someone there. You might be asking yourself why users in the local office can't check the hardware themselves. That would be nice in an ideal world, but experience has taught me that it is not always possible. Even if you have a designated contact person within the branch office who is "responsible" for the computer system, they may not necessarily be technically skilled to be able to answer all questions. Therefore, having a well-documented description saves a lot of time and trouble.

An important aspect of this documentation is a change log. As its name implies, it is a log of allchanges that are made to the system. How detailed the log is depends on you and your company. However, I believe that there is very little that should not be documented. Particularly if it is related to system administration and someone. Although I do not think it is always necessary to record the creation of a new subdirectory, I do believe you should record things like installing new software, adding users, creating printers, and so forth.

In my experience, it is not simply enough to see that a certain printer exists or a certain software has been installed. It can also be important to know exactly when certain events occurred. For example, you may notice that problems occurred after the installation of a certain piece of software. It is much easier to tell when that software was installed if you have recorded it in your change log. For example, on one Windows 95 machine, I noticed a brand new error message indicating problems in the system registry, and that the system had to be restarted so that the registry could be "reinitialized." This message started after Internet Explorer (IE)4.0 was installed. After removing IE4.0 and installing the previous version, the error messages went away. This does not prove that IE4.0 was the problem. However, once it was removed, the problem went away. In addition, it was only possible to solve this problem by noting what changes were made to the system immediately prior to the start of the problems.

User Management

Another thing that you should define is who is responsible for user management. That is, who was responsible to create and manage users and groups. Windows NT allows you to manage users and groups even if they are in different domains. Using Remote Access Server (RAS) you can even manage domains to which you do not have a 24-hour connection. The question is whether you should one on.

By having people in branch offices manage users, you relieve the headquarters of the administrative burden. On the other hand, having a centralized user management helps ensure that you do not have duplication of user names and that the polices are adhered to. Although Windows NT is able to distinguish between users and different domains, even if they have the same name, you run into trouble when these users need to communicate outside your organization.

In many organizations, the users' Internet email address is identical to their username that they use to access the system. In general, this is not problem unless you have a single Internet domain with multiple Windows NT domains. That is, the same username exists in multiple Windows NT domains. One of them will have to have a different email address.

External Help

If you're like me, you think the manual is for cowards. Any good computer hacker should not be afraid to open up the box and start feeding in disks without any regard for the consequences. You tear open the box, yank out the floppies, pop the first one in the drive and start up the file manager, double-click on SETUP.EXE and happily go through the thankless task of installing the software. After everything has been installed and your desktop icons have been created, you double-click on the icon and start your new multimedia Web Viewer. But wait! It doesn't work right. No matter how much you point and click and click again, nothing happens. In frustration, you get on the phone and frantically dial the 800 number in the back of the manual (the first time you open it).

When you finally get through to support after waiting for two hours (it was actually only five minutes), you lash out at the poor tech support representative who was unlucky enough to get your call. You spend more time ranting about poorly written software than you spent on hold. When you finally get done insulting this person's ancestry, he calmly points out that on page 2 of the manual, where it describes the installation procedure, it says that in order to get the Web Viewer to work correctly, you have to have a TCP/IP network installed. Since you decided not to install TCP/IP when you first loaded the system, there is no way for the Web viewer to work. You're embarrassed and the whole situation is not a happy thing.

The obvious solution is to read the documentation before, during, and after the installation. That tends to limit the embarrassing calls to tech support, but the world is not perfect and eventually something will go wrong. Programs are (still) written by human beings who can make mistakes, which we users call "bugs." Perhaps the QA technician who was checking your SCSI host adapter sneezed at the very moment the monitor program reported an incorrect voltage. Maybe they never tested that one rare set of circumstances that causes the program to freeze the way it did on your machine. The end result is that you've read the manual, checked and rechecked the hardware, and it still does not behave the way it is supposed to. You can't solve the problem yourself, so you need help.

Outsourcing

In order to work efficiently, you need specialists and experts. If you have your experts in-house, you need to make sure that they remain experts. In other words, you have to keep them trained. Not only do you have to give them the time to keep up-to-date, you have to send them to training. Better still is to bring the trainers to your site so that everyone gets the benefit. If your organization is small, you may not be able to afford your own support staff, so the experts may be from another company that specializes in support or could even be the vendor. This is called outsourcing.

Outsourcing is where you contract your support to an outside vendor. Even some hardware or software companies outsource the direct user support. If you have virtually no IS department, then outsourcing is a good alternative, because you can get support on a wide range of products at a fraction of what it would cost to employ someone full time.

Even if you do have your own MIS department, it might be advantageous to outsource part of your help desk, even to the extent that you have a support contract with another company for those issues that even the experts cannot solve. However, here I need to give you some warning. Remember, this other company might have a help desk built like yours. If your expert calls their first level, they may not know the answer either. This probably applies to the second-level support as well. You can often expect that *your* call is going to get escalated a couple of times before you get to someone who can answer it.

Some companies are aware of this and offer a "premium," "premier," or "first-class" service. With this you get directly to the top. However, you pay for what you get. These kinds of contracts are expensive. When we looked into the possibility of such a contract with Microsoft, they wanted $50,000 a year!

This does have an advantage in that you know what your support costs are going to be. You do not need to plan for sudden changes in the need for support; that is done by the service provider. Also, if your company is located at several sites, outsourcing provides you a way of providing support for all of your offices without having to have someone at each site.

Outsourcing has the biggest appeal to managers who are looking for ways to cut costs, at least on paper. It is, in fact, a relatively inexpensive way of getting a staff of experts in almost every imaginable field. Because they are supporting hundreds, if not thousands of customers, third-party support vendors can achieve economies of scale that are nowhere near possible for a normal company help desk. All of the money and time that you might invest training help desk analysts in the single product or component of the system can be spread out across many customers. This also enables them to keep much more current on the latest technological advances than is possible for people on an internal help desk.

Due to the sheer number of customers they have to support, third-party support providers naturally have the exposure to more different kinds of problems. This increases the likelihood that they have encountered your specific problem before and therefore immediately know the solution. Since no extra time is spent researching the problem, they can find the solution much faster and therefore you have the answer much faster.

Another aspect that is often overlooked is the natural ability of full-time help desk personnel to solve problems. This goes back to what I refer to as the "Tao of Support." The more time you spend solving problems, the greater your ability to "sense" what is wrong. Obviously, having encountered the same or a similar problem before is a key component in determining what is wrong. However, it sometimes requires that you "feel" that an apparently new problem is actually an old problem in disguise.

Another aspect affecting the efficiency of the help desk is based on the motivation of the help desk staff. Particularly if they have other duties to perform, people on an internal help desk generally have less motivation then their external counterparts. If a customer is dissatisfied with the performance of an external or outsourced help desk, he or she simply goes somewhere else. The help desk staff is therefore extremely motivated to keep the customer happy. Although it is not to say that people on an internal help desk generally do a poorer job. However, they stand to lose a lot less. Whereas it is simple enough for the internal help desk to tell the user where to read about something in the manual, this is not the best thing to do with paying customers.

Outsourcing also allows for better flexibility in staffing. During the new product rollouts, call load increases, which leads to help desk staff with much less time to do their normal duties. If you outsource your support, you may need to do nothing at all other than simply call more often. Many third-party support vendors have contracts that allow unlimited calls. Therefore, the cost to use them stays the same whether you have just made a product rollout or not.

On the other hand, you may decide that the best thing is a call pack consisting of the preset number of calls. If the product rollout or something else increases your need to call your support provider, you can simply buy more call packs. This is much easier and more cost effective than hiring the temporary help desk staff member to cover the load.

In one company where I worked, we outsourced the installation and configuration of many of our computers. Because the configuration was standardized, it was a very easy to give our support provider a self-made CD-ROM with a list of instructions on how to configure the machines. This actually worked out to be slightly more expensive then it would have been for us to do the installation and configuration ourselves. The benefit lay in the fact the support provider could install many more machines per day than we could possibly have done, which allowed us to complete our entire upgrade project in a matter of months rather than years. In addition, while the machines were being installed, we could work on other projects that were impossible to outsource.

This shows you that outsourcing need not be an all-or-nothing decision.. The day-to-day help desk activity, such as answering users' questions can still be done by the internal help desk. Larger, relatively short-term projects can be outsourced with little adverse effect.

Here again, it is important to know and document the details of your support contract. This includes things such as support hours, limits of the support, and contact information. If, for example, you end up calling during off-hours or with questions not provided for in the support contract, you end up wasting time. Therefore, it is important to know what the limitations are.

One key question to ask is how good is the supportthat the other company provides. This includes not only the expertise of the people providing the support but also how quickly they provide you with answers. It does little good for the company to know the answer but to take two weeks to give it to you. In the same vein, it does you little good to have the support rep fumble through 20 different possibilities hoping that one of them is the correct solution.

I need to emphasize that you should avoid both support organizations and consultants who do not know a product but insist they can learn it. Although this may help them in their own business, is not very likely to help you in yours. That is, it is unlikely that they will become experts fast enough to provide support for you. You should not pay to train people in the other company.

Another question to ask is what products do they support. In general, resellers that do provide support will provide it for all products that they sell. However, what about the products that they do not sell? It is rare to find a reseller that provides support for products of the products they do not sell. In general, it makes sense that they support what they sell.

This leaves you with three alternatives. First, you can find a vendor that sells and supports all of the products you need. Second, you can go to a number of different vendors. The more different products you have, the less likely you will find a vendor who sells and supports all of the products you have. If you do decide to outsource your support, this is a good reason to limit the number of products you use in-house.

This third alternative is only necessary if you cannot find a vendor that supports all of the products that you use. In some cases, it may be more cost effective to get support for these products as needed and avoid the problems of a separate support contract. For example, if only one of 50 users use your desktop publishing software, an extra support contract may not be warranted. On the other hand, if you find out that the reseller does not provide support for a product or you need a support contract, you'll either need to find a different support organization or consider using a different product.

As we talked about in the section on hardware, there are a number of advantages to having a single supplier. This also applies to suppliers of your tech support. Most likely, each will have its own set of procedures that will need to be documented and followed. You can work much more efficiently if you have only a single number to call than if you have 10.

Depending on the organization providing your support, you may end up having to provide a great deal of information about your system. That is, you may need to provide them information about all of the hardware and software components in your company. On the other hand, this information may only be required when calls are made. If you are required to provide the support organization with details about your computer systems, you may find that the management of that information takes a more time than it is worth. You need to ask yourself in advance just how much work do you have to put in yourself in order for you to get support.

It is also possible that the support provided may go to an extreme. That is, some companies may even provide remote administration of your system. For example, they will dial in via an RAS connection (or some other method) and administer your system that way. Obviously, contracts of this nature are much more expensive than contracts where you simply call in. However, they are generally a lot cheaper than having a system administrator on-staff. Which is best for your organization is something that you need to decide on your own.

External Support Contracts

Because you'll probably be supporting both hardware and software, it is useful to know what it is you're supporting. That is, you have a complete inventory of all your hardware and software. You also need to know what to do if something should break or not function properly. This is where maintenance contracts come in. Here I am not referring to contracts other departments might have with you but rather the contracts your company has with hardware and software vendors. Knowing what contracts you have and what the terms of those contracts are is an important aspect of efficient end-user support.

If you have been an efficient system administrator, you already know what hardware and software you have. Once you have that list you should compile a list of which components have support or maintenance contracts. Part of this is also determining which components actually *need* maintenance.

Not having a support maintenance contract for a particular component is not necessarily a bad thing. In some cases you do not need it. For example, if you found a single copy of a particular software package and it completely satisfies your needs, the cost of the maintenance contract may not be cost effective. If a new version comes out, you can decide then if you need it. On the other hand, if you have 500 copies of that software package, a maintenance contract may be worthwhile, because it is normally more efficient to upgrade all copies of the software package at once.

Also consider what happens if you decide wrong. With a single copy that you do not have a maintenance contract for, the worst case is you pay full price for the new version, but only for that single copy. If you end up paying full price for 500 copies, it becomes a lot more expensive.

The same thing also applies to hardware. Most hardware products have a guarantee or warranty time of about a year. You can then pay extra to extend the warranty period, often up to three years. If the hardware breaks, you get it repaired for free. Once again, it is an issue of cost. Getting blanket maintenance contracts for all of the hardware from a single vendor is more cost effective than for single pieces. Being cheaper makes the price more attractive.

However, you should consider what the effects are of not having the extended warranty and then having something break. If you have spares on hand, you can quickly replace the defective component and then return it for repairs. This is cheaper that having someone come on-site. However, this means you need to have enough spares on hand.

Part of listing the support and maintenance contracts is listing the exact details of each contract. It is not sufficient to simply say that you have a support contract for the particular component. Your help desk personnel need to know the complete scope of the support contract. For example, is it really a support contract or just a maintenance contract? That is, does it just entitle you to upgrades or do you actually get technical support? The next question is, what is the extent of the support? That is, how many calls do you get? How detailed will the support be? What aspects of the product are supported and what are not?

This will vary between the company and support contract. For example, you might get free support just for installation problems. You then have to pay a fee-per-incident for all other problems. The extension of this is determining what constitutes the "end" of the call. For example, I know some companies that say one call is a maximum of 20 minutes. That is, if your problem is not solved within 20 minutes you are charged for another call. Some companies like Microsoft have 900 numbers where you pay by the minute, even if the analyst is searching the manuals or working by trial and error. These kinds of calls can get very expensive.

Another aspect of the support contracts is who is actually providing the support. Just because you have a support contract for a particular piece of software it does not necessarily mean that the support will come from the vendor. For example there are many resellers that also provide support on the products they sell. Obviously, the person who purchases to support contract should know with whom he or she made the contract. However, this does not necessarily mean that the people using the support will know this as well. This is another aspect of good communication.

Just knowing who will provide you support is still not enough. You need to know all the contact information. Again, this might seem obvious, but I know companies that do not make this information readily available. People have to hunt for the contact information. This wastes time and money unnecessarily. I recommend that this information be available either on your company's intranet or through whatever help desk software you are using. The bottom line is that this information must be easily accessible.

Another aspect of this is the primary contact at the support provider. In some cases, you are simply given a number to call and you get to talk to the first available support representative. In some cases, you might have a single person who is responsible for your company. They may actually provide the support, or may they simply serve as an administrative contact. You need to know their function as well as their name and telephone number.

You also need to know the hours of support. For example, I have worked in support organizations that provided support to most customers from 6 a.m. to 5 p.m. For a much larger fee, they also provided support 24 hours a day and 7 days a week. The question is, what hours does your contract include?

Next you need to know what the exact steps are to take when reporting a new problem as well as making contact regarding an existing problem. Different companies will have different procedures, and if you or your support personnel are not aware of these procedures, there will be a delay in getting a solution to the problem. Therefore, it is extremely useful to have the reporting procedures well documented. This saves time by not having to redo any of the steps when you are on the phone.

Calling Support

Tech support is like any system. You put garbage in and you're likely to get garbage out. Calling in, demanding immediately results, or blaming the support rep for the problem will get probably get you one of two things. Either you'll be told that it's either a hardware problem if you've called a software company, a software problem if you've called a hardware company, or they say there is "something" else on the machine conflicting with their product, but it's your job to figure it out. You may get an answer that, yes, that board is bad and you can return it to the place of purchase to get a refund or exchange. In other words, they blew you off.

If the board was bad, getting a replacement solves the problem. If, however, there is a conflict, you will probably spend even more time trying to track it down. If the problem is caused by some program problem (conflicts or whatever), reinstalling may not fix the problem.

Rather than spending hours trying to track down the conflict or swapping out boards, you decide to call tech support. The question is, which one? If there is only one program or one board, it's pretty obvious which one to call. If the problem starts immediately after you add a board or software package, the odds are that this has something to do with it. If, however, the problem starts after you've been running it for awhile, tracking down the offender is not that easy. That's why you're going to call tech support, right? So grab that phone and start dialing.

Stop! Put that phone down! You're not ready to call, yet. There's something you need to do first. In fact, there are several things you need to do before you call.

Calling Tech Support is not as easy as picking up the phone and dialing. Many people who are having trouble with their system tend to think that it is. In many cases, this is true. The problem is basic enough that the tech support rep can answer it within a few minutes. However, if it's not, lack of preparation can turn a two-minute call into a two-hour call.

Preparation for calling tech support begins long before that first phone call or the first post to a newsgroup. In fact, preparation actually begins before you install anything on your system. I mean *anything*—before you install your first program, before you make the change to autoexec.bat to change your prompt, even before you install the operating system.

The first step is to buy a notebook and detail your system configuration. This kind of information is especially important when you need to call a hardware vendor to help track down a conflict or that the software *should* work. You may never use most of this information. However, when you do need it, you save yourself a great deal of time by having it in front of you. This is also important when you post a message to a newsgroup or CompuServe and someone asks the details of your configuration.

By knowing what products and what release you have before you call, you save yourself time when you do call. First you don't have to hunt through notes or manuals while the clock is ticking on your phone bill. Even if you can't find the release, don't guess or say "the latest." Although you can get the release number from the installation media, this may not be exactly what was used to install. The best place to look is the System icon in the Control Panel. This will give you the exact release you are running, including any service packs.

If you guess, then the support technical might have to guess too. This is important, because fixes are almost always release specific. If you say "the latest" and it isn't, and the "bug" you have was corrected in the latest service pack or hot fix, the analyst is not going to give you the fix, because he thinks you already have it. This wastes his time, wastes your time, and in the end you don't get the correct solution. More than likely if you guess and say "the latest" when posting to a newsgroup or CompuServe, you will get some "friendly" reminders that you should provide more specific details.

Should it be necessary to contact a support organization, at the very minimum you should have the following information:

- Operating system(s) and versions
- Machine type:Pentium/133, AMD K6/233, etc.
- Amount of RAM, cache RAM, plus size and type (temporary/permanent) of your paging file
- Make and model of all hardware (rarely is just the brand sufficient)
- Controller make, model, and type
- Symptoms of problem: noises, messages, previous problems
- An exact description of the error message you receive and the context in which you receive it
- Drive organization: partition sizes, special drivers
- Special devices/drivers such as disk array hardware and software
- What application software were you using when the problem occurred?

- What was the machine doing when the problem occurred?
- What was the sequence of events that preceded the problem?
- Has this problem occurred more than once? How often? Can you repeat the problem at will?
- Did you install any device drivers or additional hardware recently?
- What was the last thing that you changed?
- When did you change it and why?
- Is this a production machine and are you down now?
- If this is related to a software product you have installed, what is its exact version?
- Are there any additional packages that are not part of the standard distribution?
- How urgent is the problem?

The last question is essential to getting you the service you need. If you are not clear to the support people about the urgency of the situation, you may end up waiting for the available support analyst, or you might get the "try this and call back later" answer. By explaining the urgency to everyone you contact, you are more likely to get your answer quicker.

On the other hand, most tech support is based on the honor system. The support organizations that I have dealt with will believe you when you call in and say your system is down. (This was also the case when I worked in support.) Many of the customer service people are not in a position to judge the severity of the problem. However, the support analyst is. Saying that your company is down because you can't figure out the syntax for a batch script to check disk space usage is unfair to other people who have problems that are really more severe than yours. Simply turn the situation around, where you are the one waiting for support on a system crash and someone else is tying up the lines because he can't install a printer.

Once you have all the details about the problem you are now ready to call, right? Well, not yet. Before you actually start dialing, you need to make every effort to track down the problem yourself. The first reason is pretty obvious. If you find it yourself, then there is no need to call tech support.

This doesn't apply as much to newsgroups or CompuServe but you do save time by listing the things that you have tried. If there is no specific solution to your problem, other readers of the newsgroups will probably make suggestions. If you list what you have tried, no one is going to suggest doing something that you have already tried. Telling them what you have tried applies to tech support as well.

Most vendors have a Web site that contain answers to commonly asked questions. Unless your system won't boot at all and you have no other access to the Internet, this is always a good place to look before you call tech support. Again it's an issue of time. It is generally much easier to get into a Web site than to a support engineer. You may have to spend a little time becoming familiar with the particular interface that this company uses or how to put in the right keywords. However, once you have learned your way around, you cannot only find answers to your questions, but you often find treasures such as additional programs that are not part of the base distribution. Even if you don't find the solution, knowing that you did look on the Web site saves the support engineer a step. In addition, accessing a Web page can keep you up-to-date on patch releases.

I mentioned that some companies have fax-back services. Oftentimes answers to common questions are available. If you try the fax-back service as well as newsgroups or CompuServe, you have saved time if you need to call into support. Even if you don't get the solution to your problem, you may have gotten some of the suggestions that the tech support rep would give you. Since you already know that something doesn't work, you have saved yourself the problem of getting a "try this and call back" answer.

From the tech support perspective this is very helpful. First, there is the matter of saving time. If it takes 20 minutes just to get through the basic "sanity" checks, then that is 20 minutes that could have been used servicing someone else. Why do you care if someone else gets help instead of you? Well, if you happen to be the one waiting to talk to the support rep, you want him or her to be done with the other customer as soon as possible to be able to get to you quicker. The bottom line is that the quicker they're done with one customer, the quicker it is for everyone.

Make sure any hardware you have added or the software you have installed is supported with your version of the operating system before you call tech support. I have purchased software that explicitly said that it was for Windows 95 and **not** for Windows NT. If you install it on the wrong operating system, getting effective support is difficult at best. They may have to guess at what the problem is and possibly give you erroneous information. In many cases, you will either be referred to the hardware vendor and simply told they can't help you. Not that they won't try. The issue is usually that they don't have any information about that product, so the best they can do is work from knowledge about similar products. If the product you want to use deviates from the norm, then generic information is of little value.

If a piece of equipment is not "officially" supported, the support rep or people on the newsgroup may never have seen this before and may be unaware of quirks that this hardware has. A printer may claim to be Epson compatible, but the driver may send commands to the printer that the clone does not have. Many people will insist that this is a problem with the operating system. No one never claimed the hardware was going to work. So, if the hardware vendor claims it is 100% compatible, it is up to them to prove it.

Also try to determine if it is really an operating system problem and not specific to just one application. If you call your support vendor with a problem in an application that you got somewhere else, make sure the problem also occurs outside of that application. For example, if you can print from

WordPad but can't print from WordPerfect, it's not an operating system problem. However, if WordPad and WordPerfect both have trouble printing, then it is probably not an issue with WordPerfect.

If the problem is software and deals with configuration, make sure that all of the associated files are configured correctly. Don't expect the vendor or the people on a newsgroup to check your spelling. I had one customer who had problems configuring his mail system. He spent several minutes ranting about how the manuals were wrong because he followed them *exactly* and it still didn't work. Well, all the files were set up correctly except for the fact that he had made something plural although the manual showed is as being singular.

Even after you have gathered all the information about your system and software, looked for conflicts, and tried to track down the problem yourself, you are still not quite ready to call. Preparing for the call itself is another part of getting the answer you need.

One of the first questions you need to ask yourself is, "Why am I calling tech support?" What do you expect? What kind of answer are you looking for? In most cases, the people answering the phones are not the people who wrote the code. Unfortunately, Windows is not like Linux, where many people actually *have* spent hours digging through the source code, looking for answers or may have created a patch themselves. Therefore, Windows support people may not be in a position to tell you why the program behaves in a certain way, only how to correct it. Don't expect more than they should reasonably be expected to provide.

If you are contacting the support reps via fax, email, or any other "written" media, be sure that there are no typos. Especially when relating error messages, always make sure that you have written the text *exactly* as it appears. I have dealt with customers who have asked for help, and the error message they report is half of one release and half of another. The change required is different depending on the release you are running. This is also important to know when calling. Telling the support rep that the message was "something like . . ." may not do any good. If there are several possible errors, all with similar content, the exact phrasing of the message is important.

This is also a problem with two systems when one is having the problem and the other is not. It is not uncommon for a customer to describe the machines as "basically the same." This kind of description has little value when trying to track down a problem. I get annoyed at people who use the term when trying to describe a problem. I don't want the *basics* of the problem; I want the *details*. Often customers will use it as a filler word. That is, they say "basically," but still go into a lot of detail.

Many customers insist that the two systems are identical. If they were *identical*, then they both would be behaving the same way. The fact that one works and the other doesn't indicates that the machines are *not* identical. By trying to determine where the machines differ, you narrow down the problem to the point where tracking down the problem is much easier. You even find the problem yourself, thus avoiding the call to support.

Once you get tech support on the phone, don't have them read the manual to you. This is a waste of time for both you and the support rep, especially if you are paying for it. Keep in mind that although there may be no charge for the support itself, you may be calling a toll number. If this is during the normal business day (which it probably is), the call could still cost $20–$30. However, this is also dependent on your support contract. Many customers will pay tens of thousands of dollars a year for support so that they can have the manual read to them. They don't have the time to go searching for the answer; therefore, they pay someone else to do it for them. If you want a premium service, you have to pay a premium price.

The same applies to newsgroups. Don't waste bandwidth by asking someone to give you the option to a command. RTFM! Every version of Windows comes with some kind of on-line help.

If you do read the manual or on-line help and it still does not behave the way you expect, or you are having problems relating the documentation to the software, ensure that the manual matches the software. One customer was having trouble changing his system name. He said the documentation sucked because the software did not work the way it was described in the manual. Turns out the manual he was using was for a release that was two years old, and he never got the latest one! No wonder the manual did not match the software.

If you don't know the answer to the question, tell the support rep, "I don't know." Do not make up an answer. Above all, don't lie outright. I had a customer when I was working in support for a major UNIX vendor who was having problems running some commands on his system. They were behaving in a manner I had never seen before, even on older releases. In order to track down the problem I had him check the release his was using. None of the normal tools and files were there. After poking around awhile, I discovered that this was not our OS. When confronted with this, the customer's response was that their contract for the other operating system had run out.

Getting information from some customers is like pulling teeth. They won't give up without a fight. In order to get the right answer you must tell the analyst everything. Sometimes it may be too much, but it is much better to get too much than not enough.

When talking to support, have everything in front of you. Have your notebook open, the system running if possible, and be ready to run any command the support rep asks you. If you have a hardware problem, try to have everything else out of the machine that is not absolutely necessary to this issue. It is also helpful to try to reinstall the software prior to calling. Reinstalling is often useful, and several companies seem to use this method as their primary solution to any problem. If you have done it in advance of calling and the problem still persists, the tech support rep won't get off with that easy answer. Although I am not professing this as the standard way of approaching things, if you believe reinstalling would correct the problem and you have the opportunity, doing so either solves the problem or forces support to come up with a different solution.

Another common complaint is customers calling in and simply saying that a particular program "doesn't work right." Although this may be true, it doesn't give much information to the technician. Depending on its complexity, a program may generate hundreds of different error messages, all of which have a different cause and solution. Regardless of what the cause really is, it is almost impossible for the technician to be able to determine the cause of the problem simply by hearing you say that the program "doesn't work."

A much more effective and successful method would be to simply state what program you were trying to use, then describe the way it behaved and how you expect that it should behave. You don't even need to comment on it not working right. By describing the behavior, the technician will be able to determine one of three things: You have misunderstood the functionality of the program, you are using it incorrectly, or there really is a bug in the program.

It is a very common attitude of people calling into tech support that they are the only customers in the world with a problem. Many have the attitude that all other work by the entire company (or at least tech support) needs to stop until their problem is resolved. Most tech support organizations are on schedules. Some have phone shifts scattered throughout the day and can only work on "research" problems during specific times of the day. Other organizations have special groups of people whose responsibility it is to do such research. In any event, if the problem requires special hardware or a search through the source code, you may have to wait several hours or even days for your solution. For the individual, this may be rather annoying, but it does work out better for everyone in the long run.

The attitude that analysts need to stop what they are doing and work on this one customer's problem becomes a major issue when problems are caused by unique circumstances. The software or hardware company may not have that exact combination of hardware available. Although the combination ought to work, no one that has not tested it can guarantee there will be no problems. As a result, the support rep may have to wait until they are not working on the phone to gather that combination of hardware. It may also happen that they need to pass the problem to someone else who is responsible for problems of this type. As a result, the answer may not come for several hours, days, weeks, or even *months* depending on the priority level of the contract.

In addition to the priority of the contract, there is also the urgency of the problem. If you have a situation where data are disappearing from your hard disk, you will be given a higher priority than your contract would imply.

While I was working in support, I talked with many other support reps. Often a customer would have a support contract with their vendor, and the vendor would have the contract with us. The vendor would call us if they could not solve the problem. I had a chance to ask many of them about some of the more common problems.

There are several common complaints among tech support reps. Although it may seem like an obvious thing, many people are not in front of their machine. It's possible that the solution is easy enough that the support rep can help even without you at the machine. However, I talked to a customer who had printer problems and wanted me to help him fix things while he was driving down the freeway talking on his car phone.

Another very common issue that supports reps bring up is customers who come off as thinking they know more than tech support. When they are given suggestions, their response is usually "That won't work." Maybe not. However, the behavior exhibited by the failure often does give an indication of where the problem lies. If you are going to take the time to call support, you must be willing to try everything that is suggested. You have to be receptive to the suggestion of the support rep and willing to work with him or her. If necessary, be willing to start the problem from scratch and go over the "basics." The customers that get the best response from support are usually the ones who remain calm and are willing to try whatever is suggested.

People have called computer manufacturers to be told how to install batteries in laptops. When the support rep explains how to do this and that the directions are on the first page of the manual, one person replied angrily, "I just paid $2,000 for this damn thing, and I'm not going to read a book."

At first glance this response sounds reasonable. A computer is a substantial investment and costs a fair bit of money. Why shouldn't tech support tell you how to do something? Think about a car. A car costs more. So, after spending $20,000 for a new car, you're not going to read the book to figure out how to start it? Imagine what the car dealer would say if you called in, asking how to start the car.

The computer industry is the only one that goes to this level when supporting its products. Sometimes you get very naive customers. At least they are naive when it comes to computers. In attempting to solve a customer's problem it is often essential that we know what release of the operating system being used.

Some customers are missing some basic knowledge about computers. One customer was having trouble where we needed to know the release. Although he could boot, he was having a lot of trouble finding the Control Panel and starting the applets.

We then asked him to get the installation floppy and read us the release number off the floppy. He couldn't find it. Not the floppy, the release number. So after 10 minutes of frustration, we decided to have him photocopy the floppy and fax it to us.

Wow!" he said. "You can get information from the floppy that way."

"Sure," we said. "No problem." (What's so hard about reading a label?)

A few minutes later a fax arrived from this customer. It consisted of a single sheet of paper with a large black ring in the center of it. We immediately called him back and asked him what the fax was.

"It's the floppy." He said. "I'm still amazed that you can get information from the floppy like that. I must tell you, I had a heck of a time getting the floppy out of the case. After trying to get it out of that little hole, I had to take a pair of scissors to it." (The case was actually the plastic jacket.)

Many of us laugh at this because this is "common knowledge" in the computer industry. However, computers are the only piece of equipment where the consumer is not expected to have common knowledge. If you drive a car, you are expected to know not to fill it up with diesel when it takes normal gasoline. However, trying to load a DOS game onto Windows NT system is not unexpected.

One customer I had was having trouble installing a network card. The documentation was of little help to him because it was using a lot of "technobabble" that most "normal" people couldn't understand. The customer cannot even answer the basic questions about how his hardware was configured. He insisted that it is our responsibility to know that because we wrote the operating system and he's not a computer person. Well, I say, it's like having a car that won't start. You call the car dealership and tell them it won't start. The service department asks you what model you have. You say that they should know that. They then ask if you have the key in the ignition. You say that you are not a "car person" and don't know this technical stuff.

In the past few years, many software vendors have gone from giving away their support to charging for it. This ranges anywhere from $25 a call for application software to $300 for operating systems like Unix. As an end-user, $300 can be a bit hard to swallow. However, in defense of the software industry it really is not its fault. As more and more computers are being bought by people who have never used one, the number of calls to support organizations have gone up considerably. People treat computers differently than any other piece of equipment. Rather than reading the manual themselves, they much prefer to call support.

Would you ever call a car manufacturer and ask how to open the trunk? Would you ever call a refrigerator manufacturer to ask how to increase the temperature in the freezer? Hopefully not. However, computer tech support phones are often flooded with calls at this level, especially if their support is free or free for a specific warranty period.

The only way for a company to recover the cost of the support is either to include it with the cost of the product or to charge extra for it. The bottom line is that there is no such thing as a free lunch, nor is there free tech support. If you aren't paying for the call itself, the company will have to recover the cost by increasing the sales price of the product. The result is still money out of your pocket. In order to make the situation fairest for everyone involved, companies are charging those people who use the tech support system.

I remember watching a television program a couple of years ago on airplane accidents and how safe planes really are. The technology exists today to decrease the number of accidents and near accidents to almost zero. Improvement to airplane operations, air traffic control, and positioning could virtually eliminate accidents. However, this would result in increasing the cost of airline tickets by a factor of 10! People won't pay that much for safety. The risk is too low.

The same thing applies to software. It is possible to write code that is bug free. The professor who taught my software engineering class insisted that with the right kind of planning and testing, all bugs could be eliminated. The question is "At what cost?" Are you willing to pay 10 times as much for your software just to make it bug free? One support rep put it like this: "How can you ask us to hold up the entire product for an unknown length of time, to fix a single problem which affects few users and is not fatal? Would you expect Ford to ship their next year's model of Escort 3 months late because they found out that the placement of the passenger door lock was inconvenient for people taller than 6′ 9″?" As ridiculous as this seems, calls reporting bugs are often at this level.

After years of doing tech support, I am convinced that the statement "The customer is always right" was not coined by some businessman trying to install a customer service attitude in his employees. It must have been an irate user of some product who didn't bother to read the manual, tried to use the product in some unique way, or just generally messed things up. When this user couldn't figure out how to use whatever he bought, he decided it was the fault of the vendor and called support.

You as the customer are not always right. Granted, it is the responsibility of the company to ensure you are satisfied. This job usually falls on the shoulders of tech support, as they are usually the only human contact customers have with hardware and software vendors. However, by expecting tech support to pull you out of every hole you dig yourself into or coming across rep as a "know-it-all" or "I-am-right," you run the risk of not getting your question answered. Isn't that the reason for calling support in the first place?

Consultants

You may someday find yourself in a position where you cannot continue to try and solve problems over the phone. You need someone to come to your office to look at the problem firsthand. This is where the computer consultant comes in. Sometimes consultants are called in to evaluate and analyze the current situations and make recommendations and sometimes even to implement these recommendations.

Computer consultants are like lawyers. They often charge outrageous fees (several hundred dollars an hour) and rely on the fact that you know little or nothing about the subject. They have a service that you need and want you to pay as much as you are willing to pay. Fortunately, all you need to do to see whether a lawyer is qualified is to look on his wall. If the diploma is from Joe's Law School and Barber College, you'll probably go somewhere else. Although there are a number of different types of certifications a consultant may have, there are few laws governing who can call himself a "computer consultant." Therefore, you need to be extra careful in choosing a consultant.

I had one consultant call for a customer of his who was having trouble with a SCSI tape drive. The consultant almost got upset when I started talking about the technical issues involved, such as termination, proper cabling, etc. You see, he had a master's degree in electrical engineering and was, therefore, "fully aware" of the technical issues at hand. I asked him how much RAM his system had. He responded, "Do you mean memory? Well, there is, uh, 32, uh, what do you call them, megabytes." (No, I'm not making this up!)

Another time a customer was having a similar problem getting a network card working. Again it was the issue that the customer did not have the basic computer knowledge to know about base addresses and interrupts. In addition, the difference between thin wire and twisted pair was foreign to him. He had worked for many years on mainframes and had never had to deal with this level of problem. After over a half hour of trying to help him, it became apparent that this was really beyond what tech support is there for. I suggested he hire himself a consultant. In the long run, that would ensure he got the attention and service he needed. There was a long pause, and then he said, "I *am* the consultant."

One of my favorites is a consultant who was trying to do long distance hardware troubleshooting for a site in Alaska from his office in Texas. Despite the fact that he had a modem connection, it is often quite difficult to check hardware settings and cabling through a modem.

I once had an auto mechanic who had a PC running a DOS application written specifically for automobile workshops. Aside from the fact that the consultant had him start Windows and then click on an icon to start this DOS application, it did its job (it's the only thing the machine was used for). Recently the mechanic discovered that he was running out of hard disk space and needed a larger drive. So, the consultant came in, put in a larger hard drive, and things looked better. Since it was not part of their contract, the consultant charged them for two hours' labor to replace the drive plus 10% more than the average market price for the hard disk. So far, this seems like an acceptable practice. However, he took the smaller drive with him, even though he charged full price for the larger drive. It wasn't defective—just too small.

These stories represent four basic problems with computer consultants. First, you don't have to have studied computer science or even a related field to open shop as a computer consultant. Although electrical engineering is a related field and the person may know about the computer at the transistor level, this is comparable to saying that a chemist who knows what goes on at the molecular level inside an internal combustion engine is competent enough to fix your brakes.

The next issue is that although the person may have worked with computers for years, he knows little about PCs or operating systems. I have seen it enough times where consultants assume that all computer systems are the same. They worked for years on Windows 3.x, so they are qualified to install and support NT, right?

There is the issue of consultants not making house calls. They have to. They have to be willing to come to your site and check the situation themselves. You cannot be expected to shut down operations to bring a computer to their office, nor should you tolerate them trying to do remote support (i.e., across a modem).

Finally, if you do need to hire a consultant, make sure you know what you are paying for. When you do decide on a consultant, make sure that you know specifically what services are being provided and what other obligations the consultant has. These services include not only hardware and software, but also what work they are going to provide. If they need to replace a defective hard disk, the cost of the disk is included, but the time to replace it may not be.

The best solution is to ask your friends and other companies. If you have a good relationship with another company of similar size and product, maybe they can recommend a consultant to you. Another source is the Internet and on-line services like CompuServe. Ask people there what their experiences are. Web search engines, Like Yahoo or Alta Vista, can give you names of companies that specialize in Windows NT as well.

GETTING THE MOST FOR YOUR MONEY

Deciding that you need a consultant doesn't mean you are throwing yourself to the wolves. With a little preparation you can be ready and ensure that you don't make any costly mistakes. There are four basic steps to follow when deciding which consultant to go with:

- Define the project in detail.
- Find the right person for the job.
- Agree *in writing* exactly what the job entails and what is expect from *both* sides.
- Make sure the job gets done correctly and on time.

When you think you have found the right consultant you need to treat him like a telephone company: Get it in writing! This plus finding the right person are the two essential factors in deciding on which consultant to choose.

Let's look at the right person first. In choosing a consultant, there are several ways to go about it. First you can pick up the telephone book and find the one with the fanciest ad. Personal referrals are also a way, but this can cause a lot of problems. If the consultant is a friend or family member of the person making the recommendation, you get yourself into an awkward position when you either find he's not the right person for the job or he's not really competent and you have to get rid of him. Personally, I think recommendations from other companies are best. They have had real experiences with the consultant and (should) know his capabilities.

Part of choosing the right person is making sure that he has the skills necessary to get the job done. Never hire a consultant who doesn't know the product or issue at hand but insists he can learn it. You are paying for an expert, so that's what you should get, not someone still in training. The process is basically the same as hiring an employee. You can request a resume as well as references and then call those references. Things to ask are:

- What did they think of this consultant in general?
- What did they think of the consultant's technical abilities?
- Did he or she interact well with your employees?
- Did he follow through with commitments? Finish on time?
- When the project was finished were there any points of dispute? How well did the consultant react?
- Did they understand what the consultant did?

When you have your first meeting with the consultant, there is nothing wrong with having your expert present to "test" the consultant's knowledge. This is the same thing as an interview. You are trying to determine whether or not to hire this person. Therefore, you have the right to ask about his technical abilities.

In one company I worked for we had a very bad experience with a consultant. The company ran mostly PCs with Windows for Workgroups, but there were several UNIX servers as well as workstations. We found a consulting firm that were "experts" with Microsoft's Exchange, since we were planning to implement this on the company's intranet. We explicitly told the consulting firm that one of our goals was to get connected to the Internet. We scheduled a three-day workshop where the consultant would go through the details of configuration and give us guidance on how to implement it.

When the consultant arrived, we were pleasantly surprised that it was one of the owners. However, the pleasure was short lived after we discovered that he had no understanding of Internet mail and could, therefore, provide us no guidance on how to configure MS Exchange for the Internet. We also later discovered that he was no expert with MS Exchange, as he spent the entire afternoon on the last day trying to get a basic configuration issue to work.

This taught us two things. First, just because someone is the owner of a consulting firm does not mean he or she knows what they are talking about. Once again, there are few laws governing who can call him or herself a consultant. Second, we were not clear with what our expectations were or what the consultant was to provide. Nothing was in writing other than he would give us a "workshop." It was obviously up to him to decide whether he had achieved this goal or not.

There are many areas where a consultant is necessary. You cannot hire experts in every area. It would just be too expensive. Even if you do have people in your organization, it is often useful to have someone come in with a fresh perspective. As an employee you often have emotional responses involving your system or company that a consultant doesn't have. This is helpful to get to the core of the issue.

Another aspect is the specialization. A consultant has a particular skill set in which he knows almost everything. (At least that's what you're hoping.) Being really good at this one subject means that he or she may not be as useful to a company to hire full time. However, if the company is involved in a project that requires that skill, it is cost efficient to hire the expert and get the job done quicker. I think of setting up an Internet server as the primary example. After I had done it a few times, it became a lot easier. However, once I have done it a dozen or so times, it might become easy. Potentially, I could hire myself as a consultant to develop Internet servers. (But then again, maybe not.)

When you hire a consultant, you have to know what you want out of him. What information do you expect the consultant to impart on you or what project do you expect the consultant to complete? What does "complete" really mean? If the project is configuring a Web server, and all the consultant does is hook you up to the Internet, then the job is not done. If the project will take a long time and you expect regular status reports, have the consultant define when these reports are due. If he says every other Friday, then handing it to you on Monday is not acceptable.

You may not be able to use the correct "buzzwords" to define what you want, but you can come up with a clear idea of what you want. If the consultant uses buzzwords, make sure you understand what is meant. (I have actually seen consulting contracts that contained a glossary at the end.)

Once you have the concept of what you want, you should work with the consultant to define the project in the correct terminology. However, don't let the consultant confuse you. If you don't understand, say so. There is nothing wrong with not understanding something. If you were an expert on this subject, you wouldn't need a consultant. One thing that our MS Exchange consultant did a lot of was talk in techno-babble. He would throw out some "technical" word to make him sound like an expert. The problem was that he really didn't know much about the subject and often used the words in the wrong context. This seemed to work for the IS manager, but didn't work with the rest of us. If you get the feeling that the consultant is trying to baffle you with B.S., it's time to get another consultant.

When dealing with a consultant, there are bound to be concepts and vocabulary that are foreign to you. The question arises, what about the other way around? Will the consultant know everything about your business? If the consultant specializes in your area, you would hope so. However, you are probably hiring a computer specialist, not a legal specialist or medical specialist or wholesale distribution specialist. Therefore, there is a lot that you will have to explain to your consultant.

Do not assume that the consultant knows your business at all. Specify *every* aspect of the project. One example would be a wholesale soft drink distribution company. When buying large quantities of soda, the unit most people are familiar with is the "case." The consultant you hire to develop a tracking system may take this for granted and write the program to deal only in cases. What if you distribute containers of cola syrup as well. These are not measured in cases. If you assume that the consultant knows this and don't tell him and he programs for cases, who is responsible for paying for the changes? You said you wanted a tracking system and you got one. The project description didn't mention the kinds of units.

Don't let the consultant get away with estimates on anything. If he estimates anything, then it can be off. Just like the estimate on car repairs. Also, the more vague the job description, the easier it is for the consultant to postpone or claim that something was never agreed on. This goes for time as well as for money.

If the job will take awhile and you have said you want status reports, then these reports can be used for the basis of payment. For example, the project is to take 10 weeks with five biweekly status reports. Each time you get a status report, the consultant gets 1/5 of the total fee. Another way would be to set "milestones." Each phase of the project is to be done by a certain date. At each milestone, the consultant gets a certain percentage of the total. The idea of completion-based payment is important if you have deadlines to meet yourself. The consultant must be made aware of these as well. It is not unreasonable to make completion within the time specified be part of the contract. However, you need to be clear in contract what is to be done and by when, plus what the penalties are.

The consultant may not be working solely on your project during the time you have contracted him. This is acceptable provided he meets all his commitments. Explaining to you that he couldn't meet the deadline because of a problem at another site should tell you that his other customer is more important. They might be, so find a consultant where *you* are more important.

DID YOU GET WHAT YOU PAID FOR?

Well, that depends. Just because a consultant asks for a high rate does not mean he's good. I look at Ferrari or Jaguar as examples. These are very expensive cars. They have a "performance" comparable to their price, in that they go "fast." If you buy a Ferrari consultant, he might be done with the job in a short time. However, like the Ferrari, you might spend as much on repairs as the car originally cost.

On the other hand, a consultant's rates will get higher as he gets better. Not only does he have more technical ability, but he has the ability to do a better job and more quickly. As a result, you pay a higher rate for his time, but you pay for less time. Therefore it comes out cheaper in the long run. Even if it is not cheaper on your checkbook, having the project done faster may still save you money.

Some get paid $200 an hour, some get $1000 a day. Those are reasonable prices. Your employees (probably) don't get paid that much, so why should you pay a consultant like that? Well, first thing is that a consultant may not be "on the job" only when he or she is at your site. Depending on the project, there maybe hours, days or even weeks of preparation. Plus, there are all the administrative costs for the consultant's office. You have to pay for the people in your IS/IT department out of your own budget, but not the company receptionist. The consultant does.

LEGAL ISSUES

Remember that the consultant may have complete access to all of your data. Although I am not saying he is likely to be a spy for your competition, you need to be careful. Even if the consultant doesn't have access to your more-precious trade secrets, having him sign a nondisclosure agreement is a wise decision. This could be as simple as stating that the consultant is not to disclose *any* aspect of the job to *anyone*, or it may go into details about what is and is not to be kept secret. Talk to your lawyers about this one.

When the consultant finishes the project, who owns it? Well, you do, as far as the project within your company is concerned. The consultant is not going to charge a license fee to use the program you paid him to develop (we hope). However, what about the code itself? This was done on your time, so like the code a regular employee writes, it's yours, right? Well, it may be the case that the consultant does keep the rights to the code he has written, although the compiled, running program is yours. Make this clear in your contract. If you want the right to everything written by the consultant, make sure that part is written in the contract as well.

One important aspect of the contract is the default terms. That is, what happens if the consultant defaults on the agreement. This is especially important if you have deadlines and by not meeting them you lose money. It is not unreasonable to deduct specific amount from the total for going past the deadline. Not only does the consultant not get paid for those days past the deadline, but money is deducted from what is owed him for the other days. I have seen consultants who intentionally overextend themselves just to get a contract. They can promise to have it within a certain time but have no pressing need to unless they will be losing money.

You have to be careful with this one. If the project is a feasibility study and it turns out the project is not feasible, did the consultant do his job? Sure, he determined whether the project was feasible or not. Therefore, he did his job. Also, what happens if the cause if the delay is not the fault of the consultant? If you promised him certain resources that were not available, then you are at fault.

You might even get a consultant who has an attitude of "all or nothing." That is, if he doesn't deliver on time what is promised to you, don't pay him. However, you can guarantee that this consultant will probably have you spell out everything you want done so there is no room for discussion.

When dealing with consultants, that are some general issues to remember that will help make things easier:

- A consultant is not one of your employees. Don't insist that he arrive at a certain time or work until a certain hour. Maybe part of what he is doing can be done at his office. You're concerned with him getting the project done on time and not being physically present at your site.

- Judge the price you pay by what it would take you to do the job without the consultant. How many hours? How much money might you lose? If you would end up paying more than a "high-priced" consultant, the consultant is cheap. However, comparison-shopping is also valid for a consultant. Get a second or even a third estimate.

- Insist on some kind of proof that he knows what he's talking about. A resume is fine but references are better.

- Make sure the consultant communicates well. Can he express himself? Does he understand your needs and requirements?

- Be comfortable with the consultant. If there is something about him that you don't like, you don't need to hire him, just as it would be for considering a regular employee.

- Don't judge the consultant by personal appearance. Then again, I wouldn't hire a slob. It's okay to expect him to be clean, but don't expect a suit.

User Training

Users solving problems on their own not only means finding the answer but also being able to understand that answer. This can only be accomplished by training. Simply saying that users need training is not enough. You must also define in what areas users need training, how detailed the training should be, and how often they should have training.

For example, in one company we provided training for Microsoft Word. The company also had the documentation standard that defined, among other things, what formatting was to be used for different elements of the documentation. However, format standards were not discussed during Word training. Therefore, the users either did not know how to format the documents correctly or they did not use the proper tools. For example, many people created bullet lists by putting an asterisk at the beginning of each line. This did not look very good and it meant that each new item had to be formatted by hand. It was worse with numbered lists when an item was inserted into the middle of the list. That is, each subsequent entry had to be renumbered by hand. All this work could have been avoided by spending five extra minutes during the Word training to explain how to do numbered lists.

Training is not just for the applications but for the entire system as well. For example, I believe it is important to explain basic network or computer concepts to your end users. In one company, we noticed that at regular intervals the throughput to one of our branch offices dropped to almost zero. This is because huge files were being sent across the network and blocked out everything else. When we explained to the users how networks functioned, they understood why they shouldn't transfer files the way they did. The solution was to set up the transfer to be done in the middle of the night. We had wasted hours of time tracking down the problem that could have been prevented with five minutes of training.

I think that it is important to set up training for all new employees. Issues should include basics as well as details of how *your* computer systems are set up and basic issues such as not transferring large files in the middle of the day. Things like mapping network drives, selecting new printers, and other issues that most administrators take for granted should be also included. You might want to consider a test for all new employees to evaluate their skill levels and then assign training accordingly. For example, a fairly knowledgeable user may not need training but could be given the training materials to study on his or her own or may just need an overview of how your system works.

I firmly believe that not only should this kind of training be a *requirement* but it should enjoy the full support of the company management. This means that the training should be done on company time. This may seem like an obvious statement, but I know of companies that provide this training only after-hours, on the employees' time. Most employees did not take advantage of this, and as a result, more time was lost by the administrators who had to explain basic issues to each employee individually. This was not very cost effective.

Part of this is to *schedule* the training. This means setting aside a specific time and place for the training and ensuring that the training does take place. The training must be scheduled well in advance and made public so that users wishing to attend will be able to. Once again, it is vital that training being supported by the company management. Without training, users cannot use the computer system sufficiently and support costs go up. It is my experience that the cost of any training is offset by reduced support costs.

I worked in a company whose attitude toward training was literally "sink or swim" It was common (actually the rule) when application software was purchased, it was installed and the users were on their own to figure out how it worked. They were not even given the manuals to use, as these were kept by the system administrators in case they needed to look up something.

This is a classic case of people not understanding the total cost of ownership. The more users you have who "fight" with the software, the more expensive that software becomes. That is, the more time they spend looking for answers or doing things improperly, the less time they spend on productive work.

An added cost is that in most cases, the users do not use the full functionality of any of the software they have. Therefore, it is often more beneficial to buy a "lite" version of the same product or a different product with fewer features. One good example is MS Word versus WordPad delivered with Windows 95, Windows 98, and Windows NT. I have worked in places where hundreds of users never used any more of the functions than were provided by WordPad. The IT manager was simply caught up in Microsoft's marketing, that we just *had* to have all of the features of MS Word and always have the most recent versions. This wasted hundreds of thousands of dollars and the total value of *ownership* for MS Word was less, because we got less value out of it.

The real problem is not that users had a product of which they didn't use all of the features. Instead, the problem was that they didn't know how to use those features. In other words, they lacked the training.

It is impossible to get away from the fact that training costs money. Either you pay for outside training or someone internally needs to take the time, which costs money. The truth is that training does make sense, but the question arises of how much money are you willing to give out. The biggest cost is the person—if that cost could be eliminated or reduced, training might be more affordable.

One obvious solution is to buy copies of the manuals, or in the case of Microsoft products buying books from third-party publishers, in order to get the necessary details. Although you can get good books on many subjects for about $30, books are not always the best teachers, as they are not interactive and do not "show" you how to do something.

Fortunately, there is a solution between the active, hands-on of a human instructor and the low price of books. There are a number of vendors of training products that do an excellent job of teaching you the basics as well going into details of the various subjects.

One of the issues I encountered is that there is no one method or even one vendor that is the best in every case. Some vendors produce videos and others provide their instruction on CD-ROM. Depending on your circumstance, both are useful.

First, videos are useful for those topics where you do not need to be directly in front of the computer. These are generally limited to introductory topics, but you can watch these kinds of videos in a more-relaxed environment. Often on a rainy Saturday afternoon, I will watch one of theses videos.

Although I typically have a pad of paper next to me to write down notes, it is a low-stress way of learning something new.

If you have a large number of users, displaying the video can also be more beneficial than books as well as cheaper than hiring an instructor. If you have a classroom where the users can sit at computers to practice the things in the video, they will definitely get more out of it than watching the video alone. Although an instructor can answer questions, a well-presented video can still provide an acceptable level of training.

One limitation of the video that cannot be overcome is that it is not interactive. Interactive, hands-on training is often much more effective than videos are. Today, this is typically done with CD-ROMs, which contain the training courses. Here you play the CD directly on your workstation and can move back and forth through the instruction much more (and much quicker) than you can with a video.

In many cases, there are interactive exercises on the CD that guide you through the steps. Another key advantage is the ability of a CD to provide testing of the material. I have seen some products that have a set of questions, which are always presented in the same fashion and in some cases in the exact same order. Better products not only change the order of both the questions and the tanswers.

Unfortunately, one thing I have yet to find is a test that jumps back to the appropriate part of the lesson when you answer incorrectly. In addition, all products I have seen will tell you if your answer is incorrect, but few will tell you which answer is the right one.

Another issue that I have encountered is the style of the instruction. This refers to both the package as a whole and the person who is giving the instruction. One might think that for videos there is not much you can do with the "style." However, among the different companies that offer video training, there is a big difference in how the material is presented. In some cases, the instructor acts as if he is at gunpoint, with no enthusiasm at all. In other cases, the instructor is like an old friend, showing you something that he or she really enjoys.

Also look for the level of competence of the instructor. Although you cannot always tell if the instructor really knows what he or she is talking about, you can often see if the instructor appears to be following a script. I have seen a few videos where it was obvious that the instructor did not even understand what they were saying.

Also look at how much of the instruction has the instructor sitting there describing the material to you and how much of it is showing you the application or something related to the topic. I have seen some material that is comparable to simply making a video of an instruction in a classroom, with the instructor writing everything on a blackboard. You need a product that takes advantage of the existing technology, which means interactivity, as well as a little entertainment.

One of the key issues is reference points in the videos. You should choose a video product that has on-screen markers to tell you in what section you are currently in. If you are taking notes, you can indicate the appropriate section and find that section again, if necessary. If there are no on-screen markers, you waste a great deal of time fast-forwarding and rewinding the tape.

Some companies provide just the video, whereas others provide workbooks. Although the workbook should match the material, it does not need to be a mirror copy. I have seen some material where it is almost a transcription of what the instructor is saying; there is no supplemental information at all. Although this is useful, so you do not need to take notes, you are missing a great opportunity to get more information.

Another factor is what I call the ICR problem. ICR stands for "I Can Read" and it refers to video and CD training where the instruction simply repeats what is on the screen without explaining anything about it. For example, I remember one video where the instructor read the entries in a directory. There was almost no explanation of the function of each file and subdirectory, and the ones that were explained were generally self-explanatory.

One thing you can do with CD training that you cannot do with a video is to have interactive questions. Although a video could have a quiz at the end, the questions and answers are always in the same order. If you take the quiz repeatedly, this can lead to memorizing the order without knowing the answers. That is, you memorize that the answer to question 6 is B. However, with CD-based training, you can change the order of both the questions and the answers. To some extent it is also possible to have different incorrect choices answers each time through.

Take a look at the applications for which a particular vendor provides training material. Although it is less important than with the application software, having a consistent format is still beneficial. Therefore, you might consider going with the vendor who provides training materials for all of the applications you use, although you feel their instruction method is not optimal for your needs. On the other hand, you might want to consider choosing different vendors for the training on different products, depending on how well the information is presented.

All of the products that I will discuss have their own merits and shortcomings. As I mentioned previously, no single teaching method is valid in every circumstance. Therefore, if you plan to implement video or CD training, you should consider taking a look at one example from each company to get a feeling for the methods this company uses. In some cases, particularly with CD training, you might be able to get a demo CD from the vendor that gives you a feeling for what the training is like. You may also find that the vendor provides a money-back guarantee if you return the product within a specified period.

Some companies will lump all of their products together into one long list, whereas other separate them into (generally) two groups: applications and desktop. Often the company's definition of "desktop" is anything not immediately definable as an application. Some companies add the category "certification." These courses are designed explicitly to teach you the material needed to pass the certification programs of many vendors, such as Novell, Cisco, and Microsoft.

As the Internet grew, many companies began to add on-line training to their course offerings. Although this is intrinsically a good thing, as the training is always up-to-date, you have the disadvantage of limited bandwidth. If you are playing a training CD on your local machine or even across a local network, you typically have more bandwidth than across the Internet. If you have a relatively slow Internet connection, trying to access on-line training courses can be a bother.

Some companies have addressed this issue by limiting the material on the Internet. It may be restricted to nonvideo material and in some cases even just on-line tests. This is not necessarily a bad thing, as you constantly have new material, and the questions can reflect new or changed products much quicker than can the CDs or videos. It is just something to be aware of.

If you are thinking about on-line training, look into what corporate programs the company offers. As with other types of products, you can generally get quantity discounts. This can either be for a specific number of courses or a specific number of students. Many companies also offer corporate programs for their CD or video training courses. In addition, they may also provide free upgrades should a newer version of the course be developed during the term of your contract.

Also look at the company itself and its relationship with the vendors of the various products. Although not having a direct relationship with the vendor does not necessarily equate to a bad product, you have no guarantees of the content. Although you can judge the overall quality of the training in terms of how well it is presented, the material may not be 100% accurate, particularly if the material goes into a lot of detail that you do not test or practice yourself. Having a 1:1 relationship with the software vendor help ensure the newest and most accurate information.

Many of the training vendors are themselves official Corel Solution Partners or Microsoft Solution Providers. This generally means that one or more people employed by the training company have been certified by the software vendor. In addition, often many of the instructors on the videos and CDs are certified to instruct products from the respective vendor.

Another key aspect of helping the users to help themselves is security training. If the system is down because someone has broken into it, it does little good for your users. Therefore, users need to be aware of the different ways they can protect the system. For example, they may need to be instructed about password security. That is, how to select good passwords, not telling others with their passwords are, not writing their passwords down, and so on. Other aspects include setting permissions on files to prevent unauthorized access, password protecting documents, password protecting your screen saver, and so on.

In fact, I am a firm believer that users cannot know too much about security. Therefore, it may be in your best interest to make your users aware of all the details of security that we discussed in Chapter 6 on system security. (X-ref.) Obviously, much of that information may be too detailed for some of your users. However, it should be made available to them. On the other hand, it is possible to simplify some of the information to make it more understandable.

I worked for one company where the MIS manager didn't believe in training. It was okay for the people in the factory to get training. However, we were the high-paid techie types didn't need the training. We could get our knowledge through "learning-by-doing." It didn't matter that he never gave us time to train or that we were losing money on a daily basis because we kept having to flip through manuals to find answera and that every month came the latest software that we just had to implement. It was obvious to everyone in the department (except him) that we could save a lot of money and time by sending people to real training.

A week-long course may cost several thousand dollars, but it is insignificant compared to the losses without that course. I have seen it repeatedly where it took over a year to reach the same level as a week of training! Hours were spent flipping through the manuals and end-user efficiency is greatly decreased as they wait for the "expert" to find the answer. Remember that a down system costs an average of $5000 an hour. That is well worth the price of training courses.

If your company provides training on Windows NT to your users, you know the problems with lab machines. After users have been on the machines for the training, there is no guarantee that they will be in a completely usable state for the next class. This is not to say the users intentionally mess up the machines. However, depending on the training you give, the state of the machine is unknown. If you expect a particular state when you start the instruction, you need to return each machine to its original state.

You could reinstall each machine. This takes a great deal of time and is not cost effective. You can have the users return the machine to their original state once the training is complete. However, this requires that the users not only remember exactly what they did, but that they are capable of making the changes. The other solution is the ability to reset the system to the original settings.

Disk-cloning products are perhaps the quickest and most direct approach to this problem. It allows trainers, system integrators, resellers, and anyone else the ability to configure a large number of machines quickly and easily. This is done by creating a disk image, which contains all of the necessary information. This information is then transferred to the target system, much faster than installing it by hand.

Some products, such as RapiDeploy from Altiris Inc. increase the efficiency further by allowing you to install multiple machines at once. This is done using a multicast network address, so that all target machines receive the data simultaneously, without overloading the network. This make RapiDeploy extremely scalable as you simply broadcast to more machines.

Even when a machine is cloned, in many cases a technician needs to "touch" each machine and make the proper configuration settings. Over time, this additional work becomes a substantial part of the overall cost of the product. RapiDeploy is one of the only products that integrated the cloning process with an advanced configuration service, which is fully automatic. When the PC is first installed, RapiDeploy stores all of the unique settings within a matter of minutes, allowing you to restore them just as fast. Keep in mind that if it only take five minutes per machine to make the changes, 12 machines takes an hour.

One common problem is the unique system ID that is generated when a Windows NT machine is installed. RapiDeploy solves this by using its SIDGen program, which basically runs the same processes on the machine after it has been cloned that is done during the initial install to generate the unique ID.

Specific for lab or training environments, Altiris also provide LabExpert. It is expected, if not desired, that during training, users will make changes to the computers. As a result, when the next person sits down, there is no way of knowing if it is in a usable state. The solution for many companies is to either leave it as it is or reinstall from scratch. This is an obvious waste of time.

LabExpert solves this problem by maintaining a record of settings that can be reset at will. Since only the changes are undo, there is no need to wait as each machine is reinstalled. However, there may be cases where a reinstall is the best solution. LabExpert can manage disk images, so the machines can be reinstalled in fraction of the time.

LearnKey

LearnKey produces both video and CD training programs, which are grouped into the three main categories: Application, Desktop, and Certification training. Application training goes beyond just the major vendors like Microsoft, Corel, and Lotus, by including products like QuarkExpress, ClarisWorks, and even ActiveX. Certification training covers the major vendors as well at the A+ hardware certification from CompTIA. Desktop products include Windows, UNIX, Novell, and Internet topics. In addition, there are several programming/development courses, including one on creating an intranet.

Individual products are available as well as several different bundles. You can also get multiuser licenses for the CD products that are based on the number of students and products. For example, 100 students who each will use three different courses will required a 300-user license. This mechanism is good for users who have different schedules and therefore cannot train at the same time.

You might think you could save money by simply passing the CDs from user to user. Even if you avoided the legal problems by removing the products from each machine, you actually do not save any money. You need to consider the time to reinstall each product on the user's machine *plus* remove it when they are done. In addition, if the product is installed locally, there is no central administration function for you to monitor their progress. You also then have control over who gets access to which products.

When the program is started, each user logs in with his or her user name and password. This not only ensures that only authorized users get access but also that test scores are kept confidential.

Another useful feature is the users' management of the installed products. All of the products are accessed from a single interface. When you start the program, you choose the course you want from the list. The basic behavior of the application is then the same for each course. Figure 14-1 shows you the main window.

The upper portion is where the training video clips and tests appear. At the bottom left is an Index of the main topics in the course. On the right are

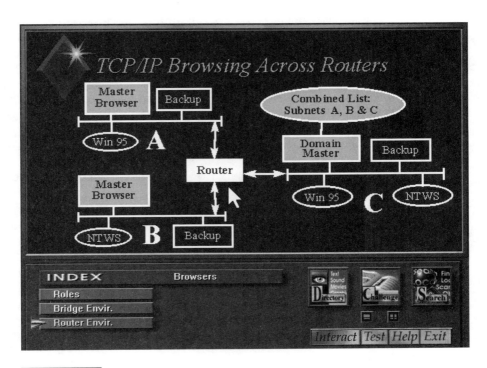

FIGURE 14-1   LearnKey Training CD main window.

several control buttons. The Directory button shows you all of the videos contained on the CD.

The Challenge button is used to access interactive exercises on the topic. You are given a list of topics that are presented in a step-by-step fashion. You are given exercises based on the material, and if you select an incorrect answer, you can choose to try it again, get "coaching," or run through the steps again.

One unique feature is the "Interact" button. This will start up the application or program currently being discussed, which allows you to try out the things you learned with the real software and not a demo.

To a limited extent, you can move back and forth through the training on a CD as much as you like. In general, each main subject is provided as a single video clip. This means you can start each of the subjects individually but not jump to specific topics within each clip. Although this *could* be accomplished with existing technology, the handling would make the product more complicated and, as a result, more expensive.

A nice feature is the on-line glossary, which is accessed through the Search button. You often encounter terms that are defined in other modules or that you are not sure what they mean. With the on-line glossary, you do not need to stop your training session to find the definition.

Like many vendors, LearnKey is moving toward on-line training. At their sister site, OnlineExpert.com, LearnKey provides on-line training geared explicitly toward professional certification, such as MCSE, CCNA, and A+. One of the key aspects is what LearnKey calls "Challenge Sessions." These include step-by-step instructions for performing tasks followed by a number of practice exercises. The exercises are not just a repeat of the steps in the training; they are designed to be challenging and really test your understanding of the material.

You also have the ability to set bookmarks. As the name implies, these mark specific locations in the training sessions, so you can start up where you left off.

In order to judge your own progress, there are both pre- and posttests. However, neither is required. I like the idea of a pretest as this gives me an idea of what aspects of the training I need to pay particular attention to. In addition, this helps me to identify the area I am already familiar with. There are a number of open-book "quizzes," which are not timed, and you are given hints as well as references of where to look for the correct answers. Here you can choose how many questions will be asked. The closed-book quizzes are designed to reflect the material and the behavior of the actual certification test.

When you have completed the tests, you can view your results, which also indicate whether your score on these practice tests would be sufficient to pass the real thing. In addition, you can save the study guide created for this test or even print it out.

The LearnKey Management Software is a tool to help the system administrator (or instructor) manage the administrative aspects of the LearnKey training packages. You can create new students and assign students to particular courses. In addition, you can view information about the students' current status and results. There are several different reporting formats, including the ability to report each student's test scores.

KeyStone Learning Systems

The depth and breadth of the training materials offered by KeyStone is truly amazing. When I first contacted them in 1998 they had over 550 different titles, and it keeps growing steadily. Their product catalog is comparable to the catalogs of many software resellers in that you would be really hard-pressed to find products that are not included (although I have a handful on my shelf that are not included).

Products range from Windows NT Server and the various components (such as MS Exchange and MS Internet Information Server) to desktop operating systems (Windows 95/98) to applications to development to Internet topics and beyond.

One key aspect is that saying there are 550 titles does not mean there are videos on 550 different software products. Instead, you may find in some cases a half dozen or more videos on a single subject. With multiple videos, the products range from beginner to advanced (sometimes five or more levels) and often have separate videos for "special features." For example, there are three levels of Excel videos with a separate one for "power features" and another just for pivot tables.

This means that you can get materials for beginning as well as advanced users who wish to take the product to its fullest potential. Because the instructors are true experts in their respective areas, you have the benefit of their experience to find the hidden tricks, shortcuts, features that many people are not aware of even after using the products for years. This applies not only to the application training but the operating system and development training as well, all of which helps increase the total value of ownership of the software dramatically.

Although all of the products are in English, KeyStone has not forgotten the rest of the world and provides the videos in NTSC as well as PAL and SECAM formats. In addition, most of the courses are now available on CD-ROM.

One of the most useful features of the videos is an unobtrusive indicator at the bottom of the screen that tells you which section you are currently viewing. On the back of the video cases, there is a complete list of "In This Video You Will Learn" topics. Each topic is marked with the same number that appears on your screen. This makes it easy to find exactly the subject you want to look at.

Accompanying each video are the KeyStone KeyNotes. These provide a handy review of the material as well as some additional information in many cases. The KeyNotes are broken into the same sections as the videos, so you know exactly where to look on the video for each topic.

I found the KeyNotes extremely useful when viewing the videos, as I did not need to write down everything myself. I simply checked to see if it was already in the KeyNotes and added a few things as appropriate. This enabled me to spend more time concentrating on the material and less time dealing with note taking.

Many of the course titles are specifically designed for the certification test of the various software vendors. The test number is included in the catalog so you know exactly what courses you need. Note that unlike some products I have seen, the material is not exclusively what you will find on the certification tests.

Products are sold separately as well as in product bundles or entire suites of products, such those necessary to complete the MCSE certification. KeyStone also offers an upgrade policy for products covering the newer version. In addition, for many products there are special upgrade videos that cover just those topics that have changed between the different releases.

ViaGrafix

ViaGrafix is another company with a wide range of video and CD-ROM instructional material. As of this writing, they provide more than 1000 training courses, which cover the entire spectrum of product types and vendors. ViaGrafix emphasizes the fact that training materials for older products are still available. Unlike some companies who only cater to the "latest and greatest," you are likely to find ViaGrafix training courses for your software without having to upgrade.

Figure 14-2 shows you the main screen of the ViaGrafix training application. On the left side of the screen you see which modules have been installed and which modules belong to the current product suite. The Contents lists the chapters in the modules along with the various topics. The Index tab lists keywords and phrases found in the module. When you double-click on an entry, you are brought to a place close to where the word or phrase is used. I say "close to" because you often need to read a couple of sentences ahead of the phrase to get it in the right context.

At any time, you can choose the Test button to either take a "Skill Builder" quiz or the comprehensive test. The quizzes are ten questions each, covering the material in a specific chapter of the module. The tests are 20 questions long and cover all of the material in that module.

One aspect of the ViaGrafix products that is emphasized in their latest marketing material is that many of their products are now "networkable," with more in the works. This simply means that a single copy of the product can be installed on a network server, and you can have as many people using the product at once as you have licenses.

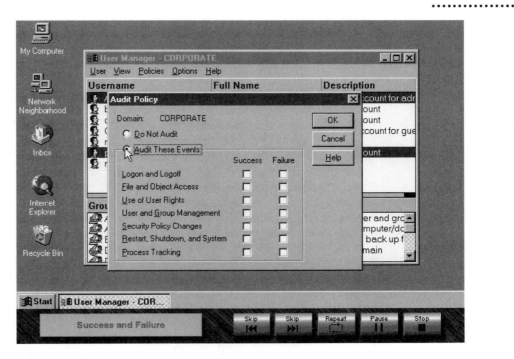

FIGURE 14-2   ViaGrafix main screen.

Detailed reporting mechanisms are provided to monitor the students' progress. This helps ensure that your training money is being put to good use and helps you identify students with potential problems.

Like the existing ViaGrafix products, the networkable products provide a simulated software environment. This presents a demonstration version of the particular application or even Windows NT. When material is presented, the mouse moves across the screen, selecting menus and clicking buttons just as it would in the real product. On occasion, video clips of the instructor appear that describe a particular topic in more detail.

One interesting aspect of the ViaGrafix line is that unlike many other products, these products are more conscious of international users. Although the videos are available only in NTSC and PAL (not SECAM), many of the courses are available in English, Spanish, German, or French.

The instructional approach emphasized in the ViaGrafix marketing materials is "hands-on" as compared to the "guided tour" of several other products. Granted, you cannot really have hands-on with a video tape, but the CD-ROM instruction provides a lot of demonstrations, simulations; and hands-on exercises.

Another aspect is how much of the material applies to the real world. I have experienced it with many other products (particularly books), where they use some off-the-wall example that one would never use in order to explain a particular topic. The instruction has far less impact because the student cannot relate the subject to his or her experience. If the topic does have real-world applications, then a real-world example should be presented. If there are no real-world applications, what's the point of bringing it up?

Although the ViaGrafix course titles are not listed in a 1:1 relationship to any specific certification (at least in the materials I found), the information provided not only helps you with real-world situations, it also help you on the examination. Each module includes a review and test, so that the student can assess his or her own progress.

As with other vendors, ViaGrafix provides their materials across the Internet as well as on CD and video. In addition, on request, ViaGrafix will develop individual, customized training.

ViaGrafix supports corporate users in several ways. Licensing of the Via-Grafix products is extremely aggressive. Licenses range from single user on single products to hundreds of users and dozens of products. There are a number of title bundles that are available, and companies can also pick and choose the titles they need for the specific number of users they have.

You can also sign up for a subscription service. This means that you have access to any upgraded training materials that are produced during the course of your subscription at no extra charge. You also have the option of exchanging material. In addition, you have the right to duplicate the material to make distribution easier.

ViaGrafix provides "ViaHelp," (Au: Is this an actual product name? Product name.) which is sold as "electronic mentoring." ViaGrafix users can email usage questions directly to ViaGrafix, who promptly sends a reply. Often these are made part of the Frequently Asked Questions list or made part of subsequent courses.

Transcender

Having the training materials is just one step of the process. You need some measure of whether the cost was effective. That is, you need some measure of whether the user learned the material they were supposed to. That means you need to test them.

Although most CD-based training products have quizzes or tests, they are always limited to the material in the training. On the one hand, this makes sense because you want to see how well the user learned *that material*. What better way than to test *that material*. The downside is that should the material not go into enough detail about the material, the user has not learned everything he or she could. If the vendor tests on material not presented in their course, the first reaction is that their training was less than adequate.

The solution is an external testing product that is independent of the training material. One company that offers these tests is Transcender Corp. Some vendors of training material realize the problems with tests and quizzes are part of their products and offer Transcender tests as part of package deals.

The Transcender tests are geared specifically toward the Microsoft certifications. This includes the operating system, application, and development certifications. Each exam can be identified with a specific Microsoft certification, so it is easy to pick the tests you are interested in.

There are actually two parts to the Transcender tests. First, there is the actual certification. Plus you have a set of flash cards, which Transcender logically calls TranscenderFlash. This is sold as a separate product and is definitely worth a look.

In all honesty, there is nothing fancy about the exams at all. You are presented with a series of questions that you have to complete within a specific period of time. For the most part, the questions are not as simple as "What domain models are there?" Instead, you are given a scenario and are expected to figure out which of the various domain models would be best.

Once you have completed the exam, it is graded instantly, and you are shown your results. I must be honest and say that the first exam I took, I failed. Aside from the fact that the exams are not easy, there are often a couple of "almost" answers that threw me off. Like on the real exam, you need to look for the best answer, not just a good one.

Figure 14-3 shows you the main window for the certification component. Here you run the exam, load previously save exams, and configure the program. However, there is not much to configure beyond changing the size of the text or changing the time limit.

I feel one of the most significant aspects of the transcendar exams and what is missing from most of the training courses is that you are not only told when an answer is incorrect, but are given a reference to the Microsoft documentation where this topic is discussed. Note that the Microsoft documentation does not always have scenarios. Instead, there is a discussion of a particular subject. Therefore, in order to transfer that material to what is asked on the exam, you actually have to understand the material and not just learn it by heart.

I find this approach much better than giving you the material and testing *exactly* what it was you were taught.Again, this forces you to understand what you just learned and can actually implement it in real-world situations.

Figure 14-4 shows you the TranscenderFlash main screen. As with real flash cards, TranscenderFlash is a series of questions and answers from the topic you choose. Although the questions are at a lower level than those in the certification, they are a fantastic way of reviewing the material.

Since TranscenderFlash behaves basically like real flash cards, there is no testing. However, there is a "self-grading" mechanism. This keeps track of what you missed and helps in reviewing the material. In addition, you can add your own information to each of the flash cards.

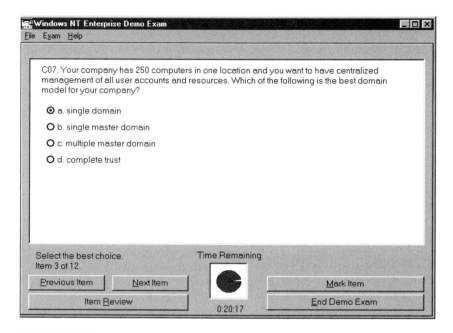

FIGURE 14-3 Transcender Certification main window.

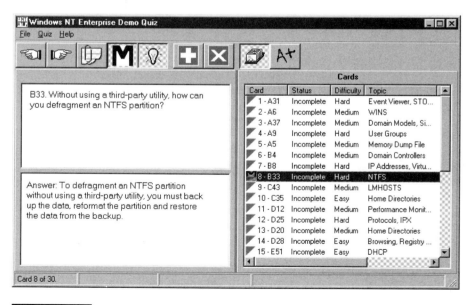

FIGURE 14-4 TranscenderFlash main screen.

....

Storing Your Knowledge

Whether you use a commercial help desk product, a database you develop yourself, or a bunch of HTML files on your company's intranet, you need to provide as much information as possible. Obviously, you can provide so much information that you do not find which you're looking for. However, you need to ensure the necessary information is available.

Among the information you need to provide is a list of contact numbers. This not only includes the numbers for your support providers; it also includes every other number you can think of. For example, the number of your Internet service provider, the service office of your local telephone company, your gas company, and any other number that might be remotely related to your computer systems and users.

Another thing to include is a list of the areas of responsibility, who is responsible for them, and exactly what is included within each area. This applies not only to areas inside your organization but to external areas as well. In one company, we had a leased-line connection from the headquarters to all of the larger branch offices. However, the connections were not all provided by the same company nor did one company provide support for the entire connection. For example, connections within the United States were provided by a one company, whereas connections between the United States and Europe or the United States.and Asia were provided by different companies. In some countries, a single company was responsible for the line from the branch office to the headquarters. However, in other countries, the local phone company might be responsible for the phone lines to the service provider and then the service provider was responsible for the rest. If the line went down, it was vital to know *exactly* who was responsible for each segment. Therefore, we had a list of the connections, who was responsible for each segment, as well as telephone and contact information.

Internally, the list of responsibilities should be used as both a guideline for solving problems and for making decisions. Depending on your organization, you may assign problems directly to the person who is responsible for a specific area. On the other hand, some companies have a support team who solvethe problems and only go to the person responsible (the expert) when necessary. For example, if the problem is too difficult for them to solve on their own they might go to the expert for help.

It is also important that the person havingthe power of decision also be listed. In some cases this is the same person as the expert. In other cases, the MIS manager makes all the decisions and it may therefore not be necessary to explicitly list his or her name. However, if different people make decisions in different areas, each area and each person need to be listed.

Included in this is a list of your hardware and software configurations. This might seem like a lot of work for you now; for example, 100 machines and 100 different configurations. However, this is exactly the case where having this list is vital to effective support of your users. For example, if the user calls in with a problem and you don't know what is on their computer, you'll waste a lot of time finding out this information. On the other hand, if you can quickly look up their computer name and determine what hardware and software it has, you're all a lot closer to finding problems and therefore the solution.

This does not necessarily mean having a complete list of all hardware and all software for each machine. If you have, for example, the number of configuration types, you can simply list that configuration for any given machine. However, you need some way of relating the configuration to the complete description. Now, this may seem to be only busywork; however, experience has taught me that the more information you have without having to ask the user for it, the quicker you can find a solution. First off, you do not need to spend the time asking the user questions. Second, you do not have to waste time when the user answers a question that is not one you asked. For example, I have asked users how much memory theyhad, who replied "2 gigabytes," referring to the size of the hard disk. In addition, there may be known problems with known solutions that relate to specific configurations. If a user were to call in with that problem, you know immediately what the solution is.

Knowledge Base

Simply put, the knowledge base is a collection of all information that is necessary to solve problems. Keep in mind that the problem solution database is just one part of the knowledge base as there are many more components that the wind to the knowledge base. It is safe to say that all the information about your computer systems and all the information that your help desk has collected to solve problems are part of your knowledge base. Among the things that go into an efficient knowledge base are:

- instruction manuals
- product documentation, such as manuals and data sheets
- training documents
- configuration information on your computer systems
- histories of previous calls
- solutions to known problems
- internal and external contact information
- troubleshooting checklists
- location of all patches in upgrades

Two of the most important characteristics of the knowledge base are its central location and common interface. Although nothing prevents you from creating a knowledge base that is spread out all over your network or requires a dozen different tools to access the information, you must consider the ease at which the information can be accessed. If the information is not easily accessible, it is of limited value.

The knowledge base should not just serve as a repository for information but should actuallyhelp to manage this information. For example, an interface needs to be available that allows you to input new documents as well as search for and review existing ones. Part of this review process is the ability to remove, or at least mark, outdated documents.

Although you can purchase commercial knowledge bases that contained a great deal ofinformation both about Windows and a large number of applications, the only way you will get company-specific information into the knowledge base is to put in there yourself. You might be able to fill it with dozens or even hundreds of different solutions. My experience as shown me that this is extremely inefficient. The best solution is to feed your database as the problems come in.

I strongly recommend that any commercial help desk software you get not only contain a call-tracking module but also a knowledge-base module. This makes integration and access from the help desk extremely efficient. Having connectivity between the problem-tracking module and the solutions module is a standard component. However, you must keep in mind that a good knowledge base consists of more than just specific solutions to specific problems. Therefore, you need a help desk product that integrates all of the components we have discussed.

All groups that are involved in the help desk process should have access to the knowledge base. Periphery groups such as those responsible for network or server maintenance are often overlooked when it comes to being given access to the knowledge base. These people need access for two important reasons. First, like the other members of the help desk team, they have the need for a central repository for their information. Second, it makes little sense to provide them tools to store information that is separate from that of the help desk. In general, both teams need access to the same information.

To be able to survive over time and to keep the knowledge base from getting disorganized, you need to have a set of procedures in place for adding to and maintaining the knowledge base. One obvious procedure is that the solution to all new problems must be put into the knowledge base as soon as possible after it has been identified. All of the better help desk products allow you to do this automatically. That is, problem descriptions and their solutions can be automatically transferred into the solutions database from the call-tracking module. If this functionality is not available, I feel it is wise to make it part of the closing procedures for all calls. If analysts are allowed to delay updating the database until they "get around to it," you can bet that many of them never will.

Although a formal review procedure is probably not necessary for this kind of problem and solution, I do feel it is extremely important for more-detailed knowledge base documents such as troubleshooting checklists and so forth. In some organizations, the review process includes the technical review by someone other than the author. If these documents are written exclusively by the expert, the technical review may seem unnecessary. However, the technical review should also ensure that the documentation is understandable as well as appropriate for the minimum skill level of the people reading it. It does little good if the information is accurate but no one other than the expert can use it because it is too difficult to understand.

If you are providing fee-based support, the reviewer needs to consider whether a document isappropriate for public consumption. The most common case is documents dealing with internal procedures of the help desk, but you might also consider limiting access to number of others. Others might describe how to exploit security holes in the system, which you obviously don't want to give everyone access to.

During the review process, the reviewer needs to ensure the documents adhere to the standards you have laid out. If there are no standards for either the appearance or the format of documents, it often makes finding the necessary information and even the review process exceedingly difficult. Among the things the reviewer needs to look for all are:

- All required elements are present.
- All items are in their proper location.
- The appropriate level of detailed is given.
- All nonstandard abbreviations are defined the first time they are used.

An important aspect of the review process is ensuring the information remains current. This means ensuring that any changes made to the software, hardware, or system as a whole are properly reflected. This may be something as basic as noting when a new server is added, or it may be something dramatic like entirely removing the documents when the software it refers to is no longer used.

A mechanism needs to be in place to allow people to make comments about the documents in the knowledge base. If certain sections of a document are unclear, the reader needs to be able to clarify these points. If something is wrong, it will affect not only the person currently reading the document but everyone in the future as well. To this end, it might be easiest to have each document numbered. The number is best when it is somewhat self-explanatory. That is, the name itself contains something about its contents. For example, Net_Print_345.doc, is the 345th document about network printers or printing.

Whether or not the users should be able to contact the author directly will depend on your users and how your help desk is organized. The greater the number of users, the greater I feel the need to limit direct contact to the help desk staff (other than through official channels like the hotline number). If users get used to having contact with the help desk staff directly for documentation issues, they will begin to contact them directly on other issues, aswell. If direct contact is not allowed, you can handle documentation issues just like any other help desk call, including problem number and so forth.

An alternative would be to store the IT administrative information for the document as well as its URL in the database. This requires slightly more effort to get the document into the database but this is compensated for by the ease in which documents can be searched for and administered. An HTML form can be quickly implemented that allows you to include this administrative information directly into the database. Using Active Server Pages you can create SQL queries that search for documents based on any criteria. Getting the basic structure of the active server page usually takes a couple of hours unless you are fairly proficient, but subsequent changes are literally made within a matter of minutes.

The simplest products use either a search tree or keyword search. The more complicated mechanism includes case-based reasoning where solutions are searched based onprevious experiences and statistical information retrieval, which evaluates both your searchcriteria and database to come up with a "statistical value." The higher the value a particularpiece of information gets, the more "likely" it is the solution.

However, the mere fact that solutions are written down and easily accessible is a major step for most companies. The most simple (and probably the cheapest) is to use some existing tool to store the problems and their solutions. Using your file system and shortcuts, you can make your data substantially more accessible. For example, you need to provide information on the use of WinChat. You could have a file /help_desk/network/tools/winchat.txt, one /help_desk/communication/tools/winchat.txt, and another /help_desk/tools/communications/winchat.txt. Maybe the directories are links or maybe just the files. When one file gets changed, they all do, as they are the same file.

Information Collection

One of the keys to an effective knowledge base is that it cannot be static, but must be ever-changing and ever-growing. Even the additions you make by simply adding the solutions from your problem of tracking database are not sufficient to create a knowledge base with the greatest potential. You need to actively a make additions as well as actively review existing documents to ensure the best quality possible.

One excellent source of information is the Internet. There are accounted sites with information ranging from tips and tricks to detailed descriptions of hardware. If you access your knowledge base through a Web browser, it is then a simple matter to create links to these other sites. All that is necessary is to categorize and then group the various sites to make finding them easier. If you manage your local documents with some kind of database, nothing is preventing you from managing these external documents in the same way. As

I previously discussed, the database contains just the administrative information about the document, including its location. There is nothing wrong with listing an external URL rather than one on your intranet.

Magazines, books, and other written documents are also on excellent source of information. These two can be managed to use the same database and the information access to use the same HTML form. Instead of listing the URL or file system path to the document, you could list the title of the book and the page number. This might seem like busywork, but even with the simplest HTML form you can add this information to your database in about 30 seconds. This saves a great deal of time later on when other people need to find the same information.

A centralized knowledge base is vital to keep users from "stockpiling" knowledge. Keep in mind that the goal of a help desk is to find answers to problems. If the answer is in someone's head or in some other location that is not easily accessible, the information is useless to the other people on the help desk.

Even before your help desk becomes operational you should make your users aware that it is coming. At the same time, you need to encourage input from users on what they expect to or would like to see in the help desk.

This is handled in one of two ways. Either you simply announce that the help desk is coming and solicit responses from those people that would like to provide them, or you actively pursue their input. Keep in mind that the help desk is for the users and is not a goal in itself. Therefore, I recommend that you actively pursue their input. Depending on the number of people within your organization, you may not be able to ask everyone individually.

However, you need to ensure that the people you ask are representative of the company as a whole. To this goal, you should try to ask people in as many departments and in as many positions as possible. The key is to find out what the users want or need and not to implement something based on your preconceptions. Depending on what the users say they need, you may end up getting more management support than you expected. That'swhy the earlier you do this kind of survey, the better. As a side note, I feel that this kind of survey should be repeated at regular intervals to determine how the users are reacting to the help desk. What better way then to ask them?

During this time, you should make the users aware of what to expect from the help desk. Once again, this is not only the services you will provide, but also those services that you explicitly do not provide. This helps setting the users' expectations, so that they are not disappointed when the help desk is implemented and get something they didn't expect.

The Help Desk

It is often a shock to people just graduating from college with degrees in information science, computer technology, or some related field. Many expect to immediately begin working on that one world-shattering application or to be involved in high-speed satellite communications. It is like a bucket of cold water poured over their head when they realize they just spent 4 years and tens of thousands of dollars training to become firefighters.

The information technology/information services (IT/IS) department in many companies is very much like fighting fires. When the alarm goes off (the telephone rings), you rush off to handle some emergency. Sometimes it is as simple as getting a cat out of a tree, and other times it is a six-alarm blaze that threatens the livelihood of the town. Without the proper equipment and training, even the simple task of getting a cat from a tree is difficult.

Whatever you call it, hotline or help desk, the principles are the same. Running a successful help desk is not simply a matter of providing users a number to call if they have computer problems, no more than dialing 911 will put out a fire. When the bell goes off, you do not know what to expect. Without the appropriate training, the necessary equipment, and the right mindset, there is no way you'll be able to effectively solve computer problems. Without the proper organization, improper equipment or insufficient personnel are sent to fight the fire with potentially disastrous results. Without the proper organization for your help desk, the results can be just as disastrous for your company.

Unless your office consists of just a handful of employees, you should strongly consider implementing some kind of help desk. Although you need not go through all of the details and effort necessary for larger organizations, your company will definitely benefit from some kind of formal procedures. Otherwise, the fires that you're called on to put out will quickly get out of control.

The larger your organization, the greater the need for a help desk and greater the need for officially defined procedures. Like any system, a help desk will function best if it is planned rather than be allowed to grow over time. Like any system, a help desk will change as the needs of your users change, but it is important for you to develop the foundation of the help desk at the beginning so that it does not change uncontrollably.

One of the first questions to answer is, "What is a help desk?" This will be different for different people and different companies. The traditional answer is that it is a group of people that the users can call to get help on computer-related problems. Sometimes, you might not even see the people; you just get a number to call.

Although this kind of answer might be sufficient for a game show on TV, it does not really get to the heart of the issue. You need to understand what the problems are that users have and what kinds of things you can do to solve them. What is a "computer-related problem?" What constitutes "help?" These are the issues that need to be addressed in order to develop an effective help desk.

That is exactly what we are going to do in the next two chapters. In this chapter, we are going to look at the issues concerning the decisions to implement a help desk or not, plus those issues you need to address when designing and developing your help desk. Then we are going to talk about the issues involved with running your help desk. Finally, in Chapter 16 we are going to talk about implementing a help desk using one of the commercially available products and how that product addresses the issues we will be discussing.

Throughout this chapter, I will be talking about the help desk as being part of the IT department. Obviously, there are dozens of different ways you can organize your company, and the help desk can fall under the jurisdiction of many different organizations. The reason I put the help desk under the IT department is to emphasize the fact that you're providing the service. You may be providing your users with technology as well as support for that technology. However, I wish to keep in the foreground the idea of service.

Another thing I need to look at briefly are those cases where the help desk really is separate from the IT department. This can bring some dangerous conflicts to the help desk. For example, you may have a situation where both sides are grabbing for power. That is, both sides are trying to solve the same problem. The other department is insisting that you are encroaching on its territory and tells you politely to back off. On the other hand, they may want to pass the buck and say that it is your responsibility and not theirs. You can prevent both of these problems by clearly defining what the responsibilities of the help desk are and have these approved and supported by the company management. There is then no way for the IT department to either lay claim to a particular issue or pass it off to you.

You must remember that this is not a battle between you and the IT department. Rather, it is a battle between you and the problem you have. It is therefore a good idea to work out with the IT department what your responsibilities are and the same time work out what exactly the responsibilities are of the IT department. If the two departments are completely separate, you may find it a lot harder to reach agreement. However, this is something that you really need to work at to ensure that none of the users' needs are overlooked.

Justifying The Help Desk

Satisfying Needs

Before you can even begin to develop your help desk, you are certainly going to need approval. Unless you are the decision maker, someone will probably need to give you the "go ahead," because this will be a very time-consuming and work-intensive project. It may also cost a fair bit of money, depending on what solutions you decide to implement.

In order to get approval, you will have to justify the time and money. This means satisfying the needs of both the users and the company management. Users want more than just having their problems solved, and management wants more than just saving money.

One of the first things in developing a help desk is to *understand* the needs of your company, both the users and management. One aspect of this is to identify what information is important for the company to maintain. More than likely, you'll need to maintain a record of the computers and software you have, as these are part of the company's assets. Here you already have a start in developing your help desk. The next step is to maintain a record of problems that you're having with particular hardware in order for you to support any warranty claims.

However, keeping records should never become a goal unto itself. There must be some logical reason for recording what you do. For example, maintaining a record of your assets is important from a financial standpoint, but it is also important when problems crop up. If the component is still under warranty, you may be able to get it serviced or even replaced for free. Knowing what SCSI host adapter is installed allows you to install the latest driver without having to open up the case. Documenting problems helps you to find the "standard solutions" more quickly or to recognize the fact that a certain brand of hard disk is always giving you problems.

For many help desks, this might be all that is necessary. However, the more personnel and equipment you have, the more problems you have and the more you need to keep track of these problems to either find their cause or provide a mechanism to keep them from repeating. (Just because you have a solution to the problem does not mean you know what caused it.)What information you need to keep track of and what services your help desk should provide will be determined by a "needs assessment." One key aspect of this is the word "need." Initially, the emphasis should be on what needs to be monitored and what services need to be provided. As your help desk grows, you can begin evaluating which services are "nice to have." These simply are those services that may or may not justify their cost. You therefore need to determine which of these services are cost effective.

To find out what the true needs of the company are, all you need to do is simply ask. Since it is the company management that will be paying your bill, you should ask them what they expect to get out of the help desk. The answers you are likely to get will range from "give the users the support they need to use their computers efficiently" to "solve users' problems so that they can return to work as quickly is possible." Therefore, you are likely to have to go into more detail about what the answer really means. Find out what "efficiently" means. Find out how quick "quickly" is.

If you have management like at places where I have worked, you may not be able to get an answer that is very specific. Many have been managers long enough not to have ever worked regularly on a PC. I have worked with some managers who have been around for so long that when they were doing the day-to-day work, it was all done with pencil and paper. Therefore, they may not have any idea of what it is like nor what the users really need. Even if they have been managers for just a few years, that is a long time as far as computers are concerned, and their knowledge of current technology may be limited.

I've worked with managers who have read in some magazine that a certain technology is "necessary." Since it appeared in print, it must be right. For example, they may not know what good a help desk can really be, but they know their competitor has one, so they should implement one as well. This attitude can be a double-edged sword in that it may give you the budget you need to implement a help desk effectively, or the lack of understanding on the part of management may prevent you getting what you need.

Even without concrete answers from management, there are a number of things that management will definitely consider important. First, it is likely they will want to keep costs as low is possible. Even if you are given a blank check, management will not take too kindly to wasting money. Therefore, it is always in your best interest to keep within the reasonable budget. Plus, the more you design versus letting it grow, the more places you can save money and thus be able to implement more features.

One way of reducing costs is to automate procedures wherever possible. There are a number of very simple ways of automating your help desk with very minimal cost. For example, both email and Web-based forms are an excellent means of automating your support. Although Web-based access has become a basic component of almost all major commercial help desk software, there are still a great many things that you can do on your own without investing a lot of money. For example, using active server pages and an MS Access database, you can provide an easy-to-use interface for users to submit problem reports or requests via Web forms. Using almost the exact same code you can create a Web page to view the input data and even sort and filter it by any criteria necessary.

From the management perspective, part of cutting costs is keeping the users working. Managers definitely do not like to see users sitting around waiting for the computer to come back on-line. Much of that is part of system administration. However, in many companies, the people running the help desk are also responsible for system administration. Therefore, anything that you can do to keep the system running efficiently means less calls to the help desk. For example, there are a number of help desk products (eg., Network associates) that are integrated with system administration tools. Not only can you monitor your system using these tools, but most of them can generate problem reports automatically. In addition, you can normally configure them to generate mail messages or some other notification when certain events occur (i.e., the hard disk becomes full).

Integration of administration tools or recording configuration information and problem reports are fairly tangible aspects of the help desk. Unfortunately, not everything is easy to define in terms of tangible benefits or savings in dollars. There are a large number of things to consider that will have a large effect on the benefit your help desk provides that are completely subjective. It almost takes a certain instinct, or sixth sense, to really understand how important these issues are.

Perhaps the most common is the increase in morale of your employees simply because they are happier when working with computers. One of the primary reasons for this is that an effective help desk convinces users that they are not completely helpless when dealing with the computer. They know that should they have a problem, there is someone there to help them. In many cases, the mere fact that they know someone is there to hold their hand gives them enough encouragement to try to solve the problem on their own. They know that should they reach a point where they can no longer continue, the help desk is there to help them further. If the help desk were not there, the user might not even try to extend the program beyond its basic functionality. Therefore, they would not be taking full advantage of the available technology.

Even if the user decides to call the help desk, its presence alone can be of benefit. One of the skills that is almost never listed as a requirement for a help desk analyst is being a fairly good psychologist. You often have to listen to the endless complaints of users going over and over things that neither of you can change. For example, it is a common occurrence on the help desk to get calls when the network connections are down. Both of you know the connections are down, and neither of you knows when they will be back up again. They usually call you just to get out the frustrations of not being able to work. You have to sit there calmly and listen to them as they go on about their problems.

This might be an exaggeration, but it is quite likely that while on the help desk, you will have to listen to the non-computer-related problems of your users. I feel that to some extent, this is part of the job.

Another aspect of your users' needs that you need to consider is their skill level. The more comfortable the users are working with computers, the less need they have to call for support. However, if you have a lot of novice users and a lot of complicated applications, you'll probably need to increase the size of your help desk. In addition, if your company decides that the help desk will provide *any* support the users require, you'll need a larger staff if the company decides the help desk is there just to solve problems.

The number of users you have and where they are located will also have an effect on the services that you can provide. Because it is much easier to give users help in programming if you can look over their shoulders, it is much easier to give them that kind of support if you are both at the same location. Issues like hardware support are almost impossible if you are spread out across multiple locations. Also, the fewer number of users in support, the less personal service you can give them.

The more diverse the technology, the more you'll have to consider restricting your support offering. This does not just involve the software products the users employ or the differentkinds of workstations they use, but also what technologies are implemented in your computer system throughout the company. First, the more diversified the hardware is, the more different kinds of problems can occur. This may limit the services you can provide, since your problem-solving abilities are spread more thinly.

Many of the problems that I have encountered while working in support or on a hotline can be solved or at least reduced by implementing a set of standards. The fewer applications you have to support, the more proficient you'll become and the more quickly you can solve problems. The fewer types of computers you own, the less time you spend looking for the right driver.

Even if the number of problems is not reduced, having standards in terms of hardware and software makes many of the issues that crop up become standard problems with standard solutions. It even gets to the point where the solutions become "common knowledge" among the help desk staff and can be solved very quickly.

What services you provide is also dependent on the priorities the users have. Here you need to be clear about the difference between what the users need and what they would like. You must evaluate the users needs in terms of how it relates to the needs of the business. Maybe your users wanted Windows 98 as soon as it was available. Some may even want Windows 2000. However, if there is no pressing business need (such as the need for higher security), switching your users to Windows NT may not be high on your list of priorities. Even the alleged greater stability of Windows 98 over Windows 95 might not warrant the expense of the new operating system and time needed to install it.

Even the kind of questions you answer will depend on the priorities you set. I have worked in places where we simply did not answer "programming"-type questions, such as creating macros. Although macros can save you a great deal of time, we did not have the personnel to invest the time needed to help people with macros. Our priorities were keeping the system running and fighting fires.

It is therefore an important aspect to establish a clearly defined set of rules in terms are what kind of support the help desk will provide. The needs of the company will be used in determining the general framework of the services you provide. The needs of the users will be used to determine the specific aspects of these services.

Defining the Objectives

A key aspect of justifying the help desk and getting approval is to develop a clearly defined set of objectives. That is, say you need to be clear on what you hope your help desk will accomplish. Specifying that the help desk is there only to solve problems allows you to say "No" if someone even helps writing a program.

One aspect that I will go into more detail about later is the need to not only define which services will be provided but to explicitly state those that you will *not* provide. This helps the user know exactly what they should expect from the help desk. However, you need to keep in mind that the goal here is not to "pass the buck" but rather to get the user closer to the solution and to provide more uniform support to all users. Often, you do not have the staff to solve every problem or to answer every question. Necessity forces you to send some users away.

Although the motivation may be different between an internal help desk and one you provide for customers, most of the basic principles are the same. An improperly run customer hotline may cost you in repeat sales. An improperly run help desk too can cost you just as much and even more in company downtime.

Although it is often easy to quantify the increased efficiency that the help desk brings in terms of dollars, one aspect that is often overlooked is the increased job satisfaction people have if they are not constantly fighting with both the computer and the IS department. This also provides the benefit for the IS department that they have to spend less time justifying their actions, since the users have less to complain about.

The current situation is not simply described by saying that users cannot solve problems efficiently. Instead, that is the most obvious outward sign of a much deeper problem. Your help desk solution needs to address the reasons why problems cannot be solved efficiently. The two biggest causes that I have found are the lack of documentation and lack of standards. In this sense, documentation is used to refer to writing down anything that would be useful in the help desk. This includes not only traditional documentation, such as on-line help files and handbooks, but also details of incoming calls and their solutions as well as the vast collective knowledge that no one has bothered to write down.

The lack of standards affects the help desk in the number of different ways. For example, lack of standardized software or hardware configuration makes tracking down the problem much more difficult. Plus, there are simply more different things to administer, which takes time away from other tasks. Lack of a documentation standard makes finding information more difficult, such as it is unclear which format the document is in, are you missing important information like the date of the last change, who the responsible person is for this document, and so forth.

Benefits from the Help Desk

Although the actual benefits that the help desk brings differs from company to company, there are a number of basic advantages for the help desk that are common. The first benefit is that users will be spending more time doing company business and less time trying to solve computer problems. Not only will the help desk provide them with a single point of contact to find answers, but the knowledge base will allow them to find answers on their own. Because the support mechanism has been formalized, there will be less time spent on the "administration" of the problem. For example, there will no longer be any time lost looking for the right contact person.

Another major advantage is that the technology will be used more efficiently. For example, users will be better able to use their applications because there is someplace that they can go to should they have problems. In addition, the help desk will be able to determine those areas where the most questions or problems occur and can include information on that subject in any training. In some cases, you can find out which applications or even hardware are being used inefficiently and replace them or move them someplace where they can be put to better use. (I have worked in places where programs like CorelDRAW were used to make simple line drawings that could be done with either MS Word Draw or even Windows Paintbrush.)

Part of the goal of the help desk is to standardize the support structure. This requires a great deal of standardization within the IT/IS infrastructure in order to work effectively. With standardized systems, it is much easier to track down recurring problems and even prevent them from occurring. For example, the recurring problem may be solved by installing an updated driver or patch to an application. Standardized hardware and software allow you to add the patch or update before the problem occurs.

There are a number of aspects of normal systems administration and the IT infrastructure that should be incorporated into the help desk. For example, system and network monitoring are easily integrated into the help desk. In fact, there are a number of help desk packages and system monitoring software that are easily integrated. Therefore, problems that originally required active monitoring on the part of the system administrator can be automatically recorded by the help desk. This may or may not make solving the problem easier, but it does make keeping track of this kind of problem much easier. The result is often detecting patterns and solving problem that you could not solve if you did not keep track of this information.

Another area that can easily be integrated is hardware maintenance. Because the help desk gets the problems first, they are in a much better position to identify a problem and take the necessary steps (such as scheduling a maintenance call). This means that the help desk would be a good place to decentralize in not only the maintenance and repair of the hardware but also the inventory. Taking this one step further, we can say that since the help desk is the primary contact for software issues, it is also the best place to centralize both maintenance and inventory of the software.

I also feel that it is important that the help desk be involved in the purchase of both new hardware and new software. This does not imply that they need to be the decisionmakers. Rather they need to be made aware of what will be coming at them. They need to know what changes are going to take place so that they can make a determination as to how it will affect the help desk in general and possibly permit them to make changes. In addition, knowing what software will be implemented allows the help desk to not only test the software in the system but also allows them to train on the product prior to it being implemented.

Some companies take this administrative function to the extreme in that the help desk becomes the approving authority. All requests for both hardware and software are first made through the help desk. In some cases, it is actually the help desk that does the purchasing; in other cases, the function of the help desk is simply to indicate whether the request is reasonable and then allow the respective department to make the purchase. Although both of these methods can be very useful, I have seen a tendency for the help desk to make decisions more in their best interest and not necessarily in the best interest of the users. Therefore, leave it in the hands of the various departments.

For the help desk to be successful it needs to be accessible to the users as well as used by them. A help desk is of little value if the users cannot find it or they do not take advantage of the services provided. It is therefore important that the help desk be well integrated into your company. This means that the help desk must be perceived as an integral part of your company and not simply a place to call when no one else can solve your problem.

Part of this is finding the appropriate place for the help desk within your organization. Because they are dealing with computer-related issues, it makes sense that the help desk be somewhere under the IT or IS organization. While this is valid reasoning, you need to be careful that it doesn't get buried. Remember that the help desk is the first group of people to hear about computer-related problems and how well the users are taking advantage of the technology. Therefore, there should be a direct route between the help desk and the company management. This allows the help desk manager to provide information to the company management without it being "filtered" by the IT manager.

Positioning the help desk in this manner will also increase the efficiency of the reporting process. The fewer people through which the information must go, the less likely it will be misinterpreted along the way. This occurred in one company where I worked when our marketing department reported problems with loading large graphics into our desktop publishing application.

Rather than buying the people in the marketing department a more powerful machine, the IT manager told the company director that marketing should simply use images with a lower resolution. Since the work they were doing was for the publication of brochures, the higher resolution had to be available. Using a lower resolution for the layout meant at least two files needed to be managed, plus it was much more difficult to create the proper aesthetic effects with a lower resolution and there was no way to enlarge the image.

This problem stemmed from the fact that the help desk staff reported the problem to the IS manager with a recommendation that new computers be purchased for the marketing department. The IS manager did not want to spend money on a new computer when the problem was easily solved by using a lower resolution (or so he thought). Marketing was told the decision and complained to the company director. He contacted the IS manager, who still did not understand the problem but still felt justified in his opinion. The company director simply repeated the answer back to the marketing department. After several phone calls and meetings between marketing and the company director, they eventually got their computers.

The question is how much time was wasted going back and forth like that? Direct contact between the help desk and the company management probably would have saved a great deal of time and money.

Difference to Paid Support

There are a number of books on the market today that deal with the subject of both customer service and help desk. Unfortunately, their primary emphasis is on running a help desk or hotline for external customers. Although this is a noble goal and the information is both valuable and well presented, these books are lacking the details that are specific to running the help desk for your own employees.

Perhaps the most dramatic difference is that in most cases, your "customers" cannot go to a different company. They are stuck with the services that you provide. In one company where I worked, the IT manager jokingly commented that if the users were not happy with their service than they can go somewhere else. He knew very well that they couldn't. In fact, he seemed to enjoy the power he had over the users, since he controlled the help desk. Such attitudes may be good for his ego, but they're not good for the company.

On the other hand, it is acceptable on a customer hotline to promote the attitude that "the customer is always right." Some customers may try to abuse this philosophy, but it is a sound business practice. You can apply the same philosophy to the customers of the internal help desk, that is, the users. However, you're in a much better position to make rules as to how things need to work.

To me, this is also valid. Your goal is to help *everyone* work as efficiently as possible, not just the single individual. If one user is dissatisfied with the "service" that you provide, he or she may complain to your supervisor. You can justify it with the statement that there are hundreds of other users that have similar needs, and that you do not have the resources necessary. (This may be a good time to ask for larger staff, but that's another story.)

Business Case

One of the biggest issues is that you'll need to make a business case for the help desk. That is, you'll need to demonstrate that the help desk has definite business value. The problem is that does not always produce any tangible object for the company. If your help desk is designed for the customers who are buying your products, at a minimum, the help desk is a necessity (or necessary evil). In some cases, like with many software vendors, the help desk or hotline actually generates revenue. However, a purely internal help desk does not have this benefit. Even if you do plan to charge other departments for your services, you do not have as strong a business case as when you're able to sell the service for hard cash.

Instead of the tangible benefits that you can see in other cases, the initial justification for the help desk may have to be built solely on nontangible benefits. Most likely, those nontangible things will be something like "time saved in solving problems" or "increased user satisfaction." However, if you already have experience with a help desk in your company, such as when updating an existing one, you probably have some tangible information that you can include. Since the justification for both a new help desk and improvement to an existing one is basically the same, let's first look at the kind of information that you might have or probably will have if you already have a functioning help desk.

The first thing to consider is whether or not your current help desk keeps accurate records of problems and their solutions; then you're in the similar situation to someone who is just starting out. That is, there is no tangible information to justify developing or expanding the help desk. However, there are certain estimates that you can make that can help you come up with some fairly accurate numbers. The most important thing for the company's management is money. Since time is money and a help desk is used to save time, the help desk can be used to save money. Therefore, a good place to start is to look at those places where a help desk will save time.

Let's assume a medium-sized company with 1,000 computer users. Let's assume further that only 10% of the users call to the help desk on any given day. This means that the help desk gets an average of 100 calls per day. If each call averages six minutes, that would be the total of 600 minutes or 10 hours per day. If you can reduce the number of calls per day to 60 and reduce the average time per call to four minutes, you'll spend just 240 minutes or three hours per day. In other words, by reducing the call load and the length of calls by just 40%, you're saved seven hours per day. If the average hourly wage is ten dollars, you save 70 dollars per day. If you figure an average of 200 work days per year, that's savings of $14,000 per year. Over two years, you are just about at what one of the better help desk products would cost.

At first glance, you might think that the help desk pays for itself within two years. However, what we didn't mention here was the work involved in getting the help desk running. On the other hand, by amortizing the help desk software over three years, you're closer to getting a reasonable return on your investment.

The most important things to note about the times I just mentioned is that I referred to them as the "average." Experience has shown me that the six minutes is much closer to a *minimum* than it is to an average. What many people fail to consider in their evaluations is the time spent either looking for or implementing the solution. Even something as mundane as resetting someone's password can take that length of time.

You need to consider the time it takes for the system administrator to start the User Manager, find that user's entry and input the new password. The time to do this is less if the User Manager is already running, but what about other issues? You need to look at all the processes in which the help desk is involved and measure how long each takes. Monitor how often each of these calls occurs in a specific period of time. It is then a fairly simple matter to get the average amount of time spent on your calls. However, don't forget to consider the calls that occur with less frequency, but take a long time to complete.

If you already have some method of recording your calls, the time it takes to do this and other administrative chores also needs to be considered when estimating the average call time. Here, you also need to consider the calls that are out of the ordinary. For example, the user calls in needing assistance in connecting to a network drive. Normally, this kind of call takes about five minutes. However, the user is a very new to computers and as a result needs the alot more "hand-holding." This means the call takes 15 minutes. (Believe me, these kind of calls happen more often then you can imagine.)

You need to be careful with what you do with these numbers. For example, the numbers you come up with might indicate savings equivalent to one or more employees. This might make you think that once the system is in place and running efficiently, you will be able to reduce your staff. However, the savings are not as tangible as with dollars. On the other hand, if you end up with tying savings equivalent to five or 10 employees, you are probably overstaffed.

Regardless of what these numbers should show, consider the many other things that need to get done in your department before you start sending out those termination notices. I have worked in departments before that never seemed to complete any significant project, because they were too busy fighting fires. By implementing some changes to their help desk, they were able to reduce the number of people working on the help desk and free people do to work on other projects.

When estimating the time it takes to solve a problem, one thing that is often not considered is how much time it takes for the user to get to the right person. This problem shows itself much more dramatically when there is not yet a help desk in place. People will look up the phone number of their favorite system administrator and give him or her a call. Even if this administrator has the skills or knowledge to solve a problem, they may not be the best choice. First, someone else could solve the problem faster. Second, he or she may be in the middle of doing something that is more important than solving this one user's problem. When the administrator redirects the user to the appropriate system administrator, all of this time is nonproductive.

In my experience too, it is rarely the case where the administrator simply says, "I am not the right person. I will transfer you," but rather a certain amount of time is spent explaining the situation to the user. Depending on how much the user begs and pleads for this administrator to help, this could add a couple of minutes to the total time it takes to solve the user's problem.

You should therefore estimate the number of such calls you get in the given period of time and multiply this number by at least two to determine the number of minutes spent redirecting calls. It may not seem like two minutes is something to worry about, but if it happens 150 times a month, that is 300 minutes or five hours.

A central data store is an important aspect of the help desk and should be mentioned in the proposal. This helps both the system administrators and the users themselves to solve problems more quickly. How much time this central store or knowledge base can save you depends on all of the factors involved in deciding on the help desk, such as technical level of your users, complexity of the programs, and so forth. However, in my experience, a well-set-up and well-maintained knowledge base can save at least half of the time spent solving problems.

Preventing problems from occurring rather then cleaning up the mess they leave is another important way to save time. Depending on the kind of problem prevention, this can even equate to saving money. For example, if you give a customer a number of files on a disk that contains a virus, your customer will probably not be pleased. This results in you losing business and therefore money. It is therefore a good idea to address the issue of system administration and monitoring tools in your help desk proposal. What things to look for in these tools is something we'll get to later.

If you have a boss like I have had, it is definitely a good idea to discuss the negative aspects of the help desk implementation in your proposal. For example, the help desk will not spring into being overnight. The knowledge base will not be magically filled with information. You obviously need to invest a certain amount of effort to get the help desk to the point where it is running efficiently. I have found that by discussing such costs in your proposal, the true costs of the help desk implementation will be clear. It is therefore easier for management to make a decision and may be more likely to get additional funds later if your boss is not "blind-sided" by the costs you failed to mention in your proposal.

Costs/Benefits Analysis

Perhaps two of the most over-used terms in recent years are total cost of ownership (TCO) and return on investment (ROI). Both of these play vital roles in determining what new computer technologies will be implemented. In essence, the TCO is not only how much it will cost to purchase a particular system but also how much it will cost to use and administer. A good analogy to computer systems would be a car. When you think of the TCO for a car, you not only have to think about the original purchase price but also recurring costs such as gasoline, insurance, maintenance, and so forth.

This same principle applies to computer systems as well. Perhaps you are not pouring gas into the back of your computer. However, you'll need to spend time configuring and monitoring it as well as a number of other administrative tasks. Since time is money, the amount of time you spend doing these tasks should also be considered in the total cost of owning the product.

Paired with the TCO is the ROI, which is basically the benefit you get from implementing a particular system. With a car, this would be the time saved going from place to place, the convenience of not having to wait for a bus, plus the ability to impress your friends with a cool-looking car. Although you're probably not to going to invest large sums of money in computer systems to impress either your friends or customers, there is still the psychological benefit of implementing certain systems. For example, an automated phone system that directs the user to the appropriate analyst may not save enough time to be worth the investment. However, users may perceive that their questions are being answered more quickly and are therefore happier with the help desk and therefore happier with their work in general.

Building a Proposal

What you need to do to get your help desk project approved will be different from company the company. In some companies, it may be possible to simply explain the situation to the boss and get approval for your help desk. In other cases, you may have to go through a more formal procedure to gain approval. As with any other kind of proposal, there are basically two parts. First, you describe the current situation in terms of cost to the company. Second, you describe the goal of your proposal (that is, the solution to the problem) along with what steps are necessary and what this solution will cost.

When describing the current situation, you need to describe the effects the current situation has on your company at every level. For example, your primary goal (at least one of them) is to efficiently solve users' problems. Therefore, the current situation includes how inefficient it is for users to get problems solved. Another issue is how hard your system administrators are trying to solve these problems. If appropriate, you might consider describing the projects that have been delayed due to manpower shortages because everyone was busy fighting fires.

Interviews with other employees provide a clear picture of how the users perceive the support they are getting. This may not be the same as how the help desk perceives the support they are providing. It would be embarrassing to insist that the support that users are getting is bad and therefore you require a larger staff, only to find out that the users are actually happy with the level of support they are getting. If that should happen, it is likely you won't get the money you're looking for. On the other hand, if you say that support is great, but the users disagree, that doesn't make you look good either.

If you are trying to expand an existing help desk, you can use the historical data to demonstrate how successful the help desk has been up to this point. If the help desk has been successful and has really demonstrated sufficient return on ROIs, you are more likely to get help to expand the system than if your project is not doing so well.

Even where you have an existing help desk and are just trying to get approval to expand it, the statistics you gather will never be 100% accurate. This is not what you are needed for. Instead, you are trying to get an overall picture of the situation.

Another key aspect of your proposal to address is how well the help desk will be able to meet changes in the future. Many managers today are getting bit by the proprietary systems implemented by their predecessors. Open systems and the ability to easily move data from one architecture to another is becoming more and more of a requirement for a company's information infrastructure.

When we were looking for approval for a help desk, one of the topics we addressed was making the help desk information available from a core database application. We demonstrated that although the goal was to eventually import the data into the company database, we could take the first steps with minimal cost and effort. This "low-end" solution also gave us the opportunity to develop and test our database design prior to importing the database.

One thing that I have found extremely useful in getting approval for projects like the help desk or an intranet is a "hands-on" demonstration of what you're proposing. You can show the current state and what processes people go through to get answers to questions. You then show how easy it could be with a properly implemented help desk.

Defining Your Service

In general, it is safe to say that for the most part, users are more or less at the mercy of the help desk. If you're not satisfied with the service there is little that you can do other than to complain. You cannot switch vendors as easily as if you are a paying customer. Although I believe that internal users should be treated like customers in many regards, there are certain issues where you do not (and should not) get the same kind of support. For example, if there are bugs in the software, the vendor is normally obligated to either provide a workaround or a fix to the bug. If the bug is detected in a product that you use in-house, then there is not the same obligations to provide a timely solution.

The Service Level Agreement (SLA)

Regardless of how your company is organized, it is very useful to establish early on what level of service you'll provide. This is referred to as a "service commitment" or "service level agreement" (SLA). Although you usually see the term SLA used in the context of (paying) customer hotlines and other external support services, I will continue to use the term throughout the chapter as any agreement between the help desk and the users.

The purpose of an SLA is so that both sides understand and agree to what level of service will be provided; hence the name. It is important to not only spell out what services will be provided but also spell out explicitly what services will *not* be provided.

The reason for implementing an SLA stems from the fact that customer satisfaction is a measure of how well their expectations are met. If you can meet or even exceed your customers' expectations, you'll have satisfied customers. It is a lot easier to meet your customers expectations if you know what they are. Therefore, developing an SLA lets both you and customer know what is expected.

Although less common in the world of external support, I believe that part of the SLA for internal support should include things that the user is expected to do. For example, if just a single person within a department is having trouble connecting to a network resource, it is reasonable to expect the user to check the cabling themselves as well as shut down the machine and start up again. This is something that would only take five minutes and would probably be recommended by the help desk in any event. By requiring that the users do it themselves before calling the help desk, you have saved yourself a call and can spend the time on more serious issues.

Getting management approval and support of the SLA is a very strong motivator for the employees when they call and haven't fulfilled their obligations. If the support analyst does not have the time, he or she can flat-out refuse to help until the user fulfils the obligation. I feel there is nothing wrong with this, because without it, you will end up wasting a lot of time.

Another thing to keep in mind is that different departments will have different needs. It is not unreasonable to expect that the engineering department be able to solve more problems on its own than the shipping department can. In this day and age, it is reasonable to expect that engineers have a certain level of expertise and experience with computers and can solve problems that the average user cannot.

Some people might think that a formal agreement within a company is unnecessary. Experience has shown otherwise. Such agreements are not designed for the majority of your calls. Instead, they are designed for the exceptions. You're bound to have users who want to exploit the help desk. Having an SLA enables you to simply say "no." Keep in mind, however, that the SLA should serve as a guideline and not a hard-and-fast rule. It is not intended as something the help desk personnel can use to get out of work. If you have the time, there is really nothing wrong with providing service beyond what is defined in the SLA.

When I was working in tech support work for a major operating system vendor, we had a port of the OmniPage optical character recognition software from the Caere Corporation. Along with it, we provided the driver for one of the few professional-level scanners available at the time. A customer called in one day because he could not get the product to work on a different scanner. He insisted that the scanner was "compatible" with the scanner that we supported. The SLA that we had for all our products said that we were obligated only to support the products on the list of supported hardware. Per the SLA, I could have simply refused to help him. Instead, it was a slow day and we tried, but we could not get the driver to work with the other scanner.

Because we were discontinuing this product, I got permission to provide him with the source code for the scanner driver. He could then access the source code directly to see if he could get it to work with the other scanner. I made it clear to him that providing source code for products wasn't part of the services we normally provided. I also made it clear to him that he was on his own in getting the driver to work with a different scanner. So, he said that he understood that and was grateful for the offer I had made.

A few days after I sent the source code to him, he called again. As you expect, he was having trouble adapting the source code to the new scanner. In fact, he had no clue as to where to begin. Despite claims he made initially, he had never written a hardware driver and therefore had no idea what he needed to do to make it work with a different scanner. So, he was hoping that we would change the code to enable it to work with the different scanner. In other words, he was expecting substantially more than what the SLA entitled him to. Plus, he was asking for much more than I had already provided *beyond* the SLA. Although we did provide support to developers, it required the different (more-expensive) support contract than this person had. At this point, I felt justified in refusing to help him further.

Aside from the fact that he was abusing my goodwill, helping and doing development work in the driver exceeded what was required in the SLA. In fact, it is possible that the amount of time and effort spent to get the driver to work with the different scanner could have cost more than his entire support contract.

A different SLA for different departments can also be very important for both developing the help desk and for planning future growth. If you know that certain departments require additional support, you might consider expanding your training to enable these departments to provide more self-help. If necessary, additional obligations on the part of the help desk may allow you to request additional personnel. Should you charge for your help desk services, knowing what each service costs allows different departments to budget in the cost for the appropriate service?

In any case, the support you provide should not only be clearly defined, the description should also be available to everyone either as a hard copy or via the company's intranet. In addition, it should have the endorsement of the company management. In some companies, this support is given simply by the fact that the IT department is allowed to make the decisions it feels are necessary. In other cases, it may be necessary to have the SLA published by the company management.

Regardless of who approves it or what levels of support you provide, there are a number of things that every SLA should contain. Among the things the SLA should include are:

- what services will be provided and explicitly what services will *not* be provided
- any exceptions to either of the above rules
- where one of level of support ends and the next one begins
- hours of support
- how to contact support, such as telephone, fax, email, and so forth
- who is authorized to call

- any limitation in terms of how many calls can be made
- description of the various priorities
- required response times
- the level of self-help on the part of the user
- what information users should provide with the call
- what the call resolution procedures are
- what the complaint procedures are and who to contact

One important aspect is to clearly state what it means to say that a problem has been "resolved." As we will get into more detail about later, call resolution does not necessarily mean that you have an answer to the users' problem. In many cases, the solution to a particular problem is not your responsibility. For external support, this may be something like a clone of a piece of hardware that your product supports. You never made the claim that your product would work with that hardware, and therefore you have no obligation to ensure that it does work. For internal support, it might be something like approving the installation of some software package. If your company policy dictates that new software must be approved by the department manager, you are not obligated to install software simply because a user requests it. You are also under no obligation to get the manager's approval should a user call. This is *their* responsibility.

So, what is supported and to what extent is very much a matter of perspective. One of my favorite stories in this regard involves the email program that we provided. This was in the days before most people had graphical interfaces to email, and so everything was done to a character-based application. I got a call from a user who insisted there was a bug in our email program. He would be typing and typing and typing and typing and never press Enter. Since he could do this in his Windows-based word processing program, he just assumed that it was also possible in our character-based Unix email program. The input buffer to the email program was only 255 characters long. What happened was that after the user had been typing for awhile, the program simply overwrote the buffer with the new characters. Granted, the program could have given a warning indicating that the buffer had overrun and had stopped accepting input. However, the key point of the dispute was the fact that the user insisted that this was a bug in the software.

In that this was a bug, he insisted that he was entitled to free support and that the "bug" be fixed.

Nowhere in the documentation did it say he could keep typing forever. In other words, he assumed certain behavior in the program, and when the program did not exhibit that behavior, he claimed the right to free support and that the "bug" should be fixed.

The key here is not those unreasonable requests by certain users but rather making it clear what the limits of your support are. If the software does not exhibit behavior that it is "common" for this particular type of program, it may be considered a bug. On the other hand, if there are no standards by which one can judge whether the behavior is correct or that the documentation clearly states the program behaves in a certain way—and it does—the user is at the discretion of the support analysts in terms of how much support he gets.

Even the issue of what constitutes call closure should be addressed in the SLA. You probably will not be able to list every single case in which the call closure becomes an issue. However, there certainly are generalizations that you can include. For example, if the problem has a known solution in terms of a work-around, it may be sufficient to say that once the customer is told of the solution and has implemented it correctly, the call is closed. However, the call may remain open until a bug fix is generated and provided to the customer. We will go into more detail about this when we talk about call tracking and escalation in the section on call management.

Support Handbook

The SLA does little good if it is not available to everyone involved. Obviously, if there are legal or other issues that require the agreement to be formalized (e.g., if you are selling support), there will be a written document. However, it can also be very useful to have the written document for the agreements that are less official. Therefore, you might find it useful to formalize your support offerings.

You can call it anything from the *Help Desk Handbook* to *The Support Services Guide,* but it should clearly state what services you're providing, how these services are obtained, and what limitations there are to the support, if any.

As with the SLA, you should discuss the details of your "help desk handbook" with your users. After all, despite the fact that they may not be paying for the service, they are still your customers, and therefore you should adjust your services to meet their needs. Granted, you're probably in a better position to dictate the limits of the support when supporting internal users. However, you should not abuse this. I have found that in most cases you can reach a reasonable compromise between what the users think you should provide and what your resources allow you to provide. If the available resources really do not allow you to provide the services necessary, it is much easier to request a larger budget from the company management than if you simply went there and asked on your own.

Your company intranet provides an excellent way of reducing the number of calls. It is the perfect medium for providing self-help information but is also the perfect way to give users up-to-the-minute information on other topics of interest. For example, where your central database has crashed, you could provide information about the nature of the problem and when it is expected to be corrected. If you do provide such information, it is important that users be *obligated* to check this information before calling the help desk.

If your company is large enough, it is possible that the help desk is as well-equipped as many commercial support providers are. You might have automatic call direction (ADC), voice mail, and many other different products. This is another technology that is often not used to its fullest. For example, if there is a larger problem affecting the large number of users, it might be a good idea to report on this fact through your ADC system. For example, when users call, the first thing they might hear could be an announcement indicating a problem with your primary database application. You can then give additional information to them such as the scope of the problem, what's being done, when it is expected to be corrected, and so forth. You can tell them to stay on the line for all other problems. Otherwise, whenever your database goes down, you'll get dozens of calls from users wanting to know when the system will be running again. Each requires 2–3 minutes to explain to the user that the problems is being worked on and an estimate of how long it will be before things are running again. This does little good.

It is especially important for an internal help desk to be as consistent as possible. If you help one user debug a program, you'll need to do it for the next one. If you loan equipment to someone, you can be assured that tomorrow someone else will call asking to borrow something else. In the first case, you may be spending hours doing something that is not your job, and in the second case, it may cost your department money if the hardware is returned broken.

Being clear on what your objectives are is not intended as carte blanche to say "No" to every request the user might have. However, you must keep in mind that your goal is to satisfy every user and not just a select few.

Written Procedures

A well-defined set of procedures is important to ensure both the efficient operation of the help desk and that you meet your SLA. In fact, you can make reference to these procedures within the SLA to ensure that both the help desk and the users work efficiently.

One aspect of this that some companies seem to miss is that the procedures need to be developed by the people working on the help desk and not by management. If these procedures are developed by people who are not directly involved with the day-to-day operation of the help desk, they tend to include things that are not reasonable. For example, one manager insisted that *all* incoming calls be recorded. The efficiency of the help desk dropped dramatically as we recorded each time a user needed his or her password reset, each time a printer was out of paper, each time users complained about the network performance, and so forth. Although much of this information may be useful in certain circumstances, we did not have the manpower to devote so much time to administrative tasks.

In my experience, the best thing is to get everyone involved. That is, you need representatives from the help desk, management, and in some cases other departments. Having other departments involved is especially important when the actual work performed is accomplished by someone else. For example, in many companies, the help desks serves as a central collection point for problems that are then passed to the responsible groups. If there are network problems, this is passed to the network group. If there are server problems, this is passed to the server group. Having the help desk decide on the procedures is just as bad as having management do it.

An obviously important aspect of these procedures is to ensure that they are accessible to everyone. To me, this means both on-line and hard copy versions of these procedures. Hard copy only means that the search time for access is longer. "On-line" means they become inaccessible when your system goes down.

Some commercial help desk products allow you to automate the work flow of the help desk to a considerable extent. In such cases, it is very easy to automate many of the procedures.

I have found that it is useful to actually create a *set* of procedures. The first set deals with how the help desk reacts to incoming calls. The second deals with the internal workings of the help desk, which does not necessarily require "other departments. For example, the internal procedures may describe how to include a new problem in the list of standard problems and solutions.

I have also found that is useful to break the procedures into two parts. The first part is a simple checklist or flow chart of the procedure. This serves as a quick reminder for those people who are already familiar with the necessary steps. These need to be short and sweet, including almost no detail. The second part are the details. This includes mundane things like which buttons to push and which values to input in the appropriate fields. One very simple solution is to use the headings of this detail section as your checklist.

Your company intranet is a good place to store this information. The Web technology of your intranet will enable you to make this information available to everyone as well as make the necessary references to other documentation through the use of hyperlinks. Most of the more-advanced help desk products include a Web interface so that all of the help-desk-related information can be accessed through a single interface (your Web browser).

Including the procedures, or any help desk information for that matter, on your intranet is a good way of ensuring that information is not duplicated. I have found that hard copies or text files tend to repeat information "just in case." Because of the inherent difficulty in searching through hard copy or word processing documents, many people tend to repeat the same information in multiple places. The ease in which references can be made using hyperlinks makes Web technology the ideal storage medium.

Among the things your procedures should include are how the call is handled in terms of both the initial contract with users and the resolution; how requests and questions are dealt with; and how to respond to emergencies, escalation procedures, and communication procedures. Here, communication means not only between the help desk and the users but also between the help desk and other organizations, both internal and external.

As with the solutions to problems, procedures are of limited value if they become outdated. Therefore, an official review and update process should be the main part of your internal procedures. The rotating schedule should be put into place to review extra and internal procedures to ensure that they are up-to-date. I recommend that this task of rotating to ensure things is not over-looked. It's human nature to read things into documents that you have read dozens of times before. Having different people read the documentation at different times, you can help to avoid the "I know what it says" syndrome.

As with all other documentation, I think it is very important to define an owner for each of the procedures. Although checking the status should be done by everyone on the help desk, one person should be designated for a specific document to ensure that the changes are made. For example, the help desk person reviewing the documentation questions the validity of a specific procedure and passes it to the owner, who then makes any necessary changes.

Planning

A help desk is not something that happens overnight. You need to plan the entire system before you implement any of it. (OK, documenting solutions is something you can start doing now.) Remember that there are a lot of hidden costs to this. There are the obvious costs of the hardware and software right up-front. However, as the help desk grows, you might need to add more functionality to it. Plus, there are the cost of staffing the help desk, training the people on the help desk system, and so on.

One thing I often see missed in calculating the cost of the help desk are the costs incurred by loss of user productivity. I worked for a company that sent out a memo with the paychecks to all the employees about the costs of leaving early, coming back from breaks late, and so on. They estimated the cost at over a million dollars a year. However, spending $10,000 for new net-work equipment to replace older outdated equipment that constantly needed to be fixed was "too expensive." When the component failed, much of the production was stopped. Plus, there was the cost of the repairs.

The initial cost of the help desk may turn out to be surprisingly high. The better help desk products start at $15,000 for five users and go up from there. $75,000 would not surprise me (although not many companies actually need something that expensive). You need to consider the fact that the re-turns will pay for themselves. It may take up to three years, but it is a reason-able investment, because user satisfaction is sure to go up, and the increased productivity as a result is hard to measure. In addition, the formalization of your support into a help desk system helps manage the costs.

Keep in mind that for the internal help desk, you are probably not gen-erating revenue. Potentially you could be charging back to the departments who use your services, but I think that's a bad idea. This makes "penny-pinching" managers upset when users use a service that was designed for them. They get upset when a problem arises that causes the end user to call support, as the call comes out of their budget. If there is no charge, people are more likely to use it. Because the help desk requires financial resources without generating revenue, often it gets the "leftovers" when it comes to the budget.

My response is to suggest that the heating be turned off, since it doesn't generate revenue either, and employees can just put on a coat. In fact, turning off the heat would cut down on fuel costs. You wouldn't expect the company to go to such drastic measures with regard to the heating, but they might when it comes to the help desk.

For an internal help desk, it is difficult to determine whether the value exceeds the costs. We can discuss the savings in time and get an estimate of what is being saved in dollars. However, just because the dollar values don't match up doesn't mean the help desk is not worth it. One "value" that needs to be considered is customer satisfaction. If your employees feel like they are being taken care of, morale is higher and they work better.

One thing that should not be overlooked but often is, is that a help desk should not be a goal unto itself. Many managers will feel that a help desk is necessary. This is probably true, but you need not invest tens of thousands of dollars, when a phone and pad of paper is enough. I have worked with managers who have read in a magazine that certain technology was "necessary." They obviously had to implement it if it was "necessary."

The costs in planning and developing your help desk need to be worth it. The best approach is to determine what the areas are where the most time is lost. My experience has been that it is always searching for solutions. In general, the amount of time implementing the solution is negligible compared to the time spent looking for it. My opinion on this is that it fits nicely into the 80–20 rule. You spend 80% of your time working on 20% of the problems. If these problems can be solved in half the time, then you have saved 40% of your work. You spend 80% of your time looking for the answers and 20% implementing them. If you reduce the search time by half, you again save 40% of your work.

Therefore, the primary focus of your help desk is the quick resolution of problems. Of the dozens of help desk products that I have looked at, the rule has been that the more expensive the product, the more effort has been invested in problem resolution. This makes sense when one considers that the technology for information retrieval is more complicated than that for information storage, such as simply tracking problem numbers.

Designing the Help Desk

A help desk works best when it is explicitly designed and not let to grow out of an existing organization. If you have an organization that you cannot simply throw away (which is often the case), then you need to control and plan the evolution toward your concept of a help desk.

Start your planning with the construction of a model of how you want your help desk to flow. The flow is more important than the way it is organized. It is much easier, in my mind, to organize the units around the flow rather than the other way around. When you see how things flow, the units build themselves according to where things are flowing.

If you don't already have a help desk system in place, the first thing you want to ask yourself is, "Do we need one?" Implementing one because "everyone else has one" is the help desk serving itself: You are not fitting the help desk to the needs of the users. If you discover that your users are constantly running into problems they cannot solve, then maybe training is a more efficient alternative.

If you already have some kind of help desk system, then it becomes a process of reengineering or tuning the existing system. Often there only needs to be a formalization of the system and nothing needs to change. In the worst cases, the whole system needs to be redesigned.

The first step is to define a mission statement. What are you trying to accomplish? Whatever your statement is, you need to stick with it. All of your activity needs to be guided by this statement. If the mission statement is, "To enable the users to work as efficiently as possible," then you are committing yourself to writing shell scripts or word processing macros for your users. That's OK! You just need to be clear on what you are offering.

If you are creating a new help desk, there may be some things that you are doing that relate to the way you want a help desk to be run. You need to look at how the users are currently being supported as well as what mechanisms are already in place. In one company, there was no formal help desk, but there was single hotline number that the users were expected to call.

This should be incorporated into any planning. What are the users' current attitudes on the support being provided? What changes would they make if they could? What technologies (hardware and software) are they using? Are they using it effectively and efficiently? One example of how users don't use technology efficiently is where they create tables of numbers in their word processing application and then do the calculation by hand, rather than using the spreadsheet. This indicates a need for either training or telling them just what tools are available.

Response Time and Resolution Time

There are two basic help desk issues that cause the greatest amount of confusion: response time and resolution time. Response time can have several different meanings depending on which environment you're working in. In essence, the response time is the time between when the help desk system becomes aware of the call until the system begins working on it. I used the word "system" here intentionally, because this also applies to automated response mechanisms. For example, your help desk system may have a mechanism for providing requests or questions through email or the Web. When the request is received by the help desk system and a response is sent to the user indicating the call has been received, it has been responded to. In such cases, the response time can be as little as 30 seconds. If you have a system where problems can be automatically added to the database, you might think that this time as zero. If no one looks in the database, the response time could be weeks! You need some mechanism to check this regularly.

In other cases, such as when the user calls the help desk, the response time is from the time the phone starts ringing until it is picked up by a person on the other end. This is where the first confusion comes in. Some people may say the response time is the time until the problem begins to be worked on. That is, a customer service representative that takes the call and assigns it to a particular help desk analyst is still included in the response time, which does not stop until the analyst begins working on the call. In other environments, a call is considered to be in the works when the customer service representative has begun taking down the necessary information or passes the call to the analysts.

The time from when the user submits the call to the time that someone actually begins working on the problem is often referred to as the *primary* response time. From the users' point of view, this is the more important of the two, since this marks the beginning of when they are starting to get help.

This all may be a simple matter of semantics. However, you need to be clear in what you are measuring. To me, both of these are valid measurements. This is especially important if any significant amount of time can be spent by the customer service representative or dispatch or to get the call to the right analyst. If you find that a significant portion of the total time spent on the call is being spent on customer service functions (even as little as 5 or 10%), this time should be reflected. You might consider creating a special category of time to reflect this customer service function. That way, when you start to measure the effectiveness of your help desk, it is easier to determine where problems are.

Last, and certainly not least, is the time until the problem is solved, the time to resolution (TTR). This is not the time when the user gets a response but rather the time until they "agree" that the problem has been resolved. Some analysts consider the issue "resolved" when they send (or in the case of an internal help desk, install) a patch. However, if the patch did not solve the problem, it has not been resolved.

The time to resolution is essentially the total time from when the call is first received until the problem has been resolved. Here, too, the actual definition is a matter of interpretation. For example, is this the time until the patch is sent or the time until the patch has been installed and recognized by the user as having solved the problem? If it takes the user two weeks to install the patch and reports that it solves the problem, this call has an extremely long time to resolution. Here, too, you might mention this in the SLA.

To avoid such problems, I feel that the best solution is to mark the problem as closed as soon as the user has been given the solution. Should that not solve the problem, the call can always be reopened, and the new time spent on the call simply added to the existing time to resolution. Therefore, the efficiency of the help desk is not adversely affected by procrastinating users.

On the other hand, when the problem is being worked on within the help desk, such as when specific equipment needs to be sent out or software installed, this time should be included in the time to resolution. If this time becomes exceptionally long, it may indicate a problem within the help desk. For example, you may need additional equipment or staff to solve such problems in a timely manner.

When planning your help desk, you need to define what the maximums are for each of these times. This goes along with setting the priorities and urgencies of each of the problem types. You also need to include the possibility that your help desk is understaffed (vacation, illness, meetings). Therefore, you should extend this maximum slightly. There may also be times when you are involved in other projects and the calls have a lower priority. Therefore, I recommend setting a low initial response time (10-20 minutes if not by phone) and a similar value for the primary response time, but leave the time to resolution open. (You have no way of knowing in advance how long the call will take.)

Help Desk Models

Properly organized and efficiently run, a help desk can function with a team of less than 1% the number of employees. Here I do not mean the size of the IT department but rather the number of people who are talking calls at any given moment. The total number of people that work on the calls is solely dependent on the call load. However, a very small number can be set on the phones. This leaves the other members to concentrate on solving other problems, whether they are problem reports or projects that they are working on.

The more spread out the projects, the greater the need for a concentrated team that mans the phones. If everyone is working on the same project, then one person being called off to handle a call is not a big deal. However, if you are the only one working on it, with constant interruptions, you never get your work done.

Choosing the Right Model

In their book *The Art of Software Support*, Francois Tourniaire and Richard Jarrell speak of two kinds of help desk models: *front-line/back-line* (FL/BL) and *touch-n-hold* (TH). Although they may be referred to by different names in different texts, these are perhaps the most common terms and are very straightforward in describing what they mean.

With the FL/BL model, your support organization is broken into two groups. As you might guess from its name, the *front line* refers to those support analysts that are in direct contact with the customers and are the first to get the problems. When they cannot solve the problem, it is passed on to the *back line*. With the TH model, the analyst who first receives the call will hang onto it until it is resolved. That is, you touch the problem and you hold it until resolution.

The structure that you choose for your help desk will be decided by which approach you're going to take to manage calls initially (i.e., when they are first received). There are two philosophies here: dispatch and resolve. The first approach, *dispatch,* is where incoming calls are dispatched to the correct place. When receiving a call to the help desk, the task of the first person who gets the call is to "dispatch" it. This could mean assigning the call to a particular queue or checking the customer's information to make sure it is accurate or to make sure they have a valid support contract (assuming support is fee based). If they don't, you could send them to customer service to get a new contract. With a result- or resolution-oriented model, the first person to get the call will also attempt to resolve the problem.

The primary advantage of a dispatch-oriented system is that the customer gets to talk to someone, usually within a relatively short time. However, this says nothing about how long it will take before they can talk to someone who will actually start to solve their problem and doesn't say anything about how long it will take to resolve the problem. That is, the time to resolution usually goes up.

On the other hand, it is generally easier for the dispatch to decide which queue is most appropriate (assuming you have a situation where different analysts solve different kinds of problems). It is very frustrating to the customer to wait on hold only to discover the person he eventually gets to talk to is not the right one to solve his problem.

Another major problem with a purely dispatch model is that the customer will often need to describe the problem more than once. Because the dispatch staff probably does not have the technical training to solve the problems, they might not even have the technical training or knowledge to even understand it. If the dispatcher is expected to write a brief description about the problem into a help desk/problem database, what comes out may not even be understandable to the analyst. The dispatcher does his or her best to write a description, but often the words are unfamiliar, so they will write what they "think" the other person said. The result is that once the customer talks with the analyst, he or she will probably need to repeat the description of the problem. This can waste time and annoy customers.

Another problem that the dispatch model creates is that customers soon learn that the dispatchers do not solve their problem and try to figure out ways to get around the system. The customer usually knows the first and last name of the analyst (particularly if they ask) and call back and ask for this person directly. If your company or organization allows incoming calls to people on the help desk, all the customers need to say is that they are a "friend" of the analyst they wish to speak to. While working in support, I received numerous calls from customers who got to me directly, claiming they were friends.

This problem can continue after you switch from the dispatch model, because the customer does not want to wait in a queue. If the analyst has a phone shift, the customer could hang up before they get to your voice mail. If you are not on the phones, people normally answer the call only to find it is a customer.

The *resolution method* is a system in which the first person to get the call will try to solve the problem. How long that person spends trying to solve the problem and what their technical expertise is differs dramatically from company to company. In many cases, they have just a rudimentary knowledge of the product and are there to deal with the very basic calls.

On the other hand, I have worked in companies where a large number of the analysts were scheduled for calls on the front line. The length of the call was limited to 5–10 minutes, after which the customer was either passed to a different engineer who would spend more time or schedule a callback (e.g., if the customer was instructed to do certain tests).

What I see as becoming more and more common in the help desk industry is a help desk model where the first analyst to get the call essentially has no time limit and will work on the call until it is resolved. If your product or the level of calls are generally very simple, this method has a very high level of customer satisfaction. The problem is the more-complicated problems where it might take hours to find a resolution. Analysts should therefore know when they are not making any progress, so that the call may be passed to a more-experienced analyst or even that they should take a break and approach the problem with a fresh mind later.

The two main advantages of the resolution-oriented approach is that the easy calls are solved on first contact, and other calls are still worked on by the analyst beginning with the first call. That means the first contact is used for problem resolution, not for administrative functions.

I would only suggest employing a dispatch-oriented model when the majority of your calls are either extremely simple or not technical at all. For example, many organizations have their hotline under the heading of "customer service." They handle the whole spectrum of calls from complaints to warranty calls to technical questions on how the product works. Complaints and warranty issues are not technical issues and generally require less training to solve. Your customer service staff can quickly sort out the calls.

There are certain modifications of each model, but the general structure stays the same. For example, I have worked as a support analyst in an organization that used the FL/BL model. However, there were actually three levels (not counting the engineering department and other companies). Analysts working on the actual front line that dealt with the customer were expected to *solve* or *pass* the problem within *15 minutes*. This resulted in quick turnover for the easy problems and also gave the back-liners a head start in working on the problem (provided the problem and the attempted solutions were documented correctly). The model was still resolution oriented, with each level providing more in-depth support than the previous one.

I have also worked as a support analyst in an organization that had a mixture of the FL/BL and TH models. The people who first answered the phones were the customer service representatives, who were given a certain amount of technical training. They would screen the calls to determine those calls that they could solve as well as those that specifically needed a patch, upgrade, and so forth. Normally they could determine this within the first couple of minutes. If not, or they determined the call actually did need a "real" analyst, the call would be passed along. Once the next person got a call, it was theirs to keep.

Advantages of the Different Models

I have some problems with certain philosophies and concepts in many help desk books. The most significant is the playing down of the FL/BL model. Granted, it does have some limitations and drawbacks, but it is extremely useful in the right circumstances. To better understand why I feel this is so, let's look at the advantages and disadvantages of both the FL/BL and TH models.

The primary advantages of the FL/BL model is the limited training that is necessary to work on the front line. You probably could not toss someone onto the phone without any special training if you were supporting a product for your customers (assuming the person did not already know the product). On the other hand, you could expect someone with a normal computer background to take calls in an internal help desk (assuming that you did not have too much specialized hardware or software). Mistakes and even guessing are acceptable. Since we are talking about supporting users, we should talk about the internal help desk. Depending on the company, I have found the FL/BL model to be very effective.

There are two primary disadvantages of the FL/BL model. The first is inevitable and that is the length of time is takes for the analyst to get the skills needed to become one of the back-liners. Although this is a major issue with customers who are paying for support, you do always have the option of having less-experienced analysts working on problems on an internal help desk. Hotline duty may be done on a rotating basis so that everyone gets his or her chance, even the experts. Since the people with less experience are not on the phone as often, they have less chance to learn (although some companies only have the new people on the phone).

Generally, people are much more patient and forgiving if the analyst is "one of their own." This also applies in reverse. A help desk analyst is generally more patient with other employees. This is usually true in smaller companies where you know the person on the other end of the phone. However, I have often seen in larger companies, where you do not know the person on the other end of the phone, that both sides can become impatient even more quickly than if it was a paying customer.

Because of the patience of other people and the fact that there is no threat that they will go to the "competition," you have more freedom in how long you can work on a problem and how many times it can be handed from one analyst to the next. This means that less-experienced analysts can work on the problem and thereby gain experience. However, when they have worked on the problem "long enough," it can be passed along to the expert with little trouble. In an environment with paying customers, they certainly do not want to pay to train your analysts, and they expect answers more quickly.

Because of customer complaints or even their own experience, companies are not willing to have the inexperienced analyst work too long on the problem in a paying environment. It is *expected* that the analyst pass it along within a certain amount of time. It may even be a contractual obligation. In many cases, the original analyst never sees the solution and therefore does not learn anything. This means it takes a lot longer to become proficient.

In one company where I worked, we had a *single* front-liner to support over 500 users. The initial reaction by most people was to think we were crazy, because that was far too many people for a single front-liner to handle. However, a "busy" day was when there were 10 incoming calls. There were two reasons for this small number of calls. First, we had an extremely limited palette of applications. We had one application that handled all of the business functions and an office suite to handle the rest Each user knew the products well enough to do to do their job. The result was that the majority of the calls were either to reset passwords, create new accounts, or to assure the user that the database was, in fact, still working, even though their request was taking an extremely long time to complete.

In this case, the front-liner was simply there to catch all of the mundane problems. On the few occasions where calls were more detailed or required more attention, they were handed off to the "expert." This freed the front-liners to do other tasks, such as change backup tapes, check log files and disk space, update the documentation, and other administrative tasks.

We found this model to be extremely effective in our particular environment. However, it requires that each responsibility be clearly defined and assigned to a particular individual or group. In addition, what type of calls are processed by the help desk and which are handed off to the experts must also be clearly defined.

One problem that this model brings with it is the increased likelihood that solutions to problems do not get documented. The front-liner has a very limited scope of problems that he or she needs to solve, and the existing documentation will rarely get updated, or the tasks are considered "common knowledge" and there is no need to document anything. When a problem is passed to one of the experts, there is often a belief that documentation is not necessary, because they will be handling this kind of call anyway. Therefore, in both cases, nothing gets documented.

Another problem is the danger that front-liners will simply toss trouble calls to the back-liners, even before they have spent time on them. I have seen this in many cases, where the support organization bases raises or promotions on the number of calls *taken* and not on the number *resolved*. A front-liner who gets a lot of calls but quickly passes them to the back-liners gets rewarded, as no record is kept of the reopened calls or calls that he or she *could* have solved. The front-liner who takes a little longer and has a high-resolution rate is not rewarded. However, customers are happier because they have a faster time to resolution.

It is both of these problems that make many companies steer away from the FL/BL model, despite the added burden of training the analysts. However, given the right circumstances, even in a company with external customers, the FL/BL model can be successfully implemented.

As already stated, the TH model has the problem of training and experience for the analyst. Either they start with the necessary skills, which is often hard to find, or there is a long period before they are "up to speed." However, in a large majority of the cases, this is compensated for by increased customer satisfaction, since there are fewer handoffs. However, there *may* be less customer satisfaction if the analyst takes too long in solving the problem. This will happen often with the newer analysts as they struggle to learn the product.

For the analyst there is also the added advantage of "satisfaction." With an FL/BL model, where they often never see the resolution, they never get the feeling of completion nor do they learn the proper solution. At least, that's what happens much of the time. With the TH model, the analyst is there (usually) from start to finish and therefore sees the resolution.

Another problem is the separation that occurs between the front-liners and back-liners. Although they are doing the same kind of job, there will always be a separation even if just due to the title. Often companies perpetuate this by "promoting" people from the front line to the back line. Therefore, the back line is perceived as being more prestigious. I have seen it where the back-liners "look down" on the front-liners. Even if subconsciously, the front-liners then "get even" by tossing over more and more calls. The back-liners have no recourse but to simply take the calls. They then get overloaded and the customer suffers.

Personally, I think these are *management problems* and not an intrinsic problem with the model. If management monitors and "corrects" analysts who pass on problems too early, this problem can be eliminated. Second, if there is a mechanism in place to inform the front-liners of the proper solutions (e.g., requiring back-liners to pass the solutions back), then this problem can be reduced (if not eliminated).

In one company I worked for, the difference between front-liners and back-liners was purely a scheduling issue, nothing more. Depending on the needs of the department, during one shift you could be a front-liner and the next shift you could be a back-liner. It all depended on where you were needed. The reason for this was to solve as many problems as quickly as possible before passing them along. Front-line calls had to be resolved within 15 minutes before they were passed to a back-liner. Since everyone could be a back-liner, it is possible that you would schedule yourself such a call for the very next hour.

Also, the calls assigned to back-liners were done so by problem area. The front-liners had spent enough time with the problem to know what it was about and would schedule it to be handled by a specialist in that area. In many cases, the specialists were *themselves*. They could solve the problem but knew it would take longer than 15 minutes.

In principle, everyone was equally skilled, so the problem of the learning curve was resolved. You got to work out the problems so you learned the answers. Since you solved the problem, you had that satisfaction. Since you could just as easily get the call yourself, there was no motivation to toss the problem off to the back-liners, as *you* could just as easily get the call.

However, you do need to be careful with this scheme. Performance should never be solely based on the total number of calls taken or resolved. If it is, then a front-liner will still have the motivation to pass the call, as it gets counted for him. The motivation is even greater if back-line calls are counted a second call. If you count resolutions, then the analysts may tend to take too long on front-line calls, as they want to be the one to get the credit for resolving them.

Dispatch or Resolve

The FL/BL model does not necessarily imply that the first person taking the call is going to try to solve it. In many support organizations, the first person to take the call will serve either in the customer service or a dispatch role. When dealing with an external help desk, the customer service aspects include things like determining whether or not the user has a support contract or the product is still under warranty.

Although this is not normally an issue for an internal help desk, there may be cases were a user is not eligible for support. Remember that one of the things you defined initially is exactly what your services are. If the user were to call in asking for something beyond these services, it seems reasonable to deny them support. Sometimes only certain users are allowed to ask certain questions (such as how to use the color laser printer). Here, too, you are justified in denying them support.

The dispatch system has the advantage that it is very efficient in getting the call to the right analyst. Even with an automatic call direction (ACD) system, users themselves are not always able to determine where the call should be directed. A dispatch system can have a negative influence on the way people perceive this success of the help desk. For example, management may see that all calls are being responded to within 30 seconds. The users have no perceived benefit in that their problems are not solved any faster. It is also conceivable that the actual resolution time for the calls *increases*. This is because additional time is spent going through dispatch.

Another problem that occurs frequently with internal help desks is that users quickly learn which administrator solves which kind of calls. The next time they have a problem, they may choose to call that person directly rather than calling the hotline. It is therefore vital that such behavior be prohibited by the company management.

If you choose a customer service or dispatch role for your front line, you are likely to find that the initial response time is fairly low. That is, users get to talk to a human fairly quickly. On the other hand, when the front line takes on the resolution role, then initial response times tend to be longer. This is due to the fact that trying to solve the problem takes longer than merely recording administrative information or directing the call. One way to decrease the response times is to put a time limit on how long the analyst should work on a problem before it is passed to the back line.

Hand in hand with the response time is the time to resolution. The total time to resolve a call will increase by the time spent by the dispatchers. However, with dispatchers you have a better chance of getting the call to the right analyst the first time. In my experience, the average time to resolution for all calls on help desks that support a large number of different products is lower when using dispatchers than when the user is expected to decide himself where the call belongs, even with an ACD system.

When a call comes in, at least a minute is spent wading through menus and listening for the right option before the user is finely placed in the right queue. If the user actually ends up in the wrong queue, it can be anywhere from 5 to 10 minutes before the user talks with the analyst, discovers he ended up in the wrong queue and is finally placed into the right queue. Even if the first analyst can place the user at the head of the queue, he will still need to wait for the next available analyst.

In one company we addressed this problem by letting the user break down their own calls into only three distinct areas: hardware, applications, and network. Users were given instructions how to determine into which area a call fell. It was then fairly easy for them to make a decision as to which button to press in the phone menu. There was obviously a great deal of overlap (such as printing from an application to network printer, which could fall into any one of the problem areas). However, the skills set that each analyst had allowed him to either solve a problem or quickly determine which was the proper queue. The percentage of calls that actually ended up in the wrong queue the first time was fairly low. This led to a comparatively short resolution time.

Another key difference between the dispatch and resolution models is the skill required. Dispatchers require only enough skill to decide where a call should go. Obviously, the skill level required for the resolution model is much higher. This has two effects. First, you need to spend more time and effort to train the front line if they are expected to resolve problems. Second, low-skill jobs have a tendency to become boring. This may lead to faster burnout than with other jobs.

To solve the problem of burnout, one company where I worked encouraged the dispatchers to improve their technical skills with the goal of eventually becoming analysts themselves. Initially this was a somewhat of an unofficial policy. However, after the first person succeeded (and fantastically so), it became official policy that all dispatchers who wished to be trained would be assigned a "mentor" from among the analysts, who would help train them. The program was so successful that eventually all dispatchers were given several weeks of training so that they could solve many of the very basic issues without the need to transfer the call to a "real" analyst.

Organization

Organizing your help desk is not just an issue of grouping your analysts into different teams. It means setting up and managing the infrastructure that helps your help desk. Here, too, we come back to the issue of savings and therefore running an *efficient* help desk. Therefore,having a properly organize help desk is vital to having one that runs efficiently.

Although the decision between a FL/BL or TH model may be considered an organizational issue, I deal with the help desk model separately, because it is such a fundamental aspect of your help desk. Here, we will begin with issues that fall much more into administrative rather than work flow areas. This means that you could use the FL/BL or T/H models with a number of different organizations.

One key element in the organization of your help desk is the organizational units (OU). This is simply the smallest level of organization within your help desk. In some instances, you might be tempted to call this a team or group. However, depending on its function and your company, an OU may consist of just a single person.

For me, the primary motivation for defining OUs that small is that the duties of your help desk need to be designed to fit to a particular job title or function rather than to a specific individual. I have experienced it before where documentation makes reference to "assign problems to Joe" or "check with Mary for clarification." This causes confusion when they no longer perform the same tasks, and it is even worse when they leave the company. Therefore, duties within the help desk (in the entire IT department for that matter) should be assigned based on the OU and not on a particular person.

As I mentioned in previous chapters, it is a good idea to have specific individuals responsible for the various aspects of your IT department: the security manager is responsible for security, the backup manager is responsible for backups, and so forth. Some of these OUs, as with the other aspects of your department, could simply be a subelement of another OU. The same thing applies to your help desk.

Perhaps the simplest method is to organize your help desk based on skill or area of responsibility. For example, you might have a network team or an applications group. Incoming calls are handled by the OU and not by any specific individual. Depending on your organization, you can break this down even further. For example, the cabling OU is part of the network OU and the Word OU is part of the applications OU.

Determining exactly which OUs you need will depend on your company, and discussing them goes beyond the scope of this book. How many people end up in each OU and how the different OUs relate to each other is something that will depend on your company. The key thing to remember is an OU is a *functional* unit and may not reflect the management organization of your company. On the other hand, I have found management functions much easier the closer the help desk organization matches the management structure.

Within a support organization, there are a number of functions that usually do not appear in other departments. For example, you may have a dedicated research group whose job it is to tackle the most difficult calls. On the other hand, I know support organizations that use the TH method, where the support analysts do their own research.

Calls that need to be researched are not necessarily the same calls that are escalated. More than likely, if you have a FL/BL model, you can consider all calls passed to the back line as having been escalated, and therefore all calls that need to be researched have at one time or another been escalated. The key difference is that calls are escalated because the person working on them is having difficulty solving them. Researched calls are those where no one can find an immediate solution.

The reason I am emphasizing the difference between the two is because in some organizations you may have separate functions that manage each of these. Often there is a great deal of interaction between the help desk and other organizations when a problem needs to be researched. This may also be the case when calls are escalated outside of the support organization. It is often necessary to have a single manager who is responsible for awarding all of this.

Even with a fairly small number of help desk personnel, you should group people into OUs. The number of units and the number of people in each unit depend on the number of different areas that you want to break up into. If you break them up by general area like networking or applications, there will be fewer units than if you break them up into network hardware, network software, word processing applications, graphic applications, and so on.

Too many units makes it hard to organize and you may miss some skills, so these problems fall through the cracks. If you have too few units, then there is less of a chance that someone is an expert, as he or she is expected to know everything about too many different things. This means that it takes longer to solve the problem.

Each unit can be broken down further into second level and third level (first level is everyone for *every* skill). The third level is *the* expert. Essentially, this is a title as well as a level of knowledge. This is the head of this unit. Depending on your organization, this could also be a team leader, but it doesn't have to be. Basically the OU expert is the one who makes the decisions about what kinds of problems get documented, how long problems should be worked on before they are escalated, and so on.

Separation between IS and the Help Desk

You also need to consider the possibility that there may be no clear distinction between the responsibilities of the help desk and those of IS. This needs to be taken into account by establishing guidelines for what to do in those cases when the clear line cannot be drawn. On the other hand, the clear separation of responsibilities is possible provided they are used for reference. For example, it is perfectly reasonable to give the help desk the responsibility for receiving and processing all problem reports. In addition, the help desk can also be responsible for solving application-related problems. For example, how to connect to a network printer may be the job of the help desk, whereas figuring out why you can't print to that same printer is a responsibility of IS.

Also, keep in mind that continuity in problem solving is a benefit for everyone concerned.

When problems are passed from help desk to IS, information can be lost. Therefore, you might want to consider having the help desk be the first line of support and have IS be the one to solve harder problems.

For me, the most efficient solution is to have a clearly defined separation of responsibilities while maintaining the attitude that no one should pass the buck. This means that both sides should try to solve problems to the best of their ability. In support of this, I feel it is important to identify the cases where problems *should* be passed to the other team, not so much passing the buck as ensuring the problem is not immediately passed back to the first group and wastes everybody's time.

The problem of defining responsibility and keeping people from passing the buck also shows itself if you have more than one support group working on the help desk. In many companies, one group would be responsible for network and system issues, for example, and another group is responsible for applications problems.

What do you do when a user cannot print from a specific application? If it is a network problem, it should be solved by the network group. If it is an application problem, it should be solved by the applications group. How do you know where the problem lies until you start working on it? Here is an example of clearly defining your goal as being to help the user. This means trying to solve a problem no matter what group you're in. If during the course of evaluating the problem, the applications group determines that it is a network problem, one alternative would be to have them query the network group themselves and not have the user do it. This provides continuity for the user and at the same time saves time by not passing the problem back and forth.

Organizing Skills

No matter what organization you choose, one of the first steps is to identify what skills you have and which are missing. This has two goals. First, you identify in what areas you need to train or hire more people. Second, it's the first step in any other kind of organization. I think you should include not only people on the help desk but also anyone you can draw on to help solve problems.

Make a table with the skills along the side and the person along the top. Fill in each cell of the table with some indication of the skill level. Regardless of how many people are in your organization, you should create the table. Even with 10 people in our system administration, we had such a table. The group was small enough that we all had a general idea of the areas in which each person was proficient. However, there was always the problem when someone was sick or on vacation. That brought up the question of who was in the best position to solve the problem.

Once you have your table, you will quickly notice that there are holes in this table. There are certain areas where there is either no one who is really good in a particular area or just one or two. This will tell you where you need to concentrate your training (maybe hire some new people). It also serves as a guide for assigning problems. Note that I said "guide." Don't assign calls strictly according to this table: How you do that, we'll get to in a moment.

There is one problem with this. You may end up with dozens of different skills. When I listed all the applications and aspects of our system, there were over 100 different entries! When trying to determine who had each of these skills, I noticed patterns. The MS Word expert was also the MS Excel expert and the DHCP expert was also the WINS expert. It was then easy (as well as logical) to combine different groups so that their labels were more generic, such as "office applications" or "Windows networking." However, be careful that you do not make them too general.

In addition, it may not always be possible to break the skills into general areas. When I was in support for a software manufacturer we had to break down skills into the more-specific units. This is necessary if you have a large number of calls. It is easy to get the call to the expert. How you do it will depend on the number of users you support, the people supporting the users, and the skills you need to have.

On the one hand, this seems like a contradiction of what I said earlier. However, I suggest that at the beginning you have as many categories as possible (at least during the planning). Once patterns develop you can begin to merge the categories. However, what happens when a new person comes into the group? They may only know MS Word, but not MS Excel. Do you create more groups or train the MS Word experts so they know MS Excel as well?

You might want to consider having a smaller number of categories that you still assign analysts to. You can then say that it is *expected* that when someone knows one area in that category, they should learn the others. With this in mind, you can immediately plan training.

Another aspect is the person's skill level: Maybe skill levels of 0-10 is too many, but you should at least have four levels: none, beginner, proficient, expert (or something similar). These levels are easier to categorize than 10, because most people would be hard pressed to find a difference between someone at level 7 and someone else at level 8.

Normally, the person who first takes the call will have enough experience to determine the complexity of the call (assuming there is no dedicated receptionist, secretary, or similar). He or she can then determine if the problem requires an expert or not and assign it appropriately.

The table with the skill levels needs to always be available to anyone assigning calls. It must be used to make the assignments. In one support organization that I worked for, we had one analyst who was an expert in a large number of areas. When he decided to learn about other areas and got himself listed in certain categories as knowing "a little," he was assigned calls in that area as if he were an expert! The people making the assignments simply assumed that he was an expert in every area.

Customer- or Product-Based Groups

Another organizational consideration is whether or not to separate the analysts by products or by customers. If you have separate queues like we discussed earlier, you have already begun to organize your help desk by products.

Even if you are dealing with internal users, you can still break down support by customers. For example, you might have separate groups who are responsible for the support of specific divisions or departments within your company. This develops a strong relationship between members of the department and their respective help desk team. You learn what their strengths and weaknesses are as well as how they do their job. This enables you to provide much better support than if you were expected to handle the entire company.

The drawback of customer-based support becomes pronounced when the products vary dramatically. If the department you support does not use a particular product, analysts probably do not get the exposure they need. For example, in one company where I worked, support was broken down by our major business application/database, technical applications, and everything else. I was in the "everything else" group, and we had to deal with the standard office applications, the servers, hardware, the network, and so forth. When people called me with issues dealing with technical applications, I could not even begin to work on the problem, because I had neither the experience nor the training to deal with the problem. In many cases, it was difficult to determine just exactly where the problem was because there was extremely little overlap of knowledge. The result was that problems often sat around waiting for the expert to get around to them.

On the other hand, product-based support gives analysts the ability to become masters in a particular area rather than a jack-of-all-trades. This can actually become a very important issue for long-term customer satisfaction. The experts are in a much better position to solve problems quickly, especially if they involve very-complex issues. On the other hand, just as customer-based support leads to a good relationship between specific customers and specific analysts, product-based support is not really conducive to building such relationships.

In general, the easier the call in general, the more you should consider customer-based support, especially for an internal help desk, if you decide to have separate groups. If the problems require any basic knowledge of the products or the solutions are easily accessible, most of your help desk staff should be able to handle the greatest range of problems. The result is that the average scale level is consistent across the different customer groups.

If the needs of the customer vary dramatically, this is another strong reason for choosing customer-based support. Just as you need to spend the time working with a particular application or other aspect of the system in order to become proficient, you need to make considerable effort to become proficient in understanding the needs of the different customer groups. Therefore, breaking the support team into groups based on the customers allows them to get a better understanding of the customer needs.

Depending on the size of your organization, its structure, and the needs of the individual departments or customers, you may want to consider dedicated support analysts in specific cases. Here, the customer has a single point of contact within the support organization; all calls from the customer are directed to that specific support analyst, who knows the details of the department.

On the other hand, if your organization does not lend itself to dedicate support analysts, it may still be necessary. Either the customer must be willing to pay for it (assuming that support is in some way fee based), or there is some pressing need to have the dedicated support analyst. In one company where I worked, I was the dedicated analyst for all technical applications in the production halls. We were a manufacturer of industrial machinery, and there were a number of special applications that were used nowhere else in the company. Since the production halls could only tolerate a much shorter downtime than the other departments, it was decided that a dedicated support analyst would be assigned to address all their problems. (Note that I did have someone who could take over for me when I was on vacation or out sick.)

Choosing the appropriate model is not always and "either-or" issue. Depending on your organization, it is conceivable that you have a combination of both, in that the groupings are just a logical separation. That is, you have elements of both a customer-based and a product-based support. This is useful if applications are concentrated by department. For example, teams can be created that support specific products and other groups created whose responsibility is to look after the needs of different departments. These groups do not need to be distinct, but rather all of the team members are drawn from the same pool of analysts.

Problems with a specific applications or other aspects of the system would be dealt with by the appropriate specialists. However, certain individuals would be responsible to ensure that the needs of the different departments are met. Keep in mind that having separate groups for products and customers can become a dangerous problem in cases where the types of applications vary dramatically between departments.

When trying to design an appropriate model, scheduling becomes a real problem with small groups. Therefore, you should only create the groups that are absolutely necessary. On the other hand, if scheduling is not an issue, "virtual groups" can be helpful. For example, in one company where I worked, different skill sets were broken into OUs. These units were the back line in the company's FL/BL model. When calls came in and could not be handled by the front line, they were assigned to the appropriate OU. Scheduling was done by including everyone and was only done for the hotline (front line). In addition, OUs were established to care for the needs of the different departments.

Specialist or Generalist?

Another consideration is the issue of generalist versus specialist. The generalist is simply a jack-of-all-trades who knows something about everything (more or less). The specialist is someone who knows everything about one specific topic (more or less). Unless you have a completely customer-based support organization, you're going to have people who are fairly well-versed in one area and not so in others. Having both is important, because the generalist can probably answer a much larger number of calls than the specialist can, especially if you have a large number of calls dealing with basic issues. Once again, the more specialized the application you use, the greater the need there is for experts.

When I was working in tech support, there was a set of topics for which everyone was expected to be a generalist. That is, at the very least they should be able to begin working on the problem in this area. Each analyst then became a specialist in one or more areas. Each analyst was then given a rating from 0 to 4 in each area. A 0 meant the analyst could not even begin working on problems in this area, and a 4 meant he was an expert. These ratings were used whenever a problem needed to be reassigned. Although we did employ a TH model, sometimes the analyst simply could not continue and needed to hand off the problem to someone else.

Generalists are good in cases where it is not immediately clear whether the problem belongs in one area or another. One group may insist that the problem belongs somewhere else because of a specific set of criteria, and the other group says it belongs to the first group based on another set of criteria. Even if the generalist does not have the authority to say once and for all to which group the problem belongs, he is still in a position to begin working on the problem in that he has experience in both areas.

However, keep in mind that these gray-area problems should be the exception and not the rule. If you find that the large number of calls are being passed to the generalist or the generalist has to make decisions, you might consider redefining the groups so that the division is much clearer.

Centralized or Decentralized?

Finally, there is the issue of centralized versus decentralized support. This can actually take two different forms. In some cases, you may have a central support organization and field representatives who solve customer problems on-site. This is different from an organization that has multiple support centers where the analysts do not go to the customer's site. Even with an internal help desk, either of these models is possible. In fact, depending on your organization and its support needs, you could have a mixture of these.

For example, I worked in one company with a few-dozen branch offices spread out across the country and throughout the world. The larger offices had their own support staff (maybe just one or two people). For the most part, they acted almost completely independent of the central support organization. The smaller offices got all of their support from either the headquarters or one of these larger branch offices, depending on the size and location of the branch office.

If the support required someone to be on-site, what was done also varied from office to office. Those offices that were within a couple of hours driving distance from either the company headquarters or one of larger branch offices got their support from that office. Those offices that were farther away got their support from a local computer supplier or some other local source.

In some cases, the users may demand it. In that same company that I just discussed, there were cases where the branch manager did not want someone from the outside to solve his problem, but rather someone from the headquarters. Obviously, if you're working in the fee-based support system and the customer is willing to pay, there is nothing wrong with sending an analyst to the remote location.

There are two important things to consider with field-based support. First, how does the field rep get access to the same tools that the others have? Recording information into your problem database may be as simple as writing down the specifics and in recording it on the rep's return. But what about your solutions database? How do field analysts get access to that? If your solutions database is stored as accessible from Web pages, it could be made available across the Internet (maybe requiring a password).

The next issue is the whole logistics of field-based support. You're going to have to deal with transportation, accommodations, and communication between the field analyst and headquarters. This is not simply a matter of giving the analyst a mobile phone so that he or she can contact headquarters whenever necessary. It includes such mundane things as whether or not someone is accessible by phone. If the time zone difference between the central support office and the branch office is large enough, the overlap of working hours can be extremely small or may be even nonexistent.

For example, if your headquarters is on the East Coast of the United States and your field analyst is in Malaysia, there is a 12-hour difference between the two. There is generally no overlap at all for normal workday. What does the field analyst do if he or she needs information from headquarters? Email is not necessarily good, because in the best case, you first get your answer the next morning. Often this is unacceptable.

Solutions to these kinds of problems are not easy. In this case, you either accept the time delay or expect that someone either start earlier or work longer in order that there be sufficient overlap between two locations.

If all the support is centralized, there is no fear of having incompatible procedures or software. However, I feel that the administrative burden is greater in this case. First, you need to ensure that communication works much more effectively, not only communication between the remote offices and the central office, but within the help desk itself. If changes are made in the remote office, everyone needs to be made aware of them. This can be a problem when you work for a multinational corporation where there is no common language.

The central office would also have the responsibility to establish and coordinate standards, not just for the help desk, but all computer system-related functions. This includes network protocols, database systems, email, and so on. The advantage is that there is one single place to call for *all* computer-related problems. It is therefore easier to coordinate the service that you provide. There will probably be fewer staff members, as you do not need experts at every site.

Defining Responsibilities

It is sometimes useful to compare the differences between an internal help desk and a customer hotline to the differences between the a full-service and a fast-food restaurant. Like the full-service restaurant, a customer hotline will provide you almost anything you ask for (within reason, of course). On the other hand, you are more limited in what you can get at the fast-food restaurant. Granted, it is likely that you can get your hamburger without ketchup or pickles, but that's about it.

The key here is that you're providing fair quality at a fair price. The success of fast-food restaurants such as Burger King and McDonald's are clear indicators that the customers are satisfied with the service. However, it is unlikely that either chain would survive very long if they decided to increase their prices to a level comparable to a full-service restaurant.

In essence, the same thing applies to your help desk. If your customers (that is, the users) are not paying as much as they would for external support, they are generally satisfied with the level of service. It is simply a matter of economics that you cannot provide the same level of support that you could for paying customers.

However, my experience has been that customers who don't pay for support are often more demanding than those who are paying for it. This is due primarily to their not understanding what the limitations are. This is because the limitations are rarely spelled out for them. When I worked in support, we provided 30 days of free "installation" support. However, the customer was never told what "installation" really meant. I often got calls where the user was having trouble installing a third-party application. Well, the word "install" was in there somewhere.

On the other hand, your users might actually be paying customers. There are organizations that have broken down each department into separate business units. In general, each business unit is a separate financial entity. Each time services are requested, the requesting department is "charged" for the service. In such cases, the customer (user) might be in a better position to make demands on the help desk.

Unofficial Support

In many books that I have read on the subject of help desks, customer service, and related topics, often there are comments about the loss of efficiency due to "informal" support systems. For example, there are usually people spread out in your company who have a higher level of computer expertise than the other employees. When this becomes common knowledge, these people end up performing help desk duties. While it is true that such informal systems may be less efficient, I think such systems can be extremely useful when they are formalized.

There are a couple of reasons for this. First, if the problem is simple enough for the department guru to solve, you have saved a call to the help desk. Even if the problem cannot be solved, having gone through the basic issues might be useful for the help desk to know. Second, someone in the department may understand the problem much better than the help desk can. At the very least, they can be helpful in making sure that the problem is understood correctly by the help desk analyst. However, you need to be careful that these people spend enough time doing their job and not just answering questions.

The Flow of the Help Desk

"Help desk" as a concept can have several meanings. This might be the team that answers the calls and at least starts to work on the problems. In many companies, that's all there is. There is no system. No multiple levels to escalate calls to. The design (if one can call it that) is simply to put out the burning fires.

It is important to understand that whatever help desk strategy is implemented, it must be a *system*. You have to be organized to be able to save yourself time and effort. For this reason, I feel it is necessary to understand the basic issues about the flow of the help desk before we talk about other things like the organization. Granted, flow and organization go hand in hand. Which flow model you choose will determine your organization or what organization you choose will determine which flow model to use.

At least this is true much of the time. There are many issues involved with the flow that are independent of what model you chose. If we simply say that a call comes to the help desk, is processed, and a response is returned to the originator, the flow can be seen as independent of any model. Here, I am going to refer to a call as any contact with the help desk, not just by phone. You could get calls by phone, fax, email, walk-ins, and so on. However, for simplicity's sake, I am going to call all of them a "call."

One key issue is to ensure that both the hotline and the users themselves can differentiate between the different types of calls. For example, if you have an automatic call direction mechanism, the number of different choices should be limited. If you've gone through an automated phone system yourself, you know how frustrating it can be if the menu choices are too complicated. It can also be a problem for the front-liners or whoever takes the call when they are trying to decide where it should go next. One of the goals of the help desk is to reduce the time to resolution of a problem. The time spent balancing around menus or handing off the problem back and forth between different groups is wasted.

The first step is identifying what the call is about. Is it a problem or just a simple question? If this is a new problem, then you might need to add it to your database. If it's an old problem, you will probably add new information or new transactions. Based on your company's policy, you prioritize the problem. System crashes may have top priority and need to be dealt with immediately, whereas problems with new fonts could be put off (even for several days). The response time for each type of problem is also something that differs from company to company or even between departments. We'll get into some suggestions about setting priorities shortly. Keep in mind that in many cases, you may not even need to have officially determined priorities.

To manage problems, you need to be able to tell them apart. Therefore, each problem needs a unique problem number if you are going to document it. Even if your management system is pen and paper, writing each problem as it comes in into a logbook will help you keep track of these problems. By the fact that each problem is recorded as it comes in, you have a chronological record to look back at, plus each problem has its own number. This number is probably more important for your users than it is for you. First, there is the psychological value of having the number. Your users know that the problem has been identified and is in the system somewhere. Even that is reassuring. For the user there is the added benefit when the problem is still not solved two weeks later, they can call back to the help desk and give them this number. The number can be looked up in the log to find out who took the call, who's working on it, its status, and so forth.

Who actually assigns the number will depend on your policy and your software. With some products, it is a matter of seconds to get the number. However, this might actually wait until the first analyst begins working on the problem. This is because on an internal help desk, you often do not record the call at all, so what's the sense in generating a number?

Once the call has been taken and given a number, it needs to be assigned. If you have a small help desk, then maybe assigning the call means that the person who took the call tries to solve it. That's OK. The important aspect is that there is someone responsible for the call. In larger systems, the person taking the call may not be the one who will eventually solve it. Maybe they are just call takers, or maybe they are not experts in that particular area, and it would be more efficient for someone else to solve the call. On the other hand, if the person taking the call can solve the problem, there is no need to specifically assign it.

In one support organization I worked for, the call takers were originally just that. They took the calls and tried to assign them as best they could. Because they did not know the system well enough, there were a number of mistakes. One suggestion was to send them to a quick training to help them better classify calls. Instead, they were sent to similar training that the new analysts got. The goal was not only to help classify the calls but potentially solve them. This worked out quite well, as many of the "quickies" never reached the analysts.

Setting Priorities

Keep in mind that for internal help desks, setting priorities, maximum TTR, and so on, is not always necessary or even desirable. You are normally not contractually obligated to provide service within a specific amount of time. A key part of this is that you are trying to provide the user with reasonable expectations, even if you are not contractually obligated. If these times are too long, the users will perceive you as being unreasonable and therefore will (probably) not yield to their expectations. Setting them to a time where both of you feel comfortable, you have a much better chance of gaining acceptance.

Setting priorities on calls is another important aspect of the help desk. The first reason for this is the same as for anything else: Without priorities, you can't figure out what work should be done first. The second reason has to do with the users' perception of the service they are getting. When priorities are defined, the user knows approximately how long it will be before the problem will get worked on. Everyone wants to have their problem worked on first, but when priorities are set (and kept), the user is more likely to understand the need to work on something more important.

The priorities you set are based on the *urgency* and *scope* of the situation. An example of a high-urgency issue with limited scope might be a report that needs to get done tomorrow. Suddenly the machine of the person who is working on the report goes down. Only one person is affected, but the urgency is great. The reverse might be the loss of the Internet connection from within the company. If no one has to get something from the Internet, then the problem is widespread, but there is no urgency. Maybe the company president, who has trouble getting the right font for the letter to his friend in Malaysia, has the highest priority of all. This depends on your company and the company president.

Setting priorities for the help desk is basically the same as for any other aspect of your business. That is, those issues that are the most critical to your business should have the highest priority of all. However, it should either be the help desk or company management and not the user who decides how important an issue is. I know from experience that every user thinks that he or she has an emergency, and their problem should be addressed first of all. The only way around it is to have clearly specified conditions that define each of the different priorities.

How upset or how desperate a user may sound should normally not be used as the criterion for determining the priority of a problem. I say "normally," because the user who is in tears and is disrupting the entire department may need immediate attention (both the problem and the user personally).

In order to set priorities, it is often useful to classify problems into one of three types: problems, requests, and questions. *Problems* are those issues that prevent a user from efficiently doing his or her work. *Requests* are those issues that do not have an immediate effect on the user's productivity, but addressing them may increase productivity in the future. Requests are also those issues that cannot be addressed immediately, such as training, new hardware, or implementation of new software. *Questions* are just as their name implies. In general, answering questions should take very little time. Even if the question needs more than just a simple yes or no answer, the response should just take a few minutes. If it takes longer, it turns into a request.

Putting a call into any one of these three categories does not necessarily imply the specific priority. Instead, I find it useful to classify a call in this way in the event it cannot be addressed immediately and therefore must be given a priority. For example, if your help desk has a constant flow of calls, you may consider only allowing questions through email or your company's intranet. These have a lower priority and therefore can be dealt with as time permits. If suddenly you have a massive influx of calls (as is common with new product releases or new hardware), requests could also be diverted to those other media.

An influx of calls after a new product release is to be expected and can be planned for. However, there are a number of cases where an increase in calls cannot be planned for. For example, a server crash will most likely generate a large number of calls. By grouping calls in this way, deciding which calls can be dealt with later is fairly straightforward.

However, one danger of all this is that problems can pile up, and those with a lower priority are pushed to the back burner. The solution to this problem is to set up maximum response times for the different kinds of problems. Table 15–1 shows suggested response times for different priorities. Obviously, these are just possibilities and should not be considered hard-and-fast rules. If the company owner wants new software installed, maybe the response time is immediate (I've worked for companies like that). Although certain occurrences (such as a computer crash) should have a "rule of thumb" as to how long the response time is, if your help desk staff has other obligations, answers may take longer than "promised."

TABLE 15–1 Example Response Times

Priority	Description	Example	Response Time
1: Emergency	Business severely affected	Server or main down database app. down	Immediate
2: Urgent	Business moderately affected	User cannot work on PC/terminal	10-20 minutes
3: Important	Business slightly affected	User needs help with usage (i.e., MS Word-processing program)	Less than one hour
4: Request	Little immediate affect on or benefit to business	Help writing shell script	One working day
5: Nice to have	Benefit to or affect on business not immediately identifiable	User wants access to specific software, has questions, etc.	Three days

• • • • • • • • • • • • • • •

To some extent, priorities *should* be hard-and-fast rules and not be delayed. However, an emergency that requires the full concentration of your entire help desk staff would prevent dealing with issues of a priority of 2. In cases where you are not working on an emergency situation but rather the workload is too high to deal with lower priority issues, you should consider some mechanism to inform users that there has been a delay in responding to calls. Most commercial help desk products have some mechanism to sort of the calls wide priority. You could then notify users whose calls have been opened for the longest time (for example, more than twice the normal response time).

I have read some help desk texts where the author set up different priority schemes for each of the call types (problems, requests, and questions). For me this causes too great a bureaucracy. That is, you end up spending more time classifying the calls and deciding on the priority of a call than you do solving it.

Instead, I find the five levels to be completely adequate, the key being how much that issue affects your business. Or in the case of paying customers, how much that issue affects the customers' business. The greater the effect on business, the higher the priority. For example, theoretically, a question could have an emergency priority if the answer to it affects a major business decision.

Keep in mind that the most important factor in determining priority is the effect that it has on *your* business. Although a single user having a problem with a single application could have the most dramatic effect on your business, this is not the most common case. Instead, you'll need to look at each call and determine how many users are affected, the work these users do, and how widespread the problem is.

Assigning Calls

If you have a dispatch model, where the person taking the call does not try to solve it, the next step is to get the call to the right person. Who that person is might depend on the priority of the call. For example, your policy says that high-priority calls are automatically passed to the expert.

The actual mechanism for assigning the call depends on two things: the way your help desk is organized and what tool you are using to keep track of the calls. The details of these we'll get to as we go along. When calls are received at the first step, a *trouble ticket* (with problem number) is generated according to the policies you establish. As mentioned, some problems may not warrant their own problem number. It all depends on what you establish. However, I recommend, for customer satisfaction, that you always give out a problem number if the user requests one. It is unlikely, however, that the user will request a problem number when they have a password reset.

Every effort needs to be made at the first step to solve the problem. However, you need to establish guidelines to determine when a call will be escalated or handed off. When problems do get escalated, they *must* have a problem number assigned to them. That should be a matter of policy.

Normally, based on how most help desk systems are organized, there is no mechanism that allows calls to be escalated without having been assigned a number. One exception might be if you could immediately hand the call off, then you could decide if a problem number is necessary. However, in most cases where the second level immediately takes the call, it is significant enough to warrant a number anyway.

One goal of your help desk is to distribute the load of calls efficiently throughout the team. "Efficiently" does not necessarily mean "equally." If 90% of the calls are network problems and you only have one network guru, spreading the calls might mean that they will take substantially longer to solve. Giving them to the guru has them solved in two minutes.

However, giving all the networking problems to the guru may not be efficient either. If the calls take a long time to solve, he or she may be bogged down and take days to get to a problem. Giving a problem to someone else may mean that it takes longer to solve the problem once he starts working in it. However, he starts working on it sooner, so it gets done sooner and the user gets his answer sooner. This is just natural. If you have less experience with an issue, it will take longer to solve. However, as you continue to work in this environment, your knowledge and experience grow. Even while you are learning, it is the *average* completion time that is important and that remains low.

When calls are assigned, the person they are assigned to becomes the "owner." Even when you decide to implement the FL/BL model, the front-liner is still the owner until the call is handed off. This makes it impossible for problems to be forgotten or swept under the rug. Since each problem has a number, the person reporting the call can refer to it.

This number then points to the owner, who needs to be able to provide a status on the call. If the user has any additional information or the problem reoccurs, there is no need to open a new call, as there is a quick reference to the first one. This mechanism also allows you to see how many calls are assigned to each person to determine if anyone is overburdened and needs help.

Multiple Support Tiers

Another way is to have several different levels or tiers of support, with expertise increasing as you go up. The person taking the call tries to solve it. This is the first level. If he or she cannot solve the problem, the call is passed to the second level. The people at the second level are not necessarily the experts but rather are those with more experience in that area. (Remember that chart I told you to make?) When these people cannot solve the problem within a predetermined time or discover it is really beyond their expertise, they escalate the call to the third level. These are the experts.

The people taking the call initially may be acting as receptionists. Your policy may be simply for them to take the call and assign it to the appropriate team or person. If they are expected to at least try to solve the problem, then their emphasis should be on *breadth* of knowledge. These are the generalists, who know a little about every product and can answer a wide range of questions.

At the second level are the specialists. Their emphasis is *depth* of knowledge. They know the details of just a few products or maybe just certain aspects of one product. Their range is limited, but they can solve problems that are much more detailed than the generalist can solve. If you do have a third level, then here are the experts. They know everything about a limited subset of issues.

This has an advantage in that the average TTR is low. More difficult calls take longer, but the average time remains low. Also, since people are exposed to more different types of calls, their knowledge naturally gets better. Therefore, in the long run, they become experts themselves and decrease the overall TTR even further. The disadvantage is that there is a certain amount of planning to come up with a scheme and mechanism to escalate the calls. You also need to define who will be placed at the second and third levels for each area. There is also a certain administration effort required to keep track of when things get escalated and who becomes the owner.

The third alternative is for the people taking the calls to escalate directly to the expert those problems that they cannot solve. Only when he or she cannot take the call (out of the office, too many calls already) will the call be assigned to someone with less experience. The advantage of this is that the calls get solved much faster when the expert works on them. That is, specific calls are solved faster. However, the average might not be better, since the expert is dealing with the easy calls first and may only get to the hard ones after a few days. Therefore, these calls have a much longer TTR. Keep in mind that some of the easy calls could be solved by someone with less experience. Added to this, overall knowledge on the help desk increases more slowly, since people are not exposed to the same level of problems.

After 15 years of working in a help desk environment, I have found that in only the smallest organization does the first alternative work (first come, first served). Here there are not enough people to make any sense in a tiered structure, plus there are so few calls. It is fairly easy to put aside a less-important call and work on something more pressing.

The second alternative (top-down) would work if there were very few calls and few people on the help desk. Calls would be assigned to the expert, since the expert is the only one who has any chance of solving the problem. This leaves us with the third alternative, bottom-up. I have found that this model has the best chance of working in most environments and the best potential for long-term improvement of the team members. Also, looking at all the help desk software that's on the market, all of them are designed with the bottom-up model. (Note that many give you the ability to design your own workflow so you can develop any model you choose.)

Any organization that is tiered in this manner has the advantage that help desk personnel can concentrate their efforts. First, when not taking calls, their energies are on other work. Also, they don't need to be knowledgeable in every area, just those in which they specialize. The more products you support, the greater the need for specialization.

Closing the Call

For the most part, closing a call should be at the discretion of the user, not the person working on it. I have seen it happen too many times where the support person arbitrarily decides the call is complete. Often the user waits a long time (weeks, even months) for a reply that will never come. He then needs to call the help desk to find out the status.

If the end user is not satisfied with the answer, it is your responsibility to find a satisfactory response. Here I want to emphasize the word *satisfactory*. By this I do not mean that the user is happy with the answer. There will be cases where the user won't be, like when the solution is too expensive or is against company policy. However, if the user is made to understand that there is nothing more that can be done, then they are satisfied, but not necessarily happy. They then agree that the problem should be closed. However, it must be their decision.

On an internal help desk, this is a two-edged sword. Company policy may dictate just how much support is provided, which sometimes is not sufficient for the user. The user may not want to close the call, because he wants more support. At times like these, it becomes an escalation issue.

Call Management

Under the heading of call tracking, you find all of the work that goes on around the call. What this work will depend on are the model and organization you choose and whether or not you decide that a certain activity should be done in the first place. Regardless of how other aspects of your help desk work, call management can be an important aspect of your help desk.

Call Tracking

The more calls you have, the greater the need to keep track of them. Call tracking is one the most tedious aspects of the help desk and one that is most likely to be ignored or not done properly. This is unavoidable, since call tracking often provides some of the greatest benefits to the user. One thing I would like to point out here is that call tracking is the primary function of all help desk software. Many are so efficient at recording the necessary information that there is essentially no time loss.

In an environment where support is being paid for by the customer, call tracking is a requirement to ensure the customer or user is getting the support that they paid for. However, in both paid and unpaid environments, one of the key benefits that call tracking provides is the ability to identify trends.

Trends can be identified at several levels. From a management perspective, keeping track of calls can be used to identify specific periods in which increased number of calls are reported to help desk. Knowing which periods result in increasing calls can enable the help desk manager to provide extra staff during the busy periods to reduce call times.

Call tracking can also be used to identify trends in the type of calls that are generated. For example, repeated calls on what the help desk may perceive as very basic issues may be the result of insufficient training on that product. Taking this one step further, repeated calls in one area may indicate an underlying problem that is not directly related to the call.

In one company where I worked, we had repeated calls from some of our branch offices indicating that the network performance to the headquarters was painfully slow. The response time in our primary business application (which ran across the network) was also significantly degraded. In most cases, by the time the office called and we began our investigations, the problem had disappeared. Tracking when the problems occurred led us to the times when our monthly newsletter was transferred to the branch office for translation. This was a huge file generated by our desktop publishing application, and transferring it basically meant nothing else could cross the line.

The cause of this problem was not insufficient bandwidth on our network but rather the press office generating the report, which was unaware of the impact transferring would have on the network as a whole. This indicated the need for training on some of the basic issues involving the network.

Among the trends that call tracking can help you identify is problems with hardware and software. For example, one company noticed recurring problems with a specific video card at higher resolutions. Calling the vendor, we discovered that this was a known problem and that an updated version of the driver was available. We were then able to distribute this driver throughout the company to prevent calls before they happened.

Other examples include repeated crashes of the specific machine (more so than is normal for Windows). Since the machine was under warranty, we could get it repaired and prevent any future crashes due to hardware problems.

Another thing that call tracking is useful for is in identifying problems you may have with specific vendors. This could indicate specific products from that vendor that are less than adequate for your needs as well as indicating products that are defective. In addition, tracking calls to vendors can also indicate problems with the vendors' support structure. For example, in one company, tracking such calls helped us to demonstrate that support from this vendor was completely inadequate.

Finally, call tracking is extremely useful when it comes time to ask for more funds to improve your help desk. Tracking calls can help demonstrate the benefits of the help desk in general as well as help you demonstrate which areas need improvement.

Commercial help desk products help you track in a number of different aspects of your help desk. These range from simply keeping track of both calls and their solutions to very complex products that can keep track of everything including hardware maintenance, software licenses, training, and even the vacation of your help desk staff. What is possible with help desk products and is necessary is something we will cover in the section on help desk software.

Escalation

There will probably be some calls that you just cannot solve, and they must be handed off to someone else. This is called *escalation*. Escalation is nothing to be ashamed about; it's a fact of life. Don't let help desk personnel (or yourself) hang on to a problem because they are embarrassed to admit they are stumped. This goes for all levels. Even if the expert cannot solve the problem and it must be passed on to the software or hardware vendor, that *will* happen.

Although the help desk cannot guarantee that the problem will be solved within a certain time, you can institute policies to ensure that it doesn't just sit on someone's desk. By forcing escalation within a certain time, you make sure that calls are being worked on efficiently. Granted, there may be calls where the help desk member can "taste" the answer and wants to continue working on it. That's okay and I encourage you to let the help desk staff hang on "just a little while longer." You just don't want them hanging on too long.

The key is that the escalation procedures are designed to move the call efficiently. Not necessarily quickly, because you want a resolution, not just numbers showing how fast you are. When the call is escalated, the user needs to be informed. This helps to assure the user that the problem is being worked on and that the help desk is not just passing the problem around. The escalation times as well as the procedures need to be part of your help desk guidelines. Everyone needs to stick to them. If possible, the help desk software should be made to do some of this automatically. Among other things you need to include are:

- Who can decide to escalate a call? If one person has it too long, can the expert simply "take" it from the other person? Can a manager *force* an escalation?

- When do you escalate? After how long and under what circumstances? Certain types of problems may automatically get escalated to the expert or even the vendor.

- How are the problems escalated and to whom? What are the procedures?

- Who has the ultimate "ownership" of the call? The first person? The last?

- Who resolves problems with the escalation process? What if you forget to address one aspect and you run into problems? Who decides how to handle it?

There are actually two different kinds of escalation. The most commonly recognized kind is a technical escalation that is passed to someone who is in a better position (technically) to solve the problem. The other kind is an administrative escalation where there is something other than a technical issue that needs to be resolved. For example, if there is some disagreement in terms of whether something is supported or not, the help desk analyst may not be in a position to make the necessary determination. A nontechnical issue is normally escalated through management channels.

If you're working in an environment where support is paid for, you often break down the nontechnical escalation issues into service-related and sales-related issues. Service-related issues are those where the customer did not get the level of support that was either promised or expected. The sales-related issue is where the customer either wishes to upgrade the product or wishes to return the existing product.

In some companies, the support representative is responsible for both technical and sales-related issues. Therefore, sales issues are not "escalated." In other companies, where these functions are separate, the call is handed off from one organization to another and can be considered to have been escalated. Obviously, if support is not paid for, there are no sales-related calls.

Being able to identify what kind of escalation is necessary is an important aspect of dealing with the call in general. As with classifying the type of problem, if you cannot properly classify the type of escalation, the call gets sent to the wrong person, which wastes everybody's time.

Keeping track of the escalations is just as important as keeping track of the problems themselves. Experience has shown me that there are a few basic causes for administrative escalations. You should therefore address these causes to ensure they do not reoccur. For example, one of the most common administrative escalations is caused by improper expectations on the part of users. That is, users expect the help desk to provide more support than what has been promised. It is quite common to have users expect you to "hold their hands." Telling the user just what the solution is is not sufficient. Instead, the help desk is expected to walk them through each step of the solution until it has been fully implemented.

If a large number of users complain that the help desk is not providing them this level of support, and it was not promised in the SLA, there are two solutions. First, it may be necessary to modify the SLA so that "hand-holding" is part of the service that is provided. However, management must be made aware of the extra burden that this will cause. The second solution is to provide additional training for the users so that hand-holding is not necessary.

If you're using a FL/BL model for your basic work flow, it may still be important to monitor at least the number of calls that are passed from the front line to the back line. If you are using the TH model, you need to decide what happens when the call is escalated. For technical issues, escalations should be less frequent with a TH model. You are expected to hold on to the call until it is resolved.

However, there will be cases where you cannot solve the problem, and it needs to be handed to someone else. The question is whether the original analyst maintains ownership of the problem. Personally, I feel that ownership should follow the call, even after escalation. If an analyst cannot solve the problem, and it needs to be escalated to someone else, the new analyst should then take over the ownership of the call. However, if the call is escalated outside of the help desk, such as to different department, ownership should be maintained by the person who has direct access to the user. (This, of course, depends on your organization.) Keep in mind that one of the major benefits of the TH model is that the analyst learns more by working on the complicated issues. If the analyst never learns what the solution is, he or she will probably need to escalate a similar call the next time. Therefore, it is extremely important that the resolution be reported back to the original analyst.

Due to their very nature, escalations often require more communication skills than are needed for normal calls, especially if analysts are dealing with nontechnical issues. With technical issues, you are likely to be spending more time with the customer and more time asking about the user's system and getting them to provide information.

With this in mind, you might find it useful to create a specific function that is responsible for *managing* the escalations. This should be someone at the management level, as they have the authority to make decisions. Granted, your help desk staff could be given that authority, but they should spend their time dealing with the technical issues and following your established procedures.

Here you need to think of economies of scale. That is, the more escalations you have, the more you need a dedicated function. If you find that escalation issues are taking time away from other duties, it is time to seriously begin thinking about a dedicated escalation manager. If you don't, analysts will either neglect their other jobs or the escalation will be handled improperly. Obviously, if you discover that there are more escalations than one person can handle, you might even consider an escalation team.

Regardless of whether or not you have a dedicated manager, you need to consider that one of the major causes of nontechnical escalations that are the results of complaints is personality differences between the user and the analyst. The escalations manager will therefore need to be part psychologist in order to resolve these personality conflicts. Therefore, communication skills are even more the requirement with the escalations manager as they are with the regular analyst.

Although the dedicated escalation function is a better position to look at the root causes objectively, an analysis can still be done by members of the help desk staff. I think it is an important part of the analysis to begin working on it as soon as possible, even before the problem has been resolved. In doing so, you cannot only help prevent repeat occurrences, but you can also help bring this call to a speedy conclusion.

For example, let's take a call that results in escalations because the user is not satisfied with the local service. If you determine early that the user is demanding more support than is provided for by the SLA, the answer to the user may be fairly straightforward. On the other hand, I know some managers who immediately declare at the beginning that the help desk analyst is not doing their job. There is no investigation, just blame. This wastes time, especially considering that next time, the analysts will probably give that user more support than they should, just to avoid getting "yelled at." Added to this is the other users who get less service than they should, because analysts are working with the "screamers."

The analysis of the escalation should include everyone involved within the help desk organization. In some cases, it may also be useful to include the user in determining the root cause. However, you must keep in mind that it is highly likely that the user will not be as objective as the people on the help desk, particularly if the escalation was caused by the user's misunderstanding of what support will be provided. On the other hand, this misunderstanding may be the catalyst for a reevaluation of the SLA.

During this analysis, there are several things that are vital to keep track of:

- the cause of the escalation
- the steps taken to resolve the problem
- problems you encounter during the resolution
- what things helped in reaching the resolution
- what might be done in the future to prevent a similar escalation

If the solution can be implemented within the help desk, it should be implemented as soon as possible. If it requires the participation or approval of someone outside the help desk (such as changes to the SLA), the escalation manager (or help desk manager) should begin working on the changes as soon as possible.

One problem that I repeatedly see during this analysis is finger pointing. Consider the escalation due to a misunderstanding of the SLA. You may think it reasonable to put the "blame" on the user for expecting more support then they are entitled to. However, is it not the "fault" of the help desk for providing an SLA that was open to such misunderstandings? On the other hand, is it then not the "fault" of the users for not specifying more clearly what kind of support they expect? This does nothing other than pass the blame back and forth across the table. The cause of the problem was a misunderstanding of the SLA, which needs to be addressed without putting the blame on anyone.

Regardless of what type of escalation it is (sales, service, technical), the call needs to be owned by the help desk, as they are the ones with the direct contact to the user. Especially in cases where the call is addressed by someone in another department, it is important that the single point of contact be maintained. For example, if the user needs a new computer and makes a request of the help desk, who in turn puts in a request to the company's purchasing department, the user should not be expected to contact purchasing to determine the status of the order. Instead, the help desk should monitor the request and keep the user informed of the status. (Obviously, this may not be feasible within your organization.)

When I was in support, I knew several engineers who would quickly rattle off the steps to solve the problem. "Do this. Do that. Do this other thing. If you have more problems feel free to call back." At first, they seemed to have a great record. In some cases, they had more than twice the calls per hour as other people. Then the department started monitoring the number of calls that were reopened, that is, the calls where the support analyst didn't solve the problem the first time. Considering those calls, these people had a much worse average. This is because the customer did not understand the answer and often was not given the chance to ask questions. As a result, when the customer started to work on the problem and discovered that the information they received from support was insufficient, they were on the phone again. This wasted time and cost money for everyone involved.

Documenting the Call

If the problem can be resolved by the first level and is not a standard problem, then the problem and resolution need to be documented. This does not need to be done immediately, but the sooner the better, as you are liable to forget details. If you are using a commercial help desk software, many have the ability to mark the record to say "this solution needs to be documented." If you develop your own system (i.e., software), then you need to include a field in the solutions table to indicate that the solution has not yet been documented. Some commercial software makes adding new solutions so easy that there is nothing gained by putting it off.

It's up to you whether calls with undocumented solutions should remain open or not. I feel that the call is not really finished until the solution is documented. However, it's your decision. As you know, the person taking the call is often not the one to solve it, even at the second level. If they go to the expert who tells them to change the settings on the LaserJet printer, then the original analyst did not solve the problem. They may also not be in a position to write an effective solution into the knowledge base. That might be the job for the expert. By marking the database to indicate the solution has not been documented, you can easily look for these solutions.

Therefore, you need a mechanism in your system to search for these undocumented solutions.The manner in which you document the solutions will depend on what means you have chosen to store them. If you choose HTML, then an editor is the tool to use. If you decide to integrate the solutions into the database, then you need to look for a mechanism within the database to add this information. Many will allow you to import text, so you can still use an editor.

When the call is escalated to the second level and the analyst decides that a problem number is warranted, I suggest that the user be notified that the call has been escalated. Tell them that the call has been escalated, who the person is that is working on it, and what the problem number is. This helps to assure the user that the problem is actually being worked on.

Communicating with Users

Communication with your users is vital to ensuring that the help desk works. The more they know about what is happening, the less likely they are to complain. When I was working in support for a major software company, I would call the customer whenever I had any new information and at a very minimum once a week.

Whenever the call needs to be escalated or handed off, the user must be informed. No matter what level it gets escalated to, you have to keep the user informed. In general, the flow to the third level is the same as for the second level. Here, too, you need to make sure that the user is informed.

Escalation to the fourth level (that is, external companies) must always have a trouble ticket. One thing that needs to get added to the problem description is the call number from the *other company* (i.e., the vendor). Without it, it's difficult to associate their call with yours. You should also ask them to include your call number in their problem description. If they call back and the person who made the call is unavailable, both sides can find the right call.

Staffing

Customer service is both a skill and a talent, whether for internal or external customers. There are certain aspects that can be trained into someone, but the personality of the person plays a key role in their success. I have worked with some very talented people that I would *never* even think about putting on the phones. They just don't have the temperament for it. They had trouble explaining things to user, as they expected them to have a comparable understanding of computers and got frustrated easily when the users could not follow the explanation.

In most cases, they would blame the user for not being able to understand. At this company we had one tenth the calls with one half the users, because the users were well trained—which is good. The other important reason was that a lot of the users were intimidated by the help desk staff.—which is not good. I personally heard comments to end users like, "Well, everyone knows that," or when asked a question they would respond, "Of course it's that way" or something similar.

Of course, it was "obvious" to someone with a computer science degree but not obvious to other people. The tone was often insulting, condescending, or both, and many people decided to either ignore the problem or find their own answers. This helps no one and costs the company money. Besides, if they really knew computers as well as the people on the help desk, they probably wouldn't need to call as often.

Among the characteristics that you need to look for in your help desk team are:

- *Forthrightness*. You have to be honest with the users and tell them both the good news and the bad news. Keep them informed of what is happening. Admit your mistakes.

- *Communications Skills*. You have to be able to express yourself clearly, even when dealing with complicated issues. If the end user cannot understand the answer, it has no value.

- *Composure*. You have to remain calm, even if you are telling the same user the same thing for the fifth time.

- *Desire to help*. This can't be just another job. You have to want to be able to help the user. Plus, you must be able to feel a certain amount of empathy. You have to be approachable and easy to talk to. Above all, you have to treat the user with courtesy and respect. They may not know as much about computers as you do, but how well do you know their area?

- *Patience*. Remember that your users generally do not know computers as well as the people on the help desk. You have to be patient with them when they do not understand the first time you explain something.

- *Aptitude and willingness to learn*. Support is not stagnant. The computer industry is constantly changing and your team members have to be able to learn new technologies.

- *Loyalty*. Don't talk badly about the company, your manager, or other team members.

and lastly:

- Technical skills.

This last point needs a bit of explaining. Saying that technical skills is the last characteristic to look for is not something I came up with, but I support it 100%. Technical skills can be trained, provided the person has an aptitude. However, the other skills can be thought of as a talent. A person can take classes and seminars and workshops, but unless that person has the personality, he or she won't work well on the help desk.

Depending on your organization, you are going to run into problems with an internal help desk. You may have hired someone who is a great technician and knows everything about the system but has the personally of a rock. If users would much rather forget the problem than talk to this person, then it may be a good idea not to have this person on the help desk. However, in one company with only 10 people, who rotated taking the calls, it was unfair to the others that this person was exempt.

It is definitely a dilemma for the help desk manager that the most important skill is also the hardest one to train. Because of this, once you have a good analyst, you had better do your best to keep him or her! It is regrettable that many help desk managers believe burnout is an undeniable consequence of work on the help desk. This is flat-out wrong!

I can speak from personal experience when I say the most significant factor of success is the company's attitude. If the company, or even the help desk manager, believes burnout is inevitable, they feel it is a wasted effort to try and prevent the burnout. I have worked on hotlines for well over a decade, and I can saying whole heartedly that this attitude cannot be further from the truth. The simplest way to prevent, or at least reduce, burnout is to limit how long each analyst spends on the phone each day. I know from experience that after about 5 hours you become fatigued and your ability to solve problems is diminished.

If you're working on the front line, where you have less of a need to solve complex problems, you still need to think. Therefore, I feel that if you want to keep your help desk staff, you must limit their phone time to 5 hours per day. Obviously, this can be extended in unusual circumstances, such as unexpected peaks. However, it should be generally kept to, at most, five.

Since any given analyst will not be on the phone for the entire day, you need to increase the help desk staffing accordingly. This extra staffing will cost money. However, the amount you save in resolving problems more than compensates for this. If, on the other hand, you decide to increase the phone hours, your analysts will burn out and you will have to hire someone new anyway. However, you won't have the advantage of having the expert to take up the slack as he just quit.

Unfortunately, there is more to it then just preventing burnout. Support can be a career, but your staff should not be forced to stay there. It is understandable that you want to keep your best people on the help desk, but you need to make sure that they do not burn out and leave the company altogether. You must *actively* work at making your help desk staff *want* to stay. For many people, money is a strong motivator. That is, you keep people on the help desk by giving a pay raise. In many cases, you'll have analysts, like myself, who can be motivated by things other than just money. Provided I make enough to feed my family and put a little something in the bank, I am usually more motivated by less-tangible things.

One thing that motivates me is training. Sending me to some specialized training, workshops, seminars, exhibitions, and so forth has important effects for me. First, there is the "warm fuzzy" that I was the one who was chosen by the department to go to these events. Second, I get several days off the phone without the stress.

Some people place a great deal of value on their position or title. Therefore, a good way to keep them is to promote them into a more-"prestigious" position. It may be that you promote them into a position that takes them off the phones. This is okay, because the knowledge and experience they have stays in the department. What would be worse is to have them quit and to take their knowledge and experience with them, maybe to a competitor.

I have found that an often-overlooked motivation tool is an employee evaluation. People obviously want praise when they are doing a good job, but many people like me want to know when we have messed things up so that we can improve our performance. One easily accomplished way is to provide career paths within support. For example, you might create special positions such as "help desk master," who may or may not handle phone calls but whose primary responsibility is to deal with more-difficult issues. You should also consider these people for management positions within the help desk organization. It is true that these people are no longer taking calls (normally), but they're still within the support organization, and their expertise can be drawn upon if necessary.

Staffing Needs

Determining your actual staffing need is not as simple as taking the number of analysts you need on the phones at any given time, multiplying by the number of hours you staff the help desk per day, and then multiplying that by the number of days per year that you are open. What this gives you is the number of "analyst hours" that you need to staff. Remember that an analyst should only be on the phone five hours a day. You need to figure in how much vacation each analyst gets, plus an estimation of how much time they will be off due to training, illness, or any other unforeseen absence. Some companies go so far as to limit the amount of sick time an employee may take. However, making them take unpaid leave when they go beyond this does little to staff your help desk.

One often-forgotten aspect is "administration time." This is the term I use to describe those functions that are necessary for the help desk but are not directly related to solving problems. For example, attending meetings, discussing problems with other analysts, responding to email, and so forth all fall into the category of administration time. You need to get an estimate of how much time is spent on such tasks in order to include this in the total time your analysts cannot be on the phone.

The key factor in deciding how many people need to be on the phones is the number of calls you get. It is therefore a logical conclusion that the more calls you have, the larger your help desk staff should be. In general, this is true. However, one simple alternative to a larger staff is to reduce the number of calls. As we discussed in the other sections, this is accomplished through better user training, more-accessible documentation, and all of the other things that provide the users the chance to help themselves.

You also need to keep in mind that all of the other factors that were used to decide whether a help desk was needed at all, also play a role in determining how large this staff should be. For example, the complexity of the applications, the extent to which the systems are standardized, the skill level of your users, and so forth all play a role in determining how large a staff is.

Another key aspect is your SLA. The more services you provide, or the more detailed these services are, the larger your staff needs to be. For example, if you provide around-the-clock service, you'll need three times as many analysts as when you provide support during a normal eight-hour business day. If you provide service on weekends and holidays, this needs to be reflected as well. If you provide support to users in other countries, one issue that is often missed is the fact that there is often very little overlap between American holidays and those in other countries. When America has a holiday, people are working in your other countries. Therefore, your staffing requirements need to reflect this.

In order to provide the necessary level of support, you will probably need to make some educated guesses about how many analysts you need at any given time. Here, the starting point is an estimate of how many calls you get per hour. However, you need to estimate the average call lengths (including administration time, like filling in your problem-tracking database) and multiply this by the average number of calls per hour. For example, ten calls that each require an hour to solve means you need ten analysts on the phone during each hour. However, ten calls per hour that each last 5 minutes means you only need a single analyst.

In determining the average call time, there is no substitute for experience. It is not something that managers can guess, but is something the analysts need to relate from their experiences. It may turn out that the analysts are spending too much time with the users, but the only way of finding that out for sure is by asking how much time they actually spend on calls. I have personally worked with managers who have felt justified in determining what the average call length was, because they knew how much time they spent themselves on the phone with analysts. Since they used a spreadsheet to do quick calculations, which were then just deleted away, it must mean everyone else did the same thing. When they call into support, it was usually about mundane issues, which were solved in a couple of minutes. Therefore, the same applies to all other users. The problem with that kind of thinking was that many of the other users would call with complicated questions on programming macros or accessing data from other programs and publishing their spreadsheets on the company's intranet. Such calls lasted much longer than the 5 minutes the manager needed.

Keep in mind that the numbers here are estimates. Your analysts are estimating what the *average* is. In addition, a more in-depth analysis of your help desk procedures may indicate too much time is being spent on each call, or perhaps not enough. However, this does give you a good starting point in determining your staffing needs.

One additional thing to consider here are the peaks. There are going to be times when the number of calls is substantially higher than what you estimate. For example, call rates go up soon after new or outdated products are installed. I have noticed a substantial increase in users requesting their password to be reset right after the Christmas holidays. Many people take vacation during this time and tend to forget their password.

You can also expect that people new to the company will be making more calls to the helpdesk. I have found this to be true even when they were already experienced computer users. In many cases, the questions all are procedural rather than technical, but it still requires the time and attention of your help desk staff. This is one good reason to formalize the nonformal support structure, such as representatives in each department who help on the basic issues.

Another thing to consider are the times when you have fewer analysts to draw from. For example, several of your analysts may be gone during a major exposition or trade fair. Although the call load probably will not increase during this period, you have fewer analysts to draw from, and scheduling may get tight. Also remember that new hires will probably not be as efficient as your old-timers. Therefore, you'll probably have to schedule more analysts during the first few weeks a new hire is on the phone.

As with the other aspects of your help desk, staffing levels and scheduling need to be monitored. You need to be able to provide the necessary level of support without having your help desk staff sit around waiting for calls. Although long wait times may indicate your help desk is understaffed, and analysts sitting around may indicate the help desk is overstaffed, you need to be careful not to overreact to temporary peaks and valleys in the number of calls.

I have worked on help desks before where the call load was so low there was just a single analyst, who had a number of other tasks such as changing the backup tapes and monitoring servers. Having a single analyst on the hotline made sure that calls were answered in a timely manner, and all of the other members of the IT department could concentrate on other work. There were times when so few calls came in that the "administrator of the day" had time to work on other projects. There were also days where so many calls came in that someone else needed to deal with the backup tapes (or take the calls).

Such dramatic changes are common with smaller help desks and are referred to as the "small-queue syndrome." Even if there are sudden surges, you need to be careful that you don't overreact and begin firing your help desks staff or hiring new analysts.

One aspect of getting the right staff and keeping them is to describe the job in detail as well as what is expected from someone working on the help desk. Although this becomes less significant when the help desk becomes just one of many task the person needs to perform, defining the job becomes essential when working on the help desk becomes a person's primary duty.

As I mentioned previously, many highly qualified people are not suited for working on the help desk. They may believe they are, since they've called tech support themselves and "know" the job is not that difficult. The biggest problem with that attitude is that they themselves are probably the only customer they have ever had to deal with. Even if they themselves got irate on the phone with tech support, they were justified in doing so, and, therefore, it was the fault of the person on the help desk or their product. Right?

As ludicrous as that attitude may seem, I have dealt with many customers who have behaved this way. Even in cases where it was obviously the customer's fault, such as trying to install explicitly unsupported hardware or any number of things that we had absolutely no obligation to support, I have been subjected to a wide range of abuses by customers. In most cases, insults were not directed at me but rather at the product and the company in general. Even so, I was a person unlucky enough to have gotten the call.

If I had responded to the customer in the same way, I would've not done anyone any good. The important thing was (and still is) to understand that the customer is most likely extremely frustrated and may be under pressure to get the problem solved quickly. Although this does not give them license to behave like a jerk, it does help you to not take the insults personally and to concentrate on that user's problem.

Unfortunately, this kind of obnoxious behavior is not just limited to customers calling in to a hardware or software vendor. Similar behavior can also be seen in your fellow employees. Although the extent to which fellow employee will let out his or her frustrations is significantly less (particularly in smaller companies), it is still likely to happen. In such cases, the danger to you should you blow up is even greater.

It takes a great deal of patience to put up with this kind of abuse, even if it does happen infrequently. In many cases, this is often compounded with a problem that is extremely difficult to solve and both sides get frustrated. Therefore, you need to at least try and find people with the appropriate mindset.

If applicable to your organization, you may want to consider allowing a perspective new hire to observe a few calls to get a feeling for what the job is like. Although the goal is not to scare off a perspective employee, doing so probably means the person was probably not suited for working on help.

A big part of the staffing requirements is determining exactly when your help desk will be running. I have worked in manufacturing companies that had multiple shifts in the production halls. However, people in the company administration only work during a traditional business day. Because of this, it was determined that the help desk need only be staffed between 7 a.m. and 6 p.m. and there only needed to be one person present before 8:00 and after 5:00.

Work Hours

Not only do you need to determine what kind of support you'll provide, you need to also determine when you will provide this support. That is, you need to decide what the hours of operation will be for your help desk. Unfortunately this is not as simple as saying that the hours of support are the normal business hours for your company. In the case of support you provide to your customers, this may not be feasible .

In one company where I worked, the headquarters as well as the support department were on the West Coast. The company's normal business day started at 8 a.m.. This meant that customers on the East Coast would not get support until 11 a.m. The solution was to start support at 6 a.m. This meant that the people on the East Coast only had to wait until 9 a.m.

Even with internal support, you may not be able to follow normal business hours. Normal business hours for the company as a whole may be 9–5. However, you may have a number of researchers or other staff that stay later or come in earlier. Maybe your sales force needs to deal with customers in different time zones and therefore they need computer support during the same times.

Keep in mind that just because you have users who work nonstandard hours does *not* necessarily mean your help desk *should* provide support during the same hours. In one company where I worked, support for most offices was provided by the headquarters. However, many of the offices were literally on the other side of the world. Providing a help desk staff for them during their business hours was extremely inefficient due to the limited number of calls they made. Most issues could be resolved using the may, and someone on the help desk staff was on call to handle the emergencies. Instead, most contact was done via email or during the couple of hours a day when we were both working at the same time.

Work Schedule

I think it's a good idea to have some kind of schedule for when people take calls. It should not be left up to whoever picks up the phone first. This tends to cause some people to ignore the phone ("Oh, I'm too busy"), and in many cases the user will call specific people directly and not the hotline.

Speaking of hotlines, there should be single phone number that the users call no matter what the problem. The people who are on duty at that time are then *required* to pick up the phone. The fewer people involved, the harder it is to pass the buck.

You also need to remember that, as we talked about before, you should spend no more than five hours a day on the phone. If you do, you'll burn out a lot faster and calls toward the end of the day will generally be far less productive than those at the beginning. Should your call load require that someone be on the phone during the entire time the help desk is active, you should obviously consider scheduling an number of people to handle the call load. Other things, such as vacation and sick leave, also need to be considered. Regardless of your organization, there are certain things that tend to increase the call load, for example, any time there is an increase in business activity, such as at the end of the month or end of the year. Not only is work being done that is not so common, but there are many more deadlines, and priorities increase exponentially. As a result, you end up with more emergencies that need to be done "immediately."

Another common cause of increased help desk calls is the introduction of new hardware or software. What these calls consist of will depend on what is being changed. However, I know from experience that you need to plan for the increase in calls well in advance of when the change is actually introduced. I found it extremely useful to test any changes to the hardware or software within the help desk to provide your help desk staff with the opportunity to become familiar with a new product or differences as well as identifying those areas that may be a problem for users. This allows you to either provide training for your users or provide instructions to your help desk staff on addressing the issues.

Administrator of the Day

I feel that one of the keys problems, and one that seems to have been missed by Tourniaire and Jarrell, is the situation within a company where you have a limited number of people in your IT organization. You may not have the luxury of having enough people to staff a TH model. In the company I described previously, we had 10 people responsible for system administration. They were not only responsible for the servers, workstations, and network, but also for all of the applications software. Plus, there were a number of projects going on at any given time.

The solution was to have an "Administrator of the Day" (AD) whose job it was to fight the fires. This meant when a user called the hotline, the AD took the call as a front-liner and tried to solve it. Since we all had our own areas of expertise, we could not solve every problem. When we got stuck we either asked the expert but still tried to solve it ourselves, or we handed the call off to the expert (who represented the back-liners). Since they were the experts, they then became the owner of the problem.

This combination of the FL/BL and TH models was very effective. As a result, we were able to efficiently support 900+ users locally and in two dozen branch offices with only the 10 people. Since we had 10 people, each had duty once every two weeks and was able to concentrate on a project or specific problem the rest of the time.

I must add a caveat here. In the larger subsidiaries (50+), there was someone locally who dealt with the mundane issues (like resetting passwords). In addition, we were more restrictive in the issues that we supported. This was part of our "missions statement," which we will get to later in this chapter. The result was that many problems that would be addressed in other companies were defined as "not supported," and the user did not even bother to call.

Another problem I have with many books is that they assume only the less-experienced analysts will be on the front line. In a commercial setting, the purpose of the front line is not to be a place to train your analysts or a place to put the people who can't handle the harder calls. Instead, it can and should be used as the place where you solve the problems with "short 'nsweet" answers. These users have their answer and can go back to work. However, with an internal help desk, you can take the extra time. In fact, it is sometimes a necessary evil.

In my opinion, this is a common misconception and perhaps one of the main reasons why the FL/BL model has such a bad reputation. I have found that when properly implemented, the FL/BL model can have much higher customer satisfaction, particularly if there is a high percentage of calls that can be solved by the front line.

However, I must point out that the analysts on the front line must have a clear understanding of which calls they can solve and which they cannot. If they know a particular call will take a relatively long time, they should *immediately* pass it on to the back line. In addition, users must be made aware of how this system works and why it is necessary. Most of the time, users can be trusted to tell the front-liner that the call is fairly complicated and requires the attention of the back line. However, once again, the key is that the front line knows which kind of problems should be passed to the back line.

Training Your Support Staff

Unfortunately for help desk staff, computer technology does not remain constant. New hardware is installed and new software is implemented, which means the help desk staff will spend a great amount of their time trying to keep current. To ensure the success of the help desk, you need to have both formal and informal training programs. Each help desk analyst should be given several hours a week to train on their own. This can be something as simple as reviewing magazines to keep up on the latest technological trends or can be something more formal such as learning new skills.

In either case, it must be supported by company management. I have experienced it myself where someone walked by my office and saw me reading a magazine. They reported it to their manager, who reported to the general manager, claiming my manager wasn't keeping track of his people. Fortunately, my manager was able to explain the situation, but it should not need to come to this.

Formal training can also have the goal of either keeping people current or training on a specific topic. The key differences are that there is an instructor and usually several people involved. In addition, formal training is typically conducted at a predetermined time and place. Depending on the number of people, a significant amount of planning is required to ensure there are no problems with staffing the phones and other issues. However, I have worked in support organizations where training was done on a one-to-one basis when both sides had the time.

One of the key places to start when determining what training is required is the skill set needed to take the calls. If you are running a FL/BL model, those people on the front line will require a much broader skill set. The people on the back line will require more specialized training. If you have a TH model, the training will need to be both broad and detailed.

One thing I would like to point out here is that it is extremely important that the training be documented. This applies not only to what training was conducted and who participated, but also the material in the training that needs to be available either on-line or in hard copy. Having the training material available like this serves two important purposes. First, it can be used as reference material when calls come in about a specific topic. Second, it can be used for informal training by the help disk analysts who either need a refresher or wish to increase their skill set.

One place where training is desperately needed and frequently overlooked is new product rollouts. I have worked in companies before where new products were installed and both the users and the help desk were on their own. In the case of upgrades for existing products, training may not be necessary depending on the skill level of your employees. However, at the very least, your help desk staff should be made aware of the major changes that have been made to the product and areas that could result in an increased number of calls.

The newer the product, the greater the need for training. For example, you may be using Microsoft FrontPage and decide to upgrade your users to the more powerful NetObjects Fusion. Although there are a great number of similarities in the functionality of these two products, the advanced features of Fusion may be lost without the proper training. If you are implementing some completely new technology, such as email or the Internet, the need for training is even greater.

I've worked in places where they never learned the value of training. With each of the product rollouts, the number of calls and complaints about the software increased dramatically. The help desk staff did not have the necessary training either, so resolution times also increased dramatically. This obviously decreased the efficiency of both the users and the help desk.

One of the greatest stumbling blocks to getting management support for training is that it is even harder to justify in terms of ROI than the help desk itself. However, an important method of reducing the number of calls is to have the users help themselves. This is done by making the necessary resources available and, as you might have guessed, giving them the necessary training.

It is unlikely that you have either the time or the money to give users all the training they need to become experts with every product. However, there are some important steps you can take to provide your users with the necessary training. For example, each employee is given the training on the basic functionality of the applications that they use the most. You can then select individuals from each group or department to get more detailed training. These will be the contacts within each department when questions arise. If they cannot solve the problem, they contact the help desk.

Another stumbling block you encounter when setting up training is scheduling problems that the training may cause. The more people you have attending training, the harder it will be to schedule phone time. In some companies, we do a "blitzkrieg." We shut down the help desk for the afternoon and everyone gets training at once. We then know that everyone has had the training, and there is relatively little impact on the company. However, this normally won't work if you have hundreds of calls a day, with thousands of users. In these cases, it might be easier to do the training in two passes, with half of the help desk attending a given session.

In essence, the same thing applies to your users. In some cases, the easiest solution is to send everyone from a specific department all the same time. Depending on the size and function of the department, it is much easier to monitor who in a department has had the training and who has not.

Training for your help desk staff should not be limited to just technical information and skill enhancement. Instead, you should also include customer service and communication skills in their training. One key aspect of this is that training customer service skills is more than just imparting factual information. Time should also be spent on addressing behavioral issues that can make or break the help desk.

Call Resolution—Solving the Problem

Believe it or not, solving problems is an important aspect of a help desk. I've worked in companies where the developing good "looking" work flow and procedures were more important than finding the answer. Here again, the help desk should not become a goal unto itself.

Unfortunately, solving the problem is not always as easy as looking up a canned answer for a specific problem. In many cases, you are going to have to work for the answer. In some cases, you are going to have to work extremely hard.

Determining the Problem

In order to properly deal with any issue, you need to make a determination of what kind of issue it is. Problems are dealt with in a different way than are requests and even simple questions. By evaluating each call as one of these three types, you can more easily determine the priority of the call and employ the proper resources. Although the work from the perspective of the help desk is pretty much the same, the steps might be slightly different. In the help desk, these steps are a vital part of the whole system.

The process begins by taking a call. Depending on your company, this can be by phone, email, fax or walk-ins. Each is considered a "call" for the purpose of this discussion.

This is typically where you begin to document the call, if that is part of your standard procedure. If users have write access to your problem database (more on that shortly), they could generate problem reports themselves. Which calls actually need to be documented is a matter of company policy. A quick reminder on how to connect to a remote printer might just need a tick mark to indicate that training is needed. Reactivating a user's account after a vacation may not require anything. On the other hand, a system crash requires as many details as possible.

Solving the Problem

Part of solving the problem is making sure that the solution is available to other people. This is especially important if it took you a long time to find the answer or if you are the expert and you realize that it is not that likely that someone else will know this answer. These problems and their solutions need to be documented and accessible to everyone.

Experience has taught me that neither well-documented solutions nor accessibility alone can make the solution useful. I've worked in places where half of the documentation was on-line, but much of it was incomplete, and the other half existed in people's heads or was buried in their personal directories and therefore not accessible to the rest of the help desk staff.

Although it may seem painfully obvious to say that the first step in solving a problem is *finding the cause,* many help desk analysts tend to forget this. Instead they try to *cure* specific symptoms of the problem without looking for the underlying cause. This manifests itself quite often when users ask for help in implementing a specific solution. They have decided that a specific solution is best for their problem, and it is up to the help desk to give them the necessary assistance in implementing that solution. The issue is that in many cases, the solution they have chosen is not the best one for the problem.

I have received many calls from users wanting to implement a particular function within their word processing program (such as MS Word) and have them get annoyed when I tell them it isn't possible. It turns out that what they are trying to accomplish is much better done from MS Excel. One of the reasons is the help desk analyst often looks for and tries to solve the symptoms rather than the underlying cause. For example, the symptom and not the problem itself is that they are having difficulty implementing something in MS Word. It is therefore extremely important that the help desk analyst understand what the goal of the user is.

One technique I find extremely useful is making sure you know what the user's problem really is. This might seem like an obvious statement, but I have worked on problems myself where I discovered that the problem I was trying to solve was not the same as the one the user had. As in the case of the user who tried to solve a problem with MS Word that was best done in MS Excel, not knowing what the problem really is leads you to the wrong answer. Here, the simplest approach is just to ask the user what they are trying to accomplish.

I have often found that if the description of their problem also includes the solution, you may not have reached the core problem. Try to get the user to describe the problem without specifying the program or any other part of the solution. For example, in the case of using MS Word to create a complicated table, the user cannot use the phrase "MS Word." Instead, the user would have to describe what they are trying to accomplish with the table. In other words, you need to press the user for more specifics.

Part of this is having the user describe what the *goal* is, what the behavior is, and what the expected behavior should be. This helps you to quickly get to those problems that are a result of either misconception or misunderstandings on the part of users. This also helps to clarify those issues where the user claims the software has a bug or just isn't working right.

When the user is done describing what is happening, repeat it back to them and asked them to confirm that this is what is actually happening. It may also be useful to modify the statements slightly (such as changing the order of phrases) so that you're not simply repeating word-for-word what the user said. This helps to ensure that you do not end up solving the wrong problem.

The goal here is to understand what the user needs. This means understanding what the problem is. I have worked on help desks myself where the first thing users do is give you a detailed list of their hardware and configuration or go into nauseating detail about a similar problem they had on another system. Although this is useful in many cases, it may become a burden when it is not relevant to the actual problem. It is up to you to *guide* the user to ensure they do not get too far off track.

The analyst needs to take control of the conversation to ensure that the user provides enough information without providing too much. Yes, as in the previous example, you can get too much information. First, too much information means you are getting things that are unrelated to the problem, and it is a waste of time to have the user provide it. Second, there is sometimes information that *may* be related, but you don't yet need it. Getting it too early in the conversation may mean you either start thinking about it prematurely or you lose track of things because of "information overload."

When you are sure you have a clearer understanding of what the problem is, you begin to see if it fits any known pattern. For example, if this problem has the exact same symptoms as something that you have encountered before, the logical approach is to try the solution that worked with the other problem. If the problems are not identical, can you find a problem that is similar? In essence, that is exactly what mechanics, doctors, physicist, or anyone else do who is trying to solve a problem or prove a theory that has a number of pieces and may have multiple solutions. Based on the evidence, you devise a theory and then investigate the system to see how well it matches your theory. If it doesn't, you revise your theory.

For those problems to which there is no easy solution, you'll have to apply a number of rules of thumb (heuristics) as well as step-by-step instructions (algorithms). For example, the rules of thumb may be to start with a simpler task and build yourself up to a more-complicated task in order to see where the behavior begins to change. Another rule of thumb may be to start with the default configuration and make changes one by one.

In dealing with problems with obvious causes or for which there is no step-by-step procedure to follow, you may need to dig for more information. The lead-off question can be something as simple as, "Just exactly what is happening?" This helps to clarify what you know about the user's understanding of the problem and at the same time gives you an idea of the technical skills of the user. This is part of ensuring that both you and the user know exactly what the problem is.

In my experience, the more accurate this description, the more technically competent the user is. Knowing the technical level of the user serves as a guide for all subsequent questions. For example, you can ask the more-detailed technical questions earlier in the conversation if the user has a stronger background in the product. For example, it is a great time-saver to be able to say, "Start the network applet in the Control Panel" versus "Click on the Start button. You now see a menu. Click on the entry labeled Settings. Now find the icon labeled Networking, . . ." and so forth.

The next step is to determine whether or not the system *ever* behaved as intended. I must admit that I have worked on number of calls where I assumed that the product was working correctly and then stopped for some reason. The emphasis on my approach was in determining what would cause this aspect of the system to stop working. This led me down the wrong path, because it never had work correctly at all. Needless to say, this wasted a lot of my time.

If the product was working before and stopped for some reason, the most likely cause is that something in the system was changed, despite what many users may try to convince you; it is unlikely that something "just stops working." Therefore, you need to find out what changes have been made in the system.

One change that is often overlooked is the physical location of the computer. How could the physical location have anything to do with the behavior of a piece of software? Well, when you moved the computer you simply forgot to plug the printer back in!

This may seem a rather mundane issue, but you would be amazed at how many hotline calls are generated because of such problems. To avoid these kind of problems, you should run through a number of "quick fixes" before you begin looking at the more complicated solutions. Despite the simplicity of the problem, loose cables generate more than their share of headaches. Loose cables seem to be the last thing that anyone checks. However, it is extremely annoying, if not embarrassing, when that is actually the cause.

If you are running an internal help desk, checking cables may be something that you can *require* of the users prior to them calling the help desk. This may require some additional training to ensure the users know how to seek the cables properly, but it is definitely worth the time in the long run. When you ask the user whether or not they have checked the cables and they say "yes," you have already saved two or to three minutes on the call. (Assuming they actually did check the cables.)

Despite the claims of Microsoft on the stability of Windows NT, I have found that sometimes the best solution is to simply reboot the machine. My success rate with using this in "solving" the problem is high enough that it has become part of my standard palette of solutions. However, keep in mind that rebooting the system like this may solve the *symptoms,* but not the *problem*.

Often just knowing what has changed is sufficient to determine the solution, particularly if what was changed was done improperly. However, it is sometimes necessary to repeat the steps on an existing, working system to see if you can recreate the problem. In order to do this, you have to be able to recreate the user's environment as closely as possible. It is therefore extremely useful to have a test environment where you can try to recreate problems.

How many different kinds of machines and different hardware are available in your test laboratory will depend on your company. The more standardized your hardware and software, the fewer different kinds of both you'll need to maintain. However, you need to remember that the purpose of the lab is to help you solve users' problems in order that they work more efficiently. If users cannot work efficiently because you cannot solve their problem due to lack of resources, then you may end up losing more money than the cost of the equipment.

If you are dealing with mostly hardware problems, you may find it almost unavoidable to have spare copies of all the different types of hardware you use. These not only can be used for test purposes but also for emergencies should the hardware break down on production machines.

One thing you may want to consider is using some kind of removable media like the SyQuest drives we discussed in the chapter on sharing resources (Chapter 12). This allows you to create an extremely large number of hardware and software combinations with substantially less real investment in hardware. In addition, this saves you on licensing fees for the software that must be licensed for each installed copy regardless of whether it used for productive use or not (such as from Microsoft).

The cost of a single SyQuest hard disk is much higher than the equivalent hard disk. However, you can install the system on the SyQuest drive, configure it to one of your standards, replace it with a different SyQuest disk, install a different standard system and so forth. Whenever you need to test a specific system, all you need to do is switch the SyQuest disk.

You might want to look into two products from KeyLabs (*www .keylabs.com*): RapidDeploy and LabExpert. RapiDeploy is used to automatically install and configure multiple machines. It addition, it creates "libraries" of standard configurations that you can use at any time. These libraries can be used to switch back and forth between configuration or for easy disaster recovery. LabExpert is intended for use in a lab or classroom environment, where changes are made to a lot of machines, and you want to return them to their original state.

Sometimes you'll find that you can actually think too hard about the problem. That is, you spend too much time analyzing the problem and the possible solutions before eventually deciding on a possible solution. I have found in many cases that the best course of action is to simply start with a number of possible solutions and see if they solve the problem. Even if the solution you try does not solve the problem, you have eliminated it from consideration, and how it fails may give you valuable insight into the cause of the problem.

One of the most common quick fixes is user error. In a way, this is similar to the user having a misconception about how the program should function. However, identifying user error is usually not as simple, as you may have to go step-by-step and examine everything the user is doing. In such cases, it is often useful to have the documentation in front of you so you can follow along as the user performs each step. The reason I say you should have the documentation in front of you is that you may know a faster way of doing something than is described in the documentation. Therefore, having the documentation in front of you helps you to ensure that you do the same steps the user is doing and that the user is doing the steps correctly.

To some extent, going through the procedure step-by-step could be considered "hand-holding." You need to know where hand holding stops and troubleshooting begins. I know many users who will call the help desk and claim they followed everything exactly as it is in the manual just so they can get someone to walk them through the procedure. It is impossible to completely avoid people like this, but with a little practice, it's easy to detect them, particularly if they keep calling with the same kinds of problems.

As I mentioned above, one of the heuristics that you can apply is getting back to basics. That is, getting the system back to use a state where you know what should work. In some cases, I've had to completely remove every card and every controller in the system and add them back one by one. Software and hardware conflicts are common causes of problems. In many cases, the simplest solution is actually to start from scratch and work your way back up. This is particularly important if you have mixed environments of Plug-and-Play, PCI, or anything else that sets the configuration automatically, plus ISA cards. Sometimes setting the cards manually is the easiest way to avoid conflicts.

Keep in mind that pulling every card out of the system may not be necessary to identify conflicts. Often you can easily identify conflicts by examining the machine's configuration.

Most users are not proficient enough to be able to provide you with the details of their system. This is where hardware inventory products such as NetSense come in extremely handy. Such products gather configuration information and store it in a central database. They can then easily be accessed by your help desk.

One stumbling block in determining the problem can often be the users themselves. If users knew everything there was to know about computers, there would probably be no need for them to call the help desk in the first place. This often results in users' description of the problem or their system being done in ambiguous and often inappropriate terms. For example, I regularly get calls from users who say they cannot "get into the screen" when they mean to say the computer will not boot.

In many cases, what the user means is obvious. However, there will definitely be a number of calls where you cannot be sure. For example, I've had calls from users who tell me how big their hard disk is when asked how much memory they have. Others may confusingly call the taskbar the toolbar.

One tool that I have found extremely useful in solving problems (not just troubleshooting help desk calls) is MindManager from MindJet, LLC (*www.mindjet.com*). Mind Manager is a tool that helps you "map your mind." In essence, you start with a central idea and map out all of the related issues. Any number of branches can lead off from that central idea, and each of these branches in turn can have any number of branches. I talked in detail about Mind Manager in the chapter on System Administration (Chapter 8).

Another tool that I find extremely useful is a flow chart software, such as Visio Standard. Although less useful than MindManager during the actual problem resolution, I find flow charts that have been included in existing problem/solutions to be extremely useful. By following the flow chart as the computer or software goes about its business, you know what it should be doing at each step and can quickly identify those places where the system is misbehaving.

Another important aspect I refer to as the "Tao of Tech Support." It cannot be taught. It is not learned. There are no words to describe it. It just is. This is the ability to go beyond the description of the physical manifestations of the problem and seek the "motivation" behind the problem. What "forces" are coming into play to make the problem manifest itself in this fashion.

You could run through a checklist of all related issues and examine each one by one, which would take an incredibe amount of time. Or you could "feel" the answer and solve the problem very quickly. This ability is obviously hard to describe and it is something that not every analyst has or even will have. However, in my experience, this ability is far more useful than an encyclopedic knowledge of the system. There are places to look for the knowledge, but the Tao of Tech Support is something you just "have."

Customer Self-Help

As commercial software vendors changed from free support to fee-based service contracts, many still felt the need to provide some level of free support to their customers. A large number of companies began making available to their customers the same database of problems and solutions that their help desk analysts had access to. This benefits not only customers who had not purchased a support contract, but it also saves a great deal of time for those paying customers who are looking for solutions to known problems.

Typically, access to the problem-solution database is made from the Internet using a standard Web browser. However, several vendors make this database available on CD-ROM, often with a proprietary interface (and usually at a cost). In addition, a number of third-party vendors provided problem-solution databases for a wide range of products. You are also going to find that the more-advanced help desk software products provide Web or even email access to the problem-solution database.

By standardizing HTML as the document format for your help desk, you can make available the same information to all of your users and not just to the help desk staff. Using active server pages that use ODBC to connect to an SQL Server or MS Access database allows users to generate their own problem reports as well as search for solutions and even check the status on existing problem reports.

Evaluating the Help Desk

With an existing help desk, you should ask yourself whether it is actually doing what it set out to do. That is, are the goals still appropriate and have you reached those goals? Your users may have gotten better or your company has expanded (or both), so the needs have changed. Also, as we all know, the technology will change, so maybe there is a new, better way of doing things. Not only do you need to evaluate the current system, but as it grows, you need to continually evaluate it.

As with any investment, you want to know whether or not your investment has paid off. This is also part of the evaluation. You need to determine if the original investment was cost effective and whether or not you should continue the way you are. Unfortunately, this kind of evaluation is not as easy as others are. Things you can look at are the average TTR as well as the average response time. If you see that calls are getting worked on 30 minutes sooner and take 5 minutes less on average to solve, that 35 minutes is a tangible savings. Multiply this by the average number of calls per pay period times the average wage and you have an estimate of your savings.

Measuring the Help Desk

After running for awhile, you may learn that the number of people on your help desk is too high for the number and type of calls. If it's too low, you probably found out a lot sooner. Consider how you should adjust this number to reflect the call load. However, you need to always plan for the worst case. That is, what happens when the call load goes up? Can you handle it quickly? Other things to look at are how the help desk is integrated into the company. Are people taking advantage of all the services you are offering? What services aren't they using? Then comes the biggest question: Are they even aware that these services exist?

If your help desk has been around for some time, you expect that most people already know about its existence. However, if you have made changes to the flow of things like adding email as a support mechanism, then maybe users don't know about them. If the database you are using permits it, you can have a field to indicate the method used to make contact. If people aren't using email, then maybe there is something they or you don't know. They may not know about its existence or you didn't training them well enough how to do it.

Part of the evaluation is determining the staffing needs. Your help desk staff can give you an idea of what the needs are, but their attitude will be prejudiced. A good way of figuring your staffing needs is to consider the number of calls you have over a specific period of time as well as what kinds of calls they are. Then figure out the average TTR for each type of call.

This is an important distinction. I worked on one help desk where the average was about ten minutes. That didn't say much, because the calls were either done in 30 seconds ("I forgot my password") or took several hours. (The database server crashed.) There were rarely any calls that came close to this average. In comparing that company to others, I found that they had half as many users but one tenth as many calls. This was partly due to the users being familiar with the products they were using.

You also need to make a determination of what work is being accomplished to solve each problem. Start with the person taking the call. This includes the receptionist or customer service person, if it's not someone who will actually work on the problem. Even if it's only a couple of minutes per call, the time and therefore costs add up. If your software has a built-in timer (many do), you can use this to add up the times. If not, I would still recommend that the help desk staff make an entry indicating how long they worked on this problem. If you have control over the database (you wrote it or the software allows it), add a field or fields to keep track of time. This can then be searched quickly and totaled. Here again, you need a breakdown by call type to get a better overview of where your money is going. (This is probably necessary if you are going to charge-back the calling department.)

With this information, you can come up with an estimate of the average time spent for each of the different types of calls. Then, using average salary as a starting point, you can quickly figure out an approximate cost for the support. If you want to get an estimate over a year you could extrapolate, but you have to be very careful. If you plan to upgrade or change products at any point during that year, the actual values are going to be off. The less training you give users on the new products, the more calls there will be, and the more these estimates will be off.

During the evaluation, you need to talk to both the help desk team and your users. Even if the help desk has been running only a short time, both groups can provide their initial reaction to the system and make valuable comments as to what is right and what is wrong. Also, both can tell you what kinds of problems are being reported to give you an indication of where potential problem areas are.

At this point, we can begin to qualify the staffing needs. We know what the average number of calls is and the average length. We also know how many people there are in the help desk or how many we would want to use. If you have an average of 100 calls a day and each takes an average of 20 minutes, then you are working 2000 minutes a day on solving problems. This works out to about 33 hours a day. With an average work day of 8 hours, this works out to 4 to 5 people per day.

Well, not quite.

The assumption here is that you put people on the phone for the full 8 hours. Once again, my recommendation is: don't. People are going to burn out. This is especially important if those on the phones are trying to solve problems. Even after 5 hours on the phone, they're not thinking as clearly. So, by the end of 8 hours they are really burnt. (I know.) You then compound the problem by doing this day after day. The result is that problems take longer to solve, and your help desk staff starts looking for other jobs.

The solution is to limit their time on the phones. Have them spend the rest of the time doing problem research, tests, training, or administration duties. Therefore, in the above example, where you estimate 4 to 5 people, you would need to increase this by at least one third (since they only spend two thirds of the time on the phone). Therefore, 6 to 7 people would be a much better number. Regardless of what number you come up with, it is always safest to round *up* to the next whole number.

Next, we need to estimate the amount of time these people are not available for phone or problem solving. There are meetings and emergencies, and every once in a while you ought to let these people go on vacation.

Then there is the possibility that one or more person will be out sick. For all of these combined, most companies use 10–15% as unavailable time. Be on the safe side and choose 15%. So, in our case, the 15% works out to one more person, totaling 7 to 8.

If you are running a small help desk, then these numbers are liable to show the greatest variance. This is normal and is referred to as the small-queue syndrome. The best tool to use instead of standard analytical tools is observation. If you see that the level of support received is regularly below what has been promised, you may need a larger staff or need to change the users' expectations. If your help desk staff has a lot of "free" time, then maybe you need less people.

Obviously, if the users are complaining that they aren't getting a quick-enough response or the help desk team is complaining that they are overburdened, you need to look at your staff. This includes the number you have as well as their behavior. Long response times may be a result of insufficient staff, but it could also mean that some of the staff just does not care and lets things slip. Therefore, you should not jump to conclusions about the cause of the problems.

If you are building up your help desk from scratch or planning major changes to the way the users interact with it, then you need to advertise before you put it into operation. The users must be made aware that changes are coming, what those changes are, and how it will affect their interaction with the help desk. For example, you may have an existing help desk but plan to start using a commercial help desk software. Since this will automatically accept email requests, you are going to change the system to where requests that do not need to be handled immediately must be sent via email. If you do not tell your users, how will they know?

An important aspect of the evaluation is defining correct metrics. The first thing most people think about measuring is the average time to resolution and number of closed calls per analyst. However, many people do not realize that both of these values are relative. A short resolution time does not mean that users get their problems solved but rather could mean that analysts are closing calls too soon. This could also be the reason for a high number of closes. Depending on the help desk model you choose, you may have a number of analysts who have longer calls will have a lower average number of closes. They are solving the real hard problems and therefore may have a higher level of customer satisfaction. However, your metrics are saying that they are not doing as good a job.

In one support organization where I worked, I remember one analyst who had almost twice as many closes than any other analyst. This looked good on paper. However, he had twice as many reopens. If the reopens were subtracted from the closes, he had a much lower average than other people.

This particular problem was solved when the organization went from the FL/BL to the T/H model. However, the analyst could still artificially pump up his average by escalating calls too soon. This problem says two things.

First, you need to be specific about what you are measuring. Simply saying the average number of closed calls is not enough. You need to define a time period. Even saying the average number per week might not be sufficient. If the average time before a call is reopened is ten days (not unreasonable), you could miss a lot of reopens.Therefore, a better metric would be to pair the number of closes and the number of reopens. If you increase closes while at the same time decrease reopens, you are doing well.

The second part of this problem is properly defining the time period you are measuring. The more long calls you have, the longer this period should be. This does not mean that you do not measure the shorter periods, but you should reflect the longer calls as well. One method is to keep a running total of weekly averages as well as monthly and quarterly averages. Tied to this should be the average length of calls as well as a breakdown of how many calls were taken over one week, two weeks, and so on.

If you have a larger number of calls that took a month to close, then your average closing time goes up and the average number of calls closed per week goes down. The reason for this kind of trend needs to be analyzed. It could be a number of things. First, you might have had too many people on vacation or a lot of people out sick during this time. Fewer people working the phones means a longer resolution time or more quick closes and reopens. This means you have to plan vacations better or increase your staff.

In one company, we had an odd occurrence in that the number of long calls increased in March, June, and December. This was independent of when new products were released, which naturally increased the number of calls. However, over a two-year period, these months were exceptionally high in long calls. A detailed analysis showed that there were specific people who had an increase in call length during this time. The reason was that these people were taking classes and had finals during this time. When they didn't have finals, they would often stay later and sometimes even come in on weekends to work on problems. However, during finals, they spent most of their free time studying.

Measuring Performance

In general, managing your help desk analysts is not too much different than managing any other group of people. Perhaps the most significant difference is the fact that like most any other service organization, the effectiveness and therefore the performance of your help desks staff is determined to great extent by people outside of your organization. In such cases, it is extremely important that the measurement criteria be clearly defined in advance.

One important thing to keep in mind is that the number of calls a particular analyst takes is not always indicative of his or her performance. I have worked with analysts before who at first glance appeared to be doing great. However, their performance rating dropped significantly when the department began keeping track of the calls that were reopened. These analysts would take the call and then get the user off quickly, so the statistics showed large number of calls. It happened quite frequently that the answer was either insufficient or not properly understood, which made the user call back. This was not very efficient for anyone concerned.

There are two important aspects to remember when defining performance goals and objectives. First, people doing similar jobs should have similar objectives. You may be able to define hiring requirements for those people who exceed the requirement. If they can reach a particular level of performance, they should be able to maintain it. However, I feel that if you find it necessary to require better performance from one or another analyst, then it might be time to change that analyst's position or title. For example, if you feel that one analyst should be taking 50% more calls than the others, giving this person to title of "senior analyst" may be in order. Keep in mind that greater responsibility should also mean more money.

This is not always as easy as it seems, because the work is not always so easy to compare. For example, you may have two analysts who take basic-level calls, one who takes network problems and another who takes applications problems. For the network analyst, it may be a simple matter of determining that a specific router has gone down. He reports it to the appropriate group and his work is done in 5 minutes. The person in the applications group may get a problem that requires a great deal of research to solve. Both of these people are doing the same job, but the requirements may be different.

The second issue is that performance should be judged based on the actual work accomplished and not any perceived accomplishments. As I mentioned previously, I worked with people who had been apparently high closure aid because they were more concerned with getting the user off the phone than solving the problem.

Addressing this problem is not always as easy as it seems. If you have an FL/BL model, where anyone could get to call, which analysts do you give the credits to? How do you determine which analysts are actually trying to help and which are just trying to get the user off the phone? If you have a TH model, the same analyst will be handling the call throughout its lifetime. Therefore, repeated closure and reopens then may indicate that the analyst is trying too hard to get the user off the phone.

If the analysts have duties other then the simply taking phone calls, this should be included in their overall performance evaluation. Here too, quality is just as important an aspect as quantity is. For example, in one company where I worked, each analyst was expected to contribute a specific number of articles to the problem-solution database every month. Some analysts were notorious for simply rewriting what existed in manuals. This helped no one and was a waste of time.

Help Desk
Software

Unless you have a very small company, you will need some kind of software to help you manage the information necessary to support your users. The simplest form would be storing all of the information in a text file or spreadsheet. Even that is better than having notes written on pieces of paper scattered all over the company.

The next step up is creating a database using something like MS Access. This enables you to create links between different tables, such as between the table containing the software that is installed on each machine and the table containing the licensing information. This enables you to see how the two interrelate and possibly find software that hasn't been licensed properly.

One thing I need to point out here is that should you decide to create a database yourself, it will have to be fairly simple. The reason is quite simply that this should not become a project on its own, which it will be if you try to do too much. Once you get started, you quickly become overwhelmed with just how much information there is to manage and how much they interrelate. The more features and functionality you add, the more you discover are missing that you "have to have."

Unfortunately, you'll find that for medium-sized and larger companies you won't be able to simply throw together a couple of tables in

MS Access and expect things to work efficiently. In other words, there actually is a lot of functionality that you *do* absolutely have to have. Once you get started, you'll find there *is* more information than you thought about originally, and it *will* become a project on its own. At first it may seem as if you are stuck with having a separate project just to create the tools to manage your help desk information. However, you're forgetting all of the tools that already exist on the market specifically designed to help you manage your help desk.

Many people shy away from prepackaged help desk products for a couple of reasons. First, many people question the validity of buying a product that is not much more than a front-end to some database. However, these same people invest millions of dollars for something like SAP, which itself could be classified as just "a front-end to a database." Granted, this is an oversimplification, but making the same statement about a help desk product is just as much an oversimplification. However, I have encountered MIS managers before who take that attitude toward help desk software.

I have also encountered MIS managers who do not feel justified in buying something that can be programmed within the department. Although this is true, you wouldn't think of buying a word processor because you could program something like that within the department. Considering the complexity of many help desk products, this is it exactly the level we are working on.

Finding the Right Product

In my experience, there is little if any reason *not* to purchase a prepackaged help desk product, even if it is one of the low-end products. The only time I would consider it is if you needed to have an interface to some existing application that the help desk product cannot handle or can only handle with some difficulty. For example, you may want to integrate the help desk functionality with the financial software to simplify processing the orders for new hardware and software. However, it might actually be simpler to forgo the direct integration and to do the ordering by and if it needs you will benefit from the other functionality of the help desk.

Another key issue is not to go overboard. Granted, you need to plan for growth, but buying a product that is more than you need might make the help desk become too big a project. Remember, a simple solution that you get fairly quickly is better than one that solves the world's problems, but we have to wait a year and have problems integrating it.

One thing to keep in mind is that no help desk software is a "Genie in a bottle." By that I mean you cannot expect to simply install the help desk software and have it solve all of your problems on the first day. Like any technology, it will take time before the technology can be used to its fullest. You can expect that regardless of how many users or what software you decide to employ, a lot of time will be spent at the beginning both configuring and "feeding" the software. You can expect that for the first few months, it may seem as if more work is being put into the help desk than you get out of it. However, you will get to a point where the database of problems and solutions can be applied to every employee.

When deciding which help desk product to buy, you need to look at more than just the "external" features the product offers. In finding the right help desk software *for your organization,* you need to remember what the goal of your help desk is in the first place. Depending on how it was set up, your help desk could be striving to manage assets more effectively, solve users problems so they can work more efficiently, and any of the other things you set out as goals for your help desk. Whatever your goals are, these need to be reflected in whatever help desk software you choose to implement.

The number of choices you have for help desk software is very much a two-edged sword. First, you won't in all likelihood find a software product that can do exactly what you need or even 95% of what you need. Therefore, making a choice can be difficult. Each takes a different approach and has a different "feel" about it, so it may be that your ultimate decision might be based purely on personal preference.

Unfortunately, part of the dilemma you will encounter is that help desk software is not so much a commodity as are word processing or photo manipulation products. The result is that help desk products are somewhat more expensive than word processors for the same level of complexity. This is completely understandable as it is true in any market that specialty goods are more expensive than your typical products. What this means is that for many companies, the cost prevents them from getting a product that fulfils close to 100% of their needs.

However, getting a help desk product that does not fulfill all of your needs is no different than getting a word processor that is missing some needed functionality. Here we come back to the issues of total cost of ownership and total value of ownership. If you buy a less-expensive help desk, which requires more administrative effort, you might be better off getting a more expensive product at the beginning. That is, the total cost of the less expensive product is actually greater in the long run. In addition, if the less expensive product is missing a very important feature, it has less value than the more expensive product.

To illustrate this point, let's take a look at what I believe to be one of the most important aspects of the help desk software: configurability. Many people will argue and say the ability to track problem numbers and manage assets are much more important than configurability. However, to me, this is comparable to saying tires and a steering wheel are much more important in evaluating automobiles than are air bags. No one would ever dream of even looking at a car where tires and a steering wheel were not standard equipment. Along the same line, in my mind, it does not make sense to look at help desk software that does not track problems or manage hardware.

Since no two organizations are alike, there is no way the programmer can consider everything every company needs. Instead, the product should be adaptable to the needs of each company. Take a look at any word processing application. Not only can you change the appearance, such as toolbars and menus, but many come with a complete programming environment. In essence, the same applies to all of the advanced help desk products. Therefore, you can start with the basic functionality and get exactly what you need.

Another aspect is that the help desk has become more than simply a place to manage user problems and keep track of hardware. Instead, the help desk has become a central aspect of the higher IS infrastructure. In many cases, it has become a central repository for all of the information related to computer systems. If this is the case in your organization, the functionality that the help desk software provides needs to reflect this.

In my experience, the less expensive the product is, the fewer things it can administer or manage. For example, the help desk will be able to manage problems and possibly the associated hardware, but many cases this is where it stops. You cannot, for example, manage maintenance contracts or software licenses. A low-end product also means you probably cannot add new tables should you wish to add to the functionality.

The more different types of information you administer, the more different types of tables you'll need. Let's take a very simple example and look at Figure 16–1. At the top, you see the incoming call. This is composed of the person making the call, the description of the problem and solution, and the associated hardware and software. Rather than storing all of these pieces of information in a single table, it is very useful to store them in separate tables. For example, it is likely that there is a separate table for user information. Although the user's name is not likely to change, he or she may move to a different department or get a new telephone number. If this information were stored along with the problem information, each time the user's telephone number changed, you'd have to change each problem report.

It is common that the description of the problem is either not sufficient to solve the problem or there may be a different underlying problem. Therefore, it is often necessary to change the problem description. In many cases, there is a common problem among many different users. It does not make sense then to input the problem description by hand. Instead, it is much more efficient to simply compare the problem to a table of known problems and solutions.

It is also useful to be able to determine if a particular piece of hardware (or software for that matter) is having problems. It is therefore useful to be able to relate problems to particular piece of hardware or software product. All you really need in the problem description is the computer name and not such things as the vendor or the size of the hard disk. All of these may be

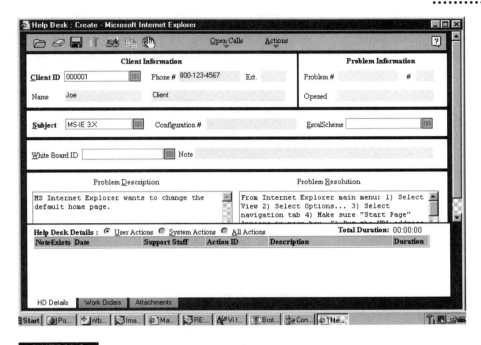

FIGURE 16–1   Magic Total Service Deskmain screen.

useful in determining the cause of the problem, but it is not necessary to store them in the same table as the problem report. Instead, the separate table containing all the details of the computer is more efficient.

Each of the elements referenced from a problem report in turn references other information. This information in turn references other information. As you can see, even with just basic information concerning a specific problem, you can have a dozen or more tables. You eventually reach a point where the only database product that can handle all of this is an enterprise-grade SQL database.

Although not obvious to some MIS managers, an important factor in choosing the right help desk product is the number of users you are supporting, which is not the same as the number of employees you have. This is an extremely important difference. For example, in one company I worked, only a third (around 500) of the employees were part of the "administration" and therefore worked on PCs. The rest worked in the production halls, and only a handful of them used PCs.

In terms of help desk products, there is a much bigger difference between 500 users and 1500 than there is between 5000 and 15,000. What this means is that a product suitable for 15,000 users will generally support 5000 without being too much of a good thing.

One primary aspect of this is the methods used to search for solutions. The most expensive products tend to have fairly complex search mechanisms that make the product more expensive. If you are dealing with thousands of problems and solutions, traditional methods such as drilldown or keyword search become impractical. However, if you only have a few hundred or even as many as a thousand problems and solutions, the extra cost for these mechanisms may not be worth it.

Although this book is dealing specifically with Windows NT, you should consider all of the platforms you work with. It is not a good idea to have multiple copies of the software running on different platforms. However, you should consider how the people are going to access the software. Modern help desk products address this issue in that access is done through a Web browser. Provided your Web browser supports the necessary features, it doesn't matter from which operating system you access the help desk. However, keep in mind there are a number of help desk products that are not supported by every browser.

Help Desk Software Requirements

Whether you buy a finished product or decide to develop your own help desk software, there are a number of functions and characteristics that you should consider. Of the dozens of different help desk products that I looked at, I have yet to find one that is suitable for every company. Granted, there are some with every imaginable feature, but these products may be out of your price range. Therefore, they are not well suited for smaller businesses, because there is no return on investment (ROI). In other words, the cost outweighs the worth of the features.

Even if you decide to go for one of the products at the lower end of the price scale, you'll still find a wide range of available features. It is therefore important for you to decide which features are most important for you.

Prior to purchasing any tool, it is a good idea to create a list of requirements. Here, I don't mean just thinking about what you need and then looking for a product that fills that need, but rather listing out a fairly detailed specification. Keep in mind that a good help desk product can cost you several thousands of dollars, so it is in your best interest to develop the proper specification.

In choosing the right product, I find it extremely useful to create a table, which has a list of potential features, along with their importance and how well the particular product addresses that issue. Be careful not to make your scale too big. On a scale of 1–10, it is difficult to classify the difference between an importance of 6 and 7, for example. A scale of 1–4 (*not needed* to *essential*) is much more realistic. In the same vein, rating how well the particular product addresses the issue should also not be too detailed. This should also have a short range, (*not present* to *exceptional*).

To get an idea of what products should be considered, you multiply the importance by how well it is addressed. For example, a characteristic with an importance of 3, but it is not present, it gets a value 0. A characteristic with an importance of 2, which is addressed exceptionally well, (with a rating of 4) would get an 8 for this characteristic. You then total all of these values to get an overall rating for the product.

However, you need to be careful not to simply look at the total and choose the product with the highest value. It is possible that a *required* feature that is not present has the same value in this evaluation as functionality that is not needed but is implemented exceptionally well. Therefore, it is a good idea to look at each characteristic individually to see if there is anything that would automatically knock out a product from consideration. For example, you might want to say that all required functionality must have at least a 2 or a 3 in order for the product to be considered.

Cost should also be listed in the table. Keep in mind that there are a number of different licensing schemes, just as there are with other kinds of applications. Some products are single seat, where you can get quantity discounts. Others are concurrent use, where you pay for the maximum number of users. You may also find products that have a base price for a specific number of users and then "packages" of users added onto that (e.g., 5, 10, 25 users). Some may charge extra for features that are included for free in others. Therefore, you may need to do a little research before you know exactly how much it will cost.

When calculating the cost of the product, do not simply list the purchase price along with the cost of maintenance and any possible add-ons. Instead, you need to include all of the costs related to implementing that particular product, including the time it will take to install the product and customize it to suit your needs.

It is also important to calculate what you expect to gain or save by implementing the product. This helps determine if it is even worth implementing. When calculating the benefit the product will be, you need to be realistic. The productivity you gain during the first several weeks will probably be just a small percentage. It is not until your help desk staff has grown used to the product and has customized it to suit their needs that you begin to see substantial increase in productivity. Also keep in mind that it is entirely possible that productivity will actually drop during the first few weeks, and it will be several months before you see any substantial increase.

Choosing the right package at the beginning is extremely important due to cost and the danger of choosing the wrong tool. Even if you do not switch tools, but simply buy an additional product, the time spent switching between the different tools may end up being far more costly than having chosen the more expensive tool in the beginning.

Spend sufficient time evaluating each step of your current processes. Consider whether or not the process can be automated and whether or not it should be. This is important, because you should not become overly concerned with automation. I have seen cases where automating a task actually takes more time in the long run than was saved by automating that task.

In addition, you need to consider whether or not the current process is worth keeping. I worked in many places where they wasted a great deal of effort for single software to fit their existing processes, because it was these processes that were the problem. You should also consider implementing new processes that are not possible using your existing tools; for example, an email interface to the help desk software.

The most important aid for the help desk is an effective help desk suite. However, there are a great many more tools that you can employ to increase your efficiency even more. One thing you need to keep in mind is that you must not get carried away with tools and automation. That is, do not simply implement a particular software product to automate certain functions just to automate them. Like the help desk itself, there must be a visible ROI for whatever tool you decide to use.

Like tools in other contexts, the help desk tool is something that enables you to do something you cannot or enables you to do something more efficiently than you could before. For example, it is unlikely that all of your help desk staff remembers the hardware configuration of them leasing the machine. You needed something to keep track of this information for you. In this case, it may be something is simple as a loose-leaf binder listing all of the necessary information.

Part of picking a product that fits into your help desk model is choosing one that does not go overboard. You want the help desk software to assist you in solving problems and not to become a problem itself. You want the help desk software to speed up access to the information, not slow it down because it is too difficult to work with. On the other hand, you want a product that can grow with your needs.

Configurability

No two companies are exactly alike, so the ability to configure the software to meet your needs is extremely important. Saying that the help desk software is configurable can mean anything from simply changing the colors on the input screen to being able to change the internal structure or the underlying database. There are even some products that provide you with a type of scripting language, which enables you to react automatically to a wide range of events.

There are actually two aspects of configurability that you will find at different levels in different software products. The first is the ability to change the outward appearance of the product. Here, I am not just talking about being able to change the colors and fonts that are used. Instead, I am referring to things like the placement of buttons or input fields on the various forms.

At first, this may seem like a rather mundane issue, but the layout of the input screens can have a dramatic effect on your proficiency. For example, in many cases, I find it easier to move between fields using the tab key so that I do not have to take my hands off the keyboard to move around. I have seen many cases where the fields I need are spread out across the screen. It is very useful for me to move all of the fields I used together and put them in the order that is most appropriate for the information I want to keep track of. The other fields are either moved to a different place on the screen or I simply remove them.

This can actually be taken one step further, in that the configuration of the screen can also include adding fields from different tables. For example, some products may have one screen to manage problems and another to manage assets. You may want to have both of these on the same screen. The question then arises whether or not the software is configurable to this extent.

Some products go even further and allow you to change the underlying database. It is entirely possible that there is information you wish to keep track of that was not foreseen by the developers of the help desk product. If you cannot add new fields or even new tables to the database, you are stuck with whatever the programmer thought of.

Logically, if you can make changes to the database, you will need to make changes to the forms to access the new fields and tables. Having this ability is not enough. You should investigate how easily it is done and to what extent you can limit users from making changes.

Here's the catch: Help desk products that are this configurable are typically much more expensive than those where the most you can configure is your fonts and colors. However, even if you have a medium-sized company, this level of configurability is definitely worth considering. Here, you are making the trade-off between a feature that you absolutely need (configurability) and the cost of the product.

Database

One of the first places to look is the database that the help desk uses. A number of products at the low end of the scale use their own proprietary database format. Others may use an existing database format, such as dBase or Microsoft Access and VisualFoxPro. At the high end, you'll find SQL databases, such is MS SQL, Informix, and Oracle.

Keep in mind that in many cases, running on top of these enterprise-level databases means that you may be required to pay the license for the database *plus* the help desk software. You therefore need to consider that in the total cost of the help desk package. Which database is right for you will depend on a number of factors.

The first thing to consider it is how many people will be accessing the database at the same time. For example, if you have just a single person inputting problems into the database and this only once or twice daily, then it does not make sense to invest in a large SQL database. On the other hand, if you have dozens of people inputting information simultaneously, then one of the low-end products that uses a small single file as its database probably won't be able to keep up.

One very useful characteristics is Open Database Database Connectivity (ODBC) support. If the help desk uses wider and access or SQL database, then this is not a problem. Sometimes it is useful to generate in trees in one more of the tables from an outside source. This is only possible if there is some interface to the database such as ODBC.

Knowledge Base

Obviously, the purpose of the help desk is not to simply record problems. As obvious as it may seem, one vital aspect is following the problems. To this goal, people on your help desk end up becoming "walking encyclopedias." That is, they are not only called on to solve problems but also to answer the full spectrum of computer-related problems (Just how safe is home banking?).

This is not necessarily a bad thing. Although your general manager might think that the purpose of your IS department is to solve computer problems as they relate to the business, solving many *personal* computer problems can be very important for the morale of the company.

If the people on your help desk are considered "walking encyclopedias," then you must have some mechanism for them to store and retrieve pieces of information. That is, it is important that they be able to find the right answer as opposed to knowing the right answer off the top of their heads. One advantage of this is that the users will be able to draw on this information themselves. So this is where the help desk's "knowledge base" comes into play. In essence, a knowledge base is the collective knowledge of the help desk, both past and present. In addition to this, a number of external sources of information can be links to your help desk.

One important aspect is the speed at which you access the solutions. The primary goal of the help desk is to save time by providing information faster. If the information is recorded in the help desk software, but you take too long to get to it, the help desk is not fulfilling its purpose.

The more products you support, the more problems you have. Repeat problems occur less frequently and therefore the average time to resolution increases. In such cases, it is extremely important that your help desk software simplify problem management and access to solutions. The more products you have, the less likely you'll find people who are proficient with all of them. As a result, the people running your help desk will end up spending more time looking for the solution. The more efficient the search mechanism needs to be.

Coupled with this is the speed at which you need to supply the answer. As I mentioned before, it is much easier to tell internal users they need to wait for the solution. Unfortunately, this does not apply to people on the road, such as a mobile sales force. If, for example, they are unable to get important information from the company headquarters, it could mean a lost sale.

Then there is the level of expertise of your users. On the one hand, more-experienced users are a good thing because they can solve a lot of problems on their own. On the other hand, when they do need to call the help desk, you can bet the problem will be uncommon and much more difficult to solve. This means you need to find out fairly quickly whether a solution for this problem already exists. This means being able to search through all of the problems fairly quickly.

Also consider the level of expertise of your help desk staff. As we discussed previously, you don't need to experience high turnover. If you do or your help desk is at the bottom of the ladder, you might have relatively inexperienced people on the help desk. This means they will naturally take longer to solve problems, which in turn means access to the solution needs to be faster.

Keep in mind that the knowledge base should contain both technical and nontechnical information. Technical references are quite simply sources of technical information. Here I am not referring to those references that are directly used to solve problems. For example, the jumper settings for your motherboard is something you probably do not need every day. However, you may need it someday, so it is worthwhile to keep track of. Granted, such information might as well be put into the knowledge base, but there is no pressing need to make the effort to do so.

Nontechnical references are sources of information that are more related to the administrative aspects of the help desk; for example, home telephone numbers, vacation plans, and similar information. Once again, it would be useful if this information was in a knowledge base or in some other way administered by your help desk software, but it is not the requirement. Nontechnical information might also be the telephone numbers and contact information regarding the services the help desk does not provide. For example, cleaning the keyboard that some user spilled coffee on may be the responsibility of some other department.

Having the information is only half the battle. You need to *find* it as well. No two users are alike, and no two problems are alike. It may be necessary to search for the answer to specific problems in different ways depending both on the problem and the person looking for the solution. For example, if you know the answer to a particular question exists within a specific Word document in a specific directory, you could very quickly navigate through the different levels of subdirectories until you found the document you are looking for. This process is called drilldown, as you start at the top and drill down to subsequent layers until you find what you are looking for. To find solutions to problems on the help desk, most help desk software provides a similar mechanism. Problems and solutions are grouped together by specific criteria starting at the top, showing your way down to the bottom.

Should you know the name of the document but not exactly where it resides in the file system, then drilldown may not be the most efficient means of finding the document. First, you start in one directory and drill down several levels, only to discover the document is not there. You then start in another directory and drill down, only to discover the file is not there either. Since you know the name of the document you can tell Windows to look for it itself. If necessary, you can even tell Word to look through every hard disk attached to your system. This is a *keyword search,* as you are looking for the set of words that someone else finds as being important to this file, such as its name. Depending on the speed of your hard disk and a number of files you need to look through, a keyword search like this may be slower than drilling down to the location if you already know where the answer is. However, if it is unclear where a file resides the search can do it much faster.

Keyword search functionality is available basically with every product that provides any kind of search mechanism. In most cases, you can even search for fairly complicated combinations of words and phrases, combining them in different ways, using AND, OR, and NOT.

Note that many word processing applications as well as help desk applications allow you to input the keywords yourself. A keyword search's advantage is that you do not need to search through the entire document. However, people often think about the problem in different ways, so the keywords they choose may be different. This can make the search harder. Some products have recognized this and allow you to create a table of synonyms. You input "floppy" in your search and it finds the correct solution, even though the original analyst used "diskette."

If you know something about its contents, such as specific words that the document contains, you can do a full text search in order to find the document in question. Since you need to look through every single document, the full text search can take a substantial amount of time. You can obviously limit the search so that the system only looks through documents or other types of files. However, the full search method takes a lot more time than either the keyword search or drilldown.

Most high-end help desk products provide additional mechanisms to search for answers. One way is doing a statistical analysis of each documented find. In this way, the program calculates the likelihood that any given document is the one you are looking for. Among the criteria that such search mechanisms use is whether or not the search phrase or part of the phrase appears in a title, how frequently the words appear in the text, and just how close together the words appear. For example, if a particular set of words that you are looking for appears in the title of the document, there is a greater likelihood that this is the document you need.

Expert systems are basically sets of rules that lead to a particular goal. For example, if the baby is crying and the diaper is wet then change the diaper. If the baby is crying and it is been more than three hours since the baby has eaten, then feed the baby. Both of these start with the same condition (the baby is crying) but have other conditions that lead to different tasks.

The same thing applies to computer problems. The initial condition might be that the printer won't print. An additional condition might be that the power cable has been pulled out. This leads to the task of plugging the cable back in. If the other condition was that no other printer in that room can print either, it might lead to the solution that there is something wrong with a print server.

Case-based reasoning is a method by which previous occurrences (or cases) are evaluated to see how well they fit the current situation. The greater the fit, the more likely that it fits the current problem. If it doesn't fit, the system evaluates the differences between the two cases in order to learn and provide new solutions.

Look to see if you can use natural language when describing the problem. For example, "the printout contains black streaks." This functionality is already present in advanced word processing systems such as WordPerfect. Basically, you type in a phrase, even as a question, and the search engine makes a determination of what you are looking for. The key is that you can use natural sentence structure to input your query.

Also look to see how well the knowledge base integrates into existing documentation. Many products allow you to create links to external files such as word processing documents. This saves you the time of not having to convert the document or store it in multiple locations.

Some help desk products take this one step further by providing connectivity to other knowledge base systems, such as Microsoft TechNet, KnowledgeBroker, and Micro House. This may be as simple as having a button on the help desk toolbar that starts the other application. However, in some cases, the problem description is imported as a query to the other application, which makes searching much quicker.

Hardware/Software Inventory

Both hardware and software inventories are definite musts for any product you implement. There are some products on the market where the inventory is contained in a separate module from the help desk. Being a separate module means you have to pay extra for it. Generally, if the asset management is contained in a separate module, it goes beyond more than just which hardware and software are installed on any given system. You generally have the ability to manage warranty and maintenance information along with contact information for the respective vendors.

All of the higher level help desk products store their information in a standard format, such as an SQL database. Many of the commercial asset tracking products also store their information in an SQL database. Therefore, if the help desk product you decide on does not have its own asset tracking module, it is beneficial to look at those products that store their information using the same database.

Asset tracking is more than just keeping track of the serial numbers of the product you have. The product must be able to keep track of who the product is assigned to, applicable license information, as well as the warranty or support status of the product. It is extremely useful when getting a problem call to be able to look up in a database to find out whether a particular product is still under warranty.

If repair of the PC is not the job of the help desk, you might think it is not necessary to have an asset management module within the help desk software. However, as I mentioned before, both groups should have access to the same tool and therefore access to the same information. It may be that the hardware and software information is managed by another group, but the help desk still has access to it. If, for example, certain problems are related to specific hardware, it becomes exceedingly difficult to track down the problem if the help desk does not have access to the hardware information.

Integration with Other Tools

I know of a number of companies that implemented other tools before they bought a help desk product. These tools had become well ingrained in the minds of the support staff and a great amount of time was spent configuring them. It was not practical to get rid of them and implement a new tool.

How the product integrates into your existing environment not only applies to operating system network protocols, existing applications, and so forth, but also to the entire help desk model. If your help desk model is based on user self-help, the help desk software should support this. For example, does the help desk product provide the interface for the users to the problem solution database? Some products allow you to send an email message to the help desk, which searches the problem-solution database and sends an appropriate solution. If the help desk is Web based, your users need to be able to search the database themselves using a standard Web browser. Keep in mind, however, you may need to pay extra for this functionality.

Many products give you the ability to start external applications. For example, it is often necessary to access the Windows NT User Manager to reset a user's password or start the Server Manager to look for problems. Rather than having to look through your menus, these programs can be started directly from the help desk. Some products take this even further by incorporating external applications within solutions to problems. For example, if the solution is to unlock the user's account, there will be a link from the solution to the User Manager.

Sometimes the solution requires more than just starting a particular program. For example, a call might be opened to request creation of a new user account. Some products provide a script language that can create the user, add the user to specific groups, create and share the home directory, and many other functions, all by simply pressing the button within the help desk.

Call Management

If tracking the calls themselves (as opposed to tracking problems) is important to you, you need to see how well the product automates this task. The first aspect of this is how quickly you can end problems when the call arrives. One way this could be sped up is by having supplemental fields filled automatically. For example, all you would need to do is to input the user's login name and the program fills in the rest. I have seen at least one program where you begin typing the user's name and as soon as the name can be uniquely identified, the rest is filled in automatically.

Each product I have seen creates a unique problem number for each incoming call. This is a *must*. However, there is often a great deal of variance in what else can be recorded. At a minimum this should include:

- real name
- login name or ID
- contact information (department, telephone, email address)
- analyst taking the call
- date call opened
- date call closed
- priority of the call
- subject of the problem
- problem description
- problem resolution
- session notes
- hardware and software information

How much of this information the analyst needs to input themselves will depend a great deal on the software. This does not mean just what fields are available to the analyst but also how the fields interrelate. For example, you may have a table consisting of just user information. By inputting the user's login name, the remaining information, such as real name, contact information, and so forth are automatically included. There might be a table containing information about each machine, such as which hardware and software are installed. All you need to do is input the computer ID, and the rest is filled in automatically.

Although not always necessary, I find it useful if there is an easy way to access the call history of the user who is calling. First, it helps to identify a specific problem the user has with certain software. Second, it helps catch users who try to open multiple calls on the exact same problem in the hopes of getting a faster response. If only a single person is taking calls, this is not an issue, but if you have several people, I know users who call in again when the analyst says they need to "research" the problem and will call back. The user is hoping that the next analyst knows the answer without having to look for it.

This *might* not be a bad thing. Remember, your goal is to solve users' problems. If a user wants to spend the time of calling in again, you might want to let them. If the second analyst does, in fact, know the answer, they will see it in the user's history and can mark the call closed.

Also investigate to what extent each of the different steps is recorded. For example, it is not sufficient just to record which analyst is currently working on the particular problem. It is also useful to know who opened the call originally and what other analysts have worked on the call before, what they did to solve the problem, and so forth. If you are the fifth analyst who worked on the problem, you don't want to waste time repeating the work someone else did. Therefore, having a record of who did what is extremely useful.

Any time a change is needed, such as reassigning, changing priority, and so forth, there needs to be an entry in the database. I know people who just love to reassign all calls, because it either makes their statistics look good or they simply do not want to be bothered with the call. If this kind of information is tracked, analysts are less likely to hand off calls without reason.

As we discussed in the previous chapter, it might be useful to define different priorities for the call. Therefore, you should see to what extent different priorities are possible within the help desk software. This goes beyond just having a field where you set the priority. Admittedly, setting priorities is available almost universally. However, what is done with these priorities is different. For example, some products simply let you sort problems by priority so you can immediately identify those with a high priority. On the other hand, there are many products that generate activity depending on the priority, such as sending email to a supervisor when a problem is overdue.

Part of call management is to escalate the calls. Therefore, you need to investigate how well or how easy it is to escalate calls from within each product. This functionality is provided by even the simplest help desk products, in that you can simply reassign a problem to a different analyst. Others provide mechanisms by which different actions are taken in different circumstances. Maybe the problems can be reassigned automatically or possibly just have their priority changed.

Managing the Help Desk Staff

If the help desk software is designed for more than one user, you will need some kind of user management within the software. On one end of the scale, this is simply a list of all help desk users, so their names can be added to the call in order to keep track of who is working on it. On the other end, there are some fairly complex user management mechanisms, such as managing contact information, permissions, schedules, and so forth.

The larger the help desk, the greater the need for all of that additional information. If your help desk is small enough, having the contact information on the help desk might not be necessary. However, permissions definitely are worth considering. For example, it may be necessary to create different input forms for different groups. You may not want the analysts themselves changing the screens, so you want a way to prevent them from making changes. Perhaps you do not want the front-liners to schedule calls directly to the experts, but rather to a group of users.

Some of the better products do allow you to define different groups. This can be as simple as just front line and back line, or you can even create groups based on products. In many cases, you need to log on to the help desk (such as when you have concurrent licensing). The username you use to log on determines the groups you belong to, what permissions you have, and so forth. Problem assignments can then be made to the different groups or even specific users.

Another important aspect is a schedule. It does little good to assign a call to an analyst who is on vacation. Therefore, the product should inform you if you try to assign a call to someone who is not there. This can even go to the extent of breaking down the schedule into individual hours. If, for example, a particular user is there, but is not on the phone for another 3 hours, you do not want to assign a call due in 1 hour.

Effective User Interface

Help desk software will be essentially useless if it cannot be used efficiently. A big part of this is the interface that is provided. One aspect is how intuitive the program is. Granted, there will be functions where you need to look in the manual. However, if you are doing this constantly, it decreases the usefulness of the program.

Also look to see if it fits known "standards" of behavior. For example, one help desk product that I looked at had a menu entry to exit the program in a very unusual place. With most programs I've ever seen running under Windows, the rightmost menu will be for help. However, with this program, the rightmost menu was to exit the program, whereas every other program has it under the "File" menu or something similar. Worse still was that it was not a pull-down menu in the normal sense. Rather, clicking the menu itself would exit the program. What was really annoying was that you are not asked if you want to exit the program or not. Clicking this menu option without so much as a "by your leave." Needless to say, when I was looking for help, I inadvertently shut down the program on a number of occasions. This was not a very effective use of my time.

Glaring lights can also reduce the efficiency of your help desk. I have noticed myself that I cannot pay as much attention in situations where a light is too bright. In addition, my eyes get tired faster. Also, if the lights are reflected off the monitors such that it makes it difficult to see the information on the screen, your users cannot work as efficiently. Granted, this problem can be solved if you can change the appearance of the product. However, that is not possible with every product.

Communication Tools

Communication tools cover a wide range of processes and refer to anything used to facilitate the flow of information. This flow can be between the help desk and other organizations or taking the communication within the help desk itself. Perhaps the most effective tool in this area is email. Email has become an almost indispensable tool in every company (at least in the United States), so why shouldn't it be used by the help desk staff to communicate? In many cases, email is so well integrated into the help desk software that users can submit problems via mail as well as search for solutions on their own.

The next step up from email is what is generally referred to as "groupware." As its name implies, groupware is software that is used within a group. Although email could fall within this category, groupware generally consists of more components. For example, the ability to post to a central location that everyone can read but is not sent to the users directly is generally considered one of the primary characteristics of groupware. Other functionality can include things like online discussions, such as what is available with Netscape Communicator. In many groupware products, the ability to carry on on-line conversation is possible with any number of participants simultaneously, unlike in chat that only allows two people to talk to each other.

The ability to post the message to a central location is similar to the old-fashioned white board. Even if you do not implement some kind of groupware product, I think the white board is a very worthwhile investment. Here I am not talking about a special kind of software, but an actual white board that you hang up on your wall. This is not only a good idea for your help desk but for your IT department as a whole. Your staff has a place to display all pertinent information in the location visible even before they log on.

One vital characteristic of the help desk software is its interface to your email system. This interface should actually go in both directions. That is, you should be able to automatically generate problem reports by sending include air. In addition, you should be able to generate answers to your customers directly from the help desk. Some products take this one step further and allow you to search the problem-solution database simply by submitting an email message.

An important part of your communication tools is the telephone systems you implement. Although you probably could not do without the telephone system in general, there are a number of aspects that are not required. For example, an automatic call distributor (ACD) is a mechanism by which users can help you distribute and manage the calls. For example, when the user calls in to the help desk, they are presented with a menu, the answers to which help direct the call. If all of your help desk staff are currently working on other calls, the ACD can place users into a queue, usually on a first-come, first-served basis. Some ACD systems are so well integrated with the help desk software that the user can input his or her user or customer ID and the call is directed accordingly. For example, which queue the user ends up in may depend on the department they are in or the service contract they have.

Depending on your needs, you can get an ACD system that is as simple as just distributing the call to the next available analyst. On the other end of the scale, an ACD device system can have several different levels of menus that are completely programmable and that maintain the very-detailed statistics on the number of calls, wait times, and even the number of calls that hang up before they reach an analyst (drops).

I have also encountered ACD products that had a limit on the number of calls they could handle. Each queue had a limited number of slots and any calls beyond that number simply disappeared. To prevent annoying users and potentially losing customers, you need to look at a product that can handle your peak call load.

If you determine you need more than a simple call direction mechanism, such as the need for a menuing system, you need to see how well your current call routing procedures can be implemented. The support business is well understood today. It is not unreasonable to require that your ACD system be able to match your call routing and procedures exactly. I'm willing to bet that if you cannot find an ACD system that is capable of matching your current procedures, then your current procedures are far too complicated.

The functionality you can expect to get includes multiple levels of branching or menus as well as the ability to automatically switch between many schemes at different times of the day. For example, you may have one set of menus during normal business hours that direct the call based on product and then have different menus during the off-hours, which simply direct calls based on an emergency or nonemergency basis.

The next thing to look at is the user interface. This includes interfacing with a unit in taking support calls as well as interfacing with the unit to program or administer. An important physical characteristic is the ability to attach the headset to the unit on the user's desk. Having your hands free when talking to users is an incredible advantage that should not be underestimated.

Another aspect is the information that can be displayed to each user. For example, can the ACD display information on how many users are waiting and in which queue? I used one product that had a light on the phone unit itself. If no one was in the queue, the light was off. Less than five people in the queue, the light was green. Between five and ten, the light was orange. Over 10, the light was red. In addition, this ACD had a software interface that allowed you to monitor all of the queues, and you could switch the use as the number of waiting calls changed.

Part of this interface is the ability to get statistics, as I previously mentioned. The question is whether or not the unit can deliver the information that is unique. Supplemental to this is the ability to monitor the current state of the ACD system. It's impossible for a supervisor or someone else to see which of the help desk staff are currently taking calls, how many calls are waiting, the number of calls taken so far that day, and so forth. As with the menu system, it's important to find out to what extent this information can be customized.

In many cases, a very simple substitute for an ACD is an answering machine. An answering machine is very valuable for nonemergency calls during off-hours. For example, you may have a number of users who worked late, but the help desk only provides services during normal business hours. Should a user encounter a problem, they can leave a message on the answering machine. Email may be a more-efficient means of communication in these cases, but it is worth the $50 for those cases where someone calls the help desk only to find it is no longer staffed.

Answering machines can also be extremely useful in the case of major system failures, when a large number of calls are expected. For example, if your database server were to go down, you can expect large number of calls. The answering machine can explain the situation and give an estimate of when the problem is expected to be corrected.

Some commercial software has the ability to automatically send an email message to the originator when the call is closed. This has the same kind of psychological effect as the problem number. Although it may not be necessary, the user has a sense of closure with the issue. In addition, if the analyst thinks the call is closed, but the user does not, this message would serve to show that there was a misunderstanding. Without it, the analyst thinks it is closed and does nothing more. The user keeps on waiting for a response that will never come.

Part of this is "multiple paths" to the help desk. Many products provide other means of generating reports than simply calling the help desk and having the analyst type in all of the necessary information. Even if the product does not have a mechanism to query the database via email, it is possible if not likely that you can submit problem reports via email. This is extremely useful for low-priority calls, which can be addressed as time permits.

Managing External Support

You may have problems that you cannot solve internally. This forces you to call some other company, such as the software or hardware vendor. It is extremely important that you do not lose the connection between your internal problem report and the call to the other company. If you have just a single person running your help desk, it may be easy for them to remember. However, as the number of employees and therefore the number of problems increase, being able to associate internal calls with external calls becomes increasingly important.

•••••••••••••••

In addition, knowing what external calls you have is important for statistical purposes. First, it may help you justify the expense of the external support contract. Repeated calls to the vendor on specific problems may also indicate a bug or other problem with that vendor's product. Unless you have a record of the problem and what external calls it generated, it is almost impossible to make that kind of determination.

Monitoring and Evaluating

All of the high-end help desk products make the work of monitoring and evaluating the success of your help desk much easier. All have sophisticated reporting mechanisms, and some will even allow you to immediately access the current statistics as well as allow you to create ad hoc views into the help desk database.

Because it is useful to see what the current call load looks like, how well particular analysts are doing, and so forth, the reporting facilities within the help desk product may be an important aspect. Many products have a number of predefined reports, which are useful in a number of different cases. However, just like the product itself, the reports need to be configurable. That is, you should have the ability to define your own reports, both in terms of what is reported and how they are displayed.

Without a good reporting mechanism, you can quickly become lost in a sea of data. A good reporting mechanism is therefore an essential help desk product. The low-end products will typically provide their own reports for you, if they provide any at all. On the other hand, the more-expensive products may include a reporting mechanism such as Crystal Reports. Should the vendor go to the trouble of providing you something like Crystal Reports, you should expect a fairly large number of available reports. For example, expecting two or three dozen different kinds of reports is not unreasonable.

The Vendor

Most vendors I have seen will either provide a demo or an evaluation version of their product. A demo is good because it provides a quick overview of the product. Although it is tantamount to judging a book by its cover, looking at the demo and deciding you don't like the way it looks is a reasonable choice. If a product is not aesthetically pleasing, it may be harder to use.

Getting an evaluation version of the product is much more time consuming, but you are in a better position to see what the product can really do. I think it is a good idea that once you have narrowed down the field of possible choices, install the evaluation version to be able to make the right choice. As far as I have seen all have a predefined database that allows you to test the functionality without having to input all of the data yourself.

Once the product is installed, pay careful attention to how easy it is to use. Here, were not only talking about the ease of moving from field to field or from screen to screen, but also how intuitive the interface is in general. If you are constantly referring back to the manual or on-line help to figure out how to perform basic functions, you would be better served by looking for a different product. If the help desk product is not easy to use, you may end up having to free a special function within the help that just answers questions about the help desk software.

As with the help desk software itself, you need to look at who is the vendor. The vendor should be able to provide you customers and in many cases contact information. If at all possible, talk to people in other companies who have implemented similar software.

In addition, it is not unreasonable to expect the vendor to answer a questionnaire. You'll be investing several thousand if not tens of thousands of dollars in the product. You want to make sure you're getting the best product for your money. On the other hand, the vendor wants to make a sale and will be willing to take the right steps to make that sale. In addition, you can reasonably expect to get an evaluation copy of the software. The company may send you the full version of the product that simply stops working after a particular length of time. Others will send you a product that has no time limit but simply send you an invoice after 60 days.

Keep in mind, however, that a test version of the software is not necessarily a good thing. You may spend several days testing a product only to discover it is missing one feature you have determined as absolutely necessary. If you had sent a questionnaire to the vendor prior to requesting the evaluation copy, you could have saved yourself a great deal of time.

Also, look to see what licensing policies the vendor has. Licenses could be done per user or per workstation. If done per user, the software will be capable of limiting access. There are also floating licenses, so you can buy enough for the maximum number of users of the software, regardless of where they are working.

The company itself is another consideration. See how long the vendor has been in business. Being new is not necessarily a bad thing, but there are probably fewer companies who use their product, so it may be harder to find references in your area. By knowing who else uses the product, you can get a general feeling for whether the product fits a company of your size. If all of the other companies are much smaller or much larger than yours, the product might not be useful for you.

You should also be careful not to just look at the age of the company but also at the age and history of the product. Take Network Associates as an example. It is a relatively young company compared with other large help desk vendors. However, it combined the technologies available in two of the most successful help desk products (from McAfee and Magic Solutions). You would do yourself a disservice if you were to avoid them simply because the company as an entity has only existed for a short time.

Also look at the training and support offered for the product. Although most vendors will offer at least six-months free tech support, you can generally expect to pay for training. In some cases, you need to go to a central training facility, while other companies do the training at your site. This is generally more expensive and borders on consultant services, as they also help you configure the product to suit your needs.

Troubleshooting Lab

One thing that often is ignored is the ability to recreate the user's environment. In one company I worked for, the help desk staff was so anxious to have the latest and greatest that they all installed Windows NT as soon as it was available. The problem was that most of the users were used to a running Windows for Workgroups. Often the user would call with a particular problem, and it was impossible for the help desk to solve that problem as they did not have the same system in front of them. This applies not only to the operating system but to the applications as well.

Being able to recreate every environment can require a lot of hard disk space. If you're a vendor, the solution is to limit the number of previous releases that you support. If you're working on an internal help desk, you can achieve the same goal by limiting the number of products you support. By this I do not mean you flat-out refuse to support certain products. However, you should limit the number of products your company uses. This has the added advantage that it reduces administrative costs to administer.

Another solution is to simply consider the likelihood that a particular configuration will be needed. So if it is extremely unlikely that someone will call with a particular configuration (perhaps they have a very old version of the software), you should look at how long it would take to recreate the environment from scratch. You might then say it is not worth the time and effort to manage this particular configuration when recreating from scratch can be so costly.

Alternatively, you could maintain various configurations on tape or other media. Should you need to create a particular environment, it would then be a fairly simple task.

Help Desk Products

Knowledge Bases

One of the biggest problems when you first implement a help desk is that it appears to take more work to administer and maintain than you save by providing fast answers. Unfortunately, that is the nature of the help desk.

One place you can save a great deal of time is in building up a problem-solution database. There are a number of products on the market that provide you with prebuilt databases, some of which can connect directly to your help desk application.

ASK.ME PRO

One such product is ASK.ME Pro from KnowledgeBrokers, which comes in three variations to suit you needs. A key aspect of ASK.ME Pro is that technically it is just a front-end to the data. The actual knowledge bases are modular, so you can install just the products you need.

In addition, there are a number of database suites, which contain the solutions to problems for a wide range of products. As of this writing, the three suites are: MS Office, Lotus Smart Suite and Corel WordPerfect Suite. Each has problems and solutions for the respective office suites, the various Microsoft operating systems, and a number of hardware topics. In addition, there are databases for Novell, OS/2, and the Internet. You can also order the database for each application separately.

Figure 16–2 shows you the main ASK.ME Pro window. On the left side is the list of available databases. By selecting an area, a list of applicable problems appears in the right window, called the "Topic Browser." In the middle are three buttons indicating the type of query you have. At the top is a button for error messages. When this is selected, a list of error messages

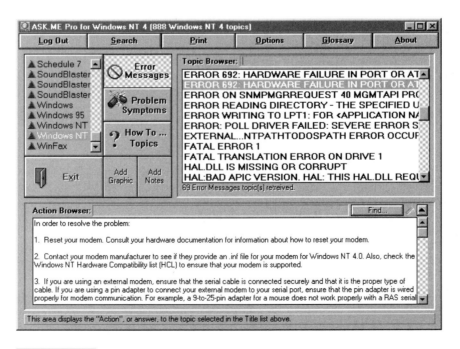

FIGURE 16–2   SupportSource main window.

will appear in the right window. In the middle is a button for problem symptoms. The right window will then show you a list of common problem descriptions. The bottom button is for "How-to" questions.

When you click on the description in the right window, the large window at the bottom of the screen (called the "Action Browser") displays the solution to the problem or the steps to take to perform the desired action. Most responses are small enough that you do not have to do much scrolling. However, you can make the Action Browser full-screen by clicking the arrow on the right side of the Action Browser. If there is still too much text, you can search within this window.

Looking for particular solutions is not just limited to looking through lists. Instead, ASK.ME Pro has a built-in mechanism to search for keywords. Using different options, you can search in the current title, all titles, or any combination. If you choose to search more than one title, the titles in which something was found are displayed in the title window.

If you do not find what you are looking for, ASK.ME Pro brings up a window of unresolved problems. This is extremely useful on a help, when you do not have the time to look for the solution. It is marked and you can then add the appropriate solution to the database when you can.

An interesting feature is called "HelpHunter," which will search any drives connected to the system (local and network) looking for help files. These are then made accessible in a list that you click on to load that particular help file. The list is updated by either starting the search process again or by adding specific entries by hand. If necessary, you can also add text files to the list. You can then search through any of the selected files for keywords that you input.

A solution database is of limited value if it cannot be expanded, and ASK.ME Pro allows you to expand in a couple of ways. First, you can add notes or graphics to existing solutions. Notes can then be searched, if you choose. That is, you can either search the existing solutions, your notes, or both. There is also a glossary of common computing terms that you can expand as needed.

In addition, you can add your own topics to the error messages, problem symptoms, or how-to sections using the KnowledgeBuilder. Here you can add entries to any existing topics as well as the ones provided with the product. You can later expand or change your own entries but not ones provided with the product. From here, you also have access to the list of unresolved problems, allowing you to simply write a solution and input it into the knowledge base. The KnowledgeBuilder also has several reporting features to give you, among other things, a list of the topics that were recently added, topics added by specific users, and so forth.

There are also several administrative functions available. For example, if you have ASK.ME Pro Custom or ASK.ME Pro Total, you can create your own knowledge-base titles. These are then accessible just like any other knowledge base, and you can distribute these custom entries to your internal users.

The administrator also has control over what functions particular users have. There are several predefined levels, and additionally, the administrator can select specific functions. For example, basic users might be able to just view the problems and solutions, more-advanced users can add entries, and only administrators can manage users and the databases.

In addition, you can also limit to which titles a user has access. For example, you can define a group of users who has MS Office and another that has MS Office Professional. Those with the standard version do not have access to the problem solutions for MS Access.

ASK.ME integrates into other products using Dynamic Data Exchange (DDE). A number of DDE functions are provided that allow you access to the knowledge bases from any application that supports DDE. In addition, there are a number of help desk products on the market that have, by default, access to the ASK.ME Pro databases.

At the entry level is the basic ASK.ME Pro. This is the standard knowledge base, which allows you to add solutions to existing titles, but not to add new titles. ASK.ME Pro Custom is one step up and allows you to add your own custom titles and even bundle these solutions with your own products.

ASK.ME Total provides all of the features of the others plus all of the available knowledge-base suites. In addition, it provides "HelpBases," which are read-only versions of the knowledge bases. These can be distributed to end users. It also includes System Viewer, which provides the users detailed information about their computer, which can be used to help solve problems or passed to the help desk staff should the users not be able to solve the problem themselves.

Support from KnowledgeBroker is not just limited to the knowledge bases on CD. They provide several different services to help you get your problems solved. First is ASK.ME OnLine, which provides on-line access to all of the knowledge bases. Since this database can be updated more often than the CDs can, you are assured of the most recent information. In addition, you can also submit problems via email and the KnowledgeBroker experts will then respond.

KnowledgeBroker also provides HelpNet, which is phone support for all of the same topics provided on the CDs. Support is available 24 hours a day, 7 days a week, on both 800 and 900 numbers. In addition to phone support, you also get access to email support. I find this extremely useful if your problem is not urgent and you don't want to deal with having to be on the phone with the technician. In addition, email provides a written record of the solution.

MICRO HOUSE

It wouldn't be quite right to call Micro House's SupportSource a problem-solution database as you could with many other products. Instead, it would be much more fitting to refer to it as a true "knowledge base." Although there are solutions to specific problems, the emphasis is on imparting knowledge and not just holding your hand through a predefined checklist. In my experience, this does not help you a long run, as you're not learning anything, just solving a problem.

SupportSource draws in knowledge of hundreds of companies, magazines, books, IT newsletters, and so forth. In many cases, you'll find complete copies of the articles, just as they appeared in the magazine or newsletter. This allows you to draw on the technical expertise of hundreds of authorities in the field of computers.

Most of this information is available from other sources—books and magazines. You may be asking yourself what the point is of getting this information from MicroHouse. The answer lies in the sheer magnitude of information available. There is anywhere from 150,000 to 200,000 entries on each CD, ranging from solutions to problems to detailed technical backgrounds on various topics.

The key is that you do not need to spend days, weeks, or even months scouting the Internet and stacks of magazines looking for this information. It is provided for you in one convenient source. Here I must emphasize the word "convenient," as accessing the information is incredibly easy.

I'll be honest and say that for the most part, I do not use SupportSource to find answers to specific problems. Instead, I use it much more frequently to research details about specific topics. In addition, I enjoy simply browsing through the numerous articles, looking for something that catches my eye.

As you can see in Figure 16–3, the SupportSource interface has a very distinct Windows look and feel about it. For those of you who have worked with Microsoft TechNet, you will be immediately familiar with the Support-Source interface. However, even without it, the interface is extremely intuitive as well as incredibly easy to use.

Like Microsoft TechNet, the main screen is broken in half. On the left side you have a Windows Explorer-like tree structure, which you can collapse and expand as needed. This is actually composed of two separate windows. The one we see here is the contents window. Clicking the tab labeled "history," you have a list of recently accessed articles. On the right-hand side you have the display window, which contains the content of the article. It also consists of two windows. Clicking on "summary" gives you details about that article, including specific products it is related to, the company that produced the article, where the article appears, the company's internal reference for the article, and so forth.

Actually, SupportSource is simply the interface to the articles. The articles themselves are packaged in what are referred to as "knowledge modules." When you load one of these knowledge modules into the Support-Source environment, it will appear in the contents window along with the other modules you have already installed.

There are four knowledge modules that you can purchase. Support on site for Networks obviously deals with networking topics. Support on site

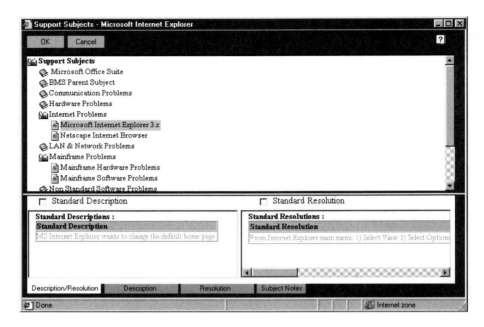

FIGURE 16-3   ASK.ME Pro main window.

for Applications covers a wide range of applications from most of the major vendors. Support on site for Hardware addresses hardware issues. The Micro House Technical Library is more of a reference work in that it provides the technical specifications on a wide range of products. This also includes the technical specifications of thousands of products, from mainboards to hard disks, networks, and beyond. This includes detailed diagrams, showing jumper and switch settings as well as other configuration information.

Make some products that run exclusively from the CD, SupportSource the view five different levels of optimization. With no optimization, only the program files are copied to the hard disk. This only takes up about 10 MBs, but results in the slowest response time. Full optimization means that everything (including indexes and documents) is copied to the hard disk and will take up over 600 MBs. If you have the hard disk space, this obviously has the fastest response time.

During installation you have the choice of one of three modes. Stand-alone is when you're not going to be providing access to the information from anywhere else other than this single workstation. You can also install it on a server, making it available to others on your network. Finally, you can install it as a client to access the information on the server. Note that a separate license needs to be obtained for each user accessing the software. You can also choose to just install specific subsets rather than the entire modules.

I have often encountered problems with products that are distributed on multiple CDs, because they expect both CDs to be in the same drive. Although workstations with multiple CD-ROM drives are not too common, it is a very common to find servers weighted dozens of CD-ROM drives. Why do some companies make it so hard to be able to access all of the CDs at the same time?

MicroHouse addresses this issue by allowing you to configure where each of the directories is located. It is therefore possible to specify different CD-ROM drives for each of the different modules. It is also possible to spread out the various files to optimize access. For example, you could store all of being documents on the central server, load the indices from the local hard disk, while pulling images off of a CD-ROM.

SupportSource is not a static tool, which only allows you to access the information MicroHouse provides. Instead, SupportSource Service as a Web browser, allowing to gather information from the Internet.

Browsing is not the only way to find the information you need. First, you can provide keywords in the "Search for" field, which will look through the articles for these words and phrases. SupportSource also provides a Query Assistant, which helps zero in quickly on the exact information.

Figure 16–4 shows you the Query Assistant with information filled in for a query on Seagate hard drives. At the top, you see several tabs for different

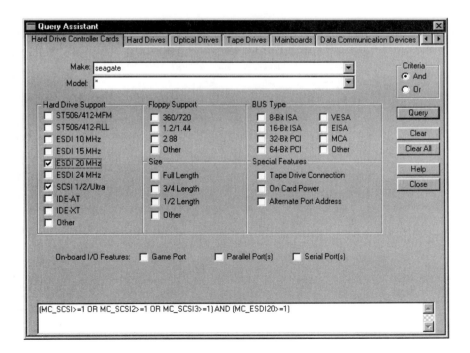

FIGURE 16–4   SupportSource Query Assistant.

kinds of hardware. At the far right are arrow keys, which allow you to move back and forth among the parents for the various kinds of hardware. There are just so many different kinds of hardware devices, it would be impossible to list all of them at once and still be able to quickly find what you are looking for.

Research options will depend on the type of device you are looking for. In this case, you can choose to look for specific capacities, average seek time, form factor, and so forth. If you want to search for motherboards, you would be able to look for this beat, BIOS, number of each kind of slot, and so forth. If you're searching in other modules, the search criteria will be different. For example, if looking for a specific article, you can search for specific publication types, publisher, range of publication dates, and so forth.

If you looking at the bottom of Figure 16–4, you will see the text equivalent of the search criteria that I inputted above. This is an example of the relatively simple, but extremely effective, query language that SupportSource provides. Although it does take a little getting used to, particularly in terms of searching for specific fields, you can come up with some fairly complex greets.

In addition to Boolean constructs such as <and>, <or>, and <not>, this query language also provides proximity operators that allow you to specify how close the words and phrases need to appear in the text. For example,

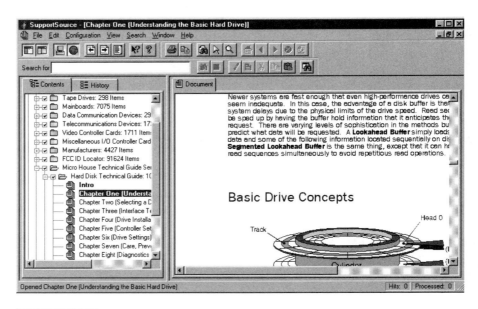

FIGURE 16–5   Example SupportSource Article.

....

the <paragraph> operator would require that two terms exist within the same paragraph.

Magic Total Service Desk

The Magic Total Service Desk (Magic TSD) from Network Associates, Inc. (NAI) is the unification of two of the most powerful and wide-spread help desk products: Magic Solution's Support Magic and McAfee's Total Service Desk. This put an end to the battle of which of these two products to implement.

I need to start off by saying that Magic TSD is not for every company. For smaller companies, it is probably more than they need. However, I want to emphasize the word "probably." Because of NAI's aggressive licensing scheme, you could implement it with just a couple of licenses and still get a very good return on your investment. In addition, the basic functionality is extremely intuitive and does not require any additional training. Therefore, for these functions it is very much "plug-n-play."

Magic TSD is more than just the fusion of two existing help desk products, but builds on new technologies to provide the next step up in help desk products. The core of the Magic TSD architecture is built on Microsoft's Windows Distributed interNet Applications (Windows DNA) architecture. Windows DNA is a multiuser, distributed application *model* that combines client-server applications in local networks and the Internet with modular application components.

One key aspect is that the Windows DNA architecture is multitiered compared with the single- or two-tiered models in previous generations of client-server applications. Windows DNA is organized around three layers, which represent the presentation or client layer, the business logic layer, and the data layer.

The client layer is what the user sees; in general, the user does not really care what goes on behind the scenes. Instead, users want the information presented in a way they can use efficiently. In addition, if new technologies are introduced to view the information, there is no need to completely rewrite the application.

The business logic layer is typically a set of rules that determine how a particular process flows or is carried out. In a help desk, this could be the rules that govern how high-priority calls are handled. Finally, the data layer contains the actual data. The business rules really do not care about how the data is stored, just what the data are. Because of this, each of these layers can exist as separate entities.

Components interact with each other using the Component Object Model (COM). This means that all of the components of Magic TSD use a common set of services and therefore do not need to include the functionality themselves. Since the interface is standardized, there is no "misunderstanding" or need to "translate" from one data type to another. Furthermore, the components are modularized, which makes repetition of code unnecessary and makes each module smaller.

Magic TSD is based on the Microsoft Internet Information Server (MIIS) and takes full advantage of MIIS's ability to process information dynamically through active-server pages. In addition, the forms used as the basis for the Magic TSD application take advantage of Dynamic HTML; the appearance of the form can be changed to fit the circumstances.

Because of the comparatively low price, Magic TSD is attractive to small businesses. Because it's based on MIIS, the Microsoft Transaction Server and MS SQL Server, you can support more than 1000 *concurrent* users, which is likely to be enough for even the largest help desk organizations.

MSTD is completely browser based, which means you do not need to install the software on every machine. The only catch is that it requires MS Internet Explorer 4.0 with at least Service Pack 1. In addition, the Web pages used rely on JScript, which is Microsoft's own version of the standard JavaScript. As a result, there are many functions that are not supported by every browser. Fortunately, this is delivered with the product, but is a problem if you have decided on Netscape Communicator as your standard communication product.

CONFIGURABILITY

One of the key aspects is the configurability. Magic TSD is by far the most configurable product I have seen. This was one of the strong points of SupportMagic and was carried over into Magic TSD. Unfortunately, the configuration of the screen is not as simple as it was with SupportMagic. This is due to the fact that everything, even the configuration of Magic TSD, is done through a Web browser. The current state of the technology is not yet to the point where you can do everything through a browser that you can using a compiled program that is run locally.

Still, configuration is done through drag and drop of the various components, the same way it was done with SupportMagic. This is done with a patent-pending technology that gives you the ability to configure all aspects of the screens, including appearance, layout, and even which fields are included. This helps you fit the help desk to the models and processes you decide are right for your company. All through a Web browser.

The primary workspace of Magic TSD (Figure 16–1) is a normal browser window with a toolbar at the top. Like the forms, the toolbar can be configured as needed. Here you can link to specific modules within Magic TSD, other Web pages, and so forth.

Customization includes the ability to configure the database to any extent you see fit. That is, you can create new fields, tables, indexes, and views into the data. Figure 16–2 shows the database administrator, which you can see has not yet been converted to the Web interface but still has the old interface used by SupportMagic. However, here you can add tables, fields, create views, and so forth.

KNOWLEDGE BASE

Magic TSD provides a number of different ways of accessing the solutions to your problems. Figure 16–2 shows you the list of "support subjects." At the top of the screen are all of the various subjects to which problems and the solutions have been documented. This is laid out in a basic tree structure, and you use drilldown to find the specific topic. Selecting that topic displays a list of standard descriptions and standard resolutions for that topic. If either one of these fits the current problem, you click on OK and the text will automatically be transferred to the call screen. This includes the subject, problem description, and the problem resolution. It is also possible that the standard description for resolution applies, in which case you need to check the one box. Should none of them apply, you can simply add your problem description and resolution.

In addition, Magic TSD supports something called Statistical Information Retrieval (SIR). This takes the text you input in the problem description and uses it to search for any appropriate solutions. One nice thing is that you can use natural language to write the problem description, and the SIR search engine will analyze the text and search through the problems and solutions in your database. SIR can also search through a number of different third-party knowledge-base products such as those from KnowledgeBroker. Once configured, SIR will search through all of the sources you configure.

In addition, SIR can also be used for external documents, such as ones you have used greeted using the word processing program or something else. It would be possible to have a list of problem-solutions on your Internet, stored as HTML, and be able to access them directly from the help desk.

ASSET MANAGEMENT

Magic TSD has a number of different modules that fall under the head of asset management. This includes the ability to track both hardware and software and who each component has been assigned to. You can also create "configurations," which are a set of hardware and software items that are standardized. You then assign a single configuration to a machine without having to assign each item individually.

The Work Orders module allows you to create a repair or maintenance order for a particular inventory item. This can then be assigned to any group or user. Note that this does not need to be maintenance in the conventional sense. It might be used to initiate the installation of an update or new software or any similar function. (Although you *could* create a new form to do any of that.)

Each item in your inventory can be recorded, including the part and serial numbers, asset tag number, vendor ID, service contract information, where it is located, when it was installed, and even the financial information such as invoice number and date. When you search for a particular inventory item, you can look for any work orders open for that particular item as well as the service history.

Service contracts can also be managed from the same interface. Here you record basic information like the contract's number and ID, vendor ID, effective dates, what response times have been guaranteed, and so forth. When you search for a particular contract's number, you'll also see which inventory items fall under that contract. The reverse is also true. That is, if you look for a particular inventory item, you can also see the service contracts that apply. And, of course, Binder information can be managed as well.

INTEGRATION WITH OTHER TOOLS

Although Network Associates provides a number of system management tools, integration with Magic TSD is not just limited to the Network Associates products, such as Sniffer Total Network Visibility. Instead, Magic TSD integrates with a wide range of third-party monitoring tools, such as Tivoli, HP OpenView, Microsoft SMS, and Cisco Works 2000. In fact, integration is relatively easy with any product that supports network standards such as SNMP, SMTP, and MAPI.

Due to the modular architecture of Magic TSD, it is possible to integrate with other products by creating the necessary objects using a number of development tools, such at Microsoft Visual Basic or C++.

CALL MANAGEMENT

Call management is simplified by Magic TSD on several levels. The most obvious is the ease with which new problems can be added to the system. Taking the simple case where a user calls in with a standard problem and solution, the call number can be generated, the solution found and recorded, and then the call closed in under 30 seconds. (This, of course, will depend on the overall system performance.) Obviously, problems for which the solution is not immediately available will take longer to solve. However, the administration time is still reduced considerably.

Magic TSD takes this one step further by allowing you to create a template for problems or actions that are recurring and which contain the same information. Once the recurring template has been created, it becomes available from the action menu on the main screen.

Calls can be prioritized using the "escalation scheme." This simply says how fast the call must be responded to. Should a user have a particular escalation scheme assigned to them, this will automatically be filled in when you input the user's name. You can also assign a particular scheme later if you need to.

A useful feature is the Whiteboard, which Network Associates lists under the heading of "Problem/crisis management." The reason is that the whiteboard is intended for the posting of important information, which may have wide-spread effects, such as a down server. Calls that relate to this problem can be automatically linked to a whiteboard entry, which speeds up the data entry process. In addition, once the problem has been resolved, all linked calls will be closed automatically.

Magic TSD is also integrated with your mail system, so you can send messages about overdue calls and so forth, using either SMTP or MAPI.

Using the Event Orchestrator, Magic TSD can be configured to automatically generate calls when certain events occur. If so configured, messages can be sent to the appropriate analyst or group. This provides them with an advanced warning of problems so they might begin working on them before the first user calls. This provides *proactive* management of help desk problems, as compared to the *reactive* nature of many help desk products.

Event Orchestrator listens for SNMP traps, which is processed according to the rules you define. Therefore, any network node (server, workstation, router, etc.) that can generate SNMP traps can generate help desk calls automatically. Based on how you configure the system, the SNMP traps can result in any number of different actions.

In support of this is a "problem-sensitive" tool linking. This provides automatic access to a number of different tools, based on what problem was reported. For example, if the analyst needs remote control access to the user's desktop, you could start Network Associates' Remote Desktop 32, for example. Network problems could launch Network Associates' Sniffer Total Network Visibility.

Magic TSD has the ability to create Service Level Agreements (SLAs). Here you define rules by which the help desk is to provide service to the users (or customers). This includes a number of the issues we discussed in the previous chapter, such as the hours that support will be provided, reaction times, who is authorized to call, which products are supported, and so forth. Although you can have multiple SLAs, all with the same condition, you assign a single SLA to each client.

Magic TSD is provided with a copy of Crystal Reports with over 150 standard reports, which satisfy most people's needs. However, if you should want to, you can create your own custom reports either from scratch or by building on one of the predefined reports. The predefined reports include many that report the status of particular users or analysts, call loads for specific periods, most common calls, and so forth. In addition, you can choose to view only calls that are opened, closed, or both, and in most cases you can define a specific range of dates.

MANAGING THE HELP DESK STAFF

There are a large number of functions available for you to manage users. First, you need to have a user name and password to log on to the system. As of this writing, it is different from your Windows NT password, but it is stored in the SQL database, which provides the access to the necessary database functions.

Users can also be put together into groups. These groups can be used to define a number of different aspects of the system, including what actions each user can perform, which desktop (default screen) they are given, call assignments, and many other things. By default, there are three groups; one for external support and two for two different internal support tiers. These have their own default configurations, which you can change as needed or create your own groups. Users can appear in any number of existing groups.

Permissions are defined primarily on the database views. For each view, you can set permissions on the four main database functions: select (view), insert, update, and delete. Each can be permitted or denied individually for specific users or specific groups. For example, it would be possible that certain groups can read the whiteboard entries, but not to create them. In addition, there are a couple of special permissions, such as the ability to close calls or work orders.

Work schedules can be defined for specific users as well as the help desk as a whole. For example, you can define holidays that are valid for everyone on the help desk or even just specific groups or individuals. By default, there are holiday schedules defined for the United States and Canada, but you can create additional schedules, which is useful if you have support people in other locations.

Prentice Hall: Professional Technical Reference

| | | | | | | | | | | |
| Back | Forward | Reload | Home | Search | Guide | Images | Print | Security | Stop |

http://www.phptr.com/

Keep Up-to-Date with

PH PTR Online!

We strive to stay on the cutting-edge of what's happening in professional computer science and engineering. Here's a bit of what you'll find when you stop by **www.phptr.com**:

@ Special interest areas offering our latest books, book series, software, features of the month, related links and other useful information to help you get the job done.

☞ Deals, deals, deals! Come to our promotions section for the latest bargains offered to you exclusively from our retailers.

$ Need to find a bookstore? Chances are, there's a bookseller near you that carries a broad selection of PTR titles. Locate a Magnet bookstore near you at www.phptr.com.

! What's New at PH PTR? We don't just publish books for the professional community, we're a part of it. Check out our convention schedule, join an author chat, get the latest reviews and press releases on topics of interest to you.

✉ Subscribe Today! Join PH PTR's monthly email newsletter!

Want to be kept up-to-date on your area of interest? Choose a targeted category on our website, and we'll keep you informed of the latest PH PTR products, author events, reviews and conferences in your interest area.

Visit our mailroom to subscribe today! **http://www.phptr.com/mail_lists**

LICENSE AGREEMENT AND LIMITED WARRANTY

READ THE FOLLOWING TERMS AND CONDITIONS CAREFULLY BEFORE OPENING THIS SOFTWARE MEDIA PACKAGE. THIS LEGAL DOCUMENT IS AN AGREEMENT BETWEEN YOU AND PRENTICE-HALL, INC. (THE "COMPANY"). BY OPENING THIS SEALED SOFTWARE MEDIA PACKAGE, YOU ARE AGREEING TO BE BOUND BY THESE TERMS AND CONDITIONS. IF YOU DO NOT AGREE WITH THESE TERMS AND CONDITIONS, DO NOT OPEN THE SOFT WARE MEDIA PACKAGE. PROMPTLY RETURN THE UNOPENED SOFTWARE MEDIA PACKAGE AND ALL ACCOMPANYING ITEMS TO THE PLACE YOU OBTAINED THEM FOR A FULL REFUND OF ANY SUMS YOU HAVE PAID.

1. **GRANT OF LICENSE:** In consideration of your payment of the license fee, which is part of the price you paid for this product, and your agreement to abide by the terms and conditions of this Agreement, the Company grants to you a nonexclusive right to use and display the copy of the enclosed software program (hereinafter the "SOFTWARE") on a single computer (i.e., with a single CPU) at a single location so long as you comply with the terms of this Agreement. The Company reserves all rights not expressly granted to you under this Agreement.

2. **OWNERSHIP OF SOFTWARE:** You own only the magnetic or physical media (the enclosed software media) on which the SOFTWARE is recorded or fixed, but the Company retains all the rights, title, and ownership to the SOFTWARE recorded on the original software media copy(ies) and all subsequent copies of the SOFTWARE, regardless of the form or media on which the original or other copies may exist. This license is not a sale of the original SOFTWARE or any copy to you.

3. **COPY RESTRICTIONS:** This SOFTWARE and the accompanying printed materials and user manual (the "Documentation") are the subject of copyright. You may not copy the Documentation or the SOFTWARE, except that you may make a single copy of the SOFTWARE for backup or archival purpose only. You may be held legally responsible for any copying or copyright infringement which is caused or encouraged by your failure to abide by the terms of this restriction.

4. **USE RESTRICTIONS:** You may not network the SOFTWARE or otherwise use it on more than one computer or computer terminal at the same time. You may physically transfer the SOFTWARE from one computer to another provided that the SOFTWARE is used on only one computer at a time. You may not distribute copies of the SOFTWARE or Documentation to others. You may not reverse engineer, disassemble, decompile, modify, adapt, translate, or create derivative works based on the SOFTWARE or the Documentation without the prior written consent of the Company.

5. **TRANSFER RESTRICTIONS:** The enclosed SOFTWARE is licensed only to you and may not be transferred to any one else without the prior written consent of the Company. Any unauthorized transfer of the SOFTWARE shall result in the immediate termination of this Agreement.

6. **TERMINATION:** This license is effective until terminated. This license will terminate automatically without notice from the Company and become null and void if you fail to comply with any provisions or limitations of this license. Upon termination, you shall destroy the Documentation and all copies of the SOFTWARE. All provisions of this Agreement as to warranties, limitation of liability, remedies or damages, and our ownership rights shall survive termination.

7. **MISCELLANEOUS:** This Agreement shall be construed in accordance with the laws of the United States of America and the State of New York and shall benefit the Company, its affiliates, and assignees.

8. **LIMITED WARRANTY AND DISCLAIMER OF WARRANTY:** The Company warrants that the SOFTWARE, when properly used in accordance with the Documentation, will operate in substantial conformity with the description of the SOFTWARE set forth in the Documentation. The Company does not

arrant that the SOFTWARE will meet your requirements or that the operation of the SOFTWARE will be ninterrupted or error-free. The Company warrants that the media on which the SOFTWARE is delivered nall be free from defects in materials and workmanship under normal use for a period of thirty (30) days om the date of your purchase. Your only remedy and the Company's only obligation under these limited arranties is, at the Company's option, return of the warranted item for a refund of any amounts paid by you r replacement of the item. Any replacement of SOFTWARE or media under the warranties shall not extend he original warranty period. The limited warranty set forth above shall not apply to any SOFTWARE which he Company determines in good faith has been subject to misuse, neglect, improper installation, repair, lteration, or damage by you. EXCEPT FOR THE EXPRESSED WARRANTIES SET FORTH ABOVE, HE COMPANY DISCLAIMS ALL WARRANTIES, EXPRESS OR IMPLIED, INCLUDING WITHOUT IMITATION, THE IMPLIED WARRANTIES OF MERCHANTABILITY AND FITNESS FOR A PAR-ICULAR PURPOSE. EXCEPT FOR THE EXPRESS WARRANTY SET FORTH ABOVE, THE COM-ANY DOES NOT WARRANT, GUARANTEE, OR MAKE ANY REPRESENTATION REGARDING HE USE OR THE RESULTS OF THE USE OF THE SOFTWARE IN TERMS OF ITS CORRECTNESS, CCURACY, RELIABILITY, CURRENTNESS, OR OTHERWISE.

IN NO EVENT, SHALL THE COMPANY OR ITS EMPLOYEES, AGENTS, SUPPLIERS, OR ONTRACTORS BE LIABLE FOR ANY INCIDENTAL, INDIRECT, SPECIAL, OR CONSEQUEN-IAL DAMAGES ARISING OUT OF OR IN CONNECTION WITH THE LICENSE GRANTED UNDER HIS AGREEMENT, OR FOR LOSS OF USE, LOSS OF DATA, LOSS OF INCOME OR PROFIT, OR THER LOSSES, SUSTAINED AS A RESULT OF INJURY TO ANY PERSON, OR LOSS OF OR DAM-GE TO PROPERTY, OR CLAIMS OF THIRD PARTIES, EVEN IF THE COMPANY OR AN AUTHO-IZED REPRESENTATIVE OF THE COMPANY HAS BEEN ADVISED OF THE POSSIBILITY OF UCH DAMAGES. IN NO EVENT SHALL LIABILITY OF THE COMPANY FOR DAMAGES WITH ESPECT TO THE SOFTWARE EXCEED THE AMOUNTS ACTUALLY PAID BY YOU, IF ANY, FOR HE SOFTWARE.

SOME JURISDICTIONS DO NOT ALLOW THE LIMITATION OF IMPLIED WARRAN-IES OR LIABILITY FOR INCIDENTAL, INDIRECT, SPECIAL, OR CONSEQUENTIAL DAMAGES, O THE ABOVE LIMITATIONS MAY NOT ALWAYS APPLY. THE WARRANTIES IN THIS AGREE-IENT GIVE YOU SPECIFIC LEGAL RIGHTS AND YOU MAY ALSO HAVE OTHER RIGHTS WHICH ARY IN ACCORDANCE WITH LOCAL LAW.

ACKNOWLEDGMENT

YOU ACKNOWLEDGE THAT YOU HAVE READ THIS AGREEMENT, UNDERSTAND IT, ND AGREE TO BE BOUND BY ITS TERMS AND CONDITIONS. YOU ALSO AGREE THAT THIS GREEMENT IS THE COMPLETE AND EXCLUSIVE STATEMENT OF THE AGREEMENT ETWEEN YOU AND THE COMPANY AND SUPERSEDES ALL PROPOSALS OR PRIOR AGREE-IENTS, ORAL, OR WRITTEN, AND ANY OTHER COMMUNICATIONS BETWEEN YOU AND THE OMPANY OR ANY REPRESENTATIVE OF THE COMPANY RELATING TO THE SUBJECT MAT-ER OF THIS AGREEMENT.

Should you have any questions concerning this Agreement or if you wish to contact the Com-any for any reason, please contact in writing at the address below.

Robin Short
Prentice Hall PTR
One Lake Street
Upper Saddle River, New Jersey 07458

ABOUT THE CD

The accompanying CD-ROM contains a few HTML pages which serve as an simple interface to the demo software on the CD. Please note that the list of hardware vendors does not represent every possible type of hardware. Instead, the list reflects the material covered in *Supporting Windows NT & 2000 Workstation & Server*.

Contents

Thumbs Plus from Cerious Software. An extremely powerful graphics manipulation and management tool.

Diskeeper from Executive Software. A product that defragments your harddisk. Diskeeper also works on the NT Filesystem (NTFS).

Undelete from Executive Software. Undeletes files on a Windows NT system. Both Workstation and Server versions are included here.

l0phtcrack from l0pht Heavy Industries. A fast and powerful password cracking program to check to see if users are adhering to good password policies.

Power Desk from Mijenix Corporation. Allows system administrators to enable users to work more efficiently.

Free Space from Mijenix Corporation. Provides more free space on your system by compressing files and directories.

Zip Magic from Mijenix Corporation. Easily creates compressed archives, as well as extracts files in all common archive formats.

MindManger from MindJet LLC. An organization and communications tool which aids in problem solving—based on the technique of "mind mapping."

Dave Anderson's PC Technology Guide Web Site. Just a few sample pages the Web site.

Transcender Certification. An example of the kinds of questions you will find in the Enterprise Certification exam.

Transcender Flash. A supplement to the certification product and functions like electronic flash cards.

Technical Support

Prentice Hall does not offer technical support for any software contained on the CD-ROM. However, if there is a problem with the media, you may obtain a replacement copy by emailing us with your problem at:
disc_exchange@prenhall.com